KOREAN COMMUNISM, 1945–1980

A Study from the Center for Korean Studies
University of Hawaii

KOREAN COMMUNISM 1945–1980

A REFERENCE GUIDE TO THE POLITICAL SYSTEM

DAE-SOOK SUH

The University Press of Hawaii / Honolulu

Library of Congress Cataloging in Publication Data

Suh, Dae-Sook, 1931–
    Korean communism, 1945–1980.

    Bibliography: p.
    Includes indexes.
    1. Korea (North)—Politics and government.
2. Communism—Korea (North)   I. Title.
JQ1729.5.A31981.S83   320.9519'3   81–12952
ISBN 0–8248–0740–5   AACR2

To Kevin Min-kul

Contents

PREFACE   xi–xiv
1. THE WORKS OF KIM IL SUNG, 1930–1980
   ON KIM'S WRITINGS   1
      Selected Works
      Complete Works
      Non–Korean Language Collections
      Topical Collections
      Pre-1945 Writings
      Writings Since 1945
      Writing Styles
   ANNOTATED BIBLIOGRAPHY   14
   SUBJECT INDEX   230
   CHRONOLOGICAL INDEX   251
   NOTES   271
2. THE WORKERS' PARTY OF KOREA, 1946–1980
   PARTY CONGRESSES AND CONFERENCES AND CENTRAL COMMITTEE
      PLENUMS   273
   AGENDAS   278
      Korean Communist Party
      Workers' Party of Korea
   PERSONNEL OF THE CENTRAL COMMITTEE AND CENTRAL
      AUDITING COMMITTEE   309
      Methods of Election
      Members of the Central Committee
      Officers of the Central Committee
      The Inspection Committee
      The Central Auditing Committee

PERSONNEL REGISTERS   315
First Congress, August 28–30, 1946
Second Congress, March 27–30, 1948
Third Congress, April 23–29, 1956
Fourth Congress, September 11–18, 1961
Fifth Congress, November 2–12, 1970
Sixth Congress, October 10–14, 1980
TABLES   337
NOTES   356
3. THE SUPREME PEOPLE'S ASSEMBLY, 1948–1980
MEETINGS OF THE SUPREME PEOPLE'S ASSEMBLY   360
AGENDAS   361
North Korean Provisional People's Committee
People's Assembly of North Korea
Supreme People's Assembly
OFFICERS AND MEMBERS OF THE ASSEMBLY   386
PERSONNEL REGISTERS   392
First Assembly, September 2–10, 1948
Second Assembly, September 18–20, 1957
Third Assembly, October 22–23, 1962
Fourth Assembly, December 14–16, 1967
Fifth Assembly, December 25–28, 1972
Sixth Assembly, December 15–17, 1977
TABLES   427
NOTES   443
4. THE ADMINISTRATION COUNCIL, 1948–1980
THE CABINET OF THE DEMOCRATIC PEOPLE'S
REPUBLIC OF KOREA   444
OFFICERS AND MEMBERS OF THE CABINET
AND ADMINISTRATION COUNCIL   448
First Cabinet, September 9, 1948
Second Cabinet, September 20, 1957
Third Cabinet, October 23, 1962
Fourth Cabinet, December 16, 1967
Administration Council, Fifth Assembly,
December 26, 1972
Administration Council, Sixth Assembly,
December 16, 1977

MINISTRIES AND COMMISSIONS OF THE REPUBLIC   456
   Cabinet Officials, by Ministry
   Cabinet Officials, Alphabetic Listing
TABLES   483
NOTES   494

5. THE CENTRAL COURT AND THE CENTRAL PROCURATOR'S OFFICE
THE JUDICIARY   495
CHIEF JUSTICES AND PRESIDENTS OF THE CENTRAL COURT   497
PROCURATORS-GENERAL   498

6. THE CONSTITUTION AND BYLAWS
THE CONSTITUTIONS OF THE REPUBLIC   499
TEXT OF THE SOCIALIST CONSTITUTION OF 1972   502
THE BYLAWS OF THE PARTY ·   522
TEXT OF THE BYLAWS OF NOVEMBER 1970   525
NOTES   544

7. STANDARD TERMS OF THE POLITICAL SYSTEM
FOR STANDARD TERMS   546
LIST OF TERMS   548
   English-Korean
   Korean-English

NAME INDEX   561
SUBJECT INDEX   585

Preface

In the three decades since its establishment, the political system of the Democratic People's Republic of Korea has undergone fundamental changes. With the advent of a new socialist constitution in 1972, emphasis seemed to shift from the party to the legitimacy and operation of the government. The government has developed from a satellite communist state to a self-reliant member of the third world. Kim Il Sung, the supreme leader for the entire period, emerged from the ruthless power struggles of the 1950s as the undisputed leader in the 1960s and was busily engaged in promoting himself as a leader of the third world in the 1970s. It is an opportune time to document the records of the political system and to put basic reference materials in order.

The most common complaint of scholars who study the North Korean communist system is the scarcity of source materials. This is due in part to the nature of the system, which publishes much propaganda but little basic information explaining the system. Another problem is the unavailability of materials in western languages. Even for serious scholars who can use non-western language materials with relative ease, sources are indeed scarce. The problem is compounded by the extreme and unconventional practices of the North Koreans, that is, secrecy, backdating, and suppression of published information.

The secrecy, at times, borders on absurdity. For example, the results of the 1977 election for the Sixth Supreme People's Assembly were kept secret. The 579 electoral districts were announced, 100 percent voter turnout for the election was reported, and the first session of the Sixth Assembly was convened, but the identities of the elected members of the Assembly were not revealed, even to the voters who elected them.

There have been a number of instances of backdating, such as the backdating of the founding congress of the Workers' Party of Korea from August 1946 to October 1945, and the continuation of such practices confuses even the most informed. The latest instance is the announcement of the change in the founding date of the Korean People's Army from February 8, 1948, to April 24, 1932. For twenty-nine years, Kim Il Sung delivered anniversary speeches once every five years on February 8 to commemorate the anniversary of the army, but this was suddenly changed to April 24 in 1978, and that date was claimed to be the celebration of the forty-sixth anniversary. April 24, 1932, is, of course, the date of the alleged founding of the old guerrilla forces of Kim in Manchuria. It was the twenty-fifth anniversary in 1973 but the forty-sixth anniversary in 1978 of the same army. There will no doubt be adjustments in the records to reflect this change of heart, and when there are several changes of this nature concerning organizations as important as the party and the army, the records are not easy for the casual observer to decipher.

The more widely publicized writings of Kim Il Sung have undergone several revisions and have been published in four different editions. The original first edition is no longer available and is neither used nor cited in the writings of North Korean scholars. From the early 1970s, alleged writings of Kim during the 1930s and the 1940s began to appear, and many of his writings of the 1950s and 1960s have been revised to conform to the political climate of the 1970s. Even the texts of the numerous interviews Kim granted to so many foreign correspondents in the 1970s were heavily edited and did not appear in the North Korean daily newspapers until one or two months after the interviews.

This study is an effort to present basic reference materials on the North Korean Communist political system of the past thirty years. Its primary purpose is the presentation of factual reference materials and not analysis of the system itself. An explanation is given in each section of the materials compiled, but it is offered to help explain the materials presented in each case and not as an analysis of the political process of the North. The analysis of the system deserves a separate study, and the information collected in this volume should be basic to any such undertaking.

The materials compiled here include an annotated bibliography of the writings of Kim Il Sung; reference materials on the Workers' Party of Korea, the Supreme People's Assembly, the Administration Council, the Central Court, and the Central Procurator's Office; the Socialist Constitution of 1972; the bylaws of the party; and approximately two hundred standard terms used in the political system.

The most important aspect of the political system is the role of the supreme leader, Kim Il Sung. All of his writings made public from 1945 to 1980, including those claimed to have been written from 1930 to 1945, are listed and annotated here and sources of the full texts are given. In most cases, more than one source is given so that different versions of Kim's writings can be found and compared. An effort has been made to cover the subject comprehensively and approximately seven hundred of his writings are annotated here. In addition, a subject index and a chronological index of the writings are provided. On the Workers' Party of Korea, the ruling Communist party of the North, all agendas of the party congresses, party conferences, and plenary meetings of the Central Committee are compiled in Chapter 2. Those plenums of the Central Committee whose agendas were kept secret are so noted, but there are only a few of these. The officers, members, and candidate members of the Central Committee and the Central Auditing Committee of the six party congresses are listed as they were originally announced in each party congress. Some of this valuable information was hitherto unavailable in English, for example, the rosters of the members of the Central Committees of the founding congresses of the Workers' Parties of North and South Korea.

In the case of the Supreme People's Assembly, the agendas of every session from the first to the sixth Assembly are known, and they are compiled in Chapter 3. The officers and members of the first five Assemblies are listed as they were originally announced. In the case of the sixth Assembly, only officers are listed because the members were not announced.

More than eighty different cabinet posts were created during the past thirty years. All ministries and commissions are briefly discussed in Chapter 4 as to their creation, development, abolition, and appointees. In addition, lists of the members of the four cabinets and two Administration Councils are presented as they were originally announced.

For the party, the Assembly, and the cabinet, more than thirty tables have been prepared to facilitate understanding of the North Korean system. These tables were made from the information provided in this study, and they reveal some startling statistical information about the system.

The operation of the Central Court and the Central Procurator's Office is briefly explained in Chapter 5, and all those who served as chief justice of the Supreme Court, president of the Central Court, and procurator-general of the Central Procurator's Office are listed.

The Socialist Constitution of 1972 is only the second constitution of the North. The first one was amended a number of times, and the process of amendment is briefly discussed in Chapter 6 with explanations of the numerous amendments. The official English text of the second constitution is reproduced here with minor editorial corrections. The bylaws of the party have also been amended several times, and the changes are explained. The latest amendment was in October 1980 at the time of the sixth party congress, but the text was not made public. The text translated and presented here is that of the bylaws amended in November 1970.

English translations of some two hundred terms used in the North Korean political organizations are offered in Chapter 7 in the hope that some measure of uniformity and standard usage may develop. Most of these are the basic and least-controversial terms, and it is hoped that their usage will be adopted by scholars studying the North Korean political system.

There are many problems in a study of this nature. One of the most obvious is the identification and use of proper primary sources. The problem is complicated because much information emanating from South Korea is intended to denigrate the North. Materials published in Japan still suffer from linguistic barriers, and the two giant Communist neighbors of the North have long been indifferent to the study of the northern political system.

The sources used for this study are all primary sources published in the North. Whenever conflicting sources dealing with the same subject have been found, the source published closer to the time of the event has been used, but the subsequent source is also cited to permit comparison.

Another problem is language. Since the late 1960s, the North Koreans have been translating their own materials into many western languages, including English. Their translations into English leave much to be desired, to say the least. However, some of the uncommon English terms originate from complicated and unusual Korean Communist jargon. Unless they are egregiously wrong in their usage of English, the North Korean translations have been followed. Many of these may sound peculiar in English, but they also sound peculiar in Korean to those who do not live under the Communist system.

Still another problem is the omission and commission of materials of the past to justify the political situations of the 1980s. The North Koreans continue to produce what Kim Il Sung is alleged to have written in the 1930s and 1940s in substantial quantity, to delete sections of his writings, and to omit entirely writings that do not conform to the politics of the 1980s. The activities of those purged in the North are deleted from the record, and at times their entire records are suppressed.

Lastly, there is the problem of coverage. This study covers only the basic organs of the state, the party, the legislature, the executive, and the judiciary, and the writings of the only leader North Korea has had. Source materials of the past three decades on the military, professional and local organizations, and diplomatic missions and statistical materials on economic development should also be collected. However, this is not an easy task, for the available materials are fragmentary and hard to find.

It is hoped that more materials will be found in the future to update this study. Furthermore, it is hoped that materials on other areas will also be found before the North Koreans revise them beyond recognition. This study was undertaken in the belief that the more information that is made available about the North, the more accurate will be our analyses of the political system of the North.

This study was conceived and the initial collection of material was begun nearly a decade ago when I was a research associate at the East Asian Institute, Columbia University. Collection, annotation, and revision of the material proceeded at a snail's pace due in part to my administrative chores at the University of Hawaii. However, it was also my work at the university's Center for Korean Studies that enabled me to locate a number of rare materials during visits to the Academies of Sciences of North Korea in 1974 and of the Soviet Union in 1978. I have also benefitted from the captured North Korean materials in the U.S. National Archives, which were declassified in 1977, and I have deliberately waited to be able to include material from the Sixth Congress of the Workers' Party of Korea, held in October 1980.

I am indebted to many scholars and colleagues both at home and abroad. They are too numerous to list here, but I want to mention only a few who directly helped me in this study. They are Dr. J. Carl Akins in Washington, Professor Masaaki Ichikawa in Tokyo, and Michael E. Macmillan in Honolulu. I also want to express my special appreciation to those who helped me at the Center for Korean Studies, Charlotte Oser, Jean Tanouye, and Debbie Ching, and to those at The University Press of Hawaii, including Stuart Kiang and Gayle Yoshida.

NOTE ON TRANSLITERATION

Except for commonly used proper names such as Kim Il Sung, Pyongyang, Park Chung Hee, and Seoul, the McCune-Reischauer transliteration system is followed. In romanizing Korean first names, the sound change in the second syllable is observed. For example, it is Ch'oe Yonggŏn and not Ch'oe Yong-kŏn, and it is Kim Tu-bong and not Kim Tu-pong.

1
The Works of Kim Il Sung
1930–1980

ON KIM'S WRITINGS

It has been more than thirty years since Kim Il Sung returned to Korea from the plains of northeast China and equally as long since he became the head of the government in the North. Through the years Kim made many speeches, gave many lectures, and wrote a few articles and theses that every citizen in the North is asked to read. The official version of his selected works has been revised twice and published in three editions. In conjunction with the efforts to glorify their leader, the North Koreans have launched a campaign to publish and republish many of Kim's writings from the late 1960s. Some of these were translated into English and other foreign languages and flooded the propaganda market in the 1970s. They have also selected and reproduced many articles and speeches on such topics as ideology, unification, revolution, the military, youth, and public health.

Beginning in the 1970s the North began to publish the alleged writings of Kim during his guerrilla days in the 1930s. To these have been added a few articles and speeches Kim is alleged to have written shortly after his return to Korea. The authenticity of these writings is highly questionable. To be sure, there is no evidence of Kim's writings in any source published prior to 1945. Under closer scrutiny it is not difficult to detect a substantial improvement in his writing style from the late 1940s to the 1970s. The alleged writings of the 1930s resemble his writings in the 1970s more than those of the late 1940s or early 1950s.

The major portion of Kim's important writings and speeches are compiled in his selected works, and they are important to the study of the North. Unlike the selected works of other Communist leaders, such as the works of Mao, which were selected and edited with considerable care and collected and published some twenty years after they were written, Kim's writings have been collected for publication with such haste that they have had to undergo embarrassing revisions and editing not just once but twice. For example, the last volume of the first edition of Kim's works, covering the materials from November 1951 to May 1953, was published in July 1953.[1] This is in sharp contrast to Mao's first volume, which covers the period from March 1926 to August 1937 and was first published in October 1951. There may be an advantage in having the collection published soon after the articles were made public, but because of the need to adjust his position to subsequent political developments, the writings of Kim have undergone substantial and at times drastic revisions. In many cases, when the revised edition is published, the earlier version is taken out of circulation. For example, the first edition of Kim's four-volume selected works is no longer available for consultation inside or outside of North Korea. In fact, North Korean scholars stopped referring to the first edition in their studies soon after the second edition appeared.

Perhaps the final edition with several future revisions will not be made until after the end of Kim's political career and will depend largely upon future political developments and the way he ends his political life, but in general the selection and compilation of his writings are made without the care and the study they deserve. Since he has led the party and the government in the North for more than three decades, what he has written and said about a particular subject at a particular place and time are important for a better understanding of the North.

This is an effort to compile a comprehensive list of Kim's writings and provide a brief annotation of each item. The list is comprehensive in the sense that all writings, speeches, reports, and other materials of substantial importance that were written by him, or alleged to have been written by him, in publicly available sources are listed and annotated here. North Korean scholars compiled a list, by title only, of Kim's writings in chronological order in 1972 in their political dictionary, *Chŏngch'i sajŏn*, published in 1973.[2] For obvious political reasons they added a few but omitted many. For the period from 1931 to 1972, they listed approximately three hundred fifty items. The items compiled here cover the period from 1930 to 1980 and number more than seven hundred. Each item is presented, in chronological order, with a brief annotation and sources of the full text. As many different sources as are available are listed so that the items appearing in different editions can be located and compared. There are a few items the texts of which are either secret or not available, and these items are so noted, giving whatever title or sources are known without annotation.

It is perhaps appropriate to discuss more fully the sources, such as the various editions of Kim's *Selected Works*, the material available in

English and other non-Korean languages, topical collections, the problems of the alleged writings of pre-1945 days, and Kim's writings since 1945. The styles of Kim's writing will also be discussed, but no attempt will be made to analyze Kim's thought and politics, for that deserves a separate study. The sources consulted to make the list and annotations are also given below.

SELECTED WORKS

The first edition of Kim's selected works was in four volumes, contained 127 items, and covered the period from December 1945 to May 1953. It was published shortly after the end of the Korean war in 1953 and carried many military orders and congratulatory messages relating to the war, particularly in the third and fourth volumes, covering the war years from June 1950 to July 1953. There were 67 items in the first and second volumes and 60 items in the third and fourth volumes. The majority of the items in the first two volumes, 47 out of 67, were reproduced in the first two volumes of the second revised edition, but most of the items in the third and the fourth volumes were dropped. The extent of revision is indicated by the fact that the third revised edition of the work included only 24 items of the 127 originally compiled in the first edition. Only the major speeches at the party congresses and the plenums of the Central Committee, the sessions of the Supreme People's Assembly, and congresses of other professional organizations were kept. Most of the routine speeches on holidays, open letters, interviews, and congratulatory messages were dropped.

More important, however, is the revision of the content of the items selected. Almost all sentences referring to the Soviet Union and China, particularly those expressing reverence or gratitude and adulation of Russian Communist leaders were deleted; at times paragraphs and pages were left out. This was an effort on the part of the North to assume a self-reliant posture in its relationship with these two quarrelous Communist neighbors. Also a major attempt was made to correct mistakes in the use of the Korean language.

The second edition was published in six volumes covering the period from 1945 to 1959.[3] The first two volumes reproduced forty-seven revised items from the first two volumes of the first edition and added twenty-one new items. The third volume of the second edition was never made public. It covered the war years from 1950 to 1953 and contained a few important items that Kim and North Korean scholars wanted to suppress; for example, Kim's speech on December 21, 1951, at the third joint plenum of the Central Committee of the party and his speech on April 4, 1951, to the political and security organization cadres. In these speeches, Kim made carping criticism of high-ranking party cadres and military generals by name for their misconduct in the war. Some of those reprimanded were expelled from the party. These items were deleted in the later edition in part because some of those expelled were later reinstated to key positions, for example Kim Il, the vice-president of the republic, Yim Ch'un-ch'u, the secretary of the Central People's Committee, and Ch'oe Kwang, the former commander-in-chief of the People's Army. For the period from the end of the war in August 1953 to 1959, fifty-six items were selected and compiled in volumes 4, 5, and 6 of the second revised edition.

Some materials that appeared in two previous editions were revised once again and reselected and compiled in the first two volumes of the newly revised third edition of Kim's work.[4] Many items from the second edition were left out in the third edition; out of 68 items in the first and second volumes only 21 items were selected, and out of 56 items in the fourth, fifth, and sixth volumes only 26 items were selected for the third edition. The first and second volumes of the third edition were published in 1967, and the third and the fourth volumes, covering the period from 1961 to 1967, were published in 1968. The fifth volume covered the three-year period from 1968 to 1972 and was published in 1972; the sixth volume covered the two-year period from 1971 to 1973 and was published in 1974. The latest volume, the seventh, covered the period from 1974 to the end of 1977.[5] There are 151 items in seven volumes.

COMPLETE WORKS

It was reported in *Nodong sinmun* on April 14, 1979, that a new collection entitled *Works of Kim Il Sung* [Kim Il Sung chŏjakchip] had been published in four volumes covering the period from June 1930 to December 1948. The first volume covered the period from June 1930 to the end of 1945 and contained fifty items; the second volume covered 1946 with seventy-nine items; the third volume covered 1947 with fifty-eight items; and the fourth volume covered 1948 with forty-six items.

This latest collection of Kim's works contains material never before revealed, but the new material seems to be work of the late 1970s rather than of the period stated.[6] It gives the impression that the North Koreans are compiling the complete works of Kim, but closer scrutiny reveals the exclusion of a number of his earlier writings, such as his letter to Marshal Stalin on September 22, 1948, expressing appreciation for the Soviet troop withdrawal from the North. Furthermore, a number of his speeches that are known to exist, such as his speech on July 27, 1946, at the Eighth Enlarged Plenum of the North Korean Branch Bureau of the Korean Communist Party, still have not been made public.

In the preface of the first volume of the latest collection, the Central

Committee of the Workers' Party of Korea stated in 1979 that this collection was published to commemorate the seventieth birthday of Kim, which is not until April 15, 1982. In April 1980, the North Korean News Agency announced the publication of the fifth volume, containing forty-eight items and covering the period from January 1949 to June 22, 1950. It is reasonable to expect that the North Koreans will publish more volumes by the time of his seventieth birthday in 1982. However, only the first four volumes of this series are included in this study.

NON-KOREAN LANGUAGE COLLECTIONS

The most commonly available work in non-Korean languages is the translation of the newly revised third edition of Kim's selected works. This version is available in many languages, including English, Japanese, Russian, and Chinese in translations done by North Korean translators and published and distributed by the Foreign Languages Publishing House in Pyongyang.

There are a few earlier versions. The earliest collection of Kim's writings was published in Japan in Japanese even before the first edition of his selected works was published in the North. What was known as the Publication Committee of the Selected Works of Kim Il Sung published a collection of his works in three volumes (volume 1, supplementary volume, and volume 2) in 1952.[7] The first volume, subtitled "The Period after the August 15 Liberation," had nineteen items covering the period from March 1, 1946, to December 25, 1947. There are three items compiled here that were not included in the first edition of the North Korean version; for example, his 1946 May Day speech. A short biographical sketch was appended to this volume, but this was hastily put together and there are numerous errors in dates and in translations. This was soon followed by a supplementary volume adding thirteen items from March 1948 to May 1950, the period prior to the Korean War. The second volume was subtitled "The Period of the Fatherland Liberation War" and covered the period from June 1950 to May 1952, compiling twenty-six items collected from newspapers, news agencies, and other published works from the North. These three volumes were published by the San-ichi Shobo of Tokyo in 1952.

The Russian version of Kim's work appeared in 1962, *Kim Ir Sen: Izbrannye stat'i i rechi*, published in Moscow. This book had a brief introduction by Kim written in April 1960. This collection of twenty-four items emphasized the postwar North Korean rehabilitation programs, covering the period from August 1953 to September 1961. The collection was an independent effort and not patterned after any North Korean version.[8]

The Chinese version of Kim's writing was published in 1963 in Peking. This was an effort to translate the second edition of Kim's selected works in six volumes. The fourth, fifth, and sixth volumes of the second edition were translated into Chinese and published,[9] but it is doubtful whether the first three volumes were ever translated or published; certainly the third volume was not because even the Korean version was not made public. Other than this, the Chinese have made no effort to publish Kim's writings in any independent collection, and the only other Chinese-language edition available today is the North Korean translation published in Pyongyang.

The first collection of Kim's writings in English was published in 1965 by the Foreign Languages Publishing House in Pyongyang.[10] It was in two volumes; the first volume, with twenty-three items, covers the period from March 23, 1946, to January 5, 1959, and the second volume, with fourteen items, covers the period from February 26, 1959, to October 10, 1965. An honest effort seems to have been made by the North Korean scholars to explain in footnotes some obscure points in English, but the translation was extremely bad, and this series has been abandoned in favor of the complete translation of the newly revised third edition of his *Selected Works*.

There are a few collections of Kim's work published in the United States, for example, *Revolution and Socialist Construction in Korea; Selected Writings of Kim Il Sung*. This was published by International Publishers in 1971 in New York and contains ten items from April 1955 to November 1970. There is no logic in this collection; it deals with many subjects without a coherent theme. Furthermore, all items compiled in this collection are excerpts except one, and in most cases the more-important parts of the articles and speeches were not excerpted.

Grossman Publishers of New York published a book on *chuch'e* in 1972 in commemoration of Kim's sixtieth birthday. It was entitled *Juche: The Speeches and Writings of Kim Il Sung* and was a collection of ten items on *chuch'e* from April 1964 to April 1970. It was edited with an introduction by a person named Li Yuk-sa, undoubtedly a pseudonym, and includes a foreword by Eldridge Cleaver. The editor explains in the introduction that he corrected the North Korean translations of Kim's work and in many instances retranslated them. However, his effort seems not to have been a serious one, because he corrected only a few articles, and if the North Korean translation was bad, his correction was worse. Moreover, his introductory essay on Korean history clearly demonstrates his ignorance of Korea, and the collection itself leaves something to be desired. For example, the first speech by Kim on the problem of *chuch'e* is the speech on December 28, 1955, but this collection begins with his speech on April 14, 1964. Eldridge Cleaver, who spent some of his exile in Pyongyang at the generous hospitality of the North Korean people, condemns the United States and praises the North in the foreword, but this, of course, was before his return to the United States and conversion to the Baptist faith.

There is still another collection, published by Guardian Associates Inc. of New York in 1976.[11] This collection is on the reunification of Korea and reproduces twenty-six items, mostly short excerpts, of Kim's speeches and interviews with reporters from August 1960 to May 1976. The difficulty with this collection is not only in the excerpted portions of Kim's originals, but also in the reproduction of the North Korean version of interviews and Kim's banquet speeches. For example, in Kim's interviews with correspondents of the *New York Times* and the *Mainichi shinbun* and the *Yomiuri shinbun* of Japan there is considerable editing of both questions and answers. The American and Japanese versions are available in English, and this collection merely reproduced the North Korean version.

There are a few other collections published in the United States, but these are mere reproductions of North Korean materials by leftist organizations. There has been as yet no serious effort to select, edit, and compile Kim's work in the United States. In fact, none in the English-speaking world. With all their shortcomings and bad translations, still the most useful for reference are the English versions published in Pyongyang by the North Koreans themselves.

TOPICAL COLLECTIONS

There are many collections of Kim's writings on specific topics such as the problems of socialist economic management, the *chuch'e* ideology, the Korean war, the South Korean revolution, youth problems, reunification problems, the tasks of the government, the People's Army, trade unions, the tasks of social scientists, the problems of agriculture, and public health. In most cases, the more-important materials in the *Selected Works* are reproduced in these collections, but to these are added new materials on the specific topic that were not made public in other collections.

The earliest such collection is perhaps the one on the Korean war published in 1954.[12] This collection compiled forty-two items from Kim's radio addresses delivered from June 26, 1950, one day after the start of the war, to July 28, 1953, when the conclusion of the cease-fire agreement that ended the war was announced. Most of the items can be found in the first edition of Kim's selected works, but only a very few important items were kept in the third edition of his work.

One of the best collections on a single topic is the four-volume collection on the problems of socialist economic management, *Sahoe chuŭi kyŏngje kwalli munje e taehayŏ*. The first three volumes were published in 1970 and the fourth in December 1977. The first volume, with sixteen items, covers the period from December 1946 to August 1960, and most of these can be found in the first edition of the *Selected Works*. However, out of forty-three items compiled in the second and third volumes, covering the period from September 1961 to October 1969, more than half, twenty-five items, are found only in this collection, and they reveal many of Kim's instructions on specific problems and methods of general economic management.

On the problems of *chuch'e* ideology, the North Koreans published a collection of thirty-two items in 1970 including more than a dozen items that were not included in the *Selected Works*. This was later expanded and published in 1975 in two volumes covering materials up to March 1974.[13] This particular collection was translated by the North Koreans into English and French: *On Juche in Our Revolution* and *A Propos du Djoutche dans Notre Revolution*. It is far superior to the one by Li Yuk-sa.

There are a number of publications on youth problems, among them one on youth and juveniles published in 1966, another on youth problems and the work of the League of the Socialist Working Youth, and the latest one in English on youth and the revolution, published in 1976.[14] Together with these publications, several English-language collections appeared in 1976, including one on reunification problems and another on the nonalignment movement. There are, of course, Korean-language publications covering these subjects, such as the one on the South Korean revolution and reunification, but at times they are different collections covering different periods.[15]

The more-important Korean-language collections were published in 1968. These include the ones on the tasks of the government, the People's Army, the trade unions, and the role of social scientists. Still others deal with agricultural workers and the problems of public health work. In the 1970s many reporters visited the North and interviewed Kim, and there is a collection of such interviews in two volumes, so far. All of these interviews were edited and in most cases only Kim's replies were published. On those rare occasions when the questions were published, only those questions that carry the highest praise of Kim were chosen.[16]

There are other unofficial collections of Kim's speeches under the more general title of *Important Documents of the Great Leader Kim Il Sung*,[17] but these are published by the North Korean front organizations in Japan and in general reproduce those already available from the North. At times, these collections tend to emphasize Kim's speeches on the role of the Koreans in Japan, but there is as yet no separate collection on the Koreans in Japan. There are still others, such as the collections of his writings on literature and art, the *Ch'ŏllima* movement, and the management of the rural economy. There will be many more editions of existing collections, and a number of new topical collections will no doubt appear in the future.

Pre-1945 Writings

The alleged writings of Kim prior to 1945 began to appear only in the 1970s. The carefully documented contents and the lucid writing style leave little doubt that these were not written by Kim prior to 1945. There is no source prior to 1945 to which these materials can be traced. In fact, there is none that even mentions such writings. Most of these writings seem to have been done in the late 1960s or early 1970s and attribute to Kim statements he might have made on earlier occasions.

The earliest such work to appear is a report on the path of Korean revolution on June 30, 1930, made public for the first time in July 1978.[18] This was followed by a speech Kim is supposed to have made at the meeting of young Communists in Mingyüehkou, Yenchi County, on May 20, 1931. The speech condemns the May 30 riot, one of the more successful Communist riots by joint Chinese and Korean forces in 1930. He gives three reasons for the failure, analyzes the result of the failure, and proposes four courses of action to be carried out in the future, all too analytically written for a young guerrilla fighter who did not participate in the riot.

In December of the same year Kim is supposed to have made another speech to the same group at the same place. Kim cites Marxism and Leninism freely in this speech, something he did not do often even after his return to Korea in 1945. He also discusses the significant labor disputes within Korea, such as the strikes at Wŏnsan, the Sinhŭng mines, the Pyongyang rubber factory, and the tenant disputes in Tanch'ŏn and Puri farms. These strikes and disputes were not well known even in Korea at this time, for the Japanese authorities wanted to suppress news of disturbances. It is indeed difficult to comprehend how a young man nineteen years of age with less than a tenth-grade education living in a remote and isolated small village in Yenchi County in Manchuria would have known of these strikes and disputes within Korea and how he would have related them to the anti-Japanese Communist armed struggle in 1931.

Other examples are more ludicrous, and the futility of such fabrication is too obvious to merit an elaborate refutation. It is safe to assume that the writings Kim claims to have done prior to his return to Korea in 1945 were in fact written in late 1960s or early 1970s.

His writings prior to 1945 advocate the general theme of an anti-Japanese armed guerrilla struggle. On occasion, he instructs his guerrillas, who were at the time fighting with a Chinese guerrilla force, to learn about Korean history, but in most cases the writings prior to 1945 are done with the benefit of historical hindsight. As of 1980, Kim claims to have written nineteen pieces during the fifteen-year period from 1930 to 1945. The most prolific year was 1937 with four speeches, but there are many years, such as 1934, 1938, 1941–42, and 1944, when he made no contributions to his writings. Or, Kim might fill these years with the writings he will do in the future.

WRITINGS SINCE 1945

Kim describes his role before 1945 as that of a revolutionary leader who engaged primarily in guerrilla activities, but his role in the North since the liberation of Korea has been that of a political leader in charge of the creation, development, and maintenance of a political system. Kim may be fabricating his writings prior to 1945, but his writings since 1945 were delivered in important meetings and on special occasions. A few were kept secret for political reasons, but among those that were made public, Kim wrote an average of twenty speeches per year from 1945 to 1980. The numbers fluctuated from year to year; the largest number was eighty in 1946, and the smallest was six in 1956.

There are many types of writings by Kim. The most common are functional speeches on special occasions, such as New Year's Day, May Day, August 15th Liberation Day, and anniversaries of the founding of the republic, the party, and the army. There are many speeches made on trips abroad, more often in the 1950s, and many welcoming addresses given to greet visitors from abroad at banquets and mass rallies in the 1970s. There are open letters to the political leaders of the Soviet Union and China and also a few widely publicized letters and messages to Koreans abroad.

The more-important writings on the direction of North Korean policy are made public through the reports delivered at the party congresses, the plenary meetings of the Central Committee, and the sessions of the Supreme People's Assembly. The most comprehensive reviews of the work of the state as well as the policy direction of the party are made at the party congresses and plenums, but even here some important writings were left out of the collections of Kim's work. For example, his report to the third party congress in April 1956 is not included in the latest revised edition of the *Selected Works*.

There are articles and theses that Kim has written over the years. For example, there are two theses Kim wrote on the socialist rural question in February 1964 and on socialist education in September 1977. There is no specific reason why Kim chose to use the term theses on these subjects. There are other ideologically oriented discourses that Kim has written—for example, on the question of the period of transition from capitalism to socialism and the dictatorship of the proletariat in May 1967 and on the theoretical problems of the socialist economy in March 1969—but these are not labeled as theses. There are also a few articles Kim has written for non-Korean journals, such as his article on the October Revolution that appeared in *Pravda* in October 1957 and two anti-American articles that appeared in the magazine, *Tricontinental*, in 1967 and 1968.

When the government of North Korea expanded its diplomatic relations with nonaligned and non-communist countries in the 1970s, Kim granted many interviews to reporters. The North Koreans have published most of these interviews after careful editing and have incorporated some of these into the collection of his writings. A few reporters from the non-communist countries asked some hard questions, and Kim revealed some of his thoughts in the interviews. A few of these interviews were printed in their entirety in non-communist papers and they are noteworthy, particularly the ones in *Asahi shinbun* of September 1971 and *Mainichi shinbun* of September 1972.

During the past thirty years or so Kim wrote and spoke most often on subjects related to the economic development of the North. More than one hundred of about seven hundred items compiled here deal with the North Korean economy. However, in the sixty or so more-serious writings he has done, Kim has dealt most often with problems relating to the party; about twenty of the sixty important writings deal with the strengthening and consolidation of the party. About fifteen items deal with economic development, and fewer than ten items deal with the state system. He has not written much on the international relations of the North nor on the military, and less on the reunification of Korea, except for the constant and perfunctory references to it in his speeches. In the case of the military, it may be that some of his writings are restricted and not made public.

A few documents and platforms are included in his *Selected Works*, obviously giving credit to Kim for authorship. The most peculiar is the inclusion of the 1972 Socialist Constitution of the Democratic People's Republic of Korea in the sixth volume of the *Selected Works*.[19]

WRITING STYLES

It is assumed that Kim has done his own writing. Some of the detailed information, technical as well as trade specialties, is provided for him, but the texts seem to have been written by him. When he speaks about what sort of nets should be used to catch a particular kind of fish and specifies the grade of machine to be used to mine certain types of minerals, it is assumed that he was provided with the trade information, but the direction and basic policy alternatives are Kim's own ideas. In fact, there is no one person who could have written for him for more than thirty years because only a few have survived the numerous purges through the years, and there are a few identifiable styles in his writings. Some of the more obvious ones are briefly discussed here.

Prolixity. Like many party leaders in Communist countries, Kim's writings are prolix and his speeches are verbose. From the very beginning in the late 1940s, his speeches before the party congresses and the Supreme People's Assembly ran for several hours at a time. Over the years Kim has learned to give shorter speeches on occasion, but this is not because he has learned to be succinct in conveying his messages, but rather because he has delegated some tasks, for example, the reports of the People's Economic Plans, to his deputies and vice-premiers. On any given subject, Kim still rambles interminably in search of things to talk about.

Statistics. Kim is a great user of statistics. He uses statistics to point out the shortcomings of the workers, to review past mistakes, and to set goals for future undertakings. In his speech to the leaders of various economic sectors on January 25, 1950, Kim urges them to use statistics. He is prone to cite statistical figures to praise economic achievements and voter participation in national elections and to compare trade figures with foreign countries. He has used statistics to such an extent that comparable numbers in absolute figures of the 1950s began to give way to percentage figures in the 1960s. However, many North Korean economic figures in the 1970s still use the statistics with both absolute and percentage figures.

At times Kim's statistics are falsified to prove a point. For example, in an effort to justify the legality of the North Korean Supreme People's Assembly, Kim said that 77.52 percent of the South Korean voters had participated in the first election of deputies in 1948. There are many examples of this kind. Kim said, for instance, that the voter turnout for the election in the liberated South was 97 to 98 percent of the eligible voters during the Korean war. He also claimed that 95,241 *chŏngbo* of land had been confiscated and redistributed to 219,980 farmers in Ch'ungch'ŏng Namdo. These are all hard-to-believe statistics in the midst of the war.

Itemization. Although Kim's writings are unnecessarily lengthy and at times repetitious, his main arguments are itemized to emphasize his points. In general, three stages of itemization occur: the first is a review of past mistakes; the second is an analysis of the present situation; and the third is the itemization of tasks for the future. From the 1960s Kim relented somewhat and began to use straight narrative form at times, but during the 1950s most of his writings contained itemized points of emphasis. Even today, Kim's writings and speeches cover a broad range of topics, and he repeats endlessly the pointless arguments from many different positions, but his steady discursive commentary usually ends with itemized points of emphasis. At times these items exceed ten points.

Metaphors. Because of his guerrilla background, Kim most often compares situations with military operations. He compares the role of a factory manager with that of a company commander, social mobilization with military maneuvers, and education with military training. North Korea is full of mottos bearing military slogans, such as the "seventy-day battle speed" for short-term objectives, and "capturing the six highlands" for long-term economic goals. Kim says that production work, the learning process, and the daily life of a party member should follow the styles of Kim's partisan guerrillas. He emphasizes that a county cooperative farm manager should know his county like a soldier knows his machine gun. Perhaps because of his lack of formal education in Korean tradition and culture, he seldom compares any particular situation to similar incidents in Korean history. He has succeeded in having Communist historians reinterpret and rewrite the rich history of Korea, but his favorite comparative norms are still those few years of anti-Japanese guerrilla struggles in Manchuria and not even the rewritten history of Korea.

Korean Language. When he first returned to Korea, there was much to be desired in Kim's usage of the Korean language. This is due in part to his Chinese educational background and lack of formal training in schools. There were not merely grammatical errors, but many difficulties in syntax, phrases, and plain Korean words. Much of his writing was reedited, and this is best displayed in the extent of editing done from the first to the second edition of his *Selected Works.* He may have refrained from using more-sophisticated phrases for the benefit of the common people, but those few he used he repeated many times, such as *yangbong ŭmwi* ("to serve in the light and betray in the dark," "double dealing") and *ŭisin chakch'ik* ("to set standards by one's own example"). He deliberately avoided using foreign words, particularly English and Russian, not only because he did not know them, but because he wanted to use Korean words. On those few occasions when he used them, his lack of understanding did not help him. For example, he called Wall Street *wŏlga* in Korean, which is not easy to decipher at first glance. He used such English words as *demagoguery* and *compressor*, for which there are Korean equivalents, and translated such words as *paper tiger* into nonexistent Korean words. Reading his writings through various editions and revisions, it is not difficult to detect a significant improvement in his writing style and usage of the language. One may single out a few items from his entire collection which have different writing styles and attribute them to someone other than Kim, but in general his writings of the past thirty years or so have a definite style that is Kim's own. They may be poor, but they are uniquely his own.

ANNOTATED BIBLIOGRAPHY

The works of Kim Il Sung are entered here in chronological order, with the title of each item following immediately after the date and the occasion for which the item was written, or on which it was delivered, explained after the title. In most cases, both the title and the occasion are given, but in a few instances only one or the other is known and that is given. If the occasion is obvious from the title, for example, a New Year address, only the title is given.

The speeches and reports made by Kim in the sessions of the Supreme People's Assembly and the congresses and plenary meetings of the Workers' Party of Korea are identified by an abbreviated notation; for example, 4SPA-1 stands for the first session of the Fourth Supreme People's Assembly, and 4WPK-18CC stands for the eighteenth enlarged plenum of the Central Committee of the Workers' Party of Korea. For more information on these meetings, see chapters 2 and 3.

Important writings, whether included in the various editions of Kim's *Selected Works* or not, are marked with an asterisk. There are, on the average, two such items per year. Some of these appeared in the *Selected Works* but were dropped from subsequent editions and suppressed.

Following the annotations, the locations of the item in the various editions of the *Selected Works* are given. Other sources of the work are then indicated in a separate line. Sources are indicated by abbreviated titles, a complete list of which appears below, followed by volume and page numbers. If only excerpts are available in a particular collection, this is noted. Pamphlets usually contain a single item under the title given; the year of publication is also shown in the citation. For example, EP77 indicates an English-language pamphlet published in 1977, and KP77 indicates a Korean-language pamphlet published in the same year. Pamphlets in English are published by the Foreign Languages Publishing House in Pyongyang, and those in Korean are, in most cases, published by the party.

The latest volume, the seventh, of Kim's *Selected Works* was published in 1978 and covers the period to the end of 1977. Works from 1977 to 1980 have been collected from various sources. These include, among others, the North Korean Yearbook, one of the most consistent source books published by the Korean Central News Agency since 1949; the official party organ, *Kŭlloja*; and an English monthly journal, *Korea Today*. These publications are not included in the list of sources below, but most issues from 1977 to 1980 were read and are cited in the bibliography. The contents of the *Selected Works* are usually drawn from articles and speeches that appear in these books and journals. *Nodong sinmun* and the *Pyongyang Times* were used to supplement the sources for works from the late 1970s, but for earlier periods, well covered by other sources, citation of newspapers was avoided.

The list that follows provides both the abbreviations used in the bibliography and, with the exceptions noted above, complete citations of all the sources used to compile the bibliography.

Abbreviations

A (1, 2)	*Answers to the Questions Raised by Foreign Journalists*, 2 vols. Pyongyang: Foreign Languages Publishing House, 1977.
CCY (49–79)	*Chosŏn chungang yŏn'gam.* Pyongyang: Chosŏn Chungang T'ongsinsa, annual from 1949. 1950, 1951–52, 1953, 1954–55, 1956, 1957, 1958, 1959, 1960, 1961, 1962, 1963, 1964, 1965, 1966–67, 1968, 1969, 1970, 1971, 1972, 1973, 1974, 1975, 1976, 1978, 1979.
CHU (1, 2)	*Uri hyŏngmyŏng esŏŭi chuch'e e taehayŏ*, 2 vols. Pyongyang: Chosŏn Nodongdang Ch'ulp'ansa, 1970.
CIK	*Chŏnhu inmin kyŏngje pokku palchŏn ŭl wihayŏ.* Pyongyang: Chosŏn Nodongdang Ch'ulp'ansa, 1956.
CJC (1–4)	*Kim Il Sung chŏjakchip.* Pyongyang: Chosŏn Nodongdang Ch'ulp'ansa, 1979.
CLM	*Ch'ŏllima undong kwa sahoe chuŭi kŏnsŏl ŭi taekojo e taehayŏ.* Pyongyang: Chosŏn Nodongdang Ch'ulp'ansa, 1970.
CSJ (1–7)	*Kim Il Sung chojak sŏnjip*, 3d ed., 7 vols. Pyongyang: Chosŏn Nodongdang Ch'ulp'ansa, 1967–1978.
DJOU (1, 2)	*A Propos du Djoutche dans Notre Revolution*, 2 vols. Pyongyang: Editions en Langue Etrageres, 1975.
EP	*English pamphlet*
FC (1, 2)	*Oeguk kijadŭl i chegihan chilmun e taedap*, 2 vols. Pyongyang: Chosŏn Nodongdang Ch'ulp'ansa, 1976.

HM   *Yŏngye kunnindŭl ŭn choguk haebang chŏnjaeng esŏ seun wihun kwa ŏpchŏk ŭl hŏttoei hajimalgo hyŏngmyŏng ŭi kotchŭl kesok p'iwŏya handa.* Pyongyang: Chosŏn Nodongdang Ch'ulp'ansa, 1968.

IPR   *For the Independent Peaceful Reunification of Korea,* rev. ed. New York: Guardian Associates, Inc., 1976.

IPRC   *For the Independent, Peaceful Reunification of the Country.* Pyongyang: Foreign Languages Publishing House, 1976.

JAP (1, supp., 2)   *Kin Nichi-sei senshu,* 3 vols. Tokyo: Sanichi Shobo, 1952.

JC   *Juche! The Speeches and Writings of Kim Il Sung.* Foreword by Eldridge Cleaver, edited and introduced by Li Yuk-sa. New York: Grossman Publishers, 1972.

JUCHE (1, 2)   *On Juche in Our Revolution,* 2 vols. Pyongyang: Foreign Languages Publishing House, 1975.

KP   *Korean pamphlet*

KW   *Chayuwa tongnip ŭl wihan chosŏn inmin ŭi chŏngŭi ŭi choguk haebang chŏnjaeng.* Pyongyang: Chosŏn Nodongdang Ch'ulp'ansa, 1954.

LA   *Uri hyŏngmyŏng esŏ munhak yesul ŭi immu.* Pyongyang: Chosŏn Nodongdang Ch'ulp'ansa, 1965.

LSWY (1, 2)   *Ch'ŏngsonyŏn saŏpkwa sahoe chuŭi nodong ch'ŏngnyŏn tongmaeng ŭi immu e taehayŏ,* 2 vols. Pyongyang: Chosŏn Nodongdang Ch'ulp'ansa, 1969.

MHJ (1–3)   *Kim Il Sung tongji ŭi chuyo munhŏnjip,* 3 vols. N.p.: Sahoe Kwahaksa, 1971.

ML   *Mark'usŭ renin chuŭi wa p'uroret'aria kukche chuŭi kich'i, panje panmi t'ujaeng ŭi kich'i rŭl nop'i dŭlgo segye hyŏngmyŏng ŭl ch'okchin haja.* Pyongyang: Chosŏn Nodongdang Ch'ulp'ansa, 1969.

NAM   *The Non-Alignment Movement is a Mighty Anti-Imperialist Revolutionary Force of Our Times.* Pyongyang: Foreign Languages Publishing House, 1976.

PH   *Pogŏn wisaeng saŏp ŭl palchŏn sik'igi wihayŏ.* Pyongyang: Chosŏn Nodongdang Ch'ulp'ansa, 1968.

PPT   *Uri hyŏngmyŏng kwa kŏnsŏl esŏ inmin chŏnggwŏn ŭi kwaŏp e taehayŏ.* Pyongyang: Chosŏn Nodongdang Ch'ulp'ansa, 1968.

RK   *For the Reunification of Korea.* N.p.: Spark Publications, n.d.

RPM   *Uriŭi hyŏngmyŏnggwa inmin kundae ŭi kwaŏp e taehayŏ.* Pyongyang: Chosŏn Nodongdang Ch'ulp'ansa, 1968.

RSC   *Revolution and Socialist Construction in Korea: Selected Writings of Kim Il Sung.* New York: International Publishers, 1971.

RUSS	*Kim Ir Sen: Izbrannye stat'i i rechi.* Moscow: Gospolit-izdat, 1962.
SAF	*Urinara sahoe chuŭi nongch'on munje wa nongŏp kŭlloja tongmaeng saŏp e taehayŏ.* Pyongyang: Chosŏn Nodongdang Ch'ulp'ansa, 1968.
SEC	*For Socialist Economic Construction.* Pyongyang: Foreign Languages Publishing House, 1958.
1SJ (1-4)	*Kim Il Sung sŏnjip,* 1st ed., 4 vols. Pyongyang: Chosŏn Nodongdang Ch'ulp'ansa, 1953-1954.
2SJ (1-6)	*Kim Il Sung sŏnjip,* 2d ed., 6 vols. Pyongyang: Chosŏn Nodongdang Ch'ulp'ansa, 1960-1964.
SK	*Namchosŏn hyŏngmyŏng kwa choguk t'ongil e taehayŏ.* Pyongyang: Chosŏn Nodongdang Ch'ulp'ansa, 1969.
SKKM (1-3)	*Sahoe chuŭi kyŏngje kwalli munje e taehayŏ,* 3 vols. Pyongyang: Chosŏn Nodongdang Ch'ulp'ansa, 1970.
SR	*For Correct Management of the Socialist Rural Economy in Our Country.* Pyongyang: Foreign Languages Publishing House, 1977.
SS	*Sahoe kwahak immu ŭi taehayŏ.* Pyongyang: Chosŏn Nodongdang Ch'ulp'ansa, 1969.
SW (1-7)	*Kim Il Sung, Selected Works,* 7 vols. English text of *Kim Il Sung chojak sŏnjip.* Pyongyang: Foreign Languages Publishing House, 1971-1979.
2SW (1, 2)	*Kim Il Sung, Selected Works,* 2 vols. English text of selected titles from *Kim Il Sung sŏnjip.* Pyongyang: Foreign Languages Publishing House, 1965.
TK	*Tang ŭi konggohwa rŭl wihayŏ.* Pyongyang: Chosŏn Nodongdang Ch'ulp'ansa, 1951.
TU	*Chigŏp tongmaeng saŏp e taehayŏ.* Pyongyang: Chosŏn Nodongdang Ch'ulp'ansa, 1968.
UNF	*Choguk t'ongil e kwanhan widaehan suryŏng Kim Il Sung tongji ŭi munhŏn* (palch'wi). N.p.: Samhaksa, 1975.
WP (1, 2)	*On the Building of the Workers' Party of Korea,* 2 vols. Pyongyang: Foreign Languages Publishing House, 1978.
WSK	*Widaehan suryŏng Kim Il Sung tongji ŭi chungyo munhŏnjip.* N.p.: Samhaksa, 1975.
WW	*Yŏsŏng tongmaeng saŏp e taehayŏ.* Pyongyang: Chosŏn Nodongdang Ch'ulp'ansa, 1967.
WY	*On the Work with Children and Youth.* Pyongyang: Foreign Languages Publishing House, 1978.
YC	*Ch'ŏngsonyŏn saŏp e taehayŏ.* Pyongyang: Chosŏn Nodongdang Ch'ulp'ansa, 1966.
YOU	*The Youth Must Takeover the Revolution and Carry it Forward.* Pyongyang: Foreign Languages Publishing House, 1976.

Z (1, 2)   *Choguk ŭi t'ongil tongnip kwa minjuhwarŭl wihayŏ*, 2 vols. Chosŏn Nodongdang Ch'ulp'ansa, 1951; Kungnip Inmin Ch'ulp'ansa, 1949.

ZA   *Chosŏn minju chuŭi inmin konghwaguk surip ŭi kil.* Pyongyang: Pukchosŏn Inmin Wiwŏnhoe, 1947.

ZB   *Minju chuŭi inmin konghwaguk surip ŭl wihayŏ.* Pyongyang: Pukchosŏn Nodongdang Ch'ulp'ansa, 1948.

ZC   *Chuch'e sasang e taehayŏ.* Pyongyang: Chosŏn Nodongdang Ch'ulp'ansa, 1977.

ZD   *Yŏngwŏnhan ch'insŏn.* Pyongyang: Chosŏn Nodongdang Ch'ulp'ansa, 1959.

ZG   *On the Building of the People's Government.* Pyongyang: Foreign Languages Publishing House, 1978.

1930

June 30
The Path of Korean Revolution.

Report delivered at officers' meeting of the Communist Youth Group and the Anti-Imperialist Youth League held in Chialun.

> This report was made public for the first time in July 1978. Kim is supposed to have said that the Korean revolution must be carried out by Korean revolutionaries. He is also said to have stressed the importance of armed struggle against the Japanese. Kim was eighteen years old at this time. The report was delivered shortly after his release from jail in the spring of 1930.
>
> *CJC 1:* 1–11.
> *KP78.*

1931

May 20
Let Us Repudiate the "Left" Adventurist Line and Follow the Revolutionary Organizational Line.

Speech delivered at the meeting of party and young Communist league cadres held at Mingyüehkou, Yenchi County.

> Kim's condemnation of the May 30 riot in Chientao. He gives reasons for its failure and things the Communists must do in the future. There is every indication that Kim did not author this at the time stated, but at a much later date.
>
> *CJC 1:* 12–26.
> *EP73; DJOU 1:* 1–17; *KP72.*

December 16
On Organizing and Waging Armed Struggle Against Japanese Imperialism.

Speech delivered at the meeting of party and young Communist league cadres held at Mingyüehkou, Yenchi County.

> Kim discusses Marxism-Leninism freely and mentions incidents that occurred in Korea. Kim urges Korean youth to wage an armed struggle and to cooper-

ate with the Chinese. From the incidents mentioned and discussed in this article, it is unmistakable that Kim did not write this at the time stated.

CJC 1: 27–48.
EP73; DJOU 1: 18–43; WSK: 1–16; KP72.

1932

April 25
On the Founding of Anti-Japanese People's Guerrilla Army.

Speech delivered at the founding conference of the anti-Japanese people's guerrilla army.

Kim says that the Korean Revolutionary Army was organized in July 1930. He urges Koreans to fight against the Japanese in cooperation with the Chinese.

CJC 1: 49–58.
KP75; EP76.

1933

March 11
To Spread and Develop the Armed Struggle into Korea.

Speech at the meeting of chiefs and political workers of underground revolutionary organizations in the Onsŏng area.

Recounting the activities of the partisans for the past year, Kim speaks of difficult struggle. Kim also says that the founding of a Communist party is an urgent task.

CJC 1: 59–70.
EP76; KP75.

March 27
On the Tasks of Strengthening and Reforming the Work of the Communist Youth Groups.

Speech delivered at the Communist youth group meeting in Wangching.

This speech was made public for the first time in June 1978. Kim reviews the work of the past year and warns the members against extremists. He tells the members to organize more young people and enlarge the Communist youth groups. He also says that the members should strengthen their ideological work and recruit more members into the Juvenile Corps.

CJC 1: 71–85.
KP78.

May 10
Fight Factionalism and Strengthen the Unity of Revolutionary Ranks.

Kim explains in the first part of this article that factionalism originates from bourgeois individualism and points out its negative impact on the development of the Korean Communist movement. In the second part he analyzes the effects of factionalism and shows the way to combat it. He says that Communists must know the strategies and tactics of factionalists and should not compromise in dealing with them. In the last part, Kim says that all members of the Communist youth groups should be armed with revolutionary ideas and fight against factionalism.

CJC 1: 86–99.
KP78.

1935

March 27
On the Dissolution of Guerrilla Bases and Advance to Larger Areas.

Speech at the officers' meeting of the Korean People's Revolutionary Army held at Yaoyingkou.

This speech was made public for the first time in 1978. Kim says that the Minsaengdan Incident must be resolved to strengthen the army. In the second part of the speech, Kim says to abandon the guerrilla bases in northern Manchuria and advance to the border areas in the south.

CJC 1: 100–110.
KP78.

1936

February 27
The Tasks of Communists in the Strengthening and Development of the Anti-Japanese National Liberation Struggle.

Report at the meeting of the political and military cadres of the Korean People's Revolutionary Army in Nanhutao.

> Kim speaks on three subjects: moving the main force of the Korean People's Revolutionary Army to the border and expanding activities within Korea; strengthening the anti-Japanese National United Front; and preparing for the creation of a Communist party. Kim mentions the directives from the Comintern, and repudiates the Comintern advocacy of separate Chinese and Korean activities.

> CJC 1: 111–26.
> KP75; EP76.

May 5
The Great Ten-Point Platform and Declaration.

Platform and declaration of the Fatherland Restoration Association.

> Kim claims authorship of this platform, but there are difficulties in this claim. The platform itself advocates Korean autonomy in Manchuria and not a communist revolution. It is in general an anti-Japanese, not a communist, document. The declaration was made public for the first time in 1978. The original declaration was signed by O Sŏng-yun and two others and not by Kim. The original texts are available in Japanese in *Shisō ihō* (March 1938).

> CJC 1: 127–33.
> CHU 1: 1–2; DJOU 1: 44–45; RSC: 9–10; PPT: 1–2; ZG: 1–2; KP78; *Nodong sinmun*, June 2, 1978.

1937

March 29
Let Us Inspire the People with Hopes of National Liberation by Advancing with Large Forces into the Homeland.

Speech delivered at the conference of the military and political cadres of the Korean People's Revolutionary Army held at Hsikiang, Fusung County.

> A speech Kim is alleged to have made in preparation for guerrilla attacks on border towns in Korea from Manchuria. Kim details strategy, showing how the attack should be made in three directions. He also cautions the guerrillas to observe strict military regulations.

> CJC 1: 134–41.
> EP77.

June 1
Proclamation.

This is basically an anti-Japanese proclamation, but it is incredible to say in June 1937, as it does, that the Japanese were using Koreans to invade China (July 1937) on their way to World War II (December 1941).

CJC 1: 142.

June 4
Let Us Fight on Staunchly for the Liberation of the Fatherland.

Speech addressed to the People of Poch'ŏnbo.

A short speech that Kim is supposed to have made when he brought his troops to the Korean-Chinese border town of Poch'ŏnbo. He says that the people of the area should keep up the Korean spirit and help his men to fight against the Japanese. Kim identifies his troops as the Korean People's Revolutionary Army and says that they have been fighting for the past six to seven years in Manchuria.

CJC 1: 143–47.
EP77.

November 10
The Tasks of Korean Communists.

Treatise published in *Sŏgwang*, organ of the Korean People's Revolutionary Army.

Kim characterizes the Korean revolution at this stage as an anti-imperialist national liberation revolution and not a socialist or bourgeois revolution. He lists four immediate tasks of the Korean Communists: to wage armed struggle, to form a united front, to strengthen solidarity with the international revolutionary force, and to work toward establishing a Marxist-Leninist party.

CJC 1: 148–84.
EP72; DJOU 1: 46–89; *WSK:* 17–43; *KP71; ZG:* 3–40.

1939

April 3
Continuously Destroy the Japanese Imperialist Invaders by Positive Counterattacks and Let Us Advance to the Fatherland.

Speech at the officers' meeting of the Korean Revolutionary Army at Puktaejŏngja.

Kim speaks about the severe cold and the Japanese operation to suppress the revolutionary army during the winter of 1938. Kim urges his officers to fight on and advance to the fatherland.

CJC 1: 185–95.

May 20
Raise the Torch of Revolution in the Fatherland.

Speech at the officers' meeting of the Korean Revolutionary Army held at Paegaebong in the Musan Area.

This is a short speech about the infiltration of Kim's forces into Korea. Along with his speech on April 3, this speech appeared for the first time in 1979.

CJC 1: 196–200.
KP 79.

May 22
Let Us Positively Participate in the Anti-Japanese Struggle to Hasten the Fatherland Restoration.

Speech to the people of Sinsadong in the Musan Area.

Kim speaks to the people (mainly forestry workers) of Sinsadong, where his soldiers have infiltrated. He tells the people to fight against the Japanese. All these speeches in 1939 appeared for the first time in 1979.

CJC 1: 201–8.
KP79.

1940

August 10
On Preparing for the Great Event of National Liberation.

Report to the meeting of military and political cadres of the Korean People's Revolutionary Army held at Hsiaohaerhpaling, Tunhua County.

Recounts the reason for the change from large-scale struggle to a small-scale operation by the Communists in Manchuria. Kim says that an agent from the Comintern stated that the reason for such a small-scale operation was not to give Japan a pretext to attack Russia. The task of Korean Communists during this small-scale operation is to strengthen the political activities of the anti-

Japanese masses. He also discusses the German invasion of Poland and France. There is no doubt that this was written long after 1940, more likely in 1970.

CJC 1: 209–22.
KP75; EP76.

1943

September 15
The Korean Revolutionaries Must Know Korea Well.

Speech delivered to the political cadres and political instructors of the Korean People's Revolutionary Army.

Kim says that Koreans must know Korea well and reviews a little bit of Korean history. He repeats the tasks of the Korean revolutionaries, i.e., to strengthen the anti-Japanese united front and to establish a revolutionary base, and he speaks of the liberation of Korea and how the Koreans must be prepared for the day of victory. There is little doubt that this was written long after the war had ended.

CJC 1: 223–49.
EP73; DJOU 1: 90–118; *WSK:* 44–62; *KP71.*

1945

August 20
For the Construction of the Party, State, and Armed Forces in the Liberated Fatherland.

Speech to the military and political cadres.

Kim speaks of three great tasks: to build the party, the state, and the armed forces after the liberation of Korea. He even lists a political platform of thirteen articles and discusses various ways to consolidate liberated Korea. This article, along with others that appeared in the early 1970s which were supposed to have been written earlier, is so involved in arguments filled with hindsight that it is obvious that it was written in the 1970s. For example, there is almost no mention of the Russian liberation of Korea, U.S. imperialists are condemned (August of 1945?), the partisans from Manchuria are glorified, and other domestic Communists are condemned.

CJC 1: 250–68.
WSK: 63–76; *DJOU 1:* 117–40; *KP71; ZG:* 41–59.

September 20
Building a New Korea and the Task of Communists.

Speech to political workers being dispatched to rural areas.

> Several points are emphasized. These include the local bases for operation, preparation for the party, establishment of the people's committees, restoration of industries, and elimination of Japanese collaborators.

> *CJC 1:* 269–79.

October 3
On Progressive Democracy.

Lecture at the Pyongyang Worker-Peasant Political Institute.

> Progressive democracy is necessary in rebuilding Korea. Kim does not elaborate on what progressive democracy is. He goes into some detail in discussing special characteristics of "our" democracy, such as self-reliance, unity, freedom and equality, and peace. Kim speaks of the work needed to establish the people's political system.

> *CJC 1:* 280–303.
> *KP75; EP76; WSK:* 77–94; *ZG:* 60–82.

October 10
On the Establishment of a Marxist-Leninist Party in Our Country and the Tasks Confronting the Party.

Report at the founding congress of the Central Organization Committee of the North Korean Branch Bureau of the Korean Communist Party (NKBB-KCP).

> Kim speaks on three subjects. First is the need to organize a Central Organization Committee of the North Korean Communist Party. Kim says that because of the American imperialist occupation of the South a unified party of the North and South is not possible and one must be organized in the North first. Secondly, Kim speaks of the principle of the organization, condemning the factionalism and opportunism practiced by the old Communists and laying down strict democratic centralism and party rule. Thirdly, Kim enumerates the political line of the party: to form a national united front, to eliminate all pro-Japanese elements, to organize people's committees, and to enlarge the party to bring in the masses.

> *CJC 1:* 304–28.
> *WSK:* 95–112.

October 13
On the Building of New Korea and the National United Front.

Speech addressed to responsible functionaries of the provincial party committees.

> In the formation of the national united front, Kim says that all those who collaborated with the Japanese must be purged and all other groups, regardless of their class and affiliation, must form a united front. This article was clearly written after the Korean war and not any earlier. It appears for the first time in the second edition of Kim's selected works.
>
> *2SJ 1:* 1–10; *CJS 1:* 1–9; *SW 1:* 1–9; *CJC 1:* 329–38.
> *WSK:* 113–19; *PPT:* 3–12; *ZG:* 82–92.

October 13
Let Us Unite and Establish a Democratic New Korea.

Speech at a banquet arranged by representatives of Pyongyang city.

> Kim emphasizes the need to train national cadres through education and to build up the armed forces in Korea. He says that these tasks should be performed under the auspices of the Communist party, which had been established three days earlier.
>
> *CJC 1:* 339–45.

October 14
Every Effort for the Building of a New Democratic Korea.

Speech delivered at the Pyongyang Welcoming Mass Meeting.

> A short speech urging the people to work toward building a new nation, to establish a people's government, and to rehabilitate an independent economy. Material is heavily edited and first appeared in 1976.
>
> *CJC 1:* 346–53.
> *KP76; EP77; ZG:* 93–99.

October 16
Decision on the Land Question.

Adopted at the first enlarged plenum of the Central Organization Committee of the North Korean Branch Bureau of the Korean Communist Party.

> This is a ten-article document on land reform. Kim is the alleged author.
>
> *CJC 1:* 354–56.

October 17
On Publishing the Party Organ.

Speech to the propaganda workers of the Central Organization Committee of the North Korean Branch Bureau of the Korean Communist Party.

Under the current circumstances the party is unable to publish daily newspapers, and therefore the party should publish a party organ. Kim suggests that the name of the organ should be *Chŏngno*.

CJC 1: 357–60.

October 18
Our Task to Build a New Democratic Nation.

Speech at the welcoming party given by the People's Political Committee of P'yŏngan Namdo.

A short speech by Kim on three tasks: to end the bad habit of factionalism, to form a united front, and to promote friendly relationships with other countries.

2SJ 1: 11–14; CJC 1: 361–64.

October 25
International and Domestic Situations and the Task of Women.

Lecture delivered to women workers in Pyongyang.

Kim urges women to participate in the work of establishing the state and to educate themselves in order to improve their understanding of ideology.

CJC 1: 365–73.

October 29
On the Organization of the Democratic Youth League.

Concluding remarks at the democratic youth activists meeting.

The need to unify various youth organizations is emphasized. Kim says that the Communist Youth League and all young people in trade unions should be united in one youth organization, the Democratic Youth League. This is the only way to enlist many young people.

CJC 1: 374–82.

November 3
On the Establishment of a University.

Talk to educators.

> The current situation does not permit the creation of many colleges and schools, and therefore the available resources should be used to establish one university. Kim suggests an education reform, emphasizing nationalistic education instead of colonialist education.
>
> *CJC 1:* 383–87.

November 5
Talk with Nationalist Leaders.

> Kim tells nationalists not to criticize Communists but to cooperate with them to build a new Korea. He downgrades Japanese collaborators and expresses his anti-American sentiments.
>
> *CJC 1:* 388–93.

November 10
Let Us Overcome the Difficulties in Establishing the State.

Speech to the workers at Pyongyang railway factories.

> Kim asks the workers to complain less and work harder. The only way to overcome difficulties is to endure hardship and reconstruct industries.
>
> *CJC 1:* 394–401.

November 15
For the Establishment of a Government by the People.

Speech at the second enlarged plenum of the Central Organization Committee of the North Korean Branch Bureau of the Korean Communist Party (NKBB-2, KCP).

> Kim says that he cannot support the Korean People's Republic (established by Yŏ Un-hyŏng) in Seoul. He accuses the leaders of that group of being reactionaries. He advocates a united front and supports the effort to win the masses. He also mentions briefly land reform and the need to transform the Communist youth group into the Democratic Youth League.
>
> *CJC 1:* 402–11.

November 17
On the Establishment of Pyongyang Hagwŏn.

Talk to the workers of the Pyongyang Hagwŏn and local party leaders in selecting a site for the institute.

> The first military-political institute to train cadres will be Pyongyang Hagwŏn. It will be established in Chiulli. The purpose of the institute is to train cadres to staff the armed forces and help establish the state.

> *CJC 1:* 412–19.

November 17
Task of Intellectuals in Establishing the State.

Speech to teachers and intellectuals in Pyongyang.

> The primary task is to rid education of all remnants of Japanese imperialistic practices and thought. Kim urges the teachers to educate the masses in the Korean tradition and to heighten the political consciousness of the people.

> *CJC 1:* 420–27.

November 19
Task of South Korean Youth at the Present Time.

Speech to the South Korean youth workers.

> The basic message is to organize a national youth organization and stop factional struggles. Kim says South Korean youth should be educated and asks them not to castigate everyone as pro-Japanese, but to punish only those who collaborated with the Japanese.

> *CJC 1:* 428–37.

November 20
To the Workers of Inspection and Security Organizations in North Korea.

> No text available.

November 26
Patriotic Youths Unite under the Democratic Banner.

Speech to the democratic youth meeting of P'yŏngan Namdo.

> Kim repeats his call for the unity of all working youth, peasant youth, and students under the banner of the Democratic Youth League.

> *CJC 1:* 438–48.

November 27
Which Path Must Liberated Korea Take?

Speech at the Sinŭiju mass meeting.

> Liberated Korea must build a democratic, independent state. Kim condemns the rioters in Sinŭiju and Yongamp'o and calls for the unity of all people. He says in answer to a question that he is a Communist.
>
> *CJC 1:* 449–58.

November 29
Let Us Build an Air Force in New Korea.

Message to the Sinŭiju branch of the Korean Aeronautic Association.

> Kim accepts the presidency of the Korean Aeronautic Association and urges the members in the Sinŭiju branch to help Korea build an air force. He quotes Stalin by saying that an air force is his hawk.
>
> *CJC 1:* 459–64.

December 7
Students Should Positively Participate in the Building of a Democratic Fatherland.

Speech to a meeting of students and youth above the intermediate school in Pyongyang.

> Youth and students must have a correct understanding of the Communist party. Kim recognizes the first creation of the party in 1925 and its dissolution in 1928. He urges the students to participate in nation-building in the North.
>
> *CJC 1:* 465–75.

*December 17
On the Work of Organizations at All Levels of the Communist Party of North Korea.

Report to the third enlarged plenum of the North Korean Branch Bureau of the Korean Communist Party (NKBB-3, KCP).

> This is the first speech by Kim after his return to Korea that is recorded in the first edition of his selected works. He speaks of Stalin in great adulation and calls Lenin "our great leader," an appellation reserved only for himself in the North today. This phrase is, of course, omitted in subsequent editions of his work.
>
> *1SJ 1:* 1–18; *2SJ 1:* 15–28; *CSJ 1:* 10–21; *SW 1:* 10–22; *CJC 1:* 476–88. *TU:* 1–2 (excerpt).

December 18
For the Strengthening of the Party.

Concluding remarks at the third enlarged plenum of the North Korean Branch Bureau of the Korean Communist Party (NKBB-3, KCP).

> A six-point directive by Kim to strengthen the organization, to end factionalism, to strengthen party rule, to educate cadres, to improve communication, and to reorganize the Communist youth group into the Democratic Youth Group.
>
> *2SJ 1:* 29–30; *CJC 1:* 489–90.

December 20
To Hŏ Hŏn.

> This is a letter to Hŏ Hŏn in South Korea. Kim claims that Hŏ had sent him a letter asking for a meeting. He too wants to meet Hŏ, but under the circumstances, he is sending this letter. He decries factional struggles in the South, and asks Hŏ to work with good leaders such as Yŏ Un-hyŏng.
>
> *CJC 1:* 491–96.

December 22
On the Problems of the Democratic United Front.

Lecture at a political lecture series of the democratic youth organizations.

> Kim says that Korea's revolution is an anti-imperialist and antifeudal democratic revolution. He speaks of the united front advocated by the Comintern in 1935 and says all youth must have a correct understanding of the united front.
>
> *CJC 1:* 497–514.
> *WSK:* 120–32; *EP76.*

December 27
Task of the P'yŏngan Namdo Organizations.

Speech to the first representative meeting of the P'yŏngan Namdo branch of the Communist Party of North Korea.

> There are approximately forty-five hundred members of the party, and the major task is to train the rank-and-file members. He stresses ideological unity and organizational discipline. He also wants to strengthen the party identity-card distribution work.
>
> *CJC 1:* 515–24.

December 28

On Incorporation of the Student League into the Democratic Youth League.

Answer to questions from students and youth.

Kim urges all student league organizations to join the Democratic Youth League as one national organization to incorporate all students and youth. This article was reported in the first edition of Kim's selected works under the title, "On the Problem of Incorporating the Student League into the Democratic Youth League, the Only Youth Organization," and was issued on December 30, 1945.

CJC 1: 525–26.

December 29

Answers to Questions by Reporters of *Seoul Sinmun.*

This is a five-question interview. Reporters from *Seoul sinmun* ask Kim for his message to the South Korean people, his photograph, the record of his struggle against the Japanese, his scheduled visit to Seoul, and others.

CJC 1: 527–31.

1946

January 1

To the People of the Entire Nation in Greeting the New Year.

The first new year address by Kim. It is a short speech emphasizing the importance of the united front and acknowledging the trusteeship decision at the Moscow foreign ministers' meeting. However, he emphasizes that Korean problems should be solved by Koreans. The text appeared only in the first edition of the selected works.

1SJ 1: 21–23; *CJC 2:* 1–3.

January 5

The Result of Three Foreign Ministers' Conference and the Task of the Korean People.

Speech delivered at the Women's League.

No text available.

January 12
Let Us Fight for the Establishment of a Truly Democratic and Independent State.

Speech at a mass meeting in Haeju.

> Had there been a united and independent government shortly after liberation, the foreign ministers of three countries would not have made a decision like the one they made in Moscow in December 1945. Kim urges the people to support the decision (trusteeship) of the conference.
>
> *CJC* 2: 4–7.

January 13
On Strengthening the Party Rank and File and Lifting the Role of the Party.

Speech to the workers of Pongsan County Committee, Hwanghaedo, of the North Korean Branch Bureau of the Korean Communist Party.

> There are only seventy to eighty Communist party members in Pongsan County. Kim says to increase the membership by training new members. He also points out the importance of the party in establishing a new government.
>
> *CJC* 2: 8–17.

January 17
On the Founding of the North Korean Committee of the Democratic Youth League of Korea.

Speech delivered at the conference of representatives of North Korean democratic youth organizations.

> This is a speech congratulating the formation of the Democratic Youth League, incorporating the former Communist Youth League. It emphasizes elimination of the remnant of the Japanese imperialists' running dogs and the importance of cadre education and correct statistical works. Text in Korean first appeared in the second edition of Kim's works.
>
> *2SJ* 1: 33–36; *CJC* 2: 18–21.
> *YOU:* 1–4; *LSWY* 1: 3–6; *YC:* 3–6; *WY:* 3–6.

January 23
The People's Political Committee Should Become a True Political Organ of the People.

Speech delivered at the first enlarged plenum of P'yŏngan Namdo People's Political Committee.

This speech supports the Moscow decision for the trusteeship of Korea. Kim condemns Cho Man-sik for opposing the trusteeship.

2SJ 1: 37–39; *CJC 2:* 22–24.

*February 8
On the Present Political Situation in Korea and the Organization of the Provisional People's Committee of North Korea (NKPPC).

Report to a consultative meeting of representatives of the democratic political parties and social organizations, administrative bureaus, and people's committees of North Korea.

Describes the formation process of the Provisional People's Committee of North Korea and lists ten items as the immediate tasks of the committee. The text has been edited twice and the edited versions omit the reference to the approval of the formation of the committee by the Soviet occupation authorities.

1SJ 1: 24–37; *2SJ 1:* 40–48; *CSJ 1:* 22–29; *SW 1:* 23–31; *CJC 2:* 25–33.
LSWY 1: 7–15; *PPT:* 13–21; *ZA:* 4–14; *ZB:* 1–14; *Z 1:* 1–14; *ZG:* 100–109.

February 11
Talk with Yŏ Un-hyŏng, Chairman of the Korean People's Party.

This is a relatively lengthy talk by Kim and Yŏ, who visited Kim in Pyongyang. Kim says that he supports the activities of Yŏ in South Korea.

CJC 2: 34–42.

*February 15
Current State and the Tasks of the Party.

Report at the fourth enlarged plenum of the Central Organization Committee of the North Korean Branch Bureau of the Korean Communist Party (NKBB-4, KCP).

Kim reviews the status of the party and points out the difficulties of factionalism, particularly in Hamgyŏng Namdo and in the propaganda activities of the party organ, *Chŏngno*. During the second part of his speech, he presents nine tasks for the party, including the need to find a solution to the food shortage.

CJC 2: 43–58.

February 20
Speech at the First Session of the North Korean Provisional People's Committee.

Kim speaks about two things: the need to strengthen the work of the committee, and the need to produce pencils so that the people can study.

CJC 2: 59–69.

February 23
Congratulating the Opening of Pyongyang Hagwŏn.

The president and the responsible officers of the institute are all former members of the guerrilla force led by Kim. Kim tells the students to train well for the future of Korea.

CJC 2: 70–80.

February 27
Let Us Become a True People's Security Force.

Speech to the security officers of Pyongyang.

Kim says to fight against all kinds of reactionaries, such as pro-Japanese collaborators, capitalists, landlords, and pro-Americans. He also instructs the officers to arrest common criminals, particularly those who steal and slaughter cattle.

CJC 2: 81–89.

February 27
On Solving the Current Food Problem.

Speech at the second session of the North Korean Provisional People's Committee.

There are considerable shortages of rice and other food stuffs, and Kim says that the three-seven system of rent (30 percent to the landlord and 70 percent to the tenant) should be strictly observed. Equal distribution of rice should also be enforced in every province.

CJC 2: 90–95.

March 1
On the Twenty-seventh Anniversary of the March First Movement.

Speech delivered at the twenty-seventh anniversary celebration of the March First movement in P'yŏngan Namdo.

Kim says that the March First uprising was a failure because of the lack of organization, leadership, and support from the Soviet Union. He enumerates six tasks that confront the North and stresses that close ties must be maintained with the Soviet Union.

2SJ 1: 49–53; *JAP 1:* 5–10; *CJC 2:* 96–100.
ZA: 15–19; Z 1: 15–20.

March 5
The Land Reform Law of North Korea.

This is a seventeen-article land reform law. Kim claims to be the author.

CJC 2: 101–4.

March 6
Tasks of the Educational Sector.

Speech at the fourth session of the North Korean Provisional People's Committee.

Six points are stressed: (1) education of teachers, (2) elimination of reactionary elements, (3) assurance of adequate learning conditions, (4) producing graduates for society, (5) strengthening of educational organizations, and (6) establishing people's education.

CJC 2: 105–12.

March 7
Decision on Pro-Japanese Collaborators and National Traitors.

Decision adopted by the North Korean Provisional People's Committee. This is a fifteen-article decision defining Japanese collaborators and national traitors.

CJC 2: 113–14.

March 9
The Announcement of the Land Reform Laws Begins with the National Welfare.

A short thesis written at the time of the announcement of the land reform laws. Lists five tasks in support of the laws.

2SJ 1: 38–40; *CJC 2:* 115–17.

March 22
Restoration of Industries and the Task of Electrical Workers.

Speech to electrical workers.

The land reform has been accomplished and it is now time to concentrate efforts on the restoration of industries. Kim says that electricity is the basis of industrial development. Kim also warns the workers to look out for reactionary elements in factories.

CJC 2: 118–24.

March 23
Twenty-Point Platform.

Radio address before the establishment of Korean interim government.

Political platforms of the new government should include twenty points enumerated here.

SW 1: 32–34; *2SW 1:* 1–3; *1SJ 1:* 41–45; *2SJ 1:* 54–57; *CSJ 1:* 30–32; *JAP 1:* 11–15; *CJC 2:* 125–27.
PPT: 22–24; *CCY 50:* 38–39; *ZA:* 20–22; *ZB:* 47–51; *Z 1:* 21–24; *ZG:* 110–13.

April 1
On Efficient Management of the State Budget and the Creation of a Peasant Bank.

Speech at the fifth session of the North Korean Provisional People's Committee.

The first state budget was passed at this session. Kim speaks about the importance of tax collection and thrifty management of the budget. The need for a bank for peasants is also emphasized.

CJC 2: 128–35.

April 5
Congratulatory Message to the North Korean People's Teacher Union.

This is a short speech congratulating the teachers for organizing their union.

CJC 2: 136–38.

April 8
On Reforming Communication Work.

Concluding remarks at the sixth session of the North Korean Provisional People's Committee.

An audit of postal offices should be performed by April 20, and the committee should set a policy for communication work by May 1.

CJC 2: 139–44.

*April 10
The Results of the Agrarian Reform and Future Tasks.

Report to the sixth enlarged plenum of the North Korean Branch Bureau of the Korean Communist Party (NKBB-6, KCP).

Historical significance, procedure and results, experiences, and shortcomings of the land reform, stipulating future tasks of the party. This report appears in all editions of his works, but it has been heavily edited, and many references to the Soviet Union's role in liberating Korea have been deleted from the original text.

SW 1: 35–55; 2SW 1: 4–24; 1SJ 1: 46–85; 2SJ 1: 58–79; CSJ 1: 33–51; CJC 2: 145–66.
EP74; KP46; ZB: 15–46; ZG: 114–36.

April 13
On the Land Reform.

Report at the first enlarged plenum of the North Korean Provisional People's Committee (NKPPC-1).

Content is same as the speech made on April 10.

JAP 1: 16–25.
ZA: 23–24; Z 1: 25–34.

April 17
Let Us Become Labor Heroes in Building a New Korea.

Speech to the workers of Hŭngnam Fertilizer Company.

Kim encourages the workers to produce more and expresses his appreciation for their hard work.

CJC 2: 167–76.

April 20
The Path Trodden by Our Party and Several Current Tasks.

Speech delivered at the enlarged plenum of the Hamgyŏng Namdo party committee.

The party has done three things: supported the Moscow decision on trusteeship, organized the North Korean Interim People's Committee, and implemented land reform. Gives statistics on party membership (increase from 4,530 to more than 6,000 members) and emphasizes increased propaganda activities to implement the land reform, political training of party members, and strengthening of party activities.

2SJ 1: 80–88; CJC 2: 177–84.

April 21
On the Tasks of People's Organizations in Hamgyŏng Pukto.

Speech at the joint meeting of party and government workers in Hamyŏng Pukto.

Kim speaks about a number of problems in the region. More specifically, he tells the workers to strengthen the government and party organizations, to catch more fish, and so on.

CJC 2: 185–92.

April 25
The Newspaper is a Forerunner of the Times and a Maker of True Public Opinion.

Congratulatory message sent to P'yŏngnam branch office of *P'yŏngbuk sinbo.*

This is a short congratulatory message that says the mission of a newspaper in liberated Korea is important.

CJC 2: 193–94.

April 29
Be an Excellent Military-Political Cadre.

Speech to the first graduating class of Pyongyang Hagwŏn.

Kim urges the graduates to continue their studies even after graduation, to win over the masses, and to observe military rules and regulations.

CJC 2: 195–98.

May 1
May Day Address.

Kim recounts the origin of the May Day celebration and reviews the world situation during and after World War II. He gives great credit to the Soviet Union for the victory in Asia against Japan. He also reviews the international situation and proposes four tasks that confront the North.

JAP 1: 26–44; CJC 2; 199–203.
Z 1: 35–36.

May 5
To Dear Children of New Korea.

Letter to all children on children's day.

A short open letter to all children of the North on children's day.

CJC 2: 204–5.
LSWY 1: 16–17; *WY*: 7–8.

May 9
On the Future Tasks of the Women's League.

Speech to the women Communist workers who are to participate in the first conference of the Democratic Women's League of North Korea.

Kim elaborates on the task of the Communist women in the Democratic Women's League, urging them to join and become leaders of the Democratic Women's League.

CJC 2: 206–19.
KP72.

May 19
For the Democratic Development and Complete Independence of Our Country.

Speech at the Pyongyang mass rally.

Condemns the United States and Kim Ku, Syngman Rhee, and Cho Man-sik for the failure of the U.S.-U.S.S.R. Joint Commission meeting in Seoul. Appeals to North Koreans to support the Moscow decision, purge Kim Ku and Syngman Rhee, support the People's Committees, maintain the friendly relationship with the Soviet Union, support the twenty-point platform, develop industries and agriculture, and promote Korean culture.

1SJ 1: 86–95; *2SJ* 1: 89–95; *CJC* 2: 220–26.

May 21
Encouraging Remarks at the Start of Pot'ong River Works.

The river works along the Pot'ong are being built in order to prevent floods in Pyongyang. Kim says that Pyongyang is the democratic capital of Korea.

CJC 2: 227–30.

May 24
Culture and Arts Should Be for the People.

Speech at the meeting of artists, culturalists, and propagandists of the provincial people's committees, party, and social organizations of North Korea.

> Points out three errors of artists and proposes five detailed tasks for the artists. The text is heavily edited in later editions, eliminating several paragraphs in reference to the Soviet and Chinese examples. The title is also changed in later editions to read "Culturalists should become Fighters in the Cultural Front."

> *1SJ 1*: 96–104; *2SJ 1*: 96–101; *CJC 2*: 231–35.
> *KP56*: Z *1*: 57–66.

May 30
Duty of the Youth in Building Democratic Korea.

Speech at the meeting of chairmen of provincial committees of the Democratic Youth League.

> Nine-point duty is given to the leaders of youth organizations. In the second edition, the ninth point was replaced with two new points, making it a ten-point duty.

> *1SJ 1*: 105–12; *2SJ 1*: 102–7; *JAP 1*: 45–50; *CJC 2*: 236–41.
> *YOU*: 5–10; *YC*: 7–12; *LSWY 1*: 18–23; *ZA*: 55–60; *Z 1*: 67–74; *WY*: 9–14.

June 3
The Central Party School is a Communist College that Educates Party Cadres.

Speech at the opening of the Central Party School.

> There are fewer than five hundred cadres, far short of the number needed. Kim tells the new students that their education period will be about two months, and that they must learn about the united front policy. Kim also says that it is wrong for trade unions to strike against the state.

> *CJC 2*: 242–57.

June 4
The Newspaper, *Minju Chosŏn*, Should Become the Correct Guide in Building a New Korea.

Congratulatory message sent to the newspaper, *Minju Chosŏn*.

This is a brief message, offering congratulations on the founding of the paper. *Minju Chosŏn* was issued as the organ of the North Korean Provisional People's Committee.

CJC 2: 258–60.

**June 20*
On the Draft of the Labor Law.

Report to the enlarged session of the Provisional People's Committee of North Korea.

A new labor law that fits the situation of Korea. Emphasizes that the proclamation of such a law is possible because of the occupation of the great Soviet armed forces in North Korea.

SW 1: 56–67; *2SW 1*: 25–36; *1SJ 1*: 113–27; *2SJ 1*: 108–20; *CSJ 1*: 52–62; *JAP 1*: 51–63; *CJC 2*: 261–72.
TU: 3–15; *ZA*: 61–73; *ZB*: 53–68; *Z 1*: 75–88.

June 24
Labor Laws on Workers and Office Workers in North Korea.

This was issued by the North Korean Provisional People's Committee and has twenty-six articles.

CJC 2: 273–79.

June 26
Let Us Enlarge and Strengthen the Democratic Forces.

Congratulatory message to the first congress of the Korean People's Party.

Kim speaks about three things: (1) unity of the democratic forces, (2) work on the democratic tasks, and (3) strengthening of the united front. Kim congratulates the members of the congress.

CJC 2: 280–82.

July 1
Democratic Cadres are the Pillars in Building a New Korea.

Speech at the opening ceremony of the Central Higher Cadres School.

Kim reemphasizes the need of more cadres at all levels of the government and the party. He gives instructions to students as well as teachers, telling the teachers to instruct students at a lower level so they can be easily understood.

CJC 2: 283–92.

July 7
Open Letter to Railway Workers.

The reasons for the mismanagement of the railways are lack of patriotism, nonobservance of labor regulations, and sabotage by remnants of the Japanese collaborators who still work for the railways. In the future, railway workers are strictly to observe labor regulations, to preserve state property, to learn railway operation techniques, and to become responsible railway workers.

CJC 2: 293–97.

July 21
To Celebrate the Completion of Pot'ong River Works.

Speech at the meeting to celebrate the completion of the Pot'ong River Works.

Many people contributed many hours of voluntary labor to complete the work on the banks of this river that runs through Pyongyang. Kim congratulates all those mobilized for this task.

CJC 2: 298–304.
Z 1: 99–106; ZA: 82–88.

July 22
On the Formation of the Democratic National United Front Committee.

Report to the meeting of the representatives of social organizations and political parties in North Korea.

Advocates the formation of a united front of all social and political organizations of the North.

1SJ 1: 128–37; 2SJ 1: 121–28; JAP 1: 64–71; CJC 2: 305–12.
LSWY 1: 24–31; ZA: 74–81; ZB: 69–80.

July 27
Report by Kim Il Sung at the Eighth Enlarged Plenum of the North Korean Branch Bureau of the Korean Communist Party (NKBB-8, KCP).

No text available.

*July 29
Present Political Situation and Our New Duties.

Speech at the joint enlarged meeting of the central committees of the North Korean Branch Bureau of the Korean Communist Party and the New People's Party of Korea.

This speech seems to be an important one, but it was made available for the first time only in 1979, and much of the text seems heavily edited to fit the party posture of the 1970s. Kim says that essential agreement to unite the two parties has been reached, and he urges both parties to refrain from factional struggles and to enhance the Democratic National United Front. On an entirely different subject (which is very strong evidence of deletion), Kim enumerates the tasks confronting the people of North Korea. He says that everyone down to the county level should support the Democratic National United Front, and he also speaks about the need to build a university in the North. Similarly, he says that the people must solve the basic food problems and all industries in the North should be nationalized.

CJC 2: 313–26.

July 30
Law on the Equality of Sexes in North Korea.

This is a decision of the North Korean Provisional People's Committee. There are nine articles.

CJC 2: 327–28.

August 5
Become a Revolutionary Fighter to Protect the Position and Ideology of the Party.

Speech at the first graduation ceremony of the Central Party School.

Refers to Syngman Rhee's provocation of a fratricidal war. Urges the graduates to work with the people. Appeared for the first time in the second edition of his work.

2SJ 2: 129–34; *CJC* 2: 329–34.

August 8
Musicians Should Contribute to the Building of a New Democratic Korea.

Speech to musicians after their performance commemorating the creation of the Central Symphony.

This is a short speech, congratulating the musicians on their performance.

CJC 2: 335–37.

August 10
Nationalization of Major Industries; The Foundation for Building an Independent, Sovereign State.

Speech delivered at the Pyongyang city mass rally held in support of the Laws on Nationalization of Industries.

In the original text this speech is said to have been delivered at the twelfth session of the Provisional People's Committee of North Korea. Although it is an identical text, the original title is "On the Promulgation of Laws concerning the Nationalization of Industries, Rail Transportation, Communication and Banks." On the occasion of the nationalization measure, Kim compares the plundering of natural resources in the South by the United States and the American practice of utilizing the remnants of Japanese cronies in the South.

SW 1: 68–73; *2SW 1:* 37–42; *1SJ 1:* 138–46; *2SJ 1:* 135–41; *CSJ 1:* 63–68; *JAP 1:* 112–18; *CJC 2:* 340–46.
EP73; ZA: 89–95; *ZB:* 81–90; *Z 1:* 107–14; *ZG:* 137–43.

August 15
Report Commemorating the First Anniversary of August 15 Liberation.

Address at the celebration rally of the first anniversary of the August 15 liberation in Pyongyang.

This is the first long speech, and it is divided into four sections. First is the recounting of the sufferings under the Japanese for thirty-six years; second is the victorious marching of the Soviet Red army against fascism; the third is the development of victorious measures in the North; and the fourth is about American exploitation and the sufferings in the South.

1SJ 1: 147–81; *2SJ 1:* 142–66; *JAP 1:* 119–48; *CJC 2:* 347–65.
KP47; ZA: 96–123; *ZB:* 91–124; *Z 1:* 115–46.

*August 29
For the Establishment of a United Party of the Working Masses.

Report to the founding congress of the Workers' Party of North Korea (1 WPK).

The report consists of four major aspects: (1) analysis of the political situation in Korea, (2) emphasis on the Democratic National United Front, (3) accounts of the coalition of the Sinmindang and the Communist party to found the Workers' Party, (4) and the tasks confronting the party. There is an original text of this speech in a pamphlet published shortly after the congress, and it has been edited four times in the successive editions of Kim's work, but the basic message and content of the report remain intact.

There are short concluding remarks by Kim, answering some questions raised during the discussion. The task confronting the Workers' Party is to realize complete democratic independence of Korea, and in order to attain such independence, the party must strengthen the revolutionary base in the North and help accomplish similar democratic reforms in the South. Kim also speaks of the united front, the youth organizations, agricultural tax-in-kind, and social organization. All Communists in the North must consolidate their strength in the mass party, the Workers' Party of North Korea. In the South, such a coalition mass party is being formed under the leadership of Yŏ Un-hyŏng. See the original text in Korean in a pamphlet entitled *Pukchosŏn nodongdang ch'angnip taehoe* (Founding Congress of the Workers' Party of North Korea). The text of the concluding remarks is in *Pukchosŏn nodongdang ch'angnip taehoe*, pp. 34–39.

1SJ 1: 182–200; *2SJ 1:* 167–82; *CSJ 1:* 69–82; *2SW 1:* 43–57; *SW 1:* 74–89; *JAP 1:* 72–87; *JAP 1:* 88–96; *CJC 2:* 366–94.
KP46; TK: 1–28.

September 6
Congratulations on the Publication of the Magazine, *Chosŏn Yŏsŏng.*

This is the first women's magazine to be published in the North, and Kim says that there are more than six hundred thousand members in the Women's League.

CJC 2: 395–97.

September 9
On the Results of the Founding Congress of the Workers' Party of North Korea.

Speech delivered at a meeting of the activists of the party organization of P'yŏngan Namdo.

Points out five reasons for success of the coalition and four shortcomings. Suggests six tasks confronting the party.

SW 1: 90–101; *1SJ 1:* 201–16; *2SJ 1:* 183–95; *CSJ 1:* 83–94; *JAP 1:* 97–111; *CJC 2:* 398–409.

September 15
To Be a Worker Devoted to the Democratic Nation-Building.

Address at the inaugural ceremony of Kim Il Sung University.

A short address emphasizing the building of Korean leaders for Korean nation-building.

1SJ 1: 217–19; *CJC 2:* 410–12.

September 18
Expose and Destroy the Reactionary Maneuvers of American Imperialists.

Concluding remarks at the sixth session of the Central Committee of the Democratic National United Front, North Korea.

This is a strong anti-American speech. Kim says that the Americans in the South are revealing their true intentions.

CJC 2: 413–17.

September 25
On the Election of the People's Committee.

Report at the second enlarged plenum of the Central Committee of the Workers' Party of North Korea (1WPK-2CC).

This speech was made public for the first time in 1979. It deals with the election of November 3, 1946, and it seems heavily edited. Kim speaks about three things: the significance of the election, the progressive election system, and the duty of party members. All citizens twenty years or older are eligible to vote and an electoral district consists of five hundred to one thousand voters.

CJC 2: 418–29.

September 26
On the Establishment of the Workers' Party of North Korea and the Question of Founding the Workers' Party of South Korea.

Reviews the development of the North and the South. Praises the North and condemns the reactionary elements in the South who oppose the coalition of three parties (Sinmindang, Inmindang, and Kongsandang) to found the Workers' Party of South Korea. Revised and edited, later version eliminates the reference to the fact that in the North, membership of the party has increased thirty thousand in one month.

SW 1: 102–20; *1SJ 1*: 220–50; *2SJ 1*: 196–214; *CSJ 1*: 95–111; *CJC 2*: 430–48.
KP55.

September 27
On Composing the National Anthem and Marching Songs of the People's Army.

Talk to the composers.

Kim speaks about composing a new national anthem and marching songs for the People's Army.

CJC 2: 449–52.

September 28

Tasks of the Learned and the Present Stage of Democratic Construction.

Speech at a joint meeting of the workers in the propaganda and culture sections of political and social organizations and People's Committees of all provinces of the North.

Kim speaks about six tasks, including illiteracy, education, participation in the People's Committees, and opposition to the American military occupation of the South.

CJC 2: 453–61.
Z 1: 147–60.

September 29

Task of Democratic Youth Organizations for Enlarging and Strengthening the Democratic Forces.

Speech at the second congress of the Democratic Youth League of North Korea.

Short speech emphasizing the coalition of all social organizations, strengthening the democratic base in the North, and calling for the support of youth in the South.

2SJ 1: 215–19; *CJC 2:* 462–66.
YOU: 11–15; *LSWY 1:* 32–36; *YC:* 13–17; *WY:* 15–19.

October 6

For the Popularization of Athletics.

A short speech emphasizing the popularization of athletic games. Kim spoke at an athletic meet in the North.

2SJ 1: 220–23; *CJC 2:* 467–70.
TU: 16–19; *LSWY 1:* 37–40; *WY:* 20–23.

October 7

For the Establishment of a Revolutionary Army.

Talk with soldiers of the first class of the security cadres training center.

The need to eliminate all Japanese collaborators is reemphasized, and the need to improve military-civilian relations is also recognized.

CJC 2: 471–78.

October 10
Let Us Strengthen the Foundation for the Construction of a Democratic Korea.

Speech at a mass meeting in Sakchu County, P'yŏngan Pukto.

> Kim is here to inspect dams on the Yalu River that will be used to electrify the North. He advocates national unity and a strong economic foundation and issues a warning against reactionary elements.
>
> *CJC* 2: 479–86.

October 10
Answers to Questions Raised by a Reporter of *Minju Chosŏn.*

> This is a brief three-question interview. The first deals with the November election; the second deals with religion. Kim says that there is freedom of religion in the North, but no religion is allowed that opposes the national policy of the state. He says that all missionaries are spies. The third question deals with his reasons for coming to Sakchu County and the Sup'ung Dam.
>
> *CJC* 2: 487–91.

October 18
On the Tasks of Scientists and Technicians of the Present Day.

Speech delivered at a meeting of scientists and technicians.

> A short three-point speech emphasizing the services of scientists and technicians to economic development, education of new scientists, and political training of scientists.
>
> *2SJ* 1: 224–29; *CJC* 2: 492–97.
> *SS:* 1–6.

October 29
Strengthen State Regulations and Establish a Central Bank in North Korea.

Concluding remarks at the eighteenth session of the North Korean Provisional People's Committee.

> Basically two different subjects are dealt with here. The first is the need to upgrade the service of state functionaries, and the second is the need to create a central bank in the North.
>
> *CJC* 2: 498–506.

October 31

Let Us Persevere in All Adverse Situations and Develop Railway Transportation.

Speech at the third meeting of bureau directors and section chiefs of the Transportation Bureau.

> The content of this speech is very similar to his open letter of July 7, 1946, to railway workers.
>
> *CJC 2:* 507–12.

November 1

On the Eve of the Historic Democratic Election.

Speech delivered at a celebration of the democratic election at Pyongyang.

> Stresses everyone's participation in the November 3 election. Urges the participation of monks, ministers, and women and assures that there is freedom of religion in the North. Those who do not participate in the election on religious grounds are spies and traitors. That portion about freedom of religion was added in the second edition.
>
> *SW 1:* 121–31; *1SJ 1:* 251–66; *2SJ 1:* 230–41; *CSJ 1:* 112–22; *CJC 2:* 513–24. *PPT:* 25–36; *ZA:* 124–36; *ZB:* 125–42; *Z 1:* 161–76; *ZG:* 144–55.

November 13

On Strengthening the Role of People's Committee Members.

Speech at the thirtieth meeting of the P'yŏngan Namdo People's Committee.

> Kim tells the members of the local People's Committee to strengthen the effort to collect tax-in-kind, to help develop industries, and to uproot the remaining Japanese collaborators.
>
> *CJC 2:* 525–34.

November 20

Task Confronting the Workers in Prosecuting and Security Organizations.

Speech at a joint meeting of provincial prosecutors-general and heads of security organizations.

> Urges protection of nation-building efforts of the Korean people and the protection of human rights. Points out six tasks for the workers in the field.
>
> *2SJ 1:* 242–48; *CJC 2:* 535–41.

November 25
Results of the Democratic Election and the Task of the People's Committee.

Speech at the third enlarged plenum of the Provisional People's Committee of North Korea (NKPPC-3).

> Gives statistics of the voting results and composition of the 3,459-member committee. Enumerates eight-point task of the People's Committee.
>
> *1SJ 1:* 267–92; *2SJ 1:* 249–68; *JAP 1:* 149–69; *CJC 2:* 542–60.
> *PPT:* 35–56; *KP47;* *ZA:* 137–57; *ZB:* 143–70; *Z 1:* 177–202; *ZG:* 156–73.

December 2
Report of Kim Il Sung to the Fourteenth Session of the Standing Committee of the Central Committee (1WPK-3CC-14SC).

> No text available.

December 3
For the Planned Supervision and Management of State Enterprises.

Speech at the meeting of directors of industries of provincial People's Committees and managers of state enterprises.

> Points out three basic difficulties of the economy: the past experience of colonial economy, the lack of technicians and skilled workers, and the lack of capital.
>
> *2SJ 1:* 269–76; *CJC 2:* 561–67.
> *SKKM 1:* 1–8.

December 5
On the Establishment of the North Korean News Agency.

> Speech at the Standing Committee of the North Korean Provisional People's Committee. Kim tells the workers of the agency to report state activities to the people.
>
> *CJC 2:* 568–72.

December 13
To One Million Koreans in Japan.

Open letter to Korean residents in Japan.

> This is a short letter urging the Korean residents in Japan to support North Korean efforts to build a state.
>
> *CJC 2:* 575–77.

December 13
To Comrade Kim Che-wŏn and Farmers of Chaeryŏng County, Hwang-haedo.

In praise of Kim Che-wŏn, who contributed thirty bushels of rice to the government.

1SJ 1: 293–94; *CJC 1:* 573–74.

December 26
On the Tasks Confronting the Democratic United Front of Today.

Speech at the eighth Central Committee meeting of the Democratic United Front.

Basically three (four in the first edition) points: (1) to strengthen the united front, (2) mass mobilization for nation-building, and (3) purchase of grains and distribution of food. Edited for the second edition.

1SJ 1: 295–304; *2SJ 1:* 277–85; *CJC 2:* 578–86.
TU: 20–22 (excerpt).

1947

January 1
To the People of the Entire Nation in Greeting the New Year.

Reassesses the achievements of the past year and proposes eight-point task for the new year. Second edition's title reflects the content of the speech, "strengthen the victories already won, and for the winning of new victories."

1SJ 1: 305–13; *2SJ 1:* 286–93; *CJC 3:* 1–8.
ZA: 158–65; *Z 1:* 203–14.

January 11
To Assure the Successful Election of Village and *Ri* People's Committee Members.

Concluding remarks at the Central Committee of the Democratic National United Front of North Korea.

Kim speaks about the details of local election procedures, including nomination methods. He also wants many women to be nominated.

CJC 3: 9–18.

January 15
Tasks of the Security Cadres Training Center.

Speech at the second meeting of officers of the Security Cadres Training Center.

> Three educational goals are emphasized: indoctrination in political thought, training in military techniques, and revolutionary unity among cadres.

> *CJC* 3. 19–29.

January 17
Reforming and Strengthening the Hamgyŏng Pukto Party Organizations.

Speech at the nineteenth Standing Committee meeting of the Hamgyŏng Pukto Committee of the Workers' Party of North Korea.

> The Hamgyŏng Pukto Provincial Party Committee is strongly reprimanded for not following the directives of the Central Committee. Kim charges that the leaders of the provincial party organizations practiced localism. He also cautions them about their cadre training work and the need to reissue party identity cards.

> *CJC* 3: 30–41.

January 18
Tasks of the Kangwŏndo Party Organizations.

Speech at the joint meeting of party activists from Wŏnsan and Kangwŏndo.

> Kim cautions that factionalists still exist in Kangwŏndo. He repeats his usual warnings and asks them to help build unity in the party.

> *CJC* 3: 42–49.

January 20
To Comrade Kim Hoe-il and All Chŏngju Railway Workers.

> Praising the workers and Kim Hoe-il of Chŏngju Railway.

> *ISJ* 1: 314–15; *CJC* 3: 50.

February 3
Report on the Policy of Strengthening and Democratizing the Powers of the People's Committees at Every Level.

Speech at the tenth Central Committee meeting of the Democratic National United Front.

> No text available.

February 7
Shortcomings of the P'yŏngan Pukto Party Organization and Several Tasks Confronting Us.

Speech at the Standing Committee, Central Committee of the Workers' Party of North Korea.

> Kim points out several shortcomings of the party cadres in P'yŏngan Pukto without really spelling out who or in what way. He tells them to be more diligent in their inspections, to instill patriotism, to lighten the burden of the people, and to correct mistakes in grain purchasing.

> *CJC 3:* 51–60.

February 8
Present Political Situation of Korea.

Report at the first anniversary of the founding of the North Korean Provisional People's Committee.

> Kim says that the people have made significant progress during the year and this is due to (1) the Russian occupation of the North, (2) the power of the people, (3) the support of the people, and (4) the united front of the people. Kim reviews the work of the Provisional People's Committee and compares it with developments in the South. Kim concludes the talk with discussion of the task of the Provisional People's Committee in the democratic construction in North Korea.

> *CJC 3:* 61–88.
> *KP47; Z 3:* 171–208; *Z 1:* 215–50.

*February 19
Report on the 1947 People's Economic Development in North Korea.

Report to the meeting of provincial, city, and county People's Committees of North Korea.

> The first extensive report on the economic development plan of North Korea. Extensive economic statistics on industries, production, coal, transportation, manufacturing, business, education, local industries, and others. A large portion dealing with Russian aid to the North is deleted in the second edition.

> *1SJ 1:* 316–54; *2SJ 1:* 294–314; *JAP 1:* 170–97; *CJC 3:* 89–108.
> *SKKM 1:* 9–28; *ZA:* 166–94; *ZB:* 209–48; *Z 1:* 251–89.

February 20
Concluding the Congress of the Provincial, City, and County People's Committees of North Korea.

Concluding remarks at a congress of the provincial, city, and county People's Committees of North Korea.

A short concluding speech. This in itself is less important than the more-revealing speech on the 1947 economic plan (1947/2/19).

SW 1: 132-36; 1SJ 1: 355-62; 2SJ 1: 315-19; CSJ 1: 123-27; JAP 1: 198-205; CJC 3: 109-13.
CHU 1: 3-7; DJOU 1: 141-46; PPT: 57-61; ZA: 195-210; ZB: 249-58; Z 1: 289-96; ZG: 174-78.

February 21
Report on the Works of the North Korean Provisional People's Committee.

Report at the first session of the People's Assembly of North Korea (PANK-1).

Commemorating the establishment of the People's Assembly of North Korea. Points out four tasks of the Provisional People's Committee: (1) land reform, (2) restoration of factories and transportation, (3) reform of people's education, and (4) purge of pro-Japanese elements and strengthening of the People's Committees. Some statistical information.

1SJ 1: 363-73; CJC 3: 114-22.
ZB: 259-70; Z 1: 297-308.

February 24
Tasks of the North Korean People's Committee.

Speech at the twenty-fifth meeting of the North Korean People's Committee.

Every bureau of the committee should do its utmost to carry out party directives. Kim repeats his usual three tasks: ideological unity, propaganda activities, and the elimination of reactionaries.

CJC 3: 123-31.

February 28
For the Efficient Administration of State Finances.

Speech delivered at the joint conference of chiefs of provincial departments and city and county financial sections and directors of the customs houses.

In this speech Kim urges the workers in the field of financial and customs affairs to be effective in their work and to be thrifty with the state treasury. He emphasizes seven points: (1) to observe strict financial discipline, (2) to strengthen checking procedures, (3) to put no other burden than taxes on the people, (4) to improve the operation of state customs houses and the tariff system, (5) to work toward the fulfillment of the 1947 economic plan, (6) to show the spirit of nation-building in the North, and (7) to become a true servant of the people.

CJC 3: 132–48.
EP77.

March 5
On the First Anniversary of the Land Reform.

This is a brief remark about the land reform on its first anniversary. Kim says that 981,390 *chŏngbo* of land were distributed to 725,000 households.

CJC 3: 149–50.
Z 1: 309–10.

March 8
Basic Task of the Farmer is to Be a Good Farmer.

Talk with farm representatives of Sinch'ŏn County, P'yŏngan Pukto.

This is a general speech encouraging farmers to produce more and be thrifty.

CJC 3: 151–55.

*March 15
On the Elimination of Shortcomings and Errors in the Work of Some Party Organizations.

Report at the sixth session of the Central Committee of the Workers' Party of Korea (1WPK-6CC).

This text seems to be heavily edited; it appeared for the first time in 1979. Kim speaks about eight shortcomings in a number of party organizations and also points out six errors. Kim repeats his emphasis on strengthening the Democratic National United Front and tells the leaders of the party to practice criticism and self-criticism. There are also concluding remarks about reforming the style of leadership, the 1947 economic plan, and criticism of the O Ki-sŏp line on trade unions.

CJC 3: 156–88.

March 22

The Election Result of the People's Committee and the Future Tasks.

Speech at the thirtieth session of the North Korean People's Committee.

Kim gives statistics and percentages of participation in the election. Voter participation was around 99 percent in local and national elections. Kim also elaborates on the tasks of the People's Committee: (1) to mobilize the people to achieve the goals of the 1947 economic plan, (2) to increase production, (3) to organize competition, (4) to upgrade the educational and cultural life of the workers, and (5) to acquire technology.

CJC 3: 189–201.
ZA: 211–21; ZB: 271–86; Z 1: 311–24.

April 6

Let Us Develop Reforestation Work into an All Mass Movement.

Talk with participants in the reforestation work in Moksubong.

Kim says that there is no need to pray to God for rain. It is more productive to mobilize the workers to water the trees. Kim wants the people to plant more trees.

CJC 3: 202–207.

April 8

To Raise the Standard of Government Workers.

Speech at the thirty-second meeting of the North Korean People's Committee.

A number of areas where government workers were doing inadequate jobs are put forward. These include the relocation of landlords and the operation of consumer goods distribution centers.

CJC 3: 208–13.

April 14

To Strengthen Transportation.

Speech at the thirty-third meeting of the North Korean People's Committee.

This speech concerns transportation, particularly cargo transportation, both in trucks and on railways. Inspection work in transportation is emphasized.

CJC 3: 214–21.

April 19
Speech to the Workers of Pyongyang Koksan Factory.

Pyongyang Koksan factory is apparently a place where daily necessities are manufactured. Kim tells the workers to work hard and recognize the importance of their work.

CJC 3: 222–28.

April 25
Duties of the Central Security Cadres School.

Talk with teachers and students of the Central Security Cadres School.

Kim inspects the school and tells the students to observe school regulations, to practice shooting, to handle arms properly, and to love their country.

CJC 3: 229–40.

April 26
On Efficient Farm Management and Reform in Government Organizations.

Concluding remarks at the thirty-fourth meeting of the North Korean People's Committee.

Two topics are dealt with: the management of the spring planting and the need to improve the quality of leadership in local government organizations.

CJC 3: 241–58.

April 30
Become a True Artist-Soldier in the Revolutionary Army.

Talk with leaders and actors of the band of the security cadre battalion.

This is a short pep talk to actors and members of the band to do a good job in order to boost the morale of soldiers.

CJC 3: 259–64.

May 5
Talk with Representatives of the Students and Youth of Pyongyang.

This is the second children's day after the liberation of Korea, and Kim speaks to youngsters about their future in the North.

CJC 3: 265–66.

May 12
Let Us Meet the Goals of the 1947 People's Economic Plan.

Concluding remarks at the thirty-sixth meeting of the North Korean People's Committee.

> Kim points out a number of shortcomings in planning, inspection, mobilization of laborers, and farm management. He orders the committee to eliminate moves of workers from one locale to another.
>
> *CJC* 3: 267–81.

May 21
To Strengthen Public Health Work.

Concluding remarks at the thirty-seventh meeting of the North Korean People's Committee.

> Kim emphasizes the importance of immunization in keeping the workers healthy.
>
> *CJC* 3: 282–90.

May 21
In Connection with the Reopening of the U.S.-U.S.S.R. Joint Commission, the Attitude of the Democratic National United Front of North Korea and the Path of the People.

At the fourteenth Central Committee of the Democratic National United Front.

> No text available.

May 29
On Reforming and Strengthening Broadcasting.

Concluding remarks at the Standing Committee of the Central Committee of the Workers' Party of North Korea.

> Kim points out several shortcomings in broadcasting and says to improve the party leadership there. He also briefly mentions the railway problems.
>
> *CJC* 3: 291–97.

June 7
Let Us Become a Good Party Worker of the Party and the People.

Speech at the first anniversary of the Central Party School.

The school was established on June 1, 1946, and this is the first anniversary. Kim tells the students to strengthen the Democratic National United Front.

CJC 3: 298–303.

June 14
What Every Political Party and Social Organization Must Demand on the Establishment of Democratic Interim Government of Korea.

Speech at the mass meeting of every political party under the Democratic National United Front.

In the wake of renewed negotiations between the United States and the U.S.S.R. on the fate of Korea, Kim enumerates political principles for a new interim government in eight categories.

1SJ 1: 374–95; *2SJ 1:* 320–36; *JAP 1:* 206–22; *CJC 3:* 304–20.
PPT: 62–77; *LSWY 1:* 41–56; *KP47;* ZA: 222–40; *ZB:* 287–312; *Z 1:* 325–48; *ZG:* 179–94.

June 20
Firmly Establish the Law and Order of the State and Strengthen Cadre Education Work.

Concluding remarks at the fortieth meeting of the North Korean People's Committee.

Kim speaks about the selection of leaders as well as the work of various judicial organs, prosecutors, and judges. He also mentions the education of judicial workers.

CJC 3: 321–32.

June 23
To the Korean Youth Before the Establishment of the Democratic Interim Government.

Speech at an athletic meet in celebration of sending representatives to the world youth meeting.

In the second edition, the title was changed to "Future Korea Belongs to the Youth." Encourages youth to be active in the construction of New Korea and compares the condition of the youth of the North and the South. Representatives were going to Prague to participate in the World Youth Congress.

1SJ 1: 396–409; *2SJ 1:* 337–46; *CJC 3:* 333–41.
YOU: 16–24; *LSWY 1:* 57–65; *YC:* 18–27; *WY:* 24–32; *ZA:* 241–51; *ZB:* 313–28; *Z 1:* 349–62.

July 4
Talk with Teachers and Students of the Second Pyongyang Elementary School.

Kim visited this school on his own and tells the students to study hard. He tells them about the future compulsory education system in the North.

CJC 3: 342–47.

July 21
Address to the Graduates of Colleges and Technical Schools.

Kim, addressing 130,000 graduates of all institutes of higher learning in the North, projects that in the future the people should get education at the expense of the government. Generally encouraging words for the graduates.

JAP 1: 223–32; *CJC 3:* 348–57.
LSWY 1: 66–75; *WY:* 33–42; *ZA:* 252–62; *Z 1:* 363–76.

July 31
On the Strengthening of Leadership in the Factory Party Organization on Production.

Concluding remarks at the Standing Committee of the Central Committee of the Workers' Party of North Korea.

These remarks are a discussion of Hwanghae Steel Mill. Kim says there are eight thousand steel workers in the mill, and the party should strengthen its leadership there.

CJC 3: 358–63.

August 1
Directives at the Third Graduation Ceremony of the Six-Month Group, Central Party School.

Kim tells the graduates to strive for four goals: (1) to work with the people, (2) to guard the party, (3) to practice what they have learned, and (4) to educate the people about the government.

CJC 3: 364–68.

*August 15
Report Commemorating the Second Anniversary of the August 15 Liberation.

Speech at the Pyongyang rally commemorating the second anniversary of the liberation of Korea.

General review of accomplishments and prospects of Korea. Divided into three segments, it reviews international relations, compares the developments in the North and South, and proposes the tasks of the North Korean people. Comprehensive document praising the North Korean accomplishments and denouncing South Korea, not the United States. Important speech, but was never reprinted in subsequent editions of his work.

1SJ 1: 410–45; *JAP 1:* 233–60; *CJC 3:* 369–91.
KP47: ZA: 263–93; *ZB:* 329–68; *Z 1:* 377–414.

August 15
Two-Year Democratic Construction.

Article in a newspaper.

The source does not say which newspaper this article appeared in. It is a short article and does not refer to any specific democratic construction or reforms during the two-year period from 1945 to 1947.

CJC 3: 392–95.

August 28
The First Anniversary of the Founding of the Workers' Party of North Korea.

Reviews the accomplishments of the past year, reaffirms the correct political and organizational policies of the party, and proposes five tasks of the party. Gives some information on party membership and definitions of bureaucratism, formalism, and liberalism, etc.

SW 1: 137–54; *1SJ 1:* 446–72; *2SJ 1:* 347–65; *CSJ 1:* 128–44; *JAP 1:* 261–70 (excerpt); *CJC 3:* 396–414.
KP47; TK: 29–68.

September 1
On Organizing Production Cooperatives.

Speech at the Standing Committee of the Central Committee of the Workers' Party of North Korea.

Such cooperatives are necessary in a developing socialist country where the nationalization of all industries is not complete. Kim says 90 percent of North Korean industries has been nationalized, but to insure the supply of daily necessities it is necessary to organize cooperatives.

CJC 3: 415–19.

September 5
On Several Problems in Reforming and Strengthening the Work of the State Granary.

Concluding remarks at the forty-seventh meeting of the North Korean People's Committee.

> The problems mentioned include the collection of tax-in-kind, the storing of grain in warehouses, and the thrift movements to conserve grain.

> *CJC* 3: 420–27.

September 7
Directives Delivered at the Joint Conference of the Heads of Propaganda Sections of Each Province.

> Kim gives five specific instructions to those in charge of the provincial propaganda sections. He says that the propaganda workers must (1) understand the problem correctly, (2) strengthen the People's Committee, (3) build on the democratic reform already won, (4) make people understand the role of the security cadres, and (5) fight against the reactionaries.

> *CJC* 3: 428–34.
> *Z* 1: 415–22.

September 16
Develop Literature and Art and Actively Promote Cultural Work for the Masses.

Concluding remarks at the Standing Committee of the Central Committee of the Workers' Party of North Korea.

> Kim repeats his call to uproot all remnants of Japanese influence in literary and art works and to promote Korean culture for the masses.

> *CJC* 3: 435–42.

September 28
Let Us Make Kŭmgangsan a Cultural Retreat for Workers.

Talk with workers of retreats in outer Kŭmgang.

> After observing many scenic places in Kŭmgangsan, Kim says that all Buddhist temples in the mountain should be preserved, not for religious purposes but as a heritage of our forefathers. All temples should observe, for example, May Day rather than April 8, Buddha's birthday.

> *CJC* 3: 443–49.

September 30
Mountainous Regions Must Utilize Mountains Well.

Talk with farmers in Kujigol, Yangdŏk County, P'yŏngan Namdo.

Kim makes a personal visit to this small town in the mountainous region of P'yŏngan Namdo and tells the farmers to make good use of the mountains. He also instructs the local party cells to educate the farmers.

CJC 3: 450–55.

October 1
Learn and Learn Again to Become an Excellent National Cadre of New Korea.

Speech delivered at the first anniversary of the founding of the Kim Il Sung University.

When the university was first opened there were 1,500 students in thirty classes, but within a year there were 3,813 students in ninety-three classes. Kim points out five tasks for the university to pursue in the future.

1SJ 1: 473–78; *2SJ 1:* 366–70; *CJC 3:* 456–60.
LSWY 1: 76–80; *Z 1:* 423–30; *WY:* 43–47.

October 5
Let Us Create a True People's Army, a Modern Regular Army.

Speech at a banquet in commemoration of the third graduating class of Pyongyang Hagwŏn.

Kim tells the graduates to prepare for the creation of a regular army and to engage in proper ideological and political preparation for such an army. He also emphasizes the training of teachers in Pyongyang Hagwŏn.

CJC 3: 461–69.

October 11
On Several Tasks of Government Workers.

Speech to the fourth graduating class of the Central Higher Cadre School.

Graduates should protect the people's government and strengthen the Democratic National United Front. When they join the government, the graduates should work to strengthen the economic foundation of the people's government and promote ideological unity.

CJC 3: 470–78.

October 12
Directives at the Opening Ceremony of the Pyongyang School for the Families of the Revolutionaries.

A short speech stipulating that the families of the revolutionaries can enjoy the educational opportunities at the above institution from elementary school to high school.

1SJ 1: 479–80; *CJC 3:* 479–81.
Z 1: 431–32.

October 13
On Strengthening the Leadership of Social Organizations.

Speech at the tenth plenum of the Central Committee of the Workers' Party of North Korea (1WPK-10CC).

Sources published in 1955 indicate that this plenum was held on September 13, 1947. Kim speaks about four problems: (1) strengthening lower party organs, (2) recognizing the special characteristics of various social organizations, (3) political and ideological training of the leaders, and (4) reforming the style of operation in social organizations.

CJC 3: 482–87.

October 20
On Strengthening the Leadership of the Women's League.

Concluding remarks at the Standing Committee of the Central Committee of the Workers' Party of North Korea.

The mainstay of women's activities should be working women, and the leadership of the women's movement should be thoroughly trained.

CJC 3: 488–95.

October 26
The Cadres of the People's Army Should Faithfully Serve the People and the Fatherland.

Speech to the first graduating class of the Security Cadres School.

Short speech encouraging the graduates to serve the country.

1SJ 1: 481–89; *2SJ 1:* 371–77; *CJC 3:* 496–502.

November 3
On the First Anniversary of the November 3 Election.

Speech to the electorate of Samdŭngmyŏn, Kangdonggun, P'yŏngan Namdo.

On this first anniversary of the November 3 election, Kim encourages the people to work harder to achieve the goals set by the government. He says that there are many farmers who voluntarily contribute grains to the government and mentions them by name. He also encourages the people to achieve great things in industrial sectors. He blames the South for the prolonged division of Korea.

CJC 3: 503–15.
Z *1:* 433–50; *ZB:* 369–87.

December 1
On the Currency Reform.

Concluding remarks at the fifty-third meeting of the North Korean People's Committee.

North Koreans have been using two currencies, one issued by the Bank of Korea under Japanese rule and the other a military currency issued by the Russian occupation authorities. The first is still used by the South Koreans, and it has complicated the economic situation in the North in the past. Both currencies were supposed to have been exchanged for a new one issued by the North Korean Central Bank, at an exchange rate of one for one.

CJC 3: 516–21.

December 3
Directives Delivered at the Ceremony Commemorating the Opening of the Third Furnace at Hwanghae Steel Mill.

A brief remark to congratulate the opening of the third furnace in Hwanghae Steel Mill. He tells the workers to work hard and produce more steel.

CJC 3: 522–23.
Z *1:* 451–52.

December 21
On the Tasks of the General Trade Union of North Korea.

Speech at the second congress of the General Trade Union.

Encourages the workers to work hard to reconstruct the country. Reviews past accomplishments and proposes six tasks for the union to pursue. In the original edition, it is dated December 17, but December 21 in the second. Korean texts are heavily edited.

1SJ 1: 490–504; *2SJ 1:* 378–87; *CJC 3:* 524–33.
TU: 23–32; *KP47; Z 1:* 453–67.

December 29
Talk with Representatives of Hŭngnam Region People's Factories.

For the first time, Kim congratulates the workers in this region on their accomplishments. He is happy with production schedules of factories in this region. He asks the workers to produce even more and to improve their production techniques.

CJC 3: 534–39.

1948

January 1
New Year Address.

A short statement to encourage further economic development.

1SJ 1: 505–10; *CJC 4:* 1–5.
Z 2: 1–6.

January 5
On Strengthening and Reforming the Work of Teachers' Colleges.

Concluding remarks at the Standing Committee of the Central Committee of the Workers' Party of North Korea.

Teachers should be properly educated. They should not read novels by reactionary writers such as Yi Kwang-su, but learn more about the revolutionary movement. College textbooks and student recruitment works should also be emphasized.

CJC 4: 6–13.

January 12
Talk with Party Members of Sinmal Cell, Anch'ang-dong, Kanggye County.

The farmers of this region should utilize fully the land awarded to them. Kim also tells the farmers that they should strengthen the work of local party cells.

CJC 4: 14–21.

January 12
What Should We Do and How Should We Work this Year?

Speech delivered at a meeting of activists of the political parties and social organizations in Kanggye county.

Seems to have been written after the Korean war. First document that is vehemently anti-American and anti-United Nations. Gives definite impression that Kim had changed his speechwriter, if he had one in the past. His writing style is different, and there is some question as to the accuracy of some statements. There is no itemization of his points, etc.

SW 1: 155–70; *2SJ 2:* 1–18; *CSJ 1:* 145–60; *CJC 4:* 22–39.
CHU 1: 8–25; *DJOU 1:* 167–69; *LSWY 1:* 81–98; *KP48;* Z 2: 7–26.

January 21
On Publishing a Newspaper of the People's Army and Editing It Well.

Talk with newspaper workers of the People's Army.

It would be good to name the paper the *Korean People's Army*, and newspaper workers should respect the people.

CJC 4: 40–46.

January 24
On the Tasks of Our Party Organizations.

Speech delivered at a conference of the organizations of Sunch'ŏn County, P'yŏngan Namdo, of the Workers' Party of North Korea.

Lauds the accomplishments of the North, points out three shortcomings, and emphasizes the strengthening of the united front. In the first edition, this speech is listed as having been delivered on January 29, 1948. The second edition is heavily edited; there are additions, such as use of the term *chuch'e* and omissions, such as deletion of the name of Kim Ku from the list of those condemned.

SW 1: 171–87; *1SJ 1:* 511–34; *2SJ 2:* 26–44; *CSJ 1:* 161–78; *CJC 4:* 47–65.
KP55; TK: 69–104.

January 25
How to Develop State Industry and How to Manage the Enterprises?

Talk with managers and technicians of state enterprises.

Instructions on how best to utilize national resources to bring economic self-sufficiency.

SW 1: 188–94; *2SJ 2:* 19–25; *CSJ 1:* 178–84; *CJC 4:* 66–72.
SKKM 1: 29–35; *Z 2:* 27–32.

February 6
Summation of the 1947 Economic Plan and on the 1948 People's Economic Development Plan.

Report at the fourth session of the People's Assembly of North Korea (PANK-4).

> This report appears only in the second edition. Recapitulates the economic accomplishments of the 1947 economic plan and sets out a new one-year economic plan for 1948. Misleading statistics, and at times different classification and calculation, are abundant, but this report gives some details of economic plans.
>
> *2SJ 2:* 45–72; *JAP supp.:* 66–89; *CJC 4:* 73–98.
> *SKKM 1:* 36–62; *KP48*; *Z 2:* 33–72.

February 8
On the Occasion of the Founding of the Korean People's Army.

Speech delivered at a review of the Korean People's Army.

> Historic speech in which Kim creates the Korean People's Army in the North. He says that the army is for the people and consists of people with experience in anti-Japanese guerrilla struggles. Later editions omitted his laudatory remarks about the Russian army and Stalin.
>
> *SW 1:* 195–203; *2SW 1:* 58–65; *1SJ 1:* 535–46; *2SJ 2:* 73–81; *CSJ 1:* 185–92;
> *CJC 4:* 99–107.
> *RPM:* 1–9; *Z 2:* 73–86; *KP50*.

February 8
Let Us Develop National Dances that Befit the Sentiments and the Needs of Our People.

Directives to the teachers and students of the Dance Research Center.

> Kim says that there is no "pure art" apart from politics. He tells the dancers to create dances for the people.
>
> *CJC 4:* 108–11.

February 9
Tasks of the Party Organizations in the Struggle for the Realization of the People's Economic Plan of This Year.

Report at the twelfth plenum of the Central Committee of the Workers' Party of North Korea (1WPK-12CC).

Repetition of his economic plan speech, but he points out three general shortcomings of the party: party members must learn about economic development, must strengthen the struggle against the pro-Japanese, and must improve leadership style. This article was not included in the first edition or third edition.

2SJ 2: 82–92; *CJC 4:* 112–22.

February 20
Let Us Train Our Soldiers to Become Sharpshooters.

Speech to the artillery officers of the 395th Company of the Korean People's Army.

This speech was made to encourage artillerymen to train themselves to be accurate when using artillery. Officers should also pay close attention to their soldiers.

CJC 4: 123–30.

February 21
On the Work of the Central Committee of the Party.

Report and concluding remarks at the second meeting of the Hamgyŏng Namdo Party Committee of the Workers' Party of North Korea.

These are two long, but perhaps heavily edited speeches. Kim reviews the work of the party. After pointing out a number of shortcomings of the Hamgyŏng Namdo Provincial Party Committee, Kim says that the provincial party committee should strengthen the internal work of the party, emphasize the work of the Democratic National United Front, strengthen the people's government, and complete the goals of the People's Economic Plan.

CJC 4: 131–64.

February 22
For the Strengthening of the Economic Base of the Fatherland.

Speech at the people's factory of Hŭngnam district.

Encouragement to the workers to carry out the economic plan, use the machinery and materials with care, and constantly be aware of subversive elements.

2SJ 2: 93–98; *CJC 4:* 165–70.
Z 2: 87–94 (excerpt).

March 9

Oppose the Unilateral Election in South Korea and Support the Unification and Self-Reliant Independence of Korea.

Speech at the twenty-fifth meeting of the Central Committee of the Democratic National United Front.

> Primarily on the topic of the United Nations decision to hold an election in South Korea to establish a government in the South. Severely condemns the United States and praises the Soviet Union. Kim opposes U.N. involvement in Korean affairs, saying that it is nothing more than a tool of the American imperialists. Slightly edited.
>
> *1SJ* 2: 1–19; *2SJ* 2: 99–112; *JAP supp.:* 90–105; *CJC* 4: 171–84.
> *SK:* 1–13; *UNF:* 1–4 (excerpt); *IPRC:* 1–14; *KP51*; *Z* 2: 95–112.

March 19

Several Tasks to Strengthen and Reform Public Health Work.

Concluding remarks at the sixty-second meeting of the North Korean People's Committee.

> The tasks include proper education of doctors and workers in the public health sector. Technological improvement in medical treatment is also emphasized.
>
> *CJC* 4: 185–91.

*March 28

Report to the Second Congress of the Workers' Party of North Korea on the Work of the Central Committee (2WPK).

> The report is divided into three sections: the international situation, the domestic situation, and the party. It is a review of the accomplishments of the one and a half years of the party. It denounces the United States, discusses accomplishments in the North, and points out the future improvement of the party. There are some significant omissions relating to the Soviet Union and editing of misquoted and miscalculated statistics. In the first edition of Kim's work, a concluding remark by Kim at the party congress is presented with this report, but in the subsequent editions the concluding remark is listed separately.
>
> *SW* 1: 204–57; *2SW* 1: 66–122; *1SJ* 2: 20–97; *2SJ* 2: 113–73; *CSJ* 1: 193–238; *CJC* 4: 192–248.
> *SK:* 14–22 (excerpt); *UNF:* 5–6 (excerpt); *KP55*; *TU:* 33–35 (excerpt); *PPT:* 78–85 (excerpt); *TK:* 105–212; *ML:* 1–12 (excerpt); *ZG:* 195–203 (excerpt).

March 29

Every Effort for the Consolidation of the Democratic Base and the Reunification and Independence of the Country.

Concluding speech delivered at the Second Congress of the Workers' Party of North Korea (2WPK).

> Contains revealing remarks on factionalism. He points out seven tasks of the party, including elimination of factionalism. He condemns O Ki-sŏp, Chŏng Tal-hyŏn, Ch'oe Yong-dal, and others. Some of the names are edited out of the subsequent editions, but this speech is most revealing of the early factional strife.
>
> *ISJ* 2: 97–110; *2SJ* 2: 174–86; *CSJ* 1: 244–54; *SW* 1: 258–269; *JAP supp.*: 7–65; *CJC* 4: 249–60.

April 21
The Political Situation in North Korea.

Report at the joint conference of the representatives of political parties and social organizations of North and South Korea.

> This speech was delivered by Kim at the joint conference of political and social organizations of North and South Korea shortly before the May 10 general election in the South under U.N. supervision. With impressive statistical evidence, Kim tells of North Korean accomplishments and condemns the United States. He calls for the establishment of a unified democratic government of all Korea. He condemns Syngman Rhee and Kim Sŏng-su, but does not mention Kim Ku and Kim Kyu-sik, who were participating in that conference.
>
> *ISJ* 2: 111–51; *2SJ* 2: 187–214; *JAP supp.*: 106–37; *CJC* 4: 261–87.
> *SK*: 23–49; *UNF*: 7–10 (excerpt); *LSWY* 1: 99–125; *PPT*: 86–103 (excerpt); *Z* 2: 113–54; *ZG*: 208–20 (excerpt).

April 29
Interview with Newspaper Reporters from South Korea.

> A short interview with South Korean reporters who accompanied political leaders to the joint conference. The interview covered several key points, but basically advocated the independent unification of Korea by the Korean people and denounced U.S. and South Korean leaders.
>
> *ISJ* 2: 152–58; *2SJ* 2: 215–19; *CJC* 4: 288–93.
> *Z* 2: 155–66.

May 3
Talk with Kim Ku.

> This is a lengthy talk with Kim Ku, who had travelled north to consult North Korean leaders on unification. Kim tells Kim Ku that he opposes the unilateral election in the South, and that all Koreans must work for a single government

in a unified Korea. Kim also returned the seal of the Korean Provisional Government in Shanghai to Kim Ku, who must have presented it to Kim Il Sung.

CJC 4: 294–304.

May 6
Talk with Hong Myŏng-hŭi.

Kim congratulates Hong on his anti-Japanese revolutionary record and on his decision to remain in the North. He stresses the importance of education in the North for a future unified Korea. Kim wishes Hong good health and a long life.

CJC 4: 305–15.

May 11
Be the Powerful People's Force in Protecting the Interests of the People and the Fatherland.

Speech at the military conference of the Independent Security Corps of the Internal Bureau.

The mission of this group, different from that of the army, is to protect the people and state from all sorts of internal as well as external enemies. Kim elaborates five tasks of the group.

2SJ 2: 220–27; *CJC 4*: 316–22.

May 22
Let Us Further Strengthen Accomplishments in the Work of Eliminating Illiteracy.

Talk with workers in the central illiteracy elimination exhibition.

Kim blames illiteracy on the Japanese education system and promises compulsory education in the 1950s.

CJC 4: 323–28.

June 7
Let Us Build the Musan Mines into a Blue Mineral Production Base.

Directives to the workers in Musan mines.

This basically encourages workers to work harder. Kim also points out the importance of safety regulations in mines.

CJC 4: 329–34.

June 18
Duties of a County People's Committee Chairman.

Directives to the participants to the workshop of city and county people's committee chairmen.

A county people's committee chairman's duties are to improve the living standards of the people, to upgrade the educational system, and to emphasize the importance of public health work.

CJC 4: 335–44.

June 20
Let Us Strengthen the Unity and Friendship with the Working Youth of the World.

Directives to the participants from the Workers' Party of Korea to the International Working Youth Congress.

This is a short speech telling the participants to learn from others.

CJC 4: 345–50.

June 29
In Connection with the Unilateral Election in South Korea, the Political Conditions of Our Fatherland and the Future Struggle Policy for the Unification of the Fatherland.

Report at the consultative council of the leaders of the political parties and social organizations of North and South Korea.

This is primarily a condemnatory speech about the May 10 election to establish a government in the South. Most of the key leaders who went to the North for the joint meeting had returned to the South by this time, and the gathering in which he spoke was a group of leaders who were sympathetic to the cause of communism in the North. He proposed a four-point policy: to simultaneously withdraw all foreign troops from Korea, to assure no internal civil strife, to convene a political conference of all Korea, and to reject any unilateral elections.

1SJ 2: 159–70; *2SJ 2:* 228–34; *CJC 4:* 351–57.
SK: 50–56; *UNF:* 11–17; *LSWY 1:* 126–32; *Z 2:* 167–78.

July 8
On the Development of Fisheries.

Concluding remarks at the Standing Committee of the Central Committee of the Workers' Party of North Korea.

Three reasons are given for the slow development of fisheries: (1) the lack of detailed study and planning, (2) the high price and inefficiency of preservation measures, and (3) the lack of interest shown by the party organizations.

CJC 4: 358–65.

July 9
On the Constitution of the Democratic People's Republic of Korea.

Report at the fifth session of the People's Assembly of North Korea (PANK-5).

The title is a bit misleading. The report consists of three parts. Part one is an analysis of the separate roads the two Koreas were taking. The second part condemns the May 10 unilateral election in the South and the resulting political conditions. In the third part, on the tasks of the people of the North, he condemns the new draft of the South Korean constitution and praises the draft constitution of the North. The report was heavily edited and rewritten in the second edition.

1SJ 2: 171–210; *2SJ 2:* 235–57; *CJC 4:* 366–87.
Z 2: 179–218; *KP48.*

July 26
Concluding Remarks at the Seventy-first Meeting of the North Korean People's Committee.

Three goals are emphasized: (1) errors in the first half of the 1948 economic plan should be corrected, (2) office work should be simplified, and (3) the two-year economic plan should be prepared.

CJC 4: 388–98.

August 7
Duties of the Thirty-eighth Parallel Border Guards.

Directives given at the time of the appointment of the Third Guard Company commander of the Internal Bureau.

Officers and men of the guard unit patrolling the thirty-eighth parallel should pay special attention in guarding the border. The officers should maintain a good unit, manage it well, and take good care of their men.

CJC 4: 399–405.

August 14
Report on the Third Anniversary of the August 15 Liberation by the Great Soviet Army.

Report at the Pyongyang rally commemorating the third anniversary of the August 15 liberation.

This report appears only in the first edition of his work. The report is divided into three sections: (1) a report on the three-year accomplishments in the North, (2) a report on the South, and (3) the future tasks of the North. The report is very laudatory of the Soviet aid to the North and has an interesting statement on the village of Ch'ŏngsalli.

1SJ 2: 211–39; *CJC* 4: 406–23.
Z 2: 219–48.

August 23
On the Election of the Supreme People's Assembly of Korea.

Speech delivered to the electorate of the Sŭngho district, Kangdonggun, P'yŏngan Namdo.

Kim was nominated by this election district to be a member of the Supreme People's Assembly. General urging of the people to participate in the election. In this speech, Kim said that some 67 million voters from the South, 77 percent of the total South Korean electorate, had participated in this election.

1SJ 2: 240–57; *2SJ* 2: 258–68; *CJC* 4: 424–32.
Z 2: 249–66; *PPT*: 104–12.

September 8
Declaration on the Transfer of Political Power.

At the first session of the Supreme People's Assembly (1SPA-1).

A short statement transferring the political power of the People's Committee of North Korea to the Supreme People's Assembly. Kim states that the People's Committee has successfully carried out the mandate of the people.

1SJ 2: 258–62; *JAP supp.*: 138–41; *CJC* 4: 433–36.
Z 2: 267–70.

*September 10
Political Program of the Government of the Democratic People's Republic of Korea.

Political program announced at the first session of the Supreme People's Assembly of the Democratic People's Republic of Korea (1SPA-1).

An eight-point program announced by Kim at the first session of the Assembly, legitimizing the North and downgrading the South. The third point states that all antipeople laws and institutions in the South are illegal and not in effect.

SW 1: 270–75; *1SJ 2:* 263–71; *2SJ 2:* 269–74; *CSJ 1:* 255–59; *JAP supp.:*
142–48; *CJC 4:* 437–42.
PPT: 113–18; *CCY 50:* 16–18; *CHU 1:* 26–28; *DJOU 1:* 167–69 (excerpt).
Z 2: 271–80; *ZG:* 231–36.

September 12
**Let Us March Forward toward the Establishment of a Democratic Korea
by Firmly Uniting around the Government of the Republic.**

Speech at the mass rally of Pyongyang in celebration of the establishment of the government of the Democratic People's Republic of Korea.

A short speech at the rally. The speech is heavily propagandistic and is of little
importance.

1SJ 2: 272–76; *2SJ 2:* 275–78; *JAP supp.:* 149–52; *CJC 4:* 443–45.
Z 2: 281–86.

September 19
Be a Faithful Security Worker of the Fatherland and the People.

Congratulatory message to the first graduating class of the Central Security School of the Ministry of Interior.

Graduates should be patriotic above all and raise the level of their political
work.

CJC 4: 446–49.

September 22
Letter to Marshal Stalin.

A short letter expressing appreciation for the Russian government decision to
withdraw military troops from Korea.

1SJ 2: 277–80.
KP48.

October 10
Let Us Educate More National Cadres.

Speech at the dedication ceremony of a new building at Kim Il Sung University.

There were 1,500 students with seventy faculty members when the university
was opened, but the faculty has doubled and the number of students has increased to 2,400.

CJC 4: 450–53.

October 14
Army Officers Should Play Important Roles in Strengthening the Fighting Forces of a Company.

Speech at the second graduating ceremony of the First Central Cadet School.

> This speech is similar to his other speeches to graduates of military schools. He emphasizes rules and regulations and education of soldiers.
>
> *CJC 4:* 454–58.

October 21
To Strengthen the Party Political Work in a Company.

Speech to the propaganda workers' meeting of guard companies.

> Kim stresses party political work in various party cells in all guard units at military and government installations as well as among those dispatched to the border.
>
> *CJC 4:* 459–77.

November 13
Ideological Education of the Youth is the Basic Task of the Democratic Youth League Organizations.

Speech delivered at the third congress of the Democratic Youth League of North Korea.

> Encouragement to youth after the establishment of the government and after the withdrawal of the Russian army from Korea. Five-point basic task in ideological education of North Korean youth.
>
> *SW 1:* 276–86; *1SJ 2:* 281–300; *2SJ 2:* 279–91; *CSJ 1:* 260–71; *CJC 4:* 478–90.
> *YOU:* 25–37; *YC:* 28–40; *LSWY 1:* 133–45; *KP49; Z 2:* 287–306; *WY:* 48–60.

November 22
Several Tasks to Improve the Material and Cultural Lives of the People.

Concluding remarks at the Standing Committee of the Central Committee of the Workers' Party of North Korea.

> Efforts should be made to produce more food, build more houses, and improve the cultural life of the common people.
>
> *CJC 4:* 491–96.

November 25
Central Tasks of the Two-Year People's Economic Plan.

Concluding remarks at the tenth cabinet meeting of the Democratic People's Republic of Korea.

> For the 1949–50 two-year economic plan, Kim tells the cabinet members to concentrate on eight tasks: building an industrial base; producing daily necessities, housing, and foodstuffs; improving transportation, schools, public health, and propaganda work.
>
> *CJC* 4: 497–504.

December 11
Become a Good Worker of the State Following the Will of Revolutionary Forerunners.

Speech to the teachers and students of Mangyŏngdae Revolutionary Family School.

> Kim claims that these are the children of those who fought with him and died in Manchuria.
>
> *CJC* 4: 505–9.

1949

January 1
New Year Address to the People of the Entire Nation in Greeting 1949.

> Kim reports that as of December 26, 1948, the Russian army had withdrawn from Korea. Condemns South Korean development and claims that 77.52 percent of voters in South Korea participated in the election of representatives to the Supreme People's Assembly in the North.
>
> *ISJ* 2: 301–17.
> Z 2: 307–24.

*February 1
The Completion of the Two-Year People's Economic Plan is the Materialistic Guarantee of the Fatherland Unification.

Speech at the second session of the First Supreme People's Assembly (1SPA-2).

> Unlike earlier economic plans, there are no statistical goals or accounting of accomplishments in this speech. The second edition is heavily edited to omit

many portions, and some are rearranged to conform to a more orderly style of presentation. Omitted are references to Kim Ku and Kim Kyu-sik. There is much condemnation of Syngman Rhee, Kim Sŏng-su, and the new premier of the South, Yi Pŏm-sŏk.

1SJ 2: 318–44; *2SJ* 2: 292–310.
SKKM 1: 63–80; *Z* 2: 325–52.

March 3
Speech at the Train Stations of Moscow and Yaroslav.

A short speech thanking the Russians for their aid, which Kim said the Korean people will never forget.

1SJ 2: 345–46.
Z 2: 353–54.

March 20
Speech before Leaving Moscow.

A short speech saying that he received assurance of economic aid from Stalin.

1SJ 2: 347–48.
Z 2: 355–56.

April 7
Reply at the Welcoming Rally of Returning Representatives of the Democratic People's Republic of Korea from the Russian Visit.

Speech at Pyongyang airport.

A short speech praising the Soviet Union and its great leader, Stalin, for giving the North economic aid and concluding a treaty of economic and cultural cooperation.

1SJ 2: 349–53.
Z 2: 357–62.

April 21
On the Works of the Government Delegation of the Democratic People's Republic of Korea on Their Visit to the Soviet Union.

Report at the third session of the First Supreme People's Assembly (1SPA-3).

A lengthy report on the conclusion of the ten-year treaty for economic and cultural cooperation between the Soviet Union and North Korea. Four other agreements were concluded: on commerce (1949–50), on a 212-million-ruble loan (1949–52) at 2 percent interest, on technical assistance, and on cultural exchange and cooperation. The second edition is heavily edited to strike out most adulatory remarks about Stalin, and there are some corrections of North Korea–Soviet Union trade statistics.

1SJ 2: 354–77; *2SJ* 2: 311–24; *JAP supp.:* 153–68.
Z 2: 363–86; *KP49.*

June 11
Report of Kim Il Sung at the Sixth Enlarged Plenum of the Central Committee (2WPK-6CC).

No text available. This plenum discussed the participation of the party in the founding congress of the Democratic Front for the Fatherland Unificiation.

August 2
On the Declaration of the Peaceful Unification of the Fatherland.

Interview with North Korean Central News Agency reporters.

Concerning the declaration issued by the Democratic Front for the Fatherland Unification. Kim condemns the attitude of the South Korean leaders and praises the unification policy of the Front.

1SJ 2: 378–82; *2SJ* 2: 325–28.
SK: 57–60; *UNF:* 18–21; *Z* 2: 387–92.

**September 9*
The First Anniversary of the Founding of the Democratic People's Republic of Korea.

Report at the fourth session of the First Supreme People's Assembly (1SPA-4).

Gives some erratic, much-edited statistics on the North Korean economy. Also attacks the South with statistics and states three tasks: to strengthen the revolutionary base, to watch out for the enemy, and to strengthen the security and armed forces.

1SJ 2: 383–417; *2SJ* 2: 329–53; *JAP supp.:* 169–80.
Z 2: 393–428.

October 31
We Must Manufacture Weapons by Ourselves and Arm Ourselves.

Talk with representatives of the Sixty-fifth factory.

This is a very short talk with munition workers, emphasizing the need to manufacture weapons in Korea. This speech was made public for the first time in 1977.

ZC: 105–9.

November 19

New Circumstances and New Conditions Require New Attitude toward Work.

Speech at the activists' meeting of industrial sectors and trade unions.

> In an effort to arouse enthusiasm for the sluggish development in the industrial sectors, Kim gives a nine-point task to reform the attitude toward work. A good speech, but was never reprinted in subsequent editions of his work.

> *1SK 2:* 418–41.
> *SKKM 1:* 81–98; *KP55; TU:* 36–53; *Z 2:* 429–52.

December 15

Let Us Be More Faithful to Marxism and Leninism and the Principles of Proletarian Internationalism.

Speech at a plenum (second joint plenum) of the Central Committee of the Workers' Party of Korea (2WPK-8CC).

> In response to the Cominform meeting held in Hungary in November 1949, Kim analyzes the reactionary forces of the United States and the democratic forces headed by the Soviet Union and discusses the five-point task of the party. Fair analysis of the international situation of the time. Heavily edited in the second edition. Condemns Tito and labels Yugoslavia a political system under murderers and spies.

> *1SJ 2:* 442–76; *2SJ 2:* 354–77.
> *KP50; TK:* 213–62; *ML:* 13–35.

December 28

Speech at the First Commencement Exercise of Physics and Mathematics Division of Kim Il Sung University.

> Z 2: 453–64.

1950

January 1

New Year Address to the Entire People of the Republic in Greeting 1950.

> Considerable emphasis on the condition of the South. Several suggestive references to strengthening the army and guerrilla forces operating in the South.

> *1SJ 2:* 477–84.
> Z 2: 465–72.

January 19
Let Us Consolidate All Patriotic Democratic Forces for the Great Task of the Fatherland Unification.

Speech at the third congress of the Ch'ŏndogyo Ch'ŏngudang.

> Invited by the Chairman Kim Tal-hyŏn to speak at the party congress of the Ch'ŏndogyo Ch'ŏngudang, Kim said that he supported trusteeship, condemned the decadence of the South, and stated that unification would not come naturally but should be won. Urged joining forces in winning the victory of the unification.
>
> *1SJ* 2: 485–96.
> Z 2: 473–84.

January 25
For Further Developing the Agrarian Management, Forestry, and Fisheries.

Speech at the joint conference of the leaders of the agrarian, forestry, and fishery sectors.

> Another speech to urge on the lagging economy. Kim is giving instruction to improve the shortcomings in the fields of agrarian management, forestry, and fisheries, and he urges leaders to improve their work. Points out seven tasks to improve work.
>
> *1SJ* 2: 497–514; *2SJ* 2: 378–91; *JAP supp.*: 188–200.
> Z 2: 485–502; *KP50.*

January 28
Address to the First Graduates of Kim Il Sung University.

> Generally encouraging speech to the first graduates of the university. Kim quotes Stalin and praises Russian accomplishments. He says that he needs cadres such as the graduates of the university to develop the North.
>
> *JAP supp.*: 181–89.

February 21
Tasks of the Transportation Workers in Carrying out the Two-Year People's Economic Plan.

Speech at the joint conference of the activists of transportation workers and workers under the Ministry of Transportation.

Pointed out two shortcomings and proposed four tasks for the workers to improve the timetable of the trains, to observe rules more strictly and to shorten the dates for returning cars, and to improve services.

1SJ 2: 515–24; *2SJ* 2: 392–98.
TU: 54–60; *Z* 2: 503–12.

February 28
On Correcting the Shortcomings in Carrying Out the People's Economic Plan.

Speech at the fifth session of the First Supreme People's Assembly (1SPA-5).

Correction of numerous mistakes and urging the representatives to be more critical in evaluating reports and in exercising their constitutional duties. Basically he pointed out six shortcomings, and he reported that there was a 1.5-billion-*wŏn* shortage in government revenues.

2SJ 2: 399–408.

March 17
On the First Anniversary of the Conclusion of the Agreement between Korea and Russia for Economic and Cultural Cooperation.

Praising the Soviet Union for its economic assistance. This article was excluded from all subsequent editions of his work. Here Kim uses statistics on North Korea–Soviet Union trade from 1946–1950 that differ from previous statistics, and he also falsifies statistics to condemn the U.S. aid to South Korea. Kim states that Russia is the closest ally, friend, and benefactor.

1SJ 2: 525–42; *JAP supp.:* 201–13.
Z 2: 513–30; *KP50.*

May
The Korean People's Struggle for the Building of a Unified Democratic Independent State.

This is a four-part article analyzing (1) the occupation of the North and South by the Soviet Union and the United States after the end of the war, (2) the situation in the North, development of the party and the state, democratic reforms, and economic development, (3) development in the South and the miseries that South Korean people face, and (4) the two different paths that North and South Korea are treading.

1SJ 2: 543–73; *2SJ* 2: 409–31; *JAP supp.:* 214–38.
SK: 61–82; *UNF:* 22–24; *PPT:* 119–40; *1PRC:* 15–37; *ZG:* 237–59.

*June 26
Every Effort for Victory in the War.

Radio address to the entire Korean people.

Outlines the North Korean effort to peacefully unify Korea and denounces the South Korean regime for starting the war. Kim calls for the people of the South to join the North in swiftly concluding the war by defeating the South.

2SW 1: 123–129; SW 1: 287–94; 1SJ 3: 1–12; CSJ 1: 272–78; JAP 2: 13–20.
KW: 1–12; SK: 83–90; CCY 51–52: 13–15; ZG: 260–68.

June 28
On the Liberation of Seoul, the Capital of our Fatherland.

Congratulatory message to the people and the Korean People's Army.

Declares that Seoul was liberated at 11:30 a.m. on June 28, 1950, and urges the people of the South to support the armies of the North.

1SJ 3: 13–14; JAP 2: 21–22.
KW: 13–15; CCY 51–52: 16.

July 5
Order No. 7 of the Supreme Commander of the People's Army of the Democratic People's Republic of Korea.

In praise of accomplishments of North Korean military units, two orders to upgrade and rename some divisions.

1SJ 3: 15–16; JAP 2: 23.
KW: 16–17; CCY 51–52: 72.

July 8
Let Us Resolutely Repulse the U.S. Imperialists' Armed Invasion.

Radio address to the Korean people.

This is the time when the military campaigns of the North are progressing well, and Kim assails the American participation in the Korean war and urges the Korean people to fight to the end for victory. Drastic changes appear in the writing style of Kim. Some minor editing was done in the subsequent editions, such as the reference to the Korean war as a "holy war."

2SW 1: 130–39; SW 1: 295–304; 1SJ 3: 17–31; CSJ 1: 279–88; JAP 2: 24–35.
KW: 18–32; CCY 51–52: 16–19.

July 23
Order of the Supreme Commander of the People's Army of the Democratic People's Republic of Korea.

Order to the People's Army advancing toward Taejŏn.

> Praises the army that liberated Taejŏn under the command of Kim Ung, Yi Hun, Yu Kyŏng-su, and Yi Kwŏn-mu.
>
> *1SJ 3:* 32–33; *JAP 2:* 36–37.
> *KW:* 33–34; *CCY 51–52:* 72.

July 27
Answers to the Question by Reporter Manian of Newspaper *Humanité*.

> An interview with a French reporter on the Korean war. Kim said that he did not want the war and could have ended the war already had it not been for U.S. intervention.
>
> *1SJ 3:* 34–39; *JAP 2:* 38–42.
> *KW:* 35–40; *CCY 51–52:* 19–21.

August 15
The Fifth Anniversary of the August 15 Liberation.

Speech at the commemoration rally by the Pyongyang City People's Committee.

> Reassessing the developments of the past five years in North and South Korea. The reason for the North Korean victory is that the North is fighting for the independence and freedom of Korea while the South is fighting for the United States and dollars. Another is the support of the war effort by the Russians and the Chinese.
>
> *1SJ 3:* 40–65; *JAP 2:* 49–68.
> *KW:* 41–66; *KP50.*

August 15
Order No. 82 of the Supreme Commander of the People's Army of the Democratic People's Republic of Korea.

> Four-item order: learn thoroughly the usage of various weapons, do not waste ammunition, lead the soldiers more efficiently, and drive out the United States and the South completely.
>
> *1SJ 3:* 66–73; *JAP 2:* 43–48.
> *CCY 51–52:* 73–74; *KW:* 67–74.

September 11

On the Second Anniversary of the Founding of the Democratic People's Republic of Korea.

Radio address.

> General statements on the war. There are statements citing false and unbelievable statistics to describe the conditions of the liberated South. He states that 97 to 98 percent of the people participated in the election of the People's Committee and gives various other statistics on confiscated lands that were distributed to the poor peasants. He also says that a petition to the Security Council of the United Nations asking it to withdraw the U.N. troops was signed by thirteen million Koreans above sixteen years of age.
>
> *ISJ 3:* 74–103; *JAP 2:* 69–91.
> *KP50.*

October 11

Radio Address, October 11, 1950.

> Acknowledges the Inch'ŏn landing of the U.N. forces and temporary setback of the People's Army. He also states that the U.N. forces are entering the North. Still he says that in the liberated area of the South there was distribution of land to the peasants and that the people participated in the election of the People's Committees.
>
> *ISJ 3:* 104–15; *JAP 2:* 92–100.
> *KW:* 75–86; *CCY 51–52:* 21–23.

December 9

Appeal of the Supreme Commander of the Korean People's Army.

> Kim's appeal to pursue the war by marching down to the South on the occasion of the liberation of Pyongyang with the assistance of the Chinese volunteers.
>
> *ISJ 3:* 116–21; *JAP 2:* 101–4.
> *KW:* 87–92; *CCY 51–52:* 23–24.

*December 21

The Present Situation and Our Tasks.

Report at the third joint plenum of the Central Committee of the Workers' Party of Korea (2WPK-9CC).

> This report is the first comprehensive analysis of the war. It is in four parts: the process of the war, the role of the party, the friendship of the fraternal Communist countries, and the future tasks of the party. There is sharp criticism of

high-ranking members, particularly the partisans, pointing out their errors. The speech seems to have been written under the influence of the Communists from the South. Some of the detailed criticism of particular incidents is omitted in the text, and at times only excerpts are presented. It is interesting to note that many North Korean leaders who fought with Kim Il Sung in Manchuria, such as Kim Il, Yim Ch'un-ch'u, and Ch'oe Kwang, are severely reprimanded and expelled from the party. All these men were later reinstated in the party, but nonpartisan leaders who were reprimanded or expelled at this time, such as Kim Yŏl and Mu Chŏng, were never reinstated.

ISJ 3: 122–73; *JAP* 2: 105–44.
CCY 51–52: 24–37; *KW:* 93–144; *KP55; TK:* 263–340.

December 24
Our Arts Should Contribute to the Victory of War.

Talk with writers, artists, and scientists.

This speech was made public for the first time in 1977, and it was heavily edited to support Kim's self-reliant thought. Kim urged the writers and artists to incite anti-U.S. sentiments in their writings and performances.

ZC: 110–20.

1951

January 1
New Year Address to the People of the Entire Nation in Greeting 1951.

Lengthy new year address, denouncing the United States and urging the people of the North to do their duty to win victory in the war. This accompanies two congratulatory telegrams to the People's Army of Korea and the Chinese Volunteer Army.

ISJ 3: 174–89; *JAP* 2: 145–57.
CCY 51–52: 37–40; *KW:* 145–46; *KP51.*

January 5
Order No. 7 of the Supreme Commander of the People's Army of the Democratic People's Republic of Korea.

An order to fire twenty-four shots from 240 cannons in commemoration of re-liberating Seoul, the capital city of the fatherland.

ISJ 3: 190–92; *JAP* 2: 158–59.
CCY 51–52: 75; *KW:* 147–49.

January 18
On the Present Situation and the Immediate Tasks of the Democratic Youth League Organizations.

Speech at the joint conference of the Central Committees of the Democratic Youth Leagues of North and South Korea.

> Kim lays down eight tasks for the youth to bring victory in the war. These include strict obedience of orders in the army, work behind enemy lines, work for reconstruction, work in transportation, work in hygienic and antiepidemic work, propaganda and agitation work, educational work, and external propaganda work.
>
> *YOU:* 38–54; *LSWY 1:* 146–63; *WY:* 61–78.

February 8
Order No. 0097 of the Supreme Commander of the People's Army of Democratic People's Republic of Korea.

> In commemoration of the third anniversary of the founding of the Korean People's Army, Kim gave a six-point order; the third point is to cooperate with the Chinese Volunteer Army, and the sixth is to fire twenty shots from 120 cannons at eight o'clock.
>
> *ISJ 3:* 193–99; *JAP 2:* 160–164.
> *KW:* 150–56; *CCY 51–52:* 75–76.

February 11
Answers to Questions by Comrade Yu Kye-ryang, Acting President of Korean Branch Bureau of the New China News Agency.

> Essentially Kim's expression of appreciation to the Chinese people for helping the Koreans.
>
> *ISJ 3:* 200–205; *JAP 2:* 165–69.
> *KW:* 157–62; *CCY 51–52:* 40–41.

February 24
Proclamation.

> Four-point proclamation on combatting spies and agents from the South.
>
> *ISJ 3:* 206–7.

March 8
Congratulatory Message.

> To two soldiers who penetrated enemy camps and had an enemy company surrender to the North. Recommended for citation as heroes of the republic.

ISJ 3: 208–9.
KW: 163–64.

March 15
Conversation with Farmers of P'yŏngan Namdo.

Essentially to urge the farmers to work harder. Three questions were asked on the war, the spring planting, and the distribution of commodities.

ISJ 3: 210–18; *JAP 2:* 170–73.
CCY 51–52: 41–43.

March 17
Letter to Marshal Stalin on the Second Anniversary of the Agreement between Korea and Russia for Economic and Cultural Cooperation.

Expression of deep respect and appreciation to Stalin for aid on the second anniversary of the agreement between the two countries.

ISJ 3: 219–21.

March 27
Congratulatory Message.

To an air force officer, Kim Ki-u, who fought gallantly against the Americans.

ISJ 3: 222.
KW: 165.

May 1
Order No. 310 of the Supreme Commander of the Korean People's Army.

Seven-point order in commemoration of May Day. Contents of the order are the usual remarks about being thrifty with weapons and ammunition and encouraging the soldiers toward victory in the war.

ISJ 3: 223–30.
KW: 166–73.

May 9
Congratulatory Messages.

Congratulating Antong 12th Regiment and the 82nd Company for receiving citations from the Supreme People's Assembly.

ISJ 3: 231–32.
KW: 174–75.

May 19
Note of Appreciation to the Patriotic Businessmen of Pyongyang.

A note of thanks addressed to Kim Ch'i-hyŏk for donating two million *wŏn* for the war.

ISJ 3: 233.

May 27
Conversation at the Reception of Investigation Group of the International Women's League.

Text of the interview was not revealed. Only Kim's remarks at the reception.

ISJ 3: 234–35.

June 14
Answer to the Request to Organize the Peace Preservation Committee by Foreign Prisoners of War at Chunggangjin Prisoner-of-War Camp in Korea.

Granting the request by American and English prisoners of war to organize a peace-preservation committee.

ISJ 3: 236–37.
KW: 176–77.

June 30
On Some Questions of Our Literature and Art.

Talk with writers and artists.

Basically four points are raised: to produce realistic art and literary works, to depict the heroes of the People's Army, to heighten hatred of the enemy, and to learn from the advanced countries, particularly the Soviet Union. Kim says here that Korean national culture can be constructed only by learning from Russia's progressive literature and art. This was omitted in later editions. Heavily edited from the original, it gives clues that his speech writers have changed many phrases.

2SW 1: 140–47; *SW 1:* 305–12; *ISJ 3:* 238–51; *CSJ 1:* 289–96; *JAP 2:* 174–84.
CCY 51–52; 43–46; *SS:* 7–16; *LA:* 1–10.

August 15
The Sixth Anniversary of the August 15 Liberation by the Great Soviet Army.

Report at the Pyongyang rally.

General condemnation of participation in the Korean War by nineteen (?) nations headed by the United States. He said he had agreed to the cease-fire because of the North Korean desire for a peaceful solution to the Korean question. North Korea will strengthen its ties with friendly nations.

1SJ 3: 252–80; JAP 2: 185–206.
KW: 178–206; CCY 51–52: 46–53; KP51.

August 15
Order No. 461 of the Supreme Commander of the Korean People's Army.

An eight-point order repeating the usual instructions to be thrifty with arms, to supply needed materials, etc. In celebration of the sixth anniversary, Kim ordered the firing of twenty rounds from 240 cannons at 8 P.M. at Pyongyang, Wŏnsan, and Hamhŭng.

1SJ 3: 281–88.
KW: 207–15; CCY 51–52: 76–78.

*November 1
On Some Defects in the Organizational Work of Party Organizations.

Report to the fourth joint plenum of the Central Committee of the Workers' Party of Korea (2WPK-10CC).

In this important report, divided into three sections, Kim discusses the defects in the organization of the party and defects in the attitude of the party members on the united front with other parties in the North, and he outlines the future tasks of the party. Apparently there was a meeting on September 1, 1951, of the Organization Committee of the Central Committee at which many party members were purged or expelled for their activities during the enemy occupation of the North. Kim urges leniency and asks the party to recruit more members to the party. He also urges the militant elements to cooperate more closely with other parties, the Democratic party and the Ch'ŏndogyo Ch'ŏngu party, and gives seven-point task for the party to follow in the future.

SW 1: 313–36; 1SJ 3: 289–327; CSJ 1: 297–319.
CCY 51–52: 53–61; KP51; TK: 341–96.

November 2
On the Improvement of the Party's Organization Work.

Concluding speech delivered at the fourth plenary meeting of the Central Committee of the Workers' Party of Korea (2WPK-10CC).

This is a concluding remark by Kim at the meeting, more or less going over the same ground covered in the speech on November 1. He discusses party development, the question of correcting party members, the united front with other parties, party cadres, and the style of work.

2SJ 1: 146–60; *SW 1:* 337–49; *CSJ 1:* 320–32; *JAP supp.:* 241–75.
SS: 17–19 (excerpt).

November 5
The October Revolution and the National Liberation Struggle of the Korean People.

A historical article surveying the Korean anti-Japanese movement, comparing the American and Russian occupation policies in Korea, tracing American imperialistic designs on Korea, and pointing out the significance of the Korean war in international relations. This article was written on the thirty-fourth anniversary of the October revolution. This is a good example of Kim's work written by others. The writing style, the examples cited in the article (such as Dennett's work on Roosevent and Russo-Japanese War), the importance put on the Korean Communist activities of the 1920s and 1930s, and other minor details indicate that this is not Kim's work. It seems to have been written by a Korean Communist educated in Japan. There are effusive tributes to the Soviet Union and Stalin, but almost no mention of Chinese assistance in the Korean war.

1SJ 4: 1–32; *JAP 2:* 207–26.
KP51.

November 30
Tasks of the Public Health Workers in the War.

Speech to public health workers.

Encourages public health workers to keep the people healthy. Urges them to increase women doctors and pharmacists.

1SJ 3: 328–34.
KP52; PH: 1–6.

December 16
Speech at the Meeting with Writers and Artists.

A short speech to a troupe of performing artists who returned from their performances at international youth festival in Germany and other socialist countries, including the Soviet Union. Remarkable lack of reference to the Chinese participation in the Korean war.

1SJ 4: 33–40.
CCY 51–52: 62–63; *LA:* 11–15.

1952

January 1
Congratulatory Messages.

Two congratulatory messages; one to the armed forces of the North and another to the Chinese Volunteer Army.

1SJ 4: 41–50; *JAP 2:* 227–33.
KW: 215–23.

February 1
The Task and the Role of Local Organizations at the Present Stage.

Speech delivered at a joint meeting of the People's Committee chairmen and leading party functionaries of provinces, cities, and counties.

A long speech outlining the basic tasks of local organizations and urging officials to do away with bureaucratism. He concludes with emphasis on five points: (1) state power is the power of the people, (2) officials must work closely with the people, (3) the country should be thrifty, (4) officials should have plans to lead the people, and (5) officials should be armed with the political ideologies of Marxism and Leninism.

SW 1: 350–70; *1SJ 4:* 51–96; *CSJ 1:* 333–53.
KP 52; PPT: 141–63; *CCY 51–52:* 63–72; *ZG:* 269–91.

February 8
Order No. 059 of the Supreme Commander of the People's Army of the Democratic People's Republic of Korea.

In commemoration of the fourth anniversary of the founding of the Korean People's Army, Kim gave six-point instructions reiterating the usual orders, including the firing of cannons.

1SJ 4: 97–102; *JAP 2:* 234–37.
KW: 224–28.

**April 4*
Speech to the Political Workers and Security Organization Cadres.

Lengthy speech detailing the correct work of the security officers, giving examples of their bad conduct, such as gambling, drinking, excessive partying, dress codes, and others. Tells them to straighten up their work to serve the people and watch out for agents and spies.

1SJ 4: 103–34.

April 16
A Letter of Appreciation.

> Letter to Stalin, thanking him for 50,000 tons of wheat.
>
> *ISJ* 4: 135–36.

April 27
Speech at the Scientists' Conference.

> Lengthy speech, quite well written, on the role of the scientists in the North. Narrative style is definitely different from his other writings, almost like his speech on November 5, 1951, on the October Revolution. Expounds the nine-point task of the scientists, after pointing out some shortcomings.
>
> *ISJ* 4: 137–84.
> *SS:* 20–42; *PH:* 7–29.

May 1
Order No. 236 of the Supreme Commander of the People's Army of the Democratic People's Republic of Korea.

> Encouraging words on May Day. There is no specific order.
>
> *ISJ* 4: 185–88.
> *KW:* 229–32.

May 1
Proletarian Internationalism and the Struggle of the Korean People.

> Another example of a different style of writing, similar to the April 27 speech. Divided into four sections, this article deals with the situation of the time, extends appreciation to those countries that gave aid to the North, denounces the United States, and urges the people to advance on this May Day.
>
> *ISJ* 4: 189–211; *JAP* 2: 238–54.
> *KP52.*

June 18
The Workers' Party of Korea is the Organizer of the Victory in the Fatherland Liberation War.

Speech to the teachers and students of the Central Party School.

> This long speech was made public for the first time in 1977. Kim said that he knew shortly after the war that it was not a civil war but an international war. He also spoke at length about the cease-fire negotiations and said that the pur-

pose of such a cease-fire was for him to regroup and smash the South and reunify the country later.

ZC: 121–44.

August 15
The Seventh Anniversary of the August 15 Liberation by the Great Soviet Army.

Speech at the commemoration rally in Pyongyang.

Divided into four sections, this speech reported on the gains of the war, on the cease-fire negotiations, on the tasks for the North, and on the ultimate victory.

1SJ 4: 212–47; *JAP supp.:* 276–98.
KW: 233–61; *KP52.*

August 15
Order No. 474 of the Supreme Commander of the People's Army of the Democratic People's Republic of Korea.

Extending appreciation to the Soviet Union and the People's Republic of China for their aid. Asking the usual firing of cannons in Pyongyang, Wŏnsan, and Hamhŭng in commemoration of the anniversary.

1SJ 4: 248–54.
KW: 262–67.

August 15
For the Freedom, Peace, and Liberation of the Korean People.

This is an article written for publication in *Pravda.* Divided into five sections, it recounts the Russian role in the liberation of Korea, the military situation of 1951–1952, the progress of the cease-fire negotiations, germ warfare, and the victory of the Korean people. Kim says that Stalin is the people's godfather and the Korean people are happy to call him the savior and father of the Korean people.

1SJ 4: 255–79.
KW: 268–87; Russian text in *Pravda,* August 15, 1952.

October 25
Our Righteous Joint Struggle Will Be Victorious.

Speech on the occasion of the second anniversary of the Chinese Volunteer Army's participation in the Korean War.

Stressed the importance of friendly socialist nations and expressed deep appreciation to the Chinese people. For the first time Kim quoted Mao and renewed his will to win in the Korean war.

ISJ 4: 280–310.
KW: 288–313; *KP52.*

December 1
Congratulatory Message to the Opening Ceremony of the Academy of Sciences.

A message sent to the first opening of the Academy of Sciences of the North.

ISJ 4: 311–12.

December 2
Reply to Congratulatory Message Sent on the Fourth Anniversary of the Founding of the Democratic People's Republic of Korea.

A letter to Watanabe Michio, a member of the Standing Committee of the Japanese Liaison Bureau of the International Trade Union.

A short letter expressing appreciation. It is difficult to understand why the reply was so late; the fourth anniversary was on September 9.

ISJ 4: 314–16.

*December 15
The Organizational and Ideological Consolidation of the Party is the Basis of Our Victory.

Report delivered at the fifth joint plenum of the Central Committee of the Workers' Party of Korea (2WPK-11CC).

One of the most important documents of the party. Kim said much about strengthening the party. He spoke of (1) the international situation, (2) economic development, with few statistics, (3) the strengthening of the party, giving information about the membership and the change in its composition and various errors committed, (4) shortcomings in organization work and the task of correcting and improving the activities of members and cadres, and (5) the strengthening of the ideological work in the party. Much revealing and down-to-earth analysis of the ills of party development.

SW 1: 371–412; *ISJ 4:* 317–407; *CSJ 1:* 354–93.
KP53; *ZG:* 292–305.

December 24
Let Us Strengthen the People's Army.

Speech at a meeting of high-ranking officers.

Divided into four sections, the speech covers the nature of the Korean war, characteristics of the People's Army, the growth of the army during the Korean war, and the shortcomings (omitted) and the tasks of the army. It is a good account of the situation and liberally quotes Stalin and adores Russian army practices. Says that the Korean army was patterned after the Russian army.

ISJ 4: 408–43.
KW: 314–43; *KP53; RPM:* 10–29.

1953

January 1
Congratulatory Messages.

Three congratulatory messages: to the officers and soldiers of the Korean People's Army, to the officers and soldiers of the Chinese Volunteer Army, and to the officers and soldiers of the 86th Regiment. New Year greetings to them.

ISJ 4: 444–50.
KW: 344–50.

February 8
Order No. 73 of the Supreme Commander of the People's Army of the Democratic People's Republic of Korea.

A six-point order in commemoration of the fifth anniversary of the founding of the Korean People's Army. Usual firing of cannons in celebration.

ISJ 4: 451–57.
KW: 351–56.

February 11
Letter of Appreciation.

Letter to the defense minister of the Soviet Union, A. Vassilievsky, in response to his congratulatory message on Kim's new title as marshal of the Democratic People's Republic of Korea.

ISJ 4: 458–59.

February 16
Letter of Appreciation.

Letter to the commander of the Chinese Volunteer Army, P'eng Teh-huai, in response to his congratulatory message on the fifth anniversary of the founding of the Korean People's Army.

1SJ 4: 460–61.

February 22
Congratulatory Message.

Congratulatory messages to Stalin and Vassilievsky on the thirty-fifth anniversary of the founding of the Russian army.

1SJ 4: 462–68.

March 6
On the Death of the Grand Marshal J. V. Stalin.

A telegram to the government and the Central Committee of the Communist Party of the Soviet Union.

Telegram of condolences to the Russian people and the party.

1SJ 4: 469–70.

March 10
Stalin is a Helper of the Struggle of the People Who Guard Their Freedom and Independence.

Glowing adulation of Stalin in this eulogy. Entirely different writing style from his usual speeches and reports.

1SJ 4: 471–85.

March 16
On the Fourth Anniversary of the Signing of the Agreement of Economic and Cultural Cooperation between North Korea and the Soviet Union.

A short letter to new premier Malenkov of the Soviet Union on the anniversary of the agreement.

1SJ 4: 486–87.

March 26
Conversation with Farmer Representatives in P'yŏngan Namdo.

A talk with representatives of farmers in P'yŏngan Namdo at the time of spring seeding. Asks all workers and office workers to work at least ten days on farms. Says that the North has received more than four hundred tractors and more than a thousand farm machines from the Soviet Union.

1SJ 4: 488–501.

March 31
Declaration concerning the Exchange of Prisoners.

Kim supports the statement issued by Chou En-lai on March 30 on the exchange of prisoners and the sick and facilitating the cease-fire in Korea.

KW: 357–59.

May 1
Order No. 269 of the Supreme Commander of the People's Army of the Democratic People's Republic of Korea.

In commemoration of May Day. There is no specific order.

1SJ 4: 502–6.
KW: 360–63.

May 11
To the Committee of the People's Peace Congress in Paris.

Letter addressed to various members of the committee.

This letter is in support of five-power (Soviet Union, United States, People's Republic of China, Great Britain, and France) peace treaty, in reply to the appeal of the World Peace Council. Kim says that 7,047,000 Koreans signed the appeal.

1SJ 4: 507–10.

July 27
Order No. 470 of the Supreme Commander of the Korean People's Army.

This order is to convey the signing of the cease-fire agreement with the enemy. Expresses sincere appreciation to the Chinese Volunteer Army.

KW: 364–66.

July 28
Broadcast Address to the Korean People on the Conclusion of the Cease-fire Agreement.

Kim claims that he has won and the intruders, headed by the U. S. imperialists, have lost the war. Kim is very proud of the fact that Stalin once called the Workers' Party of Korea the "shock troops" of national independence and freedom. In the second part of his speech, Kim says that the North won because of the high morale of the people and international assistance of the fraternal parties. He concludes by urging the rebuilding of the North both economically and in national defense.

KW: 367–90; *KP53.*

*August 5
Everything for the Postwar Rehabilitation and Development of the National Economy.

Report delivered at the sixth plenary meeting of the Central Committee of the Workers' Party of Korea (2WPK-12CC).

Policy statements concerning the three-year economic plan and future tasks to reconstruct the North. He speaks of the problems of Korean unification, all phases of economic development, problems associated with economic reconstruction, strengthening of the working class, and works in the newly liberated areas after the war.

SW 1: 413–62; *2SW 1:* 161–209; *2SJ 4:* 1–56; *CSJ 1:* 394–442; *RUSS:* 5–54. *SKKM 1:* 99–118 (excerpt); *SK:* 91–97 (excerpt); *UNF:* 25–28 (excerpt); *IPRC:* 38–44 (excerpt); *CCY 54–55:* 1–9; *EP61; TU:* 61–64 (excerpt); *KP55; CIK:* 67–104; *ZG:* 306–59; *SEC:* 1–65.

August 15
Order No. 523 of the Supreme Commander of the People's Army of the Democratic People's Republic of Korea.

A short order to the soldiers in commemoration of the August 15 liberation, the first since the cease-fire. Kim orders firing of a twenty-four gun salute for the occasion in several cities.

CCY 54–55: 9.

August 19
Speech at the Meeting of Fighting Heroes of the Nation.

Kim cites the role of hero Kim Ch'ang-gŏl, who blocked an enemy gun with his body in the 6,026 Heights. Kim encourages the heroes to be humble and contribute more to the cause of the country.

CCY 54–55: 9–11.

September 10–29
Speeches during the Visit to the Soviet Union.

Four speeches were made: at the arrival on September 10, at the Kremlin reception on September 19, at the airport in Moscow on September 25, and on arrival at Pyongyang on September 29. Basically, Kim expresses his appreciation to Malenkov, then the premier of the Soviet Union, for the aid of one billion rubles in goods and services, and for the extension, and easy terms, of earlier credit of the Soviet Union to the North.

CCY 54–55: 11–14.

October 25
Speech at the Reception of the Chinese People's Consolidation Corps on Their Third Visit to Korea.

A short speech repeating his appreciation for the aid of the Chinese people. Kim says that the Chinese people helped the Koreans with blood and also helped the Korean people in the paddy fields during the spring and the fall.

CCY 54–55: 14–15.

November 9
Speech to the Visiting Japanese People's Peace and Friendship Group in Commemoration of the Cease-fire.

The Japanese mission was headed by Oyama Ikuo. Kim speaks of the victory of the war and recovery from the devastation of indiscriminate bombing of the North.

CCY 54–55: 15–16.

November 12–27
Speeches during the Visit to the People's Republic of China.

Four speeches were made: one at the Peking railway station on arrival on November 12, one at the signing ceremony of the Economic and Cultural Cooperation Agreement between China and North Korea on November 23, one at his departure on November 25, and a lengthy one at his arrival on November 27. Kim says that China has wiped out all credits given to the North during the three-year period from the start of the war to the end of 1953 and in addition has given 800 billion *wŏn* (Chinese currency) of Chinese aid for the recovery of the North.

CCY 54–55: 16–19.

*December 20
Precious International Aid by the Peoples of the Fraternal Countries.

Report to the sixth session of the First Supreme People's Assembly on return from a visit to fraternal countries (1SPA-6).

Report of Kim's visit to the Soviet Union in September and his visit to China in October and summary report of the visit of his government delegation, headed by Yi Chu-yŏn, to Czechoslovakia, Poland, Germany, Hungary, Rumania, and Bulgaria from June to November. Detailed report of various foreign aid from these countries to the North for economic recovery from the war. Expresses sincere appreciation to these countries and condemns the U.S. aid to the South. Urges the people to make good use of the assistance for speedy recovery.

2SJ 4: 57–91.
CCY 54–55: 19–31; *KP53.*

December 29
On the Duty of Intelligence Officers.

Speech at the graduation ceremony of intelligence officers of the Korean People's Army.

RPM: 30–39.

1954

January 1
New Year Congratulatory Messages.

Two messages: one to the officers and soldiers of the Korean People's Army and another to the soldiers of the Chinese Volunteer Army. Kim says that the South is again trying to launch an invasion.

CCY 54–55: 31–32.

February 8
Order No. 63 of the Supreme Commander of the People's Army of the Democratic People's Republic of Korea.

Short three-point order to be ready for new aggression by the South, to strengthen the organization and friendship with the Chinese Volunteer Army, and to learn more on military and political strategies.

CCY 54–55: 32.

February 16
Grain is Important in Solving All Problems of the Postwar Recovery and Reconstruction.

Speech at a meeting of peasant activists who had large harvests in the country.

Kim stresses the importance of grain in postwar recovery and encourages the peasant activists gathered for the meeting to produce more.

CIK: 105–24; *SEC:* 66–78.

March 21
Defects in Industrial and Transportation Sections and on the Rectification Policy.

Report at March plenum of the Central Committee of the Workers' Party of Korea (2WPK-14CC).

A detailed report pointing out the defects in the management of industrial and transportation sectors of the economy. He covered the leadership problems in industrial sectors, recruitment problems, labor organizations and labor force, and strengthening of the party leadership in all segments.

2SJ 4: 92–142.
SKKM 1: 119–65; *CCY 54–55:* 32–46; *EP55; KP69; CIK:* 125–92; *SEC:* 79–123.

March 26
Important Tasks of Architects and Technicians in the Postwar Recovery and Reconstruction.

Speech delivered at a conference of architects and technicians.

A short speech to urge architects and technicians to work harder to rebuild the country.

CIK: 193–205; *KP55.*

May 1
In Commemoration of the May First Holiday.

Kim delivers a speech in commemoration of May Day; a general speech to encourage people to work hard for reconstruction.

CCY 54–55: 47.

May 1
Order No. 220 of the Supreme Commander of the People's Army of the Democratic People's Republic of Korea.

A short three-point order to be alert, to learn more, and to give aid to the people's efforts for reconstruction.

CCY 54–55: 46–47.

May 6
On the Task of Workers in Forestry Sectors of the Postwar Reconstruction.

Speech at a meeting of activists in the forestry sectors of the country.

Five-point speech to correct the mistakes of the workers in the forestry sectors.

2SJ 4: 143–51.
KP55; CIK: 206–17.

May 11
On the Immediate Tasks of the Transportation Workers.

Speech delivered at a conference of model workers in the transportation sector.

An eight-point speech pointing out the tasks of the transportation workers.

SW 1: 463–76; *2SJ 4:* 152–67; *CSJ 1:* 443–56.
KP68; CIK: 218–40.

July 12
The Task of the Hamgyŏng Pukto Party Organizations in the Struggle to Attain the Postwar People's Economic Reconstruction and Development Three-Year Plan.

Speech at the party activists meeting of Hamgyŏng Pukto.

Kim delivers several lengthy speeches in various provinces to bolster postwar economic reconstruction. This one is at Hamgyŏng Pukto. Kim urges the party activists to meet the goals of the three-year plan.

CIK: 241–300.

September 10
Korean People's Struggle for Postwar Recovery and Reconstruction.

Kim speaks about four subjects. The first is the basic task of completing the goals of the three-year plan, and the second is the assistance of fraternal socialist countries for postwar recovery and reconstruction. He expresses much appreciation to the Soviet Union and China in particular. The third is his review of the accomplishments of the past year in the North, and the fourth is his description of the conditions in the South. Kim praises the North Korean efforts and condemns the South.

CIK: 301–28; *KP54; SEC:* 124–42.

November 1

Speech at the November Plenum of the Central Committee (2WPK-15CC).

No text available.

*November 3

On Our Party Policy for the Further Development of Agricultural Management.

Speech delivered at November plenum of the Central Committee of the Workers' Party of Korea (2WPK-15CC).

> In three parts, this speech deals with reform in agricultural management, restructuring of agrarian sectors of North Korean economy, and the task of the party for the unification of Korea. Useful discussion of the problems and future direction of agriculture.
>
> *SW 1:* 477–500; *2SW 1:* 210–33; *2SJ 4:* 168–95; *CSJ 1:* 457–80; *RUSS:* 55–78.
> *SK:* 98–104 (excerpt); *EP64; CIK:* 329–63; *SEC:* 143–65.

December 19

Tasks of the P'yŏngan Namdo Party Organizations for the Development of Agrarian Management.

Speech at a P'yŏngan Namdo party committee meeting.

> This is another example of a speech to encourage people to work hard to meet the goals of the three-year economic plan. This one is on agrarian management in P'yŏngan Namdo. Kim gives a few specific tasks to members of the party committee here.
>
> *CIK:* 364–404.

December 23

On the Developmental Perspective of Officers and Soldiers and Making Cadres of the People's Army.

Speech at a meeting of military-political cadres of the Korean People's Army.

> General statement on strengthening the army with political thought. Claims that Pak Hŏn-yŏng told Kim during the Korean War that there were 300,000 party members in the South.
>
> *SK:* 105–33; *RPM:* 40–68 (excerpt).

1955

*April

Every Effort for the Country's Reunification and Independence and for Socialist Construction in the Northern Half of the Republic.

Theses on the character and tasks of the revolution.

> Basically a two-part thesis addressing (1) the basic question of Korean revolutionary characteristics at the time, described as anti-feudal and anti-imperialist national liberation, and (2) the strengthening of the northern half by building the revolutionary base. In the latter part of the thesis, Kim elaborates the necessity for strengthening party discipline and arming the members with Marxism and Leninism.
>
> *SW 1:* 501-17; *2SW 1:* 234-50; *2SJ 4:* 196-213; *CSJ 1:* 481-96; *RUSS:* 79-94.
> *SK:* 134-39 (excerpt); *RSC:* 13-29; *WSK:* 133-44; *KP60*; *PPT:* 164-80; *ZG:* 360-78.

*April 1

On Further Intensifying the Class Education of the Party Members.

Report delivered at April plenum of the Central Committee (2WPK-16CC).

> Divided into three parts, this report delineates the basic characteristics and basic duty of the party, the necessity to intensify the class education of the members, and the basic policy for the class education of the party. Most important, this speech directs members to study Marxism and Leninism in accordance with the interests and conditions of the Workers' Party of Korea and not to copy foreign ideas in a wholesale fashion.
>
> *SW 1:* 518-39; *2SW 1:* 251-72; *2SJ 4:* 214-37; *CSJ 1:* 497-517.
> *PPT:* 164-80; *EP61*; *KP55*; *WP 2:* 1-24.

*April 1

On Eliminating Bureaucracy.

Report delivered at April plenum of the Central Committee (2WPK-16CC).

> Kim lectures on elimination of bureaucratic tendencies in all aspects of party work. Identifies how bureaucracy is expressed, where and how it originates, and what sort of policy is needed to eliminate the bureaucratic work system.
>
> *SW 1:* 540-54; *2SW 1:* 273-87; *2SJ 4:* 238-53; *CSJ 1:* 518-31.
> *PPT:* 181-96; *KP60*; *WP 2:* 25-40; *ZG:* 379-94.

*April 4
On Some Questions of Party and State Work in the Present Stage of the Socialist Revolution.

Concluding speech delivered at April plenum of the Central Committee (2WPK-16CC).

> Kim denounces party factionalists by name, citing Pak Hŏn-yŏng, Yi Sŭng-yŏp, Pak Il-u, and Pang Ho-san, among others, and stresses unity of the party in this speech. He speaks of strengthening class education, factional elements in the party, economic thrift, the party working style, and accomplishing goals of the people's economic plan.
>
> SW 1: 555–81; 2SW 1: 288–314; 2SJ 4: 254–86; CSJ 1: 532–59; RUSS: 95–122.
> SKKM 1: 166–70 (excerpt); WP 2: 41–70.

April 15
Leninism is our Direction.

An article written on the eighty-fifth anniversary of Lenin's birthday.

> Brief survey of Korean revolutionary history based on Lenin's idea of revolution. Here for the first time Kim elaborates his partisan activities in Manchuria as an important event in the Korean revolutionary movement. This comes shortly after his denunciation of factional elements from South Korea, China, and the Soviet Union.
>
> 2SJ 4: 287–99; RUSS: 123–33.

August 14
Report at the Commemoration Rally of the Tenth Anniversary of the August 15 Liberation by the Great Soviet Army.

> A two-part report surveying the events after the liberation in the North and comparing the developments in the North and the South. He continues to speak of the unification of Korea by the Koreans and expulsion of U.S. troops from Korea.
>
> 2SJ 4: 300–24.

*December 28
On Eliminating Dogmatism and Formalism and Establishing Chuch'e in Ideological Work.

Speech to party propagandists and agitators.

> Perhaps the most important speech Kim has made so far. Here, for the first time, Kim elaborates on the now-famous idea of chuch'e, or self-reliance of Koreans in working out their own problems. Slight editing from earlier ver-

sion, but mostly a straight recounting in later edition. Many factionalists and others are condemned in this speech.

SW 1: 582-606; 2SW 1: 315-40; 2SJ 4: 325-54; CSJ 1: 560-85.
DJOU 1: 170-200; CHU 1: 29-56; WSK: 145-65; SS: 43-71; LSWY 1: 164-92; EP64; EP73; KP60; WP 2: 71-98.

1956

January 30
For Innovation in Construction Work.

Speech delivered at a national conference of architects and builders.

Detailed instruction as to how construction workers should approach the building industry. He points out the importance of reform and introduction of new methods and emphasizes standardization, mechanization, and other sundry systems, including an independent accounting system.

SW 1: 607-29; 2SJ 4: 355-81; CSJ 1: 607-29; RUSS: 134-56.
KP56; CIK: 405-42; SEC: 166-89.

February 5
The Tasks of the Party Organizations in Kaech'ŏn County.

Speech delivered at a conference of the Kaech'ŏn County party organization.

This speech was made public for the first time in a book published in 1978. It is difficult to detect from the text why this was not made public earlier except for the fact that Kim criticized a few prominent party leaders such as Pak Hŏn-yŏng in the speech. Kim speaks about three problems: (1) amendment of the party rules, (2) party work, and (3) economic and cultural work. Kim encourages the people to fulfill the goals of the three-year economic plan.

WP 2: 99-128.

April 7
Tasks of the Party Organizations in P'yŏngan Pukto.

Speech delivered at a party conference of P'yŏngan Pukto.

Sharp criticism of the party organization membership policy, organization policy, dogmatism, and formalism. Urges the party cadres to strengthen the party leadership in economic and cultural development and avoid misunderstanding of the intelligentsia class in the society.

SW 1: 630–75; 2SJ 4: 382–432; CSJ 1: 609–52.
KP56; WP 2: 129–49 (excerpt).

*April 23
Report of the Works of the Central Committee to the Third Party Congress of the Workers' Party of Korea (3WPK).

This is a major speech which is not reproduced in subsequent editions of Kim's writings. The speech is divided into three parts: international situations and North Korea, recounting the North Korean positions; domestic situations, accounting for past performances and projecting new plans; and the party, giving a short history of its development and trying to correct past mistakes in the future. This speech is revealing in many ways, for Kim frankly points out past mistakes and names those factionalists and others who were purged. In contrast to today's strong emphasis on *chuch'e*, this speech strangely lacks any mention of that idea. English text is available in a book published in 1956, a collection of documents of the third party congress, but was not reprinted in the latest edition of his selected works.

2SJ 4: 433–571; RUSS: 157–284.
SK: 140–50 (excerpt); UNF: 29–33 (excerpt); IPRC: 45–55 (excerpt); SS: 72–87 (excerpt); TU: 65–69 (excerpt); PPT: 197–200 (excerpt); KP56; PH: 30–31 (excerpt); WP 2: 150–280; ZG: 395–98 (excerpt); SEC: 190–244.

November 9
On Some Immediate Tasks of the Democratic Youth League Organizations.

Speech delivered before the newly elected members of the Central Committee of the Democratic Youth League.

This is Kim's speech shortly after the conclusion of the fourth congress of the Democratic Youth League. Kim speaks of two basic problems; one is the organizational and political work, and the other is the role the youth must play in economic construction. In the political and organizational work, Kim stresses that the Democratic Youth League must follow closely the decisions of the party central committee, organize a mass movement among the youth and children, and strengthen the united front. In economic construction, youth must learn technology and must also learn to be thrifty.

YOU: 55–80; LSWY 1: 193–219; WY: 79–105.

December 13
To Bring about a Great Revolutionary Upswing in Socialist Construction.

Concluding speech at the December plenum of the Central Committee of the Workers' Party of Korea (3WPK-2CC).

A short speech to encourage people to complete the goals of the economic plan. Kim urges miners to work hard to obtain more foreign exchange. This speech came after the August plenum, when many factionalists were purged, and Kim reiterates his calls for the elimination of factionalists from the ranks. This speech is in none of the selected works of Kim.

DJOU 1: 201–14; *EP74; KP73; CLM:* 1–12.

1957

January 21
On Some Problems of the Future Development of Agrarian Management.

Speech delivered at a meeting of managers of agricultural cooperatives of P'yŏngan Namdo.

Broadly under three headings, Kim lauds the achievements of the agricultural cooperatives of P'yŏngnam province and points out some problems in irrigation, importation of new skills, and further cooperativization of agriculture. He emphasizes that cooperativization should not be forced on farmers. He says that 79.3 percent of all farm households are already in cooperatives and 76.4 percent of arable lands are under cooperatives.

2SJ 5: 1–34.
CCY 58: 1–10; *SEC:* 245–72; *KP57.*

February 14
On the Improvement and Strengthening of Commodity Circulation.

Speech delivered at a national conference of activists in trade.

General guidelines for reform in commodity circulation in cities and countryside. Improve administrative measures for circulation.

SW 2: 1–16; *2SJ 5:* 35–52; *CSJ 2:* 1–16; *RUSS:* 285–300.
CCY 58: 10–14; *SEC:* 273–87; *KP57.*

March 26
Tasks of Hamgyŏng Namdo Party Organizations in Socialist Economic Construction.

Speech to the activists of party organizations, economic organizations, and social organizations of Hamgyŏng Namdo.

Primarily on the economic conditions of Hamgyŏng Namdo; Kim speaks of the industry, fisheries, agriculture, improvement of cooperatives, local organizations, and party work in this locale. He cites many statistics to encourage people to improve their production.

2SJ 5: 53–78.
CCY 58: 14–21; *KP57.*

April 19
On Further Development of Fisheries.

Speech at the April plenum of the Central Committee (3WPK-3CC).

Kim urges fishermen to improve skills by learning from the Russians and to catch 600,000 tons of fish. He also speaks of improving the manufacturing of fish products, and he says the government should invest more in fisheries and educate more fishermen. Fishermen should be proud of their profession, and party functionaries should strengthen party work among the fishermen.

2SJ 5: 79–96.

May 11
Speech Delivered to the Workers of the Party, Government, and Social Organizations of Hamgyŏng Pukto.

KP57 (Hambukto tang mit chŏngkwŏn kigwan sahoe tanch'e ilkun dŭl ap'esŏ chinsul han yŏnsŏl. Pyongyang: Chosŏn Nodongdang Ch'ulp'ansa, 1957).

July 5
On Strengthening the Party Organizations and Carrying Out the Party's Economic Policy.

Speech to the organization workers of the party and the provincial, city, and county workers of the party.

Efforts to educate party organization workers to carry out the party's economic policy. Kim stresses the importance of the elementary party organs and their party character *(tangsŏng).* Urges the party workers of the provincial and city levels to go among the masses. Kim elaborates what one should do in industrial construction and agrarian management.

2SJ 5: 97–123.
SKKM 1: 171–89 (excerpt).

August 2
Speech Delivered before Electorate of Mundŏk Electoral District.

Mundŏk district chose Kim to be the candidate for the Supreme People's Assembly in its second session. This speech was made before his constituents, and it is a general review of North Korean achievements and condemnation of the South.

2SJ 5: 124–43.
CCY 58: 21–26; *SEC:* 288–305; *PPT:* 201–220; *ZG:* 399–419.

August 25
Speech at the First Graduation Ceremony of Songdo Political Economy College.

Speaks primarily of Korean unification and insists that three conditions should be met for unification: success of the labor movement in the South, success in the North Korean socialist construction, and victory of fraternal socialist countries in their socialist construction. Condemns the Korean Communists in the South and accuses them of failure from the very beginning.

SK: 151–63; *KP57.*

September 11
The Development of Machine Industry is the Key to the Successful Accomplishment of the Five-Year Plan.

Speech made at the National Conference of Activists of Machine-building Industry.

General statement about the machine industry, telling workers to be thrifty and develop means to assist agriculture and other industries.

2SJ 5: 144–59.
CCY 58: 26–30; *SEC:* 306–18; *KP57.*

September 20
On the Immediate Tasks of the People's Power in Socialist Construction.

Speech delivered at the first session of the Second Supreme People's Assembly (2SPA-1).

A general speech on various points, praising the accomplishments in the North and downgrading the situation in the South. He says that the most important tasks are the peaceful unification of the country and the strengthening of the democratic base of the North for eventual unification of Korea. In international relations, he says that the North should normalize relations with Japan.

SW 2: 17–39; *2SJ 5:* 160–85; *CSJ 2:* 17–38; *RUSS:* 301–23.
SEC: 319–39; *CCY 58:* 30–36; *SK:* 164–87; *PPT:* 221–44; *KP57; ZG:* 420–45.

October 19
On Carrying Out the Party Policy in the Construction Sector.

Concluding speech made at the October plenum of the Central Committee of the Workers' Party of Korea (3WPK-4CC).

> Pointing out the errors of such people as Kim Sŭng-hwa, Pak Ch'ang-ok, and Yi Pyŏng-je, Kim stressed the development of new methods in the construction industry and also urged mobilization of all the people for construction.
>
> *2SJ* 5: 186–204.
> *SEC:* 340–54; *KP58.*

October 22
The Thought of Great October is Victorious.

An article written on the occasion of the fortieth anniversary of the October socialist revolution.

> General statement on the impact of the October revolution on Korean nation-building in the North. Laudatory remarks about the Russian contribution to the North.
>
> *2SJ* 5: 205–15.
> *KP58; Nodong sinmun,* October 29, 1958; *Pravda,* October 22, 1957; *SEC:* 355–63.

November
Friendship and Unity of the Socialist Countries.

> General statement about the Russian support for the North on the occasion of the fortieth anniversary of the October revolution and about Kim's visit to Moscow on that occasion. This is an article written for a Russian journal.
>
> Russian text is in *Muzhdunarodnaya zhizn,* no. 11 (1957): 59–67. English text is in *International Affairs,* no. 11 (1957): 65–72.
> *Nodong sinmun,* November 15, 1957; *KP58.*

November 4–21
On the Occasion of the Fortieth Anniversary of the Great October Revolution.

Speeches in Moscow.

> Five speeches: one at the airport on his arrival, one at the Central Committee of the Communist Party of the Soviet Union, one at the Supreme Soviet, one at the Moscow radio station, and one at the airport on his departure. Congratula-

tory speeches in praise of the October Revolution and its impact in Korea. He still maintains that Russia is North Korea's foremost friend.

KP58; Nodong sinmun, November 5, 8, 23, 1957.

*December 5
On the Work of the Party and Government Delegation Which Attended Celebrations of the Fortieth Anniversary of the Great October Socialist Revolution and the Meetings of Representatives of the Communist and Workers' Parties of Various Countries in Moscow.

Report at the December enlarged plenum of the Central Committee of the Workers' Party of Korea (3WPK-5CC).

> Very pro-Soviet speech. Koreans must follow Russian examples and it is the duty of the Korean Communists to follow the leadership of the Russians. Denounces the revisionists who plotted against the party in 1956. He speaks of the August plenum of 1956 (agenda of that plenum was never announced) and of exposing antiparty elements.

> *2SJ 5:* 216–49; *RUSS:* 324–63.
> *KP57; EP57; SEC:* 364–92; *CCY 58:* 37–45.

December 13
On Further Consolidating Victories Gained in the Socialist Transformation of the Rural Economy in Our Country.

Speech at a meeting of activists of farm cooperatives in Hwanghae Namdo.

> Basically a two-point speech: consolidate the cooperatives for economically productive groups and strengthen them politically. He hints that antiparty factionalists of the 1956 plot were exposed in Hwanghae Namdo party organs.

> *2SJ 5:* 250–77.
> *SEC:* 393–416; *CCY 58:* 45–53; *KP58; PH:* 32–35 (excerpt).

1958

January 29
For the Further Development of Light Industry.

Speech delivered at a meeting of activists of the Ministry of Light Industry.

> Reviews the development of light industry in the North, compares it with that of colonial Korea, and points out several tasks of the workers in light industry,

including implementation of the decision of the December plenum (1956) of the Central Committee of the Workers' Party of Korea.

SW 2: 40–63; *2SJ 5:* 278–307; *CSJ 2:* 39–63; *RUSS:* 364–87.
SEC: 417–42; *KP58.*

February 8
The Korean People's Army is the Successor to the Anti-Japanese Armed Struggle.

Speech delivered before the officers and men of the 324th Army Unit of the Korean People's Army.

Primarily an emphatic statement to stress the tradition of partisans as the only tradition inherited by the North Korean army. Points out and denounces opposition leaders who advocate other traditions. Briefly recounts economic accomplishments and reiterates Kim's position on Korean unification. Also points out the withdrawal of the Chinese Volunteer Army and the army's preparation for this event.

SW 2: 64–101; *2SJ 5:* 308–49; *CSJ 2:* 64–100.
SK: 188–94 (excerpt); *RPM:* 69–108; *LSWY 1:* 220–59; *KP73.*

February 14
Speech at Pyongyang City Mass Rally to Welcome the Government Representatives of the People's Republic of China.

This friendship visit was headed by Chou En-lai, and the speech is a general welcoming speech. This visit was preliminary to the final withdrawal of the Chinese Volunteer Army from Korea.

2SJ 5: 350–58.

*March 6
For the Successful Fulfillment of the First Five-Year Plan.

Concluding speech delivered at the first conference of the Workers' Party of Korea (WPK-IC).

The most stunning public speech after the antiparty activities of 1956. He reviewed the five-year economic plan and pointed out several tasks for the party, but more importantly he lashed out at antiparty elements who followed Russian revisionist thinking, including Kim Tu-bong, Ch'oe Ch'ang-ik, Pak Ŭi-wan, and others. The first public denunciation of the antiparty groups and revisionist tendency in the North.

2SW 1: 342–72; *SW 2:* 102–31; *2SJ 5:* 359–93; *CSJ 2:* 101–31.
DJOU 1: 215–51; *CHU 1:* 57–90; *WP 2:* 281–91 (excerpt).

*March 7
On the Reform of Party Works.

Speech before the chairmen of the People's Committees and party committees of counties, cities, and provinces.

> Perhaps one of the most important speeches on party works. Here Kim denounces his rivals, including Kim Tu-bong and others who opposed him during 1956, and presents tasks for the county and local organizations. This speech was not included in subsequent collections of his writings. Kim refers briefly to erroneous works by the judiciary branch, including the works of Chief Justice Cho Sŏng-mo, Vice-Minister of Justice Pak Yong-suk, and Hwang Se-hwan.

2SJ 5: 394–415.

March 11
Speech at the Farewell Meeting of the Returning Chinese People's Volunteer Army.

> Brief speech discussing the firm bond between the two people and how the Chinese people helped the Koreans during and after the war.

2SJ 5: 416–21.

March 19
On the Tasks of the Youth in the Socialist Construction.

Speech delivered at a national meeting of young socialist builders.

> Pointed out four tasks of youth: fulfill the first five-year plan, learn advanced technology, arm with patriotism, and hold the leadership role in the socialist construction of the country.

2SJ 5: 422–37; RUSS: 388–400.
SEC: 443–55; YOU: 81–95; LSWY 1: 260–75; YC: 41–56; KP60; WY: 106–120.

*April 29
For the Implementation of the Judicial Policy of Our Party.

Speech delivered at the national conference of judicial workers and public prosecutors.

> One of the most basic and important documents on the theory of law in the North. In response to the revisionist and anti-Russia and anti-Communist campaigns, Kim stresses the importance of the party in the judicial process. Condemns former Chief Justice Hwang and other justice ministers such as Hong Ki-ju and Yi Sŭng-yŏp and their antiparty activities.

2SW 1: 373–90; *SW 2:* 132–48; *2SJ 5:* 438–58; *CSJ 2:* 132–50; *RUSS:* 401–18.
PPT: 245–64; *ZG:* 446–64.

April 30
Speech at the Inaugural Ceremony of Number One Furnace and Coke Oven of the Hwanghae Steel Mill.

Brief speech encouraging the steel workers to produce more and meet the goals of the economic plan. Cites several workers who performed miraculous services.

2SJ 5: 459–68.

April 30
On the Preservation of Historical Ruins and Relics.

Talk with the faculty and students of Kim Il Sung University.

SS: 88–92.

May 4
On Developing the Public Health Work into the National Mass Movement.

Concluding remarks at the Standing Committee of the Central Committee of the Workers' Party of Korea.

PH: 43–47.

May 7
We Must Look After the Livelihood of the Decorated Veterans Who Spilled Blood for the People and the Fatherland.

Talk with decorated veterans at Kilchu Veterans Industrial Center.

HM: 1–7.

May 11
Tasks of the Party Organizations of Yanggangdo.

Speech to the activists of the party, political organizations, and social organizations of Yanggangdo.

Two-part speech dealing with economic and cultural construction and the tasks of the party organizations. On economic and cultural reconstruction, Kim makes a lengthy speech covering various segments of the economy and culture, including forestry, mining, agriculture, etc. On the party tasks, he stresses socialist education and revolutionary tradition, pointing out the Poch'ŏnbo battles of the mid-1930s and how to take care of antirevolutionary elements, those who flee from the south, and intellectuals.

2SJ 5: 467–511.
KP58; PH: 36–38 (excerpt); *WP* 2: 292–308 (excerpt).

June 7
On Expanding the Production of People's Consumer Goods and Reforming the Merchandise Exchange Works.

Concluding remarks at the June plenum of the Central Committee of Workers' Party of Korea (3WPK-6CC).

Speech on expanding local industry. Speaks about four topics: foodstuff manufacturing, production of daily necessities, commerce, and trade. Kim speaks of North Korean trade here by saying that the North had lost trust in the international market because the quality of goods was low and the North Koreans did not meet delivery dates. Therefore the North suffered from a shortage of foreign exchange.

2SJ 5: 518–37.
KP59.

**June 11*
Everything for the Prosperity and Development of the Country.

Speech delivered at the third session of the Second Supreme People's Assembly (2SPA-3).

General statement on the economy on the occasion of the adoption of the First Five-year Economic Plan at the Supreme People's Assembly. Reviews accomplishments and urges workers to accomplish the economic plan ahead of time.

SW 2: 149–70; *2SJ* 5: 538–63; *CSJ* 2: 151–71; *RUSS:* 419–39.
SEC: 456–77; *KP58; CLM:* 13–36.

June 23
The Decorated Veterans Must Not Blemish the Record and Honor Earned during the Fatherland Liberation War.

Talk at the Yongch'ŏn branch factory of Sinŭiju Veterans Industrial Center.

HM: 8–10.

June 23
Speech to the Leading Cadres of P'yŏngan Pukto.

> *KP59 (P'yŏngpukto chido kanbudŭl ap'esŏ han yŏnsŏl.* Pyongyang: Chosŏn Nodongdang Ch'ulp'ansa, 1959).

August 9
On Some Immediate Tasks of the City and County People's Committees.

Address at a short course session for the chairmen of the city and county People's Committees.

> General message to encourage leaders of various people's committees to heighten the spirit of socialist construction, to strengthen socialist education, to accomplish cultural and technical revolutions, to develop local industries, to reform the works of the local organizations, and to deal with a few other problems confronting the localities.

> *SW 2:* 171–92; *2SJ 6:* 1–33; *CSJ 2:* 171–92.
> *PPT:* 265–88; *PH:* 39–42; *CLM:* 37–45 (excerpt); *ZG:* 465–89.

August 12
Congratulatory Speech at the Opening Ceremony of the Haeju-Hasŏng Wide-track Railway.

> A short congratulatory speech praising a few diligent workers and citing impressive statistics.

> *2SJ 6:* 34–43.
> *SEC:* 478–86; *LSWY 1:* 276–85; *CLM:* 46–55; *WY:* 121–30.

August 18
You Must Become Advanced Combatants of the Working Masses Faithful to the Party and the Revolution.

Speech delivered at the first graduation ceremony of the three-year course of the Central Party School.

> This is another speech that was made public for the first time in a book published in 1978. Here Kim describes the struggle between conservative and progressive elements in the December plenary meeting of 1956. Kim tells the graduates to be humble and gives examples of arrogance in the work of men like O Ki-sŏp. Kim also says that the graduates of the school should wipe out formalism and subjectivism in their work.

> *WP 2:* 309–23.

August 30

Speech at the Completion Ceremony of the Reconstruction of the Sup'ung Power Station.

Commends the Russian technicians and Russian assistance in the completion of the reconstruction of the largest hydroelectric power station in Korea.

2SJ 6: 44–52.
SEC: 487–94.

September 8

Report at the Tenth Anniversary Celebration of the Founding of the Democratic People's Republic of Korea.

Divided into four parts, this report assesses the accomplishments and prospects of the republic, giving some statistical facts about the economic strides the North had made. Kim also criticizes conditions in the South, but his condemnation is too far from reality to be convincing. Lastly Kim discusses the favorable climate for the development of Communist regimes in the new international relations.

SW 2: 193–232; *2SJ 6:* 53–99; *CSJ 2:* 193–232.
SEC: 495–534; *IPRC:* 56–64 (excerpt); *SK:* 195–202 (excerpt); *UNF:* 34–36 (excerpt); *PPT:* 289–332; *KP58; ML:* 36–42 (excerpt); *ZG:* 490–533.

September 16

Against Passivism and Conservatism in Socialist Construction.

Speech at a national meeting of production innovators.

In order to achieve socialist industrialization, Kim insists that ideological and technical revolutions must be achieved. He lashes out at the conservatives, saying that there is nothing mysterious about science and that scientists and workers must cooperate to achieve the goal. There are still remnants of Japanese imperialistic thought among some scientists and intellectuals, and they tend to be contemptuous toward workers. Everyone must strengthen party character.

2SW 1: 391–403; *SW 2:* 233–45; *2SJ 6:* 100–115; *CSJ 2:* 233–46; *RUSS:* 440–52.
TU: 70–84; *LSWY 1:* 286–300; *KP59; CLM:* 56–70.

October 30

On the Strengthening of the Communist Education and the Study of the Revolutionary Tradition among Soldiers.

Speech at the conference of military school instructors of the Korean People's Army.

LSWY 1: 301–21; *KP70.*

November 20
On Communist Education.

Speech delivered at a lecture session for the agitators of the city and county party committees of the country.

> After a brief comparison of North Korean achievement with that of Japan on some selected industrial products, this speech is primarily on Communist education of party members. Kim points out seven items to strengthen party character of each individual member. He stresses that each member should strengthen his party character by studying and upgrading the educational level of the masses.

> *2SW 1:* 404–30; *SW 2:* 246–69; *2SJ 6:* 116–46; *CSJ 2:* 247–70; *RUSS:* 453–78.
> *TU:* 85–111; *WSK:* 166–85; *LSWY 1:* 322–48; *YC:* 57–87; *KP60*; *CLM:* 71–97; *WY:* 131–56; *WP 2:* 324–49.

November 21–December 10
Speeches during the Visit to China and Vietnam.

> Kim made fourteen speeches during his trip to China and Vietnam: one at Antung railway station, five in Peking, two in Shanghai, five in Hanoi, and one when he returned to Pyongyang. These were all very short banquet speeches, and Kim used one general theme of thanking the Chinese for their help in the Korean war. Kim said that he shall never forget the friendship sealed in blood with the Chinese people. He travelled to Wuhan to visit Mao there. In Hanoi, Kim emphasized that the Vietnamese and the Korean peoples have a common enemy in the United States.

> *ZD:* 4–5, 9–11, 20–26, 31–39, 83–93, 122–23, 129–30, 141–48, 152–56, 164–65, and 183–93.

December 25
For Higher Quality in Construction.

Speech delivered at a meeting of the construction workers of Pyongyang.

> A short speech on upgrading the construction industry. Points out how factional elements such as Pak Ŭi-wan and Kim Sŭng-hwa opposed the party guidelines. To improve the quality of construction, Kim insists that there must

be socialist content in planning, workers should be more responsible in the production of construction materials, the skills of workers must be improved, and the inspection system must be improved.

SW 2: 270–81; *2SJ 6:* 147–59; *CSJ 2:* 271–82.
KP59.

1959

*January 5
On the Victory of Socialist Agricultural Cooperativization and the Future Development of Agriculture in Our Country.

Report to the National Congress of Agricultural Cooperatives.

From August 1953 when the agricultural cooperatives plan was first proposed, there were three types of agricultural forms in the North, and Kim traces their development. The agricultural cooperativization is said to have been completed by August 1958. Kim also states that in October 1958, *ri* administrative district and *ri* agricultural cooperative were the same unit and *ri* people's committee chairmen were to assume concurrently the chairmanship of the cooperatives. Kim stresses the importance of agriculture in the North.

2SW 1: 431–86; *SW 2:* 282–333; *2SJ 6:* 160–221; *CSJ 2:* 283–332; *RUSS:* 479–534.
CCY 60: 1–17; *EP72; KP59.*

*January 9
For an Effective Solution of the Tasks Confronting the Agrarian Management.

Concluding remarks at the Agricultural Cooperative Conference of the Country.

KP 59 (Nongch'on kyŏngni ŭi tangmyŏn han kwaŏp ŭi sŏnggwajŏk silhaeng ŭl wihayŏ. Pyongyang: Chosŏn Nodongdang Ch'ulp'ansa, 1959).

*February 23
Congress of Communist Builders.

Report of the works of the representatives of the Workers' Party of Korea who participated in the twenty-first interim congress of the Communist

Party of the Soviet Union. The report was made at the February plenum
of the Central Committee of the Workers' Party of Korea (3WPK-8CC).

Extensive praise of Russian accomplishments and of the victory of Khruschechev and condemnation of other leaders, such as Malenkov, Bulganin, Molotov, and Kaganovich. Reference is made here to an equal rather than subser-
vient relationship among the fraternal Communist parties. Praises Russian
economic achievement by citing statistics and the eventual victory of the socialist economy.

2SJ 6: 222–46; *RUSS:* 535–55.
CCY 60: 17–23.

February 25
**Concluding Remarks at the February Plenum of the Central Committee
of the Workers' Party of Korea (3WPK-8CC).**

Reviewing the discussion of the entire meeting, Kim discusses his trip to Moscow for the twenty-first Russian party congress. Kim still maintains that all
fraternal parties must be united under the Soviet Union for the international
Communist movement. He also discusses other subjects, including the improvement of the quality of industrial goods, reforming transportation works,
and strengthening party work.

2SJ 6: 247–74.
CCY 60: 23–30.

February 26
On the Method of Party Work.

Speech at a lecture series for party organizers and chairmen of the party
committees of production enterprises and chairmen of provincial, city,
and county party committees.

Divided into four parts, the speech discusses party works, giving guidance on
how the county party chairmen and chairmen of production units must work.
Kim also speaks of the methods of party work, telling leaders not to resort to
bureaucratic and military manners of ordering people, but rather to persuade
the workers to work enthusiastically. He also stresses that each member should
try to improve himself by learning and reading party directives. Lastly he emphasizes that leaders should not doubt people, but rather guide them, particularly those who fled to the North from the South and intellectuals.

2SW 2: 1–37; *SW 2:* 334–70; *2SJ 6:* 275–316; *CSJ 2:* 333–68.
CCY 60: 30–40; *KP59; WP 2:* 350–89.

March 16
The Livelihood of the Decorated Veterans Must be Strengthened and They Must Live in Peace.

Talk with the veterans in the veterans' cooperative of daily necessities in Unggi.

HM: 11–13.

March 23
Tasks of the Party Organizations of Hamgyŏng Pukto.

Speech delivered at the enlarged plenary meeting of the Hamgyŏng Pukto Committee of the Workers' Party of Korea.

Kim had spent almost a month in this province giving personal guidance to party workers and pointed out several shortcomings in party activities, the greatest being localism. He pointed out past mistakes by the provincial party chairmen, such as Chang Sun-myŏng, Han Sang-du, Kim T'ae-gŭn, and then-chairman Sŏ Ŭl-hyŏn. He also pointed out the shortcomings in the People's Committee and emphasized elimination of bureaucratism. Other subjects included the developments in industry, agriculture, fisheries, and construction. A lengthy speech, correcting in detail the party activities in the local province.

SW 2: 371–425; *2SJ 6:* 317–79; *CSJ 2:* 369–421.
CCY 60: 40–56; *PPT:* 333–41 (excerpt); *KP68; WP 2:* 390–423 (excerpt); *ZG:* 534–42 (excerpt).

April 24
Public Health Workers Must Become True Servants of the People.

Talk with public health workers.

PH: 48–51.

June 11
For Further Development of Fisheries.

Speech delivered at a meeting of party activists in fisheries of Kangwŏn-do.

Speech primarily on fisheries. Urges the catching of large fish such as whales and dolphins to solve oil problems in the North.

SW 2: 426–49; *2SJ 6:* 380–407; *CSJ 2:* 422–445; *RUSS:* 556–78.
CCY 60: 56–63; *KP59.*

September 4

Let Us Hold Firmly the Key Handle in Solving Problems and Concentrate Our Energy.

Speech at the enlarged plenum of the Hwanghae Steel Mill Party Committee.

> Divided into three parts, the speech stressed the normalization of production patterns by improving the responsibility of each worker. Kim also stressed the assurance of the livelihood of each worker. The usual emphasis on the strengthening of the party political work was also made. Portions of this speech were omitted in his selected.works. The original text including the omitted portion that deals with the denunciation of his opposition, including Ch'oe Ch'ang-ik and Pak Ch'ang-ok, is in a pamphlet published in 1959.
>
> *2SJ 6:* 408–39.
> *SKKM 1:* 190–220; *CCY 60:* 63–70; *KP59.*

September 26

The Battlefield Friendship of the Peoples of Korea and China.

Article written on the occasion of the tenth anniversary of the People's Republic of China.

> Here Kim reveals that Korean partisans fought with the Chinese against Japan in Manchuria under the Anti-Japanese United Army. He also says that China gave the North 800 million *yuan* in aid and the trade between the two countries increased seventeen times during the five-year period from 1954 to 1958.
>
> *2SJ 6:* 440–54; *RUSS:* 579–91.
> *CCY 60:* 70–74; Chinese text in *Jen-min ji-pao*, September 26, 1959.

October 17

The Decorated Veterans Who Defended the Fatherland with Blood Must also Set Examples in the Socialist Construction.

Speech to the veterans who participated in the activists' conference of local industries and industrial cooperatives.

> *HM:* 14–25.

December 4

On Several Tasks Confronting the Socialist Economic Construction.

Concluding remarks at the December enlarged plenum of the Central Committee of the Workers' Party of Korea (3WPK-10CC).

Kim speaks of the shortcomings in the progress of the economic plan and tells the leaders to put greater efforts into political and organizational work. Han Sang-du, for example, had committed an error and confessed his mistakes in a self-criticism session. He also speaks of the important problems in 1960 and asks the local organization to reform to improve its work. Mentions the building of forestry for economic development. Lastly, the familiar emphasis on strengthening of party work. This is an important document, but was dropped in the subsequent edition of his selected works.

2SJ 6: 455–529; *RUSS*: 592–657.
SKKM 1: 221–76 (excerpt); *CCY 60*: 74–93; *KP60*.

1960

February 8
For Correct Management of the Socialist Agriculture.

Speech delivered at the general membership meeting of the party organization of Ch'ŏngsalli, Kangsŏ County.

Kim's directive on correct management of agrarian development in the North. Kim stresses ideological education for correct management. He urges doing away with conservatism and pursuing new methods in a revolutionary spirit.

SW 2: 450–83; *CSJ 2*: 446–79.
SKKM 1: 277–313; *SAF*: 1–37; *KP67*; *SR*: 1–37.

February 18
On Improving the Work Methods of the County Party Organization in Accordance with the New Circumstances.

Speech delivered at a plenary meeting of the Kangsŏ County party committee.

Kim's continued on-the-spot guidance in Kangsŏ County. Here he speaks of the shortcomings in the leadership in agrarian management. Here for the first time since December 28, 1955, Kim speaks of the *chuch'e* idea and its implementation in the party work.

SW 2: 484–511; *CSJ: 2*: 480–504.
CHU 1: 91–94 (excerpt); *DJOU 1*: 252–56 (excerpt); *SKKM 1*: 314–41; *KP68*; *WP 2*: 424–53.

*February 23
On the Lessons Drawn from Guidance to the Work of the Kangsŏ County Party Committee.

Speech at the enlarged meeting of the Standing Committee of the Central Committee of the Workers' Party of Korea (3WPK-10CC-SC).

A lengthy speech about how the local party organizations must work with the people. This speech is based on his on-the-spot guidance of the Kangsŏ county party committee. He speaks in detail as to how the county party organization must guide the people by persuasion and not by force, and how the party committee must work closely with the county people's committees. He speaks of collective leadership here repeatedly, but there is no indication that he understood what collective leadership implies in larger context. Kim seems to use the phrase in accordance with the trend of the time, but there is no specific instruction as to how this translates into the actual working relationship at the county level.

2SW 2: 38–78; *SW* 2: 512–52; *CSJ* 2: 505–42.
SKKM 1: 342–83; *KP70*.

August 11
On the Successful Accomplishment of the Technical Revolution.

Concluding speech at the August enlarged plenum of the Central Committee of the Workers' Party of Korea (3WPK-12CC).

Kim speaks of four subjects here: (1) the politico-economical significance of the technical revolution, (2) the mobilization of the masses for the technical revolution, (3) the problems in the realization of the technical revolution in all the aspects of the people's economy, and (4) the strengthening of technical personnel.

2SW 2: 79–107; *SW* 2: 553–81; *CSJ* 2: 543–70.
KP61.

August 14
Report at the Rally in Commemoration of the Fifteenth Anniversary of the August 15 Liberation, the National Holiday of the Korean People.

Kim reviews the accomplishments of the North and projects the future development in the soon-to-be-announced seven-year economic plan. This is shortly after the student revolution in the South, which he says was unsuccessful because it was not supported by the people. The new regime in the South is a rehashing of the old regime.

RUSS: 658–95.
SK: 203–19; *UNF*: 37–45 (excerpt); *IPR*: 1–15 (excerpt); *IPRC*: 65–81 (excerpt); *CCY 60*: 93–104; *KP60*.

August 22
The Riders of Ch'ŏllima Are the Heroes of Our Generation and the Red Soldiers of Our Party.

Speech at the leaders conference of the national Ch'ŏllima work group movement.

> A short speech about the workers in the Ch'ŏllima movement. This is a form of socialist competitive movement, and the North will forge ahead in economic development. Kim cites a few workers who performed outstanding work.
>
> *SKKM 1*: 384–93; *SAF*: 38–47; *LSWY 1*: 349–58; *TU*: 112–21; *CCY 61*: 1–4; *CLM*: 98–107; *KP73*; *SR*: 38–47.

August 25
The People's Army is a Communist School.

Talk with the soldiers of the 109th Division of the Korean People's Army.

> Only the fourth part of his talk is excerpted here. Kim speaks against dogmatism and revisionism and urges the soldiers to fight against the trend. He names such persons as Ch'oe Chong-hak, Pak Ch'ang-ok, and Pak Yŏng-bin as those who committed the errors of dogmatism.
>
> *CHU 1*: 95–98 (excerpt); *DJOU 1*: 257–260 (excerpt); *LSWY 1*: 359–95; *KP70*; *CLM*: 108–21 (excerpt).

September 1
For the Creation of a Modern Base for the Chemical Industry.

Speech at a meeting of the activists in the vinylon factory construction fields.

> Kim urges the workers to build the factory to produce vinylon by May Day 1961. Together with this, Kim emphasizes the need to improve the chemical industries and build a huge complex in the Hamhŭng and Hŭngnam area. Mentions several times the contribution and discussion of Dr. Yi Sŭng-gi, the inventor of vinylon.
>
> *CCY 61*: 4–8.

September 8
On the Strengthening of the Political Work in the People's Army.

Speech at the enlarged plenum of the Military Affairs Committee of the Workers' Party of Korea.

> *RPM*: 109–47; *LSWY 1*: 396–434.

November 27
Let Us Create Literature and Art Suitable to the Ch'ŏllima Age.

Talk with writers, composers, and film workers.

> Kim stresses more literary and art work on contemporary themes rather than on historical ones. He says that the traditional story of Ch'unhyang and the story about Yi Sun-sin are fine, but more anti-Japanese guerrilla and Korean war stories are desirable. He also speaks of the strengthening of the ideological content in literary works, art, and music.

> *SW 2:* 582–96; *CSJ 2:* 571–586.
> *SS:* 93–110; *KP64*; *CLM:* 122–39; *LA:* 16–33.

December 2
The Fraternal Relationship Formed in the Struggle Against the Common Enemy, American Imperialism, between the Peoples of Cuba and Korea Will Last Forever.

Speech at a banquet welcoming the economic mission of the revolutionary government of Cuba.

ML: 43–48.

1961

January 23
The Main Thing in Party Work Is to Educate, Remold, and Unite All People.

Speech delivered at the general membership meeting of the party organization of Yihyŏn-ri, Sŭngho district, Pyongyang City.

> This speech is on the party work in a local-level party organization, particularly on its agrarian work. On the work method, Kim said that the directives of the December plenum of 1956 are important. He stressed three aspects in particular: the struggle with antiparty, antipeople elements; the importance of learning party documents; and the role of the managers of the local units.

> *SW 3:* 1–26; *CSJ 3:* 1–26.
> *SAF:* 48–75; *LSWY 2:* 1–28; *KP61*; *SR:* 48–75; *WP 2:* 454–81.

April 7
On Planting Orchards through an All-People Movement.

Concluding speech at the Pukch'ŏng enlarged plenum of the Standing Committee of the Central Committee of the Workers' Party of Korea.

Brief speech about orchards. Kim was talking also about the example of the partisans.

SW 3: 27–38; *CSJ 3:* 27–39.

April 25
On the Duty of Educational Workers in the Raising of Children and Young People.

Speech delivered at a National Conference of Activists in Education.

More straight narrative compared with itemized listing of Kim's points. Kim speaks of Communist education in youth: to love collective endeavors, to be patriotic, to love labor, to teach children of the superiority of the socialist system, to teach them to be optimistic about the future, and to train them physically.

2SW 2: 108–25; *SW 3:* 39–56; *CSJ 3:* 40–59.
YOU: 96–115; *YC:* 88–110; *LSWY 2:* 29–50; *KP68.*

May 7
For the Further Development of the Chemical Industry.

Speech at Hamhŭng mass rally celebrating the completion of the construction of vinylon factory and May Day.

In commemoration of the completion of vinylon factory construction, Kim praised the invention and production of vinylon in the North. He encouraged the workers to engage vigorously in the production of vinylon.

CLM: 140–155; *KP61.*

June 7
Public Health Workers Must Become the Red Soldiers of the Party.

Speech delivered at the conference of activists in public health.

PH: 52–60.

*September 11
Report on the Work of the Central Committee to the Fourth Congress of the Workers' Party of Korea (4WPK).

Divided into five parts, this is perhaps the longest report of Kim. He sums up the works of the past five years and speaks of the prospects, primarily the record of the five-year economic plan and the prospects of the new seven-year economic plan. He goes into the details in general summation, but his statistics are not as accurate and convincing as his earlier ones. He also speaks briefly of the prospects of the peaceful unification of the country and denounces the South. Perhaps the most important part of the entire report is the fourth section, in which he speaks of the records of the party, giving membership statistics and the progress the party has made. The last part deals with North Korean international relations, but the North is still on good terms with both the Soviet Union and China, and Kim speaks of their friendship as most important to the North.

2SW 2: 126–277; *SW 3:* 57–204; *CSJ 3:* 60–203; *RUSS:* 696–842.
CHU 1: 99–183; *DJOU 1:* 261–358 (excerpt); *SKKM 2:* 1–16 (excerpt); *SK:* 220–37 (excerpt); *RSC:* 30–52 (excerpt); *UNF:* 46–50 (excerpt); *ZG:* 543–97; *IPR:* 17–32 (excerpt); *IPRC:* 82–99 (excerpt); *SS:* 111–16 (excerpt); *TU:* 122–46 (excerpt); *LSWY 2:* 51–89 (excerpt); *PPT:* 342–48 (excerpt); *KP68; PH:* 61–70; *CLM:* 156–66 (excerpt); *ML:* 49–65 (excerpt); *WP 2:* 482–643.

November 16
The Duty of Mothers in the Education of Children.

Speech at the national meeting of mothers.

Brief remarks about the education of children and the role of mothers in the socialist construction. Cites a few people for praise and encourages mothers to work hard for the state. Laments the fact that there is not yet a woman who has earned a doctorate in the North.

SW 3: 205–27; *CSJ 3:* 204–28.
PH: 71–98; *YC:* 111–40; *LSWY 2:* 90–118; *KP62; WW:* 1–32.

December 1
All Efforts for the Conquering of Six Highlands.

Concluding remarks at the second enlarged plenum of the Central Committee of the Workers' Party of Korea (4WPK-2CC).

Only those portions dealing with economic management were compiled here. Kim speaks of the 1961 economic plan and upgrading the leadership of the provincial management bureau, of the enterprises, and of the provincial party committees.

SKKM 2: 17–41 (excerpt); *PH:* 99–104 (excerpt).

December 15
On Innovation of New Economic Management System.

Speech at the enlarged meeting of the Political Committee of the Central Committee of the Workers' Party of Korea.

Detailed speech about his experience in Taean electric factory. He speaks of a new industrial management system and a new agrarian leadership system.

SKKM 2: 42–85; *KP70.*

December 16
On the Reform of the Leadership and Management in the Industries to Fit the New Circumstances.

Concluding remarks at the enlarged plenum of the Taean electric factory party committee.

Detailed management instruction in industries, based on his personal guidance experience at Taean electric factory.

SKKM 2: 86–143; *KP70.*

*December 18
On the Formation of the County Cooperative Farm Management Committee.

Talk with the leaders in Sukch'ŏn-gun, P'yŏngan Namdo.

Dividing his talk into five parts, Kim speaks of organizing the County Cooperative Farm Management Committee separate from the county People's Committee. He speaks of (1) the necessity for the committee, (2) its organization and duties, (3) the work methods, (4) the implementation of the technical revolutions, and (5) the preparations for the following year. Fairly detailed instruction on the organization and functions of this committee.

SKKM 2: 144–93; *KP70.*

December 23
For the Rapid Development of the Coal Industry.

Concluding speech at a meeting with the party nucleus of the Anju coal mine.

Kim speaks of the management system of coal mines and urges the local miners to improve their work in the party committee. Kim asks them to have a military-like organization in their work.

SW 3: 228–54; *CSJ 3*: 229–55.
SKKM 2: 194–224; *KP70.*

1962

January 1
New Year Address.

Kim recounts the accomplishments of the past year and projects the goals for the coming year. The goal for this year is the capturing of "six highlands": (1)

5 million tons of grain, (2) 250 million meters of fabric, (3) 800,000 tons of fish, (4) 200,000 residential houses, (5) 1.2 million tons of steel, and (6) 15 million tons of coal.

CCY 63: 1–3.

January 6
On the Reform of the Management Work and Economic Leadership in the Light Industry and Improving the Quality of Manufactured Goods.

Speech at the enlarged plenum of the party committee of the Pyongyang textile factory.

Kim emphasizes reform in factory management work and the role of the leadership in directing the light industrial sector of the economy. He also points out the fact that the quality of the goods manufactured is low and more and better goods should be provided. Lastly, he urges everyone to strengthen his party spirit and be faithful to the party.

SKKM 2: 225–51; *KP70.*

January 19
Decorated Veterans Must Work Well, Study Well, and Make a Good Livelihood.

Talk with decorated veterans in Sinch'ŏn veteran's food factory.

HM: 26–28.

January 22
On the Role and Duty of the County People's Committee.

Talk with chairmen and vice-chairmen of Hwanghae Namdo city and county people's committees.

PPT: 349–63.

January 26
Answers to the Questions by Editorial Bureau of Cuban Newspaper, *Revolution*, in Connection with the Foreign Ministers' Conference of the Organization of American States.

Kim condemns the foreign ministers' conference held in Punta del Este, Uruguay, on January 22, 1962, as an imperialistic action of the United States and its lackeys. Kim stresses that Cuba and North Korea have a common enemy in the United States, American imperialism.

CCY 63: 3–4.

February 1
Functionaries in the Field of Agriculture Should Acquire the Traits of a Revolutionary and Improve Their Guidance of the Rural Economy.

Speech delivered at a meeting of the management personnel of agricultural cooperatives in the Haeju area of Hwanghae Namdo.

> Another of his frequent visits to various localities for on-the-spot guidance of party work. Here Kim speaks of agrarian management and leadership reform in Haeju region.
>
> *SW 3:* 255–88; *CSJ 3:* 256–89.
> *SKKM 2:* 252–89; *SAF:* 76–113; *KP70; SR:* 76–112.

February 12
On the Strengthening of the Control Abilities of the Financial Bank Organizations on the Management Activities of the Socialist Enterprises.

Concluding remarks at the first enlarged meeting of the members of the cabinet of the Democratic People's Republic of Korea.

> Some specific remarks about banking operations in the North. The general laxity on lending capital to undertake various projects is criticized, and Kim says that the government must strengthen the control of financial institutions.
>
> *SKKM 2:* 290–304.

February 14
For Capturing the 800,000-ton Highland in Fisheries.

Speech delivered to the conference of activists in fisheries.

> Fish is a staple food of the people, and Kim says that Korean fishermen should catch all they can and reach the goal of catching 800,000 tons of fish.
>
> *KP62 (Susanmul 80mant'on kojirŭl chŏmyŏng hagi wihayŏ.*
> Pyongyang: Chosŏn Nodongdang Ch'ulp'ansa, 1962).

*March 8
On Improvising and Strengthening Organizational and Ideological Work of the Party.

Concluding speech at the third enlarged plenary meeting of the Central Committee of the Workers' Party of Korea (4WPK-3CC).

> Most important in this speech is his reference to the rising tide of revisionism in international relations of Communist countries. He speaks cautiously of the North's resistance to joining the international revisionist movement. He urges the members of the party to strengthen the party and reinforce the class struggle in the agrarian sector.

2*SW* 2: 278–321; *SW* 3: 289–330; *CSJ* 3: 290–330.
DJOU 1: 359–70 (excerpt); *CHU* 1: 184–94 (excerpt); *KP68*.

April 8
On Improving and Strengthening the Work of the Commercial Sector.

Speech delivered at a meeting of chairmen of provincial People's Committees.

This speech was made public for the first time on April 8, 1978, sixteen years after it was delivered. It deals with problems of consumer goods, marketing, deliveries, and production of daily necessities. It is a long speech, and Kim goes into a detailed explanation of various consumer needs and the supply system. This speech was published in commemoration of the eleventh anniversary of Kim's visit to Pyongyang department store on April 8, 1967.

Nodong sinmun, April 8, 1978; *Kŭlloja*, no. 5 (1978): 2–26.

May 3
On Improving the Press and Students' Education.

Talk to the men of the press and the workers of the Democratic Youth League.

In two parts, Kim speaks of how to improve the newspapers, their content and form, and he also speaks of the various activities of the Democratic Youth League and how to interest students in the league.

EP74; *LSWY* 2: 119–30; *YC*: 141–46; *KP73*; *WY*: 157–68.

August 8
Let Us Radically Improve the People's Living Standards by Strengthening the Role of the County and Further Developing Local Industry and Agriculture.

Concluding speech at the Ch'angsŏng joint conference of local party and economic functionaries.

Divided into five parts, the speech discusses the role of the county in improving living standards and commends the chairman of Ch'angsŏng County. Kim also speaks of the development of local industries (1958 June plenum, 3WPK-6CC) and of preventing rapid concentration of population in urban areas. He says this is also good for national defense. In addition he speaks of agrarian management, educational and cultural affairs, and the strengthening of the party work. He says the party needs a collective leadership.

SW 3: 331–71; *CSJ* 3: 331–71.
SKKM 2: 305–49; *PPT*: 364–408; *CCY* 63: 4–19; *PH*: 105–15 (excerpt); *KP63*.

August 15

Speech at the Seventeenth Commemoration Ceremony of the August 15 Liberation.

> The usual speech praising North Korean accomplishments and condemning the South. Kim still praises the Soviet Union here and mentions the Russian scientific accomplishments in outer space.

> *CCY 63:* 19–21.

August 30

On the Reform of the Leadership of the Control Bureaus of Ministry and on the Strengthening of the Work of the Factory Party Committee.

Speech at the party committee of Hwanghae Steel Mill.

> The production allotment for Hwanghae Steel Mill, the largest in the North, was 500,000 tons, but the work is not proceeding well, and Kim speaks of reform in the work methods of the Control Bureaus and improving the work of the factory party committee. He says that there are only 120 days left to complete the six goals set out by the party, and he urges what he terms a 120-day combat to complete the production goal of 500,000 tons of steel.

> *SKKM 2:* 350–82; *KP70.*

September 5

On Strengthening and Reforming City Management.

Speech at the chairmen's conference of the provincial People's Committee.

> This speech was made public for the first time in 1978. Kim gave some detailed instructions as to the management of the urban housing project, the drainage system, the sanitation work, the traffic system, and the park facilities.

> *KP78 (Tosi kyŏngyŏng saŏp ŭl kaesŏn kanghwa halte taehayŏ.*
> Pyongyang: Chosŏn Nodongdang Ch'ulp'ansa, 1978).

September 24

On the Further Development of the Collection Industry.

Speech to the managers and party committee chairmen of mines and coal mines.

> Kim criticizes the lagging collection industry. He says that there is not enough investment in this segment by the state and that there is a general lack of technical leadership. He speaks of the short-term goals and step-by-step accom-

plishments of these goals in metallic and coal mines. Kim says that the North must mine more not only for use in the North, but for export. He says there is nothing wrong with exporting raw materials until the domestic industries reach the stage where they can export manufactured goods.

SKKM 2: 383–422; *KP70.*

October 16
On Improving and Strengthening the Work of General Education.

Speech at the fourth plenary meeting of the cabinet of the Democratic People's Republic of Korea.

> For some unknown reason, this speech was made public for the first time in 1979. Kim speaks about the need for a good educational program to state and party officials. He emphasizes a correct attitude toward labor, the need to give living knowledge, and the need to strengthen technical education. He also points out the need to build up the ranks of teachers and treat them with respect.

EP79.

*October 23
On the Immediate Tasks of the Government of the Democratic People's Republic of Korea.

Speech delivered at the first session of the Third Supreme People's Assembly (3SPA-1).

> After a brief general survey of North Korean development since the Second Supreme People's Assembly, Kim spoke of the seven-year economic plan and its goals in terms of climbing six highlands. He also spoke of the conditions in the South and the prospects for the peaceful unification of Korea. He denounced any military effort and proposed a confederated form of government. Lastly he spoke of international relations and the position of the North among the Communist countries, particularly the equality of each Communist state, large or small, in the family of Communist states.

2SW 2: 322–74; *SW 3*: 372–422; *CSJ 3*: 372–420.
SK: 238–50 (excerpt); *UNF*: 51–60 (excerpt); *IPR*: 33–44 (excerpt); *CHU 1*: 195–215; *DJOU 1*: 371–95 (excerpt); *PPT*: 409–63; *CCY 63*: 21–40; *IPRC*: 100–113 (excerpt); *KP62*; *ML*: 66–76 (excerpt).

November 9
On Further Developing Taean Work System.

Speech at the enlarged meeting of the party committee of the Taean electrical machinery plant.

Kim explains the superior method of the Taean work system. He also explains seven points to further consolidate the Taean work system in industrial sectors of the economy.

2SW 2: 374–92; *SW 3:* 423–40; *CSJ 3:* 421–37.
EP68; TU: 147–65; *SKKM 2:* 423–41; *KP67.*

November 13
On Further Strengthening and Developing the County Cooperative Farm Management Committees.

Speech delivered at a consultative meeting of party functionaries and agricultural workers of P'yŏngan Namdo.

The County Cooperative Farm Management Committee is the unit best suited for the North because the provincial level is too large and the farm level is too small. Kim goes on to explain why this level is best suited for Korea and its advantages. Kim elaborates further on the provincial and central farm management committees.

2SW 2: 393–417; *SW 3:* 441–64; *CSJ 3:* 438–60.
SKKM 2: 442–66; *KP68; SR:* 113–38.

1963

January 1
New Year Address.

Kim says that the campaign to capture "six highlands" was successful, but he acknowledges that in housing, steel production, and coal production, the North fell short of the goal. He does not set a new goal for the new year, but encourages everyone to work hard.

CCY 64: 1–5.

January 7
Develop the Manpower Support Work on the Farms into the All-People Movement and to Correct the Leadership System in Construction.

Concluding remarks at an enlarged plenum of the Political Committee of the Central Committee of the Workers' Party of Korea.

In an effort to mobilize the labor force for agriculture, Kim points out four errors in the lack of labor force on the farms: (1) veterans were not sent back to the farms, (2) there was an appreciable increase in the non-productive work force, (3) housewives in the cities were not mobilized, and (4) there is considerable waste. He also points out three shortcomings in construction leadership: (1) planning is not well coordinated, (2) the quality of construction is low, and (3) the mechanization standards are low.

SKKM 2: 467–92; *KP70.*

*February 8

Our People's Army is an Army of the Working Class, an Army of the Revolution; Class and Political Education Should Be Continuously Strengthened.

Speech delivered to People's Army unit cadres above the level of deputy regimental commander for political affairs and the functionaries of the party and government organs of the locality.

Kim's speech on the fifteenth anniversary of the founding of the army in the North. Kim touches upon many subjects: (1) the need to strengthen class education, (2) the contents of class education, (3) the role of arts and literature in class education, (4) the strengthening of the party work, (5) the relationship of soldiers and civilians, and (6) several other problems. Kim speaks extensively of the right of each individual state to be on its own and stumbles on the cardinal elements of the idea of *chuch'e.* He says that Korea should be independent politically *(chaju)* and self-sufficient *(charip)* economically. He also speaks of the conditions in the South and how it lacks class education.

SW 3: 465–525; *CSJ 3:* 461–522.
SK: 251–61 (excerpt); *RPM:* 148–216; *TU:* 166–214 (excerpt); *LSWY 2:* 131–99; *KP69.*

March 22

The Duty of Scientists and Technicians in Carrying Out the Technical Revolution.

Speech at a conference of scientists and technicians.

Brief speech on bringing about a technical revolution and bringing scientific standards up to the world level. Various detailed instructions on mechanization, automation, application of electronics, and others.

SW 3: 526–52; *CSJ 3:* 523–50.
PH: 116–46; *SS:* 117–49; *KP70.*

April 18

For the Strengthening of Educational Work in Colleges.

Concluding remarks at the director's meeting of the Central Committee of the Workers' Party of Korea.

DJOU 1: 396–415; *KP72.*

April 27

On the Tasks of the Central-County Party Committee.

Speech to the chairmen of the Central-County Party Committees.

> For each county that has more than three central industrial enterprises, Kim proposes to establish a Central-County Party Committee to coordinate the work within the county. This is another step to strengthen the role of the last administrative organ, the county. At the time of initiation Kim proposes to establish thirty such Central-County Party Committees. Kim elaborates three tasks of the Central-County Party Committees: (1) to lead the factory party committee, (2) to strengthen the party leadership in economic fields, and (3) to cooperate with the county people's committees. Kim also elaborates the work methods of Central-County Party chairmen and urges them to go down to the villages and work with the workers.
>
> *SKKM 2:* 493–545; *KP70.*

August 13

Reply to the August 2 Letter of Chou En-lai.

> Kim's reply to Chou's letter proposing a summit conference of the heads of all nations to ban nuclear weapons. Kim says that the North supports such a meeting, and he denounces the Nuclear Test Ban Treaty signed by the United States, the Soviet Union, and Great Britain.
>
> *CCY 64:* 6–7.

August 15

In Commemoration of the Eighteenth Anniversary of the August 15 Liberation.

Speech at Hesan City.

> Kim, in Hesan City of Yanggangdo, says that it has been five years since he last visited here and speaks of economic accomplishments, particularly the forestry work in this province.
>
> *CCY 64:* 5–6.

August 15

In Commemoration of the Fifteenth Anniversary of the Founding of the Democratic People's Republic of Korea.

> General speech before representatives of various organizations and foreign guests. Kim says that he opposes the revisionists and supports the struggle of the nonaligned nations.
>
> *CCY 64:* 7–8.

August 16
Tasks of the Party Organizations in Yanggangdo.

Concluding speech at the plenary meeting of the Yanggang provincial committee of the Workers' Party of Korea.

> Basically a two-part speech on economic affairs and party work. On economic affairs, Kim speaks of agriculture, animal husbandry, forestry, local industries; and on party affairs, he urges the elimination of bureaucratism and subjectivism.

> *SW 3:* 553–97; *CSJ 3:* 551–94.
> *KP69.*

October 5
Let Us Transform Our People's Army into a Revolutionary Army and Implement the Self-Defense Policy in the National Defense.

Speech at the seventh graduating class of Kim Il Sung Military Academy.

> Kim says that there are two important tasks; one is to protect the socialist fatherland and the other is to attain national reunification and liberate the people in the South. The attainment of these revolutionary goals requires political power, economic power, and military power. Kim elaborates on the self-defense military policy, stipulating that in order to attain such goals, the People's Army must be transformed into a revolutionary army, hatred of the enemy (United States) must be built up, the entire population must be armed, the entire nation must be prepared for combat, and the quality of teachers in the military academy must be upgraded.

> *CHU 1:* 216–34 (excerpt); *DJOU 1:* 416–35 (excerpt).

November 6
On the Rewriting of the Text on "Industrial Management."

Talk with the editors of the text on industrial management.

> Kim points out errors in the draft of the industrial management text, mainly pointing out that more emphasis on political principles and Marxism and Leninism is necessary. He goes on to say what should be included in the text, pointing out five specific items.

> *SKKM 2:* 546–54; *SS:* 148–56.

November 28
On Correcting the Work of the Banking System.

Concluding remarks at a meeting of the Political Committee of the Central Committee of the Workers' Party of Korea.

Brief remark about the banking system. Kim says that the bank in the North is a government organization, and the major shortcoming is that banks lend money from the national treasury indiscriminately. Kim says it is necessary to establish a lending bank apart from the Central Bank.

SKKM 2: 555–61.

December 30
Further Develop the Role of Social Science to Suit the Necessity of Our Revolution at the Present Time.

Talk with the workers in the Department of Science and Education of the Central Committee of the Workers' Party of Korea.

A short speech telling the social scientists to develop studies on the work with people, on Communist education, on the rural-urban gap, on the problems of Korean history, on Korean languages, and others.

CHU 1: 235–40; *DJOU 1:* 436–42; *SS:* 157–62.

1964

January 1
New Year Address.

Kim reviews the accomplishments of the past year and praises the great achievements in industry and agriculture. He briefly denounces the South and projects the accomplishments to be made in the North in the coming year.

CCY 65: 1–5.

January 3
Some Problems Related to the Development of the Korean Language.

Brief talk with linguists concerning the language policy of the North. Urges the linguists to use correct Korean and control the foreign words, particularly the Chinese, in the Korean language. He also cautions against the invention of new Korean words.

SW 4: 1–13; *CSJ 4:* 1–12.
CHU 1: 241–55; *DJOU 1:* 443–58; *SS:* 163–76; *KP73.*

January 9
For the Normalization of the Basic Construction.

Speech at a council of workers in the construction sector.

A lengthy speech about the construction industry. Kim says that the industry must improve its construction planning, assure the supply of materials, upgrade the quality of construction, correctly appraise the workforce, and strengthen scientific research work, particularly such areas as port construction.

SKKM 2: 562–93; *KP70.*

January 22
On Giving Priority to Political Work and Following the Mass Line in the Field of Transport.

Speech delivered at a consultative meeting of functionaries in the field of transportation.

Kim emphasizes people-to-people work and political work in the transportation field. Kim also tells the party organizations that only provincial party organs should direct transportation work. The county party organizations should direct the agricultural cooperatives and leave the transportation work to the provincial party organs.

SW 4: 14–32; *CSJ 4:* 13–30.
SKKM 2: 594–614; *KP69.*

February 20
Tractor Drivers are Forerunners of the Agrarian Technical Revolution.

Speech delivered to a conference of tractor drivers.

KP71 (Ttŭraktorŭ unjŏnsudŭl ŭn nongch'on kisul hyŏngmyŏng ŭi sŏn'gujadŭl ida. Pyongyang: Chosŏn Nodongdang Ch'ulp'ansa, 1971).

*February 25
Theses on the Socialist Rural Question in Our Country.

Theses presented to the eighth plenum of the Central Committee of the Workers' Party of Korea (4WPK-8CC).

Most widely circulated of Kim's theses on the agrarian problems in the North. Kim said that the three basic policies on agrarian problems are (1) technical, cultural, and ideological revolution in the countryside; (2) the peasantry should be led by the working class, and, similarly, industry should assist agriculture, and urban areas should help the countryside; and (3) the establishment of an organic relationship between the state-owned (or people-owned) industries and cooperatively owned agriculture. He also reemphasized the role of County Cooperative Farm Management Committees in the construction of the socialist countryside. He pointed out a few immediate measures to strengthen the economic basis of the cooperative farms to improve the peasants' livelihood.

2SW 2: 418–69; *SW 4:* 33–83; *CSJ 4:* 31–76.
SKKM 2: 615–65; *RSC:* 53–65 (excerpt); *JC:* 67–108; *WSK:* 196–233; *SAF:* 114–63; *CCY 65:* 5–22; *EP64*; *EP68*; *PH:* 147–51; *KP67*; *SR:* 139–93.

February 27
Let Us Strengthen the Revolutionary Forces in Every Way to Achieve the Cause of Reunification of the Country.

Concluding speech delivered at the eighth plenum of the Central Committee of the Workers' Party of Korea (4WPK-8CC).

Kim speaks of three revolutionary forces—North Korean, South Korean, International—needed to attain reunification of Korea. He is very cautious about the international revolutionary forces because of the North's anti-Soviet stance in the Sino-Soviet dispute. This is the first instance where a portion of a speech is not printed in his selected works. The fifth section, dealing with the details of unification policy, is omitted.

SW 4: 84–103; *CSJ 4:* 77–96.
SK: 262–82; *WSK:* 234–49; *UNF:* 61–80 (excerpt); *KP69*.

April 22
On the Editorial Direction of Encyclopedia and Map.

Speech before the leaders of science educators.

This speech is a continuation of a talk Kim made on December 30, 1963. Here Kim speaks of the methods of encyclopedia compilation and map making. Kim insists that the encyclopedia must be made for use in Korea and must not copy other countries' encyclopedias, particularly those of capitalist countries. Kim says also that the Korean encyclopedia must include the South and it must also help strengthen the relations of the North with other countries. Kim goes into details, even suggesting the thickness of the volume, coverage, and names. Kim tells the educators to make a twenty- or thirty-volume encyclopedia by 1967. Brief remarks of a general nature on map making are also made.

CHU 1: 255–66; *DJOU 1:* 472–80 (excerpt); *SS:* 177–88.

May 1
Speech Commemorating May Day and the Construction of Kanggye Youth Development Center.

Brief speech in praise of the development and accomplishments of workers in Kanggye region of Chagangdo. This speech was delivered in Kanggye, where Kim also celebrated May Day.

CCY 65: 22–23.

*May 15
On the Tasks of the League of Socialist Working Youth.

Speech delivered at the fifth congress of the Democratic Youth League of Korea.

Urges the.youth to be faithful to the party, to participate in the building of the socialist system in the North, to push for the unification of Korea, and to become a part of the international youth movement. At this congress the Democratic Youth League of Korea (DYL) changed its name to the League of Socialist Working Youth of Korea.

2SW 2: 470–98; SW 4: 104–32; CSJ 4: 97–126.
SK: 283–89 (excerpt); CHU 1: 267–74; YOU: 116–46; YC: 147–79; CCY 65: 23–34; LSWY 2: 200–32; KP67; CLM: 167–4 (excerpt); ML: 77–81 (excerpt); WY: 169–200.

*June 23
Speech to the Delegates to the Asian Economic Seminar.

The Asian Economic Seminar was held in the North from June 13 to 23, and representatives from some thirty-four countries participated. Kim speaks of economic independence as the basis of a sovereign state for all third-world countries. Kim also thanks the delegates for holding the conference in Pyongyang. This conference was later to become the focal point of sharp exchanges with the Soviet Union. The Russians denounced the seminar, and North Korea retorted, saying that Russia was exercising big-power chauvinism.

CCY 65: 34–35; ML: 82–85.

June 26
On Improving and Strengthening the Work of the Working People's Organizations.

Concluding speech at the ninth plenum of the Central Committee of the Workers' Party of Korea (4WPK-9CC).

Created a new organization from the old Peasants' Union and named it the Union of Agricultural Working People. He spoke of the tasks of this organization as well as the shortcomings of the trade unions.

SW 4: 133–46; CSJ 4: 126–41.
TU: 215–231; SAF: 164–200; KP69; SR: 194–210.

September 9
Speech in Commemoration of the Sixteenth Anniversary of the Founding of the Republic.

Kim's speech in Sinŭiju, P'yŏngan Pukto, where Kim was touring to inspect economic development. This is a general speech to encourage people to accomplish the goals of the seven-year economic plan.

CCY 65: 35–37.

October 23–28
On the Visit of Modibo Keita, President of Mali Federal Republic.

Three short speeches on the visit of Modibo Keita and his wife. Kim stresses the rise of nonaligned nations from the yoke of imperialism.

CCY 65: 37–39.

October 29
Letter to Chou En-lai.

In replying to Chou's letter of October 29, Kim supports the Chinese government's suggestion to hold a summit conference of all nations to ban nuclear weapons.

CCY 65: 39.

November 1–4
To Welcome President Sukarno of Indonesian Republic.

Four speeches Kim made on Sukarno's visit to the North. Kim reinforces the North Korean pledge of a closer friendship with the Indonesian government. Kim also exploits the role of the third-world nations in fighting U.S. imperialism.

CCY 65: 40–43.

November 7
On Creating Revolutionary Literature and Art.

Speech to workers in the literary and art fields.

General speech to encourage artists to create more Korean art instead of copying things western. Urges writers to write a story about Kim Ch'aek. Also urges the writers to devote their efforts equally to productions concerning the socialist construction and the revolutionary struggle.

SW 4: 149–64; *CSJ 4:* 142–57.
CHU 1: 275–92; *DJOU 1:* 481–500; *SS:* 189–206; *SK:* 290–307; *LA:* 34–48.

December 19
On Enhancing the Party Spirit, Class Spirit, and Popular Spirit of Leading Functionaries and Improving the Management of the National Economy.

Concluding speech delivered at the tenth plenum of the Central Committee of the Workers' Party of Korea (4WPK-10CC).

Kim urges the leaders in the economic sector to improve their class consciousness and party spirit. He also discusses four problems in economic management, including planning, technical revolution, labor administration, and management of economic life.

SW 4: 165–190; *CSJ 4:* 158–84.
SKKM 2: 666–95; *KP69.*

1965

January 1
New Year Address.

Short speech, noting the loss of several hundred thousand tons of grain due to bad weather. Kim urges everyone to continue their struggle.

CCY 66–67: 1–5.

January 3
Let Us Eliminate Bureaucratism in State Economic Organs and Improve the Party Spirit, Class Spirit, and Popular Spirit of the Workers.

Speech at the party general meeting of the Ministry of Metal and Chemical Industries.

Lashes out at bureaucrats in the Ministry of Metal and Chemical Industries for their bureaucratic way of doing their work. Kim says that there are many in the ministry who criticize the government and do not follow directives of the party. Kim says that the party should lead the work and the role of the party in the ministry should be strengthened.

SKKM 3: 1–24; *KP70.*

January 8
Reply to the Letter of the President of the Korean Affairs Institute in Washington.

This is a reply to Kim Yong-jung, who wrote letters to both the North and South Korean presidents. Kim replied and essentially said that the unification problem is a Korean problem and the Koreans should discuss it without external influences. President Park did not reply.

2SW 2: 499–509; *SW 4:* 191–201; *CSJ 4:* 185–94.
CHU 1: 293–304; *DJOU 1:* 501–12; *SK:* 308–18; *RSC:* 66–76; *UNF:* 81–90;
IPR: 45–54; *IPRC:* 114–124; *CCY 66–67:* 37–40.

January 11–16
On the Reform of the Leadership Methods in Factories and Enterprises and on the Reform of the Management and Operation Work.

Speech at the enlarged meeting of the party committee of Hwanghae Steel Mill.

Kim repeats much of what he has been saying about the quality and methodology of cadres in leading factory work. He also speaks in detail of the tasks of 1965, the objectives of the seven-year economic plan, and five other items: (1) mobilizing the masses in planning, (2) developing large-scale production and small- and middle-scale production simultaneously, (3) developing the technical revolution, (4) strengthening political work, and (5) reforming the support and supply system.

SKKM 3: 25–66; *KP70.*

January 22
On the Reform of Ingot Production.

Speech at the party committee of Ŭnyul mines.

Kim admits the difficulties in the seven-year economic plan because of worsening international relations. In order to produce more steel and metal, the production of this second-largest mine (Ŭnyul mine) is important. Kim gives several points to improve the work in the mine: work 480 minutes per day, do not drink excessively, strengthen the party spirit, and increase military training. Kim says that in order to obtain more foreign exchange, it is important to produce more steel.

SKKM 3: 67–91; *KP70.*

January 28
On Tempering the Party Spirit of the Trade Union Workers and Firmly Upholding Self-Reliance in Foreign Trade.

Concluding remarks at the general party meeting of the Ministry of Trade.

The minister and vice-minister of trade must have been severely criticized in this meeting. Kim reiterated that no one should be spared criticism, particularly those who work in the Ministry of Trade, because they come in contact with the people in capitalist countries.

CHU 1: 305–15 (excerpt); *DJOU 1:* 513–24 (excerpt).

January 30
For Conquering the Steel Highland in the Seven-year Plan.

Speech at the enlarged plenum of the party committee of Kangsŏn Steel Mill.

Kim says that the target is 400,000 tons, and since 275,000 tons have been produced so far, there is a long way to go. Kim repeats most of the same speech urging technological innovation, improvements in manpower administration and supply work, etc. Kim says that he has directed the Ministry of Metal Industries to earn 800 million *wŏn* of foreign exchange. Kim also says that he wants to increase household earnings to 100 *wŏn* per month.

SKKM 3: 92–114; *KP70.*

February 11–14
Speeches Welcoming the Visiting Russian Delegation.

Three speeches to welcome Alexei N. Kosygin, who stopped in Pyongyang on his way back from Vietnam. Kim reassures Korean friendship with the Soviet Union.

CCY 66–67: 49–51.

February 23
On the Reform of Higher Education Work.

Speech at the party general meeting of the Ministry of Higher Education.

Only two portions of this speech are reported. These concern strengthening the *chuch'e* idea in educating professors and in scientific research work and improving the quality of cadre education. Kim says that Koreans must do most things by themselves in solving their problems. This is not to say that they should not learn from others, but the important thing is to learn from others on the basis of a Korean standpoint and Korean needs. Kim repeats his statement instituting the eight-hour work, eight-hour study, and eight-hour rest system in all fields. Kim admits that because of the rapid increase in the number of colleges (ninety colleges) the quality of professors is not as high as expected and because of the lack of labor force, even the number of college applicants is not as many as anticipated.

CHU 1: 316–42 (excerpt); *DJOU 1:* 525–52 (excerpt); *SS:* 207–45; *KP73.*

March 26
On the Reform of the Leadership and Management of the Construction to Suit New Circumstances.

Speech at the party general meeting of the State Construction Commission.

> A lengthy speech about reform of the work of the State Construction Commission. Kim says that four years have passed since the inauguration of the seven-year economic plan, but the State Construction Commission has never fulfilled its target in any year. Kim discusses the shortcomings of the commission and asks the leaders not to question the party policy, to reorganize the various organs of the commission, to revise the planning work, to improve technological leadership, and to mechanize the work.

> *SKKM 3:* 115–62; *KP70.*

*April 14
On Socialist Construction in the Democratic People's Republic of Korea and the South Korean Revolution.

Lecture at the Ali Archam Academy of Social Sciences of Indonesia.

> Kim's visit to Indonesia, a third-world country, at the height of the Sino-Soviet dispute had significant impact in many aspects. In this lecture Kim reviewed the developmental process of the socialist construction in the North, efforts to establish the socialist system, and also the socialist economic system in the North. But throughout his lecture the most important message is Kim's clear implication that the North had done what it had done on its own; fraternal countries helped, but their assistance, for example, 5.5 billion dollars in total economic aid, was small compared to Korean efforts. Here Kim expounded for the first time the full context of *chuch'e* (self-reliance in ideology, independence in politics, self-sustenance in economics, and self-defense in national defense). He said the North is trying hard to fight dogmatism and revisionism and to resist all those who want to influence the North Korean economy through aid. Kim said that political work comes before anything else in the North, and because of military spending, the seven-year economic plan was being delayed. Kim spoke briefly of the South Korean revolution and repeated his earlier remark about the three forces of Korean unification: the North Korean revolutionary base, South Korean revolutionary strength, and the international revolutionary forces.

> *2SW 2:* 510–60; *SW 4:* 202–51; *CSJ 4:* 195–240.
> *CHU 1:* 343–55; *DJOU 1:* 553–67 (excerpt); *SKKM 3:* 163–75 (excerpt); *SK:* 319–33 (excerpt); *RSC:* 77–110 (excerpt); *JC:* 23–64; *WSK:* 250–86; *CCY 66–67:* 19–35; *SS:* 246–58 (excerpt); *KP67; CLM:* 175–87 (excerpt).

April 19
Answer to the Questions by Tatsuo Sakai and Michio Fuse, Reporters of *Nihon Keizai Shinbun*.

General answers to three questions on talks to normalize relations between South Korea and Japan. North Korean policy toward unification and toward Japan were discussed.

CCY 66–67: 42–43; *FCI:* 23–29; *ML:* 86–91.

April 21
Answers to the Questions by Kiyoshi Iwamoto, Officer of Japanese Kyodo News Agency.

Seven questions were asked on the Vietnamese question, the Sino-Soviet dispute, South Korean dispatch of troops to Vietnam, the Japan-Korea talks, North Korean policy toward Japan, and others relating to Japan-North Korea relations. Kim gives general answers, condemning the United States. Kim says that the South Korean soldiers of fortune cannot compete with the people's struggle for their own country.

CCY 66–67: 41–42; *FCI:* 30–31 (excerpt).

May 25
Speech to the Leaders of the Party and Government and Members of the Supreme People's Assembly.

PH: 152–56.

July 1
Concluding Remarks at the Eleventh Plenum of the Central Committee of the Workers' Party of Korea (4WPK-11CC).

In the first part of his speech, Kim speaks primarily of prevention of waste in power and electricity and of strengthening their management. In the second part, Kim speaks of the reform of higher education and scientific research work. Kim speaks of two problems; one is revolutionizing the intellectuals, and the other is to eliminate flunkeyism and establish *chuch'e* in academic work. Kim says to intensify the party life and the study of Marxism and Leninism so that all intellectuals can be revolutionized.

SKKM 3: 176–86; *CHU 1:* 356–72; *SS:* 259–75; *PH:* 157–73.

July 6
Answers to the Questions by Reporters from Cuba.

Six questions were asked about the unification of Korea, Cuba-Korean relations, Vietnam War, American involvement in Santo Domingo, and others.

Kim gives carping condemnation of the United States in all these questions and promotes the unity of anti-U.S. forces.

CCY 66–67: 43–46; *FCI:* 32–45.

August 15
Speech in Commemoration of the Twentieth Anniversary of the August 15 Liberation.

Kim is in Wŏnsan city of Kangwŏndo and gives a short speech in commemoration of the national holiday. Kim also praises the accomplishments of the people of Kangwŏndo.

CCY 66–67: 35–37.

August 26–29
Speeches Welcoming Alfonse Massamba Deba, President of the Republic of Congo, Brazzaville.

Three speeches by Kim, essentially to promote the solidarity of nonaligned nations and to denounce the United States.

CCY 66–67: 55–58.

September 2
On the Tasks of the Organization Workers of the Women's League.

Speech delivered at the third congress of the Democratic Women's League of Korea.

WW: 33–45.

September 14
Answers to the Questions by Reporters from the United Arab Republic.

Five questions concerning unification of Korea, the Sino-Soviet dispute, the Vietnamese question, and the North Korea and UAR relationship. Kim says that the North is ready to send troops or any assistance to Vietnam. He insists that one socialist country has a right to assist another, acknowledges sending assistance of weapons and other materials, and says that he is ready to send troops to Vietnam if requested by the North Vietnamese government.

CCY 66–67: 46–48; *FCI:* 46–54; *ML:* 92–99.

September 23

For the Exhibition of Great Vitality of the Unified and Detailed Planning of the National Economy.

Speech delivered at a general meeting of the party organization of the State Planning Commission.

Kim's effort to boost the sagging economy by better planning and greater enthusiasm. He points out the shortcomings of the national planning commission. He urges planners not to make a great plan, but rather to carry out what has been planned. He speaks openly about the difficulties in his seven-year economic plan due to the changes in international and domestic conditions.

SW 4: 252–90; *CSJ 4:* 241–78.
SKKM 3: 187–228; *KP69.*

October 4–10

Speeches to Welcome Norodom Sihanouk, Head of State of the Cambodian Kingdom.

Four speeches, including two at the airport, supporting the struggle of the Cambodian people against the United States. Kim speaks of the need for solidarity among the nonaligned states against the United States.

CCY 66–67: 58–61.

*October 10

On the Occasion of the Twentieth Anniversary of the Founding of the Workers' Party of Korea.

Report delivered at the celebration of the twentieth anniversary of the founding of the Workers' Party of Korea.

In this report Kim (1) reviews the pre-World War II Communist movement, (2) summarizes postliberation developments in the North, (3) discusses the post-Korean war economic recovery process in the North together with the ultimate emergence of North Korea's *chuch'e* idea and independence, (4) makes usual condemnatory remarks about developments in the South, (5) examines the precarious position of the North in international relations and professes general proletarian internationalism, and (6) proposes a few tasks confronting the party. Kim urges party members to strengthen the party and work hard to accomplish the goals of the seven-year plan.

2SW 2: 561–602; *SW 4:* 291–331; *CSJ 4:* 279–316.
SK: 334–40 (excerpt); *CCY 66–67:* 5–18; *KP65; CLM:* 188–99 (excerpt); *ML:* 100–104 (excerpt).

November 15–17

On the Strengthening of Party Work and Organizing State Affairs.

Speech delivered at the twelfth plenum of the fourth party (4WPK-12CC).

PH: 174–79; *PPT:* 464–77 (excerpt).

1966

May 14

For Maintaining National Characteristics in Korean Language.

Talk with Korean linguists.

Kim's perception of what the language should keep and discard. This speech is technical and seems to have been written by a linguist to tell other linguists the North Korean policy on Korean language. In general Kim says that Korean linguists should use and preserve the Korean language.

CHU 1: 373–90; *DJOU 1:* 585–603; *SS:* 276–93; *KP69.*

June 5

On the Guidance of Works in the Juvenile Corps.

Talk with leaders of the League of Socialist Working Youth on the twentieth anniversary of the founding of the Juvenile Corps.

Kim urges the members and instructors of the Juvenile Corps to do their work properly.

KP69; WY: 201–10.

*October 5

The Present Situation and the Tasks of Our Party.

Report to the second conference of the Workers' Party of Korea (WPK-IIC).

This report is basically a statement of the North Korean position in the Sino-Soviet dispute. Kim says that all fraternal parties should stop fighting each other and put forces together to fight the U.S. imperialists. He says that the North is ready to send troops to Vietnam if requested by Vietnam. Each party is independent and each state is sovereign so that no domestic intervention can be allowed in the fraternal socialist countries. Some accuse the North of being opportunist, but Kim says that the North has her own chair to sit in rather than stretch out uncomfortably in two non-Korean chairs. Kim says that the North has experienced big-power chauvinism, but rebuffed it. This report is the strongest statement so far on the North's international position in the Sino-Soviet dispute. Kim also speaks of the socialist construction and development of the revolutionary base in the North and, in addition, repeats the usual condemnation of the South, particularly after the Japan-Korea normalization treaty.

SW 4: 332–420; *CSJ 4:* 317–403.
CHU 1: 391–465; *DJOU 1:* 604–84 (excerpt); *SK:* 341–62 (excerpt); *RSC:* 111–45 (excerpt); *UNF:* 91–93 (excerpt); *SS:* 294–389; *TU:* 232–327; *RPM:* 217–312; *EP68; CCY 66–67:* 99–130; *KP66; LSWY 2:* 233–328; *CLM:* 200–95; *ML:* 105–44 (excerpt).

October 16
Let Us Develop Our Art into a Revolutionary Art with Nationalistic Form and Socialist Content.

Talk with artists at the ninth national art exhibition.

> After explaining a few paintings of the exhibition, Kim says that Korean art should have nationalistic form and socialistic content in its expression. All forms of capitalistic bourgeois paintings such as abstract paintings should be avoided. Kim says that he prohibits such abstract paintings from coming into the North.

CHU 1: 466–74; *DJOU 1:* 685–94; *SS:* 390–98; *KP69.*

*October 18
On the Elimination of Formalism and Bureaucracy in the Party Work and Revolutionizing the Functionaries.

Speech to the functionaries of the Department of Organization, Leadership, Propaganda, and Agitation of the Central Committee of the Workers' Party of Korea.

> An important speech to party functionaries on strengthening revolutionary thought among party members. Divided into three parts, the speech discusses the elimination of formalism in economic guidance work, intensifying the ideological revolution, and proposed steps to eliminate formalism and bureaucracy in the party work.

SW 4: 421–58; *CSJ 4:* 404–41.
SKKM 3: 229–41 (excerpt); *TU:* 328–69; *LSWY 2:* 329–70; *KP69.*

October 20

The Communist Upbringing of Children is a Glorious Revolutionary Duty of Nursery School and Kindergarten Teachers.

Address to the national congress of nursery school and kindergarten teachers.

> Work with children is important, and the party should improve the quality of teachers. Kim also urges elimination of formalism in nursery schools. He says that there are 870,000 children in nurseries and 790,000 children in kindergartens.
>
> *SW 4:* 459–72; *CSJ 4:* 442–55.
> *PH:* 180–94; *WW:* 46–62.

October 20

The Socialist Medicine is a Preventive Medicine.

Talk with the leaders in the Ministry of Public Health.

> *PH:* 195–200.

October 26

We Will Always Cooperate with Fraternal Cuban People.

Speech at a banquet welcoming the party and government delegation of Cuba.

> ML: 145–49.

1967

January 4

Reply to the President of the Korean Affairs Institute in Washington.

> Kim reiterates the North Korean position in this letter, replying to the second letter, dated November 12, 1966, from Kim Yong-jung. Kim emphasizes that the South Koreans must get rid of all foreign influences.
>
> *SK:* 363–74; *CCY 68:* 33–38.

February 2

On Revolutionizing the Peasants and Carrying Out the Decisions of the Party Conference in the Agrarian Sector.

Speech delivered at a national congress of agricultural functionaries.

This is a fairly detailed instruction in agriculture. In addition to his emphasis on simultaneous development of economic construction and national defense, Kim states a ten-point task of the leadership in agrarian production and another ten-point task in cooperative farm management.

SW 4: 473–500; *CSJ 4:* 456–82.
SKKM 3: 242–56 (excerpt); *SAF:* 201–30; *KP69; SR:* 211–40.

*May 25
On the Questions of the Period of Transition from Capitalism to Socialism and the Dictatorship of the Proletariat.

Speech delivered before the party ideological workers.

Kim speaks of the period of transition and the dictatorship of the proletariat. He says that just defeating capitalism and establishing socialism does not mean the end of the period of transition and that the attainment of socialism and communism does not mean the end of the dictatorship of the proletariat. The transition period continues even after all peasants have joined the ranks of the workers and the socialist state is well under way. The dictatorship of the proletariat continues even after one nation attains the communist state so long as there are capitalist states in the world. Kim also speaks of class struggle, which should continue within the socialist state, although it is a different kind of class struggle.

CHU 1: 475–92; *JUCHE 2:* 1–17; *JC:* 111–24; *WSK:* 293–305; *SS:* 399–416; *EP68; KP69.*

June 6
On Developing the Pharmaceutical Industries and Medical Equipment Industries.

Concluding remarks at the Political Committee of the Central Committee of the Workers' Party of Korea.

PH: 201–205.

June 13
Let Us Make a Good Factory like the Hamhŭng Decorated Veterans' Daily Necessities Factory.

Talk with the decorated veterans of Ch'ŏllima Hamhŭng Daily Necessities Factory.

HM: 29–30.

July 3
For a Great Revolutionary Upsurge in the Present Economic Work and for the Improvement and Strengthening of Manpower Administration.

Concluding speech delivered at the sixteenth plenum of the Central Committee of the Workers' Party of Korea (4WPK-16CC).

> Kim urges workers to show greater enthusiasm for economic development. In the second section of his speech, where he speaks of labor administration, Kim points out many defects in the workers and urges them to work 480 minutes (eight hours) per day, study eight hours, and rest eight hours. He tells the workers to work hard to accomplish the tasks set forth in the economic plan.

> *SW 4:* 501–37; *CSJ 4:* 483–518.
> *SKKM 3:* 257–96; *KP70; CLM:* 296–305 (excerpt).

August 12
Let Us Intensify the Anti-Imperialistic, Anti-U.S. Struggle.

An article published in the first issue of the magazine, *Tricontinental,* organ of the Organization of Solidarity of the Peoples of Asia, Africa, and Latin America.

> Brief anti-U.S. article. Kim speaks of the solidarity of the peoples in Asia, Africa, and Latin America. He says that when Africa and Latin America are not free, Asia is not free.

> *SW 4:* 538–45; *CSJ 4:* 519–26.
> *JC:* 265–71; *WSK:* 287–92; *RPM:* 313–21; *CCY 68:* 30–33; *EP68; KP68; ML:* 150–57.

October 24
Speeches to Welcome President Moktar Ould Daddah, Head of State of the Republic of Mauritania.

> Two speeches Kim made to welcome President Daddah. The North began her diplomatic relations with Mauritania in November 1964, and Kim repeats his usual battle cry of the solidarity of the people of the third world.

> *CCY 68:* 42–44; *ML:* 158–63.

October 28
Open Letter.

> This letter is to let the North Korean people know that he has accepted the nomination to the Supreme People's Assembly from the electoral district of

Songnim. This open letter seems to have been necessary because Kim was nominated by so many electoral districts.

CCY 68: 38.

November 15
Students Must Acquire a Communist Attitude Toward Labor and Learn Science and Knowledge to Serve the Interests of the Korean Revolution.

Speech at a meeting with students of universities and higher technical schools; participants in the rebuilding of the capital.

Generally an instructive speech to the students, saying that all intellectuals and students must love labor. These students were mobilized to work in the reconstruction of the capital after the flood in Pyongyang. Kim urges that all students must establish *chuch'e* in their study in all fields.

CHU 1: 493–505; JUCHE 2: 18–29; SS: 417–29; LSWY 2: 371–84; KP69; WY: 211–22.

November 17
Congratulatory Message.

This message is to all the workers, technicians, and office workers of factories and enterprises where the 1967 economic goal was fulfilled before the twenty-second anniversary celebration of the founding of the party (October 10). This is a general congratulatory message.

CCY 68: 40–42.

*December 16
Let Us Embody the Revolutionary Spirit of Independence, Self-Sustenance and Self-Defense More Thoroughly in All Fields of State Activity.

Political program of the government of the Democratic People's Republic of Korea announced at the first session of the Fourth Supreme People's Assembly (4SPA-1).

This is a ten-point political program adopted at the first session of the fourth Supreme People's Assembly. The ten points are: (1) to implement the idea of *chuch'e*, (2) to bring about unification, (3) to incorporate all people into the working class under the leadership of the party, (4) to eliminate bureaucracy and mobilize the revolutionary mass, (5) to bring about technical revolution in the industrialization of the economy, (6) to step up the development of science and technology, (7) to increase defense capabilities, (8) to further trade with other countries, (9) to look after the interests of the Koreans abroad, and (10) to be friendly with other nations under the principle of equality and fraternity.

SW 4: 546–610; *CSJ 4:* 527–86.
CHU 1: 506–73; *JUCHE 2:* 30–100; *SKKM 3:* 297–301 (excerpt); *SK:* 375–90 (excerpt); *JC:* 151–205; *NAM:* 1–71; UNF: 94–97 (excerpt); *CCY 68:* 1–29; *IPRC:* 125–40 (excerpt); *IPR:* 55–68 (excerpt); *SS:* 430–96; *TU:* 370–437; *PPT:* 478–544; *RPM:* 322–88; *EP67; PH:* 206–11 (excerpt); *LSWY 2:* 385–452; *KP67; CLM:* 306–72; *ML:* 164–70 (excerpt).

December 25
Congratulatory Message.

Similar to November 17 message, but this one is for the miners, technicians, and office workers of Sŏnghŭng Mines. Kim says that these workers have successfully met the tasks that the party has given them.

CCY 68: 39–40.

1968

February 2
Congratulatory Messages to Soldiers and Officers of the 661st Division of the Korean People's Army and Soldiers and Officers of the 2423rd Division of the Korean Coast Guard.

Two messages congratulating their gallant and successful work in carrying out their duty. Although it is not directly mentioned in these messages, they refer to the capture of the American spy ship *Pueblo*.

CCY 69: 53–69; *KP68.*

February 8
On the Twentieth Anniversary of the Founding of the Korean People's Army.

Speech at a banquet given in honor of the twentieth anniversary of the founding of the Korean People's Army.

Stresses that the Korean People's Army is a successor to the anti-Japanese armed guerrillas and partisans and that they are well-armed both mentally and physically. He speaks of the intrusion of the *Pueblo* and condemns it.

SW 5: 1–10; *CSJ 5:* 1–9.
CCY 69: 36–39; *EP68; KP68.*

February 14

On the Correct Realization of Small Group Management System and on the Attainment of New Heights in Farm Production.

Concluding remarks at the national farm workers meeting.

> Kim praises the accomplishments of the past year in grain production and urges the farm workers to repeat the performance. He goes into small details to arouse the farmers to attain new heights in their production. Kim says that by producing greater amounts of grain, the North can save foreign exchange. He also says that farmers should be prepared for war in view of the *Pueblo* incident, etc.
>
> *SKKM 3:* 302–20; *KP68.*

February 16

Congratulatory Message to All Farm Workers and Agricultural Managers.

> General congratulatory message for successfully carrying out farm work for the past year.
>
> *CCY 69:* 59–62.

March 14

Let Us Educate and Train the Students to Be the True Reserves in the Socialist and Communist Construction.

> *SS:* 497–527; *KP69*; *LSWY 2:* 453–83.

March 26

On the Strengthening of the Struggle with Communicable Diseases.

Talk with leaders of the Ministry of Public Health.

> *PH:* 212–26.

April 13

Youth Must Become the Vanguard on All Fronts of Economic and Defense Construction to Bring Our Revolution to Final Victory.

Speech at a meeting of the National Youth General League.

> General speech to boost morale of the youth in the North. Kim touches on the *Pueblo*, conditions of the North and the South, the duties of the League of the Socialist Working Youth, and other subjects. Kim supplements his talk with interesting examples.
>
> *SW 5:* 11–43; *CSJ 5:* 10–44.
> *YOU:* 147–181; *LSWY 2:* 484–522; *KP69*; *WY:* 223–59.

May 11
Let Us Develop the Ch'ŏllima Workteam Movement in Depth, a Great Impetus to Socialist Construction.

Speech delivered at the second national meeting of the vanguards of the Ch'ŏllima Workteam Movement.

Kim revealed that it was Chin Ŭng-wŏn of Kangsŏn Steel Mill who first started the Ch'ŏllima movement. Kim said that the central tasks of the Ch'ŏllima Workteam Movement are: (1) ideological revolution, (2) technological revolution, and (3) cultural revolution.

SW 5: 44–73; CSJ 5: 45–75.
JUCHE 2: 101–32; SKKM 3: 321–54; TU: 438–71; LSWY 2: 523–57; KP68; CLM: 373–406; SR: 241–72.

*May 27
On Strengthening the Guidance of the Party Life of Party Members and Properly Implementing the Cadre Policy of Our Party.

Speech to the heads of the organizational and personnel departments of provincial party committees.

Divided into four parts, the speech gives some instruction on party work at the provincial level. First he speaks of the duties of the chairman of the organization department, which include participation in party meetings and meeting with cadres. Secondly he speaks of the duties of the chairman of the personnel department, who must meet with the workers in administration and economic sectors. Kim also spoke of the proper selection and allocation of cadres and of continued education of the cadres.

SW 5: 74–97; CSJ 5: 76–98.
KP71.

June 4–5
To Bring About New Progress in the Development of Fisheries.

Speech delivered at a council of fishery workers of the eastern sea.

KP69 (Susanŏp palchŏn esŏ saeroun piyak ŭl irŭk'igi wihayŏ. Pyongyang: Chosŏn Nodongdang Ch'ulp'ansa, 1969).

June 14
On Correctly Implementing Our Party's Policy towards Intellectuals.

Speech to intellectuals in Hamgyŏng Pukto.

Kim says that the party policy is to revolutionize intellectuals. The duties of the intellectuals are to possess a revolutionary world view and to arm themselves with revolutionary ideas and the idea of *chuch'e*.

SW 5: 98–129; *CSJ 5:* 99–132.
CHU 1: 574–96; *JUCHE 2:* 133–53 (excerpt); *SS:* 528–64; *KP72.*

June 22–24
Speeches to Welcome President Julius K. Nyerere, Head of the State of Tanzania.

Three speeches welcoming President Nyerere, who visited the North. The usual call for the unity of the nonaligned nations is made.

CCY 69: 47–51; *ML:* 171–74.

August 25
Speech to Welcome a Delegation of the Japanese Communist Party.

On the occasion of the visit of the general secretary of the Japanese Communist party, Kenji Miyamoto, Kim speaks very cordially of cooperation between the Japanese Communist party and the North.

CCY 69: 51–52.

**September 7*
The Democratic People's Republic of Korea is the Banner of Freedom and Independence for Our People and a Powerful Weapon for Building Socialism and Communism.

Report at the twentieth anniversary celebration of the founding of the republic.

A long report on the accomplishments of the North. Divided into three major sections, the report reviews the achievements of the North from the liberation, the war, economic recovery, and planning. Secondly, Kim speaks of the further consolidation of the socialist system in the North, and lastly, Kim urges destruction of the United States to accomplish the unification of Korea. In this speech, Kim gives no credit to Russia for the liberation of Korea, nor does he mention Chinese volunteers in the Korean war.

SW 5: 130–99; *CSJ 5:* 133–200.
CHU 1: 597–620; *JUCHE 2:* 154–78 (excerpt); *SK:* 391–409 (excerpt); *RSC:* 146–58 (excerpt); *MHJ:* 1–37; *UNF:* 98–100 (excerpt); *TU:* 472–546; *SS:* 565–639; *CCY 69:* 1–33; *LSWY 2:* 558–632; *KP68; CLM:* 407–81; *ML:* 175–249.

September 24
On Speeding up Construction of Socialism in the Countryside and Solidly Developing the Counties.

Speech delivered at a consultative meeting of chief secretaries of the city and county committees of the Workers' Party of Korea.

> Kim speaks of the importance of the counties in solving the problems of the countryside. Kim says that it is important to eliminate the rural-urban gap in rapidly developing the countryside. Kim also emphasizes the role of counties in developing the rural areas.
>
> *SW 5:* 200–221; *CSJ 5:* 201–22.
> KP71; SR: 273–96.

October 2
Let Us Strengthen the Training of Technical Personnel to Meet the New Requirements of Socialist Construction.

Speech to the faculty and students of the Kim Ch'aek Polytechnic Institute.

> Kim speaks of technical education, particularly in the electronic and light metal industries, and of general emphasis on natural science and technical science over the social sciences. Kim says here that it is the party policy to send high school graduates to the army for a few years before sending them to college.
>
> *SW 5:* 222–35; *CSJ 5:* 223–37.
> *JUCHE 2:* 179 94; *KP71.*

October 8
The Great Anti-Imperialist Revolutionary Cause of the Asian, African, and Latin American Peoples is Invincible.

The treatise published on the occasion of the first anniversary of the death of Che Guevara in battle, in the eighth issue of *Tricontinental*, theoretical organ of the Organization of Solidarity of the Peoples of Asia, Africa, and Latin America.

> General condemnation of the United States and American imperialism. Kim says that revolution in each country is a part of the world revolution, but each revolution is conducted in accordance with the objective conditions of each nation.
>
> *SW 5:* 236–49; *CSJ 5:* 238–51.
> *SK:* 410–24; *MHJ 3:* 38–45; *WSK:* 306–16; *NAM:* 72–86; *CCY 69:* 40–46;
> *KP68; ML:* 250–64.

October 31
On Strengthening the Capacity and the Role of Finances in the Socialist Construction.

Talk at the council of workers in the finance sectors.

Kim speaks in detail of daily life and necessities of the families together with the principle of socialistic financial management. He attempts to lay down several rules of distribution and capital accumulation in a socialist economy, but the principle is not convincing. More important are the revelations that there are few consumer goods in the North and that such daily necessities as sugar and other foodstuffs are not selling because of high prices. He also speaks of the lack of curtains in the houses of workers and even speaks of how to make buttons.

SKKM 3: 355–78; *KP70.*

November 16
On Relieving the Strain on Transport.

Concluding speech at the eighteenth enlarged plenum of the Central Committee of the Workers' Party of Korea (4WPK-18CC).

Kim speaks against what he terms the departmentalism in railway transportation. He says that there is considerable waste because each department or area-station wants to control its section. He also says that discipline should be strict, almost like that of the military, that every transportation section should be militarized, and that transport workers should be exempt from the military draft. All local party organs should not interfere with transportation work.

SW 5: 250–75; *CSJ 5:* 252–79.
KP72.

November 16
Some Problems of Manpower Administration.

Concluding speech at the eighteenth enlarged plenum of the Central Committee of the Workers' Party of Korea (4WPK-18CC).

The most important work in manpower administration is political work. In the North it is not material incentive that induces people to work, but rather it is the love of one's country that makes them work. Korean workers, Kim said, are happy to work as long as the state guarantees their livelihood. Kim also emphasized the use of women in the labor force and their gradual replacement of men.

SW 5: 276–93; *CSJ 5:* 280–98.
SKKM 3: 379–406; *KP72.*

1969

February 7
On Further Developing the Socialist Agrarian Construction.

Speech at a national farm workers meeting.

> Kim praises the farm production of the past year in spite of the bad weather. In this lengthy speech Kim goes into the details of his three revolutions (ideological, technical, and cultural) on the farms. In the second part of his speech he enumerates how the unsuccessful cooperative farms can be helped. Thirdly he speaks of how, in the next year, farming plans can be helped through irrigation, advanced farm techniques, support materials, and efficient labor administration.
>
> *SKKM 3:* 407–80.

February 15
P'yŏngan Namdo Must Head All Fronts in the Socialist Construction.

Concluding remarks at a P'yŏngan Namdo representative meeting of the Workers' Party of Korea.

> Only the third part, dealing with manpower administration, is excerpted here. Much of what Kim says repeats what he has been saying about correct administration of manpower management. Here Kim speaks, in conjunction with the farm manpower administration, of mobilization for forty days of military personnel, office workers, students, and workers on the farms. In correcting some aspects of manpower administration, Kim says that college students were mobilized to build military installations, but the supply of building materials was incorrectly carried out, thus wasting the manpower.
>
> *SKKM 3:* 481–94 (excerpt).

*March 1
On Some Theoretical Problems of the Socialist Economy.

Answers to the questions raised by scientific educational workers.

> Kim tackles three problems related to economic development. The first is his contention that there is no correlation between the size of the economy and the rate of growth in a socialist society. The problem of a relatively lower growth rate in an advanced economy is a phenomenon of a capitalist and not a socialist economy. The second is the problem of whether the means of production is a commodity. Kim contends that when the means of production is a commodi-

ty, the theory of value applies. The third is the ways with which to abolish the peasant market in a socialist society.

SW 5: 294–319; *CSJ 5:* 299–323.
JUCHE 2: 209–36; *SKKM 3:* 495–521; *RSC:* 159–82; *JC:* 127–47; *MHJ 3:* 46–59; *WSK:* 317–36; *SS:* 640–66; *CCY 70:* 1–12; *KP69; CLM:* 482–91 (excerpt); *EP75.*

June 30
On the Thrift and Care of State Properties and Further Development of Fisheries.

Concluding remarks at the nineteenth plenum of the fourth session of the Workers' Party of Korea (4WPK-19CC).

Only the first part, on state properties, is excerpted here. Kim speaks of proper care and tighter control of state properties, improvement of cooperative production, elimination of unplanned work, upgrading of the quality of products, and prevention of destruction of state properties. In his discussion of these six items, Kim reveals some of the vices the people are engaged in, such as illicit prescription of drugs, illegal sales of eggs for personal profit, construction of unplanned buildings for personal profit, and deliberate destruction of state properties, that need to be corrected.

SKKM 3: 522–81.

July 1
Answers to the Questions Raised by the Iraqi News Agency.

Three-question interview; questions on unification, the Arab people's struggle against Zionism, and the Iraqi revolution of July 17, 1968, were asked. Kim gives a general answer in support of his three points on the revolution, his support for the Arab people, and support for the new revolutionary regime in Iraq.

JC: 221–26; *CCY 70:* 20–22; *FCI:* 55–63.

July 1
Answers to the Questions Raised by Abdel Hamid Ahmed Hanrouche, General Manager of *Dar-El-Tahrir* Publishing Company of the United Arab Republic.

Four questions were asked, one about the self-resuscitation efforts of North Korea, two pertaining to the Sino-Soviet dispute, and one about the people of the United Arab Republic. Kim says that disputes among the socialist countries are different from those between the socialist and capitalist countries.

When asked why the North is not participating in the conference held in Moscow this year, Kim says that when the conditions are not right for the North, it does not participate.

CHU 1: 621–35; *JUCHE 2:* 195–208; *CCY 70:* 23–29; *FCI:* 64–81.

July 2
For the Further Development of a Uniform Planning System.

Speech at a meeting of workers in the planning sector.

Kim speaks of four items here: (1) creation of a state planning section in each factory and enterprise as a branch of the district planning committee to facilitate uniform planning, (2) introduction of a new planning method, (3) planning city management and commodity flows, and (4) planning quickly the goals of the next year's people's economic plan. Kim tries to correct the imbalance in planning, thus slowing down work and eliminating confusion in carrying out the goals of the plan. The newly created state planning section, consisting of three or four men or five or six men, is to serve the higher-echelon planning committee, the district planning committee.

SKKM 3: 582–608; *KP70.*

September 2
Answers to the Questions Raised by the Delegation of the Democratic Youth League of Finland for *Kansan Uutiset*, the Central Organ of the Communist Party of Finland.

Seven questions were asked on U.S. violations of North Korean territory, increase in the South Korean military, chances of the outbreak of a total war, U.S. suppression of the national liberation movement in the South, the unification of Korea, the efforts of the youth, and the Vietnamese question. Kim repeats his earlier stands on most of these questions and reaffirms his conviction that the North will eventually win regardless of U.S. provocations and threats in the South. He also reasserts his belief that the Vietnamese people's struggle will succeed.

JC: 243–62; *CCY 70:* 30–40; *FCI:* 82–110.

September 18
Progressive Journalists of the Five Continents, Wield Your Powerful Revolutionary Pen and Sternly Condemn U.S. Imperialism.

Congratulatory remarks at the international conference on the tasks of journalists of the world in their fight against the aggression of U.S. imperialism.

Strong anti-U.S. statements at the international conference of journalists held in Pyongyang. Kim expressed appreciation to the conference for voting Kim Chong-t'ae an international journalist award.

SW 5: 320–33; *CSJ 5:* 324–36.
JC: 229–40; *MHJ 3:* 60–67; *NAM:* 87–101; *CCY 70:* 13–19; *KP69; FCI:* 1–17.

September 27
Speeches to Welcome N. Adassi, Head of State of Syria.

Four speeches to welcome Premier Adassi of Syria. The usual welcoming speech denouncing the United States and advocating the solidarity of the two countries. His visit lasted until October 3.

CCY 70: 47–51.

October 11
On Some Experiences of the Democratic and Socialist Revolutions in Our Country.

Lecture to cadres of party and state organizations.

Brief discussion of three aspects of North Korean socialist revolution, the agrarian reform, the Agricultural Cooperative Farm movement, and the socialist transformation in trade and industries. This is a general review, only revealing a few facts, such as isolating the rich peasants during the land reform period, helping those who chose to join the cooperativization movement, etc. There is no clear indication of the purpose of this lecture.

SW 5: 334–59; *CSJ 5:* 337–63.
WSK: 337–57; *EP73; KP72.*

October 21
Several Problems in the Reform of the Socialist Statistics Work.

Speech at the Political Committee of the Central Committee of the Workers' Party of Korea.

In an effort to set a uniform standard in statistical work, Kim says that: (1) statistics must be correct, scientifically computed and objective; (2) statistics must be prepared within a reasonable time without delay; and (3) the party must work toward solving the problems in statistical work.

KP76; Nodong sinmun, January 27, 1976.

November 4
Popularize Athletics and Prepare the Entire People for Work and National Defense.

Speech delivered at a national athletes meeting to popularize various sports and build strong athletes and healthy people who can in turn serve the country.

KP70 (Ch'eyuk ŭl taejunghwa hayŏ chŏnch'e inmindŭl ŭl nodonggwa kukbang e t'ŭnt'ŭnhi chunbi sik'ija. Pyongyang: Chosŏn Nodongdang Ch'ulp'ansa, 1970).

November 19
Speech Welcoming the Norwegian Communist Party Delegation Headed by Chairman Reidar Larsen.

A short speech confirming the friendship and cordial relationship of the two parties. Kim denounces the United States and hopes for closer ties with the Norwegian Communist party. This visit by Chairman Larsen was a result of an invitation from the Central Committee of the Workers' Party of Korea.

CCY 70: 52–54.

November 22
Answers to the Questions Raised by Ali Balout, Correspondent of the Lebanese Newspaper *Al Anwar.*

Five questions were raised, asking about the prospects of North Korean development, the possibilities of a U.S. attack, the Sino-Soviet dispute, the Middle Eastern crisis, and advice to the people of Arab countries. Kim says that the North is trying hard to complete the seven-year economic plan, repeats his noncommittal stand on the Sino-Soviet dispute, and expresses strong support for the Arab cause, including the Palestine Liberation movement.

JUCHE 2: 237–49; *CHU 1:* 636–48; *CCY 70:* 41–46; *FCI:* 111–25.

1970

February 17
Education, Literature and Art Should Contribute to Equipping People with a Revolutionary World Outlook.

Speech at a consultative meeting of workers in science, education, literature, and art.

Kim reveals a little bit of his boyhood life. He claims that he read up on Marxism and Leninism. He urges the artists and literary writers to concentrate on producing works of the anti-Japanese guerrilla days and gives the specific example of *P'ibada* (Sea of blood), which was made into a musical later.

EP73; KP72.

February 27
Let Us Develop Local Industry and Bring About a Fresh Upswing in the Production of Mass Consumer Goods.

Speech at a national conference of workers in local industry.

To meet the rising demand of workers, Kim urges the workers in light industry and local industries to produce more and improve the quality of consumer goods to such an extent that they can be exported. Kim encourages local industries, telling them to use women laborers, reduce the rural-urban gap, and decentralize the population away from the cities.

SW 5: 360–89; *CSJ 5:* 364–95.
KP72.

March 31
On Further Developing the Poultry Industry.

Address to a national meeting of poultrymen.

All about poultry; how to raise chickens, the production of eggs, prevention of disease, etc.

SW 5: 390–407; *CSJ 5:* 396–415.
KP72.

April 5–7
Speeches Welcoming Premier Chou En-lai of the People's Republic of China.

Four speeches welcoming Chou. Kim repeats his gratitude for the Chinese people's support for the North during the Korean war and renews the friendship sealed with blood. Kim says that they have discussed many problems of mutual interest.

CCY 71: 68–72.

April 16
The Great Idea of Lenin on the National Liberation Struggle in Colonies in the East is Triumphant.

Article published in *Pravda* on the centenary of the birth of V. I. Lenin.

Kim praises Lenin's idea of national liberation struggle in colonial countries and reviews the Asian struggle from Chinese Communist victories to the struggles of the Vietnamese, Laotian, and other peoples. Kim says that Korean revolution also was guided by Lenin's idea, and after the liberation the Korean Communists were able to build a strong, self-reliant state in the North. Kim says that Korea is still fighting U.S. imperialism and Japanese militarism, and he vows eventual victory for socialism in Korea and pledges close friendship with the Russians.

JC: 209–11; *CCY 71;* 63–67; *KP70.*

June 15
Speeches Welcoming Samdech Norodom Sihanouk, Head of the State of Cambodia and Chairman of the Cambodian National Unification Front.

This is the second visit of Sihanouk, and Kim renews his support for the Cambodian people's anti-U.S. struggle. Sihanouk stayed in the North until July 1 and returned to the North many times following this visit.

CCY 71; 73–80.

August 13–16
Speeches Welcoming Gaafar Mohamed Nimeri, President of the Revolution Command Council and Prime Minister of the Democratic Republic of Sudan.

After the May 1969 revolution in Sudan, Nimeri visited China and came to Korea for talks with Kim. Kim made a general statement about the need for solidarity of nonaligned nations and supported the African people's struggle for independence.

CCY 71; 81–86.

*November 2
Report to the Fifth Congress of the Workers' Party of Korea on the Work of the Central Committee (5WPK).

Divided in into five parts, this report is one of the most comprehensive summaries of the 1960s. (1) Kim first reviews the accomplishments in the process of transformation into a socialist industrial state, the cultural revolution, ideological unity, all-people defense system, and socialist economic management. (2) Kim outlines the basic tasks of the new six-year economic plan in the socialist construction, the cultural revolution, ideological revolution, strengthening of national defense capabilities, and improving living standards. (3) He speaks of the reunification of Korea and the revolution in South Korea. (4) He speaks of international relations to strengthen solidarity with the revolutionary forces of other countries. (5) He speaks of the ideological unity with the thought of *chuch'e* in the North. This is a lengthy report, and there is much revealing information and many statistics in this report.

SW 5: 408–526; *CSJ 5:* 416–529.
JUCHE 2: 250–320 (excerpt); *RSC:* 183–214 (excerpt); *MHJ 3:* 68–129; *NAM:* 102–13 (excerpt); *UNF:* 101–4 (excerpt); *IPR:* 69–82 (excerpt); *IPRC:* 141–56 (excerpt); *CCY 71:* 1–62; *KP70; SR:* 297–368 (excerpt).

1971

January 1
New Year Address.

Kim's praise for the accomplishments of the past year, and his encouragement to workers to attain the goal of the new six-year plan.

CCY 72: 1–5; *KP71.*

January 28
Congratulatory Message.

This message is to the ninth congress of the Korean Resident's Association in Japan (Chōsōren), an organization supported by and sympathetic to the North. Kim praises the accomplishments of the four years since the eighth congress was held. He urges Korean residents in Japan to wage an anti-U.S. struggle.

CCY 72: 46–47.

February 3
On Further Invigorating the Work of the League of Socialist Working Youth to Suit the Character of Young People.

Speech at the conference of the heads of the youth affairs sections of the party committees and the chairmen of the League of Socialist Working Youth Committees of provinces, cities, counties, factories, enterprises, and the institutes of higher learning.

Kim speaks on three subjects: first on improving the organizational work, second on intensifying the ideological and cultural work, and third on the implementation of the decisions of the fifth party congress. Here Kim tells the LSWY to limit the age of members to twenty-nine and no one over forty years of age must be a member of the league. Kim also urges young people to learn foreign languages, but to learn them so that they can use them during the conflict with Japan or the United States. Kim asks women not to marry early and urges them to help complete the goals of the economic plan.

CSJ 6: 1–47; SW 6: 1–44.
YOU: 182–229; KP71; WY: 260–308.

February 12
On the Tasks of Tractor Operators in the Rural Technical Revolution.

Speech at a national meeting of tractor operators.

> Kim says that the North needs eighty thousand to ninety thousand tractors, and this means that they have to produce sixty thousand more tractors to completely mechanize agriculture. Kim tells the tractor drivers to work more efficiently and be thrifty in using oil and gasoline. He points out the need to train more drivers and strengthen their party spirit.

CSJ 6: 48–59; SW 6: 45–55.
SR: 369–80.

June 6
Speech to Welcome the Delegation of the Chilean Socialist Party Headed by Carlos A. Orego.

> Kim congratulates the victory of President Salvador Allende and welcomes the delegation for their visit to the North. Kim denounces U.S. imperialism in Latin America and praises the struggle of the Cuban and Chilean peoples.

CCY 72: 26–27; KP71.

June 6
Congratulatory Message.

> This message is to all members of the Youth Corps of the North on the twenty-fifth anniversary celebration of the founding of the Youth Corps. Kim gives ten-point task to the youngsters: (1) to strengthen the organizational life, (2) to be good students, (3) to love the socialist system and be thrifty with national property, (4) to hate the enemy of the revolution, (5) to enhance the collective spirit, (6) to have communist morality, (7) to love work and help build socialism, (8) to be active in socialist political work, (9) to help bring about unification, and (10) to promote friendship with youth of the world.

CCY 72: 14–18; KP71; WY: 309–18.

June 9–15
Speeches Welcoming the Party and Government Delegation of the Romanian Socialist Republic Headed by Comrade Nicolae Ceausescu.

> Five speeches were given, two at the airport, two at each other's banquet, and one at a Pyongyang mass rally, all in support of friendship between the Romanian government and North Korea. Kim denounced the United States and ex-

pressed concern about the rise of Japanese militarism and their encroachment into South Korea. A joint communique was issued during this visit.

CCY 72: 27–36.

June 24
The Youth Must Take Over and Carry Forward the Revolution.

Speech delivered at the sixth congress of the League of Socialist Working Youth of Korea.

Kim is encouraging socialist youth to master technology and propagate technical skills to other youth, thus avoiding what he terms as mysticism of science. He praises the struggle by the South Korean youth and denounces the United States.

CSJ 6: 60–73; *SW 6:* 56–69.
YOU: 230–45; *CCY 72:* 19–25; *EP71; KP71; WY:* 319–34.

August 6
The Revolutionary Peoples of Asia Will Win in Their Common Struggle against U.S. Imperialism.

Speech at the Pyongyang mass meeting welcoming Samdech Norodom Sihanouk, Head of the National United Front of Kampuchea.

Kim says that the North is ready to take any measures necessary to help the Cambodian people. Kim condemns the United States and its efforts in Southeast Asia and calls Nixon's trip to China, not the march of a victor but a trip of the defeated. Kim speaks of the eight-point unification program advanced in April of 1970 and claims that the South is afraid to speak to the North. Kim made two other speeches in connection with this third visit of Sihanouk to the North. One was at Kim's banquet for Sihanouk on July 22 and the other at Sihanouk's banquet for Kim on August 8.

NAM: 114–30; *UNF:* 105–7 (excerpt); *IPR:* 83–85 (excerpt); *IPRC:* 157–74; *CCY 72:* 6–13; *KP71; RK:* 1–15.

*September 25 and October 8
On Several Questions of Domestic and International Policies of the Workers' Party of Korea and the Government of the Republic.

Talk with the editor of the Japanese *Asahi shinbun* and reporter of the Kyodo News Agency.

Kim speaks on a wide range of problems and answers eight questions. First, on the prospects of the six-year plan of the North, Kim repeats his three ideological, technical, and cultural revolutions in the North to attain the goals of the plan. Secondly, he speaks of the unification problem and says that the South Koreans are dragging their feet in the Red Cross talks. Thirdly, Kim denounces the unjust resolutions of the United Nations and says the United Nations is nothing but a tool of the U.S. imperialists. Fourthly, Kim addresses himself to the Korean residents in Japan, saying these people should be assured of their rights and educational opportunities. Fifth, on Japanese-North Korean relations, Kim says that the Japanese government is very hostile to the North, and sixth, he says he fears the rebirth of Japanese militarism. On the Nixon visit to China (seventh), Kim says that it is the visit of the defeated and there is no change in North Korean foreign policy. Lastly, Kim says that the North will help resolve the Sino-Soviet dispute, but the dispute is a difference of opinion between fraternal parties and there is no basic contradiction in the Communist international order.

CSJ 6: 74–111; *SW* 6: 70–104.
WSK: 358–87; *UNF:* 108–18 (excerpt).

October 7
On Revolutionizing and "Working-Classizing" Women.

Speech at the fourth congress of the Democratic Women's Union of Korea.

Kim gives a few instructions to women to strengthen the organizational work, the social work, the educational work, and other tasks assigned to women. He urges them to be thrifty and prepare themselves for the eventual unification of Korea.

CSJ 6: 112–35; *SW* 6: 105–26; *KP72.*

October 11
Answers to the Questions Raised by the Iraqi Journalists' Delegation.

Answering a question about the most important achievement by the North, Kim says that it is the establishment of the idea of *chuch'e.* Others are general questions relating to the support of the Vietnamese people against the United States and the Arab people against the Zionists.

JUCHE 2: 321–26; *EP71; CCY* 72: 41–45.

November 15
Report at the Third Session of the Central Committee of the Workers' Party of Korea (5WPK-3CC).

No text available.

December 2

On Improving and Strengthening the Training of Party Cadres.

Speech delivered before the teachers of party cadre-training institutions.

> Kim speaks on two basic points: to teach the cadres revolutionary work methods and to teach the rich experiences of the party. Kim tells them to correct the administrative methods of the leaders and to rid their work of bureaucratic methods and subjectivism. Do not expand work unnecessarily, finish it on time, try not to hog the work for oneself, and give appropriate directives to specialists.
>
> *CSJ* 6: 136–63; *SW* 6: 127–54.

December 14

On the Character and Tasks of the Trade Union in Socialist Society.

Speech at the fifth congress of the General Federation of Trade Unions of Korea.

> Kim reemphasizes the transforming of all workers into the working class, what he calls "working-classization." He also speaks of revolutionization of all, meaning to arm all with the revolutionary spirit. Kim makes a remark about the Red Cross dialogue between the North and the South and claims that the North proposed it and the South had no choice but to accept. Kim says that the South's proposal about finding lost families is not that important, but they agreed to do it. However, the South is not agreeing to the North's proposition for free travel, postal exchanges, and others.
>
> *CSJ* 6: 164–93; *SW* 6: 155–83.
> *JUCHE* 2: 327–56; *EP74*; *KP72*.

December 27

On the Thorough Implementation of the Principles of Socialist Pedagogy in Education.

Speech delivered at a national meeting of teachers.

> General slogans of Kim's speech during the early 1970s are what he calls "working classization" and "revolutionarization" of the people. He urges the educators to follow suit. He also mentions that the classics of communism and early progressive literary works have certain limitations because the time is different. Today, it is important to emphasize both economic determinism and ideological training. Repeats Ma Tong-hŭi's mother story. Kim says that the North has nine-year compulsory education, but he hopes for ten-year compulsory education soon.
>
> *CSJ* 6: 194–226; *SW* 6: 184–213.
> *JUCHE* 2: 357–89; *EP73*; *KP72*.

1972

January 1
New Year Address.

General review of the accomplishments of the past year and expression of hope for the coming year. Condemns the South, the South Korean leaders, the United States, and Japan and renews his conviction that the Communists in Vietnam, Cambodia, Laos, and everywhere else will triumph. Briefly mentions the Red Cross talks between the North and the South, but makes carping criticism of the South Korean leaders.

UNF: 119–22 (excerpt); *IPR:* 87–94 (excerpt); *IPRC:* 175–83 (excerpt); *CCY 73:* 1–9; *EP72; KP72.*

January 10
On Present Political and Economic Policies of the Democratic People's Republic of Korea and Some International Problems.

Answer to the questions raised by newsmen of the Japanese newspaper, *Yomiuri shinbun.*

Kim speaks on five topics: *Chuch'e* ideology, the six-year plan, the reunification of Korea, international relations, and Korea-Japan relations. Kim basically repeats what he has been saying of the idea of *chuch'e*, and on the economic plan, Kim reemphasizes the technical, cultural, and ideological revolutions and three major objectives of the technical revolution. Kim speaks badly of the South in connection with the Red Cross talks and disparages U.S. policy in Asia. Kim says that Japan should abrogate the South Korea and Japan treaty and normalize relations with the North.

JUCHE 2: 390–424; *WSK:* 388–414; *UNF:* 123–27 (excerpt); *IPR:* 95–100 (excerpt); *IPRC:* 184–89 (excerpt); *CCY 73:* 30–45; *KP72.*

February 16
On the Central Tasks of the Union of Agricultural Working People.

Speech delivered at the second congress of the Union of Agricultural Working People of Korea.

Kim speaks on five subjects: (1) accelerate the technical revolution, (2) step up the ideological revolution, (3) boost the cultural revolution, (4) improve management of the cooperative farms, and (5) upgrade the organizations of the Union of Agricultural Working People.

CSJ 6: 227–52; *SW 6:* 214–38.
SR: 381–407.

April 5
Speeches at Banquets to Welcome Prince Norodom Sihanouk.

Kim congratulates enthusiastically the victories of the Cambodian people's struggle against the United States and its stooges. This is Sihanouk's fourth visit, and his visits became not only frequent but also lengthy. This time Sihanouk stayed about one month and went to Hŭich'ŏn, Chagangdo, where Kim gave him another banquet on April 11. Kim spoke primarily on domestic issues at this banquet, congratulating the production of ten thousand machines in this factory. Other delegates from China and Korean residents in Japan also participated. Sihanouk gave two banquets for Kim on April 26 and May 4. Kim repeated his usual attack on the United States and his hope for ultimate victory of the Cambodian people.

CCY 73: 92–101.

May 14
Talk with the Delegation of the All-Japan Revolutionary Mayors Association.

Kim answers essentially six questions: (1) on international situations, (2) fairly detailed discussion on local administration, its functions and structures in the North, (3) on the educational systems in the North, (4) on the close cooperation between Japanese citizens and Korean residents in Japan, (5) on the promotion of mutual friendship and sister relationship between Japanese and North Korean cities, (6) on the return of Okinawa to Japan.

CCY 73: 46–56; *KP72.*

May 18–23
Speeches to Welcome President Mohamed Siad Barre of Somalia.

Two speeches (one at Kim's banquet and another at Barre's banquet) on the close cooperation between the two countries. Kim thanks Barre for Somalia's support for the North in the United Nations.

CCY 73: 101–3.

May 26
Talk with Journalists of the U.S. Newspaper, *New York Times.*

Kim explains to Harrison Salisbury the anti-U.S. sentiment in the North. The relations between the United States and the North can be improved, and this depends very much on the attitude of the United States. Kim reiterates his position on the reunification of Korea, the independent and peaceful reunification formula. He also touches on Japan-North Korea relations, and this too depends on the attitude of the Japanese government. Replying to a question about the most difficult task the North has faced since the liberation, Kim says that it was recovery from the Korean war.

IPR: 101–16; *UNF:* 128–36 (excerpt); *IPRC:* 190–206; *CCY 73:* 56–64; *KP72*; *RK:* 16–31; *New York Times*, May 31, 1972.

June 1
Talk with the Representatives of the Japanese Communist Party.

On the reunification question, Kim repeats his stand on independent and peaceful unification of Korea without interference from other countries. Kim assails the hostile attitude of the Japanese government and insists on the withdrawal of the American forces in the South.

UNF: 137–42 (excerpt).

June 21
Talk with a Correspondent of the *Washington Post*.

At the request of Selig S. Harrison to make a new proposal, Kim says that the North is interested in reducing armed forces by 150,000 or 200,000 men and ultimately bringing the armed forces to the level of 100,000 men or less. He also proposes a peace treaty between the North and the South, thus effecting the withdrawal of the U.S. troops from the South. Kim also says that he is willing to meet with Park Chung Hee if Park wishes to see him. On the Korean reunification question, Kim says that there is no need for U.N. supervision, and if the South abrogates its security agreements with foreign powers, the North can abrogate its treaties in favor of the peaceful unification of Korea. Kim repeats his stands on other questions raised.

UNF: 143–49 (excerpt); *Washington Post*, June 26, 1972.

June 30
Let Us Introduce Innovations in Heat Supply.

Speech delivered at a national meeting of heat supply workers.

Brief speech about the reforms in the heat supply operation. Kim proposes a few policies, such as to make boilers to fit the needs of various different ferrous metals and to improve the management of the heat structures. Kim says to be thrifty in coal consumption and manpower utilization.

CSJ 6: 253–67; *SW* 6: 239–52.

July 1
Report at the Fourth Session of the Central Committee of the Workers' Party of Korea (5WPK-4CC).

No text available.

July 28
Speech Welcoming the Government Delegation of the Arab Republic of Yemen, Headed by Premier Mohsin Ahmed Al Aini.

Very general speech to welcome the delegation to the North. Kim says that the prospects for unification of Korea are bright, and he is happy that talks between the North and South have begun.

CCY 73: 105–7.

*September 17
On Some Problems of Our Party's *Chuch'e* Idea and the Government of the Republic's Internal and External Policies.

Answers to the questions raised by journalists of the Japanese newspaper, *Mainichi shinbun.*

Kim answers previously submitted questions on four topics: (1) *Chuch'e*, (2) North Korea's Foreign Policy, (3) the unification of Korea, and (4) Korea-Japan relations. In general, Kim speaks very openly on all subjects. He reiterates his theory of *chuch'e*, but he says that this is not his idea but the idea of Marxism and Leninism. He merely emphasized it. On the question of foreign policy, he says that he is willing to submit the question of Korean unification to the United Nations, and he condemns the South for its efforts to block it. His position here is quite different from his earlier statements about the United Nations having nothing to do with Korean unification. Thirdly, on peaceful unification, Kim speaks of the joint statement and the progress the North and the South have made, and he proposes the confederation formula. Kim proposes to open both sides to journalists, sportsmen, artists, and others to travel freely on both sides of the parallel. Kim seems to be unaware of how tight a country he runs in the North. Lastly, on the Korea-Japan relationship, Kim says that it is Japan that prevents a friendly relationship with the North, and he condemns Japan's economic agreements with the South as economic imperialism and a step toward Japan's subjugation of Korea.

CSJ 6: 268–95; *SW 6:* 253–80.
JUCHE 2: 425–36 (excerpt); *WSK:* 415–37; *UNF:* 150–56 (excerpt); *IPR:* 117–43; *IPRC:* 207–37; *CCY 73:* 65–78; *EP72; KP72; RK:* 32–38.

October 6

Talk with the Managing Editor of the Japanese Politico-Theoretical Magazine, *Sekai*.

Kim is questioned on the idea of *chuch'e* and repeats more or less the same answers. He also touches on the problems of pollution and economic relations between Japan and the North. On the diplomatic relationship between North Korea and Japan, Kim says that it is unrealistic to discuss normalization of relations between the two countries until after Japan abrogates its relationship with the South, particularly pointing out Article 3 of the treaty between the South and Japan, stipulating that Japan considers the Republic of Korea, the South Korean government, as the only legal government in Korea.

JUCHE 2: 437–51; *CCY 73:* 78–91; *EP72; KP72.*

October 23

Report at the Fifth Session of the Central Committee of the Workers' Party of Korea (5WPK-5CC).

No text available.

November 4

Speeches at Banquets to Commemorate the Fiftieth Birthday and the Visit of Prince Norodom Sihanouk.

This was Sihanouk's fifth visit, and Kim repeated his congratulation of the Cambodian people's victories and denounced the United States. Kim, of course, congratulated Sihanouk's fiftieth birthday and wished him long life. Sihanouk returned the favor and held a banquet on December 1 at which Kim again spoke for the Cambodian people and against the United States. Kim said that Sihanouk was invited again next year, and Sihanouk accepted his invitation.

CCY 73: 107–15.

November 7

Speech to Welcome the Delegation of the Spanish Communist Party, Headed by Secretary-General Santiago Carillo.

Kim denounces Franco and his regime and vows fraternal relationship of the two parties. A routine speech to welcome the visitors.

CCY 73: 110–12.

December 5

Some Tasks in Developing Our Country's Science and Technology.

Speech delivered at a consultative meeting of natural scientists.

This was the occasion of the twentieth anniversary of the founding of the Academy of Sciences of the North, and Kim says that they started the Academy with only ninety-seven intellectuals. Compared to social sciences, the natural science fields are lagging far behind, and Kim urges them to improve on many aspects of daily life, including environmental studies.

CSJ 6: 296–325; *SW 6:* 281–308.

December 18
Speech to Welcome the Government Delegation of the Republic of Guinea, Headed by Prime Minister Lansana Beavogui.

Kim praises the struggle of the Guinean people under the leadership of President Seku Tourre and welcomes the delegation headed by Beavogui. Kim pledges fraternal and cordial friendship between the two countries.

CCY 73: 115–17.

*December 25
Let Us Further Strengthen the Socialist System of Our Country.

Speech at the first session of the Fifth Supreme People's Assembly of the Democratic People's Republic of Korea (5SPA-1).

This is a general review of the state of the country. Kim speaks on four items. The first is a review of the development of the North Korean efforts to build socialism and their socialist revolution. The second is to argue various advantages of the socialist system, in which Kim makes the bold claim that political freedoms of speech, assembly, and even demonstrations are guaranteed. The third is his explanation of the main content of the new constitution adopted in this session. The fourth is the task of the people to consolidate and develop the socialist system in the North. This speech may be considered Kim's explanation of the new constitution, but there is no detailed explanation. Most of his references are general in nature, going over the same ground of three revolutions and three technical revolutions, *chuch'e*, and others.

CSJ 6: 326–69; *SW 6:* 309–53.
JUCHE 2: 452–500; *WSK:* 438–71; *CCY 73:* 10–29; *KP72.*

December 27
Socialist Constitution of the Democratic People's Republic of Korea.

This is the constitution of the North, and it is difficult to see why this document is included in Kim's selected works. There is no reference to the fact that Kim authored this constitution.

CSJ 6: 370–91; *SW 6:* 354–80.

1973

January 1
New Year Address.

Kim reviews the accomplishments of the past year and compliments the work of the entire population. Kim also says that there has been a significant development in the unification effort in organizing the North-South Coordination Committee. Kim emphasizes for the new year that the North must develop more rapidly mining work, which is the basis for industrial development.

CCY 74: 1–4.

*February 1
On Some Problems for the Improvement of the Management of the Socialist Economy.

Concluding speech at the enlarged meeting of the Political Committee of the Central Committee of the Workers' Party of Korea.

Here Kim says for the first time that materialistic incentive is as important as political incentive for workers to perform their best. Kim says that political incentives and material incentives must be properly combined. Kim goes on to point out a few deficiencies in management, such as the supply of materials and an independent accounting system.

CSJ 6: 392–407; *SW 6:* 381–96.

February 8
Unity Based on Revolutionary Comradeship is the Source of the Invincibility of the People's Army.

Speech at a banquet given in honor of the twenty-fifth anniversary of the founding of the Korean People's Army.

Brief remarks about comradery of the soldiers in the army. Kim says that he left his parental care at the age of fourteen and received the love of his revolutionary comrades.

CSJ 6: 408–14; *SW 6:* 397–403.
EP75; CCY 74: 5–8.

*February 21
On the Development of Ideological Revolution, Technological Revolution, and Cultural Revolution in the Farming Villages.

Speech at the Three-Revolution Team Council on agriculture.

Kim discusses the recent decision of the political committee of the party central committee to create the three-revolutionary teams and dispatch them to farm villages to boost agricultural production. Kim says that these small teams should go to villages and implement the three revolutions in ideology, technology, and culture. It is only at the end of the speech that Kim mentions that the members of these teams are college students and they should stay in the village from the time of planting the paddy fields to the harvest. Kim acknowledges that this long stay in the villages away from study would hamper education, but, he says, this is a living education and they should help the farmers.

CCY 74: 8–24.

March 14

Let Us Further Develop the Ideological Revolution, Technological Revolution, and Cultural Revolution.

Speech at the Kangsŏ enlarged plenum of the Political Committee of the Central Committee of the Workers' Party of Korea.

Because of the inefficiency and waste in many segments of the economy, Kim urges the workers to carry out more efficiently the three revolutions that the party has advocated since February 1964. Kim also tells them of the need for the work of three great revolution teams and urges them to cooperate with these young men to produce more. Kim goes into the details of each revolution by citing examples and how they should improve.

CSJ 6: 415–45.
CCY 74: 25–39.

April 14–16

Let Us Completely Frustrate U.S. Imperialist Aggression and Intervention in Asia.

Speech delivered at a mass meeting in Pyongyang to welcome Samdec Norodom Sihanouk, Head of State of Cambodia and Chairman of the National United Front of Kampuchea.

Kim denounces U.S. intervention in the North-South negotiations and asks the South to observe the spirit of the July 4 joint statement of 1972. Kim proposes that representatives of social organizations and other groups should participate in the North-South Coordination Committee.

IPRC: 238–45 (excerpt); *CCY 74:* 40–49.

*June 23
Let Us Prevent a National Split and Reunify the Country.

Speech at the Pyongyang mass rally to welcome the party and government delegation of the Czechoslovak Socialist Republic.

> This is an important speech. After short welcoming remarks Kim lays down five points for the reunification of Korea: (1) end military confrontation and alleviate tension; (2) multi-faceted cooperation and interchange between the North and the South; (3) participation of all people in national reunification work; (4) a proposed Confederal Republic of Koryŏ; and (5) opposition to entering the United Nations separately and a proposal to dismantle the United Nations Commission for the Unification and Rehabilitation of Korea and the U.N. forces in Korea.

> *EP73; UNF:* 157–64 (excerpt); IPR: 145–51; *CCY 74:* 50–58; *RK:* 39–49.

*June 25
On the Five-Point Policy for National Reunification.

Speech at an enlarged meeting of the Political Committee of the Central Committee of the Workers' Party of Korea.

> Kim says that he had made his five-point policy public two days earlier to counter the South Korean special statement of June 23. Kim explains the five-point policy: (1) to remove military confrontation and lessen tensions between the North and South, (2) to realize many-sided cooperation and interchange between the North and South, (3) to convene a Great National Congress comprising representatives of people of all strata, political parties, and social organizations from the North and South, (4) to institute a North and South Confederation under the nomenclature of Confederal Republic of Koryŏ, and (5) to enter the United Nations under a single national identity.

> *CSJ 6:* 446–53; *SW 6:* 404–11.
> *JUCHE 2:* 501–9; *WSK:* 472–77; *UNF:* 165–72; *IPRC:* 246–54; *EP77.*

July 21
The Government and the People of the Democratic People's Republic of Korea Enthusiastically Congratulate the Result of Prince Norodom Sihanouk's Visit to Many African and European Countries.

> Kim congratulates Sihanouk once more after his return for the seventh time. Sihanouk, with a delegation from Cambodia, visited eleven countries and drummed up support for the Cambodian people's struggle against the United States. Sihanouk remained in the North and gave Kim a banquet on August 12, and Kim made another speech at this banquet.

> *CCY 74:* 58–60, 77–78.

August 1–3
Speeches to Welcome Major Marien N'gouabi, President and Head of State of the People's Republic of Congo.

Two speeches by Kim to welcome President N'gouabi. Kim repeats his usual greetings and hopes for a fraternal and cordial relationship between the two countries.

CCY 74: 60–64.

August 9
Let Us Attain New Height in Agricultural Production.

Speech at a meeting of activists in agriculture of the nation.

Kim thanks the workers for their hard work and good harvest and gives some of the reasons for the good results. He repeats ideological, technological, and cultural revolutions to attain new goals in the coming years and also tells them the tasks of the agrarian management sectors. Here Kim reveals some of the detailed tasks, which include more cutting of grass to use as fertilizer. Kim also says that in order for the entire population to be self-sufficient in rice, they should increase rice paddy fields to 700,000 *chŏngbo*, and he tells them to irrigate more lands for that purpose. Kim also speaks of a movement to earn more foreign exchange by increasing, for example, silk worm production. Lastly Kim says that for the next year grain production should reach 6.5 or 7 million tons.

CSJ 6: 454–77; *SW 6:* 412–35.
CCY 74: 65–76; *SR:* 408–33.

August 31
On the Tasks Facing the Educators of Chōsōren

Speech to the members of the visiting groups of Korean educators and music and sports circles of Chosŏn University in Japan.

Kim is giving instructions to upgrade the educational efforts of Korean children in Japan. Among many points Kim makes, he says that the educators in Japan must revolutionize their own thinking and work not only on the children, but on the parents of the children by each teacher's taking on five families to guide them.

CSJ 6: 478–93; *SW 6:* 436–51.

September 9
Speech at the Banquet to Commemorate the Twenty-fifth Anniversary of the Founding of the Democratic People's Republic of Korea.

Short speech to commemorate the twenty-fifth anniversary. Kim projects that the goals of the six-year plan can be attained by 1975 if North Korean workers proceed at the current pace.

CCY 74: 79–91.

September 19
Talk with the Executive Director and Chief Editor of Iwanami Publishing House in Japan.

Kim's interview with Midorikawa Touru, who visited the North on the occasion of the twenty-fifth anniversary celebration of the founding of the DPRK. Kim speaks on six subjects: (1) he reviews the development of the republic in both internal and external affairs, (2) he reviews the prospects of the six-year plan and boasts that the plan will be accomplished one year ahead of time, (3) he repeats the condemnation of the United States and South Korea on the issue of reunification and the role of the United Nations, (4) he elaborates his idea of confederation, (5) he maintains his opinion that contact and dialogue in the North and South Coordination Commission should continue, and (6) he says that he wants better and friendlier relations between Japan and North Korea.

JUCHE 2: 510–28; *UNF:* 173–79 (excerpt); *CCY 74:* 82–91.

October 11
Let Us Strengthen the Company of the People's Army.

Speech at a meeting of company commanders and company political commissars of the Korean People's Army.

Kim says that a company unit is like a cell in a human body, and this basic unit must be strengthened. He gives ten specific tasks: be brave, strong, responsible, etc. Kim also says that a soldier must be prepared politically, physically, and militarily.

CSJ 6: 494–523.

October 28
Let Us Achieve National Reunification and World Peace through Struggle.

Speech at a mass meeting in Pyongyang to welcome the party and government delegation of the Bulgarian People's Republic.

This is the visit of Todor Zhivkov, the president of Bulgaria. Kim repeats his rejection of the "two Korea" proposal of the South and demands that the United Nations vote down the proposal. Kim claims the support of the third world nations and advocates peaceful unification of Korea. Kim also blames the United States for the troubles throughout the world, in Chile, the Middle

East, Southeast Asia, and Africa. He vows long friendship and close relations between Bulgaria and the North. There are two more speeches, one at Kim's banquet and the other at Zhivkov's banquet, pledging the solidarity of the two countries.

CCY 74: 92–100; *IPRC:* 255–66; *RK:* 50–59.

1974

January 1
New Year Address.

Kim reviews the accomplishments of the past year and states that the North Korean economy is on firm ground even at a time when other countries are suffering from the fuel crisis. He also outlines what needs to be accomplished this year and urges people to work with Ch'ŏllima speed and Pyongyang speed. An interesting item is his insistence on stepping up the shipbuilding industry to boost the foreign trade of the North.

CCY 75: 1–6; *EP74; Kŭlloja* (no. 1, 1974): 2–8; *Korea Today* (no. 2, 1974): 2–8.

*January 10
Let Us Further Consolidate and Develop the Great Successes Achieved in the Building of a Socialist Countryside.

Speech delivered at the National Congress on Agriculture.

Kim claims that production in agriculture has more than doubled during the past year compared with 1972. Kim goes into details about the livelihood of the people in the countryside and touches upon cleanliness, the supply of drinking water, paving streets, reforming the antiquated social norms in weddings and funerals, etc. Lastly he speaks of the increased role of the counties in the management of agrarian cooperatives.

CSJ 7: 1–26; *SW 7:* 1–24.
CCY 75: 6–19; *EP74; SR:* 434–60; *Kŭlloja* (no. 1, 1974): 9–23; *Korea Today* (no. 3, 1974): 2–12.

January 14
On the Duty of *Ri* Party Secretaries.

In this speech to the *ri* party secretaries, Kim says that the *ri* is the administrative unit and represents 1/4,000 of the country. Kim gives ten tasks of *ri* secretaries ranging from participation in party meetings to opposition to non-*chuch'e* ideas.

CSJ 7: 27–49; *SW 7:* 25–46.
CCY 75: 19–30.

January 29
Answers to the Questions Raised by *L'UNITA*, **Organ of the Italian Communist Party.**

Altogether four questions of superfluous character, and Kim answers them with the usual rhetoric. Kim says that the South has disregarded the North and South Joint Statement from the day after it was signed.

UNF: 180–83; *IPR:* 153–56 (excerpt); *CCY 75:* 30–35; *EP74; FC 2:* 1–12; *A 2:* 1–12; *Korea Today* (no. 6, 1974): 2–8; *RK:* 60–64 (excerpt).

February 11
On the General Mobilization for the Great Socialism Construction Works.

Report at the eighth session of the Central Committee of the Workers' Party of Korea (5WPK-8CC).

No text available.

February 22
Answers to Questions Put by the Chief Editor of the Yugoslav Newspaper *Vecernje Novosti.*

Five questions of general nature and Kim's answers are of repetitious character. Kim says that the basic causes of the rapid development in the North are the leadership of the Workers' Party of Korea and the *chuch'e* idea.

JUCHE 2: 529–38; *NAM:* 131–35 (excerpt); *IPR:* 157–60 (excerpt); *A 2:* 13–22; *IPRC:* 267–71 (excerpt); *CCY 75:* 36–39; *EP74; FC 2:* 13–21; *Külloja* (no. 3, 1974): 26–30; *Korea Today* (no. 5, 1974): 2–6; *RK:* 65–68 (excerpt).

March 4
The Peoples of the Third World Who Advance under the Uplifted Banner of Independence Will Certainly Win Their Revolutionary Cause.

Speech at the Pyongyang mass rally to welcome Houari Boumedienne, president of the Council of Revolution and chairman of the Council of Ministers of the Algerian Democratic and People's Republic.

Effusive praise for Boumedienne as the leader of the third world and sharp anti-Israeli statements. Kim repeats rhetorical statements about his dealing with the South, and he says that if the South wants serious negotiations with the North it must retract the June 1973 special statement stipulating the two-Korea idea and simultaneous admission to the United Nations. Kim says that the South Korean suggestion of a "non-agression pact" is ridiculous because it is not the South but the United States that is in command in the South. Kim suggests that a Great National Congress or a North and South Political Consultative Meeting should be convened quite apart from the North and South Coordination Commission.

EP74; JUCHE 2: 539–52; *NAM:* 136–49; *IPR:* 161–66 (excerpt); *RK:* 69–74 (excerpt); *IPRC:* 272–85; *CCY 75:* 40–50; *Kŭlloja* (no. 3, 1974): 2–9; *Korea Today* (no. 4, 1974): 2–9.

March 7
On Attaining New Heights in the Socialist Economic Construction.

Speech at the National Industrial Convention.

Kim speaks on three subjects: (1) attaining the goals of the six-year economic plan earlier than the target date, (2) the targets of ten items in the socialist economic construction as proposed by the eighth plenum of the Central Committee of the fifth session of the Workers' Party, and (3) the duties of factory and enterprise managers. On the goals of the ten items, Kim enumerates the amount and items, such as 12 million tons of steel, 20 million tons of cement, etc.

CSJ 7: 50–75; *SW 7:* 47–71.
CCY 75: 50–63; *Kŭlloja* (no. 3, 1974): 10–25; *Korea Today* (no. 7, 1974): 2–16.

April 12
Speech at the Banquet in Honor of Prince Norodom Sihanouk, Head of State of Cambodia and Chairman of the National United Front of Kampuchea and Madam Princess Monique Sihanouk.

Kim makes two speeches on this eighth visit of Sihanouk. Kim urges the United States to accept the North's peace proposals and not to provoke other incidents.

CCY 75: 63–67; *IPR:* 167–68.

April 25
Answers to the Questions Raised by the Chief Editor of *Al Sahafa*, Organ of the Sudanese Government.

Questions submitted to Kim in advance and answered in the usual manner with no revelations or important statements. He speaks briefly of Middle Eastern issues, condemning the Zionists.

NAM: 150–61; *EP74; IPR:* 169–74; *IPRC:* 286–93 (excerpt); *RK:* 75–77 (excerpt); *CCY 75:* 67–73; *A 2:* 23–34; *FC 2:* 22–34; *Kŭlloja* (nos. 5–6, 1974): 2–7; *Korea Today* (no. 9, 1974): 2–7.

May 13–15
Speeches to Welcome Leopold Sedar Senghor, President of the Republic of Senegal.

Two speeches at banquets on May 13 (Kim's) and May 15 (Senghor's); Kim advocates the cooperation of third world countries against the super powers and the strength of the nonaligned states in the bright new world.

CCY 75: 73–77; *Korea Today* (no. 8, 1974): 2–4

June 2
Talk with the Editor-in-Chief of the Peruvian Newspaper *Expreso* and His Wife.

Impressed with the North Korean education system, the Peruvian editor asked about the educational system. Kim says that the North is making great efforts, but he also says that humanistic studies in the North are restricted (30 percent) in favor of science. Kim lauds Peru's claim of 200 miles as its territorial waters. He also mentions that the North follows an independent policy and does not meddle in other countries' internal affairs. Kim gives an example of the U.S. economic blockade against the North by citing a blast furnace that he intended to purchase from Japan but could not. He also denounces the practice of flunkeyism in South Korea.

NAM: 162–75; *CCY 75:* 77–83; *FC 2:* 35–49; *A 2:* 35–48; *Kŭlloja* (no. 12, 1974): 2–9; *Korea Today* (no. 4, 1975): 2–9.

June 13
Answers to the Questions Raised by the Secretary-General of the Peru-Korea Institute of Culture and Friendship.

The usual five-question interview, touching upon the unification issue, Peru-Korean relations, *chuch'e*, and others. No important ideas are revealed in this interview.

CCY 75: 84–91; *EP74; FC 2:* 50–67; *A 2:* 49–67; *RK:* 78–86 (excerpt); *Korea Today* (no. 11, 1974): 2–11.

June 16
Answers to Questions Raised by Editorial Bureau of Magazine *Korea Focus* and the Executive Committee of the American-Korean Friendship and Information Center.

Kim speaks of five problems: (1) the rising influence of the third-world force in the national liberation struggle, (2) Korean unification, (3) the reasons for the success of North Korean foreign relations, (4) the present stage of U.S.-North Korean relations, and (5) the role of progressive elements in the United States.

FC 2: 68–82; A 2: 68–82.

July 31
On Further Strengthening of the Party Work.

Letter to the participants of the party organization lectures.

Four major topics are discussed. Kim calls for strengthening of the party cadres and masses in the party organizational work, thorough implementation of the mass line of the party, and involvement of party members and cadres in the economic construction of the country. Lastly Kim repeats his favorite topics: bureaucratic work methods should be eliminated and cadres should go into the midst of workers in directing their work.

CSJ 7: 76–95; SW 7: 72–92.
CCY 75: 92–101.

August 21
Answers to the Questions Raised by the Delegation of the National Association of Senegalese Journalists.

Answers to six questions on Senegal-Korean relations, youth problems, interaction of agriculture and industry in a developing nation, Korean reunification, decolonization of the African continent, and Kim's visit to Senegal. No new revelations here, except to point out that Kim said that a developing country must develop industry first and then strive to develop agriculture.

CCY 75: 102–8; NAM: 176–90: EP74; FC 2: 83–97; A 2: 83–97; RK: 87–90; Kŭlloja (no. 10, 1974): 29–35; Korea Today (no. 12, 1974): 2–9; WY: 335–39.

September 1
Talk with the Panamanian Journalist Delegation.

Kim speaks on three topics: education policy, reunification, and the influence of *chuch'e*. Kim says that the North has instituted compulsory eleven-year education and hopes to accomplish what he calls "intellectualization." He continues his criticism of the South, citing the past Japanese affiliation of Park Chung Hee and the jailing of students, poets, politicians, and religious leaders.

EP74; NAM: 191–208; CCY 75: 108–17; FC 2: 98–117; A 2: 98–115; RK: 91–94 (excerpt); Kŭlloja (no. 11, 1974): 19–27; Korea Today (no. 3, 1975): 14–23.

September 7
Speech to Welcome President Gnassiugbe Eyadema, the Head of State of the Republic of Togo.

Kim says that Togo and the North established diplomatic relations in January 1973, and both countries have a cordial relationship. Kim lashes out at the United States and expresses appreciation for Togo's support in the twenty-ninth U.N. session in support of the withdrawal of U.S. troops from South Korea.

CCY 75: 117–20; *Korea Today* (no. 11, 1974): 12–15.

September 18
Answers to Questions Raised by Reporters from Argentina.

This is a six-question interview; Kim answers on various problems, including the future course for Latin American people, third-world cooperation, Argentine-North Korean cooperation, Korean unification, and the idea of *chuch'e*. In answer to a question about the greatest and most rewarding experience of his socialist construction, Kim says that it is the establishment of *chuch'e* in the North.

FC 2: 118–30; *A 2:* 116–27.

September 19
Talk with the Director of *Daho Express*, Official Newspaper of the Dahomeyan Government.

This is the second visit of this man and Kim calls him a propagandist for the North. Kim speaks of Korea and Dahomey relations and the third world, about African people, and his favorite subject, *chuch'e*. Kim speaks of the deadlocked North and South negotiations, reunification issues, and the North Korean socialist construction.

EP74; NAM: 209–19; *UNF:* 184–87 (excerpt); *CCY 75: 120–29; FC 2:* 131–52; *A 2:* 128–48; *RK:* 95–98 (excerpt); *Kŭlloja* (no. 11, 1974): 8–18; *Korea Today* (no. 1, 1975): 11–21.

September 21–22
Speeches to Welcome President Moktar Ould Daddah, the Head of State of The Islamic Republic of Mauritania.

This is the second visit of the Mauritanian president. The first visit was in 1967 after Mauritania severed relations with the South in 1964. Kim speaks generally of the solidarity of the third-world countries against U.S. imperialism.

CCY 75: 130–34; *Korea Today* (no. 12, 1974): 10–13.

*September 24
On the Situation of Our Country and Tasks of the League of Korean Youth in Japan.

Speech to the home-visiting group of art and sports delegates of Korean youth in Japan, the second home-visiting group of Korean high school students in Japan.

Divided into two parts, the speech deals with the situation in the North and the tasks of the Korean youths in Japan. Kim speaks of the three tasks the party has undertaken in the North: socialist construction, strengthening of the revolutionary forces in the South, and the united struggle in the international arena with nonaligned nations. On the domestic front, Kim speaks of the three revolutions of ideology, technology, and culture and also of the three technological revolutions. About South Korea, Kim repeats his usual denunciations, including the August 15 incident in which the wife of Park Chung Hee was killed, and says that the incident was contrived by the South and had nothing to do with the residents in Japan. He also attacks for the first time the fascist system, more than the leaders of the system, of the South. In the international arena, Kim says that the North is supported by the nonaligned nations. In the second part of his talk on the tasks of the League of Korean Youth in Japan, Kim says that the League should make all Koreans in Japan defenders of the North, defend the democratic and national rights of Korean citizens in Japan, support the democratic revolutionary movement in the South, and cooperate with the democratic forces and Japanese people in Japan.

CSJ 7: 96–129; *SW 7:* 93–125.
CCY 75: 135–51; *EP74; Kŭlloja* (no. 10, 1974): 2–19; *Korea Today* (no. 1, 1975): 2–19; *WY:* 340–75; *RK:* 127–47 (excerpt).

October 1
U.S. Imperialist Army of Aggression Must Withdraw Unconditionally from South Korea.

Speech at a mass rally in Pyongyang to welcome the party and government delegation of the Syrian Arab Republic.

To welcome President Hafez Al Assad, Kim denounces Zionism and Israel. Then he speaks of the North Korean efforts at the United Nations and repeats his policy of removing the American troops stationed in the South under U.N. auspices. Kim mentions his three principles of independence, peaceful reunification, and great national unity for the North and South negotiations. Two other speeches to welcome Assad were made, one on September 28 at Kim's banquet and another on October 1 at Assad's banquet.

NAM: 220–31; *UNF:* 188–91 (excerpt); *IPRC:* 294–99; *Kŭlloja* (no. 11, 1974): 2–7; *Korea Today* (no. 1, 1975): 20–25; *RK:* 99–108.

October 9

Talk with the President of Ecuadorian Publishing Company, Burundat.

After briefly thanking him for bringing a gift (does not mention what it is except to say that it is 15 kg.), Kim speaks of two problems, the cooperation of Latin American countries with the North and Korean unification. Kim denounces the South, mentioning Kim Dae-jung, Kim Chi-ha, and the August 15 shooting incident. Kim reiterates his three principles of unification.

FC 2: 153–68; *A* 2: 149–62.

November 4

Answers to Questions Raised by Australian Reporters.

Kim speaks of six problems: the philosophical basis of the *chuch'e* idea, objectives of the six-year plan, the North Korean abolition of the taxation system, unification problems, North Korea-Japan relations, and North Korean-Australian relations.

FC 2: 169–82; *A* 2: 163–75.

November 6

Answers to Questions Raised by the Head of *Al Kabas*, Newspaper of Kuwait.

Five-question interview covering unification, the North Korean position on the Palestine Liberation Movement, future economic relations with Arab countries, and the experience of North Korean development.

FC 2: 183–96; *A* 2: 176–89.

November 18–21

Speeches to Welcome the Delegation of the Democratic People's Republic of Yemen, Headed by Salem Rubaya Ali.

Two speeches pledging solidarity between the two countries. Kim sees this visit as the rise of the people of the third world against U.S.imperialism.

CCY 75: 162–66.

*November 29

Problems Arising from the Thorough Implementation of the Agrarian Theses.

Speech at the fourth session of the Fifth Supreme People's Assembly (5SPA-4).

Several delegates suggested at this session changing the cooperative farms into state property owned by the entire people. The distribution of grains and moneys reflects the earnings of each cooperative, but under the new arrangement the farmers would be paid wages just as in any other industry. Kim says that this proposal is premature for two reasons. One is that to institute this system, people should be prepared to rid themselves of their individualism and egotism completely and to arm themselves with collectivism, and this is not realistic in the North yet. Another reason is that mechanization of the farms should be highly developed before this system can work, and there are as yet not enough machines and mechanization. However, some experimental, highly mechanized cooperatives should try this system.

CSJ 7: 130–48; *SW* 7: 126–43.
CCY 75: 166–75.

December 2–6
Speeches to Welcome Norodom Sihanouk of Cambodia.

Two speeches on December 2 and December 6 at each other's banquets. Kim refers to Sihanouk's frequent visits to North Korea as a sign of mutual friendship between the peoples of Cambodia and the North. This is Sihanouk's ninth visit to the North. Kim says that the United Nations is discussing both Cambodian and Korean problems at the current session.

CCY 76: 175–79.

December 15
The New-Emerging Forces Should Unite under the Banner of Independence against Imperialism.

Speech at the Pyongyang mass rally to welcome President of the Republic of Zaire Mobutu Sese Seko Kuku Ngbendu Wa Za Banga.

A short welcoming speech by Kim. Kim stresses the independence of newly emerging nations in Africa, Asia, the Middle East, and Latin America and emphasizes the unity of these nations against imperialism.

NAM: 232–41; *CCY* 75: 179–85; *EP74*; *Kŭlloja* (no. 1, 1975): 11–15; *Korea Today* (no. 4, 1975): 10–14.

December 16
Answers to Questions Raised by Reporters from Zaire.

Six questions were raised: two related questions on Kim's impression of Mobutu and Zaire, two related questions on economic recovery and success, one on the role of culture in Korea, and lastly one on unification problems. Kim vows the solidarity of the third-world nations economically as well as politically and wants to promote mutual cooperation with Zaire.

FC 2: 197–208.

1975

January 1
New Year Address.

Kim encourages the people to work toward the goals set by the eighth plenum of the Central Committee of the fifth party congress. He briefly reviews the accomplishments in industries, agriculture, and culture. Kim says that 1975 is the year of the thirtieth anniversary of the founding of the Workers' Party of Korea and everyone should continue to make his best efforts toward the socialist construction, particularly in the field of transportation.

CCY 76: 1–7; *Kŭlloja* (no. 1, 1975): 2–15; *Korea Today* (no. 2, 1975): 2–10.

January 15
All Efforts to Attain the Goal of Eight Million Tons of Grain.

Speech at the National Agricultural Congress.

Kim urges farmers to produce more grains. He says that grain output increased more than 30 percent last year and urges them to produce eight million tons this year. He speaks a great deal about the production of maize and says combined ideological and scientific efforts make the attainment of the goal possible. Kim also speaks of the importance of grain reserves if war breaks out.

EP75; CCY 76: 8–17; *Kŭlloja* (no. 2, 1975): 2–13; *Korea Today* (no. 3, 1975): 2–13.

February 17
Report at the Tenth Session of the Central Committee of the Workers' Party of Korea (5WPK-10CC).

No text available.

**March 3*
Further Assist the Socialist Construction by Developing the Three Revolutions.

Speech at a meeting of industrial activities.

Dividing his talk into four parts, Kim speaks of the historical necessity of the three revolutions (ideological, technological, and cultural), how the three-revolution teams were begun, what the teams have accomplished, and the tasks in assisting the socialist construction. This speech seems to indicate that there was a need to boost the North Korean economy and Kim's answer was to dispatch a work team to reincite the enthusiasm for work in all segments of the North Korean economy. In this speech Kim makes some bold statements, such as that the North Korean per capita income in American dollars is more than $1,000. Kim also says that the North must trade with nonaligned nations and capitalist nations to develop its economy, and in order to develop the trade, the North must upgrade the quality of its goods, establish trust in international markets, and use shipping more efficiently.

CSJ 7: 149–87; *SW* 7: 144–82.
KP75; *CCY 76*: 17–36; *Kŭlloja* (no. 3, 1975): 2–22; *Korea Today* (no. 5, 1975): 2–23.

April 8
On Developing a Local Budget System.

Speech at the fifth session of the Fifth Supreme People's Assembly (5SPA-5).

> After discussing several advantages of the local budget system, Kim traces the brief history of its development from the 1950s. The local budget system should boost local industries. He points out three problems of local factories: the lack of technical development, the support from major industries, and the need to build basic chemical factories to serve local industries.

CSJ 7: 188–202; *SW* 7: 183–96.

April 10
For the Successful Introduction of Universal Compulsory Eleven-Year Education.

Speech at the fifth session of the Fifth Supreme People's Assembly (5SPA-5).

> Kim proclaims that eleven-year compulsory education will be put into practice from September 1, 1975. There are 3.5 million children in nurseries and kindergartens and 4.7 million students in schools, and a total of 8.2 million students study in the North at government expense. Kim also says that those teachers in junior high and high schools who do not have normal college degrees should work to earn their degrees. In all education, Kim says that everyone should observe the principle of socialist education.

CCY 76: 37–43; *EP77*; *KP76*.

April 13
Answers to the Questions Raised by the Chairman of the Costa Rica-Korea Association of Friendship and Culture Who is Chairman of the Costa Rica Socialist Party and Chairman of the Costa Rica Journalists Union.

> Five questions of general nature, praising North Korean achievements and solidifying the ties of the third-world nations. There is nothing of importance

here, and the interview is very similar to most previous interviews with representatives of third-world nations.

EP75; NAM: 242–47; *IPR:* 195–203 (excerpt); *IPRC:* 300–303 (excerpt); *A 2:* 190–201; *FC 2:* 209–20; *KP75; CCY 76:* 37–43; *Külloja* (no. 6, 1975): 2–8; *Korea Today* (no. 7, 1975): 2–7; *RK:* 109–17.

April 18
Speech Delivered at a Banquet Given at the Great Hall of the People in Peking by the Central Committee of the Communist Party of China and the State Council of the People's Republic of China in Honor of the Party and Government Delegation of the Democratic People's Republic of Korea.

Kim speaks of the solidarity of the Chinese and Korean people and reaffirms his conviction of future cooperation. Kim lauds Chinese accomplishments and speaks of the progress made in the North. Kim also makes remarks about the great transformation in the East, citing the successes of the Cambodian people, the Vietnam struggle, the Arab people, and the African continent. He says that the struggle of the third-world people will succeed. Kim says that the question of war in Korea depends on the attitude of the United States and if it ignites war, it will lose.

Peking Review, no. 17 (April 25, 1975): 14–17; *IPR:* 175–83; *CCY 76:* 49–54; *Korea Today* (no. 6, 1975): 2–8.

April 25
Speech Delivered at a Banquet Given at the Great Hall of the Chinese People in Peking on the Visit of the Party and Government Delegation of the Democratic People's Republic of Korea to the People's Republic of China.

Reaffirmation of the Korean people's militant friendship with the Chinese people. Emphasis was placed upon the vitality of the joint struggle in the future of the two people against imperialist aggressors.

Peking Review, no. 18 (May 2, 1975): 11–12; *IPR:* 185–87; *CCY 76:* 54–56.

May 21
Speech Delivered at a Banquet to Welcome Prince Norodom Sihanouk and His Wife.

A brief welcoming speech. Kim says that it has been ten years since they first met.

CCY 76: 56–58.

May 22, 24, 26
Speeches Delivered during the Visit to the Romanian Socialist Republic.

Basically Kim expresses his appreciation for the warm welcome and vows close cooperation between the two countries. Kim also extends thanks for Romanian assistance during the Korean war and current efforts at the United Nations in behalf of the North. President Ceausescu visited the North in June 1971.

IPR: 189–94; *EP76; CCY 76:* 58–66; *Korea Today* (no. 8, 1975): 2–5.

May 26, 27, 28
Speech Delivered at Mass Meeting in Algiers to Welcome the Party and Government Delegation of the Democratic People's Republic of Korea.

Four speeches during his visit to Algeria. Kim was awarded an honorary doctorate. Kim thanks President Houari Boumedienne for making him an honorary citizen of Algiers. He commends the progress the Algerian people have made and offers thanks for Algerian support for the cause of Korean unification in the United Nations and in the forum among the nonaligned nations. He vows firm friendship between the two peoples.

NAM: 248–58; *IPR:* 195–203 (excerpt); *EP76; CCY 76:* 66–79; *Korea Today* (no. 8, 1975): 18–23.

May 29
Answers to the Questions Raised by a Journalist of *El Moudjahid*, Official Newspaper of the Government of the Algerian Democratic and People's Republic.

Four-question interview, going over many points previously covered: the accomplishments of the Workers' Party of Korea, new war threat by the United States, North Korean reunification policy, three principles and five policies, and capitalist economic exploitation.

NAM: 259–70; *UNF:* 192–95 (excerpt); *IPRC:* 304–9 (excerpt); *EP75; A 2:* 202–13; *FC 2:* 221–32; *CCY 76:* 79–84; *Kŭlloja* (no. 6, 1975): 9–15; *Korea Today* (no. 8, 1975): 30–35; *RK:* 118–21 (excerpt).

May 31
Answers to the Questions Raised by an AFP Correspondent (France).

Three-question interview covering the Asian situation, the future of divided Korea, and Kim's impression of Africa on his recent visit.

NAM: 271–77; *UNF:* 196–201 (excerpt); *IPRC:* 310–16 (excerpt); *EP75; FC 2:* 233–42; *Kŭlloja* (no. 7, 1975): 2–6; *Korea Today* (no. 9, 1975): 2–6; *RK:* 122–26.

May 31
The Mauritanian People Have Made a Big Advance in the Struggle to Build a New Society and a Vast Prospect is Open Ahead of Them.

Speech made at the Nouakchott mass meeting in Mauritania.

> Kim praises the Mauritanian people and vows friendship between the two countries. He endorses the cause of the African people and thanks President Moktar Ould Daddah of Mauritania.

> *Korea Today* (no. 8, 1975): 36–38.

June 2, 3, 4, 5
Speeches Delivered during the Visit to the Bulgarian People's Republic.

> Kim makes five speeches expressing his appreciation for the warm welcome. Mentions Todor Zhivkov's visit to the North in 1973 and extends thanks for Bulgarian support for the North in the United Nations.

> *EP76; CCY 76:* 85–95; *Korea Today* (no. 8, 1975): 43–45.

June 6, 7, 9
Speeches Delivered during the Visit to the Socialist Republic of Yugoslavia.

> Three short speeches by Kim expressing his thanks to Tito. The speeches are not as enthusiastic as those given in other countries. Perhaps his past condemnation of Tito as a revisionist and Tito's failure to visit the North may have had something to do with this.

> *IPR:* 205–8 (excerpt); *EP76; CCY 76:* 95–100; *Korea Today* (no. 8, 1975): 52.

August 6
Answers to Questions Raised by the Chief Editor of *Indian Weekly*.

> Kim speaks of four problems: the idea of *chuch'e*, the South Korean revolution, the nonaligned movement, and the accomplishments of the six-year economic plan.

> *CCY 76:* 100–106; *FC 2:* 243–56; *A 2:* 214–27.

August 13
Answers to Questions Raised by the Chief Editor of Peruvian Newspapers, *Expreso* and *Extra*.

> Five questions concerning the U.S. troop withdrawal, nonaligned nation conference in Lima, Peru, economic development problems of the nonaligned na-

tions, and other questions. Kim gives a general comment, not much different from his earlier positions.

CCY 76: 106–9; *FC 2:* 257–65; *A 2:* 228–36.

August 20
Speech at the Banquet Held for Kim Il Sung by Norodom Sihanouk.

Brief speech congratulating the victory of the Cambodian people and the leaders of the struggle, including Kieu Sampan.

CCY 76: 110–11.

September 11
Answers to Questions Raised by Representatives of *La Nouvelle Critique,* Organ of the Central Committee of the French Communist Party.

Two-question interview, one on the prospects of North Korean economic development after the successful completion of the six-year plan and the other on prospects for the unification of Korea. Kim says that Korea will continue to pursue the three-revolution campaign and that prospects for peaceful unification are good when the U.N. forces withdraw from Korea.

CCY 76: 112–16; *FC 2:* 266–75; *A 2:* 237–46.

September 28
Answers to Questions Raised by the Chief Editor of *Yomiuri Shinbun,* a Japanese Newspaper.

Six questions were asked concerning (1) the dissolution of the United Nations Command in Korea, (2) Kim's expectations of Japan in the security of East Asia, (3) North Korean invasion of the South, (4) the Japan-U.S. Security Treaty, (5) a trip to Moscow, and (6) the prospects of economic development. Kim reiterates his usual position favoring the dissolution of the U.N. command and the withdrawal of U.S. forces, disavows any intent to invade the South, opposes the Japan-U.S. treaty, and says he hopes to visit Moscow soon. Kim speaks of the difficulty in North Korean trade due to the problems arising from the shipping industries.

CCY 76: 116–22; *FC 2:* 276–88; *A 2:* 247–60.

*October 9
On the Occasion of the Thirtieth Anniversary of the Founding of the Workers' Party of Korea.

Report delivered at the commemoration of the thirtieth anniversary of the founding of the Workers' Party of Korea.

Kim speaks on four topics here. First is the struggle of the party for sovereignty, independence, and socialist construction. He recounts the history of the party and makes a few interesting statements, such as those concerning the first genuine Communist revolutionary organization and backdating the *chuch'e* idea to the anti-Japanese guerrilla movement. Second he speaks of the three revolutions: the ideological, technological, and cultural revolutions. Thirdly, he reiterates his position on the reunification of Korea and says that the South is antagonistic. Lastly, Kim speaks of the North's expanded diplomatic activities in the third-world countries. Except for the first few statements about *chuch'e* and party origins, the speech is routine.

CSJ 7: 203–36; *SW* 7: 197–232.
EP75; *WSK*: 478–504; *NAM*: 278–316; *UNF*: 202–8 (excerpt); *IPR*: 209–15 (excerpt); *IPRC*: 317–31 (excerpt); *CCY* 76: 122–39; *Kŭlloja* (no. 11, 1975): 2–22; *Korea Today* (no. 11, 1975): 2–21; *RK*: 148–54 (excerpt).

October 10
Speech at the Banquet Commemorating the Thirtieth Anniversary of the Founding of the Workers' Party of Korea.

General congratulatory speech remembering those who fought for the party. In this speech Kim says that the party has grown from a membership of a few thousand to a party of two million members. He also cites the foreign guests who were at the banquet.

CCY 76: 139–42; *Kŭlloja* (no. 11, 1975): 23–27.

October 13
Answers to Questions Raised by the General-Secretary of the Italian International Relations Research Center.

Kim speaks of four problems here: (1) the future struggle of the party and the pursuance of the three great revolutions, (2) on *chuch'e*, (3) the reasons for the rapid development of socialist construction in Korea, and (4) the problems of unification of Korea. Kim says that the rapid development in the North is due to the leadership exercised by the Workers' Party of Korea.

CCY 76: 143–46; *FC* 2: 289–97; *A* 2: 261–69.

October 17
Speech at the Banquet Welcoming Prince Norodom Sihanouk and His Wife of Cambodia.

Kim says that Sihanouk left the North in August to return triumphantly to Cambodia and then travelled to New York to participate in the thirtieth session of the United Nations, and returned again to the North in celebration of the thirtieth anniversary of the founding of the Workers' Party of Korea.

CCY 76: 147–49.

October 21
Talk with Wilfred Burchett, Australian Writer and Reporter.

Kim speaks of five problems: (1) the as-yet unaccomplished targets (steel and cement production) of the six-year plan, (2) the impact of the victory in Indochina on Korea, (3) Korean questions at the United Nations, (4) the prospects of unification, and (5) the significance of North Korean membership in the nonaligned nations.

CCY 76: 149–60: *FC 2:* 298–322; *A 2:* 270–92.

October 28
Speech at a Banquet for Kim Il Sung by Prince Norodom Sihanouk.

Brief speech expressing appreciation for the party; Kim pledges North Korean friendship with Cambodia.

CCY 76: 160–61.

November 6
Talk with Japanese Scholars.

Kim remembers Midorikawa Touru and Yasue Ryosuke of magazines *Iwanami* and *Sekai*. Kim answers questions on six problems dealing with the history of the party, problems with the six-year economic plan, three-great-revolution workteam, the problems of unification, his impression of the third world, and Korea-Japan relations. Nothing revealing in this talk; Kim reiterates his previous positions here.

CCY 76: 162–72; *FC 2:* 323–45; *Sekai* (no. 2, 1976): 186–97; *A 2:* 293–314.

November 16
Answers to Questions Raised by the Chairman of Research Planning and Information Section of Dahomey.

This is a five-question interview, and Kim reiterates his usual positions, surveying the thirty-year history of the party, its prospects, and its contribution to proletarian internationalism. Kim praises new Dahomey revolutionary group for severing diplomatic relations with the South.

CCY 76: 172–76; *FC 2:* 346–55; *A 2:* 315–24.

November 21

Remarks at the Eleventh Session of the Central Committee of the Workers' Party of Korea (5WPK-11CC).

No text available.

November 25

Interview with Gomi Mitsuo, Managing Editor of *Mainichi Shinbun*, **Japan.**

Kim answers questions concerning the likelihood of a new war in Korea, now that the Vietnam war is over, on reunification of Korea, withdrawal of American troops from Korea, exchanges of reporters between the United States and the North, difficulties in foreign exchange, North Korean education, and the *Shosei maru* incident. Kim admits that there are some difficulties in foreign trade, but says that they are temporary in nature, and as soon as enough ships are built to carry goods abroad, the difficulties will be dissipated.

Mainichi Daily News, November 29, 1975; *FC* 2: 356–88; *CCY 76:* 176–90; *A* 2: 325–54.

December 16

The Nonalignment Movement is a Mighty Anti-Imperialist Revolutionary Force of Our Times.

Treatise published in the inaugural issue of the Argentine magazine, *Guidebook to the Third World.*

Very short article noticing the fact that the North was admitted to the non aligned nations group at the foreign ministers meeting held in Lima, Peru, in 1975. Kim urges political and economic cooperation among the nonaligned nations.

CSJ 7: 237–41; *SW* 7: 233–37.
EP75; *NAM:* 317–22; *CCY 76:* 191–93; *Kŭlloja* (no. 5, 1976): 2–4; *Korea Today* (no. 3, 1975): 2–4; *KP76.*

December 25

Speech at the Banquet for Manuel Pinto Da Costa and His Wife of Sao Tome and Principe.

Kim expresses appreciation for the first visit of President Da Costa after independence in July of this year and vows his friendship to this country. Kim says that he is happy to see that this newly independent nation is one of the nonaligned nations of the third world and is following its own independent foreign policy.

CCY 76: 193–95; *Korea Today* (no. 2, 1976): 2–4.

1976

January 1
New Year Address.

Kim says that the North has attained the goals of the industrial sector in the six-year plan one year and four months ahead of schedule. Kim also alleges that while the capitalist countries suffer from the world economic crisis, the North has accomplished an economic miracle and developed its economy. Kim also speaks of the North's achievements in diplomatic circles among the nonaligned nations. Kim urges complete success in attaining the goals of every segment of the six-year plan during this year.

EP76; KP76; Külloja (no. 1, 1976): 2–5.

March 28
Talk with the Editor-in-Chief of the Japanese Politico-Theoretical Magazine, *Sekai.*

Kim's interview with Yasue Ryosuke. Kim speaks of reunification, the North and South Joint Statement, the peace agreement that he proposed to the United States, North Korea-Japan relationship, and the North Korean foreign policy toward the nonaligned nations. There is nothing really new in the talk. Yasue asks about various subjects, including the Confederal Republic, nuclear weapons, and the question of cross recognition. Kim says that the North does not plan to have any nuclear weapons and will never agree to any form of cross recognition because it is a method to divide the country permanently.

CSJ 7: 242–64; *SW* 7: 238–58.
EP76; IPR: 217–35 (excerpt); *Külloja* (no. 6, 1976): 2–15; *Korea Today* (no. 7, 1976): 2–13; *Nodong sinmun,* May 14, 1976.

April 29
On Further Developing the Nursing and Upbringing of Children.

Speech delivered at the sixth session of the Fifth Supreme People's Assembly (5SPA-6).

Kim says that there are 3.5 million children in nurseries and kindergartens and 5,090,000 students, a total of 8.6 million students in schools in the North. The purpose of passing this law on the nursing and upbringing of children is to rear the new generation as a Communist type of man from a very young age and to free women for labor. Kim says that women comprise 48 percent of the labor force in the North. Kim says at the end of the speech to stop making speeches and go out to work because this is a busy farming season.

EP76.

May 14

Speech at a Banquet Arranged in Honor of His Excellency Moussa Traore, Chairman of the Military Committee of National Liberation, Head of State, and Prime Minister of the Government of the Republic of Mali.

Kim thanks Traore for his visit and also congratulates Madame Mariam Traore for her second visit to the North. Kim also thanks them for their votes in the conference of foreign ministers of nonaligned nations and the thirtieth session of the United Nations General Assembly. He reiterates the cause of the peoples of Asia, Africa, and Latin America in their fight against the old colonial powers.

Korea Today (no. 8, 1976): 7–8.

May 21

Speech at a Banquet Arranged in Honor of His Excellency Prime Minister Sulfikar Ali Bhutto of the Islamic Republic of Pakistan.

Kim says that this is his second meeting with Bhutto. They met first in Djakarta, Indonesia, in 1965. Kim says that it was only after Bhutto came to power in Pakistan that diplomatic relations between the two countries were established. He mentions that Pakistan withdrew from the United Nations Commission for the Unification and Rehabilitation of Korea and congratulates the independent diplomatic posture of Pakistan.

Korea Today (no. 8, 1976): 11–12.

May 27

Talk with Journalists of the Islamic Republic of Pakistan.

This interview covered many questions, but contained nothing new. Kim gave general answers to most of the questions on South Asia, Pakistan and Bangladesh, Pakistan and the North. He spoke at length of Korean reunification problems and the summit conference of nonaligned nations to be held in Colombo. Kim said that the North must participate.

EP76; IPR; 237–44 (excerpt); *Kŭlloja* (no. 7, 1976): 7–14; *Korea Today* (no. 9, 1976): 2–8; *Nodong sinmun,* June 14, 1976.

May 29

Answers to the Questions Put by the Foreign Editor of the Yugoslav News Agency, *Tanjug.*

A short five-question interview concerning the role of nonaligned nations and the fifth summit conference to be held in Colombo, Sri Lanka, in August. In answer to a question about North Korean-Yugoslavian relations, Kim praises Tito as the great leader of Yugoslav people and an intimate friend of the Korean people.

EP76; IPR: 245–46; *Kŭlloja* (no. 8, 1976): 2–7; *Korea Today* (no. 8, 1976): 2–6; *Nodong sinmun*, June 30, 1976.

June 4
Speech at a Banquet Arranged in Honor of His Excellency Didier Ratsiraka, President of the Democratic Republic of Madagascar.

Kim says that Ratsiraka had visited the North four years ago, and this is the second visit. Kim also congratulates the revolutionary transformation to socialism in Madagascar. Kim speaks of the forthcoming fifth summit conference of nonaligned nations and stresses its importance.

Korea Today (no. 9, 1976): 9–11.

June 5
Members of the Juvenile Corps, Let Us Become Young Communist *Chuch'e* Revolutionaries Complete with Knowledge, Virtue, and Physical Strength.

Congratulatory message sent to the members of the Juvenile Corps on the thirtieth anniversary of the Korean Juvenile Corps.

Kim encourages the youngsters to love the party, the socialist system, and the work and urges them to build Communist moral character. Kim also encourages them to observe the rules and regulations of schools and help the socialist construction of the country.

Kŭlloja (no. 7, 1976): 2–6.

July 7
On Some Experiences of the Financial Operations in the Rural Areas.

Talk with workers of the party and economic organizations.

Kim reviews the history of the Peasant Bank in the North, how it was started, and how it was operated. Farmers deposited money in the bank, and the state prevented usurers from exploiting the farmers. Lending from the Peasant Bank, however, was operated by the Central Bank until 1964, when the Industrial Bank was created to take over the lending function. Loans are made both to individual farmers and to cooperatives, but not to any other enterprises.

EP76.

July 10
Speech at a Banquet Given in Honor of Party and Government Delegation of the People's Republic of Benin Led by His Excellency President Mathiew Kerekou.

Kim congratulates the visit of Kerekou and also his socialist programs in Benin. Kim says that he supports the struggles of the African people, particularly those of Zimbabwe, Namibia, and Azania. He thanks him for the votes on the admission of the North to the nonaligned nations conference in 1975 and also in the thirtieth session of the United Nations General Assembly. He also says that when Kerekou came into power diplomatic relations between the North and Benin were established, and Kerekou severed relations with the South, established by the former regime in Benin.

Korea Today (no. 10, 1976): 3–4.

October 14
On Vigorously Promoting Projects to Remodel Nature for the Ten-Million-Ton Grain Goal.

Concluding remark at the twelfth plenary meeting of the Central Committee of the Fifth Party.

Kim raises five points to produce more grains: (1) complete irrigation of farm lands, (2) build many small-patch fields in the mountains, (3) rebuild farm lands, (4) work on the mountains and streams, and (5) irrigate the delta lands.

CSJ 7: 265–77; *SW* 7: 259–71.
KP76.

November 28
To Reform and Further Strengthen the Cadre Education Work.

Speech delivered to the faculty of Kim Il Sung University.

The occasion is the thirtieth anniversary of the founding of Kim Il Sung University, and Kim praises the past work of the university in producing many able leaders of the country. Kim points out two important tasks for the future; one is to raise the quality of education by employing highly qualified scholars, and another is to reeducate those who are already graduates of the University.

KP77 (Minjok kanbu yangsŏng saŏp ŭl tŏuk kaesŏn kanghwa halte taehayŏ. Pyongyang: Chosŏn Nodongdang Ch'ulp'ansa, 1977).

1977

January 1
New Year Address.

Kim briefly recounts the economic achievenents in both industry and agriculture and speaks of the threat by the United States in the Panmunjŏm incident on August 18. More important, however, is Kim's effort to boost the economy by saying that during the new year the North must ease the strains created in some branches of the economy, particularly in transportation and mining. The new year is the year to improve all land and sea transportation and produce moe in mining. This seems a tacit admission that the six-year plan is not all that successful.

EP77; Kŭlloja (no. 1, 1977): 2–8; *Korea Today* (no. 2, 1977): 2–8.

February 25
Tasks of the League of Socialist Working Youth Organizations.

Speech delivered at the Central Committee meeting of the League of Socialist Working Youth.

In this speech, Kim says for the first time that students must learn foreign languages well and concentrate on the study of subjects in science. Kim also says that students must develop a healthy body by participating in athletic programs, and they must also be armed with monolithic ideology.

CSJ 7: 278–94; *SW 7:* 272–87.
KP77.

April 5
On the General Mobilization of the Party, the Army, and the People to Fight Against the Dangers of Drought Caused by the Cold Front.

Concluding remarks at the thirteenth plenum of the Central Committee (5WPK-13CC).

A speech on prevention of drought damages due to unusually bad weather during the winter. Kim urges the mobilization of the entire population to work on irrigation and preservation of water for the fields. The goal of producing 8.5 million tons of grain should be attained regardless of the weather.

CSJ 7: 295–317; *SW 7:* 288–308.
KP77.

April 23
Talk with Executive Managing Editor of Japanese *Yomiuri shinbun* and His Party.

Kim comments on a number of questions. Since the editor came to the North on the occasion of Kim's birthday with gifts, Kim thanks him but says that he does not celebrate his birthdays *(sic)*. On education, Kim says that there are more than eight million, nearly half of the population of the North, in schools. On economic development, Kim says that they have now fully fulfilled the goals of the six-year economic plan and are preparing to launch the second seven-year economic plan that covers the period from 1978 to 1984. On Carter's administration, Kim says that he is not sure of Carter's campaign pledges and whether he will in fact carry out his pledges. On the question of the reunification of Korea, Kim condemns the South for obstructing the unification efforts of the North. Kim says that he is willing to deal with new leaders of the United States, China, and Japan, but he is not sure of the Japanese leaders. He is willing to work out an agreement with Japan on fisheries and to set up a Japanese liaison office in the North.

EP77; *Korea Today* (no. 7, 1977): 2–7; *Kŭlloja* (no. 5, 1977): 2–8.

*April 29
On the Land Law.

Speech delivered at the seventh session of the Fifth Supreme People's Assembly.

Kim says that the new land law is a comprehensive rule governing the ownership, development, conservation, and administration of the land. Proper administration of the land policy is important, and this should control all phases of land utilization, such as the location of villages and the building of cities, factories, canals, and railways. Kim says that the scholars in the universities in the North have devised a plan to build a canal(?) across the North from the East to the West. Pollution control, irrigation of nonpaddy fields, mountain terrace fields, forestation, and standardization of all paddy and nonpaddy fields, and also tideland development should be conducted in accordance with a comprehensive plan based upon this land law.

CSJ 7: 318–32; SW 7: 309–22.
EP77; KP77.

*April 30
Speech to Welcome Arthur Chung of Guyana and His Wife to Our Country.

This is a short speech to welcome Arthur Chung and members of his government delegation from Guyana to North Korea. Kim praised the role of Latin American countries in the nonaligned movement.

CCY 78: 92–93.

*May 9–11
Speeches to Welcome El Hadj Omar Bongo of Gabon and His Wife to Our Country.

There are two short speeches; one is to welcome El Hadj Omar Bongo of Gabon to North Korea, and the other is Kim's speech at Bongo's banquet to honor Kim. In both speeches Kim congratulates the role played by Gabon in the nonaligned movement.

CCY 78: 93–96.

June 13
Speech to Welcome Kaysone Phomvihane of Laotian People's Democratic Republic and the Party and Government Delegation.

This is a short speech to welcome Kaysone Phomvihane of Laos. Kim pledges his friendship to the Laotian people.

CCY 78: 96–98.

June 20
Talk with the Editor-in-Chief of the French Newspaper *Le Monde.*

Kim touched upon the reunification question, emphasizing the confederation formula. Kim denounced the U.S. troop withdrawal by saying that the group troop withdrawal is not the same as total withdrawal. On Korea-France relations, Kim said that he hopes to further the good relations between the two countries. He also commented briefly on Euro-communism, the Sino-Soviet dispute, and the trade deficit of the North in Europe. Kim said that the economic difficulties are temporary and placed the blame on the oil crisis. Lastly Kim said that he wanted to be the servant of the people throughout his life.

EP77; Korea Today (no. 9, 1977): 2–7; *Kŭlloja* (no. 8, 1977): 2–7; *KP77.*

July 3
Answers to Questions Raised by N.H.K. Reporters.

Kim answers familiar questions about the U.S. troop withdrawal and the economic difficulties of the North. Kim says that the United States is not keeping Carter's campaign promise by leaving the air force and the navy in Korea. He also says that he hopes for brisk trade with Japan. Kim touches upon the problems of Japanese fishermen fishing within the 200-mile economic zone of the North and expresses hope for solution of the problem. The North Korean version is an abridged account of the interview.

EP77; Korea Today (no. 9, 1977): 8–12; *Kŭlloja* (no. 8, 1977): 8–13; *KP77.*

July 19
On Problems in the Development of the Machine Industry.

Concluding remarks at a conference of workers in the machine industry.

The machine industry is the heart of industrial development and the basis for the technical revolution. Kim says to improve the quality of the machine industry and its facilities, and urges the workers to achieve modernization, automation, and specialization in various machine industries.

KP77 (Kigye kongŏp ŭl palchŏn sik'igi wihayŏ nasŏnŭn myŏtkaji munje e taehayŏ. Pyongyang: Chosŏn Nodongdang Ch'ulp'ansa, 1977).

August 20
On Further Development of Machine Industries.

Speech delivered at the national conference of activists in machine industries.

> Emphasis is placed upon farm machinery production. In other segments, Kim says that large-scale facilities, modernized machines, and high-speed production machines must be developed in mining industries. Bigger machines and larger facilities must be made for the transportation industries. In all these efforts, Kim emphasizes the role of the party and the renewed efforts of the party to develop machine industries.

> *CSJ* 7: 333–54; *SW* 7: 323–43.
> *KP77.*

August 28
The Nonaligned Countries and All the People of the World Advocating Independence Should Form a United Front Against All Forms of Dominating Forces.

Speech at a mass meeting to welcome Josip Broz Tito.

> A short speech to welcome Tito to Korea. Kim says that Yugoslavia and Korea are on the same side of the socialist countries and fight for one Korea against those who advocate a two-Korea solution. Kim calls Tito an intimate friend of Korea and hails his effort toward the nonalignment movement.

> *Korea Today* (no. 11, 1977): 29–31.

*September 5
Theses on Socialist Education.

Speech delivered at the fourteenth plenary meeting of the fifth Central Committee of the Workers' Party of Korea (5WPK-14CC).

> Divided into five parts, the speech discusses the educational policy of the North. (1) Kim proposes four principles of socialist pedagogy: Have party spirit and class spirit, establish *chuch'e*, have revolutionary practice, and be responsible for education. (2) Socialist education must contain political and ideological education, scientific and technological education, and physical education. (3) The methods of education must be heuristic teaching, combine theoretical and practical teachings, combine school and societal education, and also have continuous education from preschool to adult education. (4) Kim describes the socialist educational system, pointing out the eleven-year compulsory education, the system of universal free education, the system of studying while working, and the education of children. (5) Kim points out the duties of the educational institutions, describing the duty of schools, role of

teachers, party guidance, and the state guarantee and social support for educational work. All in all, it is tightly controlled education in which the state examines every aspect of the educational process; the educational system, the content of teaching, and study and working duties, the state support, and all are controlled by the party.

CSJ 7: 355–402; *SW 7*: 344–92.
EP77; *Korea Today* (no. 11, 1977): 6–28; *Kŭlloja* (no. 10, 1977): 2–29; English pamphlet by World View Publishers of New York in 1977; *KP77*.

September 5–7
Concerning the Theses on Socialist Education.

Speeches delivered at the fourteenth plenary meeting of the fifth Central Committee of the Workers' Party of Korea.

These are two other speeches Kim delivered at the meeting; one is to introduce the theses on September 5 and the other to encourage party members to implement the directives in the theses on September 7. Both speeches are relatively shorter than the main speech on the theses. Kim merely points out the highlights of the theses.

CCY 78: 34–37, 67–71.

September 15–17
Speeches to Welcome Maie Nguema Biyogo Negue Ndong of Equatorial Guinea.

There are two speeches: one at the banquet given by Kim to welcome the President and government delegation of Equatorial Guinea and the other at the banquet given by the president of Equatorial Guinea to honor Kim.

CCY 78: 103–5.

September 20–22
Speeches to Welcome U Ne Win, President of Burma.

There are two speeches by Kim; one is to welcome President U Ne Win of Burma, and the other is to express appreciation for the banquet given by Ne Win to honor Kim. Kim reiterates the solidarity of the third-world countries.

CCY 78: 106–8.

October 7
Speech at the Pyongyang Mass Rally to Welcome the Party and Government Delegation of Democratic Kampuchea Headed by Comrade Pol Pot, Secretary of the Central Committee of the Communist Party of Kampuchea and Prime Minister of the Government of Democratic Kampuchea.

A short speech to welcome Pol Pot of Cambodia. Kim has a special interest in Cambodia because of his long friendship with Sihanouk, but he does not mention him at all. He calls for the unity of nonaligned nations and resistance to all kinds of intervention by imperialists and big powers in the affairs of the small independent nations.

Korea Today (no. 12, 1977): 2–5.

November 30
Let Us Build Up the Strength of the People's Army Through Effective Political Work.

Speech at the seventh congress of agitators of the Korean People's Army.

Kim speaks about three party policies pertaining to the Korean People's Army. They are: (1) policy on the independent and peaceful unification of the country, (2) policy on the strengthening of political work in the People's Army, and (3) the ten-point rule of the People's Army for soldiers to observe. Kim stresses the need to establish a fine tradition of the army.

CSJ 7: 403–25; *SW* 7: 393–413.

December 10
Speech at the Pyongyang Mass Rally to Welcome the Party and State Delegation of the German Democratic Republic Headed by Comrade Erich Honecker, General Secretary of the Central Committee of the Socialist Unity Party of Germany and Chairman of the Council of State of the German Democratic Republic.

Kim condemns the division of Germany and the West German government, and he enthusiastically endorses the Socialist Unity Party of Germany. He says that the situations in Germany and Korea are different. Germany wants to remain divided and Korea does not. Germany was a sovereign state prior to the division, and Korea was a colonial state. Germany was a defeated nation, and Korea was an occupied nation. He says that he rejects any measure to perpetuate the division of the country, such as simultaneous U.N. membership and cross recognition. Kim asks the United States to withdraw its troops completely from Korea. Kim expresses deep appreciation for the help the German government gave to Korea during the Korean war.

Korea Today (no. 1, 1978): 29–32.

December 13
Concluding Remarks at the Fifteenth Plenary Meeting of the Central Committee of the Fifth Party (5WPK-15CC).

No text available.

*December 15
Let Us Further Strengthen the People's Government.

Speech delivered at the first session of the Sixth Supreme People's Assembly of the Democratic People's Republic of Korea (6SPA-1).

> Kim speaks about three subjects. The first is that the working people are the masters of the state and society. The second is Kim's own version of democracy. Kim defines socialist democracy as the true demoracy and the democracy practiced in the capitalist countries as bogus democracy. Under the same topic, Kim stresses that the issue of human rights advocated by the capitalist countries is a hypocritical maneuver to disparage socialist democracy. Thirdly, Kim says that they must completely uproot bureaucratism, the remnant of the old society in the North. He says that government functionaries must go to the people and work in the interest of the people, applying Ch'ŏngsalli methods and the Taean work system. He also outlines the second seven-year economic plan and urges the members of the Assembly to work hard toward the goals of the plan.

> *CSJ* 7: 426-46; *SW* 7: 414-34.
> *EP77*; *Korea Today* (no. 1, 1978): 6-17; *Kŭlloja* (no. 1, 1978): 7-19.

December 17
On the Second Seven-Year Plan for the Development of the National Economy of the Democratic People's Republic of Korea.

Adopted as law of the Supreme People's Assembly of the Democratic People's Republic of Korea.

> This is an official document, but presented under the name of Kim Il Sung, president of the republic. The basic tasks of the plan are to strengthen the economic basis of socialism in the North, to raise the standard of living of the people, and to modernize the society. Specific tasks are divided under the topics of Industry, Agriculture, Transportation and Communications, Capital Construction, Education, Science and Culture, and the People's Living Standards.

> *CSJ* 7: 447-65; *SW* 7: 435-56.
> *Korea Today* (no. 1, 1978): 18-28.

1978

January 1
New Year Address.

> This is a short speech. Kim reviews the accomplishments of 1977 in transportation, mining, agriculture, and government operations. This is the first year

of the second seven-year plan, and Kim emphasizes the mining industry, transportation works, and agriculture, encouraging the people to work hard to accomplish the goals set in the plan. He points out the important work in strengthening the people's government as outlined in the first session of the sixth Supreme People's Assembly and urges the people to reject easy life and indolence in order to achieve the goals set by the government.

EP78, Kǔlloja (no. 1, 1978): 2–6; *Korea Today* (no. 2, 1978): 2–5; *CCY 79:* 1–4.

January 27
Let Us Make New Progress in Agricultural Production by Thoroughly Implementing the *Chuch'e* **Agrarian Law.**

Speech at a national meeting of agricultural workers.

Kim raised a number of points about boosting production. He emphasized that agriculture should be mechanized, chemical fertilizers should be adequately distributed, scientific research on agriculture should be carried out, and cultural revolution should be brought about in farming villages. He also pointed out a number of tasks confronting farmers and urged them to prepare for a new year of productive farming.

CCY 79: 4–13.

April 21–26
Speeches to Welcome Prime Minister Linden Forbes Sampson Burnham of Guyana.

Kim makes two speeches: one at this banquet to welcome Prime Minister Burnham and another at the banquet arranged by Prime Minister Burnham for Kim. Both speeches are routine congratulatory remarks with little substance.

Pyongyang Times, April 29, 1978; *CCY 79:* 88–91.

April 28–May 1
Speeches to Welcome Bokassa the First, Emperor of Central Africa.

Kim makes two speeches; the first one is at a banquet arranged by Kim to welcome Bokassa, and the second is at a ceremony for the signing of the treaty of friendship and cooperation between North Korea and the Empire of Central Africa. The treaty is a short ten-article agreement of friendship and economic cooperation for ten years, automatically renewable for another ten years at the end of 1988.

Pyongyang Times, May 3, 1978; *CCY 79:* 91–94.

May 4
Speech at the Banquet to Welcome the Government Delegation of the Republic of Seychelles Headed by President France Albert Rene.

Kim congratulates President Rene for his victory in the June 1977 revolution and the socialist road the government of Seychelles has chosen. Kim says that one of the important questions facing the countries in the Indian Ocean is to dismantle foreign military bases on Diego Garcia Island. The Korean and Seychelles peoples should join hands in driving imperialism out of the region.

Pyongyang Times, May 6, 1978; *CCY 79*: 94–96.

May 5–9
Speech at Pyongyang Mass Rally to Welcome Hua Kuo-feng.

Kim welcomes Hua to the North at the Moranbong stadium. He congratulates Hua for solving the difficult domestic problems of the Gang of Four and gives blessings for the bright future of China. Kim recalls the Chinese assistance during the Korean war and vows eternal friendship between the two governments. He denounces the United States for the permanent division of Korea and demands that the U.S. forces withdraw from Korea. Kim also makes two short speeches at banquets hosted by Hua and himself.

Peking Review (no. 19, 1978): 9–12; *Korea Today* (no. 7, 1978): 21–24; *CCY 79*: 96–103.

May 14–18
Speeches to Welcome Samora Moises Machel, President of the People's Republic of Mozambique.

There are two speeches, one at the banquet Kim arranged for Machel on May 14 and another at the banquet arranged by Machel for Kim on May 18. Kim expresses his appreciation to Machel for recognizing the North as the only legitimate government in Korea. He condemns South Africa and Rhodesia, supported by the United States and Britain, and expresses his support for the Frelimo Party of Mozambique along with the struggles of Tanzania, Zambia, Angola, and Botswana. In the second speech, Kim says that North Korea and Mozambique have concluded a treaty of friendship and cooperation and a number of agreements. Kim vows the solidarity of the third-world countries.

Pyongyang Times, May 20, 1978; *CCY 79*: 103–7.

May 20–21
Speeches to Welcome Nicolae Ceausescu, General Secretary of the Romanian Communist Party and President of the Romanian Socialist Republic.

Kim makes two speeches to welcome Ceausescu and his wife at a banquet on May 20 and at a grand Pyongyang mass rally held at Moranbong Stadium on May 21. Kim expresses his appreciation to Ceausescu for his support for the peaceful reunification of Korea and for support of North Korean policy in the international arena. In his second speech Kim repeats his praise of Ceausescu's help of the North in international relations, and goes further by praising Ceausescu's leadership. Kim attacks imperialism and other forces that try to dominate the third-world countries, and he emphasizes the independence of each socialist country.

Korea Today (no. 8, 1978): 3–6; *CCY 79*: 107–12.

May 25–28
Speech to Welcome Joachim Yhomby-opango, Chairman of the Council of Ministers of the People's Republic of the Congo.

Kim condemns the assassination of President Marien Ngouabi and blames it on "the imperialists." He welcomes the successor, President Yhomby-opango, and reaffirms his support for him and for a close relationship between the two countries. Kim attends two banquets and makes two short speeches.

Nodong sinmun, May 29, 1978; *CCY 79*: 112–15.

June 14–16
Speeches to Welcome Habyarimana Juvenal, President of the Republic of Rwanda.

Two speeches were made by Kim at his own and President Juvenal's banquets. Kim congratulates the proclamation of the second republic under the leadership of President Juvenal, and he also encourages President Juvenal's efforts in the liberation struggle of other African people in Zimbabwe, Zambia, and South Africa. In the second speech, Kim promises close cooperation between the two countries and says that this was their first meeting, but he hopes for a long and durable relationship between the two countries.

Nodong sinmun, June 17, 1978; *CCY 79*: 115–19.

July 28
On Several Experiences in Solving the Agrarian Problems in Our Country.

Talk with workers in economic fields.

Kim speaks about four subjects: (1) the importance of agrarian problems in the development of industries, (2) the reform of agrarian management ahead of technological reforms, (3) carrying out ideological, technological, and cultural revolutions, and (4) the role of the county in solving agrarian problems.

KP78; *CCY 79*: 14–46.

September 7 and 20
Speeches to Welcome Didier Ratsiraka, President of the Democratic Republic of Madagascar.

Kim expresses appreciation to President Ratsiraka for visiting the North on the occasion of the thirtieth anniversary of the founding of the republic. He later makes a similar speech of welcome at a banquet arranged by Ratsiraka in his honor.

CCY 79: 119–20, 125–26; *Nodong sinmun,* September 21, 1978.

September 8–10
Speech to Welcome Ziaur Rahman, President of the People's Republic of Bangladesh.

This is one of the shortest speeches Kim has made to welcome any head of state. Kim merely said that this trip would contribute to the friendship of the two countries, and he regretted that the visit was so short. Kim made another short speech when Rahman left the country.

Nodong sinmun, September 11, 1978; *CCY 79:* 121–22, 124–25.

*September 9
Let Us Step Up Socialist Construction Under the Banner of the *Chuch'e* Idea.

Report delivered at the thirtieth anniversary celebration of the founding of the Democratic People's Republic of Korea.

Kim said that the North Korean people had made significant progress during the past thirty years. The country is at the height of its prosperity, and the people are enjoying the fruits of their long struggle. He said that the people should subscribe to the *chuch'e* idea more thoroughly and carry on ideological, technological, and cultural revolutions in the North. On the question of reunification, Kim said that it was the South that plotted to divide the country, and he urged the people of Korea to smash the two-Korea plot and peacefully reunify the country. On North Korean foreign relations, Kim said that the newly emerging countries should unite their forces and fight resolutely against imperialism and any form of domineering forces. This speech seemed clearly to imply, although they were not mentioned in the text, that the North Koreans did not approve Cuban activities in Africa.

KP78; EP78; Pyongyang Times, September 9, 1978; *Külloja* (no. 10, 1978): 2–19; *Korea Today* (no. 10, 1978): 7–25; *CCY 79:* 47–61.

October 1
Let Us Bring About a New Turnaround in Educational Work, Thoroughly Carrying Through the Theses on Socialist Education.

Speech delivered at a national meeting of educational functionaries.

Kim points out several tasks in fulfilling the goals set in the Theses on Socialist Education. He says that the quality of education must be improved and the state must insure the material conditions for education by providing adequate laboratories and libraries. He also repeats his emphasis on the studying-while-working program to educate the whole society and urges the strengthening of the party guidance in educational work.

Kŭlloja (no. 11, 1978): 2–14; *CCY 79:* 61–71.

October 21
Talk with Managing Editor of Japanese Politico-Theoretical Magazine, *Sekai.*

This is still another interview with Yasue Ryosuke, who visited Pyongyang to participate in the thirtieth anniversary celebration of the founding of the republic. Kim said that the prospects of the North were bright and the end of the cold war era had come. He said that the Sino-Japanese Peace Treaty was a normal development and emphasized his opposition to dominationism in the international socialist movement. He condemned Carter's policies toward Korea on both the troop withdrawal question and the human rights issue. He spoke at length about the Japan-Korea relationship and reiterated his opposition to the idea of cross recognition.

EP78; KP78; Sekai (no. 1, 1979): 146–57; *CCY 79:* 72–79.

December 23
Let Us Step Up Socialist Construction by Effective Financial Management.

Speech at a national meeting of financial and bank workers.

Kim reviewed past accomplishments and congratulated the workers for their hard work. He gave five specific instructions to correct past mistakes, however. They were: Apply a proper cost accounting system, emphasize financial discipline, prevent waste, strengthen the local budgetary system, and enhance the role of banking organization by hiring more women.

Nodong sinmun, December 26, 1978; *Pyongyang Times*, December 30, 1978; *Korea Today* (no. 2, 1979): 12–20; *CCY 79:* 80–87.

1979

January 1
New Year Address.

Kim expresses his appreciation for the accomplishments of various sectors of the society in 1978. For the New Year, Kim says that the important task is to achieve the national economic goal set for the year. He mentions briefly the coal mining industry, foreign trade, chemical industry, transportation, and grain production.

Nodong sinmun, January 1, 1979; *Kŭlloja* (no. 1, 1979): 2–7; *Pyongyang Times,* January 6, 1979; *Korea Today* (no. 2, 1979): 7–11.

January 11
Let Us Advance Our Socialist Agriculture onto a New Stage.

Speech delivered at National Congress of Agriculture.

Kim speaks about four problems in the agrarian sector of the North: (1) the problem of raising the level of scientific and technical knowledge of the agricultural workers, (2) the way to improve planning work in agriculture, (3) the improvement of the organization and guidance of farm production, and (4) better utilization of land.

Nodong sinmun, January 13, 1979; *Kŭlloja* (no. 2, 1979): 2–9; *Pyongyang Times,* January 13, 1979; *Korea Today* (no. 3, 1979): 7–14.

March 20
Speech to Welcome Jean-Baptiste Bagaza, President of Burundi.

Kim honors President Bagaza of Burundi and expresses his appreciation for the visit. Kim pledges fraternal friendship between the peoples of Korea and Africa.

Nodong sinmun, March 21, 1979; *Pyongyang Times,* March 24, 1979.

May 5
Talk with a Japanese Visitors' Group.

Two members of the Liberal Democratic Party of Japan, Kuno Chuji and Antaku Tsunehiko, visited the North. Kim thanks them for their visit, and talks about the thirty-fifth world table tennis match that was going on at the time. He derides South Korea in the North-South dialogue and mentions briefly U.S.-North Korean and Japan-North Korean relations.

Pyongyang Times, July 7, 1979; *Korea Today* (no. 8, 1979): 7–11.

May 20
Speech to Welcome Samdech Norodom Sihanouk.

Kim thanks Sihanouk for his work for North Korea in the international arena and says that he is happy to see him after such a long absence from the North. North Korea was among the first to recognize the royal government of Kampuchea as the legitimate government.

Pyongyang Times, May 26, 1979.

May 26
Speech to Welcome Comrade Teng Ying-ch'ao (Deng Yingchao), Member of the Political Committee of the Chinese Communist Party.

Teng Ying-ch'ao (Deng Yingchao) came to Korea to participate in the unveiling of Chou En-lai's statue in the North. Kim pledges Sino-North Korean solidarity.

Pyongyang Times, June 2, 1979.

June 19
Talk with a Nepalese Journalist Delegation.

Kim met the delegates in his tour of the countryside, a place away from Pyongyang. Kim answers questions on the *chuch'e* idea, on the prospects of the second seven-year plan, on reunification of Korea, and on Nepal-North Korea relations.

Korea Today (no. 9, 1979): 7–10.

June 30
Answers to Questions Raised by Director of the Research and Planning Department of the Ministry of Internal Security and National Orientation of the People's Republic of Benin.

Kim answers questions on many topics, including the prospects of economic progress in the North, the idea of *chuch'e*, expectations concerning the nonaligned nation conference to be held in Cuba, and the reunification of Korea.

Korea Today (no. 10, 1979): 7–12; *Pyongyang Times*, August 4, 1979.

September 27
Let Us Thoroughly Abide by the Socialist Labor Law.

Speech delivered at a meeting of labor administration workers.

Saying that the North has a superior socialist labor law, Kim comments on four problems in the implementation of the law. He emphasizes (1) the need to improve political work by the labor administration workers and also points out that (2) all working people should be made to love labor. He recognizes (3) the need to improve the socialist principle of distribution and the socialist system of labor remuneration. Finally he says that (4) the labor administration workers should not give bureaucratic orders high-handedly, but should go down among the workers to achieve the projected goal.

Nodong sinmun, September 29, 1979; *Kŭlloja* (no. 11, 1979): 2–10; *Korea Today* (no. 12, 1979): 7–13; *Pyongyang Times*, October 6, 1979.

October 9
Speech to Welcome Ahmed Sekou Toure, President of Guinea.

Sekou Toure visited the North after the sixth nonaligned nations summit conference in Cuba. Kim pledges the usual fraternal and mutual support for the peoples of the two countries.

Nodong sinmun, October 10, 1979; *Pyongyang Times*, October 13, 1979.

November 1
Speech to Welcome Luiz Cabral, President of Guinea-Bissau.

Kim expresses appreciation for the support of Luiz Cabral on the reunification question and pledges a fraternal relationship between the two countries. A treaty of friendship and cooperation of eleven articles is concluded between the two countries.

Nodong sinmun, November 2, 1979; *Pyongyang Times*, November 10, 1979.

1980

January 1
New Year Address.

Kim reviews the accomplishments of 1979 in coal mines and other heavy industries, transportation work, foreign trade, agriculture, and scientific work. For the new year, Kim repeats the message of continuous growth in all sectors of the economy, and urges workers in a few specific segments, such as fisheries and electric power plants, to renew their resolve. Kim expresses his concern over the South Korean people during the transitional stage, but his emphasis is more on the South Korean revolution. Kim speaks about the glorious occasion for the convocation of the sixth party congress in 1980.

Nodong sinmun, January 1, 1980; *Külloja* (no. 1, 1980): 2–8; *EP80*; *Korea Today* (no. 2, 1980): 7–12; *Pyongyang Times*, January 1, 1980.

April 5
Speech to Welcome Kenneth David Kaunda, President of Zambia.

Kim says that the present international situation is extremely tense and complicated and the united stand of the nonaligned nations is important for both countries.

Pyongyang Times, April 12, 1980; *Nodong sinmun*, April 6 and 9, 1980.

April 23

Speech to Welcome Comrade Enrico Berlinguer, General Secretary of the Italian Communist Party.

The Italian Communist Party actively supports the North Korean stand on the Korean reunification question, and Kim expresses his appreciation to Berlinguer. Kim mentions briefly the great occasion for the historic sixth party congress to be held in October 1980.

Pyongyang Times, May 3, 1980; *Nodong sinmun*, April 24, 1980.

May 12

Speech at a Banquet in Romania.

On his way back from the funeral service of Tito in Belgrade, Kim spoke at a banquet in his honor arranged by Nicolae Ceausescu in Bucharest. He reaffirmed the fraternal relationship between Romania and North Korea.

Pyongyang Times, May 17, 1980.

September 22

Speech to Welcome France Albert Rene, President of Seychelles.

This is the second visit of President Rene to North Korea, but is the first after the Republic of Seychelles broke off diplomatic relations with South Korea in May 1980. The two leaders renewed their friendship, and Kim expressed his appreciation for the diplomatic act.

Pyongyang Times, September 27, 1980.

October 8

Speech to Welcome Ahmed Sekou Toure, President of the Guinean Revolutionary People's Republic.

This is the third meeting of Kim and Toure; the first was in 1979 in Pyongyang, the second in May 1980 in Belgrade, and the third in Pyongyang. President Toure visits Kim on the occasion of the sixth party congress.

Pyongyang Times, October 12, 1980.

October 9

Speech to Welcome Robert G. Mugabe, Prime Minister of the Republic of Zimbabwe.

The Republic of Zimbabwe broke diplomatic relations with South Korea in May 1980. Kim congratulates Mugabe for the action and reassures his friendship with Mugabe. His visit to Pyongyang was on the occasion of the sixth party congress.

Pyongyang Times, October 12, 1980.

*October 10
Report on the Work of the Central Committee of the Workers' Party of Korea Delivered at the Sixth Congress of the Party.

It took Kim more than five hours to deliver this report, which is divided into five parts: (1) past accomplishments in the three revolutions, (2) North Korean society under the *chuch'e* idea, (3) the reunification question, (4) strengthening of the nonalignment policy, and (5) the future tasks of the party. Kim analyzes the past accomplishments in the three revolutions (ideological, technological, and cultural revolutions) and recounts the consolidation of the state system under the 1972 constitution. On the domestic front, he emphasizes the *chuch'e* idea, and efforts to remold the country into a revolutionary, working-class, intellectual, modern, and scientific construction in the 1980s. Major portions of his speech, however, deal with the problem of South Korea and the reunification problems, giving some details of his idea about the Democratic Confederal Republic of Korea. He says that the Korean people should join and work toward nonalignment. Lastly, Kim repeats many of his past directives to improve future work of the party, such as the establishment of the monolithic ideological system, the revolutionary work system, and the strengthening of party life.

Pyongyang Times, October 11, 1980; *Nodong sinmun*, October 11, 1980.

SUBJECT INDEX

This index is arranged as outlined below, with items listed in chronological order under each heading. The dates are given in the order: year, month, day; thus, 46/08/29 means August 29, 1946. Most items are listed only once and not cross-indexed, but the more-important works, marked with an asterisk, usually cover more than one subject and should be consulted in searching for material on any topic. The works that were not available or were not annotated are indicated by (na).

1. Party
   a. Party congresses and conferences
   b. Party Central Committee plenums
   c. Local party organizations
2. Political thought and theses
3. State system of the republic
   a. On the state
   b. Reunification problems
4. Economy
   a. General
   b. Agriculture
   c. Industries
5. Military and security
   a. Security and armed forces
   b. Korean war
6. International relations
   a. General
   b. Kim's travels abroad
   c. Visitors to the North
   d. Interviews
   e. Letters
7. Education, culture, and arts
8. Youth, women, and public health
9. Commemoration addresses
   a. New Year's Day
   b. May Day
   c. National Liberation Day
10. Pre-1945 writings

1. PARTY

a. **Party Congresses and Conferences**

*46/08/29   Founding Congress of the Workers' Party of Korea

*48/03/28   Second Congress of the Workers' Party of Korea
*56/04/23   Third Congress of the Workers' Party of Korea
*58/03/06   First party conference
*61/09/11   Fourth Congress of the Workers' Party of Korea
*66/10/05   Second party conference
*70/11/02   Fifth Congress of the Workers' Party of Korea
*80/10/10   Sixth Congress of the Workers' Party of Korea

b. **Party Central Committee Plenums**

45/10/10   Establish a Communist party
*45/12/17   Organization work of the party
45/12/18   Strengthening of the party
*46/02/15   Task of the party
46/07/01   Central Higher Cadre School
46/07/22   For the national united front
46/07/27   North Korean Branch Bureau (na)
*46/07/29   Merger of two parties
46/09/25   At the second enlarged plenum
46/09/26   On the Workers' Party of South Korea
46/12/02   At the fourteenth session of the Standing Committee (na)
47/03/15   At the sixth enlarged plenum
47/08/28   First anniversary of the founding of the party
47/10/13   Leadership of social organizations
49/06/11   Sixth enlarged plenum (na)
*50/12/21   War situation and the tasks of the party
*51/11/01   Defects in the organization work
51/11/02   Improve the organization work
*52/12/15   Organizational and ideological consolidation
54/11/01   November plenum (na)
*55/04/01   Class education of party members
*55/04/04   Factional struggles within the party
58/08/18   Graduation ceremony of the central party school
65/07/01   Strengthening the party life
*65/10/10   Twentieth anniversary of the party
65/11/15-17   Strengthening the party work (na)
*66/10/18   Elimination of formalism and bureaucracy
68/11/16   Manpower administration
69/10/11   Experiences of the socialist revolution
71/11/15   Third plenum of the Central Committee (na)
*71/12/02   Training of party cadres
72/07/01   Fourth plenum of the Central Committee (na)
72/10/23   Fifth plenum of the Central Committee (na)

74/07/31	Strengthening of the party work
75/02/17	Tenth plenum of the Central Committee (na)
*75/10/09–10	Thirtieth anniversary of the party
75/11/21	Eleventh plenum of the Central Committee (na)
77/12/13	Concluding remarks at the fifteenth plenary meeting (na)

c. **Local Party Organizations**

45/10/13	United front in the provincial party committees
45/12/27	P'yŏngan Namdo party organization
46/01/13	Strengthening party rank and file
46/04/20	Hamnam party committee
46/04/21	Hamgyŏng Pukto people's organizations
46/09/09	P'yŏngnam party committee
47/01/17	Hamgyŏng Pukto party organizations
47/01/18	Kangwŏndo party organizations
47/02/07	P'yŏngan Pukto party organizations
48/01/12	Kanggye local party members
48/01/24	P'yŏngnam party committee conference
48/02/21	Central Committee of the party
54/07/12	Hambuk party organizations
56/02/05	Kaech'ŏn County party organization
56/04/07	P'yŏngbuk party organizations
57/05/11	Hambuk party organizations (na)
*58/03/07	On the reform of party work
58/05/11	Yanggang provincial party organizations
58/06/23	P'yŏngbuk party cadres (na)
59/02/26	On the method of party work
59/03/23	Hambuk party organizations
*60/02/23	Role of local party in agrarian management
61/01/23	Work of the local party organizations
63/04/27	On the central-country party committee
63/08/16	Yanggang provincial party organizations
*68/05/27	Cadre policy of the party
74/01/14	*Ri* party secretaries

2. POLITICAL THOUGHT AND THESES

See also Party, State, International Relations, and Economy

45/10/03	On democracy
*55/04	Character of Korean revolution
*55/04/01	On bureaucracy
55/04/15	On Leninism
*55/12/28	On self-reliant attitude of *chuch'e*

*62/03/08   Ideological work against revisionism
*64/02/25   Theses on the socialist rural question
 66/10/18   Formalism and bureaucracy in party work
*67/05/25   Transition from capitalism to socialism
*67/12/16   Political program of the republic
*69/03/01   Theoretical problems of the socialist economy
 73/03/14   Ideological, technological, and cultural revolution

3. State System of the Republic

See also Party and Economy

a. **On the State**

45/08/20   Preparation for a state
45/09/20   Building of new Korea
45/10/13   Establish democratic new Korea
45/10/14   Work toward the establishment of a state
45/10/18   To build a new democratic state
45/11/05   Nationalist leaders
45/11/10   Establishing the state
45/11/15   Establishing the government
45/11/17   Intellectuals and the state
45/11/27   Path for liberated Korea
46/01/12   Democratic and independent state
46/01/23   P'yŏngnam Political Committee
*46/02/08   Founding of the North Korean Provisional People's Committee
46/02/20   Provisional People's Committee
46/03/01   Twenty-seventh anniversary of the March First incident
46/03/07   Traitors and collaborators
46/03/23   Twenty-point platform
46/05/19   For complete independence of Korea
46/06/26   Korean People's Party
46/11/01   On the November 3 election
46/11/13   People's Committee
46/11/25   Task of the Provisional People's Committee
46/12/26   Democratic United Front
47/01/11   People's Committee elections
47/02/03   Powers of the People's Committee (na)
47/02/08   General political situation
47/02/20   People's committee meetings
47/02/21   First session of the People's Assembly of North Korea
47/02/24   North Korean People's Committee
47/03/22   Election results

47/06/14	On the democratic interim government
47/06/20	Law and order in judicial organs
47/11/03	First anniversary of the November 3 election
48/06/18	County People's Committee
48/07/09	On the constitution of the republic
48/08/23	On the election for the Supreme People's Assembly
48/09/08	Transfer of power
*48/09/10	Political programs of the republic
48/09/12	Commemoration of the establishment of the republic
*49/09/09	First anniversary of the republic
50/09/11	Second anniversary of the republic
52/02/01	Local organization works
57/08/02	Mundŏk electoral district speech
57/09/20	Tasks of the people's power
*58/04/29	Judicial policy of the party
58/08/09	City and county people's committees
58/09/08	Tenth anniversary of the republic
62/01/22	Hwangnam County People's Committee
62/09/05	City management
*62/10/23	Tasks of the republic
63/08/15	Fifteenth anniversary of the founding of the republic
64/09/09	Sixteenth anniversary of the founding of the republic
65/05/25	Leaders of the Supreme People's Assembly
*65/12/16	Political programs of the republic
*68/09/07	Twentieth anniversary of the founding of the republic
*72/12/25	Review of the socialist system
72/12/27	Constitution of the republic
73/09/09	Twenty-fifth anniversary of the founding of the republic
*77/12/15	On the people's government
*78/09/09	Thirtieth anniversary of the republic

b. **Reunification Problems**

See also Party, State, Interviews, and Education

48/03/09	Oppose South Korean election
48/03/29	Democratic base for the unification
48/04/21	Unified government of North and South Korea
48/06/29	Oppose unilateral election in South Korea
49/08/02	Declaration of the peaceful unification
50/01/19	Ch'ŏndogyo Young Friends Party
50/05	Struggle to establish a united Korea
*50/06/26	Every effort for victory in the war
*53/08/05	Postwar recovery

*54/11/03   Party policy on agricultural management
54/12/23   Cadres of the People's Army
*55/04   On character of Korean revolution
*56/04/23   Third party congress
57/08/25   At the graduation ceremony of Songdo College
57/09/20   Tasks of the people's government
58/02/08   On the People's Army
58/09/08   Tenth anniversary of the republic
60/08/14   Fifteenth anniversary of the national liberation
*61/09/11   Fourth party congress
*62/10/23   On the tasks of the government
*63/02/08   On the People's Army
64/02/27   Reunification of the country
*64/05/15   Youth and the unification
64/11/07   On literature and arts
65/01/08   Letter to Kim Yong-jung on unification
*65/04/14   On the South Korean revolution
*65/10/10   Twentieth anniversary of the party
*66/10/05   On the struggle of the South Korean people
67/01/04   Letter to Kim Yong-jung on unification
*67/12/16   For a self-reliant Korea
*68/09/07   To oust the United States and unify the country
68/10/08   The nonalignment movement
*73/06/25   Five-point reunification plan

4. ECONOMY

See also Party, State, and International Relations

a. General

46/04/01   State budget and Peasant Bank
46/10/29   Central Bank
*47/02/19   1947 economic plan
47/02/28   On state finance
47/04/08   Standard of government workers
47/04/19   Pyongyang Koksan Factory workers
47/05/12   1947 economic goals
47/08/15   Two-year democratic construction
47/12/01   Currency reform
47/12/21   Second congress of the General Trade Union
*48/02/06   1948 economic plan
48/02/09   Role of the party in economic development
48/07/26   North Korean People's Committee
48/11/22   Improve material and cultural lives

48/11/25	Two-year economic plan
*49/02/01	Two-year economic plan
50/02/28	Correcting shortcomings in the economic plan
*53/08/05	Three-year economic plan, postwar recovery
54/09/10	Postwar recovery
57/03/26	Hamnam party organizations
57/07/05	Strengthen the party organs for economic development
*58/06/11	First five-year economic plan
*59/12/04	Shortcomings in economic construction
60/08/22	Ch'ŏllima movement
61/12/01	To conquer six highlands
62/08/08	Urbanization problems
63/01/07	Manpower support for farm and construction
*64/06/23	Delegates to the economic seminar in Pyongyang
64/06/26	Union of Agricultural Working People and the trade unions
64/12/19	Improving economic management
65/09/23	Greater enthusiasm for economic work
67/07/03	Manpower administration to work 480 minutes
67/11/17	Congratulatory messages for 1967 economic goals
68/05/11	Ch'ŏllima workteam movement
68/09/24	Role of counties in the countryside
69/02/15	Manpower administration
*69/03/01	Theoretical problem of socialist economy
69/07/02	Uniform planning system
69/10/21	Reform in the statistics work
*73/02/01	Materialistic incentives and management
74/02/11	General mobilization (na)
75/04/08	Local budget system
76/07/07	Financial operation in the rural areas
77/12/17	On the second seven-year plan
78/12/23	Financial management

b. Agriculture

45/10/16	Land question
46/02/27	Food problems
46/03/05	Land reform law
46/03/09	Land reform laws
*46/04/10	Agrarian reform
46/04/13	Land reform
47/03/05	First anniversary of the land reform
47/03/08	Basic task of the farmer
47/04/06	Reforestation work

47/04/26   Farm management and government organizations
47/09/05   State granary work
47/09/30   Mountainous regions in P'yŏngan Namdo
50/01/25   Agrarian management, forestry, and fisheries
54/02/16   Grain harvest (na)
*54/11/03   Party policy on agricultural management
54/12/19   P'yŏngnam agricultural management
57/01/21   Problems of agrarian management
57/12/13   Hwanghae farm cooperatives
*59/01/05   Agricultural cooperatives
59/01/09   Agrarian management (na)
60/02/08   Agrarian management
60/02/18   Kangsŏ County agrarian management
61/04/07   Orchards at Pukch'ŏng
*61/12/18   County cooperative farm management committee
62/02/01   Haeju agricultural cooperatives
62/11/13   P'yŏngnam County cooperative farm management
            system
64/02/20   Tractors and agrarian technical revolution (na)
*64/02/25   Theses on the socialist rural question
67/02/02   Leaders of agrarian sectors
68/02/14   Small group management system
68/02/16   Messages to farm workers
69/02/07   Socialist agrarian construction
72/02/16   Task of the Union of Agricultural Working People
*73/02/21   Three revolutions in farm villages
73/08/09   On agricultural production
*74/01/10   Building of the socialist countryside
*74/11/29   Problems in agrarian theses
75/01/15   Eight million tons of grain
76/10/14   Nature remaking and ten million tons of grain
77/04/05   To prevent drought damages
*77/04/29   On the land law
78/01/27   Agricultural production
78/07/28   Agrarian problems
79/01/11   Socialist agriculture

c. **Industries**

46/03/22   Restoration of industries
46/04/08   Communication work
46/04/17   Labor heroes
46/05/21   Pot'ong River works
*46/06/20   On labor laws

46/06/24	Labor laws
46/07/21	Completion of Pot'ong River project
46/08/10	Nationalization of major industries
46/10/10	On electricity in Sakchu County
46/10/31	Railway transportation
46/12/03	Management of state enterprises
47/04/14	Transportation works
47/07/31	Factory party organization on production
47/09/01	Production cooperatives
47/12/03	Third Hwanghae steel mill
47/12/29	Hŭngnam people's factories
48/01/25	Management of state industries
48/02/22	Hŭngnam factory
48/06/07	Musan mines
48/07/08	Fisheries development
49/11/19	New attitude toward work
50/02/21	Transportation workers
54/03/21	Shortcomings in industrial and transportation sectors
54/03/26	Architects and technicians
54/05/06	Forestry sector
54/05/11	Tasks of transportation workers
56/01/30	Construction architects and builders
56/12/13	Upswing in the socialist construction
57/02/14	Commodity circulation and trade
57/04/19	On fisheries
57/09/11	Machine industries
57/10/19	Party's policy on construction
58/01/29	Light industry development
58/04/30	Hwanghae steel mill
58/06/07	Consumer goods production and exchange
58/08/12	Haeju-Hasŏng railway
58/08/30	Sup'ung power station
58/09/16	Against passivism and conservatism
58/12/25	For higher quality in construction
59/06/11	Fisheries
*59/09/04	Hwanghae steel mill party committee
60/08/11	On technological revolution
60/09/01	Chemical industry
61/05/07	Hamhŭng chemical industry (na)
61/12/15	Taean electric factory
61/12/16	Taean industrial management system
61/12/23	Coal industry at Anju mines

62/01/06	Light industry and quality of manufactured goods
62/02/12	Financial bank organizations
62/02/14	80,000-ton fisheries
62/04/08	Consumer goods
62/08/30	Hwanghae steel mill leadership reform
62/09/24	Mining industries
62/11/09	Taean work system
63/11/28	Banking system
64/01/09	On construction industry
64/01/22	Transportation work
65/01/03	Metal and chemical industries
65/01/11–16	Hwanghae steel mill
65/01/22	Ŭnyul mines ingot production
65/01/28	Trade union works and foreign trade
65/01/30	Kangsŏn steel mill
65/03/26	Works of the State Construction Commission
67/12/25	Congratulating Sunhŭng mine workers
68/06/04–05	Fisheries
68/10/31	Role of finances
68/11/16	On relieving the strain in transportation
69/06/30	Care for state properties and fisheries
70/02/27	Local industry and consumer goods
70/03/31	Poultry industry
71/02/12	Tractor operators in rural areas
71/12/14	Trade unions in the socialist construction
72/06/30	On heat supply
74/03/07	New heights in economic construction
*75/03/03	Development of three revolutions
77/07/19	Development of the machine industry
77/08/20	Further development of machine industries
*79/09/27	Socialist labor law

5. MILITARY AND SECURITY
See also Party and State

a. **Security and Armed Forces**

45/11/17	For Pyongyang Hagwŏn
45/11/20	Inspection and security organization workers (na)
45/11/29	Air force in new Korea
46/02/23	Opening of Pyongyang Hagwŏn
46/02/27	People's security force
46/04/29	Military-political cadre

46/10/07	Revolutionary army
46/11/20	Internal security organizations
47/01/15	Security Cadres Training Center
47/04/25	Central Security Cadres School
47/04/30	Artist-soldiers in the army
47/10/05	Modern people's army
47/10/26	First security cadre graduation
48/01/21	People's Army newspapers
*48/02/08	Founding of the Korean People's Army
48/02/20	Soldiers to sharpshooters
48/05/11	Security Corps conference
48/08/07	Thirty-eighth parallel border guards
48/09/19	Security workers
48/10/14	Army officers and fighting force
48/10/21	Political work in guard companies
49/10/31	Manufacture weapons
52/06/18	Cease-fire negotiations
53/08/15	Order no. 523
53/08/19	Citation for hero Kim Ch'ang-gŏl
53/12/29	Intelligence Corps graduation ceremony (na)
54/02/08	Order no. 63
54/05/01	Order no. 220
54/12/23	Cadres of the People's Army
58/02/08	People's Army and the anti-Japanese struggle
58/03/11	For the returning Chinese Volunteer Army
58/05/07	Veterans of the Kilchu Industrial Center (na)
58/06/23	Sinŭiju Veterans Industrial Center (na)
58/10/30	Military school instructors (na)
59/03/16	Livelihood of the veterans
59/10/17	Veterans must set examples
60/08/25	Talk with 109th Division
60/09/08	Political works in the People's Army (na)
62/01/19	Sinch'ŏn Veterans Food Factory (na)
*63/02/08	Fifteenth anniversary of the founding of the People's Army
63/10/05	Self-defense policy in national defense
67/06/13	Hamhŭng Veterans Factory
68/02/02	Congratulating the capture of the *Pueblo*
68/02/08	Twentieth anniversary of the founding of the People's Army
73/02/08	Twenty-fifth anniversary of the founding of the People's Army

| 73/10/11 | Strengthening the company units of the army |
| 77/11/30 | People's Army and political work |

b. **Korean War**

*50/06/26	Every effort for victory in the war
50/06/28	The liberation of Seoul
50/07/05	Order no. 7
50/07/08	Repulse the U.S. forces
50/07/23	Advance to Taejŏn
50/08/15	Order no. 82
50/10/11	Inch'ŏn landing of the U.N. forces
50/12/09	Liberation of Pyongyang
51/01/05	Order no. 7
51/02/08	Order no. 0097
51/02/24	Proclamation on spies
51/03/08	Congratulatory messages
51/03/27	On air force officer Kim Ki-u
51/05/01	Order no. 310
51/05/09	Citation for Antong 12th Regiment
51/06/14	Peace Preservation Committee
51/08/15	Order no. 461
52/02/08	Order no. 059
*52/04/04	Security organization cadre works
52/05/01	Order no. 236
52/08/15	Order no. 474
52/10/25	Chinese participation in the war
52/12/24	Strengthen the People's Army
53/02/08	Order no. 73
53/03/31	Exchange of prisoners
53/05/01	Order no. 269
53/07/27	Order no. 470
53/07/28	Cease-fire agreement

6. INTERNATIONAL RELATIONS
   See also Party and State

a. **General**

46/01/05	Three Foreign Ministers' conference (na)
46/09/18	American imperialists
47/05/21	Reopening of the U.S.–U.S.S.R. Joint Commission (na)
*47/08/15	On the second anniversary of the Korean liberation
49/04/21	Ten-year treaty with the Soviet Union

49/12/15	Proletarian internationalism
50/03/17	First anniversary of the treaty with the Soviet Union
51/11/05	The October Revolution and the Korean national liberation
52/08/15	Freedom, peace, and liberation of the Korean people
53/03/10	On the death of Stalin
*53/12/20	Aid to the North by Communist countries
57/10/22	Fortieth anniversary of the October Revolution
57/11	Russian support for the North
*57/12/05	Pro-Russian speech to downgrade factionalists
59/02/23	Relationship with the Soviet Union
59/09/26	Relationship with China
*66/10/05	Independent line of the North in the Sino-Soviet dispute
67/08/12	Anti-imperialist and anti-U.S. struggles
68/10/08	Asian-African-Latin American people's cause
69/09/18	International journalists' conference
70/04/16	Centenary of Lenin's birth
71/01/28	Korean residents in Japan
75/12/16	The nonalignment movement

b. **Kim's Travels Abroad**

49/03/03–20	Russia: First visit for economic aid
49/04/07	Pyongyang airport
53/09/10–29	Russia: To express appreciation for aid
53/11/12–27	China: Economic and cultural cooperation agreement
57/11/04–21	Russia: On the fortieth anniversary of the October Revolution
58/11/21–12/10	China and Vietnam: Friendship visits
59/02/25	Russia: Twenty-first congress of the Communist Party of the Soviet Union
*65/04/14	Indonesia: Ali Archam Academy of Indonesia
75/04/18–25	China: To visit Mao Tse-tung
75/05/22–26	Romania: To visit N. Ceausescu
75/05/26–28	Algeria: To visit H. Boumedienne
75/05/31	Mauritania: To visit Moktar Ould Daddah
75/06/02–05	Bulgaria: To visit T. Zhivkov
75/06/06–09	Yugoslavia: To visit J. Tito
80/05/12	Romania: On his way back from Tito's funeral

c. **Visitors to the North**

53/10/25	Chinese People's Consolidation Corps
53/11/09	Japanese People's Peace and Friendship group

58/02/14	Government delegation of the People's Republic of China
60/12/02	Cuban economic mission (na)
64/10/23–28	Modibo Keita of Mali
64/11/01–04	Sukarno of Indonesia
65/02/11–14	Alexei N. Kosygin of the Soviet Union
65/08/26–29	Massamba Deba of Congo, Brazzaville
65/10/04–10	Sihanouk of Cambodia
66/10/26	Cuban government delegation
67/10/24	Moktar Ould Daddah of Mauritania
68/06/22–24	Julius K. Nyerere of Tanzania
68/08/25	Miyamoto Kenji of the Japanese Communist Party
69/09/27	N. Adassi of Syria
69/11/19	Reidar Larsen of the Norwegian Communist Party
70/04/05–07	Chou En-lai of China
70/06/15	Sihanouk of Cambodia
70/08/13–16	G. M. Nimeri of Sudan
71/06/06	Carlos A. Orego of Chilean Socialist Party
71/06/09–15	Nicolae Ceausescu of Romania
71/08/06	Sihanouk of Cambodia
72/04/05	Sihanouk of Cambodia
72/05/18–23	Mohamed Siad Barre of Somalia
72/07/28	Mohsin Ahmed Al Aini of the Arab Republic of Yemen
72/11/04	Sihanouk of Cambodia
72/11/07	Santiago Carillo of Spanish Communist Party
72/12/18	Lansana Beavogui of Guinea
73/04/14–16	Sihanouk of Cambodia
*73/06/23	Government delegation of Czechoslovakia
73/07/21	Sihanouk of Cambodia
73/08/01–03	Marien N'gouabi of the Republic of Congo
73/10/28	Todor Zhivkov of Bulgarian People's Republic
74/03/04	H. Boumedienne of Algeria
74/04/12	Sihanouk of Cambodia
74/05/13–15	L. S. Senghor of Senegal
74/09/07	G. Eyadema of Togo
74/09/21–22	Moktar Ould Daddah of Mauritania
74/10/01	H. Al Assad of Syria
74/11/18–21	Salem Rubaya Ali of the Democratic People's Republic of Yemen
74/12/02–06	Sihanouk of Cambodia
74/12/15	Mobutu of Zaire
75/05/21	Sihanouk of Cambodia

75/08/20	Sihanouk of Cambodia
75/10/17–28	Sihanouk of Cambodia
75/12/25	Manuel Pinto Da Costa of Sao Tome and Principe
76/05/14	Moussa Traore of Mali
76/05/21	Ali Bhutto of Pakistan
76/06/04	Didier Ratsiraka of Madagascar
76/07/10	Mathiew Kerekou of Benin
77/04/30	Visit of Arthur Chung of Guyana
77/05/09–11	Visit of El Hadj Omar Bongo of Gabon
77/06/13	Kaysone Phomvihane of Laos
77/08/28	Josip Broz Tito
77/09/15–17	Ndong of Equatorial Guinea
77/09/20–22	U Ne Win of Burma
77/10/07	Pol Pot of Kampuchea
77/12/10	Erich Honecker of East Germany
78/04/21–26	Linden Forbes Sampson Burnham of Guyana
78/04/28–05/01	Bokassa the First, Emperor of Central Africa
78/05/04	France Albert Rene of Seychelles
78/05/05–09	Hua Kuo-feng, People's Republic of China
78/05/14–18	Samora Moises Machel of Mozambique
78/05/20–21	Nicolae Ceausescu of Romania
78/05/25–28	Joachim Yhomby-opango of Congo
78/06/14–16	Habyarimana Juvenal of Rwanda
78/09/07–20	Didier Ratsiraka of Madagascar
78/09/08–10	Ziaur Rahman of Bangladesh
79/03/20	Jean-Baptiste Bagaza of Burundi
79/05/05	Japanese visitors
79/05/20	Sihanouk of Cambodia
79/05/26	Deng Yingchao of China
79/10/09	Sekou Toure of Guinea
79/11/01	Luiz Cabral of Guinea-Bissau
80/04/05	Kenneth David Kaunda of Zambia
80/04/23	Enrico Berlinguer of Italy
80/09/22	France Albert Rene of Seychelles
80/10/08	Ahmed Sekou Toure of Guinea
80/10/09	Robert G. Mugabe of Zimbabwe

d. Interviews

45/12/29	Reporters of *Seoul sinmun*
46/02/11	Talk with Yŏ Un-hyŏng
46/10/10	Interview with *Minju Chosŏn*
48/04/29	South Korean reporters

48/05/03	Talk with Kim Ku
48/05/06	Talk with Hong Myŏng-hŭi
49/08/02	North Korean reporters
50/07/27	Reporter of *Humanite* of France
51/02/11	Reporter of the New China News Agency
51/03/15	P'yŏngnam farmers
51/05/27	International Women's League
53/03/26	P'yŏngnam farmers
62/01/26	Reporters from *Revolution* of Cuba
65/04/19	Sakai Tatsuo and Fuse Michio of *Nihon keizai shinbun*
65/04/21	Iwamoto Kiyoshi of Kyodo News Agency
65/07/06	Reporters from Cuba
65/09/14	Reporters from the United Arab Republic
69/07/01	Iraqi News Agency
69/07/01	Abdel Hamid Ahmed Hanrouche of the United Arab Republic
69/09/02	Reporter from *Kansan Uutiset* of Finland
69/11/22	Ali Balout of Lebanon
*71/09/25	Reporters from *Asahi shinbun* and Kyodo News Agency of Japan
71/10/11	Iraqi journalist delegation
72/01/10	Reporters from *Yomiuri shinbun* of Japan
72/05/14	Japanese Mayors Association
72/05/26	Harrison Salisbury of the *New York Times*
72/06/01	Representatives of the Japanese Communist Party
72/06/21	Selig S. Harrison of the *Washington Post*
*72/09/17	Reporters from *Mainichi shinbun* of Japan
72/10/06	Editor of *Sekai* of Japan
73/09/19	Midorikawa Touru of Iwanami Shoten of Japan
74/01/29	Reporter from *L'Unita* of Italian Communist Party
74/02/22	Chief Editor of *Vecernje Novosti* of Yugoslavia
74/04/25	Chief Editor of *Al Sahafa* of Sudan
74/06/02	Reporter from *Expreso* of Peru
74/06/13	Secretary-general of the Peru-Korea Friendship group
74/06/16	Editorial bureau of *Korea Focus* from the United States
74/08/21	Journalists from Senegal
74/09/01	Journalists from Panama
74/09/18	Reporters from Argentina
74/09/19	Director of *Daho Express* of Dahomey
74/10/09	Reporters from *Burundat* of Ecuador
74/11/04	Reporters from Australia
74/11/06	Reporters from *Al Kabas* of Kuwait

74/12/16	Reporters from Zaire
75/04/13	Chairman of Costa Rica-Korea Friendship group
75/05/29	Journalist of *El Moudjahid* of Algeria
75/05/31	Reporter from AFP
75/08/06	Chief Editor of *Indian Weekly*
75/08/13	Chief Editor of *Expreso* and *Extra* of Peru
75/09/11	Reporter from *La Nouvelle Critique* of France
75/09/28	Reporters from *Yomiuri shinbun* of Japan
75/10/13	Italian International Relations Research Center
75/10/21	Wilfred Burchett of Australia
75/11/06	Midorikawa Touru and Yasue Ryosuke of *Iwanami* and *Sekai* of Japan
75/11/16	Chairman of Research Group of Dahomey
75/11/25	Gomi Mitsuo of *Mainichi shinbun* of Japan
76/03/28	Editor of *Sekai*
76/05/27	Journalists of Pakistan
76/05/29	Editor of *Tanjug*, Yugoslavia
77/04/23	Editor of *Yomiuri shinbun*
77/06/20	Editor of *Le Monde*
77/07/03	N.H.K. reporters
78/10/21	Yasue Ryosuke of *Sekai*
79/06/20	Nepalese reporters
79/06/30	Benin journalists

e. Letters

45/12/20	Letter to Hŏ Hŏn
46/07/07	Railway workers
46/12/13	One million Koreans in Japan
46/12/13	Farmer Kim Che-wŏn for contribution
47/01/20	Kim Hoe-il for his work in railways
48/09/22	Marshal Stalin for Russian troop withdrawal
51/03/17	Marshal Stalin on the economic aid treaty
51/05/19	Businessman Kim Ch'i-hyŏk for contribution
52/04/16	Marshal Stalin for wheat
52/12/02	Watanabe Michio on the fourth anniversary of the republic
53/02/11	Defense Minister Vassilievsky of the Soviet Union
53/02/16	P'eng Teh-huai of the Chinese Volunteer Army
53/02/22	Stalin and Vassilievsky on thirty-fifth anniversary of Russian army
53/03/06	To the Soviet Union on the death of Stalin
53/03/16	Malenkov on the fourth anniversary of the treaty

53/05/11	Peace congress in Paris to end the war
63/08/13	Chou En-lai to ban nuclear weapons
64/10/29	Chou En-lai to ban nuclear weapons
65/01/08	Kim Yong-jung of Washington
67/01/04	Kim Yong-jung of Washington
67/10/28	Open letter to North Korean people

7. EDUCATION, CULTURE, AND ARTS

See also Party and State

45/10/17	Party organ publication
45/11/03	On university
46/03/06	Education sector
46/04/05	Teachers union
46/04/25	*P'yŏngbuk sinbo*
46/05/24	People's culture and arts
46/06/03	Central Party School
46/06/04	*Minju Chosŏn*
46/08/05	First graduation of the Central Party School
46/08/08	Musicians and composers
46/09/15	Inauguration of Kim Il Sung University
46/09/27	National anthem and marching songs
46/09/28	Role of intellectuals (na)
46/10/06	Popularization of athletic programs
46/10/18	Role of scientists and technicians
46/12/05	North Korean News Agency
47/05/29	Broadcasting work
47/06/07	Good party worker
47/07/04	Teachers and students of Pyongyang
47/07/21	College and technical school graduates
47/08/01	Central Party School graduation
47/09/07	Directives to propaganda sections
47/09/16	Literature and arts
47/09/28	Kŭmgangsan cultural retreats
47/10/01	First anniversary of Kim Il Sung University
47/10/11	Government workers
47/10/12	Pyongyang School for Revolutionary Families
48/01/05	Teachers' college reform
48/02/08	National dance
48/05/22	Elimination of illiteracy
48/10/10	Education of national cadres
48/12/11	Revolutionary family school

49/12/28 Physics and mathematics graduates (na)
50/01/28 First graduation at Kim Il Sung University
50/12/24 Writers and artists for the war
51/06/30 Talk with writers and artists
51/12/16 Artist troops performed in Europe
52/04/27 Scientists on their work
52/12/01 Academy of Sciences opening ceremony
57/08/25 Graduation ceremony of Songdo College
58/04/30 Preservation of historical relics (na)
58/11/20 On Communist education
60/11/27 Writers and composers of Ch'ŏllima Age
62/10/16 On general education
63/03/22 Duties of scientists in technical revolution
63/04/18 Reinforcing the educational work
63/11/06 Industrial management textbooks
63/12/30 Role of the social scientists
64/01/03 On Korean language
64/04/22 Encyclopedia and maps
64/11/07 Revolutionary literature and arts
65/02/23 On the reform of higher education
66/05/14 Policy on Korean language
66/10/16 Revolutionary art
68/03/14 Train students for construction (na)
68/06/14 Party's policy on intellectuals
68/10/02 Technical personnel training
69/11/04 Popularization of athletic programs
70/02/17 Role of education, literature, and arts
71/12/27 Socialist pedagogy in education
72/12/05 Science and technology development
73/08/31 Task of Ch'ongnyŏn educators
75/04/10 Universal compulsory education
76/11/28 Cadre education work
*77/09/05 Theses on socialist education
77/09/05–07 Concerning the education theses
78/10/01 Educational work

8. Youth, Women, and Public Health

See also Party and State

45/10/25 Task of women
45/10/29 Youth league
45/11/19 South Korean youth

45/11/26	Patriotic youth
45/12/07	Student participation in the state
45/12/22	For Democratic United Front
45/12/28	Student League into Democratic Youth League
46/01/17	Founding of the Democratic Youth League
46/05/05	For children
46/05/09	On the Women's League
46/05/30	Duty of the youth
46/07/30	Equality of sexes
46/09/06	*Chosŏn yŏsŏng*
46/09/29	Second congress of the Democratic Youth League
47/05/05	Students and youth of Pyongyang
47/05/21	Public health works
47/06/23	World youth meeting
47/10/20	Women's League
48/01/12	Kanggye County social organizations
48/03/19	Public health work
48/06/20	World youth groups
48/11/13	Ideological education of the youth
51/01/18	Role of the youth in the war
51/11/30	Role of public health in the war
56/11/09	Tasks of the Democratic Youth League
58/03/19	Youth in the socialist construction
58/05/04	Public health work (na)
59/04/24	To become true servants (na)
61/04/25	Education of youth and children
61/06/07	Red soldiers of the party (na)
61/11/16	Role of mothers in child education
62/05/03	Improving the press and student education
*64/05/15	Tasks of the League of Socialist Working Youth
65/09/02	On the organization work of the Women's League (na)
66/06/05	On the Youth Corps
66/10/20	Nursery and kindergarten teachers
66/10/20	Preventive medicine (na)
67/06/06	Pharmaceutical industries (na)
67/11/15	Communist attitude of students
68/03/26	Communicable diseases (na)
68/04/13	Youth must become the vanguard
71/02/03	Character of the young people
71/06/06	Congratulatory messages to youth organizations
71/06/24	Youth must takeover
71/10/07	Revolutionizing the women

*74/09/24   Role of the Korean youth in Japan
76/04/29   Upbringing of children
76/06/05   To the members of the Juvenile Corps
77/02/25   League of Socialist Working Youth

9. COMMEMORATION ADDRESSES

a. **New Year's Day**

1946, 1947, 1948, 1949
1950, 1951, 1952, 1953, 1954
1962, 1963, 1964, 1965
1971, 1972, 1973, 1974, 1975, 1976, 1977, 1978, 1979, 1980

b. **May Day**

1946
1952, 1954
1964

c. **National Liberation Day, August 15**

1946, 1947, 1948
1950, 1951, 1952, 1953, 1955
1960, 1962, 1963, 1965

10. PRE-1945 WRITINGS

30/06/30   Path of revolution
31/05/20   On the May 30 incident
31/12/16   Armed struggle
32/04/25   Founding of the guerrilla forces
33/03/11   Underground organizations
33/03/27   Strengthening of youth groups
33/05/10   Fight factionalism
35/03/27   Dissolution of guerrilla bases
36/02/27   Anti-Japanese Communist struggle
36/05/05   Ten-point platform and declaration
37/03/29   Armed forces into Korea
37/06/01   Anti-Japanese proclamation
37/06/04   Fatherland liberation
37/11/10   Task of the Korean Communists
39/04/03   Destroy the Japanese invaders
39/05/20   Fatherland revolution
39/05/22   Restoration of fatherland
40/08/10   Preparation for the fatherland liberation
43/09/15   Learning about Korea

CHRONOLOGICAL INDEX

1930
June 30   Path of revolution

1931
May 20   On May 30 incident
December 16   Armed struggle

1932
April 25   Founding of the guerrilla forces

1933
March 11   Underground organizations
March 27   Strengthening of youth groups
May 10   Fight factionalism

1935
March 27   Dissolution of guerrilla bases

1936
February 27   Anti-Japanese Communist struggle
May 5   Ten-point platform and declaration

1937
March 29   Armed forces into Korea
June 1   Proclamation
June 4   Fatherland liberation
November 10   Tasks of the Korean Communists

1939
April 3   Destroy Japanese invaders
May 20   Fatherland revolution
May 22   Restoration of fatherland

1940
August 10   Preparation for the fatherland liberation

1943
September 15   Learning about Korea

1945
August 20   Preparation for a state
September 20   Building of New Korea
October 3   Political thought: On democracy
October 10   Establish a Communist party
October 13   United front in the provincial party committees

October 13	Establish democratic new Korea
October 14	Work toward the establishment of a state
October 16	Land question
October 17	Party organ publication
October 18	To build a new democratic state
October 25	Task of women
October 29	Youth league
November 3	On university
November 5	Nationalist leaders
November 10	Establishing the state
November 15	Establishing the government
November 17	For Pyongyang Hagwŏn
November 17	Intellectuals and the state
November 19	South Korean youth
November 20	Inspection and security organization workers (na)
November 26	Patriotic youth
November 27	Path for liberated Korea
November 29	Air force in new Korea
December 7	Student participation in the state
*December 17	Organization of the party
December 18	Strengthening of the party
December 20	Letter to Hŏ Hŏn
December 22	For the Democratic United Front
December 27	P'yŏngan Namdo party organization
December 28	Student League into Democratic Youth League
December 29	Reporters of *Seoul sinmun*

1946

January 1	New Year address
January 5	Three Foreign Ministers' Conference (na)
January 12	Democratic and independent state
January 13	Strengthening party rank and file
January 17	Founding of the Democratic Youth League
January 23	P'yŏngnam political committee
*February 8	Founding of the North Korean Provisional People's Committee
February 11	Talk with Yŏ Un-hyŏng
*February 15	Task of the party
February 20	Provisional People's Committee
February 23	Opening of Pyongyang Hagwŏn
February 27	People's security force
February 27	Food problems

March 1	Twenty-seventh anniversary of the March First incident
March 5	Land reform law
March 6	Education sector
March 7	Traitors and collaborators
March 9	Land reform laws
March 22	Restoration of industries
March 23	Twenty-point platform
April 1	State budget and Peasant Bank
April 5	Teachers union
April 8	Communication work
*April 10	Agrarian reform
April 13	Land reform
April 17	Labor heroes
April 20	Hanam party committee
April 21	Hamgyŏng Pukto people's organizations
April 25	*P'yŏngbuk sinbo*
April 29	Military-political cadre
May 1	May Day speech
May 5	For children
May 9	On the Women's League
May 19	For complete independence of Korea
May 21	Pot'ong River works
May 24	People's culture and arts
May 30	Duty of the youth
June 3	Central Party School
June 4	*Minju Chosŏn*
*June 20	On labor laws
June 24	Labor laws
June 26	Korean People's Party
July 1	Central Higher Cadre School
July 7	Railway workers
July 21	Completion of Pot'ong River project
July 22	For the national united front
July 27	North Korean Branch Bureau (na)
*July 29	Merger of two parties
July 30	Equality of sexes
August 5	First graduation of the Central Party School
August 8	Musicians and composers
August 10	Nationalization of major industries
August 15	National Liberation Day speech
*August 29	Party congress: The founding congress
September 6	*Chosŏn yŏsŏng*

September 9	P'yŏngnam party committee
September 15	Inauguration of Kim Il Sung University
September 18	American imperialists
September 25	Second enlarged plenum
September 26	On the Workers' Party of South Korea
September 27	National anthem and marching songs
September 28	Role of intellectuals
September 29	Second congress of the Democratic Youth League
October 6	Popularization of athletic programs
October 7	Revolutionary army
October 10	On electricity in Sakchu County
October 10	Interview with *Minju Chosŏn*
October 18	Role of scientists and technicians
October 29	Central Bank
October 31	Railway transportation
November 1	November 3 election
November 13	People's committee
November 20	Internal security organizations
November 25	Task of the provisional people's committee
December 2	At the fourteenth session of the Standing Committee (na)
December 3	State enterprises management
December 5	North Korean News Agency
December 13	Letter to farmer Kim Che-wŏn for contribution
December 13	One million Koreans in Japan
December 26	Democratic United Front

1947

January 1	New Year address
January 11	People's Committee elections
January 15	Security Cadres Training Center
January 17	Hamgyŏng Pukto party organizations
January 18	Kangwŏndo party organizations
January 20	Letter to Kim Hoe-il for his work in railways
February 3	Powers of the People's Committee (na)
February 7	P'yŏngan Pukto party organizations
February 8	General political situation
*February 19	1947 economic plan
February 20	People's Committee meetings
February 21	First session of the People's Assembly
February 24	North Korean People's Committee
February 28	On state finance

March 5	First anniversary of the land reform
March 8	Basic task of the farmer
*March 15	At the sixth enlarged plenum
March 22	Election results
April 6	Reforestation work
April 8	Standard of government workers
April 14	Transportation works
April 19	Pyongyang Koksan Factory workers
April 25	Central Security Cadres School
April 26	Farm management and government organizations
April 30	Artist-soldiers in the army
May 5	Students and youth of Pyongyang
May 12	1947 economic goals
May 21	Public health works
May 21	Reopening of the U.S.–U.S.S.R. Joint Commission (na)
May 29	Broadcasting work
June 7	Good party worker
June 14	On the democratic interim government
June 20	Law and order in judicial organs
June 23	The world youth meeting
July 4	Teachers and students of Pyongyang
July 21	College and technical school graduates
July 31	Factory party organization on production
August 1	Central Party School graduation
*August 15	On the second anniversary of the Korean liberation
August 15	Two-year democratic construction
August 28	First anniversary of the founding of the party
September 1	Production cooperatives
September 5	State granary work
September 7	Directives to propaganda sections
September 16	Literature and arts
September 28	Kŭmgangsan cultural retreats
September 30	Mountainous regions in P'yŏngan Namdo
October 1	First anniversary of Kim Il Sung University
October 5	Modern People's Army
October 11	Government workers
October 12	Pyongyang School for Revolutionary Families
October 13	Leadership of social organizations
October 20	Women's League
October 26	First security cadre graduation
November 3	First anniversary of the November 3 election
December 1	Currency reform

December 3	Third Hwanghae steel mill
December 21	Second congress of the General Trade Union
December 29	Hŭngnam people's factories

1948

January 1	New Year address
January 5	Teachers' college reform
January 12	Kanggye local party members
January 12	Work of Kanggye County political and social organizations
January 21	People's Army newspapers
January 24	P'yŏngnam party committee conference
January 25	Management of steel industries
*February 6	1948 economic plan
*February 8	Founding of the Korean People's Army
February 8	National dance
February 9	Role of the party in economic development
February 20	Soldiers to sharpshooters
February 21	Central Committee of the party
February 22	Hŭngnam factory
March 9	Oppose South Korean election
March 19	Public health work
*March 28	Party congress: Second congress
March 29	Democratic base for the unification
April 21	Unified government of North and South Korea
April 29	Interviews with South Korean reporters
May 3	Talk with Kim Ku
May 6	Talk with Hong Myŏng-hŭi
May 11	Security Corps conference
May 22	Elimination of illiteracy
June 7	Musan mines
June 18	County people's committee
June 20	World youth groups
June 29	Oppose unilateral election in South Korea
July 8	Fisheries development
July 9	On the constitution of the republic
July 26	North Korean People's Committee
August 7	Thirty-eighth parallel border guards
August 14	National Liberation Day speech
August 23	On election for the Supreme People's Assembly
September 8	On transfer of power
*September 10	Political programs of the republic

September 12   Commemoration of the establishment of the republic
September 19   Security workers
September 22   Letter to Stalin for Russian troop withdrawal
October 10   Education of national cadres
October 14   Army officers and fighting force
October 21   Political work in guard companies
November 13   Ideological education of the youth
November 22   Improve material and cultural lives
November 25   Two-year economic plan
December 11   Revolutionary family school

1949
January 1   New Year address
*February 1   Two-year economic plan
March 3   Kim's travel to Russia
March 20   Kim's travel to Russia for economic aid
April 7   Back from Russia at Pyongyang airport
April 21   Ten-year treaty with the Soviet Union
June 11   Sixth enlarged plenum
August 2   Declaration of the peaceful unification
*September 9   First anniversary of the republic
October 31   Manufacture weapons
November 19   New attitude toward work
December 15   On proletarian internationalism
December 28   Physics and mathematics graduates (na)

1950
January 1   New Year address
January 19   Ch'ŏndogyo Young Friends Party
January 25   Agrarian management, forestry, and fisheries
January 28   First graduation at Kim Il Sung University
February 21   Transportation workers
February 28   Correcting the shortcomings in the economic plan
March 17   First anniversary of the treaty with the U.S.S.R.
May   Struggle to establish a united Korea
*June 26   For victory in the war
June 28   The liberation of Seoul
July 5   Order no. 7
July 8   Repulse the U.S. forces
July 23   Advance to Taejŏn
July 27   Interview with reporter of *Humanite* of France
August 15   Order no. 82
August 15   National Liberation Day address

September 11   Second anniversary of the republic
October 11   Inch'ŏn landing of the U.N. forces
December 9   Liberation of Pyongyang
December 21   War situation and the task of the party
December 24   Writers and artists for the war

1951
January 1   New Year address
January 5   Order no. 7
January 18   Role of the youth in the war
February 8   Order no. 0097
February 11   Interview with reporter of the New China News Agency
February 24   Proclamation on spies
March 8   Congratulatory messages to two soldiers
March 15   Interview with P'yŏngnam farmers
March 17   Letter to Marshal Stalin on the economic aid treaty
March 27   Air force officer Kim Ki-u
May 1   Order no. 310
May 9   Citation for Antong 12th Regiment
May 19   Letter to Kim Ch'i-hyŏk for contribution
May 27   Interview with International Women's League
June 14   Peace Preservation Committee
June 30   Talk with writers and artists
August 15   National Liberation Day speech
August 15   Order no. 461
*November 1   Defects in the organization work
November 2   Improve the organization work
November 5   The October Revolution of Russia
November 30   The role of public health in the war
December 16   Artist troops performed in Europe

1952
January 1   New Year address
February 1   Local organization work
February 8   Order no. 059
*April 4   Security organization cadre works
April 16   Letter to Marshal Stalin for wheat
April 27   Scientists on their work
May 1   May Day address
May 1   Order no. 236
June 18   Cease-fire negotiations
August 15   National Liberation Day speech
August 15   Order no. 474

August 15   Freedom, peace, and liberation of the Korean people
October 25   Chinese participation in the war
December 1   Academy of Sciences opening ceremony
December 2   Letter to Watanabe Michio on the fourth anniversary
*December 15   Organizational and ideological consolidation
December 24   Strengthening the People's Army

1953
January 1   New Year address
February 8   Order no. 73
February 11   Letter to Defense Minister Vassilievsky of the Soviet
                 Union
February 16   Letter to P'eng Teh-huai of the Chinese Volunteer Army
February 22   Letters to Stalin and Vassilievsky on thirty-fifth anni-
                 versary
March 6   Letter to Russia on the death of Stalin
March 10   On the death of Stalin
March 16   Letter to Malenkov on the fourth anniversary of the
                 treaty
March 26   Interview with P'yŏngan farmers
March 31   Exchange of prisoners
May 1   Order no. 269
May 11   Letter to peace congress in Paris to end the war
July 27   Order no. 470
July 28   Cease-fire agreement
*August 5   Three-year economic plan, postwar recovery
August 15   National Liberation Day speech, Order no. 523
August 19   Citation for hero Kim Ch'ang-gŏl
September 10–29   Kim's travel to Russia to express appreciation for
                 aid
October 25   Visit of the Chinese People's Consolidation Corps
November 9   Visit of a Japanese People's Peace and Friendship group
November 12–27   Kim's travel to China for an economic and
                 cultural agreement
*December 20   Economic aid from Communist countries
December 29   Intelligence Corps graduation ceremony (na)

1954
January 1   New Year address
February 8   Order no. 63
February 16   Grain harvest
March 21   Shortcomings in industrial and transportation sectors
March 26   Architects and technicians

May 1	May Day address
May 1	Order no. 220
May 6	Forestry sector
May 11	Tasks of transportation workers
July 12	Hambuk party organizations
September 10	Postwar recovery
November 1	November plenum of the Central Committee (na)
*November 3	Party policy on agricultural management
December 19	P'yŏngnam agricultural management
December 23	Cadres of the People's Army

1955

*April	Political Thought: Character of Korean revolution
*April 1	Class education of party members
*April 1	Political Thought: On bureaucracy
*April 4	Factional struggles within the party
April 15	Political Thought: On Leninism
August 14	National Liberation Day speech
December 28	Political Thought: Self-reliant attitude of *chuch'e*

1956

January 30	Construction architects and builders
February 5	Kaech'ŏn County party organization
April 7	P'yŏngbuk party organization
*April 23	Party congress: Third congress
November 9	Task of the Democratic Youth League
December 13	Upswing in the socialist construction

1957

January 21	Problems of agrarian management
February 14	Commodity circulation and trade
March 26	Hamnam party organizations
April 19	On fisheries
May 11	Hambuk party organizations (na)
July 5	Party organs for economic development
August 2	Mundŏk electoral district speech
August 25	Graduation ceremony of Songdo College
September 11	On machine industries
September 20	Task of the people's power
October 19	Party policy on construction
October 22	Fortieth anniversary of the October Revolution
November	Russian support for the North
November 4–21	Kim's travel to Russia, October Revolution anniversary

*December 5   Pro-Russian speech against factionalists
December 13   Hwanghae farm cooperatives

1958
January 29   Light industry development
February 8   People's Army and the anti-Japanese struggle
February 14   Visit of the government delegation of China
*March 6   Party conference: First party conference
*March 7   On the reform of party work
March 11   For the returning Chinese Volunteer Army
March 19   Youth in the socialist construction
*April 29   Judicial policy of the party
April 30   Hwanghae steel mill
April 30   Preservation of historical relics (na)
May 4   Public health work (na)
May 7   For the veterans of Kilchu Industrial Center (na)
May 11   Yanggang provincial party organizations
June 7   Consumer goods production and exchange
*June 11   First five-year economic plan
June 23   P'yŏngbuk party cadres
June 23   Veterans of the Sinŭiju Industrial Center (na)
August 9   City and county people's committee
August 12   Haeju-Hasŏng railway
August 18   Graduation ceremony of the Central Party School
August 30   Sup'ung power station
September 8   Tenth anniversary of the republic
September 16   Against passivism and conservatism in construction
October 30   Military school instructors (na)
November 20   On Communist education
November 21–December 10   Trip to China and Vietnam
December 25   For higher quality in construction

1959
*January 5   Agricultural cooperatives
January 9   Agrarian management (na)
February 23   Relations with the Soviet Union
February 25   Kim's travel to Russia for the Twenty-first Congress of
                   the CPSU
February 26   On the methods of party work
March 16   Livelihood of veterans
March 23   Hambuk party organizations
April 24   To become true servants in public health work (na)
June 11   On fisheries

*September 4   Hwanghae steel mill party committee
September 26   Relations with China
October 17   Veterans must set examples
*December 4   Shortcomings in economic construction

1960
February 8   Agrarian management
February 18   Kangsŏ County agrarian management
*February 23   Role of local party in agrarian management
August 11   On technical revolution
August 14   National Liberation Day speech
August 22   Ch'ŏllima movement
August 25   Talk with 109th Division
September 1   Chemical industry
September 8   Political work in the People's Army (na)
November 27   Writers and composers of the Ch'ŏllima Age
December 2   Visit of the Cuban economic mission (na)

1961
January 23   Work of the local party organizations
April 7   Orchards at Pukch'ŏng
April 25   Education of youth and children
May 7   Hamhŭng chemical industry (na)
June 7   Red soldiers of the party in public health work (na)
*September 11   Party congress: Fourth congress
November 16   Role of mothers in child education
December 1   To conquer six highlands
December 15   Taean electric factory
December 16   Taean industrial management system
*December 18   County Cooperative Farm Management Committee
December 23   Coal industry at Anju coal mines

1962
January 1   New Year address
January 6   Light industry and quality of manufactured goods
January 19   Sinch'ŏn Veterans Food Factory (na)
January 22   Hwangnam County People's Committee
January 26   Interview with reporters from *Revolution* of Cuba
February 1   Haeju agricultural cooperatives
February 12   Financial bank organizations
February 14   80,000-ton fisheries
*March 8   Ideological work against revisionism
April 8   Consumer goods

May 3	Improving the press and student education
August 8	Urbanization problems
August 15	National Liberation Day speech
August 30	Hwanghae steel mill leadership reform
September 5	City management
September 24	Mining industries
October 16	On general education
*October 23	Tasks of the republic
November 9	Taean work system
November 13	P'yŏngnam County cooperative farm management system

1963

January 1	New Year address
January 7	Manpower support for farm and construction
*February 8	Fifteenth anniversary of the People's Army
March 22	Duties of scientists in technical revolution
April 18	Reinforcing the educational work
April 27	On the central county party committee
August 13	Letter to Chou En-lai to ban nuclear weapons
August 15	National Liberation Day speech, fifteenth anniversary speech
August 16	Yanggang provincial party organizations
October 5	Self-defense policy in national defense
November 6	Industrial management textbooks
November 28	Banking system
December 30	Role of social scientists

1964

January 1	New Year address
January 3	On Korean language
January 9	On construction industry
January 22	Transportation work
February 20	Tractor and agrarian technical revolution (na)
*February 25	Theses on the socialist rural question
February 27	Reunification of the country
April 22	Encyclopedia and maps
May 1	May Day address
*May 15	Tasks of the League of Socialist Working Youth
*June 23	Delegates to the economic seminar in Pyongyang
June 26	Union of Agricultural Working People and the Trade Unions
September 9	Sixteenth anniversary of the founding of the republic

October 23–28 Visit of Modibo Keita of Mali
October 29   Letter to Chou En-lai to ban nuclear weapons
November 1–4 Visit of Sukarno of Indonesia
November 7   Revolutionary literature and arts
December 19   Improving economic management

1965
January 1   New Year address
January 3   Metal and chemical industries
January 8   Letter to Kim Yong-jung of Washington
January 11–16 Hwanghae steel mill
January 22   Ŭnyul mines ingot production
January 28   Trade union works and foreign trade
January 30   Kangsŏn steel mill
February 11–14 Visit of Alexei N. Kosygin of the Soviet Union
February 23   On the reform of higher education
March 26   Works of the State Construction Commission
*April 14   Kim's travel to Indonesia: Ali Archam Academy speech
April 19   Interview with Sakai and Fuse of *Nihon keizai shinbun*
April 21   Interview with Iwamoto Kiyoshi of Kyodo News Agency
May 25   Leaders of the Supreme People's Assembly
July 1   Strengthening the party life
July 6   Interview with reporters from Cuba
August 15   National Liberation Day speech
August 26–29 Visit of Massamba Deba of Congo, Brazzaville
September 2   On the organization work of the Women's League
September 14 Interview with reporters from the United Arab Republic
September 23 Greater enthusiasm for economic work
October 4–10 Visit of Sihanouk of Cambodia
*October 10   Twentieth anniversary of the party
November 15–17 Strengthening the party work

1966
May 14   Policy on Korean language
June 5   On the Youth Corps
*October 5   Party conference: Second party conference
October 16   Revolutionary art
*October 18   Elimination of formalism and bureaucracy
October 20   Nursery and kindergarten teachers
October 20   Preventive medicine (na)
October 26   Visit of the Cuban government delegation

1967
January 4   Letter to Kim Yong-jung of Washington
February 2   Leaders of agrarian sectors
*May 25   Political Thought: Transition from capitalism to social-
                   ism
June 6   Pharmaceutical industries (na)
June 13   Hamhŭng Veterans Factory
July 3   Manpower administration to work 480 minutes
August 12   Anti-U.S. and anti-imperialist struggles
October 24   Visit of Moktar Ould Daddah of Mauritania
October 28   Open letter to North Korean people
November 15   Communist attitude of students
November 17   Congratulatory messages for 1967 economic goals
*December 16   Political program of the republic
December 25   Congratulating Sinhŭng mine workers

1968
February 2   Capture of *Pueblo*
February 8   Twentieth anniversary of the People's Army
February 14   Small group management system
February 16   Congratulatory messages to farm workers
March 14   Train students for construction (na)
March 26   Communicable diseases (na)
April 13   Youth must become the vanguard
May 11   Ch'ŏllima workteam movement
*May 27   Cadre policy of the party
June 4–5   Fisheries
June 14   Party's policy on intellectuals
June 22–24   Visit of Julius K. Nyerere of Tanzania
August 25   Visit of Miyamoto Kenji of the Japanese Communist
                   Party
*September 7   Twentieth anniversary of the founding of the republic
September 24   Role of the counties in the countryside
October 2   Technical personnel training
October 8   Cause of the Asian-African-Latin American peoples
October 31   Role of finances
November 16   Manpower administration in the party
November 16   On relieving the strain in transportation

1969
February 7   Socialist agrarian construction
February 15   Manpower administration
*March 1   Theoretical problems of the socialist economy

June 30   Care for state properties and fisheries
July 1   Interview with Abdel Hamid Ahmed Hanrouche of the UAR
July 1   Interview with Iraqi News Agency
July 2   Uniform planning system
September 2   Interview with reporter from *Kansan Uutiset* of Finland
September 18   International journalists' conference
September 27   Visit of N. Adassi of Syria
October 11   Experiences of the socialist revolution
October 21   Reform in the statistics work
November 4   Popularizing the athletic programs
November 19   Visit of Reidar Larsen of the Norwegian Communist Party
November 22   Interview with Ali Balout of Lebanon

1970
February 17   Role of education, literature, and arts
February 27   Local industry and consumer goods
March 31   Poultry industry
April 5–7   Visit of Chou En-lai of China
April 16   Centenary of Lenin's birth
June 15   Visit of Sihanouk of Cambodia
August 13–16   Visit of G. M. Nimeri of Sudan
*November 2   Party congress: Fifth congress

1971
January 1   New Year address
January 28   Korean residents in Japan
February 3   Character of the young people
February 12   Tractor operators in rural areas
June 6   Messages to youth organizations
June 6   Visit of Carlos A. Orego of Chilean Socialist Party
June 9–15   Visit of Nicolae Ceausescu of Romania
June 24   Youth must takeover
August 6   Visit of Sihanouk of Cambodia
*September 25 and October 8   Interview with reporters from *Asahi shinbun* and Kyodo News Agency
October 7   Revolutionizing the women
October 11   Interview with Iraqi journalist delegation
November 15   Third plenum of the Central Committee (na)
*December 2   Training of party cadres
December 14   Trade unions in the socialist construction
December 27   Socialist pedagogy in education

1972

January 1	New Year address
January 10	Interview with *Yomiuri shinbun* of Japan
February 16	Task of the Union of Agricultural Working People
April 5	Visit of Sihanouk of Cambodia
May 14	Interview with Japanese Mayors Association
May 18–23	Visit of Mohamed Siad Barre of Somalia
May 26	Interview with Harrison Salisbury of the *New York Times*
June 1	Interview with representatives of the Japanese Communist Party
June 21	Interview with Selig S. Harrison of the *Washington Post*
June 30	On heat supply
July 1	Fourth plenum of the Central Committee (na)
July 28	Visit of Mohsin Ahmed Al Aini of the Arab Republic of Yemen
*September 17	Interview with reporters from *Mainichi shinbun* of Japan
October 6	Interview with editor of *Sekai* of Japan
October 23	Fifth plenum of the Central Committee (na)
November 4	Visit of Sihanouk of Cambodia
November 7	Visit of Santiago Carillo of Spanish Communist Party
December 5	Science and technology development
December 18	Visit of Lansana Beavogui of Guinea
*December 25	Review of the socialist system
December 27	Constitution of the republic

1973

January 1	New Year address
*February 1	Materialistic incentives and management
February 8	Twentieth anniversary of the People's Army
*February 21	Three revolutions in farm villages
March 14	Ideological, technical, and cultural revolution
April 14–16	Visit of Sihanouk of Cambodia
*June 23	Visit of the government delegation of Czechoslovakia
*June 25	Five-point reunification plan
July 21	Visit of Sihanouk of Cambodia
August 1–3	Visit of Marien N'gouabi of the Republic of Congo
August 9	On agricultural production
August 31	Tasks of Ch'ongnyŏn educators
September 9	Twenty-fifth anniversary of the republic
September 19	Interview with Midorikawa Touru of Iwanami Shoten of Japan

October 11	Strengthening of the company units of the army
October 28	Visit of Todor Zhivkov of Bulgarian People's Republic

1974

January 1	New Year address
*January 10	Building of the socialist countryside
January 14	*Ri* party secretaries
January 29	Interview with reporter from *L'Unita* of Italian Communist Party
February 11	General mobilization (na)
February 22	Interview with chief editor of *Vecernje Novosti* of Yugoslavia
March 4	Visit of H. Boumedienne of Algeria
March 7	New heights in economic construction
April 12	Visit of Sihanouk of Cambodia
April 25	Interview with chief editor of *Al Sahafa* of Sudan
May 13–15	Visit of L. S. Senghor of Senegal
June 2	Interview with reporter from *Expreso* of Peru
June 13	Interview with the Peru-Korea Friendship group
June 16	Interview with editorial bureau of *Korea Focus* of the U.S.A.
July 31	Strengthening of the party work
August 21	Interview with journalists from Senegal
September 1	Interview with journalists from Panama
September 7	Visit of G. Eyadema of Togo
September 18	Interview with reporters from Argentina
September 19	Interview with director of *Daho Express* of Dahomey
September 21–22	Visit of Moktar Ould Daddah of Mauritania
*September 24	Role of the Korean youth in Japan
October 1	Visit of H. Al Assad of Syria
October 9	Interview with reporters from *Burundat* of Ecuador
November 4	Interview with reporters from Australia
November 6	Interview with reporters from *Al Kabas* of Kuwait
November 18–21	Visit of Salem Rubaya Ali of the DPR of Yemen
*November 29	Problems in agrarian theses
December 2–6	Visit of Sihanouk of Cambodia
December 15	Visit of Mobutu of Zaire
December 16	Interview with reporters from Zaire

1975

January 1	New Year address
January 15	Eight million tons of grain
February 17	Tenth session of the Central Committee (na)

*March 3	Development of three revolutions
April 8	Local budget system
April 10	Universal compulsory education
April 13	Interview with chairman of Costa Rica-Korea Friendship group
April 18–25	Kim's travel to China to visit Mao Tse-tung
May 21	Visit of Sihanouk of Cambodia
May 22–26	Kim's travel to Romania to visit N. Ceausescu
May 26–28	Kim's travel to Algeria to visit H. Boumedienne
May 29	Interview with a journalist of *El Moudjahid* of Algeria
May 31	Interview with a reporter from AFP
May 31	Kim's travel to Mauritania to visit Moktar Ould Daddah
June 2–5	Kim's travel to Bulgaria to visit T. Zhivkov
June 6–9	Kim's travel to Yugoslavia to visit J. Tito
August 6	Interview with chief editor of *Indian Weekly*
August 13	Interview with chief editor of *Expreso* and *Extra* of Peru
August 20	Visit of Sihanouk of Cambodia
September 11	Interview with reporter from *La Nouvelle Critique* of France
September 28	Interview with reporters from *Yomiuri shinbun* of Japan
*October 9	Thirtieth anniversary of the party
October 10	Concluding remarks at the anniversary
October 13	Interview with Italian International Relations Research Center
October 17–28	Visit of Sihanouk of Cambodia
October 21	Interview with Wilfred Burchett of Australia
November 6	Interview with Midorikawa and Yasue of *Iwanami* and *Sekai*
November 16	Interview with chairman of Research Group of Dahomey
November 21	Eleventh plenum of the Central Committee (na)
November 25	Interview with Gomi Mitsuo of *Mainichi shinbun* of Japan
December 16	The nonalignment movement
December 25	Visit of Manuel Pinto Da Costa of Sao Tome and Principe

1976
January 1	New Year address
March 28	Interview with editor of *Sekai*

April 29	Upbringing of children
May 14	Visit of Moussa Traore of Mali
May 21	Visit of Ali Bhutto of Pakistan
May 27	Interview with journalists of Pakistan
May 29	Interview with editor of *Tanjug*, Yugoslavia
June 4	Visit of Didier Ratsiraka of Madagascar
June 5	To the members of the Juvenile Corps
July 7	Financial operation in the rural areas
July 10	Visit of Mathiew Kerekou of Benin
October 14	Nature remaking and ten million tons of grain
November 28	Cadre education work

1977

January 1	New Year address
February 25	League of Socialist Working Youth
April 5	To prevent drought damages
April 23	Interview with editor of *Yomiuri shinbun*
*April 29	On the land law
April 30	Visit of Arthur Chung of Guyana
May 9–11	Visit of El Hadj Omar Bongo of Gabon
June 13	Visit of Kaysone Phomvihane of Laos
June 20	Interview with editor of *Le Monde*
July 3	Interview with N.H.K. reporters
July 19	Development of the machine industry
August 20	Further development of machine industries
August 28	Visit of Josip Broz Tito
*September 5	Theses on socialist education
September 5–7	Concerning the education theses
September 15–17	Visit of Ndong of Equatorial Guinea
September 20–22	Visit of U Ne Win of Burma
October 7	Visit of Pol Pot of Kampuchea
November 30	People's Army and political work
December 10	Visit of Erich Honecker of East Germany
December 13	Concluding remarks at fifteenth plenary meeting (na)
*December 15	On the people's government
December 17	On the second seven-year plan

1978

January 1	New Year address
January 27	Agricultural production
April 21–26	Visit of Linden Forbes Sampson Burnham of Guyana
April 28–May 1	Visit of Bokassa the First, Emperor of Central Africa
May 4	Visit of France Albert Rene of Seychelles

May 5–9	Visit of Hua Kuo-feng, People's Republic of China
May 14–18	Visit of Samora Moises Machel of Mozambique
May 20–21	Visit of Nicolae Ceausescu of Romania
May 25–28	Visit of Joachim Yhomby-opango of Congo
June 14–16	Visit of Habyarimana Juvenal of Rwanda
July 28	Agrarian problems
September 7 and 20	Visit of Didier Ratsiraka of Madagascar
September 8–10	Visit of Ziaur Rahman of Bangladesh
*September 9	Thirtieth anniversary of the republic
October 1	Educational work
October 21	Interview with Yasue Ryosuke of *Sekai*
December 23	Financial management

1979

January 1	New Year address
January 11	Socialist agriculture
March 20	Visit of Jean-Baptiste Bagaza of Burundi
May 5	Japanese visitors
May 20	Visit of Samdech Norodom Sihanouk
May 26	Visit of Deng Yingchao of China
June 19	Interview with Nepalese journalists
June 30	Interview with journalists from Benin
*September 27	Socialist labor law
October 9	Visit of Sekou Toure of Guinea
November 1	Visit of Luiz Cabral of Guinea-Bissau

1980

January 1	New Year address
April 5	Visit of Kenneth David Kaunda of Zambia
April 23	Visit of Enrico Berlinguer of Italy
May 12	Travel to Romania
September 22	Visit of France Albert Rene of Seychelles
October 8	Visit of Ahmed Sekou Toure of Guinea
October 9	Visit of Robert G. Mugabe of Zimbabwe
*October 10	Report to sixth party congress

NOTES

1. *Kim Il Sung sŏnjip, che sagwŏn* (Pyongyang: Chosŏn Nodongdang Ch'ulp'ansa, 1953). The last article in this selection is dated May 11, 1953; the book was published July 31, 1953

2. *Chŏngch'i sajŏn* (Pyongyang: Sahoe Kwahak Ch'ulp'ansa, 1973).

3. *Kim Il Sung sŏnjip*, 2d ed., 6 vols. (Pyongyang: Chosŏn Nodongdang

Ch'ulp'ansa, 1960–1964). Compare the first and second editions of Kim's selected works, for example, the first volumes of *Kim Il Sung sŏnjip*, published in 1953 and 1960.

4. *Kim Il Sung chŏjak sŏnjip*, 2 vols. (Pyongyang: Chosŏn Nodongdang Ch'ulp'ansa, 1967–1968).

5. The latest volume is the seventh, covering the period from January 10, 1974, to December 17, 1977. It was published in 1978 in Korean and in English in 1979.

6. *Kim Il Sung Chŏjakchip*, 4 vols. (Pyongyang: Chosŏn Nodongdang Ch'ulp'ansa, 1979).

7. *Kin Nichi-sei senshu*, 3 vols. (Tokyo: Sanichi Shobo, 1952).

8. *Kim Ir Sen: Izbrannye stat'i i rechi* (Moscow: Gospolitizdat, 1962).

9. *Chin Jih-cheng hsuan-chi*, vols. 4–6 (Peking: Jen-min Ch'upan-she, 1953).

10. *Kim Il Sung, Selected Works* (Pyongyang: Foreign Languages Publishing House, 1965).

11. *For the Independent Peaceful Reunification of Korea*, rev. ed. (New York: Guardian Associates, 1976).

12. *Chayuwa tongnip ŭl wihan choson inmin ŭi chŏngŭi ŭi choguk haebang chŏnjaeng* (Pyongyang: Chosŏn Nodongdang Ch'ulp'ansa, 1954).

13. *On Juche in Our Revolution*, 2 vols. (Pyongyang: Foreign Languages Publishing House, 1975). For the latest Korean version, including some revisions, see *Chuch'e sasang e taehayŏ* (Pyongyang: Chosŏn Nodongdang Ch'ulp'ansa, 1977).

14. See, for example, *Ch'ŏngsonyŏn saŏp e taehayŏ* (Pyongyang: Chosŏn Nodongdang Ch'ulp'ansa, 1966); *Ch'ŏngsonyŏn saŏpkwa sahoe chuŭi nodong ch'ŏngnyŏn tongmaeng ŭi immu e taehayŏ*, 2 vols. (Pyongyang: Chosŏn Nodongdang Ch'ulp'ansa, 1969); *The Youth Must Takeover the Revolution and Carry It Forward* (Pyongyang: Foreign Languages Publishing House, 1976).

15. Compare, for example, *Namchoson hyŏngmyŏng kwa choguk t'ongil e taehayŏ* and *For the Independent Peaceful Reunification of the Country*.

16. *Oeguk kijadŭl i chegihan chilmun e taedap*, 2 vols. (Pyongyang: Chosŏn Nodongdang Ch'ulp'ansa, 1976).

17. *Kim Il Sung tongji ŭi chuyo munhŏnjip*, 3 vols. (n.p.: Sahoe Kwahaksa, 1971).

18. *Choson hyŏngmyŏng ŭi chillo* (Pyongyang: Chosŏn Nodongdang Ch'ulp'ansa, 1978).

19. *Kim Il Sung, Selected Works* (Pyongyang: Foreign Languages Publishing House, 1975), 4: 354–380.

2

The Workers' Party of Korea 1946–1980

PARTY CONGRESSES AND CONFERENCES AND CENTRAL COMMITTEE PLENUMS

The highest party organization is the party congress, but since it is supposed to meet only once in four years (less often in practice) the Central Committee of the party manages the work of the party between congresses. The bylaws of the first party congress stipulated annual party congresses,[1] but this rule was never followed and was later amended. Daily activities of the party are administered by secretaries, and policies are directed by the Political Committee, at times known as the Standing Committee, of the Central Committee. There are three other committees, the Inspection Committee, the Military Committee and the Central Auditing Committee. The Inspection Committee is organized by the Central Committee and enforces party rules and regulations and supervises party activities. The Military Committee sets policies on military affairs. The Central Auditing Committee is organized, and its members elected, by the party congress; it reviews the financial affairs of the party.

The bylaws of the party are specific in enumerating the functions of the party congress. The congress hears, discusses, and approves the reports of the Central Committee, the Central Auditing Committee, and other central party organizations. It has the power to amend the bylaws and to set the basic policy of the party. The party congress also elects the members of the Central Committee and the Central Auditing Committee. The members of the Inspection Committee are elected by the Central Committee. Information on the Military Committee was never revealed.

The Central Committee is to meet once every six months. The first bylaws stipulated that the committee meet once in three months. This was later amended to once in four months, but these provisions were seldom followed. When it is considered necessary, the Central Committee can convene party conferences between party congresses to discuss pressing problems and can dismiss the delinquent and elect new members of the Central Committee. However, such expulsion or addition of members can not exceed one-fifth of the total membership of the Central Committee. The North Koreans have not reported any such expulsion or addition at either of the two party conferences they have had.

The party has, so far, held six congresses: the first in August 1946, the second in March 1948, the third in April 1956, the fourth in September 1961, the fifth in November 1970, and the sixth in October 1980. The second congress was held less than two years after the first, but the third congress was not held until eight years after the second. The Korean war explains the large gap. The fourth congress was held five years after the third, the closest approximation of the four-year rule. The party congresses have followed closely the completion of the economic plans in the North, for example, the three-year plan from the end of the war to 1956 and the five-year plan from 1957 to 1961. The fifth congress, held in 1970, was due in part to the extension of the seven-year economic plan of 1961–1967 to ten years, or to 1970. At the time of each party congress, the party launched a new economic plan and followed the practice of holding a party congress at the completion of the plan. The fifth congress launched a six-year economic plan ending in 1976. The second seven-year plan of 1978–1984 is the first major economic plan launched without a party congress.

As the party grew, each successive party congress was held for longer duration than the previous one until the fifth congress; the first congress was held for three days, the second for four days, the third for seven days, the fourth for eight days, the fifth for twelve days, and the sixth congress was held for four days. Each party congress heard a lengthy report by the chairman of the party reviewing the work of the party. There was also a report by the chairman of the Inspection Committee and the unveiling of a new economic plan. New members of the Central Committee and the Central Auditing Committee were elected, but in general the party congresses unanimously approved prepared lists of the members of these committees. The major portion of each party congress has been spent in discussion of the chairman's review of party activities by various delegates to the congress. Over the years, the discussion became lengthier and the discussants more numerous.

The North Koreans claim October 10, 1945,[2] as the date of the founding of the Workers' Party of Korea, but this is a bit misleading and needs explanation. The founding congress of the North Korean Branch Bureau of the Korean Communist Party was held from October 10 to 13, 1945. It was the merger at a meeting held from August 28 to 30, 1946, of this

Branch Bureau and another party, the New Democratic Party, that created what was known as the Workers' Party of North Korea. A similar process took place in the South. Three parties, the Korean Communist Party, the New Democratic Party, and the People's Party, merged to found the Workers' Party of South Korea on November 23–24, 1946. The merger of the two resulting parties created the Workers' Party of Korea in 1949. Since Communist activities were outlawed in the South and the Workers' Party of South Korea was an underground organization and eventually fled to the North, the unified party represented the absorption of the South Korean organization by the Workers' Party of North Korea more than a merger of equals. The official merger was not made until June 11, 1949, at the sixth enlarged plenum of the Workers' Party of North Korea.[3] For a long time, the North Koreans claimed the founding congress of the Workers' Party of North Korea in August 1946 to be the founding of the Workers' Party of Korea, but since the mid-sixties they have backdated the founding to October 10, 1945.

Two party conferences have been held, one in March 1958 between the third and fourth party congresses and another in October 1966 between the fourth and fifth party congresses. The significance of the first party conference was in the strengthening of the party ranks by elimination of several factional elements, although no official expulsions from or additions to the membership were announced. It also signified the rapid realization of the goals of the first five-year plan. The second party conference was held to declare the self-reliance and independent position of North Korea in international relations, particularly in the Sino-Soviet dispute. Another reason for the second conference was to report the three-year extension of the seven-year economic plan, which failed to meet its goal in seven years. The conference also adopted a resolution in support of the struggle of the Vietnamese people.

The bylaws of the party, as amended at the time of the third party congress, stipulated that the agenda of the party congress must be announced two months before the congress convenes. This rule was later amended at the time of the fourth party congress in September 1961 to three months, and the amended rule was followed at the fifth party congress. The records of the party congresses and conferences are published in pamphlet or book form shortly after each congress. Except for the first two congresses, source materials for the congresses and conferences are available in many languages.

In contrast to the party congresses and conferences, the agendas for the Central Committee meetings are not announced. Most of the agendas are later reported in the party organ, but some are kept secret. Except for reports to the party congresses, the agendas and meetings of the Central Auditing Committee and the Inspection Committee are never announced or reported.

The Central Committee of the first party met twelve times from August 1946 to February 1948. The bylaws of the first congress stipulated that the Central Committee meet at least once in three months (Article 16). It met eight times in 1947, most frequent meeting in any year. The agendas for all meetings except the fifth and ninth plenums are known. Even the exact dates of the fifth and ninth plenums are unknown. The fifth plenum was held sometime in February and March of 1947, and the ninth plenum was held sometime between July and September of the same year.

The Central Committee of the second party met seventeen times from March 1948 to December 1955. After the merger of the North and South Korean parties in June 1949, the Central Committee meetings were called joint plenums until after the Korean war. During the war, from June 1950 to July 1953, only three plenums were held, and from 1954 each plenum was referred to according to the month in which it was held, for example, the March plenum, which was held March 21–23, 1954. This practice continued throughout the remainder of the second party period and during the third party. The agendas of all plenums of the second party are known except that of the fourth plenum, which was held sometime in October 1948 and January 1949.

The Central Committee of the third party met thirteen times from April 1956 to September 1961, and this committee was perhaps most consistent in holding its meetings, averaging three per year. Agendas for every plenum of the committee are known except one, the August plenum of 1956. It is commonly alleged that a group of antiparty factionalists was purged at this time, and North Korean sources later revealed that this plenum discussed the expulsion of antirevolutionary elements from the party.[4] Later sources deleted that portion of the agenda and merely listed the report of the government delegation on its trip abroad.

The Central Committee of the fourth party met twenty times from September 1961 to December 1969, averaging about two meetings per year. This committee reverted to the practice of numbering its meetings in chronological order. Agendas for three plenums were not announced. These are the fourth plenum, which was held sometime in the summer of 1962, and the fifteenth and sixteenth plenums, which were held in the winter of 1966 and the spring of 1967. There is no clue to the secrecy of the fourth plenum, but the fifteenth and sixteenth plenums must have concentrated on discussion of the expulsion of many generals and party functionaries because it was shortly after these two plenums that many partisans and generals of Kim Il Sung's own group were expelled from the party.[5]

The Central Committee of the fifth party met twenty times from November 1970 to October 1980 and more or less regularized its meetings to twice per year in the spring and the autumn. It met three times in 1972, but only once the following year. For reasons not yet clear, the agenda for the ninth plenary meeting, held in the autumn of 1974, was not announced. Speculation centers on the work of the three-revolution workteam movement and more prominently on the problem of succession.

The Central Committee meetings are attended by the members and candidate members of the committee. The members of the Inspection Committee and Central Auditing Committee also participate in the meetings. Depending upon the agenda and subjects of discussion, members of the party who are directly involved in the matter under discussion are invited to participate in the meetings. For an enlarged plenum, representatives of government organizations, such as cabinet ministers, members of the Standing Committee of the Supreme People's Assembly, and military personnel also participate in the meetings. However, only regular members of the Central Committee have the right to vote in the meetings. In general, many decisions are made before the meetings and voted unanimously. The Central Committee meetings are held for three to four days, and speeches are made on the subjects on the agenda by leaders of the party. The participants at the meetings discuss the problems in support of the major speech made on the subject.

In general, the plenums of the Central Committee discuss important matters of the party and the state, and the agendas of the meetings reflect the pressing issues of the time. Those meetings where the agenda and the meeting itself are kept secret may have involved more important, if not controversial, issues facing the party. However, there have been few of these compared to the total number of meetings of the Central Committees. The agendas of only eight of eighty plenums have been kept secret. It is possible to make rational conjectures on some of the agendas that are kept secret, such as the August plenum of the third Central Committee, when the expulsion of antiparty reactionaries was discussed, and the fifteenth and sixteenth plenums of the fourth Central Committee, when a large number of generals were expelled from the party.

Some of the agendas of the Standing Committee have been made public after the meetings, but such information is hard to collect systematically. A few agendas of the Standing Committee of the first and third Central Committees are cited in the notes to this chapter to give some idea of the nature of its sessions. In general, the agendas of the Standing

Committee and Political Committee of the Central Committee are kept secret.

At the time of the sixth party congress in October 1980, many provisions of the party bylaws were amended, and while the text of the new bylaws was not made public, a number of changes were discernible immediately. The most obvious were the changes in the names of central organizations of the party. For example, the Political Committee was renamed the Politbureau, and the Standing Committee within the Political Committee was named the Presidium, not to be confused with the Standing Committee of the Supreme People's Assembly. Other committees were renamed commissions; for example, the Inspection Committee became the Control Commission, the Central Auditing Committee was changed to Central Auditing Commission, and the Military Committee was renamed the Military Commission. For the first time, they also revealed the members of the Military Commission.

In addition to the top-level organizational changes, there must have been a number of changes that were long overdue, such as the incorporation of the *chuch'e* idea into the party bylaws, provisions for joint meetings of the Politbureau and the Central People's Committee of the state, recomposition of the party rank and file with workers and intellectuals, and the succession problems. However, these changes will not become clear until after the complete text of the new bylaws is made public.

AGENDAS

The agendas are arranged in chronological order under the following headings:

Korean Communist Party
1. North Korea
   First to eighth plenums of the North Korean Branch Bureau
2. South Korea
   First to sixth plenums of the Korean Communist Party

Workers' Party of Korea
1. Period of the First Congress of the Workers' Party of Korea, August 1946–March 1948
   Party congress and twelve plenums of the Central Committee
2. Period of the Second Congress of the Workers' Party of Korea, March 1948–April 1956
   Party congress and seventeen plenums of the Central Committee

3. Period of the Third Congress of the Workers' Party of Korea, April 1956–September 1961
   Party congress, first party conference, and fourteen plenums of the Central Committee
4. Period of the Fourth Congress of the Workers' Party of Korea, September 1961–October 1970
   Party congress, second party conference, and twenty plenums of the Central Committee
5. Period of the Fifth Congress of the Workers' Party of Korea, October 1970–October 1980
   Party congress and nineteen plenums of the Central Committee
6. Period of the Sixth Congress of the Workers' Party of Korea, October 1980–

The following abbreviations are used in the agendas:

CC	Central Committee (of the Workers' Party of Korea)
8CC	Eighth plenum of the Central Committee
KCP	Korean Communist Party
NKBB	North Korean Branch Bureau (of the Korean Communist Party)
SC	Standing Committee (of the Central Committee)
WPK	Workers' Party of Korea
5WPK	Fifth Congress of the Workers' Party of Korea
5WPK-8CC	Eighth plenum of the Central Committee of the Fifth Party Congress of the Workers' Party of Korea
WPSK	Workers' Party of South Korea

KOREAN COMMUNIST PARTY
Period of the Korean Communist Party, August 1945–November 1946.

1. North Korea
NKBB-1. October 10–13, 1945.
Founding Congress of the North Korean Branch Bureau of the Korean Communist Party.

North Korean sources[6] claim this as the founding congress of the Workers' Party of Korea. According to this version, seventy representatives participated and the agenda included:
a. Report of Kim Il Sung on organizational problems.
b. Election of the members (17) of the Organization Committee.

South Korean sources of the late 1940s reported that this meeting was held on October 13, 1945, and was attended by the leaders of the five northern provinces of the Korean Communist Party. The agenda included:

a. Founding of the North Korean Branch Bureau of the Korean Communist Party. (The bureau was recognized by the headquarters of the Korean Communist Party in Seoul on October 23, 1945.)
b. Election of party secretaries, Hyŏn Chun-hyŏk and O Ki-sŏp.

NKBB-2. November 15, 1945.
Second Enlarged Plenum of the North Korean Branch Bureau of the Korean Communist Party.

a. Problems of enlarging and strengthening the Democratic National United Front.
b. Reorganization of the Communist Youth League into a Democratic Youth League.
c. Election of party secretary. (Hyŏn was assassinated and Kim Yong-bŏm was elected to succeed Hyŏn as secretary.)

NKBB-3. December 17–18, 1945.
Third Enlarged Plenum of the North Korean Branch Bureau of the Korean Communist Party.

a. Report of Kim Il Sung on the errors and shortcomings of the Communist activities in North Korea.
b. Election of party secretary. (Kim Il Sung was elected as Secretary.)

NKBB-4. February 15, 1946.
Fourth Enlarged Plenum of the North Korean Branch Bureau of the Korean Communist Party.

Strengthening of the Interim People's Committee of North Korea.

NKBB-5. Date unknown.
Fifth Plenum of the North Korean Branch Bureau of the Korean Communist Party.

No data available.[7]

NKBB-6. April 10, 1946.
Sixth Enlarged Plenum of the North Korean Branch Bureau of the Korean Communist Party.

Report of Kim Il Sung: General summation of the land reform and the future tasks.

NKBB-7. June 22–23, 1946.
Seventh Enlarged Plenum of the North Korean Branch Bureau of the Korean Communist Party.

No data available.

NKBB-8. July 27–29, 1946.
Eighth Enlarged Plenum of the North Korean Branch Bureau of the Korean Communist Party. Joint session with the Central Committee of the New Democratic Party.

   a. Reports of Kim Tu-bong and Kim Il Sung.
   b. Discussion on the drafts of the platform and the bylaws of a new coalition party.
   c. Issuance of "Declaration Concerning the Coalition of the New Democratic Party and the North Korean Branch Bureau of the Korean Communist Party to Found the Workers' Party of North Korea."

2. South Korea

KCP-1. August 16, 1945.
Meeting of the Changan group, former Seoul-Shanghai and M. L. groups, to found a Communist party in Seoul.

KCP-2. August 20, 1945.
Meeting of the Korean Communist Party Reestablishment Preparation Association, former Tuesday Association, and Communist groups, to found a Communist party in Seoul.

KCP-3. September 8, 1945.
Joint meeting of the Changan group and the Korean Communist Party Reestablishment Preparation Association group.

KCP-4. September 11–14, 1945.
Founding Congress of the Korean Communist Party.

   a. Discussion of the draft Declaration of the Korean Communist Party.
   b. Problems of organization and election of the officers of the party. (Pak Hŏn-yŏng was elected chairman.)

KCP-5. September 4, 1946.

No data are available on subsequent meetings of the party until September 4, 1946, when a joint meeting of the People's Party, the New

Democratic Party, and the Communist Party was held to prepare for the founding congress of the Workers' Party of South Korea.

WPSK. November 23–24, 1946.

First day, November 23.
a. Opening remarks by Hŏ Hŏn.
b. Election of Interim Executive Committee (fourteen men were elected).
c. Report by Yi Ki-sŏk on the merger of the People's Party, the New Democratic Party, and the Communist Party to found the Workers' Party of South Korea.
d. Passage of draft platform and the bylaws of the party.
e. Report by Ku Chae-su on the international and domestic political situation.
f. Congratulatory messages from Yŏ Un-hyŏng (read by Cho Han-yong) and Pak Mun-gyu, representing the Democratic United Front.

Second day, November 24.
a. Congratulatory messages by Kim Kye-rim (Central People's Committee), Hyŏn Tong-uk (All-Nation Agrarian League), Cho Hŭi-yŏng (Youth League), and Kim Chŏng-hong (Korean residents in Japan).
b. Acceptance of message drafted by Yi Kyŏng-hŭi to be sent to the U.S.S.R.-U.S. Joint Commission.
c. Reading of message from the Workers' Party of North Korea (Ch'oe Wŏn-t'aek).

WORKERS' PARTY OF KOREA
1. Period of the First Congress of the Workers' Party of (North) Korea, August 1946–March 1948.

1WPK. August 28–30, 1946.
First Congress of the Workers' Party of (North) Korea.[8]

First day, August 28.
a. Opening of the founding congress.
b. Reading of congratulatory messages.
c. Proposal and passage of the agenda of the congress.

Second day, August 29.
a. Report of Kim Il Sung on the founding of the Workers' Party of North Korea.
b. Report of Kim Tu-bong on the founding of the Workers' Party of North Korea.

c. Discussion and adoption of the decision to found the Workers' Party of North Korea.

d. Report of Pak Il-u on the credentials of the representatives.

Third day, August 30.

a. Adoption of the platform and the bylaws of the Workers' Party of North Korea.

b. Report of Ch'oe Ch'ang-ik on the coalition of three democratic political parties of South Korea.

c. Adoption of a declaration to the people of all Korea.

d. Adoption of a decision to publish the organ of the party, *Nodong sinmun.*

e. Election of the members of the Central Committee and the Central Inspection Committee. Subsequent election and announcement of the chairman, vice-chairmen, and members of the Political Committee of the Central Committee.

1WPK-1CC. August 31, 1946.
First meeting of the Central Committee.

Election of members to the various organs of the party, including thirteen members to the Standing Committee, editor of the party organ, *Nodong sinmun*, and officers of the Central Inspection Committee.

1WPK-2CC. September 25, 1946.[9]
Second Enlarged Plenum of the Central Committee.

Report of Kim Il Sung on the election of the members of the People's Committee.

1WPK-3CC. November 28, 1946.[10]
Third Enlarged Plenum of the Central Committee.

a. Discussion on the present task of the party.

b. Discussion on the democratic election on November 3 in North Korea.

c. Concerning the strengthening of the organizational and political education projects and the growth of the party.

1WPK-4CC. February 2, 1947.
Fourth Enlarged Plenum of the Central Committee.

Discussion on the election of the People's Committee on the *myŏn* and *ri* levels.

1WPK-5CC. Date unknown.
Fifth Plenum of the Central Committee.

No data available.

1WPK-6CC. March 15, 1947.[11]
Sixth Enlarged Plenum of the Central Committee.

a. Report of Kim Il Sung on a practical and cooperative policy at every level of the party organization for realization of the projected goals of the 1947 people's economic reconstruction and development plan in North Korea.
b. Discussion on the duty of the party in strengthening the people's political rights.
c. Report concerning the elimination of grave errors and shortcomings committed by some party organizations in party projects.

1WPK-7CC. June 16, 1947.
Seventh Enlarged Plenum of the Central Committee.

a. Discussion on participation in and cooperation with the U.S.S.R.-U.S. Joint Commission on Korea on the establishment of an interim government of Korea.
b. Election of Kim Il Sung to represent North Korea to the U.S.S.R.-U.S. Joint Commission on Korea.
c. Election of an *ad hoc* committee to draft a reply to the questionnaires of the U.S.S.R.-U.S. Joint Commission on Korea. (On June 23 a reply was presented, discussed, and approved by the Political Committee of the Central Committee.)

1WPK-8CC. July 1, 1947.[12]
Eighth Plenum of the Central Committee.

a. Discussion of the resolutions of the U.S.S.R.-U.S. Joint Commission on Korea.
b. Approval of the reply to the questionnaires on Article 5, Principles and Organizations of the Interim Government, and Article 6, Policies of the Interim Government.

1WPK-9CC. Date unknown.
Ninth Plenum of the Central Committee.

No data available.

1WPK-10CC. September 13, 1947.
Tenth Plenum of the Central Committee.

Discussion on the party's leadership role in the projects of the mass organization.

1WPK-11CC. December 23, 1947.
Eleventh Plenum of the Central Committee.

a. Concerning the projects of every leadership organ of the party.
b. Convocation of the second party congress.
c. Election of the members of the committee to amend the platform and the bylaws of the party.
d. Concerning the cooperative policy of all levels of party organization for the realization of the goals of the first and the fourth periods of the 1948 people's economic plan.
e. Concerning the problems of organization.

1WPK-12CC. February 9, 1948.
Twelfth Plenum of the Central Committee.

a. Report by Kim Il Sung concerning the tasks of every party organization for the realization of the 1948 people's economic plan.
b. Discussion on the draft of the interim constitution of Korea.
c. Discussion on the postponement of the convocation date of the second party congress.

2. Period of the Second Congress of the Workers' Party of (North) Korea, March 1948–April 1956.

2WPK. March 27–30, 1948.
Second Congress of the Workers' Party of (North) Korea.[13]

First day, March 27.
a. Opening of the congress.
b. Passage of the agenda of the congress.

Second day, March 28.
Report of Kim Il Sung on the work of the Central Committee of the Workers' Party of North Korea.

Third day, March 29.
a. Discussion of Kim Il Sung's report.

b. Report of the Credentials Committee.

c. Report on the amendments to the bylaws of the party.

Fourth day, March 30.

a. Decision on Kim Il Sung's report.

b. Decision on the bylaws.

c. Election of the central leadership of the party.

2WPK-1CC. March 31, 1948.
First Meeting of the Central Committee.

Election of the officers of the Central Committee.

2WPK-2CC. July 12, 1948.
Second Meeting of the Central Committee.

Report on the task of the party organization in the general election of the Supreme People's Assembly and the promulgation of the Democratic People's Republic of Korea.

2WPK-3CC. September 24–25, 1948.
Third Meeting of the Central Committee.

a. Tasks of the party organizations and the election results of the Supreme People's Assembly of the Democratic People's Republic of Korea.

b. Discussion on the tasks of the party organizations in collection of textile tax and increased production of agricultural grains in 1949.

c. Concerning the organizational problems of the party.

(1) Election of the new vice-chairman of the party, Hŏ Ka-i.

(2) Expansion of the Standing Committee to seventeen members. Election of two additional members, Kim Yŏl and Pak Yŏng-sŏn.

(3) Decision to establish an Organization Committee in the Central Committee. Election of members to the Organization Committee.

(4) Election of chairmen of the Inspection Committee and the Auditing Committee.

(5) Discussion on the farewell ceremony for the Russian forces in North Korea.

2WPK-4CC. Date unknown.
Fourth Meeting of the Central Committee.

No data available.

2WPK-5CC. February 12–13, 1949.
Fifth Meeting of the Central Committee.

   a. Concerning the strengthening of the party leadership. General sum-
      mation of the lower-level party organization projects during the last
      nine months.
   b. Discussion of the tasks presented to the party in the realization of
      the people's economic reconstruction and development plans during
      1949 and 1950 in the Democratic People's Republic of Korea.
   c. Discussion of the report on the task of the party organization in the
      election of the representatives of the People's Committee on the pro-
      vince, city, county, and district levels.
   d. In connection with the establishment of Chagang-do and the
      organization of administrative districts, decision to establish a
      Chagang-do provincial party committee and other county-level par-
      ty committees in accordance with the reorganized administrative
      districts.

2WPK-6CC. June 11, 1949.
Sixth Enlarged Plenum of the Central Committee.

   a. Report of Kim Il Sung concerning the participation of the party in
      the founding congress of the Democratic Front for the Fatherland
      Unification.
   b. Discussion on the establishment of the Workers' Party of Korea by
      unifying the Workers' Parties of the North and the South.

2WPK-7CC. June 24, 1949.
First Joint Plenum of the Central Committees of the Workers' Parties of
North and South Korea.

   a. Decision to establish a united Workers' Party of Korea.
   b. Election of new officers of the party (Kim Il Sung, chairman, Pak
      Hŏn-yŏng and Hŏ Ka-i, vice chairmen).
   c. Reorganization of the committees within the Central Committee.

2WPK-8CC. December 15–18, 1949.
Second Joint Plenum of the Central Committee.

   a. Concerning the revised policy of the party organization in the indus-
      trial sector of the two-year people's economic plan.
   b. Report of Pak Hŏn-yŏng concerning the tasks of the party organiza-
      tions in strengthening the ideological education of the members.
   c. Discussion on the problems of organization.

Speech by Kim Il Sung: Let Us Be More Faithful to Marxism and Leninism and the Principles of Proletarian Internationalism.

2WPK-9CC. December 21–23, 1950.
Third Joint Plenum of the Central Committee.

    a. Report of Kim Il Sung: The Present Situation and Our Tasks.
    b. Unification problems of the workers' organizations in North and South Korea.
    c. Discussion on the problems of organization.

2WPK-10CC. November 1–4, 1951.
Fourth Joint Plenum of the Central Committee.

    a. Report of Kim Il Sung: On Some Defects in the Organization Work of Party Organizations
    b. On organizational problems: Election of Pak Chŏng-ae, secretary of the Central Committee, to membership in the Political Committee of the Central Committee. Election of Pak Ch'ang-ok as a secretary of the Central Committee. Election of Pak Yŏng-bin as chairman of the Organization Section and election of Kim Ch'ŏn-hae as chairman of the Social Affairs Section.

Concluding Speech by Kim Il Sung: On the Improvement of the Party's Organizational Work.

2WPK-11CC. December 15–18, 1952.
Fifth Joint Plenum of the Central Committee.

    a. Report of Kim Il Sung: The Organizational and Ideological Consolidation of the Party is the Basis of our Victory.
    b. Report of Pak Chŏng-ae: Concerning the Problems of Organization.

2WPK-12CC. August 4–6, 1953.
Sixth Joint Plenum of the Central Committee.

    a. Report of Kim Il Sung: Everything for the Postwar Rehabilitation and Development of the National Economy.
    b. Report of Pak Chŏng-ae on the recent antiparty and antistate spy activities of Yi Sŭng-yŏp, Pae Ch'ŏl, Pak Sŭng-wŏn, Yun Sun-dal, Cho Il-myŏng, Yi Kang-guk, and others, and the incident of Hŏ Ka-i, who cowardly committed suicide after committing antipeople and antiparty activities.
    c. Problems of organization.
        (1) The following are expelled from membership in the Central

Committee: Chu Yŏng-ha, Chang Si-u, Pak Hŏn-yŏng, Kim O-sŏng, An Ki-sŏng, Kim Kwang-su, Kim Ŭng-bin. Kwŏn O-jik, a candidate member, is expelled from the Central Committee.

(2) The following who were not faithful and sacrificial in their services to the party and state during the war of fatherland liberation are expelled from the Central Committee: Ku Chae-su, Yi Ch'ŏn-jin, Cho Pok-ye, Yi Chu-sang.

(3) The following are elected to the Central Committee: Yi Yŏng-sŏm, Hwang T'ae-sŏng, Pak Kyŏng-su, Yu Ch'uk-un, Yun Hyŏng-sik.

(4) Abolition of the Organization Committee of the party and the election of the new Standing Committee of the Central Committee. The following are the new members of the Standing Committee: Kim Il Sung, Kim Tu-bong, Pak Chŏng-ae, Pak Yŏng-bin, Ch'oe Wŏn-t'aek, Ch'oe Ch'ang-ik, Chŏng Il-yong, Kim Hwang-il, Kang Mun-sŏk, Kim Sŭng-hwa, Kim Kwang-hyŏp, Pak Kŭm-ch'ŏl, and Nam Il.

(5) Election of the following to the Political Committee of the Central Committee: Kim Il Sung, Kim Tu-bong, Pak Chŏng-ae, Pak Ch'ang-ok, Kim Il.

(6) Chang Sun-myŏng and Yi Ki-sŏk, chairman and vice-chairman of the Inspection Committee, are relieved of their positions, and Kim Ŭng-gi is elected as new chairman of the Inspection Committee.

(7) Abolition of the secretary system of the Central Committee. Election of Pak Chŏng-ae, Pak Ch'ang-ok, and Kim Il as vice-chairmen of the Central Committee.

(8) Election of the following members to the party bylaw revision committee: Kim Il Sung, Pak Chŏng-ae, Pak Ch'ang-ok, Kim Il, Pak Yŏng-bin, Yi Ki-sŏk, Kim Kwang-hyŏp, Yi Kwŏn-mu, Han Sŏl-ya, Kang Mun-sŏk, Hwang T'ae-sŏng, Kim Yŏl, Ko Pong-gi, Kim Sŭng-hwa, and Pak Kŭm-ch'ŏl.

(9) The following are elected to positions in the Central Committee: Kim Ch'ang-man, chairman of Propaganda and Agitation Section; Kim Min-san, chairman of Society Section; Yi Ch'ŏng-wŏn, chairman of Social Science Section.

2WPK-13CC. December 18–19, 1953.
Seventh Joint Plenum of the Central Committee.

a. Report of Vice-chairman Kim Il: Concerning the Strengthening of the Work of the Democratic Front of the Fatherland Unification.

b. Report of Vice-chairman Pak Chŏng-ae: General Report on Every

Party Leadership Organization in the Coming Election, January-April 1954.

2WPK-14CC. March 21–23, 1954.
March Plenum of the Central Committee.

   a. Report of Kim Il Sung: The Present Task of the Party, State, Economic Organization, and the Workers to Rectify New Shortcomings in Industry and Transportation Sectors.
   b. Report of Kim Il Sung on organization problems.
   Pak Yŏng-bin and Pak Kŭm-ch'ŏl were elected as vice-chairmen of the Central Committee. Two newly appointed vice-premiers of the cabinet, Pak Ch'ang-ok and Kim Il, were relieved from the vice-chairmanship of the party.

2WPK-15CC. November 1–3, 1954.
November Plenum of the Central Committee.

   a. Speech by Kim Il Sung: On the Unification of Korea with the Correct Understanding of the Fatherland Unification.
   b. Report of Kim Il: Concerning the Future Policy of the Workers' Party of Korea to Struggle for the Rapid Reconstruction and Development of Agricultural Management.
   c. General report on the role of every party organization in the election.
   d. Reorganization and election of the party platform draft committee of twenty-five members.
   e. Concerning the organization problems of the party.
   f. Speech by Kim Il Sung: On Our Party Policy for the Further Development of Agricultural Management.

2WPK-16CC. April 1–4, 1955.
April Plenum of the Central Committee.

   a. Report of Kim Il Sung: On Further Intensifying the Class Education of Party Members.
   b. Report of Kim Il Sung: On the Elimination of Bureaucratism of Some Workers in the Party and the Government.
   c. Report of Pak Ch'ang-ok: On the Strengthening of the Struggle for Economic Thrift Rules for Financial and Material Statistics, Anti-corruption, and Antiwaste.
   d. Discussion on the problems of discipline.
   e. General concluding remarks by Kim Il Sung: On Some Questions of

Party and State Work in the Present Stage of the Socialist Revolution.

2WPK-17CC. December 2–3, 1955.
December Plenum of the Central Committee.

a. Concerning the decision of the November plenum, November 1954, on the rapid reconstruction and development of agricultural management.
b. Concerning the convocation of the third party congress:
   Decision to hold the third party congress in April 1956. The agenda of the party congress: (1) Report of the activities of the Central Committee by Kim Il Sung. (2) Report of the work of the Central Inspection Committee by Yi Chu-yŏn. (3) Report on the revision of the bylaws of the party by Pak Chŏng-ae. (4) Election of officers of the party.
c. Discussion on the organization problems of the party.

3. Period of the Third Congress of the Workers' Party of Korea, April 1956–September 1961.

3WPK. April 23–29, 1956.
Third Congress of the Workers' Party of Korea.[14]

First day, April 23.
a. Opening of the congress by Kim Il Sung.
b. Election of officers of the congress.
c. Passage of the following agenda of the congress:
   (1) Report of the Central Committee by Kim Il Sung.
   (2) Report of the Central Inspection Committee by Yi Chu-yŏn.
   (3) Report of the party bylaw revision committee by Pak Chŏng-ae.
   (4) Election of the officers of the party.
d. Report of Kim Il Sung: Report of the Central Committee to the third congress of the Workers' Party of Korea.

Second day, April 24.
a. Discussion on the report of the Central Committee by Yi Song-un, Kang Yŏng-ch'ang, Ko Pong-gi, Chŏng Chun-t'aek, Yi T'ae-hwa, Sŏ Ch'un-sik, Kim Pyŏng-su, Kim Tu-bong, Yi Chong-ok, Kim Kwang-hyŏp, and Yu Kwang-yŏl.
b. Congratulatory speeches by the representatives of the Communist parties of friendly countries, including the U.S.S.R. and the People's Republic of China.

Third day, April 25.
a. Report of the Central Inspection Committee by Yi Chu-yŏn.
b. Report of the Credentials Committee by Yim Hae.
c. Discussion on the reports of the Central Committee and the Central Inspection Committee by Ha Ang-ch'ŏn, Nam Il, Pak Ŭi-wan, Ch'oe Yong-gŏn, Mun Man-uk, Kim T'ae-gŭn, and Kim Tu-sam.
d. Election of a nineteen-member committee to draft a declaration of the party.
e. Congratulatory speeches by the representatives of the Communist parties of friendly countries, including Poland and Indonesia.

Fourth day, April 26.
a. Discussion on the reports of the Central Committee and the Central Inspection Committee by Kim Il, Yi Il-gyŏng, Ko Yŏng-ja, Paek Pong-gwan, Kim Chae-ha, Hyŏn Chŏng-min, Kim Ki-ju, Kim Ch'ang-man, Yu Ch'ŏl-mok, Yi Chae-yŏng.
b. Congratulatory speeches by the representatives of the Communist parties of friendly countries, including Japan and Romania.
c. Congratulatory speeches by the leaders of other parties in North Korea: Speeches by Hong Ki-hwang and Kim Tal-hyŏn.

Fifth day, April 27.
a. Discussion on the reports of the Central Committee and the Central Inspection Committee by Han Sang-du, Kim Kwang-t'aek, Pak Yong-guk, Yu Sun-sik, Ch'ŏn Ch'i-ok, Paek Sun-jae, Pak Nae-su, Song Ch'ang-yŏm, Chŏng T'ae-sik, P'i Ch'ang-nin, Kim Sang-hae, Yu Ch'uk-un, Kim Nak-hŭi, and Yi Ch'ŏng-wŏn.
b. Congratulatory speeches by the representatives of the General Federation of Koreans in Japan.

Sixth day, April 28.
a. Continued discussion on the reports of the Central Committee and the Central Inspection Committee by Han Sŏl-ya and Pak Kŭm-ch'ŏl (total number of discussants, 47).
b. Adoption of the reports of the Central Committee and the Central Inspection Committee.
c. Report by Pak Chŏng-ae of the party bylaw revision committee.
d. Discussion on the reports of Pak Chŏng-ae by Cho Yŏng, Kim Wŏn-p'ung, Kim Chin-t'ae, Ch'oe Chong-hak, Chŏng Kye-rak.

Seventh day, April 29.
a. Election of the officers of the party.
b. Closing of the party congress.

3WPK-1CC. August 30–31, 1956.[15]
August Plenum of the Central Committee.

a. Report of the government delegation that visited the fraternal countries and report on the tasks confronting our party.
b. On the reform and strengthening of public health works.

3WPK-2CC. December 11–13, 1956.
December Plenum of the Central Committee.

a. Concerning the 1957 people's economic plan.
b. On the work of the Hambuk party organization in the development of agricultural management.

Concluding speech by Kim Il Sung: To Bring about a Great Revolutionary Upswing in Socialist Construction.

3WPK-3CC. April 18–19, 1957.
April Plenum of the Central Committee.

a. Report of Kim Il Sung: On Further Development of Fisheries.
b. Decision to solve the basic problems of food, housing, and clothing of the workers during the first five-year plan.

3WPK-4CC. October 17–19, 1957.
October Plenum of the Central Committee.

a. Report of Pak Kŭm-ch'ŏl: On the Revision of the Basic Construction Projects.
b. Discussion on the convocation of the first conference of the party.

Concluding speech by Kim Il Sung: On Carrying Out the Party Policy in the Construction Sector.

3WPK-5CC. December 5–6, 1957.
December Enlarged Plenum of the Central Committee.

Report of Kim Il Sung: On the Work of the Party and Government Delegation Which Attended the Celebration of the Fortieth Anniversary of the Great October Revolution and the Meetings of Representatives of the Communist and Workers' Parties of Various Countries in Moscow.

WPK-IC. March 3–6, 1958.
First Conference of the Workers' Party of Korea.

a. Report of Yi Chong-ok: Concerning the First, Five-Year Plan, 1957–61, of the People's Economy.
b. Report of Pak Kŭm-ch'ŏl: Concerning the Strengthening of the Union and Cooperation of the Party.
c. Concerning the organization problems of the party.
d. Concluding speech by Kim Il Sung: For the Successful Fulfillment of the First Five-Year Plan.

3WPK-6CC. June 5–7, 1958.
June Plenum of the Central Committee.

a. On revision and strengthening of the foodstuff manufacturing industry and the production of daily necessities.
b. Discussion on revision and strengthening of the domestic industries and the external trade.

Concluding remarks by Kim Il Sung: On Expanding the Production of People's Consumer Goods and Reforming the Merchandise Exchange Works.

3WPK-7CC. September 26–27, 1958.
September Plenum of the Central Committee.

a. Concerning further enlargement of the irrigated fields for agriculture.
b. Discussion on the promotion of metal industry development.

3WPK-8CC. February 23–25, 1959.
February Plenum of the Central Committee.

a. Report of Kim Il Sung: Participation of the Workers' Party of Korea in the twenty-first congress of the Communist party of the Soviet Union.
b. On improving the quality of manufactured goods and industries.
c. Concerning the strengthening of transportation and transport works.
d. Concerning the various projects of the party.

Concluding remarks by Kim Il Sung.

3WPK-9CC. June 27–30, 1959.
June Plenum of the Central Committee.

a. Further development of animal husbandry.
b. Further promotion of the electrical industries.

3WPK-10CC. December 1–4, 1959.[16]
December Enlarged Plenum of the Central Committee.

   a. Concerning the 1960 people's development plan.
   b. Concerning revising and strengthening the local organizations.
   c. On the realization of the all-people's economic movement.

   Concluding remarks by Kim Il Sung: On Several Tasks Confronting the Socialist Economic Construction.

3WPK-11CC. April 21, 1960.
April Plenum of the Central Committee.

   a. An appeal to the people of South Korea: "To the People of South Korea."
   b. Concerning the 4-19 demonstration.

3WPK-12CC. August 8–11, 1960.
August Enlarged Plenum of the Central Committee.

   a. Concerning the technical revolution movement in all segments of the people's economy.
   b. Concerning strengthening the training programs of technical personnel.
   c. Concluding speech by Kim Il Sung: For the Successful Accomplishment of the Technical Revolution.

3WPK-13CC. December 20–23, 1960.
December Enlarged Plenum of the Central Committee.

   a. General report of the 1960 agricultural management sector and the task of the party in 1961.
   b. On the 1961 people's economic development plan.
   c. Concerning the conferences of the representatives of the Workers' Party of Korea and other Communist organizations.

3WPK-14CC. March 20–22, 1961.
March Plenum of the Central Committee.

   a. Concerning the convocation of the Fourth Congress of the Workers' Party of Korea.
   b. Concerning the realization of the decisions of the 1958 June plenum of the Central Committee (3WPK-6CC) and the task of the party in the foodstuff manufacturing industry and the production of daily necessities.

    c. On further strengthening of the basic construction projects of each sector.

4. Period of the Fourth Congress of the Workers' Party of Korea, September 1961–October 1970.

4WPK. September 11–18, 1961.
Fourth Congress of the Workers' Party of Korea.[17]

    a. General review of the work of the Central Committee of the Workers' Party of Korea. Report of Kim Il Sung.

    b. General review of the work of the Central Inspection Committee of the Workers' Party of Korea. Report of Kim Kye-rim.

    c. On the seven-year economic plan (1961–67) of the Democratic People's Republic of Korea. Report of Kim Il.

    d. Election of officers to the leadership organs of the Workers' Party of Korea.

First day, September 11.
a. Opening remarks by Ch'oe Yong-gŏn.
b. Report of Kim Il Sung on the general review of the work of the Central Committee of the Workers' Party of Korea.

Second Day, September 12.
a. Report of Kim Kye-rim on the general review of the work of the Central Inspection Committee of the Workers' Party of Korea.
b. Discussion on Kim Il Sung's report by Yi Chae-yun, Yun Sŭng-gwa, Kim Mun-hwa, Pak Kŭm-ch'ŏl, Kim Hwak-sil, Han Ki-ch'ang, and Kim Sŏk-bong.
c. Congratulatory remarks by Russian delegate F. L. Kozlov, Chinese delegate Teng Hsiao-p'ing, German delegate Alfred Krehler, and Japanese delegate Kenji Miyamoto.

Third day, September 13.
a. Discussion on reports of Kim Il Sung and Kim Kye-rim by Mun Chŏng-suk, Kim Su-bok, Yi Ch'ang-sun, Kim Ch'ang-man, P'i Ch'ang-nin, and Yi Yong-gu.
b. Congratulatory remarks by delegates from Romania, Mongolia, Bulgaria, Albania, Vietnam, Hungary, Czechoslovakia, Poland, and Cuba.
c. Report of the Credentials Committee by Kim Ik-sŏn. Adoption of Kim Ik-sŏn's report.

Fourth day, September 14.

a. Congratulatory remarks by delegates representing Communist parties of New Zealand, Malaya, France, Venezuela, Switzerland, Spain, Ceylon, Syria, and Italy.

b. Discussion on reports of Kim Il Sung and Kim Kye-rim by Yi Chong-ok, Kim Kwang-hyŏp, Pak Chŏng-ae, Kang Ch'il-yong, and Kim Wal-su.

Fifth day, September 15.

a. Congratulatory remarks by delegates representing Communist parties of Indonesia, England, Austria, Algeria, Canada, Thailand, and the Netherlands.

b. Congratulatory remarks by Kim Ŭn-sun, representing the Koreans in Japan, Kang Yang-uk, representing the Democratic party, and Pak Sin-dŏk, representing the Ch'ŏndogyo Ch'ŏngu-dang.

c. Discussion on reports of Kim Il Sung and Kim Kye-rim by O Che-ryong, Kim Pyŏng-su, Yi Hyo-sun, Yim Kye-ch'ŏl, Yi Kwang-sil, Han Sŏl-ya, Kim Ok-sim, and Yi Il-gyŏng.

d. Adoption of a Declaration for the Peaceful Unification of Korea, a letter to be sent to South Korea.

Sixth day, September 16.

a. Discussion on reports of Kim Il Sung and Kim Kye-rim by Nam Il, Kim Wal-yong, Han Ch'ang-sun, Sŏ Pyŏng-sik, Ch'oe Ch'ang-sŏk, O Hyon-ju, Yi Sŭng-gi, and Kim T'aek-yong.

b. Report of Kim Il on the seven-year economic plan (1961–67) of the Democratic People's Republic of Korea.

Seventh day, September 17.

a. Discussion on Kim Il's report by Chŏng Chun-t'aek, Ch'oe Yong-jin, Chang Yun-p'il, Kim Yŏng-ch'ang, Kim Chong-hang, Yi Chu-yŏn, Kim Hong-gwan, Kim Wŏn-muk, Han Sang-du, Kim Kyŏng-sŏk, Yi Chae-yŏng, Yi Kwang-u, Kim Sun-bok, Yi Hong-gyun, Chŏn Ho-sŏn, Kim Pyŏng-sik, Kim Myŏng-sŏng, Kim Chin-sŏn, Yi Sŏk-chong, Han Tae-yŏng, Kim Hoe-il, and Cho Sun-yong.

b. Adoption of the decision of the Central Committee, economic statistics of the seven-year economic plan, and the declaration of the peaceful unification of Korea.

c. Election of fifty-five-member nominating committee for the election of the members of the Central Committee and its organs.

Eighth day, September 18.

a. Discussion and adoption of the amendment to the bylaws of the Workers' Party of Korea.

b. Election of the members of the Central Committee.
c. Closing remarks by Kim Il Sung.

4WPK-1CC. September 18, 1961.
First Plenum of the Central Committee.

Election of the officers of the party.

4WPK-2CC. November 27–December 1, 1961.
Second Enlarged Plenum of the Central Committee.

a. Report of the representative corps of the Workers' Party of Korea after participation in the twenty-second congress of the Communist Party of the Soviet Union.
b. On the 1962 economic development plan.
c. On the construction of 600,000 residential houses in villages.
d. Election of Hyŏn Mu-gwang as a candidate member of the Political Committee of the Central Committee.

Concluding remark by Kim Il Sung: All Efforts for the Conquering of Six Highlands.

4WPK-3CC. March 6–8, 1962.
Third Enlarged Plenum of the Central Committee.

a. Discussion on the party organization in Hwanghae Namdo in accordance with the directives of Kim Il Sung in Ch'ŏngsalli.
b. Concerning the strengthening of the thought education in the party.
c. Concluding speech by Kim Il Sung: On Improving and Strengthening the Organizational and Ideological Work of the Party.

4WPK-4CC. Date unknown.
Fourth Plenum of the Central Committee.

No data available.

4WPK-5CC. December 10–14, 1962.
Fifth Plenum of the Central Committee.

a. On further strengthening the national defense forces in view of the current situation.
b. General review of accomplishments of the 1962 people's economic plan and on the 1963 people's economic development plan.

4WPK-6CC. May 13–15, 1963.
Sixth Plenum of the Central Committee.

a. Further strengthening of the work of the party committees in factories and industries.

b. Strengthening of the *Ch'ŏllima* workteam movement.

4WPK-7CC. September 3–5, 1963.
Seventh Plenum of the Central Committee.

a. Preliminary report of the 1963 people's economic development plan and concerning the 1964 people's economic plan.

b. Concerning improvement in animal husbandry.

4WPK-8CC. February 25–27, 1964.
Eighth Plenum of the Central Committee.

a. Report of Kim Il Sung: Theses on the Socialist Agrarian Questions in our Country.

b. The present situation of South Korea and the task of our party for the unification of our fatherland.

c. On further strengthening of the work of the masses.

Concluding speech by Kim Il Sung: Let Us Strengthen the Revolutionary Forces in Every Way to Achieve the Cause of Reunification of the Country.

4WPK-9CC. June 25–26, 1964.
Ninth Plenum of the Central Committee.

a. Concerning the organization of a conference for the agrarian workers of Korea.

b. Discussion on the reorganization of the trade unions.

Concluding remarks by Kim Il Sung: On Improving and Strengthening the Work of the Working People's Organizations.

4WPK-10CC. December 14–19, 1964.
Tenth Plenum of the Central Committee.

a. Preliminary report on the 1964 economic plan.

b. Discussion on various policies to successfully complete the 1965 people's economic plan.

Concluding speech by Kim Il Sung: On Enhancing the Party Spirit, Class Spirit, and Popular Spirit of Leading Functionaries and Improving the Management of the National Economy.

4WPK-11CC. June 29–July 1, 1965.
Eleventh Plenum of the Central Committee.

   a. Report of Kim Il: On the Revision and Strengthening of Power and
   Electricity Management.
   b. Report of Kim Ch'ang-man: On the Revision and Strengthening of
   Higher Education and Scientific Research Projects.

   Concluding remarks by Kim Il Sung.

4WPK-12CC. November 15–17, 1965.
Twelfth Plenum of the Central Committee.

   Report by Kim Il Sung: On Further Strengthening of the Party Leadership in All Sectors of the People's Economy and the County Party
   Committees.

4WPK-13CC. March 28–April 4, 1966.
Thirteenth Plenum of the Central Committee.

   a. Preliminary report of the work based on the decision of the twelfth
   plenum of the Central Committee (4WPK-12CC).
   b. Report of Kim Kwang-hyŏp: On the Convocation of the Second Party Conference.

WPK-IIC. October 5–12, 1966.
Second Conference of the Workers' Party of Korea.

   a. Report of Kim Il Sung: The Present Situation and the Tasks of Our
   Party.
   b. Report of Kim Il: The Present Problems of the Socialist Economic
   Development.
   c. Resolution of the party on the problem of the Vietnam conflict.

4WPK-14CC. October 12, 1966.
Fourteenth Plenum of the Central Committee.

   a. Adoption of the decisions of the second conference of the party.
   b. Reorganization problem of the party.

4WPK-15CC. May 4–8, 1967.
Fifteenth Plenum of the Central Committee.

   No data available. There is a reference to this plenum in a speech by
   Kim Il Sung on October 11, 1969. Kim said that party propaganda activities had increased since this plenum.

4WPK-16CC. June 28–July 3, 1967.
Sixteenth Plenum of the Central Committee.

No specific agenda reported for this plenum. Discussion centered on the realization of the decisions of the second party conference.

Concluding speech by Kim Il Sung: For a Great Revolutionary Upsurge in the Present Economic Work and for the Improvement and Strengthening of Manpower Administration.

4WPK-17CC. April 22–25, 1968.
Seventeenth Plenum of the Central Committee.

a. On the 1968 people's economic development plan to further strengthen the economic and military construction in view of the current situation.
b. On rapid development of animal husbandry.

4WPK-18CC. November 11–16, 1968.
Eighteenth Plenum of the Central Committee.

a. Report of Kim Il: On the Strengthening of the Railway Transportation and the General Transportation Works, Particularly the Automobile Transport Works.
b. Discussion on the interim report of the decisions of the sixteenth plenum of the Central Committee on the labor administration of the workers. Efficient utilization of 480-minute, 8-hour, work day.

Concluding speech by Kim Il Sung: On Relieving the Strain on Transport.

4WPK-19CC. June 27–30, 1969.
Nineteenth Plenum of the Central Committee.

a. On strengthening the struggle to be thrifty and preserve state properties in all segments of the people's economy.
b. Concerning the new reform in the development of the fishing industries.

Concluding speech by Kim Il Sung: On the Thrift and Care of State Properties and On the Further Development of Fisheries.

4WPK-20CC. December 1–5, 1969.
Twentieth Plenum of the Central Committee.

a. Concerning strengthening the activities of the League of Socialist Working Youth.

b. Concerning strengthening the party leadership role in educational work.

c. Concerning the convocation of the fifth congress of the Workers' Party of Korea.

5. Period of the Fifth Congress of the Workers' Party of Korea, November 1970–October 1980.

5WPK. November 2–13, 1970.
Fifth Congress of the Workers' Party of Korea.[18]

a. General review of the work of the Central Committee of the Workers' Party of Korea.

b. General review of the work of the Central Inspection Committee of the Workers' Party of Korea.

c. On the six-year economic plan (1971–76) of the Democratic People's Republic of Korea.

d. Election of officers to the leadership organs of the Workers' Party of Korea.

First day, November 2.
a. Report by Kim Il Sung on the general review of the work of the Central Committee of the Workers' Party of Korea.

Second day, November 3.
a. Report by Kim Kuk-hun on the general review of the work of the Central Inspection Committee of the Workers' Party of Korea.
b. Discussion of Kim Il Sung's report by Pak Sŏng-ch'ŏl, O Chin-u, Yŏn Hyŏng-muk, and Kim Man-gŭm.

Third day, November 4.
a. Discussion of Kim Il Sung's report by Kim Il, Yang Hyŏng-sŏp, Hŏ Tam, Kim Yun-yong, and Kim Kuk-t'ae.

Fourth day, November 5.
a. Discussion of Kim Il Sung's report by Kim Chung-nin, Song Sŏng-p'il, Chŏng Chun-t'aek, Hwang Chang-yŏp, Yi Hu-gil, Ch'oe Chin-sŏng, Kang Yang-uk, and Pak Sin-dŏk.

Fifth day, November 6.
a. Discussion of Kim Il Sung's report by Chŏn Ch'ang-ch'ŏl, Pyŏn Ch'ang-bok, Han Sŭng-gyŏm, Yi Chin-su, Chŏng Chun-gi, Yi Chung-nin, and Pak Su-dong.

Sixth day, November 7.
a. Discussion of Kim Il Sung's report by Kim Tong-gyu, Hyŏn Mu-
   gwang, Yi Chŏng-sun, Yi Myŏn-sang, Sin Sŏng-u, Nam Il, O Ki-
   ch'ŏn, Yi Rim-su, Chŏn Ha-ch'ŏl, Chŏng Kyŏng-sik, An Ch'ang-se,
   An Ch'an-su, Chin Ch'ang-hu, Sŏ Ch'ŏl, Kang Sŏng-san, Kim T'ae-
   hyŏn, Kim Ŭi-sun, Kim I-hun, Sin Su-gŭn, Chŏng Hŭi-ch'ŏl, Kang
   T'ae-hŭi, Chang Kuk-chin, Kwak Tae-hong, Han Pyŏng-yong, Ko
   Yun-suk, Yi Kyŏng-sŏp, and Han P'il-hwa.

Seventh day, November 8, Sunday - Holiday.

Eighth day, November 9.
a. Report by Kim Il on the six-year economic plan (1971–76) of the
   Democratic People's Republic of Korea.
b. Continuation of discussion on Kim Il Sung's report by Ch'oe
   Ch'ang-gwŏn, Ŏm Sang-il, Yang chŏng-t'ae, P'i Ch'ang-nin, Chang
   Sam-son, Chŏn Pyŏng-ch'ae, Chu Chun-il, Yi Pong-gyu, Hwang
   Tae-yŏn, Yu Ŭl-sam, and Yi Un-jŏn.

Ninth day, November 10.
a. Discussion on Kim Il Sung's report by Yun Ki-bok, Hong Wŏn-gil,
   Yi Kil-song, Kim Chong-sŏng, Yi Ch'ang-jun, Ch'oe Hyŏn-gyu, Pak
   Sŏn-gyun, Mun Ki-sŏp, Kim Sang-mun, and Kim Pok-sil.

Tenth day, November 11.
a. Discussion on Kim Il Sung's report by Kim Yŏng-yŏl, Kim Hak-sun,
   Yi Hyŏng, Yi Ho-hyŏk, Kim Yŏng-hak, Son Kyŏng-jun, and Ch'oe
   Chae-gon.

Eleventh day, November 12.
a. Discussion on Kim Il Sung's report by Chŏng Il-yong, Hong Si-hak,
   Yim Kye-ch'ŏl, Chang Yun-p'il, An Sŭng-hak, No Pyŏng-u, Kim
   Kŭm-ch'ŏl, Yi Nak-pin, No U-yong, Yi Pong-yong, and Yun Yong-
   muk.

Twelfth day, November 13.
a. Election of officers to the party central leadership organs.
b. Continuation of discussion on Kim Il Sung's report by Pak Yŏng-
   sun, Kye Hyŏng-sun, Kim Su-dŭk, Kim Se-hwal, Ch'oe Yun-su, O
   Sŏng-yŏl, Pak Yŏng-sin, Pak Yong-sik, Kim Ch'ang-bok, Kim Nak-
   hŭi, Kim Ch'ŏl-hun, Pak Pok-sun, Yi Hwan-sam, and Pak Tae-sŏp.

5WPK-1CC. November 13, 1970.
First Plenum of the Central Committee.

   Election of the officers of the party.

5WPK-2CC. April 19–23, 1971.
Second Plenum of the Central Committee.

    a. On the present international situation and the self-reliant unification of the fatherland.
    b. On the technical revolution of orchard works and the present economic problems.
    c. On the party guidance of the people's health programs.

5WPK-3CC. November 15–23, 1971.
Third Plenum of the Central Committee.

    a. On several problems of the international situation.
    Report by Kim Il Sung: Revolutionary Solidarity of the International Situation and the Emphasis on the Self-Reliant Unification of the Fatherland.
    b. Report by Kim Il on the three great technical revolutionary systems. Emphasis on the development of the main force of machine tool industry, electronic industry, and automation industry.
    c. On the manufacturing of consumer goods.
    Report by Pak Sŏng-ch'ŏl.
    Emphasis on strict regulations and on the strengthening of Communist education of the workers for the quality production of consumer goods.
    Emphasis on the ideological struggle to accomplish the above tasks.

5WPK-4CC. July 1–6, 1972.
Fourth Plenum of the Central Committee.

    a. On the party policy for the peaceful unification of the fatherland.
    Report of Kim Il Sung: The General Unity Transcending the Differences in Thought, Ideologies, and Systems for the Self-Reliant and Peaceful Unification of the Fatherland without External Interference.
    b. On the institution of general ten-year compulsory education of middle and high schools.
    Report of Kim Il on instruction of detailed plans and realization of the system from 1972.

5WPK-5CC. October 23–26, 1972.
Fifth Plenum of the Central Committee.

    a. On the socialist constitution of the Democratic People's Republic of Korea.
    Report of Kim Il Sung.

   b. Concerning the 1973 people's economic development plan.
     Report by Ch'oe Chae-u.
   c. On the execution of the reissuing of party identity cards of the
     Workers' Party of Korea.

5WPK-6CC. December 22–25, 1972.
Sixth Plenum of the Central Committee.

   a. On the socialist constitution of the Democratic People's Republic of
     Korea.
   b. Important conclusion on the constitution by Kim Il Sung.

5WPK-7CC. September 4–17, 1973.
Seventh Plenum of the Central Committee.

   a. On carrying out the three revolutions of ideology, technology, and
     culture set forth by the Fifth Congress of the party.
     Discussion of the problems by the local party, factory, and indus-
     trial workers.
   b. On correctly enforcing the cost-accounting system in accordance
     with the great Taean work system.
     Report by Yang Hyŏng-sŏp.

5WPK-8CC. February 11–13, 1974.
Eighth Plenum of the Central Committee.

   a. On the general mobilization for the great socialism construction
     work.
     Report by Kim Il Sung.
   b. On the complete abolition of taxes and reducing the prices of indus-
     trial products.

5WPK-9CC. Date unknown.
Ninth Plenum of the Central Committee.

   No data available.

5WPK-10CC. February 11–17, 1975.
Tenth Plenum of the Central Committee.

   a. On the guidance work for the realization of the tasks of the three
     great revolutions of ideology, technology, and culture as proposed
     by the great leader Kim Il Sung.
   b. On the proclamation of the party Central Committee on the occa-

sion of the thirtieth anniversary of the establishment of the Workers' Party of Korea.

c. Concluding remarks by Kim Il Sung.

5WPK-11CC. November 19–21, 1975.
Eleventh Plenum of the Central Committee.

a. Discussion on the 1976 people's economic plan.
Report by the organs of the Central Committee of the Workers' Party of Korea.

b. Concluding remarks by Kim Il Sung.
Adoption of Kim Il Sung's conclusion.

5WPK-12CC. October 11–14, 1976.
Twelfth Plenum of the Central Committee.

a. On reviewing the results of farming in 1976.
b. On attaining ahead of time the goal of 10 million tons of grain by thoroughly implementing the five-point policy of nature remaking set forth by our party.

Concluding remarks by Kim Il Sung.

5WPK-13CC. April 4–6, 1977.
Thirteenth Plenum of the Central Committee.

a. On waging a powerful struggle to prevent drought damage under the influence of the cold front through a general mobilization of the whole party, the whole army, and the entire people.
b. On the review of the fulfillment of the decision of the eighteenth plenary meeting of the fourth Central Committee of the party on the work in the domain of transport and future tasks.

Concluding remarks by Kim Il Sung.

5WPK-14CC. September 5–7, 1977.
Fourteenth Plenum of the Central Committee.

a. Theses on Socialist Education.

Speech by Kim Il Sung and discussion of the theses by members of the party.

5WPK-15CC. December 13, 1977.
Fifteenth Plenum of the Central Committee.

a. On the second seven-year plan for the development of the national economy (1978–84) to be deliberated at the first session of the sixth Supreme People's Assembly. Report by Hong Sŏng-yong, chairman of the State Planning Commission.
b. Organizational affairs.

Concluding speech by Kim Il Sung.

5WPK-16CC. January 8, 1978.
Sixteenth Plenum of the Central Committee.

a. Letter of the Central Committee of the party to all party members.

Concluding speech by Kim Il Sung.

5WPK-17CC. November 27–28, 1978.
Seventeenth Plenum of the Central Committee.

a. On the 1979 plan for the development of the national economy.

Concluding speech by Kim Il Sung.

5WPK-18CC. June 13–15, 1979.
Eighteenth Plenum of the Central Committee.

a. On the results of the implementation of the decision of the thirteenth plenary meeting of the fifth Central Committee of the party to carry through the policy of applying three transport methods and on the tasks of rapidly developing transportation to suit the demand of the high stage of socialist economic construction.

5WPK-19CC. December 1–12, 1979.
Nineteenth Plenum of the Central Committee.

a. On the 1980 plan for the development of the national economy.
b. On leading the entire party, the entire army, and the entire people to a vigorous campaign to build dams across rivers and extensively construct hydro-power stations in order to prevent flood damage and increase electricity output.
c. On the convocation of the sixth congress of the Workers' Party of Korea.

6. Period of the Sixth Congress of the Workers' Party of Korea, October 1980–

6WPK. October 10–14, 1980.
Sixth Congress of the Workers' Party of Korea.[19]

    a. Summing-up of the work of the Central Committee of the Workers' Party of Korea.

    b. Summing-up of the Central Auditing Commission of the Workers' Party of Korea.

    c. On the revision of the rules of the Workers' Party of Korea.

    d. Election of central leading bodies of the Workers' Party of Korea.

First day, October 10.
a. Report by Kim Il Sung on the work of the Central Committee of the Workers' Party of Korea.

Second day, October 11, Saturday, no meeting held.

Third day, October 12.
a. Report by Yi Nak-bin on the work of the Central Auditing Commission.
b. Discussion of Kim Il Sung's report by Yi Chong-ok, Kim Yŏng-nam, Hwang Chang-yŏp, O Kŭk-yŏl, Hŏ Tam, Kim Ki-nam, Kye Ŭng-t'ae, Kang Sŏng-san, Yi Kil-song, Cho Ch'ang-dŏk, Yi Chi-ch'an, Yi Chae-yun, Chu Hwa-jong, Chi Chae-ryong, Chi Ch'ang-ik, Chŏn Chong-hyŏk, Pak Yŏng-ch'ŏl, Kim Chin-hyŏk, Kim Yŏng-nan, and Yi Hwa-sun.
c. Congratulatory speeches by Yi In-gi of the Revolutionary Party for Reunification and by Kang Yang-uk of the Korean Democratic Party.

Fourth day, October 13.
a. Report by Sŏ Ch'ŏl of the Credentials Committee.
b. Discussion of Kim Il Sung's report by Kim Chung-nin, Paek Hyŏng-gi, Kong Chin-t'ae, T'ae Chŏng-su, Kim Tu-yŏng, Paek In-jun, Son Kyŏng-jun, Sŏ Yun-sŏk, Chang Kuk-ch'an, Yi Chin-su, Kim Pyŏng-yul, Maeng T'ae-ho, Paek Pŏm-su, Kim Chong-sŏng, Kang Chŏm-gu, Ko Yŏng-sŏn, Ko Chŏng-sik, Sin Su-gŭn, Kim Ho-gyŏng, and Kang Sŭng-hwan.
c. Discussion of the revision of the rules of the Workers' Party of Korea and adoption of the revised bylaws.
d. Congratulatory speeches by Sŏ Man-sul from the General Association of Korean Residents in Japan and Chŏng Sin-hyŏk of the Ch'ŏndogyo Young Friends Party.

Fifth day, October 14.
a. Election of members of the central organizations.
b. Closing remarks by Kim Il Sung.

PERSONNEL OF THE CENTRAL COMMITTEE
AND THE CENTRAL AUDITING COMMITTEE

The number of the party members has grown from about forty-five hundred in 1945 to more than two million in 1975, an increase of approximately 425 times during the past thirty years. Party members constitute approximately 14 percent of the population, the highest of all Communist parties. Until the fifth party congress in 1970, the precise number of party members was given at each party congress. But since the fifth congress neither the number of party members nor any of the other usual statistical information (such as the composition of the delegation and the number of basic cell organizations) has been announced. The latest figure on party membership comes from Kim's speech on October 10, 1980, when he said that the sixth party congress was attended by 3,220 delegates, each representing 1,000 members, approximately 3.2 million members.

The party bylaws stipulate that the number of delegates to the party congress is determined by the Central Committee, but do not say what sort of rule is used to determine the number. In the past, the delegates chosen were not proportionate to the membership of the party. For example, there were 999 delegates to the second party congress, when the party had a membership of 725,762, while there were only 916 delegates at the third party congress, when the membership of the party had increased to 1,164,945. The bylaws also stipulate that the delegates to the party congress are elected at the lower-level party organizations, but there is no provision for the representation of top party leaders.

The delegates to the party congress elect the members of the Central Committee and the members of the Central Auditing Committee. The officers of the Central Committee (such as chairman, vice-chairman, and secretaries) and members of other committees within the Central Committee (such as Political, Inspection, and Standing committees) are elected by the members of the Central Committee. The bylaws of the first party, later amended, stipulated that the chairman and vice-chairmen of the party be elected by the members of the Political Committee. The chairman and vice-chairmen of the Central Auditing Committee are elected by the members of that committee.

At the time of the first party congress, the function of the Central Auditing Committee was performed by what was known as the Central Inspection Committee, which combined the work of both the inspection and auditing of the party. This committee reported directly to the party congress, and the members were elected by the party congress, but this was soon divided into two committees, the Central Auditing Committee, which reports to the party congress, and the Inspection Committee, which belongs to the Central Committee. The bylaws were amended, and the functions of these two committees were separated from the second party congress on.

METHODS OF ELECTION

The methods used to elect the members of the Central Committee varied from party congress to party congress. The first party congress voted on a prepared list of nominees, and it was not revealed who or how many people served on the nominating committee. Since the first party congress was the founding congress, bringing together the leaders of the Korean Communist Party and the New Democratic Party, leaders of the two parties were heavily represented on the nominating committee.

The delegates of the second party congress voted on the individual nominees of the Central Committee, and it was reported that all nominees received unanimous approval except one; O Ki-sŏp was reported to have received 5 negative votes.[20] In the election of candidate members of the Central Committee, it was reported that all except one received unanimous approval; Kim Tu-yong was reported to have received 18 negative votes. Out of 999 delegates chosen for the second party congress, only 990 attended and voted in the congress. Five or 18 negative votes out of 990 may not be significant numerically, but it is important to note such negative votes, particularly because there has been no such show of disapproval of any nominee since the second party congress. It is also important to note that such negative votes had little effect in the ranking of these individuals within the Central Committee. O was ranked forty-second in the sixty-seven-member Central Committee, and Kim Tu-yong was ranked sixteenth of twenty candidate members of the Central Committee. O was reelected to the third party Central Committee, but Kim was not.

Article 26 of the revised bylaws of the third party stipulated that the election of members to various party committees and leadership organizations must be by secret ballot, and each nominee must be voted on separately. The delegates of the party congress had the right to discuss, approve, or disapprove the nominee. It also referred to a separate regulation for the election of the members of party leadership organizations. There is no detailed information as to how the members of the Central

Committee were chosen for the third party, and the separate regulation was not made public.

The fourth party congress selected a fifty-five-member Nominating Council on the seventh day of the congress, September 17, 1961, and a slate of nominees to various offices within the Central Committee was presented to the congress. The delegates unanimously approved the slate. The details of the Nominating Council and the margin of approval of each of the nominees were not made public.

Of all party congresses, the fifth and the sixth provided the least basic information, such as the total number of party members and the methods used to elect the members and candidate members of the Central Committee. Examining the list of the Central Committee members of the fifth party, one can easily speculate on the work of a Nomination Council similar to that of the fourth party congress. The Nomination Council of the fifth congress seems to have recommended a list of candidates which was unanimously approved.

All members and candidate members of the Central Committee are presented in rank order in all six party congresses, but the work of a nominating council in the fourth, the fifth, and the sixth party congresses suggests a grouping of certain professions, for example, military personnel, artists, and educators. There is no doubt that the rank order is important for the first twenty to thirty members, but thereafter representation of various professions in the Central Committee seems equally important.

Because of the interval between party congresses, at times nine years (from the fourth in 1961 to the fifth in 1970) and ten years (from the fifth to the sixth), there were many efforts to update the original list of the Central Committee, deleting those who were purged and those who had passed away and promoting those who had gained prominence, but the party has not issued an official list of the members of the Central Committee between party congresses. Even when there were opportunities to do so in the two party conferences held in 1958 and 1966, the party did not announce a new list of the members of the Central Committee. The party bylaws provide that new members can be added and delinquent members can be expelled from the Central Committee, not exceeding one-fifth of the total number, at the time of a party conference, but no such action, if it has occurred, has been officially announced.

Only once throughout the plenums of the Central Committee held between party congresses has the party announced the addition of members to the Central Committee. This came shortly after the Korean war at the sixth joint plenum in August 1953, when five members were added at a time when a large number of people were purged and many changes were reported in the rank and file of the party. There have been many occasions when officers of the Central Committee and members of various committees within the Central Committee have been replaced, and the plenums in which such changes were made have announced the newly elected officers, but no new slate of the members of the Central Committee has been announced other than at the regular party congresses.

MEMBERS OF THE CENTRAL COMMITTEE
The first party congress elected 43 members, the second party congress 67 members, the third party congress 71, the fourth party congress 85, the fifth party congress 117 members, and the sixth party congress 145 members of the Central Committee, a total of 528 members. Of these, only two served in all six congresses. None served five congresses, and only nine served four times, while 28 members served three times, 118 members served twice, and the majority, 160 members, served once. The actual number of persons who served as regular members of the Central Committee in six party congresses is 317. Except for the first party congress, the number of members reelected to the subsequent party congress is very low; in fact, fewer than half of the members have been reelected to the Central Committee. Thirty out of 43 members of the Central Committee of the first party congress were reelected, but only 29 out of 67 members were reelected from the second to the third, 28 out of 71 members from the third to the fourth, 31 out of 85 members from the fourth to the fifth, and 69 out of 117 members from the fifth to the sixth party congress.

The records of the candidate members of the Central Committee are worse. There were no candidate members to the first party congress. The second party congress elected 20, the third party congress 45, the fourth party congress 50, the fifth party congress 55, and the sixth party congress 103, a total of 273. No one served all five Central Committees as a candidate member; only one served three times, twenty served twice, and the rest, 230, served only once. The actual number of persons who served as candidate members in six party congresses is 251. This tendency to short service in the Central Committee is not due to the promotion of candidate members to regular membership in the subsequent Central Committees. The record of promotion of candidate members to regular membership is equally low, meaning most of the candidate members are neither promoted to regular membership nor remain in the Central Committee as candidate members. Only 5 of 20 candidate members were promoted from the second to the third party, 12 of 45 from the third to the fourth, 15 of 50 from the fourth to the fifth, and 12 of 55 from the fifth to the sixth party congress.

OFFICERS OF THE CENTRAL COMMITTEE

Unlike the members and candidate members of the Central Committee, officers of the committee often have been replaced between party congresses, and such changes have been reported and the new slate of officers announced. To simplify the explanation, some of the significant changes made in three major plenums are presented in the list of officers in addition to the changes at the regular party congresses. These are the first joint plenum of the Central Committees of the Workers' Parties of North and South Korea, June 24, 1949; the sixth joint plenum of the Central Committee, held August 4–6, 1953, shortly after the Korean War; and the fourteenth plenum of the Central Committee of the fourth party, October 12, 1966, shortly after the second party conference. In addition, the officers and members of the Workers' Party of South Korea elected at the founding congress, November 23–24, 1946, are presented in the list of officers.

As far as the chairmanship of the party is concerned, all major changes have come between party congresses. The first chairman of the party during the first and second party congresses was Kim Tu-bong, and his South Korean counterpart was Hŏ Hŏn. Kim Il Sung assumed the chairmanship of the party when the North and South Korean parties merged June 24, 1949, at the first joint plenum of the party between the second and third party congresses. The post of chairman was abolished and the office of general secretary was instituted at the fourteenth plenum of the fourth party on October 12, 1966, and Kim Il Sung became the general secretary of the party.

Seventeen persons were elected as chairman, general secretary, vice-chairman, or secretary at the regular party congresses; only Kim Il Sung served in all six congresses. No one served four times. The late Ch'oe Yong-gŏn served three times. Only five were elected twice, and the rest were elected only once. If those who were elected between party congresses are included, the number is substantially increased, but the tendency is the same: more people serving fewer times in these positions, except Kim Il Sung.

The same is true of membership in the key committees within the Central Committee, such as the Political, Standing, and Organization committees. A total of fifty-eight persons were elected to these committees in six regular party congresses, but more than half, thirty-three persons, served only once; seventeen served twice; five served three times; one served four times; none served five times and only two served all six congresses. These two men, Kim Il and Kim Il Sung, are also the only two who served all six congresses as members of the Central Committee.

When those elected to these committees between party congresses are added to the members elected at regular party congresses, the tendency remains the same. There were more people who were not reelected to the subsequent committee than who remained on the committee. Only three or four top party leaders maintained continuity throughout the party congresses and important plenums between party congresses. For example, only four of ten secretaries who were elected at the fourteenth plenum of the fourth party congress in October 1966 were reelected in the fifth party congress. These are Kim Il, Kim Il Sung, Ch'oe Yong-gŏn, and Kim Yŏng-ju.

THE INSPECTION COMMITTEE

Similarly in the Inspection Committee, only three of forty-three people who ever served in the committee were reelected. The overwhelming majority, forty, served only once. The function of this committee is to keep discipline, to enforce the rules and regulations of the party, and to hear appeals and decide upon the penalties for those who violate the party bylaws. However, the rate of turnover in this committee is the highest among all the committees of the Central Committee, including membership in the Central Committee itself. At least two explanations can be made. The first is that the committee takes its job seriously and enforces the rules to the letter, criticizing the majority of the members of the Central Committee and thus creating a high rate of turnover, even in its own committee. The second is that this committee is not different from other committees, that appointment is political, and that performance is rather perfunctory, carrying out the wishes of the supreme leader of the party.

THE WORKERS' PARTY OF SOUTH KOREA

At its founding congress, November 23–24, 1946, in Seoul, one chairman, two vice-chairmen, eight members of the Political Committee, and fourteen members of the Standing Committee were elected. Only four men (Pak Hŏn-yŏng, Yi Sŭng-yŏp, Hŏ Hŏn, and Kim Sam-yong) remained in leadership positions when the North and South Korean parties merged in June 1949. By the time of the sixth joint plenum in August 1953, shortly after the Korean war, none of these men survived. Only two men from the Workers' Party of South Korea were recruited into the Standing Committee of the sixth joint plenum: Ch'oe Wŏn-t'aek, who was the chairman of the Inspection Committee, and Kang Mun-sŏk, who ranked eighth in the Central Committee of the Workers' Party of South Korea. By the time of the third party congress in 1956, none survived as an officer of the Central Committee.

From the first joint plenum of the North and South Korean parties of June 1949 to the seventh joint plenum in December 1953, all but a few of the officers and members of the Central Committee of the South Korean party were purged. From March 1954 on, the Central Committee plenums were no longer referred to as joint plenums, but were called after the month in which they were held. Of twenty-eight members of the Central Committee of the Workers' Party of South Korea, only four were elected to the Central Committee of the third party congress in 1956.

THE CENTRAL AUDITING COMMITTEE

While the function of the Central Auditing Committee was performed by the Central Inspection Committee at the first party congress, the auditing of the party became independent from the inspection function of the Central Committee at the time of the second party congress. The number of the members on this committee increased from seven at the second party congress to seventeen in the third and the fourth party congresses, but this number was reduced at the fifth and sixth party congresses to fifteen. None of the members of the Central Inspection Committee of the first party was reelected to the Central Auditing Committee of the second party congress, but some continuity was maintained when three of seven members of the committee, including the chairman, Yi Chu-yŏn, were reelected to the Central Auditing Committee of the third party congress. The fourth party's Central Auditing Committee, however, elected all new members except one, Kim Kye-rim, from the third party congress. Of the seventeen members of the fourth party, only three were reelected to the Central Auditing Committee of the fifth party, and similarly three members from the fifth were reelected to the sixth. The total number who served in the Auditing Committees of the second, third, fourth, fifth and sixth parties is seventy-one; only ten served twice, and the rest, fifty-one members, served only once. In view of the turnover in this committee, which must require technical skill in auditing financial matters, the criteria for election to the committee seem to be based upon factors more political than technical. Unless, of course, the party has such a simple financial accounting system that technical skills are not required, or the party has so many skilled accountants that it can afford to replace all of them at will.

PERSONNEL REGISTERS

I. First Congress of the Workers' Party of (North) Korea, August 28–30, 1946
   1. Officers of the Central Committee
   2. Members of the Central Inspection Committee

3. Members of the Central Committee
4. Officers of the Workers' Party of South Korea
5. Members of the Central Committee of the Workers' Party of South Korea

II. Second Congress of the Workers' Party of (North) Korea, March 27–30, 1948
    1. Officers of the Central Committee
    2. Members of the Central Committee
    3. Candidate members of the Central Committee
    4. Members of the Central Auditing Committee
    5. Officers of the first joint plenum, June 24, 1949
    6. Changes after the Korean war: Sixth joint plenum, August 4–6, 1953

III. Third Congress of the Workers' Party of Korea, April 23–29, 1956
    1. Officers of the Central Committee
    2. Members of the Central Committee
    3. Candidate members of the Central Committee
    4. Members of the Central Auditing Committee

IV. Fourth Congress of the Workers' Party of Korea, September 11–18, 1961
    1. Officers of the Central Committee
    2. Members of the Central Committee
    3. Candidate members of the Central Committee
    4. Members of the Central Auditing Committee
    5. Changes after the second party conference: Fourteenth plenum, October 12, 1966

V. Fifth Congress of the Workers' Party of Korea, November 2–12, 1970
    1. Officers of the Central Committee
    2. Members of the Central Committee
    3. Candidate members of the Central Committee
    4. Members of the Central Auditing Committee

VI. Sixth Congress of the Workers' Party of Korea, October 10–14, 1980
    1. Officers of the Central Committee
    2. Members of the Central Committee
    3. Candidate members of the Central Committee
    4. Members of the Central Auditing Commission
    5. Members of the Military Commission

FIRST CONGRESS OF THE WORKERS' PARTY OF (NORTH) KOREA, AUGUST 28–30, 1946[21]

1.Officers of the Central Committee

Chairman
  Kim Tu-bong

Vice-Chairmen
  1. Kim Il Sung
  2. Chu Yŏng-ha

Members of the Political Committee
1. Kim Tu-bong
2. Kim Il Sung
3. Chu Yŏng-ha
4. Hŏ Ka-i
5. Ch'oe Ch'ang-ik

Members of the Standing Committee
1. Kim Tu-bong
2. Kim Il Sung
3. Chu Yŏng-ha
4. Hŏ Ka-i
5. Ch'oe Ch'ang-ik
6. Pak Il-u
7. Kim Ch'ang-man
8. Kim Ch'aek
9. Pak Chŏng-ae
10. Pak Hyo-sam
11. Pak Ch'ang-sik
12. Kim Il
13. Kim Chae-uk

2. **Members of the Central Inspection Committee**[22]

1. Kim Yong-bŏm, chairman
2. Chin Pan-su
3. Pang U-yong
4. Kim Sŭng-hun
5. Yi Tong-hwa
6. Kim Ch'an
7. Ch'oe Yong-dal
8. Pak Ŭng-ik
9. Pak Ch'un-sŏk
10. Kim Ch'ae-ryong
11. Yu Yŏng-gi

3. **Members of the Central Committee**

1. Kim Tu-bong*
2. Kim Il Sung*
3. Chu Yŏng-ha*
4. Ch'oe Ch'ang-ik*
5. Hŏ Ka-i*
6. Kim Ch'ang-man
7. Hŏ Chŏng-suk*
8. Kim Yŏng-t'ae
9. Pak Ch'ang-sik*
10. Pak Chŏng-ae*
11. Kim Ch'aek*
12. Mu Chŏng*
13. Yi Ch'un-am
14. An Kil
15. Kim Ye-p'il
16. Kim Il*
17. Pak Hyo-sam*
18. Chang Sun-myŏng*
19. Kim Yŏl*
20. Kim Chae-uk*
21. Yun Kong-hŭm
22. Han Il-mu*
23. T'ae Sŏng-su*
24. Han Sŏl-ya*
25. Ch'oe Kyŏng-dŏk*
26. Kang Chin-gŏn*
27. Chang Si-u*
28. Chŏng Tu-hyŏn*
29. Yim To-jun
30. Yim Hae*
31. O Ki-sŏp*
32. Kim Uk-chin
33. Yi Sun-gŭn*
34. Kim Kyo-yŏng*
35. Myŏng Hi-jo
36. Han Pin

37. Yi Chong-ik*
38. Chŏn Sŏng-hwa
39. Kim Wŏl-song
40. Chang Chong-sik

41. Kim Min-san*
42. Pak Hun-il*
43. Pak Il-u*

*Reelected to the Central Committee of the second party congress. There were thirty.

4. Officers of the Workers' Party of South Korea, November 23–24, 1946[23]

Chairman
 Hŏ Hŏn

Vice-Chairmen
 1. Pak Hŏn-yŏng
 2. Yi Ki-sŏk

Members of the Political Committee
 1. Hŏ Hŏn
 2. Pak Hŏn-yŏng
 3. Yi Ki-sŏk
 4. Kim Sam-yong

 5. Yi Chu-ha
 6. Yi Sŭng-yŏp
 7. Ku Chae-su
 8. Kim Yong-am

Members of the Standing Committee
 1. Hŏ Hŏn
 2. Pak Hŏn-yŏng
 3. Yi Ki-sŏk
 4. Kim Sam-yong
 5. Yi Chu-ha
 6. Yi Sŭng-yŏp
 7. Ku Chae-su

 8. Kim Yong-am
 9. Yi Hyŏn-sang
 10. Kang Mun-sŏk
 11. Ko Ch'an-bo
 12. Yu Yŏng-jun
 13. Kim O-sŏng
 14. Song Ŭl-su

Members of the Inspection Committee
 1. Ch'oe Wŏn-t'aek, chairman
 2. Kim Hyŏng-sŏn, vice-chairman
 3. Yi Sŏk-ku, vice-chairman
 4. Yun Il-chu
 5. Hong Sŏng-u

 6. Hong Tŏk-yu
 7. O Yŏng
 8. Nam Kyŏng-hun
 9. Han Yŏng-uk
 10. Yi Yŏng-uk
 11. Yi Chŏng-hwan

5. Members of the Central Committee of the Workers' Party of South Korea

 1. Hŏ Hon
 2. Pak Hŏn-yŏng

 3. Yi Ki-sŏk
 4. Yi Sŭng-yŏp

5. Ku Chae-su
6. Kim Sam-yong
7. Kim Yong-am
8. Kang Mun-sŏk
9. Yu Yŏng-jun
10. Yi Hyŏn-sang
11. Ko Ch'an-bo
12. Kim O-sŏng
13. Song Ŭl-su*
14. Yi Chae-nam
15. Kim Sang-hyŏk
16. Kim Yŏng-jae

17. Kim Kye-rim
18. Kim Kwang-su
19. Chŏng No-sik
20. Sŏng Yu-gyŏng
21. Chŏng Yun
22. Kim Chin-guk
23. Hyŏn U-hyŏn
24. Hong Nam-p'yo
25. Pak Mun-gyu*
26. Yi Chu-ha
27. Kim T'ae-jun
28. Hŏ Sŏng-t'aek*

*Reelected to the Central Committee of the third party congress. There were only three.

SECOND CONGRESS OF THE WORKERS' PARTY OF (NORTH) KOREA, MARCH 27–30, 1948.[24]

1. **Officers of the Central Committee**

Chairman
Kim Tu-bong

Vice-Chairmen
1. Kim Il Sung
2. Hŏ Ka-i[25]

Members of the Political Committee
1. Kim Tu-bong
2. Kim Il Sung
3. Hŏ Ka-i
4. Kim Ch'aek

5. Ch'oe Ch'ang-ik
6. Pak Il-u
7. Chu Yŏng-ha

Members of the Standing Committee
1. Kim Tu-bong
2. Kim Il Sung
3. Hŏ Ka-i
4. Kim Ch'aek
5. Ch'oe Ch'ang-ik
6. Pak Il-u
7. Pak Chŏng-ae
8. Pak Ch'ang-ok
9. Kim Il

10. Kim Chae-uk
11. Chin Pan-su
12. Ki Sŏk-bok
13. Chŏng Chun-t'aek
14. Chŏng Il-yong
15. Chu Yŏng-ha
16. Kim Yŏl[26]
17. Pak Yŏng-sŏn

Members of the Organization Committee
1. Kim Il Sung
2. Hŏ Ka-i
3. Kim Yŏl
4. Pak Ch'ang-ok
5. Pak Yŏng-sŏn

Members of the Inspection Committee
1. Chang Sun-myŏng, chairman[27]
2. Chang Hae-u
3. Kim Ko-mang
4. Pang Hak-se
5. Chang Ch'ŏl
6. Yi Chong-ik

2. Members of the Central Committee[28]

1. Kim Tu-bong*
2. Kim Il Sung*
3. Hŏ Ka-i
4. Chu Yŏng-ha
5. Kim Ch'aek
6. Ch'oe Ch'ang-ik*
7. Pak Il-u
8. Pak Chŏng-ae*
9. Kim Kyo-yŏng
10. Chŏng Chun-t'aek*
11. Pak Ch'ang-ok*
12. Kim Il*
13. Kim Chae-uk
14. Kim Hwang-il*
15. Kim Yŏl
16. Ch'oe Kyŏng-dŏk
17. Kim Min-san
18. Ch'oe Suk-yang
19. Chin Pan-su*
20. Kang Chin-gŏn*
21. Han Il-mu*
22. Pak Hun-il*
23. Ch'oe Chae-rin
24. Han Sŏl-ya*
25. Yi Hŭi-jun
26. Kang Kŏn
27. Kim Sŭng-hwa
28. Ki Sŏk-bok
29. Hŏ Chŏng-suk*
30. Yi Chung-gŭn
31. T'ae Sŏng-su
32. Chang Sun-myŏng
33. Kim Ŭng-gi*
34. Kim Ko-mang
35. Mu Chŏng
36. Pak Ch'ang-sil
37. Yi Puk-myŏng
38. Pak Hyo-sam
39. Kim Sang-ch'ŏl*
40. Chang Si-u
41. Chŏng Tu-hyŏn
42. O Ki-sŏp*
43. Song Che-jun
44. Kim Chik-hyŏng*
45. Yi Sun-gŭn
46. Kim Kwang-hyŏp*
47. Yi Chong-ik
48. Chang Hae-u
49. Yi Tong-hwa
50. Yim Hae*
51. Chŏng Il-yong*
52. Pang Hak-se*
53. Cho Yŏng*
54. Kim Ung
55. Pak Mu*
56. Kim Yŏng-su
57. Chang Ch'ŏl
58. Kim T'ae-ryŏn
59. Yi Kwŏn-mu*
60. Kim Kyŏng-sŏk*

61. Kim Han-jung
62. Pak Yŏng-sŏn
63. Yi Yu-min*
64. Kim Kwang-bin

65. Yi Song-un*
66. Pak Kŭm-ch'ŏl*
67. Kim Ch'an

*Reelected to the Central Committee of the third party congress. There were twenty-nine.

3. Candidate Members of the Central Committee[29]

1. Pak Wŏn-sul
2. Yi Yŏng-hwa
3. Kim Chin-yŏ
4. Ch'ae Kyu-hyŏng
5. Ha Ang-ch'ŏn*
6. Pak Yŏng-hwa
7. Pak Tong-ch'o
8. Kang Yŏng-ch'ang*
9. Ch'oe Kwang-yŏl
10. Yi Kyu-hwan**

11. Nam Il*
12. Chang Wi-sam
13. Ko Pong-gi*
14. Kim T'ae-hwa
15. Kye Tong-sŏn
16. Kim Tu-yong
17. Yi Hyo-sun*
18. Yi Chi-ch'an**
19. Yi Yŏng-sŏm
20. Ch'oe Pong-su

*Elected to full membership in the Central Committee of the third party congress. There were five.
**Remained as a candidate member of the Central Committee of the third party congress. There were only two.

4. Members of the Central Auditing Committee[30]

1. Yi Chu-yŏn
2. Kim Sŏ-ho
3. Hyŏn Ch'il-chong
4. Ch'a Sun-ch'ŏl

5. Yu Mun-hwa
6. Han Hŭng-guk
7. Yang Yŏng-sun

5. Officers of the First Joint Plenum, Unifying the Workers' Parties of North and South Korea, June 24, 1949

Chairman
  Kim Il Sung

Vice-Chairmen
  1. Pak Hŏn-yŏng
  2. Hŏ Ka-i

Secretaries
  1. Hŏ Ka-i, first secretary
  2. Yi Sŭng-yŏp, second secretary
  3. Kim Sam-yong, third secretary

Members of the Political Committee
1. Kim Il Sung, chairman
2. Pak Hŏn-yŏng, vice-chairman
3. Kim Ch'aek
4. Pak Il-u
5. Hŏ Ka-i
6. Yi Sŭng-yŏp
7. Kim Sam-yong
8. Kim Tu-bong
9. Hŏ Hŏn
    Pak Chŏng-ae[31]

Members of the Organization Committee
1. Kim Il Sung
2. Pak Hŏn-yŏng
3. Kim Ch'aek
4. Pak Il-u
5. Hŏ Ka-i
6. Yi Sŭng-yŏp
7. Kim Sam-yong
8. Kim Tu-bong
9. Hŏ Hŏn
10. Ch'oe Ch'ang-ik
11. Kim Yŏl

6. Changes after the Korean War: Sixth Joint Plenum of the Central Committee of the Second Congress, August 4–6, 1953.

Chairman
   Kim Il Sung

Vice-Chairmen
1. Pak Chŏng-ae
2. Pak Ch'ang-ok[32]
3. Kim Il
4. Pak Yŏng-bin
5. Pak Kŭm-ch'ŏl

Members of the Political Committee
1. Kim Il Sung
2. Kim Tu-bong
3. Pak Chŏng-ae
4. Pak Ch'ang-ok
5. Kim Il

Members of the Standing Committee
1. Kim Il Sung
2. Kim Tu-bong
3. Pak Chŏng-ae
4. Pak Yŏng-bin
5. Ch'oe Wŏn-t'aek
6. Ch'oe Ch'ang-ik
7. Chŏng Il-yong
8. Kim Hwang-il
9. Kang Mun-sŏk
10. Kim Sŭng-hwa
11. Kim Kwang-hyŏp
12. Pak Kŭm-ch'ŏl
13. Nam Il

THIRD CONGRESS OF THE WORKERS' PARTY OF KOREA, APRIL 23–29, 1956[33]

1. Officers of the Central Committee

Chairman
   Kim Il Sung

Vice-Chairmen
1. Ch'oe Yong-gŏn
2. Pak Chŏng-ae
3. Pak Kŭm-ch'ŏl
4. Chŏng Il-yong
5. Kim Ch'ang-man

Members of the Standing Committee
1. Kim Il Sung
2. Kim Tu-bong
3. Ch'oe Yong-gŏn
4. Pak Chŏng-ae
5. Kim Il
6. Pak Kŭm-ch'ŏl
7. Yim Hae
8. Ch'oe Ch'ang-ik
9. Chŏng Il-yong
10. Kim Kwang-hyŏp
11. Nam Il

Candidate Members of the Standing Committee
1. Kim Ch'ang-man
2. Yi Chong-ok
3. Yi Hyo-sun
4. Pak Ŭi-wan

Members of the Organization Committee
1. Kim Il Sung
2. Ch'oe Yong-gŏn
3. Pak Chŏng-ae
4. Pak Kŭm-ch'ŏl
5. Chŏng Il-yong
6. Kim Ch'ang-man

Members of the Inspection Committee
1. Kim Ik-sŏn, chairman
2. Hŏ Sŏng-t'aek, vice-chairman
3. Yun Ŭng-yong, vice-chairman
4. Yi Hyo-sun
5. Kim Yŏ-jung
6. Ch'oe Ton-gŭn
7. Hŏ Hak-song

2. Members of the Central Committee[34]
1. Kim Il Sung*
2. Kim Tu-bong
3. Ch'oe Yong-gŏn*
4. Pak Chŏng-ae*
5. Kim Il*
6. Pak Kŭm-ch'ŏl*
7. Pak Ch'ang-ok
8. Ch'oe Ch'ang-ik
9. Pak Ŭi-wan
10. Chŏng Il-yong*
11. Han Sang-du*
12. Ha Ang-ch'ŏn*
13. Kim Hwang-il
14. Pak Hun-il
15. Yi Hyo-sun*
16. Pak Il-yŏng
17. Yi Il-gyŏng*
18. Han Sŏl-ya*
19. Sŏ Hŭi
20. Yim Hae
21. Kim Ch'ŏn-hae
22. Yi Chong-ok*
23. Nam Il*
24. Chŏng Chun-t'aek*
25. Chin Pan-su
26. Pang Hak-se
27. Kim Ch'ang-man*
28. Yu Ch'uk-un

29. Kim Hoe-il*
30. Mun Man-uk
31. Chŏng Sŏng-ŏn
32. Hŏ Sŏng-t'aek
33. Pak Mun-gyu*
34. Hŏ Chŏng-suk
35. Kim Sŭng-hwa
36. Kang Yŏng-ch'ang*
37. Kim Kwang-hyŏp*
38. Ch'oe Hyŏn*
39. Ch'oe Chong-hak
40. Han Il-mu
41. Yi Kwŏn-mu
42. Yu Kyŏng-su
43. Yi Rim
44. Kim Kyŏng-sŏk*
45. Yi Yŏng-ho*
46. Kim Ch'ang-dŏk*
47. Kim Yong-jin
48. Hyŏn Chŏng-min
49. Ko Pong-gi
50. Cho Yŏng

51. Yi Yu-min
52. Song Pong-uk
53. Yi Song-un*
54. Kim Tŏk-yŏng
55. Kim Man-gŭm*
56. Yi In-dong
57. O Ki-sŏp
58. Kang Chin-gŏn*
59. Kim Wŏn-bong
60. Ch'oe Wŏn-t'aek*
61. Hŏ Pin
62. Han Chŏn-jong
63. Kim Tu-sam
64. Kim Sang-hyŏk
65. Kim Ik-sŏn*
66. Song Ŭl-su
67. Kim Chik-hyŏng
68. Yun Kong-hŭm
69. Pak Mu
70. Kim Sang-ch'ŏl
71. Kim Ŭng-gi

*Reelected to the Central Committee of the fourth party congress. There were twenty-eight.

3. **Candidate Members of the Central Committee**[35]

1. Yu Ch'ŏl-mok
2. Kim T'ae-gŭn*
3. Pak Yong-guk*
4. Kang Tŏk-il
5. Chŏng Tu-hwan*
6. Sŏ Ch'un-sik
7. Yang Kye
8. Ch'oe Ch'ŏl-hwan
9. Yi Tal-chin
10. Paek Hong-gwŏn
11. Chŏng Yŏn-p'yo
12. Ch'oe Il
13. Yi Chae-ch'ŏn
14. O Tong-uk*
15. Yi Ch'ŏng-wŏn

16. Chang Ha-il
17. Yi Mun-il
18. Kim Hyŏn-bong
19. Ko Hŭi-man
20. Sŏk San*
21. O Chin-u*
22. Chang P'yŏng-san
23. Ch'oe Kwang*
24. Kim Pong-yul
25. Ch'oe Yong-jin*
26. Yi P'il-gyu
27. Cho Hun
28. Kim Ch'ang-bong*
29. Ch'oe Sŏn-gyu
30. Pak Kwang-hŭi

31. Ch'oe Ton-gŭn	39. Yi Sang-jo
32. Chŏng Ch'il-sŏng	40. Sŏ Ch'ŏl*
33. Yi Chi-ch'an**	41. Hŏ Kuk-bong
34. Yi Ch'ŏn-ho	42. Yi Kyu-hwan
35. Kim Ch'ŏl-u	43. Yi Puk-myŏng*
36. Yu Ch'ŏl-sŭng	44. Paek Nam-un*
37. Paek Sun-jae	45. Ko Kyŏng-in
38. Yi T'ae-hwa	

*Elected to full membership in the Central Committee of the fourth party congress. There were twelve.
**Remained as a candidate member of the fourth party congress.

4. Members of the Central Auditing Committee[36]

1. Yi Chu-yŏn, chairman	10. Kim Min-san
2. Pak Hyo-sam	11. Kim Kye-rim, vice-chairman
3. Pak Ch'ang-sik	12. Yu Yŏn-hwa, vice-chairman
4. Kim Kyo-yŏng	13. Chŏng Mok
5. Hwang Se-hwan	14. Kim Yŏng-su
6. Chŏng No-sik	15. Yi Sun-gŭn
7. Hyŏn Ch'il-chong	16. Cho Sŏng-mo
8. Kim Ch'ang-hŭp	17. Yu Mun-hwa
9. Yi Hŭi-jun	

FOURTH CONGRESS OF THE WORKERS' PARTY OF KOREA, SEPTEMBER 11–18, 1961[37]

1. Officers of the Central Committee

Chairman
Kim Il Sung

Vice-Chairmen

1. Ch'oe Yong-gŏn	4. Kim Ch'ang-man
2. Kim Il	5. Yi Hyo-sun
3. Pak Kŭm-ch'ŏl	

Members of the Political Committee

1. Kim Il Sung	7. Pak Chŏng-ae
2. Ch'oe Yong-gŏn	8. Kim Kwang-hyŏp
3. Kim Il	9. Chŏng Il-yong
4. Pak Kŭm-ch'ŏl	10. Nam Il
5. Kim Ch'ang-man	11. Yi Chong-ok
6. Yi Hyo-sun	

Candidate Members of the Political Committee

1. Kim Ik-sŏn
2. Yi Chu-yŏn
3. Ha Ang-ch'ŏn
4. Han Sang-du

Members of the Inspection Committee

1. Kim Ik-sŏn, chairman
2. Hwang Wŏn-bo, vice-chairman
3. Kim Ch'ang-dŏk, vice chairman
4. Pak Ch'un-hyŏk, vice-chairman
5. Yi Min-su
6. O Yŏng-bong
7. Yi Sŭng-u

2. Members of the Central Committee[38]

1. Kim Il Sung*
2. Ch'oe Yong-gŏn*
3. Kim Il*
4. Pak Kŭm-ch'ŏl
5. Kim Ch'ang-man
6. Yi Hyo-sun
7. Pak Chŏng-ae
8. Kim Kwang-hyŏp
9. Chŏng Il-yong
10. Nam Il*
11. Yi Chong-ok
12. Kim Ik-sŏn
13. Yi Chu-yŏn
14. Ha Ang-ch'ŏn
15. Han Sang-du
16. Chŏng Chun-t'aek*
17. Sŏ Ch'ŏl*
18. Ch'oe Hyŏn*
19. Sŏk San
20. Kim Kyŏng-sŏk
21. Kim Ch'ang-bong
22. Hŏ Pong-hak
23. Ch'oe Yong-jin*
24. Pak Sŏng-ch'ŏl*
25. O Chin-u*
26. Chŏn Mun-sŏp*
27. Han Sŏl-ya
28. Yi Yŏng-ho
29. Chŏn Ch'ang-ch'ŏl*
30. Yi Song-un
31. Ch'oe Kwang
32. An Yŏng
33. Han Ik-su*
34. Kim Tae-hong*
35. Kang Chin-gŏn
36. Ch'oe Wŏn-t'aek*
37. Paek Nam-un*
38. Yi Il-gyŏng
39. Kang Yŏng-ch'ang
40. Kim Tong-gyu*
41. Kim Yŏng-ju*
42. Pak Yong-guk
43. Kim To-man
44. Hyŏn Mu-gwang*
45. Kim T'ae-gŭn
46. Kim Man-gŭm*
47. Chŏng Tu-hwan
48. Ko Hyŏk
49. Kang Hŭi-wŏn*
50. No Su-ŏk
51. Pak Yŏng-sun*
52. Kim Wal-yong
53. Ch'oe Ki-ch'ŏl
54. O Paek-yong*
55. Yang Kun-ok*
56. Sin Tae-sik
57. Kim Chong-hang
58. Yim Kye-ch'ŏl

59. Pak Se-ch'ang
60. Pak Mun-gyu*
61. Kwŏn Yŏng-t'ae
62. Kim Pyŏng-sik
63. O Hyŏn-ju
64. Kim Hoe-il*
65. Kim Ch'ang-dŏk
66. Hŏ Sŏk-sŏn
67. Kim Ok-sun
68. Yim Ch'ŏl*
69. Ch'oe Min-ch'ŏl
70. Kim Chwa-hyŏk*
71. Chi Pyŏng-hak*
72. Yi Chang-su

73. Hŏ Hak-song
74. O Che-ryong
75. Yim Chin-gyu
76. Yi Chae-yun
77. P'i Ch'ang-nin*
78. Yi Chae-yŏng
79. Yi Kwang-sil
80. No Yong-sam
81. Chŏng Chi-hwan
82. Ch'ae Hŭi-jŏng
83. No Ik-myŏng
84. Yi Puk-myŏng
85. O Tong-uk*

*Reelected to the Central Committee of the fifth party congress. There were thirty-one.

3. Candidate Members of the Central Committee[39]

1. Paek Hak-nim*
2. Kim Chung-nin*
3. Han Tae-yŏng
4. Ch'oe Ch'ang-sŏk
5. Kim Ŭng-sang
6. Pak Ung-gŏl
7. Ch'oe Chae-u*
8. No T'ae-sŏk*
9. Song Ch'ang-nyŏm
10. Kim Kwan-sŏp**
11. Yi Kŭn-mo*
12. O T'ae-bong*
13. Yi Myŏn-sang*
14. Hwang Wŏn-bo
15. Yŏm T'ae-jun*
16. An Sŭng-hak*
17. Yu Ch'ang-gwŏn
18. Kim T'ae-hyŏn
19. Chang Yun-p'il*
20. Paek Sŏn-il**
21. T'ae Pyŏng-yŏl*
22. Pak T'ae-jin
23. Pak U-sŏp

24. Chŏng Pyŏng-gap
25. Ch'oe Chong-gŏn**
26. Yŏm Sang-gi
27. Kim Sŏng-gŭn
28. Yi Yang-suk
29. Yi Kuk-chin
30. Yi Tŏk-hyŏn
31. Ch'oe Hak-sŏn
32. Hwang Sun-hŭi*
33. Pak Hyŏng-suk
34. Yŏm Ŭi-jae
35. Yi Yŏng-sun
36. Kim Myŏng-gŏn
37. Yi Hong-gyun**
38. Yun Ch'ang-sun
39. Han Kyŏng-suk
40. Song Pok-ki*
41. Kim Yong-sŏk
42. Kim Hong-gwan**
43. Kim Ki-du
44. Kim Pyŏng-sam**
45. Pak In-hyŏk
46. Kim Hyŏng-sam

47. Hong Wŏn-gil*
48. Yang Ch'ung-gyŏm**

49. Yi Chi-ch'an*
50. Kim Pyŏng-su

*Elected to full membership in the Central Committee of the fifth party congress. There were fifteen.
**Reelected to candidate membership in the fifth party congress. There were seven.

4. Members of the Central Auditing Committee[40]

1. Kim Yŏ-jung, chairman
2. Kim Kye-rim, vice-chairman
3. Song Yŏng
4. Yun T'ae-hong
5. Yi Pong-su
6. Yim Ch'un-ch'u
7. Kim Cha-rin
8. Yang T'ae-gŭn
9. Chŏng Tong-ch'ŏl
10. Kim Se-bong
11. Kim Kuk-hun
12. Pae Ki-jun
13. Kang Sŏk-san
14. Yi Ho-ch'ŏl, vice-chairman
15. Kim Hong-ok
16. Hwang Hae-yŏng
17. Yi Sang-un

5. Changes after the Second Conference of 1966: Fourteenth Plenum of the Central Committee, October 12, 1966.[41]

General Secretary
Kim Il Sung

Secretaries
1. Ch'oe Yong-gŏn
2. Kim Il
3. Pak Kŭm-ch'ŏl
4. Yi Hyo-sun
5. Kim Kwang-hyŏp
6. Sŏk San
7. Hŏ Pong-hak
8. Kim Yŏng-ju
9. Pak Yong-guk
10. Kim To-man

Members of the Political Committee
1. Kim Il Sung
2. Ch'oe Yong-gŏn
3. Kim Il
4. Pak Kŭm-ch'ŏl
5. Yi Hyo-sun
6. Kim Kwang-hyŏp
7. Kim Ik-sŏn
8. Kim Ch'ang-bong
9. Pak Sŏng-ch'ŏl
10. Ch'oe Hyŏn
11. Yi Yŏng-ho

Candidate Members of the Political Committee
1. Sŏk San
2. Hŏ Pong-hak
3. Ch'oe Kwang
4. O Chin-u
5. Yim Ch'un-ch'u
6. Kim Tong-gyu
7. Kim Yŏng-ju
8. Pak Yong-guk
9. Chŏng Kyŏng-bok

FIFTH CONGRESS OF THE WORKERS' PARTY OF KOREA, NOVEMBER 2–12, 1970[42]

1. Officers of the Central Committee

General Secretary
  Kim Il Sung

Secretaries
  1. Ch'oe Yong-gŏn
  2. Kim Il
  3. Kim Yŏng-ju
  4. O Chin-u
  5. Kim Tong-gyu
  6. Kim Chung-nin
  7. Han Ik-su
  8. Hyŏn Mu-gwang
  9. Yang Hyŏng-sŏp

Members of the Political Committee
  1. Kim Il Sung
  2. Ch'oe Yong-gŏn
  3. Kim Il
  4. Pak Sŏng-ch'ŏl
  5. Ch'oe Hyŏn
  6. Kim Yŏng-ju
  7. O Chin-u
  8. Kim Tong-gyu
  9. Sŏ Ch'ŏl
  10. Kim Chung-nin
  11. Han Ik-su

Candidate Members of the Political Committee
  1. Hyŏn Mu-gwang
  2. Chŏng Chun-t'aek
  3. Yang Hyŏng-sŏp
  4. Kim Man-gŭm

Members of the Inspection Committee
  1. Kim Yŏ-jung, chairman
  2. O Yŏng-bong, vice-chairman
  3. Yi Yong-nin
  4. An Pae-ok
  5. Yi Kwang-p'il
  6. Chŏng Myŏng-yong
  7. Yi Yŏng-nin

2. Members of the Central Committee[43]

  1. Kim Il Sung*
  2. Ch'oe Yong-gŏn
  3. Kim Il*
  4. Pak Sŏng-ch'ŏl*
  5. Ch'oe Hyŏn*
  6. Kim Yŏng-ju
  7. O Chin-u*
  8. Kim Tong-gyu
  9. Sŏ Ch'ŏl*
  10. Kim Chung-nin*
  11. Han Ik-su
  12. Hyŏn Mu-gwang*
  13. Chŏng Chun-t'aek
  14. Yang Hyŏng-sŏp*
  15. Kim Man-gŭm*
  16. Nam Il
  17. Ch'oe Yong-jin*
  18. Hong Wŏn-gil
  19. Chŏng Kyŏng-hŭi*
  20. Kim Yŏ-jung
  21. O Paek-yong*
  22. Chŏn Ch'ang-ch'ŏl*

23. Chŏng Tong-ch'ŏl*
24. Hwang Sun-hŭi*
25. Pak Yŏng-sun*
26. Paek Nam-un
27. Ch'oe Wŏn-t'aek
28. Yu Chang-sik
29. Hŏ Tam*
30. Kim Pyŏng-ha
31. Chŏn Mun-sŏp*
32. Kim Hyŏk-ch'ŏl*
33. Yu Chŏng-suk*
34. Yim Ch'un-ch'u*
35. Kim Chwa-hyŏk*
36. Chi Pyŏng-hak
37. Kim Tae-hong
38. Yim Ch'ŏl
39. T'ae Pyŏng-yŏl*
40. Paek Hak-nim*
41. Pak Mun-gyu
42. O Tong-uk
43. Pang Hak-se*
44. Chu To-il*
45. Yi Tu-ik*
46. Yi Ŭl-sŏl*
47. Kim Ch'ŏl-man*
48. O Chae-wŏn*
49. Chŏn Mun-uk*
50. Ch'oe In-dŏk*
51. Kim Ik-hyŏn
52. Kang Hyŏn-su*
53. Yi Yong-mu
54. Yi Kŭn-mo*
55. Hong Si-hak*
56. No Pyŏng-u
57. Yun Ki-bok*
58. Ch'oe Chae-u*
59. Song Pok-ki
60. O T'ae-bong
61. Kim Kuk-t'ae*
62. Chŏng Chun-gi*
63. Yŏn Hyŏng-muk*
64. Pak Su-dong*
65. Kang Sŏng-san*
66. Yi Pong-gil*
67. Kim Sŏng-ae*
68. O Suk-hŭi
69. Yi Sŏn-hwa
70. Yu Sun-hŭi
71. Ch'oe Yun-su
72. Kang Hŭi-wŏn*
73. Kye Ŭng-t'ae*
74. P'i Ch'ang-nin
75. Chang Yun-p'il*
76. Hyŏn Ch'ŏl-gyu
77. Ch'oe Yŏng-nim*
78. Han Yŏng-hak
79. Kim Hoe-il*
80. Kim Yŏng-nam*
81. Kim Yun-sŏn
82. Kim Sŏk-hwan
83. Sim Kyŏng-ch'ŏl*
84. Yang Man-ch'ŏl
85. Yi Chi-ch'an*
86. Yu Sŭng-nam
87. Pae Sŭng-hyŏk
88. Ch'oe Ch'ang-gwŏn
89. Kim Ch'ŏng-yong*
90. Chŏn Chae-bong*
91. Kim Chang-gwŏn
92. Pak Yong-sŏk*
93. Kim Pyŏng-yul*
94. Yi Kil-song*
95. Yi Yong-ik*
96. Yim Su-man*
97. Yi Tong-ch'un*
98. Kim I-hun
99. No T'ae-sŏk
100. Kim Kyŏng-yŏn*
101. Kim Su-dŭk
102. Hwang Chang-yŏp*
103. Yi Myŏn-sang*
104. Yang Kun-ok
105. Yŏm T'ae-jun*
106. Yi Min-su

107. Yi Kyŏng-sŏk
108. Kim Kye-hyŏn
109. O Kŭk-yŏl*
110. Kim Kuk-hun*
111. Kim Si-hak*
112. Ch'oe Ch'ang-hwan

113. An Sŭng-hak*
114. Yi Kŏn-il
115. Chŏn Yŏng-hŭi
116. Kim Nak-hŭi
117. Pak Hae-gwŏn

*Reelected to the Central Committee of the sixth party congress. There were sixty-nine.

3. Candidate Members of the Central Committee[44]

1. Cho Myŏng-sŏn*
2. Kim Yong-yŏn**
3. Kim Sŏng-guk
4. Pak Sŏn-gyun
5. Kye Hyŏng-sun**
6. Kim Ŭng-sam**
7. Chŏn Ha-ch'ŏl**
8. Son Sŏng-p'il
9. Yim Hyŏng-gu*
10. Yi Rim-su
11. Kim Ŭi-sun
12. Yi Pong-wŏn*
13. Pak Yŏng-sin
14. Paek Pŏm-su*
15. Yi Si-wŏn
16. Sim Ch'ang-wan*
17. Kim Ch'ang-bok
18. Son Kyŏng-jun*
19. Chŏn Pyŏng-ho*
20. Kim Hyŏng-bong**
21. Ch'oe Chin-sŏng*
22. Chu Kyu-ch'ang**
23. Ch'oe Chong-gŏn
24. Yang Ch'ung-gyŏm
25. Kim Pyŏng-sam
26. Yi Chang-su
27. Paek Sŏn-il
28. Yi Hong-gyun

29. Kim Hong-gwan
30. Sin Chin-sun**
31. Ch'ŏn Se-bong*
32. Kim Kwan-sŏp*
33. O Yong-bang**
34. Sŏ Ch'ang-nam
35. Yi Pong-sŏp
36. Pak Ki-sŏ**
37. An Myŏng-ch'ŏl
38. Kim Chae-yong
39. Kim Nŭng-il
40. Yi Pong-gyŏm
41. Hyŏn Ch'ang-yong
42. Chu Ch'ang-bok**
43. Pak Ch'un-sik
44. Kim Ki-sŏn*
45. Yi Ch'ŏl-bong**
46. Kim Kwang-guk
47. O Kyŏng-hun
48. Yi Ch'ŏng-il
49. Hŏ Ch'ang-suk**
50. Wang Ok-hwan**
51. Chang Ch'ŏl**
52. Kim Kŭm-ok
53. Hŏ Yŏn-suk
54. Yi P'il-sŏng
55. Sŏ Yun-sŏk*

*Elected to full membership in the Central Committee of the sixth party congress. There were twelve.

**Reelected to candidate membership in the sixth party congress. There were fourteen.

4. Members of the Central Auditing Committee[45]

1. Kim Se-hwal, chairman
2. Yu Chong-yŏl
3. Chŏng Tu-hwan
4. Yi Nak-bin, vice-chairman
5. Kim Kŭm-ch'ŏl
6. Kim Tu-sam
7. Kim Hong-ok
8. Ŏm Sang-il, vice-chairman
9. Kim Ch'i-gu
10. Ch'oe Man-guk
11. Chŏng Kyŏng-sik
12. Kim Un-suk
13. Yang T'ae-gŭn
14. Kim Se-bong
15. Song Kŭm-sun

SIXTH CONGRESS OF THE WORKERS' PARTY OF KOREA, OCTOBER 10–14, 1980[46]

1. Officers of the Central Committee

General Secretary
  Kim Il Sung

Secretaries
1. Kim Chŏng-il
2. Kim Chung-nin
3. Kim Yŏng-nam
4. Kim Hwan
5. Yŏn Hyŏng-muk
6. Yun Ki-bok
7. Hong Si-hak
8. Hwang Chang-yŏp
9. Pak Su-dong

Members of the Presidium of the Politbureau
1. Kim Il Sung
2. Kim Il
3. O Chin-u
4. Kim Chŏng-il
5. Yi Chong-ok

Members of the Politbureau
1. Kim Il Sung
2. Kim Il
3. O Chin-u
4. Kim Chŏng-il
5. Yi Chong-ok
6. Pak Sŏng-ch'ŏl
7. Ch'oe Hyŏn
8. Yim Ch'un-ch'u
9. Sŏ Ch'ŏl
10. O Paek-yong
11. Kim Chung-nin
12. Kim Yŏng-nam
13. Chŏn Mun-sŏp
14. Kim Hwan
15. Yŏn Hyŏng-muk
16. O Kŭk-yŏl
17. Kye Ŭng-t'ae
18. Kang Sŏng-san
19. Paek Hak-nim

Alternate Members of the Politbureau
1. Hŏ Tam
2. Yun Ki-bok
3. Ch'oe Kwang
4. Cho Se-ung

5. Ch'oe Chae-u
6. Kong Chin-t'ae
7. Chŏng Chun-gi
8. Kim Ch'ŏl-man
9. Chŏng Kyŏng-hŭi
10. Ch'oe Yŏng-nim

11. Sŏ Yun-sŏk
12. Yi Kŭn-mo
13. Hyŏn Mu-gwang
14. Kim Kang-hwan
15. Yi Sŏn-sil

Members of the Control Commission

1. Sŏ Ch'ŏl, chairman
2. Kim Chwa-hyŏk, vice-chairman
3. Chu Ch'ang-bok, vice-chairman

4. Kim Ch'ang-hwan
5. Chŏng Kwan-yul
6. Yi Yong-mo
7. Han Sŏk-kwan

2. Members of the Central Committee of the Sixth Congress[47]

1. Kim Il Sung
2. Kim Il
3. O Chin-u
4. Kim Chŏng-il
5. Yi Chong-ok
6. Pak Sŏng-ch'ŏl
7. Ch'oe Hyŏn
8. Yim Ch'un-ch'u
9. Sŏ Ch'ŏl
10. O Paek-yong
11. Kim Chung-nin
12. Kim Yŏng-nam
13. Chŏn Mun-sŏp
14. Kim Hwan
15. O Kŭk-yŏl
16. Kye Ŭng-t'ae
17. Kang Sŏng-san
18. Hŏ Tam
19. Yŏn Hyŏng-muk
20. Yun Ki-bok
21. Ch'oe Kwang
22. Cho Se-ung
23. Ch'oe Chae-u
24. Kong Chin-t'ae
25. Chŏng Chun-gi
26. Kim Ch'ŏl-man
27. Chŏng Kyŏng-hŭi

28. Ch'oe Yŏng-nim
29. Sŏ Yun-sŏk
30. Yi Kŭn-mo
31. Hyŏn Mu-gwang
32. Paek Hak-nim
33. Kim Kang-hwan
34. Yi Sŏn-sil
35. Hong Si-hak
36. Pak Su-dong
37. Hwang Chang-yŏp
38. Sŏ Kwan-hŭi
39. Kim Tu-yŏng
40. Kim Kyŏng-yŏn
41. Chŏng Tong-ch'ŏl
42. Kim Kuk-t'ae
43. T'ae Pyŏng-yŏl
44. Pyŏn Ch'ang-bok
45. No Myŏng-gŭn
46. Yim Ho-gun
47. Kim Pyŏng-ha
48. Yi Chin-su
49. Kim Ki-nam
50. Kim Kwan-sŏp
51. Yang Hyŏng-sŏp
52. Yi Chŏng-yong
53. Chŏn Ch'ang-ch'ŏl
54. Hŏ Chŏng-suk

55. Yi Ch'ang-sŏn
56. Yim Hyŏng-gu
57. Chang Kuk-ch'an
58. Cho Ch'ang-dŏk
59. Kim Yun-hyŏk
60. Yi Chi-ch'an
61. Yun Ho-sŏk
62. Yŏm Chae-man
63. Yim Kye-ch'ŏl
64. Ko Chŏng-sik
65. Kim Il-dae
66. Kim Yŏng-ch'ae
67. Ch'oe Chŏng-gŭn
68. Pang Hak-se
69. Yi Chae-yun
70. Kim Pyŏng-yul
71. Paek Pŏm-su
72. Ch'oe Mun-sŏn
73. Yi Tong-ch'un
74. Kim Ki-sŏn
75. Kang Hŭi-wŏn
76. Yi Kil-song
77. Yim Su-man
78. Chang In-sŏk
79. Sim Ch'ang-wan
80. Pak Yong-sŏk
81. Kim Ch'i-gu
82. Pak Yŏng-sun
83. Hwang Sun-hŭi
84. Yi Ŭl-sŏl
85. Cho Sun-baek
86. Chu To-il
87. Yi Tu-ik
88. Yang Yong-gyŏk
89. Chang Sŏng-u
90. Cho Myŏng-nok
91. Kim Il-ch'ŏl
92. Ch'oe Sang-uk
93. Yi Chŏng-bae
94. Kim Yong-un
95. Cho Hŭi-wŏn
96. Yi Ha-il
97. Yi Pong-wŏn
98. Han Yŏng-ok
99. Ch'oe In-dŏk
100. O Chae-wŏn
101. Chŏn Mun-uk
102. Yi Tu-ch'an
103. Kim Si-hak
104. Chang Yun-p'il
105. Kim Sŏng-ae
106. Ch'ŏn Se-bong
107. Yi Myŏn-sang
108. Cho Myŏng-sŏn
109. Chŏn Pyŏng-ho
110. Yi Pong-gil
111. Mun Sŏng-sul
112. Yi Wŏn-bŏm
113. Yi Ch'an-sŏn
114. Hyŏn Chun-gŭk
115. Kim Yong-sun
116. Hong Sŏng-yong
117. Kim Hoe-il
118. Ch'oe Chin-sŏng
119. Kim Chwa-hyŏk
120. Yu Chŏng-suk
121. Yi Tong-ho
122. Kim Kuk-hun
123. Yi Kyŏng-sŏn
124. Kim Tu-nam
125. Chŏn Hŭi-jŏng
126. Yi Hwa-yŏng
127. Kim Yun-sang
128. Wŏn Tong-gu
129. Kim Man-gŭm
130. Kang Hyŏn-su
131. Yi Yong-ik
132. Yŏm T'ae-jun
133. An Sŭng-hak
134. Hong Ki-mun
135. Hong Sŏng-nam
136. Ch'oe Yong-jin

137. Yi Chong-mok
138. Son Kyŏng-jun
139. Chu Kil-bon
140. Kim Hyŏk-ch'ŏl
141. Pae Ch'ŏl-u

142. Kim Ch'ŏng-yong
143. Chŏng Ch'ŏl
144. Sim Kyŏng-ch'ŏl
145. Chŏn Chae-bong

3. **Candidate Members of the Central Committee of the Sixth Congress**[48]

1. Kang Sŏk-sung
2. T'ae Chong-su
3. Pang Ch'ŏl-gap
4. Kim Ŭng-sang
5. Cho Ch'ŏl-jun
6. Tong Min-gwang
7. Hŏ Sun
8. Yi Yang-suk
9. Sŏ Chae-hong
10. Chŏng Song-nam
11. Ch'oe Man-hyŏn
12. Kim T'ae-gŭk
13. Ch'ae Hŭi-jŏng
14. Pak Myŏng-bin
15. Yun Ki-jŏng
16. Sin Sang-gyun
17. Kim Pong-yul
18. Pak Chung-guk
19. Kim Kwang-jin
20. Yi Pyŏng-uk
21. Kim Yŏng-ch'un
22. Kim Yi-ch'ang
23. Chŏn Chin-su
24. Han Ch'ang-su
25. Yŏ Ch'un-sŏk
26. Yi Chong-u
27. Pak Ki-sŏ
28. O Yong-bang
29. Yi In-dŏk
30. Yun Ch'i-ho
31. Ok Pong-nin
32. Chŏng Wŏn-gyo
33. Kim Yong-hyŏn
34. Kim Chae-mun

35. Wŏn Myŏng-gyun
36. Kwŏn Sŏng-nin
37. Kim Pong-ju
38. Son Sŏng-p'il
39. Chi Ch'ang-ik
40. Kim Sŏng-gŏl
41. Kim Yu-Sun
42. Kim Chu-yŏng
43. Pyŏn Sŭng-u
44. Yŏm Ki-sun
45. Yi Sŏng-bok
46. Yi Hwa-sŏn
47. Kil Chae-gyŏng
48. Yi Wan-gi
49. Chu Ch'ang-bok
50. Pang Ch'ŏl-ho
51. Kim Chang-gwŏn
52. Yi Ch'ŏl-bong
53. Kim Hyŏng-bong
54. Han Sŏng-yong
55. Ch'oe Sang-yŏl
56. Chu Kyu-ch'ang
57. Pak Si-hyŏng
58. Ch'oe Ŭng-nok
59. Chang Ch'ŏl
60. Kim Chae-bong
61. Sin Chin-sun
62. Kim Man-guk
63. Han Sang-gyu
64. Kwŏn Hŭi-gyŏng
65. Chŏn Myŏng-su
66. Sin In-ha
67. Kim Yong-yŏn
68. Yim Nok-chae

69. Hŏ Ch'ang-suk
70. Wang Ok-hwan
71. Yi Su-wŏl
72. Kim Ŭng-sam
73. Yi Ho-hyŏk
74. Chŏn Ha-ch'ŏl
75. Kim Nak-hŭi
76. Yi Kwang-han
77. Hong In-bŏm
78. Yi Hwan-sam
79. Pak Pong-ju
80. Sin Tong-hwan
81. Ko Hak-ch'ŏn
82. Chŏn Che-ha
83. Pak Im-t'ae
84. Hŏ Min-sŏn
85. Ko T'ae-ŭn
86. Kye Hyŏng-sun

87. Ch'oe Myŏng-ch'ŏl
88. Kim Ch'ang-ho
89. Song Pok-ki
90. Ch'oe Pyŏng-ho
91. Han Kyu-p'al
92. Yu Chae-hwa
93. Pak Su-bŏm
94. Yun Myŏng-gŭn
95. O Hyŏn-ju
96. Yi Sun-gŭn
97. Ch'oe Ch'ang-hwan
98. Yi Chŏng-do
99. Kwak Yŏng-ho
100. Pak Yong-myŏn
101. Wŏn Tal-sik
102. Pak Sŏl-hŭi
103. Pak Yŏng-ch'ŏl

4. Members of the Central Auditing Commission[49]

1. Yi Nak-bin, chairman
2. Kang Chŏm-gu
3. Kim Chong-sŏng
4. Chu Hwa-jong
5. Pang Ki-yŏng
6. Chŏng Tu-hwan
7. Song Kwan-jo
8. Kang Chung-han

9. Ch'oe Ch'i-sŏn
10. Yi Chŏng-sik
11. Sin Sang-yun
12. Pak Yŏng-ch'an
13. Sŏ Sŏn-ch'il
14. Yi Yong-sun
15. Song Kŭm-sun

5. Members of the Military Commission[50]

1. Kim Il Sung, chairman
2. O Chin-u
3. Kim Chŏng-il
4. Ch'oe Hyŏn
5. O Paek-yong
6. Chŏn Mun-sŏp
7. O Kŭk-yŏl
8. Paek Hak-nim
9. Kim Ch'ŏl-man
10. Kim Kang-hwan

11. T'ae Pyŏng-yŏl
12. Yi Ŭl-sŏl
13. Chu To-il
14. Yi Tu-ik
15. Cho Myŏng-nok
16. Kim Il-ch'ŏl
17. Ch'oe Sang-uk
18. Yi Pong-wŏn
19. O Yong-bang

TABLES

2.1 Central Committee Chairmen, General Secretary, Vice-chairmen, and Secretaries Elected at Party Congresses

2.2 Persons with Repeated Service as Chairman, Vice-chairman, and Secretary of the Party Central Committee

2.3 Central Committee Chairman, Secretary, Vice-chairman, and Secretaries Elected between Party Congresses

2.4 Members of the Politbureau and Political, Organization, and Standing Committees of the Party Central Committee

2.5 Candidate Members of the Political and Standing Committees and Alternate Members of the Politbureau, Third through Sixth Party Congresses

2.6 Persons with Repeated Service in the Political, Organization, and Standing Committees and Politbureau of the Party Central Committee

2.7 Members and Candidate Members of the Political, Organization, and Standing Committees Elected between Party Congresses (Including the Workers' Party of South Korea)

2.8 Officers and Members of the Inspection Committee and the Control Commission

2.9 Patterns of Reelection to the Party Central Committee

2.10 Members Elected to the Party Central Committee More Than Three Times

2.11 Patterns of Reelection to Candidate Membership in the Party Central Committee

2.12 Persons Reelected More Than Twice to Candidate Membership in the Party Central Committee

2.13 Patterns of Promotion from Candidate Membership to Membership in the Party Central Committee

2.14 Candidate Members Promoted to the Party Central Committee

2.15 Patterns of Reelection to the Central Auditing Committee

2.16 Members Reelected to the Central Auditing Committee

2.17 Party Membership and Composition of Party Congresses

TABLE 2.1

*Central Committee Chairmen, General Secretary,
Vice-chairmen, and Secretaries Elected at Party Congresses*

	First Cong.	Second Cong.	Third Cong.	Fourth Cong.	Fifth Cong.	Sixth Cong.
Ch'oe Yong-gŏn			vc-1	vc-1	sec-1	
Chŏng Il-yong			vc-4			
Chu Yŏng-ha	vc-2					
Han Ik-su					sec-7	
Hong Si-hak						sec-7
Hwang Chang-yŏp						sec-8
Hyŏn Mu-gwang					sec-8	
Kim Ch'ang-man			vc-5	vc-4		
Kim Chŏng-il						sec-1
Kim Chung-nin					sec-6	sec-2
Kim Hwan						sec-4
Kim Il				vc-2	sec-2	
Kim Il Sung	vc-1	vc-1	c	c	g. sec	g. sec
Kim Tong-gyu					sec-5	
Kim Tu-bong	c	c				
Kim Yŏng-ju					sec-3	
Kim Yŏng-nam						sec-3
O Chin-u					sec-4	
Pak Chŏng-ae			vc-2			
Pak Kŭm-ch'ŏl			vc-3	vc-3		
Pak Su-dong						sec-9
Yang Hyŏng-sŏp					sec-9	
Yi Hyo-sun				vc-5		
Yŏn Hyŏng-muk						sec-5
Yun Ki-bok						sec-6

c - chairman; vc - vice-chairman; g. sec - general secretary; sec - secretary.
Numbers indicate rank order.

TABLE 2.2

Persons with Repeated Service as Chairman,
Vice-chairman, and Secretary of the Party Central Committee

Six times	Kim Il Sung
Five times	none
Four times	none
Three times	Ch'oe Yong-gŏn
Two times	Kim Ch'ang-man, Kim Chung-nin, Kim Il, Kim Tu-bong, Pak Kŭm-ch'ŏl
One time	Eighteen persons served only once

Total number of persons serving: 25

TABLE 2.3

Central Committee Chairman, General Secretary, Vice-chairman,
and Secretaries Elected between Party Congresses

	Workers' Party of South Korea	Joint Session June 1949	Joint Plenum August 1953	14th Plenum Oct. 1966
Ch'oe Yong-gŏn				sec-1
Hŏ Hŏn	c			
Hŏ Ka-i		sec-1		
Hŏ Pong-hak				sec-7
Kim Il			vc-3	sec-2
Kim Il Sung		c	c	g. sec
Kim Kwang-hyŏp				sec-5
Kim Sam-yong		sec-3		
Kim To-man				sec-10
Kim Yŏng-ju				sec-8
Pak Ch'ang-ok			vc-2	
Pak Chŏng-ae			vc-1	
Pak Hŏn-yŏng	vc-1	vc-1		
Pak Kŭm-ch'ŏl			vc-5	sec-3
Pak Yŏng-bin			vc-4	
Pak Yong-guk				sec-9
Sŏk San				sec-6
Yi Hyo-sun				sec-4
Yi Ki-sŏk	vc-2			
Yi Sŭng-yŏp		sec-2		

c - chairman; vc - vice-chairman; g. sec - general secretary; sec - secretary.
Numbers indicate rank order.

TABLE 2.4
*Members of the Politbureau and Political, Organization,
and Standing Committees of the Party Central Committee*

	1st Cong.		2d Cong.			3d Cong.		4th Cong.	5th Cong.	6th Cong.
	P	S	P	S	O	O	S	P	P	P
Chin Pan-su				11						
Ch'oe Ch'ang-ik	5	5	5	5			8			
Ch'oe Hyŏn									5	7
Ch'oe Yong-gŏn						2	3	2	2	
Chŏn Mun-sŏp										13
Chŏng Chun-t'aek				13						
Chŏng Il-yong				14		5	9	9		
Chu Yŏng-ha	3	3	7	15						
Han Ik-su									11	
Hŏ Ka-i	4	4	3	3	2					
Kang Sŏng-san										18
Ki Sŏk-bok				12						
Kim Chae-uk		13		10						
Kim Ch'aek		8	4	4						
Kim Ch'ang-man		7				6		5		
Kim Chŏng-il										4
Kim Chung-nin									10	11
Kim Hwan										14
Kim Il		12		9			5	3	3	2
Kim Il Sung	2	2	2	2	1	1	1	1	1	1
Kim Kwang-hyŏp							10	8		
Kim Tong-gyu									8	
Kim Tu-bong	1	1	1	1			2			
Kim Yŏl					3					
Kim Yŏng-ju									6	
Kim Yŏng-nam										12
Kye Ŭng-t'ae										17
Nam Il							11	10		
O Chin-u									7	3
O Kŭk-yŏl										16
O Paek-yong										10
Paek Hak-nim										19
Pak Ch'ang-sik		11								
Pak Ch'ang-ok				8	4					

TABLE 2.4—*Continued*

	1st Cong.		2d Cong.			3d Cong.		4th Cong.	5th Cong.	6th Cong.
	P	S	P	S	O	O	S	P	P	P
Pak Chŏng-ae	9	7				3	4	7		
Pak Hyo-sam	10									
Pak Il-u	6		6	6						
Pak Kŭm-ch'ŏl						4	6	4		
Pak Sŏng-ch'ŏl									4	6
Pak Yŏng-sŏn					5					
Sŏ Ch'ŏl									9	9
Yi Chong-ok								11		5
Yi Hyo-sun								6		
Yim Ch'un-ch'u										8
Yim Hae						7				
Yŏn Hyŏng-muk										15

P - Politbureau and Political Committee; S - Standing Committee; O - Organization Committee. Numbers indicate rank order.

TABLE 2.5

Candidate Members of the Political and Standing Committees and
Alternate Members of the Politbureau, Third through Sixth Party Congresses

	3d Congress	4th Congress	5th Congress	6th Congress
	CS	CP	CP	AP
Cho Se-ung				4
Ch'oe Chae-u				5
Ch'oe Kwang				3
Ch'oe Yŏng-nim				10
Chŏng Chun-gi				7
Chŏng Chun-t'aek			2	
Chŏng Kyŏng-hŭi				9
Ha Ang-ch'ŏn		3		
Han Sang-du		4		
Hŏ Tam				1
Hyŏn Mu-gwang			1	13
Kim Ch'ang-man	1			
Kim Ch'ŏl-man				8
Kim Ik-sŏn		1		
Kim Kang-hwan				14
Kim Man-gŭm			4	
Kong Chin-t'ae				6
Pak Ŭi-wan	4			
Sŏ Yun-sŏk				11
Yang Hyŏng-sŏp			3	
Yi Chong-ok	2			
Yi Chu-yŏn		2		
Yi Hyo-sun	3			
Yi Kŭn-mo				12
Yi Sŏn-sil				15
Yun Ki-bok				2

CS - candidate member of the standing committee; CP - candidate member of the political committee; AP - alternate member of the politbureau. Numbers indicate rank order.

TABLE 2.6

Persons with Repeated Service in the Political, Organization,
and Standing Committees and Politbureau of the Party Central Committee

Six times	Kim Il, Kim Il Sung
Five times	none
Four times	Pak Chŏng-ae
Three times	Ch'oe Ch'ang-ik, Ch'oe Yong-gŏn, Chŏng Il-yong, Kim Ch'ang-man, Kim Tu-bong
Two times	Seventeen persons served twice
One time	Thirty-three persons served once

Total number of persons serving: 58

TABLE 2.7

Members and Candidate Members of the Political, Organization,
and Standing Committees Elected between Party Congresses
(including the Workers' Party of South Korea)

	Workers' Party of South Korea		Joint Session June 1949		Joint Plenum August 1953		14th Plenum Oct. 1966	
	P	S	P	O	P	S	P	CP
Ch'oe Ch'ang-ik				10		6		
Ch'oe Hyŏn							10	
Ch'oe Kwang								3
Ch'oe Wŏn-t'aek						5		
Ch'oe Yong-gŏn							2	
Chŏng Il-yong						7		
Chŏng Kyŏng-bok								9
Hŏ Hon	1	1	9	9				
Hŏ Ka-i			5	5				
Hŏ Pong-hak								2
Kang Mun-sŏk		10				9		
Kim Ch'aek			3	3				
Kim Ch'ang-bong							8	
Kim Hwang-il						8		
Kim Ik-sŏn							7	
Kim Il					5		3	
Kim Il Sung			1	1	1	1	1	
Kim Kwang-hyŏp						11	6	
Kim O-sŏng		13						
Kim Sam-yong	4	4	7	7				
Kim Sŭng-hwa						10		
Kim Tong-gyu								6
Kim Tu-bong			8	8	2	2		
Kim Yŏl			10	11				
Kim Yong-am	8	8						
Kim Yŏng-ju								7
Ko Ch'an-bo		11						
Ku Chae-su	7	7						
Nam Il						13		
O Chin-u								4
Pak Ch'ang-ok					4			
Pak Chŏng-ae					3	3		
Pak Hŏn-yŏng	2	2	2	2				

TABLE 2.7—*Continued*

	Workers' Party of South Korea		Joint Session June 1949		Joint Plenum August 1953		14th Plenum Oct. 1966	
	P	S	P	O	P	S	P	CP
Pak Il-u			4	4				
Pak Kŭm-ch'ŏl						12	4	
Pak Sŏng-ch'ŏl							9	
Pak Yŏng-bin						4		
Pak Yong-guk								8
Pak Yŏng-sŏn			11					
Sŏk San								1
Song Ŭl-su		14						
Yi Chu-ha	5	5						
Yi Hyo-sun							5	
Yi Hyŏn-sang		9						
Yi Ki-sŏk	3	3						
Yi Sŭng-yŏp	6	6	6	6				
Yi Yŏng-ho							11	
Yim Ch'un-ch'u								5
Yu Yŏng-jun		12						

P - Political Committee; S - Standing Committee; O - Organization Committee; CP - candidate member of the Political Committee

TABLE 2.8
Officers and Members of the
Inspection Committee and the Control Commission

	First Cong.	Second Cong.	Third Cong.	Fourth Cong.	Fifth Cong.	Sixth Cong.
An Pae-ok					4	
Chang Ch'ŏl		5				
Chang Hae-u		2				
Chang Sun-myŏng		1				
Chin Pan-su	2					
Ch'oe Ton-gŭn			6			
Ch'oe Yong-dal	7					
Chŏng Kwang-yul						5
Chŏng Myŏng-yong					6	
Chu Ch'ang-bok						3
Han Sŏk-kwan						7
Hŏ Hak-song			7			
Hŏ Sŏng-t'aek			2			
Hwang Wŏn-bo				2		
Kim Chae-ryong	10					
Kim Ch'an	6					
Kim Ch'ang-dŏk				3		
Kim Ch'ang-hwan						4
Kim Chwa-hyŏk						2
Kim Ik-sŏn			1	1		
Kim Ko-mang		3				
Kim Sŭng-hun	4					
Kim Ŭng-gi		1*				
Kim Yŏ-jung			5		1	
Kim Yong-bŏm	1					
O Yŏng-bong				6	2	
Pak Ch'un-hyŏk				4		
Pak Ch'un-sŏk	9					
Pak Ŭng-ik	8					
Pang Hak-se		4				
Pang U-yong	3					
Sŏ Ch'ŏl						1
Yi Chong-ik		6				
Yi Hyo-sun			4			
Yi Kwang-p'il					5	
Yi Min-su				5		

TABLE 2.8—*Continued*

	First Cong.	Second Cong.	Third Cong.	Fourth Cong.	Fifth Cong.	Sixth Cong.
Yi Sŭng-u				7		
Yi Tong-hwa	5					
Yi Yong-mo						6
Yi Yong-nin					3	
Yi Yŏng-nin					7	
Yi Yŏng-gi	11					
Yun Ŭng-yong			3			

*Elected chairman at the sixth joint plenum in August 1953.

Only three (Kim Ik-sŏn, Kim Yŏ-jung, and O Yŏng-bong) were elected twice; the rest served only once. The total number elected to the committee is forty-three.

TABLE 2.9

Patterns of Reelection to the Party Central Committee

	First Cong.	Second Cong.	Third Cong.	Fourth Cong.	Fifth Cong.	Sixth Cong.
First Congress	43	30	12(2)[a]	5(1)[a]	2	2(1)[b]
Second Congress		67	29	11(1)[c]	3(1)[d]	2
Third Congress			71	28	10	6(1)[e]
Fourth Congress				85	31	13(3)[f]
Fifth Congress					117	67
Sixth Congress						145

a. Kim Ch'ang-man and Yun Kong-hŭm were not reelected to the Second, but to the Third Congress. Of the two, only Kim was reelected to the Fourth Congress.

b. Hŏ Chŏng-suk was elected to the First, Second, Third, and Sixth Congresses, but was not reelected to the Fourth and Fifth Congresses.

c. Yi Puk-myŏng was elected to the Second and Fourth Congresses, but not the Third.

d. Pang Hak-se was elected to the Second, Third, Fifth, and Sixth Congresses, but not to the Fourth Congress.

e. Yi Chong-ok was elected to the Third, Fourth, and Sixth Congresses, but not to the Fifth Congress.

f. Ch'oe Kwang, Yi Chae-yun, and Yim Kye-ch'ŏl were elected to the Fourth and Sixth Congresses, but not to the Fifth Congress.

TABLE 2.10

Members Elected to the Party Central Committee More Than Three Times

	First Cong.	Second Cong.	Third Cong.	Fourth Cong.	Fifth Cong.	Sixth Cong.
Six times (two)						
Kim Il	16	12	5	3	3	2
Kim Il Sung	2	2	1	1	1	1
Five times (none)						
Four times (nine)						
Ch'oe Hyŏn			38	18	5	7
Chŏng Chun-t'aek		10	24	16	13	
Han Sŏl-ya	24	24	18	27		
Hŏ Chŏng-suk	7	29	32			54
Kang Chin-gŏn	26	20	58	35		
Kim Hoe-il			29	64	79	117
Kim Man-gŭm			55	46	15	129
Pak Chŏng-ae	10	8	4	7		
Pang Hak-se		52	26		43	68
Three times (twenty-eight)						
Ch'oe Ch'ang-ik	4	6	8			
Ch'oe Wŏn-t'aek			60	36	27	
Ch'oe Yong-gŏn			3	2	2	
Ch'oe Yong-jin				23	17	136
Chŏn Ch'ang-ch'ŏl				29	22	53
Chŏn Mun-sŏp				26	31	13
Chŏng Il-yong		15	10	9		
Han Il-mu	22	21	40			
Hyŏn Mu-gwang				44	12	31
Kang Hŭi-wŏn				49	72	75
Kim Ch'ang-man	6		27	5		
Kim Chwa-hyŏk				70	35	119
Kim Kwang-hyŏp		46	37	8		
Kim Kyŏng-sŏk		60	44	20		
Kim Tu-bong	1	1	2			
Nam Il			32	10	16	
O Chin-u				25	7	3
O Ki-sŏp	31	42	57			
O Paek-yong				54	21	10
Pak Hun-il	42	22	14			
Pak Kŭk-ch'ŏl		66	6	4		

TABLE 2.10—*Continued*

	First Cong.	Second Cong.	Third Cong.	Fourth Cong.	Fifth Cong.	Sixth Cong.
Pak Mun-gyu			33	60	41	
Pak Sŏng-ch'ŏl				24	4	6
Pak Yŏng-sun				51	25	82
Sŏ Ch'ŏl				17	9	9
Yi Chong-ok			22	11		5
Yi Song-un		65	53	30		
Yim Hae	30	50	20			

Twice (118)

Once (160)

Total number elected: 528. Absolute number of persons: 317.

Numbers indicate rank order in the Central Committee.

TABLE 2.11

Patterns of Reelection to Candidate Membership
in the Party Central Committee

	First Cong.	Second Cong.	Third Cong.	Fourth Cong.	Fifth Cong.	Sixth Cong.
First Congress						
Second Congress		20	2	1		
Third Congress			45	1		
Fourth Congress				50	7	
Fifth Congress					55	14
Sixth Congress						103

TABLE 2.12

Persons Reelected More Than Twice
to Candidate Membership in the Party Central Committee

	First Cong.	Second Cong.	Third Cong.	Fourth Cong.	Fifth Cong.	Sixth Cong.
Chang Ch'ŏl					51	59
Ch'oe Chong-gŏn				25	33	
Chŏn Ha-ch'ŏl					7	74
Chu Ch'ang-bok					42	49
Chu Kyu-ch'ang					22	56
Hŏ Ch'ang-suk					49	69
Kim Hong-gwan				42	29	
Kim Hyŏng-bong					20	53
Kim Kwan-sŏp			10	32		
Kim Pyŏng-sam			44	25		
Kim Ŭng-sam					11	72
Kye Hyŏng-sun					5	86
O Yong-bang					33	28
Paek Sŏn-il			20	27		
Pak Ki-sŏ					36	27
Sin Chin-sun					30	61
Wang Ok-hwan					50	70
Yang Ch'ung-gyŏm			48	24		
Yi Chi-ch'an		18	33	49		
Yi Hong-gyun			37	28		
Yi Kyu-hwan		10	42			

Numbers indicate rank order.

TABLE 2.13

Patterns of Promotion from Candidate Membership to
Membership in the Party Central Committee

	First Cong.	Second Cong.	Third Cong.	Fourth Cong.	Fifth Cong.	Sixth Cong.
First Congress						
Second Congress		20	5	4	1	
Third Congress			45	12	5	3
Fourth Congress				50	15	11
Fifth Congress					55	12
Sixth Congress						103

TABLE 2.14
Candidate Members Promoted to the Party Central Committee

	First Cong.	Second Cong.	Third Cong.	Fourth Cong.	Fifth Cong.	Sixth Cong.
An Sŭng-hak					113	133
Chang Yun-p'il					75	104
Cho Myŏng-sŏn						108
Ch'oe Chae-u					58	23
Ch'oe Chin-sŏng						118
Ch'oe Kwang			31			
Ch'oe Yong-jin			23		17	136
Chŏn Pyŏng-ho						109
Ch'ŏn Se-bong						106
Chŏng Tu-hwan				47		
Ha Ang-ch'ŏn			12	14		
Hong Wŏn-gil					18	
Hwang Sun-hŭi					24	83
Kang Yŏng-ch'ang			36	39		
Kim Ch'ang-bong				21		
Kim Chung-nin					10	11
Kim Ki-sŏn						74
Kim Kwan-sŏp						50
Kim T'ae-gŭn				45		
Ko Pong-gi			49			
Nam Il			23	10	16	
No T'ae-sŏk					99	
O Chin-u				25	7	3
O T'ae-bong					60	
O Tong-uk				85	42	
Paek Hak-nim					40	32
Paek Nam-un				37	26	
Paek Pŏm-su						71
Pak Yong-guk				42		
Sim Ch'ang-wan						79
Sŏ Ch'ŏl				17	9	9
Sŏ Yun-sŏk						29
Sŏk San				19		
Son Kyŏng-jun						138
Song Pok-ki					59	
T'ae Pyŏng-yŏl					39	43
Yi Chi-ch'an					85	60

TABLE 2.14—*Continued*

	First Cong.	Second Cong.	Third Cong.	Fourth Cong.	Fifth Cong.	Sixth Cong.
Yi Hyo-sun			15	6		
Yi Kŭn-mo					54	30
Yi Myŏn-sang					103	107
Yi Pong-wŏn						97
Yi Puk-myŏng		37		84		
Yim Hyŏng-gu						56
Yŏm T'ae-jun					105	132

Numbers indicate rank order in the Central Committee after promotion.

TABLE 2.15
Patterns of Reelection to the Central Auditing Committee

	First Cong.	Second Cong.	Third Cong.	Fourth Cong.	Fifth Cong.	Sixth Cong.
First Congress						
Second Congress		7	3			
Third Congress			17	1		
Fourth Congress				17	3	
Fifth Congress					15	3
Sixth Congress						15

TABLE 2.16
Members Reelected to the Central Auditing Committee

	First Cong.	Second Cong.	Third Cong.	Fourth Cong.	Fifth Cong.	Sixth Cong.
Chŏng Tu-hwan					3	6
Hyŏn Ch'il-chong		3	7			
Kim Hong-ok				15	7	
Kim Kye-rim			11	2		
Kim Se-bong				10	14	
Song Kŭm-sun					15	15
Yang T'ae-gŭn				8	13	
Yi Chu-yŏn	1	1				
Yi Nak-bin					4	1
Yu Mun-hwa	5	17				

Only ten were reelected; the rest served only once.

Total number elected: 71. Absolute number who served: 61.

Numbers indicate rank order.

TABLE 2.17
Party Membership and Composition of Party Congresses

	First Congress	Second Congress	Third Congress	Fourth Congress	Fifth Congress	Sixth Congress
Party membership	366,339	725,762	1,164,945	1,311,563	1.6 million	3 million
Percentage of population	4%	8%	10%	12.2%	13%	17%
Cell organizations	12,000	29,763	58,259	65,000	---	---
Number of delegates to congress	801	999	916	1,657	1,734	3,220
Occupation of delegates						
worker	183	466	439	944	---	---
peasant	157	270	192	451	---	---
officer worker	385	234	246	191	---	---
others	76	29	39	71	---	---

NOTES

1. For the text of the bylaws of the first party congress, see *Pukchosŏn nodongdang ch'angnip taehoe* [The Founding Congress of the Workers' Party of Korea] (Pyongyang: Pukchosŏn Nodongdang Chungang Ponbu, 1946), pp. 48–56.

2. October 10 is a national holiday. See, for example, Kim's speech on October 10, 1965, claiming it as the twentieth anniversary of the founding of the party. *Kim Il Sung chŏjak sŏnjip* (Pyongyang: Chosŏn Nodongdang Ch'ulp'ansa, 1968), 4: 278–316.

3. *Haebanghu simnyŏn ilchi* [Ten-Year Diary After the Liberation] (Pyongyang: Chosŏn Chungang T'ongsinsa, 1955), p. 45.

4. Ch'oe Ch'ang-ik and Pak Ch'ang-ok were the top antiparty factionalists expelled at this plenum. See the reference in Paek Pong, *Minjok ŭi t'aeyang Kim Il Sung changgun* [The Sun of the Nation, Marshal Kim Il Sung] (Pyongyang: Inmun Kwahaksa, 1969), 2: 403–5.

5. The generals included Kim Kwang-hyŏp, Sŏk San, Kim Ch'ang-bong, Hŏ Pong-hak, Ch'oe Kwang, and Yi Yŏng-ho.

6. There are many sources, but one of the earliest sources to claim this is Sŏnu Mong-yŏng, *Inmin chŏggwŏn ŭi surip kwa kŭŭi konggohwa rŭl wihan chosŏn nodongdang ŭi t'ujaeng* [The Establishment of the People's Power and the Struggle of the Workers' Party of Korea to Strengthen It] (Pyongyang: Chosŏn Nodongdang Ch'ulp'ansa, 1958), pp. 1–21.

7. Reference to this plenum is in Kim Il Sung's speech on April 10, 1946.

8. For details of the First Congress, see *Pukchosŏn nodong ch'angnip taehoe hoeŭirok* [Minutes of the Founding Congress of the Workers' Party of North Korea] (n.p., n.d.).

9. Between the second and third Central Committee meetings, a Standing Committee meeting was reported.

    1WPK-2CC-11SC. November 16, 1946.

    Eleventh Session of the Standing Committee of the Central Committee.

    Concerning the Socialist Workers' Party in South Korea.

10. Several Standing Committee meetings were reported.

    1WPK-3CC-SC. December 2, 1946.

    Fourteenth Session of the Standing Committee of the Central Committee.

    Kim Il Sung's report: Development of Struggle for Thought Reform.

1WPK-3CC-SC. December 15, 1946.

A Session of the Standing Committee of the Central Committee.

Decision to support the resolution of the peasant meeting in Charyŏng County, Hwanghae Province, to contribute grains and to develop a grain purchase project assurance movement. Adopted a decision to enlarge and organize the movement throughout North Korea.

1WPK-3CC-SC. January 20, 1947.
A Session of the Standing Committee of the Central Committee.

> Decision to support the coal mining movement of the Chŏngju transportation workers, and to popularize such a patriotic movement among all people.

11. Another Standing Committee meeting was reported.
1WPK-6CC-SC. March 28, 1947.
A Session of the Standing Committee of the Central Committee.

> Concerning the strengthening of democratic culture: (1) elimination of the remnants of the old feudalistic and colonial thought patterns, (2) disclosure of bureaucratism, formalism, and factionalism, (3) strengthening of class consciousness of the toiling masses.

12. Another Standing Committee meeting was reported.
1WPK-8CC-SC. July 7, 1947.
A Session of the Standing Committee of the Central Committee.

> a. Concerning the increased production movement of the workers of Hŭngnam fertilizer factory and Suan mines in commemoration of the second anniversary of the liberation of Korea.
> b. Decision to promulgate increased production movement throughout Korea.

13. For the details of the Second Congress, see *Puk chosŏn nodongdang che ich'a chŏndang taehoe hoeŭirok* [Minutes of the Second Congress of the Workers' Party of North Korea] (Pyongyang: Pukchosŏn Nodongdang Chungang Wiwŏnhoe, n.d.).

14. *Chosŏn nodongdang che samch'a taehoe munhŏnjip* [Collection of Documents of the Third Party Congress of the Workers' Party of Korea] (Pyongyang: Chosŏn Nodongdang Ch'ulp'ansa, 1956).

15. Sources subsequent to this plenum indicated that the plenum was held to discuss:

> a. Elimination of sectarian factionalists from the party.
> Expulsion of Ch'oe Ch'ang-ik and Pak Ch'ang-ok and other antiparty factionalists from the party.
> b. Strengthening of Leninism in the party work.

16. Several Standing Committee meetings were reported.
3WPK-10CC-SC. December 15, 1959.
A Session of the Standing Committee of the Central Committee.

> On strengthening the party's thought-education project.

3WPK-10CC-SC. January 15, 1960.
A Session of the Standing Committee of the Central Committee.

> On strengthening of party leadership in the local party organizations, particularly in the provincial party committees.

3WPK-10CC-SC. April 1, 1960.
A Session of the Standing Committee of the Central Committee.

 a. On strengthening the political, economic, military, and revolutionary democratic bases in North Korea.
 b. On the correct understanding of the party by the masses.
 c. On strengthening the revolutionary forces around the party.

 17. *Chosŏn nodongdang che sach'a taehoe munhŏnjip* [Collection of Documents of the Fourth Party Congress of the Workers' Party of Korea] (Pyongyang: Chosŏn Nodongdang Ch'ulp'ansa, 1961). This is also available in English, *Documents of the Fourth Congress of the Workers' Party of Korea* (Pyongyang: Foreign Languages Publishing House, 1961).

 18. For the report on the Fifth Congress of the Workers' Party of Korea, see *Chosŏn chungang yŏn'gam, 1971* (Pyongyang: Chosŏn Chungang T'ongsinsa, 1971), pp. 157-71.

 19. For the report on the Sixth Congress of the Workers' Party of Korea, see *Nodong sinmun*, October 11-16, 1980, and *Pyongyang Times*, October 11-16, 1980.

 20. For the voting record, see *Pukchosŏn nodongdang che ich'a ch'angnip taehoe hoeŭirok*, pp. 232-39.

 21. Information on the First Congress is from *Pukchosŏn nodongdang ch'angnip taehoe, che chaeryo* (Pyongyang: Pukchosŏn Nodongdang Chungang Ponbu, 1946), pp. 72-74. The minutes of the First Congress *(Pukchosŏn nodongdang ch'angnip taehoe hoeŭirok)* lists (41) Kim Min-san, (42) Pak Hun-il, and (43) Pak Il-u between (22) Han Il-mu and (23) T'ae Sŏng-su, giving them the rank order of 23, 24 and 25, and pushing everyone from T'ae Sŏng-su down three numbers. However, both lists are the same as to the members of the Central Committee.

 22. The bylaws of the first party provided for the Central Inspection Committee, which performed the function of both the Inspection Committee and the Central Auditing Committee, and the Central Inspection Committee reported directly to the party congress. This provision was amended to provide two separate committees: the Inspection Committee, to become a part of the Central Committee, and the Central Auditing Committee, which reports directly to the party congress.

 23. For the officers and members of the Workers' Party of South Korea, see *Chosŏn yŏn'gam, 1948* (Seoul: Chosŏn T'ongsinsa, 1947), p. 441.

 24. *Pukchosŏn nodongdang che ich'a chŏndang taehoe che chaeryojip* [Source Materials of the Second Congress of the Workers' Party of Korea] (Pyongyang: Pukchosŏn Nodongdang Chungang Ponbu, 1948), pp. 121-32.

 25. Hŏ was added at a third meeting of the Central Committee in September 1948.

 26. Kim Yŏl and Pak Yŏng-sŏn were added at the third meeting of the Central Committee in September 1948.

 27. The original record of the party congress showed that Hŏ Ka-i was chairman and Chang Sun-myŏng was vice-chairman, but Hŏ must have yielded the position to devote himself to the newly created Organization Committee. Chang

Sun-myŏng was dismissed from the Inspection Committee along with Yi Ki-sŏk, who was elected to the Inspection Committee after the merger of the Workers' Party of North and South Korea, and Kim Ŭng-gi was elected chairman of the Inspection Committee at the sixth joint plenum in August 1953.

28. *Pukchosŏn nodongdang che ich'a chŏndang taeho che chaeryojip* (Pyongyang: Pukchosŏn Nodongdang Chungang Ponbu, 1948), pp. 121–32.

29. Ibid.

30. Ibid.

31. Pak was elected to the Political Committee at the fourth joint plenum in November 1951.

32. At the March plenum of the Central Committee in 1954, Pak Ch'ang-ok and Kim Il were relieved of their positions, and Pak Yŏng-bin and Pak Kŭm-ch'ŏl were elected.

33. *Chosŏn nodongdang che samch'a taehoe munhŏnjip*, pp. 539–44. See also *Nodong sinmun*, April 30, 1956.

34. Ibid.

35. Ibid.

36. Ibid.

37. *Chosŏn nodongdang che sach'a taehoe munhŏnjip*, pp. 415–19. See also *Nodong sinmun*, September 18, 1961.

38. Ibid.

39. Ibid.

40. Ibid.

41. *Nodo. g sinmun*, October 13, 1966. See also *Minju Chosŏn*, October 13, 1966.

42. *Nodong sinmun*, November 14, 1970.

43. Ibid.

44. Ibid.

45. Ibid.

46. *Nodong sinmun*, October 15, 1980.

47. Ibid.

48. Ibid.

49. Ibid.

50. Ibid.

3

The Supreme People's Assembly
1948–1980

MEETINGS OF THE SUPREME PEOPLE'S ASSEMBLY

The Supreme People's Assembly exercises exclusive legislative power in the Democratic People's Republic of Korea. It was established in September 1948 with the creation of the republic in the North, and during the past thirty years, six different assemblies have met. Prior to the creation of the republic and during the Russian occupation of the North, two interim organizations performed more or less similar functions. The first was the North Korean Provisional People's Committee, which came into existence in February 1946. This committee met three times during 1946 and passed laws governing elections, land reforms, and administrative redistricting of counties and provinces. The committee dissolved itself to create the People's Assembly of North Korea in February 1947, and this assembly performed interim legislative functions until the Supreme People's Assembly was formally declared in September 1948. This assembly held five sessions, meeting on the average once in four months, and passed various statutes. There were 237 representatives to this assembly; it elected the chairman of the People's Committee, chief procurator, and chief justice of the Supreme Court. It performed important legislative functions, such as passing tax laws, drafting a provisional constitution, and approving the national budgets for 1947 and 1948.

The first session of the Supreme People's Assembly was held from the second to the tenth of September 1948. It adopted a constitution by September 8 and declared the birth of the republic on September 9, 1948. The First Assembly lasted for approximately ten years, but succeeding assemblies were convened every five years. There is no constitutional provision for the convening of a new Assembly every five years, but the practice has been followed. The term of the elected members is four years. The First Assembly was in session from 1948 to 1957, and one can attribute the length of this session to the Korean war. The Second Assembly was in session from 1957 to 1962, the Third from 1962 to

1967, the Fourth from 1967 to 1972, and the Fifth from 1972 to 1977. The Sixth Assembly began its first session in December 1977.

The First Assembly had thirteen sessions, meeting on the average twice per year. During the Korean war, the Assembly did not meet at all for three years from 1950 to 1953. The constitution of September 1948 stipulated that the Assembly should have two regular sessions each year; this was amended to one or two sessions per year in the 1972 constitution. The Second Assembly held eleven sessions, averaging twice per year, and the Third Assembly held seven sessions, averaging once per year. Both the Fourth and Fifth Assemblies held six sessions, and the meetings were more or less regularized to once per year in either March or April.

Agendas for all sessions are reported and known. It is obvious from the agendas that the first two Assemblies were engaged in more discussion of various legislative problems of the time than were the Third and Fourth Assemblies. By the time of the Fifth Assembly, the meetings had become sessions to hear reports and approve the annual budget of the state. The Assembly has legislative, elective, and recall powers. It has authority to elect and recall top officers of the state, establish basic principles of domestic and foreign policies, and decide questions of war and peace. Each session lasts from three to five days, and few legislative functions are performed except unanimous and enthusiastic approval of the reports or proposals on the agenda. Although the constitution guarantees the inviolability of the members of the Assembly and only a simple majority is needed to pass any legislation, all sessions are attended by almost all members and the votes are, without exception, unanimous.

A much smaller body of fewer than twenty members, the Standing Committee of the Assembly, exercises most of the legislative functions. The agendas for this committee are never reported. The committee has the right to decide on bills, amend laws and ordinances, and even interpret laws, subject to the approval of the regular sessions of the Assembly. However, at no time has a regular session of the Assembly failed to approve the decisions of the Standing Committee. There is no record of questioning or discussion, except praise, on any decision. The Standing Committee can also convene an extraordinary session of the Assembly, but no extra sessions have ever been called. In fact, even the regular sessions have become merely an annual formality.

AGENDAS

The agendas are arranged in chronological order under the following headings:

North Korean Provisional People's Committee
  February 8, 1946–February 17, 1947
  Founding congress and three enlarged plenums

People's Assembly of North Korea
  February 17, 1947–September 2, 1948
  First congress and five sessions of the Assembly

Supreme People's Assembly
  1. Period of the First Supreme People's Assembly
     September 2, 1948–September 18, 1957
     Thirteen sessions of the Assembly

  2. Period of the Second Supreme People's Assembly
     September 18, 1957–October 22, 1962
     Eleven sessions of the Assembly

  3. Period of the Third Supreme People's Assembly
     October 22, 1962–December 14, 1967
     Seven sessions of the Assembly

  4. Period of the Fourth Supreme People's Assembly
     December 14, 1967–December 25, 1972
     Six sessions of the Assembly

  5. Period of the Fifth Supreme People's Assembly
     December 25, 1972–December 15, 1977
     Seven Sessions of the Assembly

  6. Period of the Sixth Supreme People's Assembly
     December 15, 1977–

Abbreviations:

DPRK	Democratic People's Republic of Korea
NKPPC	North Korean People's Provisional Committee
PANK	People's Assembly of North Korea
SPA	Supreme People's Assembly
1SPA	First Supreme People's Assembly
5SPA-7	Seventh session of the Fifth Supreme People's Assembly

NORTH KOREAN PROVISIONAL PEOPLE'S COMMITTEE
Period of the North Korean Provisional People's Committee, February 8, 1946–February 17, 1947.

NKPPC. February 8, 1946.
Founding Congress of the North Korean Provisional People's Committee.

   a. Report of Kim Il Sung on the present political situation of Korea and the establishment of the North Korean Provisional People's Committee.
   b. Adoption of a resolution to establish the North Korean Provisional People's Committee.

NKPPC-1. April 13, 1946.
First Enlarged Plenum of the North Korean Provisional People's Committee.

   Report of Kim Il Sung on land reform in North Korea.

NKPPC-2. September 5, 1946.
Second Enlarged Plenum of the North Korean Provisional People's Committee.

   a. Election laws of the villages, counties, cities, and provincial People's Committees in North Korea.
   b. Proclamation of the election laws.
   c. Laws on the governance of the special city of Pyongyang.
   d. Decision to incorporate the city of Wŏnsan, the counties of Anbyŏn and Munch'ŏn into Kangwŏn-do.
   e. Organization of the Central Election Committee.

NKPPC-3. November 25, 1946.
Third Enlarged Plenum of the North Korean Provisional People's Committee.

   Report of Kim Il Sung on the democratic election in North Korea and the tasks of the People's Committee.

People's Assembly of North Korea
Period of the People's Assembly of North Korea, February 17, 1947–September 2, 1948.

PANK. February 17–20, 1947.
First Congress of the People's Assembly of North Korea.

   February 17:
   a. Passage of the agenda of the congress.

b. Congratulatory messages by the representatives of the parties and other social organizations.

February 18:

a. Report of the Credentials Committee.

b. Approval of all laws passed by the North Korean Provisional People's Committee.

February 19:

a. Report of Kim Il Sung on the North Korean people's economic development of 1947.

b. Report on the establishment of the People's Assembly of North Korea.

c. Election of a committee to draft rules and regulations concerning the election and the People's Assembly.

February 20:

a. Passage of the rules and regulations concerning the election and the People's Assembly.

b. Election of 237 representatives of the People's Assembly.

c. Concluding remarks by Kim Il Sung.

PANK-1. February 21–22, 1947.

First Session of the People's Assembly of North Korea.

February 21:

a. Report of Kim Il Sung: Report of the North Korean Provisional People's Committee to the People's Assembly of North Korea.

b. Passage of laws on the People's Committees, courts, and procurator's offices in North Korea.

c. Election of Kim Il Sung as the chairman of the People's Committee, Chang Hae-u as the chief procurator, and Ch'oe Yun-ok as the chief justice of the Supreme Court.

February 22:

a. Passage of Kim Il Sung's report on the People's Committee of North Korea.

b. Approval of the elections of chief procurator and chief justice.

c. Proclamation of a declaration of the People's Assembly of North Korea.

d. Approval of a telegram to be sent to Molotov.

e. Adoption of a congratulatory message to the Russian soldiers on the occasion of the founding day of the Soviet army.

PANK-2. May 15–16, 1947.
Second Session of the People's Assembly of North Korea.

May 15:

Report of the chairman of the Agriculture and Forestry Bureau of the People's Committee of North Korea on the revision of tax-in-kind.

May 16:

a. Congratulatory telegrams to the Soviet Union and the United States on the Occasion of the Reconvening of the U.S.S.R-U.S. Joint Commission on Korea.
b. Passage of a national budget totaling 6.7 billion *wŏn* for the fiscal year 1947.
c. Adoption of North Korean tax laws.
d. Adoption of laws concerning the change in the administrative district in P'yŏngan Namdo.
e. Election of two judges to enlarge the Supreme Court from seven to nine members.
f. Speech by Kim Il Sung on the occasion of the reopening of the U.S.S.R.-U.S. Joint Commission on Korea and the path of the Korean people.

PANK-3. November 18–19, 1947.
Third Session of the People's Assembly of North Korea.

November 18:

a. Report of Kim Tu-bong on the preparation for the drafting of the provisional constitution of Korea.
b. Discussion of Kim Tu-bong's report.

November 19:

a. Election of a committee to draft a provisional constitution of Korea under the chairmanship of Kim Tu-bong.
b. Discussion and election of a twenty-four-member committee to draft laws of Korea.
c. Approval of decrees issued by the People's Committee of North Korea during the period between the second and third sessions of the People's Assembly of North Korea.
d. Approval of the decisions passed by the Standing Committee of the People's Committee during the period between the second and third sessions of the People's Assembly of North Korea.

e. Decision to enlarge the Supreme Court to fourteen members and election of additional judges.

PANK-4. February 6–7, 1948.
Fourth Session of the People's Assembly of North Korea.

February 6:
a. Report of Kim Il Sung on the result of the 1947 people's economic plan and the projection of the 1948 people's economic plan.
b. Report on the national budget for the 1948 fiscal year.

February 7:
a. Discussion and passage of the 1948 national budget.
b. Report of Vice-chairman Kim Ch'aek and the approval of the decrees issued by the People's Committee of North Korea during the period between the third and fourth sessions of the People's Assembly of North Korea.
c. Approval of the decisions passed by the Standing Committee of the People's Assembly during the period between the third and fourth sessions of the People's Assembly of North Korea.
d. Report of Chairman Kim Tu-bong of the provisional constitution draft committee. Decision to have a nationwide discussion on the draft constitution and to convene a special session of the People's Assembly of North Korea during March 1948 to examine and adopt the draft constitution.

PANK-5. July 9–10, 1948.
Fifth Session of the People's Assembly of North Korea.

July 9:
Report of Kim Il Sung on the promulgation of the constitution of the Democratic People's Republic of Korea adopted at the special session of the People's Assembly.

July 10:
a. Discussion on the report of Kim Il Sung and the promulgation of the constitution in the territory of North Korea.
b. Decision to elect representatives to the Supreme People's Assembly.

SUPREME PEOPLE'S ASSEMBLY
Period of the Supreme People's Assembly, September 2, 1948–

1. Period of the First Supreme People's Assembly.
1SPA. September 2, 1948–September 18, 1957.

1SPA-1. September 2–10, 1948.
First Session of the First Supreme People's Assembly.

September 2:
a. Passage of the agenda of the session.
b. Election of Kim Tu-bong as chairman of the committee to draft a constitution of the Democratic People's Republic of Korea.
c. Election of Kang Yang-uk as chairman of the Rules Committee defining the rights and duties of the representatives.
d. Election of members to the Credentials Committee.

September 3:
Discussion on the draft constitution of the Democratic People's Republic of Korea by Kim Ch'aek, Yi Sŭng-yŏp, Song Pong-uk, Pak Hŏn-yŏng, Chu Yŏng-ha, Hŏ Hŏn, Hong Myŏng-hŭi, Chŏng Chun-t'aek, and others.

September 4:
a. Decision to accept the report of the Credentials Committee.
b. Reading of congratulatory messages.
c. First reading of the draft constitution.

September 5:
Second reading and discussion of the draft constitution.

September 6:
a. Report of Kim Tu-bong, chairman of the committee to draft a constitution of the Democratic People's Republic of Korea.
b. Discussion of the draft constitution, 20 chapters and 104 articles.

September 7:
Continued discussion of the draft constitution.
End of discussion of the draft constitution.

September 8:
a. Adoption by unanimous vote of the draft constitution as the constitution of the Democratic People's Republic of Korea.
b. Election of Kim Tu-bong as chairman of the Standing Committee and election of twenty representatives as members of the Standing Committee of the Supreme People's Assembly.
c. Declaration of Kim Il Sung on the transfer of authority.
d. Discussion on the organization of the government and election of

Kim Il Sung as premier of the Democratic People's Republic of Korea.

September 9:
a. Approval of new cabinet proposed by Kim Il Sung.
b. Election of the justices to the Supreme Court of the DPRK.
c. Appointment of chief procurator of the DPRK.
d. Organization of a Legislative Committee.
e. Adoption of a regulation concerning the rights and duties of the representatives of the Supreme People's Assembly of the DPRK.
f. Election of a committee to draft a statement requesting simultaneous withdrawal of both Russian and American troops from Korea.

September 10:
a. Report of Kim Il Sung on the political platform of the DPRK.
b. Decision on amnesty in the DPRK.
c. Adoption of a statement requesting simultaneous withdrawal of both Russian and American troops from Korea.
d. Approval of the selection of a delegate by the government to represent North Korea to the United Nations for future discussion of the Korean question.

1SPA-2. January 28–February 1, 1949.
Second Session of the First Supreme People's Assembly.

January 28:
a. Passage of the agenda of the session.
b. Report of chairman Chŏng Chun-t'aek of the State Planning Commission: On the Results of 1948 Economic Plan and the 1949–50 Economic Plan for the People's Economic Rehabilitation and Development in the Northern Half of the DPRK.

January 29:
a. Election of a twenty-five-member Basic Committee headed by Kim Il Sung to draft a bill on results of the 1948 economic plan and the 1949–50 economic plan for the economic rehabilitation and development of the northern half of the DPRK.
b. Report of Pak Hŏn-yŏng, foreign minister, on the foreign policy of the DPRK.

January 31:
a. Discussion and adoption of the report of Pak Hŏn-yŏng.
b. Report on the elections of the provincial, municipal, county, and village People's Committees.

c. On the changes in the administrative districts; creation of Chagang-do and Najin County of Hamgyŏng Pukto.

d. Report on the general amnesty. Discussion and adoption of the report on the general amnesty.

e. Election of a justice to the Supreme Court and election of a twenty-member jury.

February 1:

a. Passage of a Bill entitled, "On the Results of 1948 Economic Plan and the 1949–50 Economic Plan for the Economic Rehabilitation and Development in the Northern Half of the DPRK."

b. Concluding speech by Kim Il Sung on completion of the two-year people's economic plan: Completion of the Two-year People's Economic Plan is the Materialistic Guarantee of Fatherland Unification.

1SPA-3. April 19–23, 1949.
Third Session of the First Supreme People's Assembly.

April 19:
Report of Ch'oe Ch'ang-ik: Report on the national budget for the 1948 fiscal year and the proposed national budget for the 1949 fiscal year.

April 20:
Discussion of Ch'oe Ch'ang-ik's report.

April 21:
Report of Kim Il Sung: Report of the Delegates of the Democratic People's Republic of Korea on Their Visit to the Soviet Union.

April 22:
Discussion and approval of Kim's report.

April 23:
Passage of the national budget. Approval of the decision on the election of the provincial, municipal, county, and district People's Committees.

1SPA-4. September 8–10, 1949.
Fourth Session of the First Supreme People's Assembly.

September 8:
Report of Kim Il Sung: Report on the First Anniversary of the DPRK.

September 9:

a. Approval of a statement in support of government policies as reported by Kim Il Sung.

b. Approval of a committee headed by Hong Myŏng-hŭi to draft a law on compulsory elementary education.

September 10:

a. Discussion by eleven members of the Assembly on the law.
   Passage of the compulsory education law.

b. Passage of several bills: Defining punishment for the usage of counterfeit currencies, revision of income taxes, and others.

1SPA-5. February 25–March 3, 1950.
Fifth Session of the First Supreme People's Assembly.

February 25:
   Report of Chŏng Chun-t'aek: Report on the 1949–50 Economic Plan for the Development and Rehabilitation of People's Economy.

February 26:
   No meeting was held on this day.

February 27:
   Approval of various decrees issued by the government.

February 28:

a. Report of Ch'oe Ch'ang-ik on the national budget for the 1949 fiscal year and the proposed national budget for the 1950 fiscal year.

b. Discussion on the report of the budget by the representative Kim Che-wŏn, proposing a state bond in the amount of 1.5 billion *wŏn* to cover the deficit.

c. Election of an investigation committee headed by Kim Il Sung to examine the proposed national budget for the 1950 fiscal year.

March 1:

a. Report of the investigation committee on the proposed national budget for the 1950 fiscal year. Discussion and passage of the report.

b. Report of the organization laws of the courts. (The third item of the agenda.) Passage of the above law.

c. Report on the criminal laws and the criminal appeals laws of the DPRK.

March 2:
   Discussion and passage of the criminal laws, 23 chapters and 301 articles.

March 3:

a. Discussion and passage of the criminal appeals laws, 25 chapters.

b. Report of Han Sŏl-ya: Approval of the Peace Preservation Statement by the World Peace Preservation Congress.

c. Approval of the decrees issued by the Standing Committee of the Supreme People's Assembly.

1SPA-6. December 20–22, 1953.
Sixth Session of the First Supreme People's Assembly.

December 20:
Report of Kim Il Sung: On the Work of the Delegates of the Democratic People's Republic of Korea Dispatched to the U.S.S.R., the People's Republic of China, and other Friendly Countries.

December 21:
Discussion of Kim Il Sung's report.

December 22:

a. Discussion and approval of Kim's report.

b. Approval of the decrees issued by the Standing Committee of the Supreme People's Assembly.

c. Concerning the changes in the membership of the Standing Committee of the Supreme People's Assembly.

1SPA-7. April 20–23, 1954.
Seventh Session of the First Supreme People's Assembly.

April 20:
Report of Pak Ch'ang-ok: On the Three-year, 1954–56, Economic Plan of the DPRK.

April 21:
Discussion of the report of Pak Ch'ang-ok.

April 22:

a. Report of Ch'oe Ch'ang-ik on the national budget for the 1950, 1951, 1952, and 1953 fiscal years, and the proposed national budget for the 1954 fiscal year.

b. Election of a twenty-five-man investigation committee to examine the national budget.

April 23:

a. Approval of the three-year, 1954–56, economic plan.

b. Report of Kim Ch'ang-jun, chairman of the investigation committee on the national budgets for the 1950, 1951, 1952, and 1953 fiscal years and the proposed national budget for the 1954 fiscal year.

c. Approval of the report on the national budget.

d. Report of Kang Yang-uk on the decrees issued by the Standing Committee of the Supreme People's Assembly during the period between the sixth and seventh sessions of the Assembly. Approval of the decrees reported by Kang Yang-uk.

e. Passage of a law to amend and add provisions to Article 37, Paragraph 8, and Article 58 of the constitution of the DPRK.

1SPA-8. October 28–30, 1954.
Eighth Session of the First Supreme People's Assembly.

October 28:

Report of Foreign Minister Nam Il: On the Work of the Delegates of the DPRK at the Geneva Conference for the Peaceful Settlement of the Korean Question.

October 29:

Discussion and approval of Nam Il's report.

October 30:

a. Passage of a declaration of the Supreme People's Assembly of the DPRK to be sent to the National Assembly, political parties, social organizations, leaders of society and the people of South Korea.

b. Discussion of the draft laws of the regional organization of the DPRK. Passage of laws to amend Article 36 and Chapter 5 of the constitution.

c. Discussion of the division of a province and changes in the city, county, village, and workers' districts in the northern half of the DPRK. Passage of a law to divide Hwanghaedo into Hwanghae Namdo and Hwanghae Pukto and to create Yanggangdo.

d. Approval of the decrees issued by the Standing Committee of the Supreme People's Assembly during the period between the seventh and eighth sessions of the Assembly.

1SPA-9. March 9–11, 1955.
Ninth Session of the First Supreme People's Assembly.

March 9:

a. Discussion of the declaration of the second meeting of the fourth Supreme Soviet of the U.S.S.R. Election of a thirteen-member committee headed by Representative Pak Chŏng-ae to draft a declaration of the Supreme People's Assembly.

b. Report of Yi Chu-yŏn on the national budget for the 1954 fiscal year and the proposed national budget for the 1955 fiscal year. Discussion of the report of Yi Chu-yŏn and election of an investigation committee on the national budget.

March 10:

a. Approval of the report of the investigation committee on the national budget.
b. Report of Paek Nam-un, minister of education: On the Massive Training Program of Scientific and Technical Cadres for the Postwar People's Economic Development and Rehabilitation Plan and Preparation for General Compulsory Elementary Education.

March 11:

a. Discussion and passage of the report of Paek Nam-un.
b. Remarks by Kim Il Sung on the peaceful unification of our fatherland and other problems.
c. Report of Hong Ki-ju, minister of justice, on the revision of Articles 2, 3, 48, 53, 58, and 83 of the constitution of the DPRK. In connection with the revision of Article 58, a cabinet organization law was approved.
d. Approval of the decrees issued by the Standing Committee of the Supreme People's Assembly.
e. Election of a new chief justice, Cho Sŏng-mo, to replace Chief Justice Kim Ik-sŏn.
f. In connection with the declaration issued by the second meeting of the Fourth Supreme Soviet of the U.S.S.R., a declaration of the Supreme People's Assembly was approved.

1SPA-10. December 20–23, 1955.
Tenth Session of the First Supreme People's Assembly.

a. Report of Kim Il, vice-premier and minister of agriculture, on further development of agricultural management.
b. Report of Pak Chŏng-ae on the agricultural tax-in-kind.
c. Report of Yi Chu-yŏn, minister of finance, on a citizen income tax.
d. Approval of the decrees issued by the Standing Committee of the Supreme People's Assembly.

1SPA-11. March 10–13, 1956.
Eleventh Session of the First Supreme People's Assembly.

March 10:

a. Report of Finance Minister Yi Chu-yŏn on the proposed national budget for the 1956 fiscal year.

b. Election of the members of an investigation committee on the national budget.

March 12:
Discussion and approval of the proposed national budget for the 1956 fiscal year.

March 13:
a. Report of Vice-minister of Finance Yun Hyŏng-sik on a system of local self-government tax and discussion and approval of the report.
b. Approval of the decrees issued by the Standing Committee of the SPA.
c. Election of a chief justice of the Supreme Court of the Democratic People's Republic of Korea, Hwang Se-hwan.

1SPA-12. November 5–7, 1956.
Twelfth Session of the First Supreme People's Assembly.

a. Report by delegates of the Supreme People's Assembly of the DPRK on their visit to the Soviet Union.
b. Concerning an appeal from the Supreme Soviet of the U.S.S.R. to the congresses of all nations for the reduction of armaments.
c. Approval of the decrees issued by the Standing Committee of the SPA.

1SPA-13. March 14–16, 1957.
Thirteenth Session of the First Supreme People's Assembly.

a. On the final accounting of the national budget for the 1955 fiscal year and the proposed national budget for the 1957 fiscal year.
b. Approval of the decrees issued by the Standing Committee of the SPA.

2. **Period of the Second Supreme People's Assembly.**
   2SPA. September 18, 1957–October 22, 1962.

2SPA-1. September 18–20, 1957.
First Session of the Second Supreme People's Assembly.

a. Organization of the Credentials Committee.
b. Establishment of Standing Committees of the SPA congress.
c. Approval of decrees issued by the Standing Committee of the SPA.
d. Election of members of the Standing Committee of the SPA.
e. Organization of the cabinet.
f. Appointment of the chief procurator.
g. Election of the chief justice of the Supreme Court.

September 18:
Organization of the Credentials Committee of seven members.
Establishment of committees of law and rule, national budget, and foreign affairs as standing committees of the SPA congress.

September 19:
Decision to accept the report of the Credentials Committee.
Approval of the decrees issued by the Standing Committee of the SPA.
Adoption of Pak Chŏng-ae's proposal to entrust the organization of the new cabinet to Kim Il Sung.

September 20:
Election of a twenty-one-member Standing Committee of the SPA.
Election of Kim Ha-un as the chief justice of the Supreme Court.
Election of Pak Se-ch'ang as the chief procurator.
Kim Il Sung's address: On the Immediate Tasks of the People's Power in Socialist Construction.

2SPA-2. February 17–19, 1958.
Second Session of the Second Supreme People's Assembly.

a. On the accounting of the national budget for the 1956 fiscal year, and the proposed national budget for the 1958 fiscal year.
b. Concerning the decision of the Supreme Soviet of the Union of Soviet Socialist Republics and the proposals of the government of the Union of Soviet Socialist Republics on "The Easing of International Tension" and "The Establishment and Maintenance of World Peace."
c. Approval of the decrees issued by the Standing Committee of the Supreme People's Assembly.

2SPA-3. June 9–11, 1958.
Third Session of the Second Supreme People's Assembly.

a. On the first five-year plan, 1957–1961, for the development of the people's economy.
b. Approval of the decrees issued by the Standing Committee of the Supreme People's Assembly.
c. Kim Il Sung's address: All for the Prosperity and Development of the Fatherland.
d. Adoption of laws of the five-year economic plan.
e. Adoption of a letter to China; proposal of Pak Chŏng-ae.
f. Organization of a committee to draft an amendment and supplement to the constitution; proposal of Hŏ Chŏng-suk.

2SPA-4. October 1–2, 1958.
Fourth Session of the Second Supreme People's Assembly.

  a. On the nationwide enforcement of a system of compulsory secondary education, and the preparation of a system of compulsory technical education.
  b. Approval of the decrees issued by the Standing Committee of the Supreme People's Assembly. Dismissal of Kim Wŏn-bong and Hyŏn Ch'il-chong from the vice-chairmanship of the Standing Committee of the SPA, and election of Han Sŏl-ya and Ko Chun-t'aek as vice-chairmen of the Standing Committee of the SPA.

2SPA-5. February 19–21, 1959.
Fifth Session of the Second Supreme People's Assembly.

  a. On the national budget for the 1957 fiscal year and the proposed budget for the 1959 fiscal year.
  b. On the agricultural tax-in-kind.
  c. Approval of the decrees of the Standing Committee of the SPA.

2SPA-6. October 26–28, 1959.
Sixth Session of the Second Supreme People's Assembly.

  a. Report of Vice-Premier and Foreign Minister Nam Il on the peaceful unification of the fatherland.
  b. On the reorganization of the people's education system.
  c. Approval of the decrees issued by the Standing Committee of the SPA.
  d. Election of Kim Kyŏng-sŏk and Pak Sin-dŏk as members of the Standing Committee of the SPA.
     Recall of Kim Ha-un and election of Hŏ Chŏng-suk as chief justice of the Supreme Court.
     Election of Kang Yang-uk to replace Ko Chun-t'aek as vice-chairman of the Standing Committee of the SPA, and election of Pak Mun-u to replace Kang Yang-uk as the secretary-general of the SPA.

2SPA-7. February 15–27, 1960.
Seventh Session of the Second Supreme People's Assembly.

  a. On the accounting of the national budget for the fiscal year 1958 and the proposed national budget for the fiscal year 1960.
  b. On strengthening the people's public health programs.

c. Approval of the decrees issued by the Standing Committee of the SPA.

2SPA-8. June 19–24, 1960.
Eighth Session of the Second Supreme People's Assembly.

a. Report of Ch'oe Yong-gŏn on the peaceful unification of the fatherland.
b. Report of Yi Chong-ok on the general accomplishments of the first five-year economic plan, 1957-61.
c. Approval of the decrees issued by the Standing Committee of the SPA.
d. Election of Kim Ik-sŏn to replace Hŏ Chŏng-suk as chief justice of the Supreme Court.
e. Adoption of a letter addressed to the National Assembly and political parties of the Republic of Korea concerning a plan for the realization of economic and cultural interchange and cooperation and the self-sustaining development of national economy in South Korea.
f. Report of Yi Chu-yŏn: Let's Realize the Economic Interchange and Cooperation Between the South and the North as Soon as Possible in Order to Relieve South Korea from Economic Bankruptcy.
g. Report of Pak Sŏng-ch'ŏl: Let's Fight Against the Imperialists for the Peaceful Unification of the Fatherland and the Eternal Peace of the World.

2SPA-9. March 23–25, 1961.
Ninth Session of the Second Supreme People's Assembly.

a. On the accounting of the national budget for the fiscal year 1959 and the proposed national budget for the fiscal year 1960.
b. Approval of the decrees issued by the Standing Committee of the SPA.
c. Election of Paek Nam-un to replace Yi Kŭk-no as a vice-chairman of the Standing Committee of the SPA.

2SPA-10. April 5, 1962.
Tenth Session of the Second Supreme People's Assembly.

a. Concerning the accounting of the national budget of the 1961 fiscal year, and proposed national budget for the 1962 fiscal year.
b. Approval of the decrees issued by the Standing Committee of the SPA.

2SPA-11. June 20–21, 1962.
Eleventh Session of the Second Supreme People's Assembly.

    a. On waging a national struggle for the withdrawal of American troops from South Korea.
    b. Approval of the decrees issued by the Standing Committee of the SPA.

3. Period of the Third Supreme People's Assembly.
3SPA. October 22, 1962–December 14, 1967.

3SPA-1. October 22–23, 1962.
First Session of the Third Supreme People's Assembly.

    a. Organization of the Credentials Committee of the SPA.
    b. Establishment of the permanent committees of the SPA.
    c. Approval of the decrees issued by the Standing Committee of the SPA.
    d. Election of members of the Standing Committee of the SPA.
    e. Organization of the cabinet of the DPRK.
    f. Appointment of the chief procurator.
    g. Election of the chief justice of the Supreme Court of the DPRK.

October 22:
    a. Organization of the Credentials Committee; Ch'oe Yong-jin and five other members.
    b. Establishment of the committees on law and regulations, national budget, and foreign affairs as standing committees of the SPA.
    c. Approval of the decrees issued by the Standing Committee of the SPA.

October 23:
    a. Election of the members of the Standing Committee, SPA.
    b. Approval of the organization of the cabinet.
    c. Appointment of Pak Se-ch'ang as the chief procurator.
    d. Election of Kim Ik-sŏn as the chief justice of the Supreme Court.
    f. Kim Il Sung's speech: Problems Confronting the DPRK.

3SPA-2. May 9–11, 1963.
Second Session of the Third Supreme People's Assembly.

    a. On the accounting of the national budget of the 1962 fiscal year, and the proposed national budget for the 1963 fiscal year.
    b. Approval of the decrees issued by the Standing Committee of the SPA.

3SPA-3. March 26–28, 1964.
Third Session of the Third Supreme People's Assembly.

Discussion of Kim Il Sung's Theses on the Socialist Agrarian Problems in Our Country.

a. On strengthening the economic foundations of collective farms and improving the standard of living of farmers. Report of Vice-Premier Kim Il.
b. On crushing the Korea-Japan conference and accelerating the peaceful unification of the fatherland. Report of Foreign Minister Pak Sŏng-ch'ŏl.
c. Concerning the accounting of the national budget for the fiscal year 1963 and the proposed national budget for the 1964 fiscal year.
d. Approval of the decrees issued by the Standing Committee of the Supreme People's Assembly.

3SPA-4. May 20–23, 1965.
Fourth Session of the Third Supreme People's Assembly.

a. On the positive support of the righteous struggle of the Vietnamese people against U.S. imperialist aggression.
b. On the crushing of the criminal Korea-Japan talks by uniting all people.
c. On the accounting of the national budget for the 1964 fiscal year and the proposed national budget for the 1965 fiscal year.
d. Approval of the decrees issued by the Standing Committee of the SPA.

3SPA-5. April 27–29, 1966.
Fifth Session of the Third Supreme People's Assembly.

a. On the accounting of the national budget for the 1965 fiscal year and the proposed national budget for the 1966 fiscal year.
b. Concerning the complete abolishment of the agricultural tax-in-kind. Report of Kim Kwang-hyŏp.
c. On the struggle against the dispatch of South Korean troops to South Vietnam.
d. On supporting the proclamation of the People's Assembly of the DPRK.
e. Approval of the decrees issued by the Standing Committee of the SPA.

Election of Yi Yŏng-ho as vice-chairman of the Standing Committee and Pak Mun-gyu as a secretary-general of the SPA.

3SPA-6. November 22–24, 1966.
Sixth Session of the Third Supreme People's Assembly.

    a. On the general implementation of a system of compulsory nine-year technical education. Report of Vice-Premier Kim Il.

    b. Approval of the decrees issued by the Standing Committee of the SPA.

3SPA-7. April 24–26, 1967.
Seventh Session of the Third Supreme People's Assembly.

    a. Concerning the accounting of the national budget of the 1966 fiscal year and the proposed national budget for the 1967 fiscal year.

    b. Approval of the decrees issued by the Standing Committee of the SPA.

4. Period of the Fourth Supreme People's Assembly.
4SPA. December 14, 1967–December 25, 1972.
4SPA-1. December 14–16, 1967.
First Session of the Fourth Supreme People's Assembly.

    a. Organization of the Credentials Committee of the SPA.

    b. Establishment of the permanent committees of the SPA.

    c. Election of members of the Standing Committee of the SPA.

    d. Organization of the cabinet of the DPRK.

    e. Appointment of the chief procurator.

    f. Election of the chief justice of the Supreme Court of the DPRK.

4SPA-2. April 25–27, 1968.
Second Session of the Fourth Supreme People's Assembly.

    Concerning the accounting of the national budget of the 1967 fiscal year and the discussion of the proposed national budget for the 1968 fiscal year. Report of Finance Minister Yun Ki-bok.

4SPA-3. April 24–26, 1969.
Third Session of the Fourth Supreme People's Assembly.

    Concerning the accounting of the national budget of the 1968 fiscal year and the discussion of the proposed national budget for the 1969 fiscal year.

4SPA-4. April 20–23, 1970.
Fourth Session of the Fourth Supreme People's Assembly.

Concerning the accounting of the national budget of the 1969 fiscal year and the discussion of the proposed national budget for the 1970 fiscal year. Report of Finance Minister Ch'oe Yun-su.

4SPA-5. April 12–14, 1971.
Fifth Session of the Fourth Supreme People's Assembly.

- a. On the promotion of self-reliant unification of the fatherland and the current international situation.
- b. Concerning the accounting of the national budget of the 1970 fiscal year and the discussion of the proposed national budget for the 1971 fiscal year.

4SPA-6. April 29–30, 1972.
Sixth Session of the Fourth Supreme People's Assembly.

- a. Speech by Norodom Sihanouk on the struggle of the Cambodian people.
- b. Concerning the accounting of the national budget of the 1971 fiscal year and the discussion of the proposed national budget for the 1972 fiscal year.

5. Period of the Fifth Supreme People's Assembly.
5SPA. December 25, 1972–December 15, 1977
5SPA-1. December 25–28, 1972.
First Session of the Fifth Supreme People's Assembly.

- a. Concerning the socialist constitution of the DPRK.
- b. Concerning the election of central state organizations of the DPRK.

December 25:
Opening remarks by Ch'oe Yong-gŏn.
Report by Kim Il Sung: Let Us Strengthen the Socialist System of Our Country.
Reading of the draft by Kim Il of the socialist constitution of the DPRK.

December 26:
Discussion on the draft constitution by Pak Sŏng-ch'ŏl, Han Ik-su, Yang Hyŏng-sŏp, Chŏng Chun-ki, Hŏ Tam, Yun Ki-bok, Pak Sin-dŏk, Pak Hun, Yang Sun-do, Hwang Chang-yŏp.
Report of the Credentials Committee of the Supreme People's Assembly by Kim Tong-gyu.

December 27:
Discussion on the report of Kim Il Sung by Kim Chung-nin, Chŏng

Chun-t'aek, Kang Yang-uk, Hŏ Chŏng-suk, Yi Sŭng-gi, Pyŏn Ch'ang-bok, Ch'oe Ik-kyu, Yi Yŏng-bok, Kang Sŏng-san, Kim Pok-sin, Son Sŏng-p'il, Pak Ch'un-sik, Yi Cha-sŏn, Kim Sŏk-hwa, Pak Pok-sun, Kim Sŏk-hyŏng.

December 28:

Election of the president of the DPRK. Nomination speech by Kim Il.

Discussion on the nomination by O Chin-u, Yŏm T'ae-jun, Kim I-hun, Kim Tŭk-nan.

Election of vice-presidents of the DPRK; secretary and members of the Central People's Committee of the DPRK; chairman, vice-chairmen, and members of the Standing Committee of the Supreme People's Assembly; premier of the State Administration Council; vice-chairmen of the National Defense Commission; chairman and members of the Auditing Committee of the Supreme People's Assembly; chief justice of the Supreme Court of the DPRK.

Appointment of chief procurator of the Central Procurator's Office of the DPRK.

5SPA-2. April 5–10, 1973.
Second Session of the Fifth Supreme People's Assembly.

a. Concerning the ending of foreign intervention in domestic politics for the promotion of the self-reliant peaceful unification of the fatherland. (Proposal of the State Administration Council of the DPRK)
Report by Kim Il. Discussion by Kim Tong-gyu, Kim Sŏng-yul, Yi Ch'ang-do, Yŏm T'ae-jun, Kim I-hun, Kim Tŭk-nan, and Pak Chae-ro.

b. Concerning the realization of general ten-year middle and high school and one-year preschool compulsory education. (Proposal of the State Administration Council of the DPRK)
Report by Pak Sŏng-ch'ŏl. Discussion by Hong Wŏn-gil, Kim Su-dŭk, Hŏ Ryŏn-suk, Yi Kŭn-mo, Sin Chŏng-hŭi, Hyŏn Ch'ang-sin, Kim Se-bong, Kim Ok-sun, Kim Ch'ae-yŏn, Yu Kŭm-sŏn, and Yi Yong-gyu.
Adoption of the letter to be sent to the Congress of the United States and parliaments of every country in the world.

c. On the accounting of the national budget for the 1972 fiscal year and on the proposed national budget for the 1973 fiscal year. (Proposal of the State Administration Council of the DPRK) Report of Kim Kyŏng-yŏn.

Report of the result of the Auditing Committee by O T'ae-bong.
Discussion by Ch'oe Chae-u, Kang Sŏng-san, Chŏng Yong-t'aek, Ko
Kŭm-sun, Pak Im-t'ae, Kim Kye-hwan, Song Pok-ki, Cho Se-ung, O
Ik-hwan, and Ch'oe Hyŏn-gi.

5SPA-3. March 20–25, 1974.
Third Session of the Fifth Supreme People's Assembly.

a. Concerning the complete abolition of the tax system. (Proposal of
the State Administration Council of the DPRK) Report by Yi
Kŭn-mo.
Discussion by Chŏng Chun-gi, Yi Cha-sŏn, Kim Sŏk-hyŏng, Hong Si-
hak, Kim Chŏng-sun, Han Yong-bo, and Kim Yu-hun.

b. On the accounting of the national budget of the 1973 fiscal year,
and on the proposed national budget for the 1974 fiscal year.
(Proposal of the State Administration Council of the DPRK) Report
by Kim Kyŏng-yŏn.
Report of the Auditing Committee by O T'ae-bong.
Discussion by Tong Sun-mo, Kim Hŭi-jun, Ko Yun-suk, Pak Chong-
i, Kim Hak-sun, and Kim Se-yun.

c. Concerning the preparation of premise to promote self-reliant
peaceful unification of the fatherland and to eliminate the emergency situation in Korea. (Proposal of the State Administration Council
of the DPRK) Report by Hŏ Tam.
Discussion by Kim Tong-gyu, Kim Sŏng-yul, Kang Chang-su, and
Kim Sŏng-gŭn.

5SPA-4. November 27–30, 1974.
Fourth Session of the Fifth Supreme People's Assembly.

a. General review and future tasks of Kim Il Sung's Theses on Socialist
Agrarian Problems of Our Country. (Proposal of the State Ad-
ministration Council of the DPRK) Report by Kim Il.
Discussion by Kim Kŭm-ok, Chŏng T'ae-hwang, Chŏng Yong-t'aek,
Han Pong-nyŏ, and Yi Chun-ho.

b. Concerning the election of vice-president of the DPRK.
Election of Kim Tong-gyu as vice-president of the DPRK.

5SPA-5. April 8–10, 1975.
Fifth Session of the Fifth Supreme People's Assembly.

a. On the accounting of the national budget of the 1974 fiscal year,
and on the proposed national budget for the 1975 fiscal year.

(Proposal of the State Administration Council of the DPRK) Report of Kim Kyŏng-yŏn.

Discussion by Pak Sŏng-ch'ŏl, Kim Pyŏng-yul, No Se-bŏm, Ch'oe Yŏl-hŭi, Kang Sŏng-san, Kim Kwan-su, Yang Yong-gŏn, Cho Yŏng-suk, Pang T'ae-uk, and Ch'oe Han-gil.

b. Concerning the general review of the law on the general eleven-year compulsory education. (Proposal of the State Administration Council of the DPRK) Report of Kim Sŏk-ki.

Discussion by Yi Chŏng-sun, T'ae Ch'ang-am, Kim Hong-wŏn, Yi Chin-gyu, O Ch'un-gyŏng, and Yi Sun-bong.

5SPA-6. April 27–29, 1976.
Sixth Session of the Fifth Supreme People's Assembly.

a. On the accounting of the national budget of the 1975 fiscal year, and on the proposed national budget for the 1976 fiscal year. (Proposal of the State Administration Council of the DPRK) Report of Kim Kyŏng-yŏn.

Discussion by Ch'oe Chae-u, Yi Ŭm-sŏn, Kim Kuk-hun, Yi Kil-song, and Ch'oe Nam-hyang.

b. Concerning further strengthening and developing the progressive nursery system for children established in our country. (Proposal of the State Administration Council of the DPRK) Report by Chŏng Chun-gi.

Discussion by Yi Kyŏng-suk, Yu Kŭm-sŏn, Cho Kyŏng-hŭi, and Yi Ŭn-sun.

Report by Kim Il Sung: On Further Developing the Nursing and Upbringing of Children.

c. Organization Problem.

Election of Comrade Kim Il as the first vice-president and election of Comrade Pak Sŏng-ch'ŏl as the premier of the State Administration Council of the DPRK.

5SPA-7. April 26–29, 1977.
Seventh Session of the Fifth Supreme People's Assembly.

a. On the accounting of the national budget of the 1976 fiscal year, and on the proposed national budget for the 1977 fiscal year. Report by Kim Kyŏng-yŏn.

b. On the adoption of the land law of the DPRK. Report by Yang Hyŏng-sŏp.

Speech by Kim Il Sung on the land law.

6. Period of the Sixth Supreme People's Assembly.
6SPA. December 15, 1977–

6SPA-1. December 15–17, 1977.
Period of the Sixth Supreme People's Assembly.
First Session of the Sixth Supreme People's Assembly.

   a. Election of president of the DPRK.
   b. Election of leading state organs of the DPRK.
   c. On the results of the fulfillment of the six-year plan and on the second seven-year plan (1978–84) for the development of the national economy.

December 15:
   Opening remarks by Kim Il.
   Nomination for the office of the president of the republic as authorized by the Political Committee of the Central Committee of the Workers' Party of Korea.
   Kim Il Sung was elected.
   At the recommendation of Kim Il Sung, the session elected members of various leading state organs of the republic.
   The new premier, Yi Chong-ok, took oath before Kim Il Sung.
   Kim Il Sung made a speech entitled, "Let Us Further Strengthen the People's Government."

December 16:
   Discussion of Kim's speech by Chŏng Chun-gi, Hŏ Tam, Hwang Chang-yŏp, Hyŏn Mu-gwang, Hong Si-hak, Hŏ Chŏng-suk, Kim Ch'ŏl-min, Pyŏn Ch'ang-bok, and Ch'oe Wŏn-ik.
   Yi Chong-ok's report on the results of the fulfillment of the six-year plan and on the second seven-year plan (1978–84) for the development of the national economy.

December 17:
   Discussion of Yi's speech by Kye Ŭng-t'ae, Cho Chŏng-dok, Yun Ho-sŏk, Sŏ Kwan-hŭi, Hong Ho-sik, Kye Hyŏng-sun, Pak Im-t'ae, Yi Ok-sang, Kang Sŏng-san, Yi Chi-ch'an, Ch'ong Ch'un-sil, Kim Il-dae, Pak Yong-sŏk, Yi Hwa-sun, Kim Pun-ok, Han Sang-gyu, Han In-hwan, Chin Ch'ang-hu, Pak Myŏng-bin, Wŏn Tong-gu, Yi Chae-gon, Yim Wŏn-sang, Ko Chŏng-sik, Kim Hyŏng-hae, Kim Sun-p'il, Chŏn Myŏng-sim, and Kim Ch'i-se.
   Report by Yim Ch'un-ch'u, chairman of the Credentials Committee.
   Yim's report approved.

Closing remarks by Chairman Hwang Chang-yŏp of the Standing Committee.

6SPA-2. April 18–20, 1978.
Second Session of the Sixth Supreme People's Assembly.

a. On the adoption of the socialist labor law of the DPRK.
b. On the result of the execution of the state budget for 1977, and the state budget for 1978 of the Democratic People's Republic of Korea.

Speech by Kim Il Sung.

6SPA-3. March 27–29, 1979.
Third Session of the Sixth Supreme People's Assembly.

a. On the results of the fulfillment of the state budget for 1978 and on the state budget for 1979.

6SPA-4. March 2, 1980.
Fourth Session of the Sixth Supreme People's Assembly.

a. On the adoption of the public health law of the DPRK.
b. On the result of the execution of the state budget for 1979, and on the state budget for 1980 of the DPRK.

OFFICERS AND MEMBERS OF THE ASSEMBLY

The political climate at the time the first Supreme People's Assembly convened was such that both the National Assembly of the South and the Supreme People's Assembly of the North claimed sovereignty over all Korea. While the South left almost one-third of its assembly seats vacant so that representatives from the North could eventually be present in the South, the Supreme People's Assembly of the North claimed a fictitious election in the South and filled the seats allocated to the southern half with representatives, in name only in most cases, from the South.

Of 572 representatives who constituted the First Supreme People's Assembly 360 were supposed to have been elected from the South, while 212 were elected in the North. It was claimed that an incredible 99.97 percent of the voters turned out and that the 212 members in the North were elected from 227 nominees. In subsequent elections for the Supreme People's Assembly, the North claimed a 100 percent turnout of the voters for nominees who were exactly the same in number as those elected. For the first two Assemblies, each member represented 50,000 people.

Statistics on the members of the Assembly were issued, for example, their social and occupational backgrounds, their revolutionary records, age, sex, and education, but in the case of the First Assembly, it is difficult to rely on these statistics because more than one half of the members of the Assembly were from the South and served in name only. According to these figures, the First Assembly was in general composed of workers and peasants who worked for political parties, who were young males with good educations, and who had records of less than five years of imprisonment for their revolutionary activities during the Japanese occupation of Korea.

Unlike the party Central Committee, officers and members of the Assembly represent various political parties, such as Ch'ŏndogyo Young Friends Party and the Democratic Party, and include some with no party affiliation. The most powerful committee within the Assembly for the first four Assemblies was the Standing Committee. Many of the functions of the Standing Committee were assumed by the Central People's Committee by the Fifth Assembly under the new constitution. Under the old constitution, the Assembly had one chairman and two vice-chairmen who presided over Assembly meetings. These men, however, should not be confused with the more-powerful chairman and vice-chairmen of the Standing Committee. The membership of the Standing Committee was fixed at twenty-one in the constitution, but this provision was amended even before the 1972 constitution to give more flexibility. Under the new constitution, the chairman and vice-chairmen of the Assembly were replaced with a president and vice-presidents of the republic. The chairman and vice-chairmen of the Standing Committee served concurrently as chairman and vice-chairmen of the Assembly. The new post of secretary-general of the Central People's Committee in addition to the Standing Committee of the Assembly was also created.

The First Assembly lasted for ten years from September 1948 to September 1957, twice as long as any subsequent session. Since the Korean war, the Assembly has undergone some changes. New officers of the Assembly as well as new officers and members of the Standing Committee were announced at the sixth session of the First Assembly in December 1953, replacing the casualties of the Korean war. However, there was no new election for members of the First Assembly

From the Second Assembly on, all seats allocated to representatives from the South were eliminated, and the number of members was reduced from 572 to 215. There were 212 representatives from the North in the First Assembly, so the net increase was only 3. The electoral districts in the North were apportioned at this time in nine provinces and two cities, and while the absolute number of districts in each province has increased, this apportionment in nine provinces and two cities is still maintained. Candidates are allowed to run for seats in any electoral district of their choice, but nominations are carefully screened and selected by the party. In addition to the Standing Committee, the Second Assembly elected members to four functional committees: the Bills, Budget, Foreign Affairs, and Credentials Committees. As in the First Assembly, the sixth session of the Second Assembly announced a new lineup of officers in October 1959. It is coincidental that these changes also occurred in the sixth session, but these are the only two sessions in which changes in the leadership of the Assembly were reported.

The Third Assembly was held in October 1962, five years after the second, and all subsequent Assemblies have been held at five-year intervals. The constitution provides for a new Assembly every four years, but this provision has not been followed. In the Third Assembly, the membership was increased from 215 to 385, an increase of 68. This was the result of a reapportionment of electoral districts that reduced the ratio of representation from 50,000 to 30,000 population. Article 35 of the first constitution was amended to effect this change.

There was also a sharp change in the characteristics of the members of the Assembly. The members were in general from the working class and not from the usual worker and peasant class, were middle-aged people with secondary educations, and had been heavily decorated by the North Korean regime. Their records in the anti-Japanese revolutionary movement were not even mentioned, and fewer than 10 percent of the members were females. From the Third Assembly on, the officers served out their terms, and even when there were vacancies in the committees, new lineups for the committees were not announced.

The Fourth Assembly was held in December 1967, and the membership increased from 383 to 457. Little explanation was given for the increase of 74 members. The ratio of representation remained the same at one member per 30,000, and it is assumed that the North had begun to adjust for the increase in its population, an increase of approximately two million in the five years from 1962 to 1967. In contrast to the increase in the membership of the Assembly, the membership of the Standing Committee was reduced from 23 in the Third Assembly to only 15 in the fourth.

A new constitution was adopted at the Fifth Assembly, changing the structure of the Assembly. In addition to the Standing Committee, which lost some of its important functions, the constitution provided for the offices of president, vice-presidents of the republic, and secretary-general of the Central People's Committee. The new Central People's Committee consisted of twenty-five members and exercised most of the important functions of the state. Compared with the old Standing Committee, which represented many parties and social organizations, the new Central People's Committee consisted of more party leaders and political figures and had direct control of the executive branch of the republic.

The membership of the Assembly has once again jumped by 84 members, from 457 in the fourth to 541 in the fifth, while the ratio of representation remained the same. This may or may not indicate another jump in the population of 2.5 million in the five years from 1967 to 1972; it is difficult to believe that the North Korean population, which was estimated at less than 12 million in 1962, increased by 4.5 million in the ten years from 1962 to 1972. The characteristics of the members remained the same, except that female representatives jumped from fewer than 10 percent in the Third Assembly to more than 20 percent in the Fifth Assembly.

The Sixth Assembly was held in December 1977, and there was only a modest increase in membership, the number rising to 579, an increase of only 38. The electoral districts for the election of members to the Sixth Assembly were listed in accordance with the districts apportioned for the Second Assembly, nine provinces and two cities. Although the number of representatives in the Sixth Assembly was more than two and one half times those in the Second Assembly, the percentage of the representatives from each province remained more or less the same. This signifies that there was very little change in the dispersion of the population and that the population increase was proportionate throughout the North. In the two cities, Pyongyang and Kaesŏng, however, the population doubled in twenty years, indicating slight urbanization, but not at an alarming rate in the modern world (Table 3.1).

In the Sixth Assembly, both the Central People's Committee and the Standing Committee were reduced to fifteen members, a considerable reduction in the case of the Central People's Committee, which formerly had twenty-five members. The Standing Committee was reduced from nineteen to fifteen members. In addition, some of the functional committees of the Assembly seem to have been eliminated. For example, the Foreign Affairs Committee was abolished and its functions taken up by the Foreign Policy Commission of the Central People's Committee. In the case of the Credentials Committee, only the chairman gave a report on the work of the committee and its membership was not announced.

The number of representatives reelected to successive Assemblies is in general very small. The First Assembly had 572 members, but only 13 percent, 75 members, were reelected to the Second Assembly. Even among the 212 members who represented the northern half of Korea in the First Assembly, only 35 percent were reelected. The situation worsened from the Second to the Third Assembly; only 70 members, 33 percent of the 215 members, were reelected to the Third Assembly. However, the situation improved drastically from the Third to the Fourth Assembly. Of 383 members of the Third Assembly, 225 members, 59 percent, were reelected to the Fourth Assembly, reflecting one of the most stable periods in the North in the 1960s. The number was reduced again after the Fourth Assembly with only 177 of 457 members of that Assembly, 39 percent, being reelected to the Fifth Assembly. For the first time, the elected members of the Sixth Assembly were not announced.

Except for the Fourth Assembly, which had 225 returning representatives, the rate of reelection in all Assemblies was less than 40 percent. In all cases, including the Fourth Assembly, each Assembly consisted of more new members than reelected members. In other words, newly elected members constituted a majority in each new Assembly. In most cases, new representatives constituted more than two-thirds of the new Assembly (Table 3.2). This pattern is similar to the pattern of reelection in the Central Committee of the Workers' Party of Korea. This may seem insignificant when one considers that there is no competitive voting on contested issues in the Assembly, but it is a fact worth noting, particularly when nomination to the Assembly comes not from the people but from the party.

All members who were reelected to subsequent Assemblies, thus serving in the Assembly twice, are marked with an asterisk in the list of the members of each Assembly. From the first to the Fifth Assembly, ninety-one persons were elected three times, and thirty-two were elected four times. Only nine members were elected to all five Assemblies (Table 3.3). Since the members of the Sixth Assembly were not disclosed after the election on November 11, 1977, there is no accurate account of those who may have served more than five times. Only the list of officers of the Sixth Assembly was announced at the first session of the Assembly on December 15, 1977. On the basis of this list, only three of the above nine were reelected to the Assembly. They are Kang Yang-uk, Kim Il, and Kim Il Sung.

As to the rate of reelection in the Standing Committee, it is also quite similar to the pattern established in the Standing Committee and Political Committee of the Workers' Party of Korea. Reelection to a subsequent Standing Committee is an exception rather than a rule. Of fifty-two members who served as committee chairman, as vice-chairman of the Assembly, or as a member of the Standing Committee from the First to the Sixth Assembly, only three served four times: Kang Yang-uk, chairman of the Democratic Party; Pak Sin-dŏk, chairman of the Ch'ŏndogyo Young Friends Party; and Yi Ki-yŏng, a prominent literary writer who fled to the North from the South. Seven members served three times, twenty-one members served twice, and the rest served only once (Table 3.5).

The rate of reelection in the Central People's Committee is also low. Only nine of twenty-five were reelected from the Fifth to the Sixth Assembly, a mere 36 percent. The case of the Standing Committee members from the Fifth to the Sixth Assembly is similar (Table 3.6); only seven of nineteen were reelected (Table 3.5).

The rate of reelection in other functional committees is worse. For example, in the Bills Committees from the Second to the Sixth Assembly, only two, Kim Ik-sŏn and Kim Kuk-hun, of a total of thirty-nine members were reelected (Table 3.7). In the case of the Budget Committee, a few were reelected from the Third and Fourth Assemblies, and one member, Chang Yun-p'il, was elected three times, but the entire membership of the Budget Committee of the Fourth Assembly was replaced in the Fifth, and still another completely new group was elected for the Sixth Assembly (Table 3.8).

A similar pattern is also evident in both the Foreign Affairs Committee and the Credentials Committee. During the Second, Third, and Fourth Assemblies, only two, Kim Ok-sun and Pak Yong-guk, served on the Foreign Affairs Committee twice (Table 3.9). No one served on the Credentials Committee twice (Table 3.10). This is in sharp contrast with the National Defense Commission, the chairman and vice-chairmen of which were all reelected from the Fifth to the Sixth Assembly. In the case of the National Defense Commission, only officers were reported and members of the commission were not announced.

In general, the memberships of all functional committees are becoming smaller; for example, members of the Budget Committee were reduced from nine in the Second Assembly to six in the Sixth Assembly. It is interesting to note that while the membership of the entire Assembly has more than doubled from 215 in the Second Assembly to 579 in the Sixth Assembly, membership of the various functional committees has at times been reduced to less than half of the original number.

As to the general membership of the Assembly, the listings of the elected members varied from Assembly to Assembly. The First Assembly just announced that 212 members were elected from the North and 360 members were elected from the South. There was no indication of any electoral districts from which each member was elected, and the list seems to have followed some sort of rank order. All important political figures were listed within the first fifty of the total of 572 members.

However, for the Second Assembly, successful candidates were announced together with electoral districts, divided in accordance with the administrative division of nine provinces and two cities. The members of the Second Assembly were listed in accordance with the electoral districts and no rank order was observed.

In the Third and Fourth Assemblies, the members were listed with the districts from which they were elected, but the electoral districts were not divided into the nine provinces and two cities, and the list was prepared and announced in rank order. For the Fifth Assembly election, each electoral district was numbered, and neither the rank order nor the electoral district formula was followed. The members of the Fifth Assembly were listed at random.

The Sixth Assembly returned to the formula of the Second Assembly by dividing the electoral districts into nine provinces and two cities and numbering each district, but it was decided not to do the most important thing, that is, to announce the names of those elected.

PERSONNEL REGISTERS

The officers and members of each Supreme People's Assembly except the Sixth are given below. For the Sixth Assembly, only the names of the officers are available. Additional background information on the members of the Assembly is given in Table 3.11.

FIRST SUPREME PEOPLE'S ASSEMBLY, SEPTEMBER 2–10, 1948
Officers of the First Assembly[1]

Chairman
   Hŏ Hŏn[2]

Vice-chairmen
   1. Kim Tal-hyŏn
   2. Yi Yŏng

Standing Committee[3]

1. Kim Tu-bong, chairman	11. Chang Sun-myŏng
2. Hong Nam-p'yo,[4] vice-chairman	12. Chang Kwŏn
3. Hong Ki-ju, vice-chairman	13. Yu Yŏng-jun
4. Kang Yang-uk, secretary-general	14. Pak Yun-gil
5. Kang Chin-gŏn	15. Na Sŭng-gyu
6. Sŏng Chu-sik	16. Ch'oe Kyŏng-dŏk
7. Ku Chae-su	17. Yi Nŭng-jong
8. Yi Ku-hun	18. Kim Pyŏng-je
9. Pak Chŏng-ae	19. Yi Ki-yŏng
10. Kim Ch'ang-jun	20. Kang Sun
	21. Cho Un

Changes at the Sixth Session of the First Assembly after the Korean War, December 20–22, 1953[5]

Chairman
Yi Yŏng

Vice-chairmen
1. Yi Yu-min
2. Hong Ki-hwang

Standing Committee
1. Kim Tu-bong, chairman
2. Kim Ŭng-gi, vice-chairman
3. Yi Kŭk-no, vice-chairman
4. Kang Yang-uk, secretary-general
5. Kang Chin-gŏn
6. Sŏng Chu-sik
7. Yi Ku-hun
8. Pak Chŏng-ae
9. Kim Ch'ang-jun
10. Chang Sun-myŏng
11. Chang Kwŏn
12. Yu Yŏng-jun
13. Na Sŭng-gyu
14. Kim Pyŏng-je
15. Yi Ki-yŏng
16. Ch'oe Wŏn-t'aek
17. Wŏn Hong-gu
18. Kang Ŭng-jin[6]
19. Chŏn Yun-do
20. Yu Hae-bung
21. Mun Tu-jae

Members of the First Assembly[7]
1. Kim Il Sung*
2. Kim Tu-bong*
3. Hŏ Hŏn
4. Kim Tal-hyŏn*
5. Yi Yŏng*
6. Hong Nam-p'yo
7. Hong Ki-ju
8. Pak Hŏn-yŏng
9. Hong Myŏng-hŭi*
10. Kim Ch'aek
11. Kang Yang-uk*
12. Kang Sun
13. Kang Chin-gŏn*
14. Ku Chae-su
15. Kim Pyŏng-je*
16. Kim Ch'ang-jun*
17. Na Sŭng-gyu*
18. Yu Yŏng-jun*
19. Yi Ku-hun
20. Yi Ki-yŏng*
21. Yi Nŭng-jong
22. Pak Yun-gil
23. Pak Chŏng-ae*
24. Sŏng Chu-sik*
25. Chang Kwŏn
26. Chang Sun-myŏng
27. Cho Un
28. Ch'oe Kyŏng-dŏk
29. Chŏng Chun-t'aek*
30. Ch'oe Yong-gŏn*
31. Kim Wŏn-bong*
32. Pak Il-u
33. Pak Mun-gyu*
34. Chang Si-u
35. Chu Yŏng-ha
36. Ch'oe Ch'ang-ik

*Reelected to the second Supreme People's Assembly. Seventy-five were reelected.

37. Paek Nam-un*
38. Kim Chŏng-ju
39. Yi Sŭng-yŏp
40. Hŏ Chŏng-suk*
41. Hŏ Sŏng-t'aek*
42. Yi Pyŏng-nam*
43. Yi Yong
44. Yi Kŭk-no*
45. Chang Hae-u*
46. No Chin-han
47. Kim Il*
48. Pak Hun-il
49. Hŏ Ka-i
50. Pak Ch'ang-sik*
51. Kim O-sŏng
52. Ko Hŭi-man*
53. Pang Hak-se*
54. Kang Kŏn
55. Kang Ŭng-jin
56. Yi Man-gyu*
57. Kim Sam-yong
58. Pak Se-yŏng
59. Kim Sŏng-gyu
60. Yun Haeng-jung
61. Kang Mun-sŏk
62. Song Ŭl-su*
63. Kim Sang-hyŏk*
64. Yi Tong-hwa*
65. Han Hyo-sam
66. Chŏng Il-yong*
67. Yun Hyŏng-sik
68. Yi Ki-sŏk*
69. Song Pong-uk*
70. Kim Ŭng-gi*
71. Kim Chae-uk
72. Hong Ki-hwang*
73. Yi Sŏk-bo
74. Kim Yŏng-su*
75. Nam Il*
76. Yi Pyŏng-je
77. Yi Yŏ-sŏng*

78. T'ak Ch'ang-hyŏk
79. Cho Yong-se
80. Yi Sang-jun
81. Kim Ki-do
82. Kim Kwang-su
83. Ch'oe Ik-han
84. Yu Hae-bung
85. Ch'oe Chun-yŏng
86. Kim Yŏl
87. Yi Hong-yŏl*
88. Kim Ch'an
89. Yun Chŭng-u*
90. Ch'oe Wŏn-t'aek*
91. Chŏng Sŏng-ŏn*
92. Yi Sik
93. Kim Hwang-il*
94. Kim Ki-ju
95. Yi Chong-man*
96. Pak Yŏng-sŏng
97. Yi Yu-min*
98. Pak Ch'ang-ok
99. Yi Yŏng-jun
100. Yi In-dong*
101. Cho Chung-gwang
102. Yu Ki-sŏp
103. Yi Chŏm-sun
104. Chŏng No-sik*
105. Han Sang-muk
106. Kim Yŏng-jae
107. Kim Yong-dam
108. O Chae-yŏng
109. Kim Ok-bin
110. Ch'oe Pong-su*
111. Hwang T'ae-sŏng
112. Han Il-su
113. Kim Yŏng-wan
114. T'ae Sŏng-su
115. Yi Chu-yŏn*
116. Kim Sang-ch'ŏl*
117. Pak Sang-jun
118. Kim Min-san

119. Kim Yun-gŏl
120. Chŏn Ch'an-bae
121. Cho Hi-yŏng
122. U Pong-un
123. Yi T'ae-sŏng
124. Hwang Uk
125. Yi Chu-ha
126. Chŏng Paek
127. No Sŏk-kwi
128. Sŏ Kap-sun
129. Cho Pŏm-gu
130. Han Sŏl-ya*
131. Chu Hwang-sŏp*
132. Han Il-mu*
133. Pak Ch'i-ho
134. Kim Ch'ung-gyu
135. Yi Mun-hwan
136. Ok Yŏng-ja
137. Hong Myŏn-hu
138. Kim Sŏn-gil
139. Ham Ik-nok
140. Kim Wŏn-hyŏng
141. Pak Il-yŏng
142. Kim Sŏng-ok
143. Kim Nam-ch'ŏn
144. Wŏn Ho-sun
145. Song Myŏng-hŏn
146. Ch'oe Sŏn-gyu
147. Pak Chun-yŏng
148. Song Kyu-hwan
149. Yi Wŏn-il
150. Chŏng Tae-sŏk
151. Ch'ae Chun-sŏk
152. Yi Yŏng-sŏm
153. Kim Su-hyŏn
154. Wŏn Man-su
155. Chŏng Ch'ŏl
156. Kim Il-ch'ŏng
157. Kim Sŭng-hyŏn
158. Kim Hyŏng-gŏn
159. Kim Myŏng-sŏk

160. Kim Sŏng-hak
161. Chŏng Un-yŏng
162. Pak Yong-han
163. Yi Kang-guk
164. O Ki-sŏp*
165. Kim Hae-ch'ŏn
166. Yi Sang-sun
167. Kim Sang-ju
168. Chu Hae
169. Yun Su
170. Yi Hyŏk-yŏng
171. Pak Ki-ho
172. Sin Nam-ch'ŏl*
173. Chŏng Chu-gyŏng
174. Yi Sul-chin
175. Sin Yong-bok
176. Ch'oe Yong-dal
177. Kim Sŭng-mo
178. Chŏng Chong-sik
179. Cho Chae-han
180. Kim Chae-rok
181. Yi Tong-yŏng
182. Wŏn Hong-gu*
183. Kim Paek-tong
184. Hŏ Nam-hŭi
185. Paek Pong-sŏn
186. Ch'oe Ŭng-yŏ
187. Yi Sŏn-jae
188. Yŏm Chŏng-gwŏn
189. Yu Tong-yŏl
190. Chang U-uk
191. Ch'oe Sŏng-hwan
192. Yang Hong-ju
193. Yi Ch'il-sŏng
194. Sŏn Tong-gi
195. Paek Pyŏng-ik
196. Yi Chae-yŏng
197. Ch'oe Sŏn-ja
198. Kang Chun-sam
199. Min Hyŏk-cho
200. Chŏng Ch'il-sŏng*

201. Kye Tong-sŏn
202. Kim Ho-sun
203. Ch'oe Yun-ok
204. Ch'oe Sŭng-hŭi*
205. Pak Wŏn-jun
206. Yi Ch'ŏng-song
207. Kim Kil-su
208. Chŏn Pok-chin
209. Kim Yŏng-yun
210. Yi Chŏng-yŏl
211. Yu Hyŏng-gyu
212. Yi Sang-in
213. Ham Se-dŏk
214. Yim Chae-yŏng
215. Sin Chin-u
216. Yi Tong-gŭn
217. Yi Hong-yŏn
218. Ham To-gyŏm
219. Kim Tŏk-hŭng
220. Sŏ Pyŏng-su
221. Cho Yŏng-nae
222. Kim Hae-jin*
223. Kim Han-il
224. Yi Ch'ang-gyu
225. Pak Sang-sun
226. Kim Tong-il
227. Kim Mu-sam
228. Yi Man-su*
229. Wŏn Ch'ŏn-jun
230. Hŏ Sin
231. Yi Tu-san
232. Yu Yŏng-yun
233. Mun Ok-sun
234. Hong Kwang-jun
235. Maeng Tu-ŭn
236. Yang Po-hyŏn
237. O Ki-ok
238. O Yŏng
239. Yi Ch'ŏl
240. Yun Sang-man
241. Yi Ch'ang-ha
242. Chŏn Suk-cha
243. Kim Wan-gŭn
244. Kang Yun-wŏn
245. Kwak Chu-sŏk
246. Yi Ch'un-su
247. Chŏng Yŏn-t'ae
248. Ch'ae Paek-hŭi
249. Kim Sun-il
250. Kim Se-yul*
251. Song Wan-sŏk
252. Kim Kye-rim
253. Kim Hyŏn-gŭk
254. Ko Chun-t'aek*
255. Yi Pong-nyŏn
256. Chŏng Se-yŏl
257. Cho Pok-nye
258. Yi Chae-hyang
259. Kil Wŏn-p'al
260. Yi Sun-jŏ
261. Mun Tong-yong
262. Yi Uk
263. Chŏng Se-ho
264. Kim Ho-yŏng
265. Kim Han-ung
266. Kim Hak-chong
267. Kwŏn Pyŏng-ch'ŏl
268. Sŏl Pyŏng-ho
269. Hong Sŭng-guk
270. Ko Sŏk-hwan
271. Kim Su-il
272. Pak Chŏng-hyŏn
273. Yi Sang-hun
274. An Yŏng-il
275. Chang Kil-yong
276. Kim Yu-yŏng
277. Hwang T'ae-yŏl
278. An Sin-ho
279. Paek Nak-yŏng
280. Chŏn Yŏng-gi
281. Yi Suk-kyŏng
282. An Yŏng-gil

283. Kim Yong-guk
284. Kim Sun-nam
285. Hong Sŏn-u
286. Chang Chun
287. Yi Kyu-hŭi
288. Kim Myŏng-hwan
289. Hyŏn Hun*
290. Ch'oe Sŏk-sun
291. Kim Ch'ŏl-ho
292. Kim T'ae-hong
293. Pak Si-yun
294. An Si-do
295. Yi Yong-dŏk
296. Kim Si-yŏp
297. Kim Hyŏng-t'ae
298. Yi Chae-yŏng
299. Pak Chong-t'ae
300. Mun Sang-jik
301. Kim Ta'e-ja
302. Yi Tong-t'ak
303. Yi In-gyu
304. O Sin-nam
305. Yi Sŏk-sung
306. Ch'oe Kŭm-bok
307. Yi Hwan-gi
308. Cho Chung-gon
309. Yi Chin-gŭn
310. Yi Chi-ch'an
311. Han Ch'un-yŏ
312. Pak Ch'an-hyŏk
313. Kim Chŏm-gwŏn
314. Yu Chin-yŏng
315. Yi Hae-su
316. Yi Chŏng-suk*
317. Yim Sang-sun
318. Yi Chin
319. Song Ŏn-p'il
320. Kim T'ak
321. Ch'oe Kwan-yong
322. Yi Pong-nam
323. Yi Pyŏng-ho

324. Pak Ch'i-hwa
325. Kim Yu-t'ae
326. Yun Sang-yŏl
327. Kim Pyŏng-je*
328. Kim Ŭi-su
329. Pak Ch'ŏl
330. Sŏ Ch'ang-sŏp
331. Pak Pok-cho
332. Chŏng Sin-hyŏn
333. Ch'oe Sŏn-bi
334. Mun Ŭi-sok
335. Yi Hun
336. Yun Pyŏng-gwan
337. Kim Nanju-hwa
338. Chŏn Yŏng-uk
339. Cho T'ae-u
340. Pak Sŭng-gŭk
341. Hong Myŏn-ok
342. Yi Chong-myŏng
343. Kim Yŏng-sŏp
344. An Yŏng-muk
345. Chang Ch'ŏl
346. Mun Hong-gi
347. Chŏng Kil-sŏng
348. Kim Ki-su
349. Chu Ch'ang-sŏn
350. Ch'oe Ki-nam
351. Cho Kŭm-sŏng
352. Kim Ch'ŏl-su
353. Yi Pyŏng-hŭi
354. Yi Tu-wŏn
355. Chŏng Nam-jo
356. Pak Ch'ang-gu
357. O Ch'ŏl-chu
358. Kim Pong-sŏn
359. Sŏng Chae-ch'ŏl
360. Kwŏn Yŏng-ju
361. Kim P'il-chu
362. Ch'a Chi-hun
363. Pak Pong-u
364. Chŏng In-sŏk

365. Hyŏn Sŭng-gap
366. Yi Hi-bong
367. Kang In-gŏl
368. Pak Pyŏng-jik
369. Pak Mun-sun
370. Ha Yŏng-suk
371. Yun Chae-bong
372. Hong Chŭng-sik*
373. Yi Kŭn-u
374. Ko Ch'ŏl-u
375. Kil Chin-sŏp
376. Yi Ch'ang-su
377. Ch'oe Ka-ma
378. Kim Han-jung
379. Yi Po-yŏl
380. O Chae-il
381. Ok Mun-hwan
382. Hwang Un-bong
383. Kim On
384. Chang Sang-bong
385. Kim T'ae-sŏng
386. Min Ki-wŏn
387. Cho Sŏng-gyu
388. Kim Ch'ang-nok
389. Ch'oe Kwang*
390. Kim Nak-to
391. Hong Ki-mun
392. Yi Song-jŏng
393. Chŏn Chung-hak
394. Yi Chin-suk
395. Paek Ŭng-yŏp
396. Yun In-yŏng
397. Kim Ŭi-sun
398. Yi Min-yong
399. Chu Chin-hwang
400. No Myŏng-hwan
401. Chang Ki-uk
402. Yi Sang-ho
403. Na Yun-ch'ul*
404. Song Chong-gŭn
405. Pak Sŏng-ok

406. Pak Kŭn-mo
407. Song T'ae-jun
408. Chŏn Pyŏng-gi
409. Kim Pyŏng-mun
410. Ma Chong-hwa
411. Yi Kang-mu
412. Hŏ Ha-baek
413. Kim Si-gyŏm
414. Sin Hyŏn-u
415. Yi Sŏng-baek
416. Kim Myŏng-ni
417. Yi Yong-jin
418. Chŏn Chŏng-il
419. Mun Tu-jae
420. Kim Yong-hŭi
421. Kim T'ae-ryŏn
422. Yim Chŏng-sun
423. O Ho-sŏk
424. Yi Yong-sŏn
425. Yi Tong-sŏn
426. Pak Chin-hong
427. Yi Chŏng-gu
428. Chŏn Kap-sun
429. Ko Ch'ang-nam
430. Kim Sŏn-ch'o
431. Ch'oe Han-ch'ŏl
432. Kang Kyu-ch'an
433. Han Yang-ŭl
434. Yi Chong-gwŏn
435. Han Yŏng-gyu
436. Kwŏn Ŭn-hae
437. Kang Ch'ŏl
438. Yi Kwan-sul
439. Yu Myŏng-sŏk
440. Han Chong-su
441. Kwŏn O-jik
442. Sŏng T'ae-rae
443. An Ki-sŏng
444. Kim Che-wŏn
445. Hwang Il-bo
446. Ŏm Aeng-gwan

447. Yim Tong-uk
448. Kim Mun-hwan
449. Kim Kwang-jun
450. Cho Yŏng*
451. Yu Sŏk-kyun
452. Kang Sin-u
453. Mun Min-un
454. Pyŏn Ki-ch'ang
455. Ch'oe In
456. Yi Pok-ki
457. Hŏ Chun
458. Ko Chin-hŭi
459. Kim Tal-sam
460. Song Sŏng-ch'ŏl
461. Yi Myŏn-hong
462. Kim Pyŏng-ju
463. Kim Man-jung
464. Chŏn Pong-hwa
465. Ko Kyŏng-in*
466. An Hŭi-nam
467. Chŏng Chin-sŏp
468. Kim Ki-t'aek
469. Sin Paek-hyŏn
470. Yi Sang-gap
471. Pak Ŭn-sŏng
472. Ch'oe San-hwa
473. Kim T'ae-bong
474. Ch'oe Suk-yang
475. Yu Kŭm-bong
476. Kim To-sŏng
477. Kim Chŏng-sun
478. Kim Ŭng-yul
479. Son Tu-hwan
480. Son Chong-yŏl
481. Kim Yong-ho
482. Kim Yong-uk
483. Cho Wŏn-suk
484. Kim Ch'ang-han
485. Yang Wŏn-mo
486. An Se-hun
487. Han Ch'ang-gyo

488. Han Chang-su
489. Chu Man-sul
490. Yim T'aek*
491. Han Chang-ho
492. Hŏ Man-ho
493. Han Kyŏng-su
494. Paek P'a
495. Yŏ Un-ch'ŏl
496. Pak Hyŏng-uk
497. Cho U-bang
498. Chŏng Chae-sŏn
499. Yi Pyŏng-il
500. Yim P'ung-wŏn
501. Kang In-gyu
502. Pak Ch'un-ŏn
503. Yi Pyŏng-no
504. Yi Chong-wan
505. Pak Po-ok
506. Kim Po-p'ae
507. Yi Ho-je
508. Pak P'il-hwan
509. Sin Sun-ye
510. Yi Ki-hwan
511. Song Chun-ho
512. O Che-hong
513. Yu Yong-sang
514. Kim Ŭn-han
515. Kim In-bae
516. Pak Kŏn-byŏng
517. O Ok-byŏl
518. Yi Sŏ-un
519. Yi Sŏ-hyang
520. Kang Sŏng-jae
521. Yi Ch'ang-bin
522. Song Chae-hyŏn
523. Cho Pok-ae
524. Hyŏn Po-yŏl
525. Chŏng In-ch'ul
526. Sin Sun-jik
527. Kim Chae-yong
528. O T'ae-yŏng

529. Ch'oe Wŏl-sŏng
530. Kim Ki-nam
531. Kim Il-sŏn*
532. Mun Ch'i-hwa
533. Kim Tŭk-nan*
534. Ch'oe Han-sik
535. Hong Ch'ŏl-hŭi
536. Kim Yŏn-p'il
537. Kim Hyo-wŏn
538. Kim Yong-wŏn
539. Kim Chŏng-ae
540. Pae Hyŏng-han
541. Song Kŭm-ae
542. Ko Kwang-han
543. Yi Suk-yŏ
544. Kang Yŏng-sun
545. Yi Yŏng-ju
546. Ha P'il-wŏn
547. Hong Chin
548. Kim Hong-gi
549. Kim Chin-ho
550. Yi Kyŏng-dong

551. Kim Sang-sun
552. Chang Ha-myŏng
553. Chŏn Yun-do
554. Kim Man-su
555. Ch'ae Ki-ok
556. Yi Sŏk-ha
557. Kim Sŏng-yul
558. Sŏk T'ae-ryong
559. Sin Sang-dong
560. Kim Chae-ŭl
561. Yun Yong-jun
562. Chŏng Chu-ha
563. Ch'ŏn Sŏng-ok
564. Yŏm Ŭi-hyŏn
565. Cho Tong-sŏk
566. Kim Ŏp-tol
567. Yun Hŭi-gu
568. Kim Nak-chin
569. Pak Chae-sŏp
570. Kim Yŏng-ŭn
571. Kwŏn T'ae-bong
572. Sin Sang-hun

*Reelected to the second Supreme People's Assembly. Seventy-five were reelected.

SECOND SUPREME PEOPLE'S ASSEMBLY, SEPTEMBER 18–20, 1957

Officers of the Second Assembly[8]

Chairman

Ch'oe Wŏn-t'aek

Vice-chairmen

1. Yi Ki-yŏng
2. Kim Ch'ang-jun

Standing Committee

1. Ch'oe Yong-gŏn, chairman
2. Yi Kŭk-no, vice-chairman
3. Hyŏn Ch'il-chong, vice-chairman
4. Kim Wŏn-bong, vice-chairman
5. Kang Yang-uk, secretary-general
6. Pak Chŏng-ae
7. Kang Chin-gŏn
8. Sŏng Chu-sik
9. Kim Pyŏng-je
10. Wŏn Hong-gu
11. Yi Man-gyu
12. Yi Song-un
13. Han Sang-du

14. Kim Ch'ang-dŏk
15. Chŏng No-sik
16. Kim Ch'ŏn-hae
17. Ha Ang-ch'ŏn

18. Chang Hae-u
19. Kye Ŭng-sang
20. Yi Myŏn-sang
21. Song Yŏng

Changes at the Sixth Session of the Second Assembly, October 26–28, 1959

Chairman
Ch'oe Wŏn-t'aek

Vice-chairmen
1. Yi Ki-yŏng
2. Kim Tŭk-nan

Standing Committee
1. Ch'oe Yong-gŏn, chairman
2. Yi Kŭk-no,⁹ vice-chairman
3. Han Sŏl-ya, vice-chairman
4. Kang Yang-uk, vice-chairman
5. Pak Mun-gyu, secretary-general
6. Pak Chŏng-ae
7. Kang Chin-gŏn
8. Kim Pyŏng-je
9. Wŏn Hong-gu
10. Yi Man-gyu

11. Yi Song-un
12. Han Sang-du
13. Kim Ch'ang-dŏk
14. Chŏng No-sik
15. Kim Ch'ŏn-hae
16. Ha Ang-ch'ŏn
17. Chang Hae-u
18. Kye Ŭng-sang
19. Yi Myŏn-sang
20. Song Yŏng
21. Kim Kyŏng-sŏk
22. Pak Sin-dŏk

Other Committees

Bills Committee
1. Kim Ik-sŏn, chairman
2. Kim Yong-jin
3. Sin Nam-ch'ŏl
4. Cho Yŏng
5. Yu Ch'ŏl-mok

6. Ch'oe Chong-hak
7. Yi Yu-min
8. Hŏ Hak-song
9. Han In-sŏk

Budget Committee
1. Song Pong-uk, chairman
2. Paek Nam-un
3. Chŏn T'ae-hwan
4. Kim Sang-ch'ŏl
5. Chŏng Tu-hwan
6. Kim Tŭk-nan

7. Hyŏn Hun
8. Song Ch'ang-nyŏm
9. Yi Chae-ch'ŏn
10. Hwang Sun-ch'ŏn
11. Ch'oe Ch'ŏl-hwan
12. Chang Yun-p'il

13. Chŏng Yŏn-p'yo
14. Mun T'ae-hwa
15. Sŏ Ch'un-sik

16. Kim Mun-gŭn
17. Yim Kŭn-sang

Foreign Affairs Committee
1. Kim Ch'ang-man, chairman
2. Kim Man-gŭm
3. Kim Yŏng-su
4. Hong Chŭng-sik

5. Hŏ Pin
6. Pak Yong-guk
7. Ko Kyŏng-in

Credentials Committee
1. Yi Hyo-sun, chairman
2. Kim T'ae-gŭn
3. Kim Wŏn-bong
4. Yi Hong-yŏl

5. Sin Hong-ye
6. Pak Ch'ang-sik
7. Pak Yong-t'ae

Members of the Second Assembly[10]

Pyongyang city
1. Kim Kwang-hyŏp*
2. Kim Tu-bong
3. Kim Myŏng-jun
4. Yi Nam-i
5. Yi Song-un*
6. Yi Chŏng-suk*
7. Pak Yŏng-sŏp

8. Pak Yŏng-sin*
9. Yu Sŏng-hun
10. Chŏng Yŏn-p'yo
11. Chu Pyŏng-sŏn
12. Ch'oe Kyŏng-hwi
13. Ch'oe Sang-hwa*
14. Hong Ki-hwang

P'yŏngan Namdo
15. Kang Yang-uk*
16. Kang Chun-guk*
17. Kang Chin-gŏn
18. Kim Tu-sam
19. Kim Nak-hŭi
20. Kim Man-gŭm*
21. Kim Il Sung*
22. Kim Ch'ang-dŏk*
23. Yu Su-yŏn
24. Yu Ch'uk-un
25. Yu Hyŏn-gyu
26. Yi Ki-yŏng*
27. Yi Man-gyu*
28. Yi Yŏng
29. Yi Il-gyŏng*

30. Yi Chae-ch'ŏn
31. Yi Chong-man
32. Yim Kŭn-sang
33. Pak To-hwa
34. Pak Mu
35. Pak Sŏng-guk*
36. Pak Yong-guk*
37. Song Yŏng*
38. Yun Pong-jin
39. Yun Ch'i-il
40. Chang Yun-p'il*
41. Chang P'yŏng-san
42. Chang Hae-u
43. Chŏng Tu-hwan*
44. Chŏng Chun-t'aek*

*Reelected to the third Supreme People's Assembly. Seventy-one were reelected.

45. Ch'oe Tu-ch'an
46. Ch'oe Sŭng-hŭi
47. Ch'oe Ch'ŏl-hwan

48. Han Il-mu
49. Han Tong-baek*
50. Hong Chŭng-sik

P'yŏngan Pukto
51. Kang Yŏng-ch'ang*
52. Kye Ŭng-sang*
53. Ko Chun-t'aek*
54. Kwŏn O-gil
55. Kim Tŭk-nan*
56. Kim Sŏk-yong*
57. Kim Sŏng-mun
58. Kim Se-yul
59. Kim Hoe-il*
60. Na Sŭng-gyu
61. Yang Sin-yŏng
62. No Yŏng-se*
63. Yi Tong-hwa
64. Yi Myŏn-sang*
65. Yi Sŭng-gi*

66. Yi Ch'ŏn-ho
67. Sŏ Ch'un-sik
68. Sin Pong-hyŏn
69. An Pyŏng-su
70. Ŏ Han-sang
71. Wŏn Hong-gu*
72. Yun Chŭng-u
73. Chŏng No-sik
74. Chŏng Ch'il-sŏng
75. Cho In-guk
76. Ch'oe Yong-gŏn*
77. Ha Ang-ch'ŏn*
78. Han In-sŏk
79. Han Chŏn-jong
80. Hyŏn Hun

Chagangdo
81. Kim Ki-jun
82. Kim Pyŏng-sŏn
83. Kim Sang-ch'ŏl
84. Kim Wa-ryong
85. Kim Yong-jin
86. Kim Il-sŏn
87. Yi Man-su

88. Yi Hyo-sun*
89. Yim T'aek
90. Pak Ch'ang-sik
91. Sin Hong-ye
92. Chŏng Il-yong*
93. Ch'oe Kwang*

Hwanghae Namdo
94. Ku Cha-sŏng
95. Kim Tŏk-yŏng
96. Kim Sang-sin
97. Kim Wŏn-gyu
98. Kim Ŭng-gi
99. Kim Chŏng-hyŏk
100. Kim Ch'ang-jun
101. Kim Hae-jin
102. Yi Sang-ch'un
103. Yi Chu-yŏn*
104. Pak Kwi-nyŏ
105. Mun Man-uk

106. Pak Mun-gyu*
107. Pak Chŏng-ae*
108. Paek Nam-un*
109. Sin Nam-ch'ŏl
110. Sin Chung-sun*
111. An Tal-su*
112. Yu Man-ok*
113. Yu Ch'ŏl-mok
114. Chŏn T'ae-hwan
115. Chŏng Sŏng-ŏn*
116. Ch'oe Wŏn-t'aek*
117. Han Kwan-ok

Hwanghae Pukto
118. Kim Pyŏng-je*
119. Kim Il*
120. Kim Hwang-il
121. Yi Kwŏn-mu
122. Yi Rim
123. Yi Sŏk-nam*
124. Yi Si-ha
125. Yi Ch'an-hwa*
126. Yi Ch'ang-do*

127. Son Ch'ŏl
128. Song Pong-uk
129. O Ki-sŏp
130. Cho Sŏng-mo
131. Ch'u Sang-su*
132. Han Kil-yong
133. Hŏ Pin
134. Hyŏn Ch'il-chong
135. Hwang Ch'ŏl

Kangwŏndo
136. Kang Tŏk-yŏ*
137. Kim Myŏng-gyun
138. Kim Wŏn-bong
139. Kim Ch'ŏn-hae
140. To Pong-sŏp
141. Yi Kye-san*
142. Yi Chong-ok*
143. Yi Hong-yŏl
144. Mun T'ae-hwa

145. Pang Hak-se
146. O Che-yŏng
147. Yu Kyŏng-su
148. Yu Kwang-yŏl
149. Chŏng Un-bok
150. Ch'oe Chae-ha
151. Ch'oe Chong-hak
152. Ch'oe Hyŏn*

Hamgyŏng Namdo
153. Kang Ch'o-sun*
154. Ko Hŭi-man
155. Kim Tal-hyŏn
156. Kim Mun-gŭm
157. Kim Pyŏng-je
158. Kim Yŏng-su
159. Kim Wŏn-bong
160. Na Yun-ch'ul
161. Yi Kyu-ho
162. Yi Pyŏng-nam
163. Yi Pong-ch'un
164. Yi Yŏ-sŏng
165. Yi Yu-min
166. Yi In-dong
167. Yi Hwa-sŏp

168. Pak Kŭm-ch'ŏl*
169. Pak Ŭi-wan
170. Sŏng Chu-sik
171. Yu Kyŏng-sam
172. Yun Ki-ho
173. Chŏn Sang-gŏn
174. Cho Chŏng-hyŏn
175. Chu Hwang-sŏp
176. Chin Pan-su
177. Ch'oe Yong-jin*
178. Han Sŏl-ya
179. Han Hubang-nyŏ*
180. Hyŏn Chŏng-min
181. Hong Myŏng-hŭi*
182. Hwang Myŏng-jong

Hamgyŏng Pukto
183. Kang T'ae-mu
184. Kwŏn Yŏng-u*
185. Kim Pok-chin

186. Kim Sang-hyŏk
187. Kim Ik-sŏn*
188. Kim Ch'ang-man*

189. Kim T'ae-gŭn*
190. Kim Hu-nam
191. Kim Hŭng-il*
192. Nam Il*
193. Yu Yŏng-jun
194. Yi Kŭk-no*
195. Yi Ki-sŏk
196. Yi Nam-yŏn
197. Pak Yong-t'ae

198. Paek Saeng-gŭm
199. Song Ŭl-su
200. Ch'oe Pong-su
201. Han Sang-du*
202. Hŏ Sŏng-t'aek
203. Hŏ Chŏng-suk
204. Hwang Sun-ch'ŏn
205. Hwang Chung-ŏp*

Yanggangdo
206. Ko Kyŏng-in
207. Kim Pyŏng-yŏn
208. Yim Hae
209. Song Ch'ang-nyŏm*

210. Kim Sŭng-do
211. Cho Yŏng
212. Ch'u Yun-yŏp

Kaesŏng city
213. Kim Myŏng-ho*
214. Chŏng Nak-sŏn
215. Hŏ Hak-song*

*Reelected to the third Supreme People's Assembly. Seventy-one were reelected.

THIRD SUPREME PEOPLE'S ASSEMBLY, OCTOBER 22–23, 1962
Officers of the Third Assembly[11]

Chairman
Ch'oe Wŏn-t'aek

Vice-chairmen
1. Yi Ki-yŏng
2. Kim Tŭk-nan

Officers and members of the Standing Committee
1. Ch'oe Yong-gŏn, chairman
2. Pak Chŏng-ae, vice-chairman
3. Hong Myŏng-hŭi, vice-chairman
4. Kang Yang-uk, vice-chairman
5. Paek Nam-un, vice-chairman
6. Pak Kŭm-ch'ŏl,[12] vice-chairman
7. Yim Ch'un-ch'u,[13] secretary-general
8. Yi Hyo-sun
9. Ha Ang-ch'ŏn
10. Hyŏn Mu-gwang
11. Pak Sin-dŏk
12. Ch'oe Hyŏn
13. Yi Yŏng-ho
14. Kim Wal-yong
15. Kim Ok-sun

16. No Ik-myŏng
17. Kim Ch'ang-dŏk
18. Song Yŏng
19. Yi Man-gyu

20. Yi Myŏn-sang
21. Kye Ŭng-sang
22. Yi Chae-bok
23. To Yu-ho

Other Committees

Bills Committee

1. Kim Ik-sŏn, chairman
2. Hŏ Pong-hak
3. Kim Tong-gyu
4. Ch'oe Ki-ch'ŏl
5. Yi Chae-yŏng

6. Kim Hŭi-jun
7. No Ik-myŏng
8. Kim Kuk-hun
9. Kim Si-jung

Budget Committee

1. Yim Kye-ch'ŏl, chairman
2. Kang Hŭi-wŏn
3. Chŏng Sŏng-ŏn
4. O Che-ryong
5. Yi Ch'an-sŏn
6. Chŏng Chong-gi
7. Chang Yun-p'il
8. Yi Ch'ang-bok

9. Kim Mu-hoe
10. Pak Sŭng-hŭp
11. Chu Wŏn-saeng
12. Chi Chang-gŏn
13. Yun Yŏn-hwan
14. Chŏn Kyŏng-hwa
15. Yi Sŏk-sim

Foreign Affairs Committee

1. Pak Yong-guk, chairman
2. Kim Wal-yong
3. Hŏ Sŏk-sŏn
4. Yu Kŏn-yang

5. Chŏng Kwang-nok
6. Kim Ok-sun
7. Ch'oe Hak-sŏn

Credentials Committee

1. Ch'oe Yong-jin, chairman
2. Pak Ung-gŏl
3. Han Tong-baek
4. Yi Chae-yun

5. Yu Ki-ik
6. Ch'u Sang-su
7. No Yŏng-se

Members of the Third Assembly[14]

1. Kim Il Sung*
2. Ch'oe Yong-gŏn*
3. Kim Il*
4. Hong Myŏng-hŭi*
5. Pak Kŭm-ch'ŏl
6. Kim Ch'ang-man
7. Yi Hyo-sun

8. Kim Kwang-hyŏp*
9. Chŏng Il-yong*
10. Nam Il*
11. Yi Chong-ok*
12. Pak Chŏng-ae*
13. Yi Chu-yŏn*
14. Kim Ik-sŏn*

*Reelected to the fourth Supreme People's Assembly; 225 were reelected.

15. Ha Ang-ch'ŏn
16. Han Sang-du*
17. Chŏng Chun-t'aek*
18. Hyŏn Mu-gwang*
19. Kang Hŭi-wŏn*
20. Hŏ Pong-hak*
21. Yŏm Kyŏng-jae
22. Sin Chung-sun
23. Kim Kuk-hun*
24. Ch'oe Ch'ang-sŏk
25. Ch'oe Un-hak*
26. Yi Song-un
27. Pak Se-ch'ang
28. Pak Kyŏng-suk*
29. Kang Yang-uk*
30. Kim Pyŏng-sik*
31. Song Tŏk-hun*
32. Yi Chŏng-suk
33. T'ae Pyŏng-yŏl*
34. Yi Ch'ang-do*
35. Yi Ŭng-wŏn*
36. Yi Chae-bok*
37. Yun Pyŏng-gwŏn*
38. Paek Ŭi-myŏng*
39. Kim Wŏn-bin*
40. Chŏn Kyŏng-hwa
41. Kim Su-bok
42. Ch'oe Sang-hwa
43. Ko Hyŏk
44. Kim T'ae-hyŏn*
45. Hwang Sun-hŭi*
46. Ch'oe Kwang*
47. Kim Ch'ang-bong*
48. Kim Chong-hang
49. Kwŏn Yŏng-t'ae
50. Kim Ŭng-sang*
51. Chŏn Ch'ang-ch'ŏl*
52. Pak Kŭm-ok
53. Kim Tong-gyu*
54. O Tong-uk*
55. Kim Sŏng-yul*
56. Yang Chŏng-t'ae*
57. Pak Sŏng-guk*
58. Han Tong-baek
59. Pak Sin-dŏk*
60. To Yu-ho
61. Song Yŏng*
62. Kim Wŏn-jŏm*
63. Hwang Chae-sŏn*
64. Chi Chang-gŏn*
65. O Rye-sŏn
66. Kang Wi-jun*
67. Ch'oe Hyŏn*
68. Kim Sang-hwan
69. Kim Wŏn-jŏn
70. Ko Chŏng-ik
71. Mun Chŏng-suk*
72. Yim Yun-sik*
73. Kim Kŭm-san*
74. Chŏng Pyŏng-gap*
75. Yu Ki-ik
76. O T'ae-bong*
77. Yi Man-gyu*
78. Ko Chun-t'aek*
79. Yŏm T'ae-jun*
80. Pak Kwang-sŏn*
81. No Ik-myŏng*
82. Hwang Chung-ŏp*
83. Pak Yong-guk*
84. Kim Ch'ang-jun*
85. Ch'oe Ch'ang-do*
86. An Chae-sŭng
87. Kim Man-gŭm*
88. Yi Yŏng-ho*
89. Kim Pyŏng-su
90. Kang Chun-guk
91. Pak Yŏng-sun*
92. Ch'oe Ch'un-sŏp*
93. Han Ch'an-ok*
94. Kim Nak-hŭi*
95. Kim Hyŏn-su
96. Kim Yŏng-ju*
97. Cho Myŏng-hwa*
98. Son Wŏn-dong
99. Yi Chŏng-sam
100. Yi Ch'ang-bok*

101. An Suk-yong*
102. Yi Min-su*
103. Cho Ŭng-sŏp
104. Chŏng Tu-hwan*
105. Chin Pyŏng-mu*
106. Kim Kwan-sŏp
107. Yi T'ae-u
108. Pak Sŏng-ch'ol*
109. Kang Chung-yŏn
110. Ch'oe T'ae-sŏn
111. Pak Tong-gwan*
112. Chi Myŏng-gwan
113. Ch'oe Ki-wŏn
114. Yi Il-gyŏng
115. Yi Tŏk-hyŏn
116. Hyŏn Ch'ang-yong*
117. Kim Sŏk-yong*
118. Paek Sŏn-il*
119. O Paek-yong*
120. Kim Tŭk-nan*
121. Yi Tan*
122. Kim Ch'un-sŏng
123. Sŏk San*
124. Yi Ch'un-yong
125. Ko Kŭm-sun*
126. Kim Yang-yul
127. Kim Sŏk-hyŏng*
128. Han Tae-yŏng
129. Han Ik-su*
130. Chŏng Chi-hwan
131. Kye Ŭng-sang
132. Yi Ch'an-sŏn*
133. Kim Yong-ho*
134. Sŏ Ch'ŏl*
135. Yi Wŏn-jun
136. Yim Pong-ŏn
137. No Yŏng-se
138. Kim Tŏk-bok
139. Ko In-gŏl*
140. Kim Sŭng-wŏn*
141. Yim Kye-ch'ŏl*
142. Yu Myŏng-ho
143. Kim Myŏng-gyŏng

144. Kim T'ae-ryŏn
145. Sŏk Ch'il-bo*
146. Kim Pong-sŏn*
147. Kim Sŏng-ch'ŏl
148. Kang U-sik*
149. Kang Chung-han
150. Kang Ho-sin
151. Hwang Wŏn-t'aek*
152. Han Yŏng-ok
153. Yim Yŏng-gyun
154. Chang Myŏng-jun
155. Kim Yŏng-uk*
156. Wŏn Hong-gu*
157. Kim Mu-hoe*
158. Kim Chae-un*
159. Kim Ch'ŏn-hwang*
160. Yu Rak-chong*
161. Ch'oe Ch'ang-gŏl
162. Yang T'aek-kŏn*
163. Nam Sŏn-ok*
164. Sŏ Ŭl-hyŏn
165. Kim Sŏk-man*
166. Kang Un-sŏng*
167. Yu Kŏn-yang
168. Yi Yong-sŏn*
169. Yŏn Pok-kil
170. Cho Tong-sŏp
171. Kim Chung-nin*
172. Kim Wŏn-ch'ŏng*
173. Kim Tong-sik
174. Song Ch'ang-nyŏm
175. Kim Pyŏng-mo
176. Kim Tal-chun
177. Han Sŭng-un
178. Yu Yŏng-sŏp
179. Chang Kyŏng-sun
180. Kim Wa-ryong
181. O Kyŏng-ae*
182. Kim Ok-chun
183. Han Sang-sun
184. Kim Wŏn-sŏl
185. Kim Wŏn-sam*
186. Yim Chin-gyu*

187. Paek Sŏng-hak*
188. Kim Pyŏng-sun
189. Chŏng Tong-ch'ŏl*
190. Ch'oe Sŏng-nak
191. Kim Wŏn-hyŏng
192. Chang Ch'ŏng-t'aek
193. Han Su-hyŏn*
194. Pak Chŏng-yŏl
195. Ch'oe Pong-sun
196. Mun Ch'ang-sŏk
197. Paek Sŏng-guk
198. Ch'oe Pong-san*
199. Kim Chin-hwa*
200. Chu Wŏn-saeng
201. Hŏ P'il-su
202. Yang Pok-wŏn
203. Kim Se-bong
204. Kim Ok-sun*
205. Kim Hak-sun
206. Yi Chae-gŭn
207. Ch'oe Chung-sŏk
208. Kim Hŭng-il*
209. Kim Sang-guk*
210. Hong Si-hak*
211. Hwang Hwa-bok*
212. Kim Tong-hyŏk
213. Yi Pyŏng-bu*
214. Yu Ch'ang-gwŏn*
215. Yang T'ae-gŭn
216. Han Ki-ch'ang*
217. Chŏng Kwang-nok*
218. Mun Sŏng-sul*
219. Kim Wal-yong
220. Yi Yang-suk*
221. Yi Kwang-sŏn
222. Pak Yong-sŏng
223. Ch'oe Ki-ch'ŏl
224. To Chong-ho
225. Yi Ki-ch'ŏl*
226. Yang Ch'ung-gyŏm
227. Ch'oe Chung-san*
228. Kang Ch'o-sun*
229. Yi Sang-un

230. Ko Min-sun*
231. Ch'oe Ch'il-gap*
232. Yi Song-yŏn
233. Yun Ki-bok
234. Yi Pong-nam
235. Kim Hoe-il*
236. Kang Yŏng-ch'ang
237. Yi Kuk-chin*
238. Yun Yŏn-hwan*
239. Yi Yŏn*
240. Yim Ch'un-ch'u
241. Yi Yŏng-gu*
242. Ch'oe Yong-jin*
243. Kwŏn Yun-il*
244. Ch'oe Sang-ŭl*
245. Yang Hyŏng-sŏp*
246. Pak Hong-sun
247. Pak Hong-gŏl*
248. Chu Sŏng-il*
249. Pak Pong-jo*
250. Yi Sŭng-gi*
251. Ch'oe Chŏng
252. Yi Tong-sŏng
253. Ch'oe Min-hwan*
254. Chŏn Cha-ryŏn*
255. Kim Mun-gŭn*
256. Yŏ Kyŏng-gu*
257. An Sŭng-hak*
258. Yi Hak-pin*
259. Kim Kyŏng-hoe
260. Yi Kyŏng-yong
261. Yi Kwang-sil*
262. Kim Ki-su
263. Yi Chae-yun*
264. Kim Yang-ch'un*
265. Han Hubang-nyŏ*
266. Chŏng Chong-gi*
267. Pak Sŭng-sŏ
268. Han Su-dong
269. Kim I-sun
270. Ch'oe Hak-sŏn
271. Kim Yŏ-jung*
272. Kim Tong-hyŏn

273. Kim Hi-jun
274. Hwang Wŏn-bo
275. Yu Chae-hun
276. Sim Sang-ŭi
277. Chang Pyŏng-su
278. Yi Mae-ch'un*
279. Kang Tŏk-yŏ*
280. Chŏng Ki-hwan
281. Kim Ch'ŏl-man*
282. Hwang Wŏn-jun
283. No Su-ŏk*
284. Yi Sŏng-nam*
285. Pak Yŏng-sin*
286. Yi Man-ik*
287. Pak Sŭng-hak*
288. Hwang Chang-yŏp
289. Han Ch'ang-sun*
290. Yi Myŏn-sang*
291. Kim Chwa-hyŏk*
292. Yu Pyŏng-yŏn*
293. Pak T'ae-jin
294. Yi Ki-yŏng*
295. Yang Chun-hyŏk*
296. O Chin-u*
297. Nam Ch'un-hwa
298. Kim Pong-yul*
299. O Che-ryong*
300. Yi Ŭl-sŏl*
301. Kim Ŏk-su
302. Yi Kye-san*
303. Chang Chŏng-hwan*
304. Ch'oe Sŏng-jip*
305. Yi Sun-yŏng*
306. Yi Tu-ik*
307. Pae Ki-jun
308. Chŏng Ki-man*
309. Kim Kŭm-sil*
310. Pak Mun-gyu*
311. Kim Chae-gu
312. Han Hong-sik
313. Pak Yŏng-su*
314. Sim Hyŏng-sik*
315. Pak Chŏng-gŭn

316. Ch'ae Hŭi-jŏng
317. Chŏn Mun-sŏp*
318. Pak Ch'an-je*
319. Yi Ch'an-hwa*
320. An Yŏng*
321. Yun Yŏng-gyŏng
322. Yi Sŏk-nam*
323. Chŏng Chŏng-man
324. Ch'oe Man-guk*
325. Yi Chae-yŏng
326. Kim Ch'ang-dŏk
327. Pak Chae-p'il
328. Yi Tal-yŏng
329. Sŭng Sin-bŏm*
330. Ch'oe Sun-nam*
331. Yim Kwi-bin*
332. Kim Tae-hong*
333. Chu Chong-myŏng*
334. Kim To-man
335. Kang Uk-kŭk*
336. Pak Sŭng-hŭp
337. Ch'u Sang-su*
338. Yim Sun-nyŏ*
339. Yi Yŏng-sun*
340. Hŏ Sŏk-sŏn
341. Kim Kyŏng-in
342. Yu Man-ok*
343. Kim Si-jung
344. Paek Nam-un*
345. Chŏn Man-yŏng*
346. Yi Ch'ang-jun*
347. Hŏ Hak-song
348. Hong To-hak*
349. Chŏng Wŏl-san*
350. Yi Kŭk-no*
351. Kim Sŏk-t'ae
352. O Hyŏn-ju*
353. Pak Pyŏng-guk*
354. Yi Kŭn-song*
355. Ch'oe Chae-u*
356. Chang Yun-p'il*
357. Kim Pyŏng-je
358. Yi Hwa-yŏng

359. An Tal-su*
360. Chŏng In-sŏn*
361. Sin Myŏng-ch'ŏl
362. Sin Ko-song
363. Pak Kyŏng-sun
364. Chu To-il*
365. Ch'oe Wŏn-t'aek*
366. Kim T'ae-gŭn*
367. Chŏng Sŏng-ŏn
368. Yi Sŏk-sim
369. Kim Ki-sŏn*
370. Chu Ch'ang-jun
371. Hwang Wŏn-nam*

372. Sin Chin-sik
373. Kim Pyŏng-ik*
374. Kwŏn Yŏng-u*
375. Ch'oe Ŏk-chun*
376. Kim Ŭi-hwan*
377. Yi Yŏng-sun
378. Yun Hyŏng-sik*
379. Pak Ung-gŏl
380. Kim Chae-suk
381. Chi Pyŏng-hak*
382. Kim Myŏng-ho
383. Yi Ch'ang-sun*

*Reelected to the fourth Supreme People's Assembly; 225 were reelected.

Fourth Supreme People's Assembly, December 14–16, 1967

Officers of the Fourth Assembly[15]

Chairman

Paek Nam-un

Vice-chairmen

1. Yi Ki-yŏng
2. Kim Tŭk-nan

Officers and members of the Standing Committee

1. Ch'oe Yong-gŏn, chairman
2. Hong Myŏng-hŭi, vice-chairman
3. Pak Chŏng-ae, vice-chairman
4. Kang Yang-uk, vice-chairman
5. Yi Yŏng-ho, vice-chairman
6. Pak Mun-gyu, secretary-general
7. Ch'oe Hyŏn
8. Hŏ Pong-hak
9. Kim Yŏng-ju
10. Yi Kuk-chin
11. Ch'oe Kwang
12. O Chin-u
13. Kim Tong-gyu
14. Pak Sin-dŏk
15. Kim Yŏ-jung

Other Committees

Bills Committee

1. Kim Yŏ-jung, chairman
2. Yi Yong-gu
3. Kim Chwa-hyŏk
4. Paek Hak-nim
5. Yi Rim-su
6. Yŏm T'ae-jun
7. Kim Ch'ang-bok
8. Yi Sŭng-gi
9. Kim Kuk-hun

Foreign Affairs Committee
1. Sŏ Ch'ŏl, chairman
2. Chŏn Ch'ang-ch'ŏl
3. Kim Ok-sun
4. Ch'oe Chung-gŭk
5. O Ki-ch'ŏn
6. O Hyŏn-ju
7. Yi Yun-do

Budget Committee
1. Yim Kye-ch'ŏl, chairman
2. Kang Hŭi-wŏn
3. O Che-ryong
4. Yi Wŏn-bŏm
5. Chang Yun-p'il
6. Kim Sŏk-hyŏng
7. Yi Chong-guk
8. Yun Yŏn-hwan
9. Ch'oe Ch'un-sŏp
10. Han Chŏng-gi
11. Kim Nak-hŭi

Credentials Committee
1. Yi Kuk-chin, chairman
2. Kim Sŏk-yong
3. Kim Yong-ho
4. Yim Hyŏng-gu
5. Ch'oe Chong-gŏn
6. Yi Tal-yong
7. Yi Kye-san

Members of the Fourth Assembly[16]
1. Kim Il Sung*
2. Ch'oe Yong-gŏn*
3. Kim Il*
4. Kim Kwang-hyŏp
5. Hong Myŏng-hŭi
6. Nam Il*
7. Yi Chong-ok*
8. Pak Chŏng-ae
9. Yi Chu-yŏn
10. Ch'oe Hyŏn*
11. Kim Ch'ang-bong
12. Pak Sŏng-ch'ŏl*
13. Kim Ik-sŏn
14. Yi Yŏng-ho
15. Sŏk San
16. Hŏ Pong-hak
17. Kim Yŏng-ju*
18. Yi Kuk-chin
19. Chŏng Chun-t'aek*
20. Ch'oe Yong-jin*
21. Han Sang-du
22. Hyŏn Mu-gwang*
23. Ch'oe Kwang
24. O Chin-u*
25. Kim Tong-gyu*
26. Chŏng Kyŏng-bok
27. Hwang Sun-hŭi*
28. Ch'oe Chong-gŏn
29. Chŏn Hŭi
30. Ch'oe In-dŏk*
31. Chang Hŭi-do
32. Kim Sang-jin*
33. Yi Sŏn-bi
34. Ch'oe Un-hak
35. An Sang-ch'un
36. Yang Ho-jae
37. Kim Yun-sŏn*
38. Song Tŏk-hun

*Reelected to the fifth Supreme People's Assembly; 178 were reelected.

39. Ch'oe Ch'ae-ryŏn
40. Kim Sŏng-guk
41. Yi Tong-il
42. Kim Yŏng-ch'ae*
43. Kim Yŏng-ho
44. Kim Myŏng-suk
45. Yi Ŭng-wŏn*
46. Yi Myŏng-wŏn*
47. Pak Su-bom
48. Hwang Chi-ryŏp*
49. Kang Chae-wŏn
50. Yun Pyŏng-gwŏn*
51. Yi Che-jin
52. Pak Nam-sun*
53. Paek Ŭi-myŏng*
54. Yi Tan
55. O Myŏng-sŏp
56. Han Hyŏng-ho
57. Pak Sŏng-guk
58. Yi Pong-gyŏm
59. Kim Chŏng-t'ae
60. Kang Hŭi-wŏn*
61. Chŏng Yŏng-yŏl
62. Kim Pok-sŏn
63. Chi Pyŏng-hak*
64. Yi Yong-hŭi
65. Hŏ Paek-san*
66. Chu Ho-sun
67. Kim Po-ok
68. An Yŏng-hwan
69. Chang Sŏk-ha
70. Kim Pyŏng-sik*
71. Sŏ Kwan-hŭi*
72. Kim Sŏng-yul*
73. Sin Yong-sik*
74. Cho Ch'un-sam*
75. Kim Chwa-hyŏk
76. Kim Sŏng-yŏn
77. Yi Ch'ang-bok
78. Paek Chong-hŭp
79. Yu Ch'ang-gwŏn
80. Yi Sun-nam
81. Kye Ch'un-yŏng*
82. Han T'ae-ryong
83. Pak Kwan-sun
84. Chi Chang-gŏn
85. Wŏn Hong-gu
86. Kim In-ch'ŏl
87. Yi Hyŏn-muk
88. Chŏng Pyŏng-gap
89. Mun Chŏng-suk
90. Han Tŏk-su*
91. O Hyŏn-ju*
92. Kim Tong-yŏn
93. Yim Yun-sik*
94. Kang Wi-jun
95. Yi Tu-ch'an*
96. Chu To-il*
97. Hwang Chung-ŏp
98. Kim Pyŏng-sik
99. Hwang Chae-sŏn*
100. Ch'oe Ch'ang-do*
101. Kim Ch'ang-jun*
102. Kang Yang-uk*
103. Yi Pyŏng-sik
104. Pak Ki-t'aek
105. Song Kwan-jo*
106. Kim T'ae-hyŏn
107. Yi Sun-yŏng
108. Kim Yŏng-sik
109. Kim Nak-hŭi*
110. Ch'oe Ch'un-sŏp
111. Ch'oe Kyŏng-hu
112. Yi Chae-bok
113. Kim Wŏn-jŏm
114. Hong Nae-gŭn*
115. Yi Yŏng-suk*
116. Kim Sŏk-yong*
117. Pak Kwang-sŏn
118. Kim Kŭm-san*
119. An Ch'ang-se*
120. Chu Kil-sun*
121. Han Ch'an-ok*
122. Chin Pyŏng-mu*

123. Ch'oe Rin-bŏm
124. Kim Kuk-hun*
125. Kim Pyŏng-han
126. Cho Myŏng-hwa
127. Kim Tae-hong
128. Kim Yong-ho*
129. Kim Pyŏng-bin*
130. Yi Min-su
131. Kim T'ae-gŭn
132. Pak Tong-gwan*
133. O Tong-uk
134. Yi Chang-su
135. Yi Kuk-kwŏn*
136. Ch'oe Ch'ang-yong
137. Kim Ch'ang-bok
138. Yi Yang-suk
139. Yi Yu-sŏp
140. Pak Kyŏng-suk
141. Yi Yŏng-gu*
142. Kang Chong-gŭn
143. Ch'oe Wŏn-t'aek
144. Han Chŏng-gi*
145. Yi Myŏn-sang*
146. Han T'ae-suk
147. Kim Tŏk-wŏn*
148. Sŭng So-il
149. Kim Yŏ-jung
150. Yi Man-gyu
151. Yun Pong-gu
152. An Yŏng
153. Chang Chŏng-hwan*
154. Hong Si-hak*
155. Kim Kyŏng-myŏng*
156. Hong Yu-bok
157. Kim Kye-hyŏn
158. Kim Myŏng-ok
159. An Sŭng-hak
160. Yi Ch'ang-do*
161. Yi Ch'un-bal
162. Tokko Mun-hŭng
163. Kim Sŭng-wŏn*
164. Yi Chun-sil*
165. Kang Yŏng-suk*

166. Yun Kyŏng-ja
167. Yi Pong-nyŏ
168. Song Yŏng
169. Pak Mun-gyu
170. Yang In-gil*
171. Kim Pong-sŏn*
172. Kim Pyŏng-ik
173. Ko In-gŏl
174. Pak Sin-dŏk*
175. Cho Kwan-ha
176. Sŏk Ch'il-bo
177. Kang U-sik
178. Chang Il-gyŏng*
179. Yi Kŭm-nyŏ*
180. Yŏm Chae-man
181. Hwang Wŏn-t'aek
182. Ko Kŭm-sun*
183. Kim Tŭk-nan*
184. Kim Kap-sun
185. Yang Chong-go*
186. Kim Sŏk-hyŏng*
187. Kim Yŏng-uk
188. No Pyŏng-u
189. Yang Chae-il
190. Kim Chae-hŭng
191. Nam Sŏn-ok
192. Kim Mu-hoe
193. Kim Ch'ŏn-hwang
194. Kim Sŏng-do
195. Yu Rak-chong*
196. Ch'oe Kŭm-nyŏ
197. Yu Chang-sik*
198. Kim Chae-un
199. Yang T'aek-kŏn
200. Yi Wŏn-bŏm
201. Kim Sŏk-man
202. Kim Wŏn-ch'ŏng*
203. Yŏn Hyŏng-muk*
204. Yang Ok-nyŏ*
205. Yi Yong-sŏn*
206. Paek Kŏn-sa
207. Han Chŏng-hŏn
208. Hong Wŏn-gil*

209. Paek Sŏng-hak
210. Chŏn Hak-su
211. Kim Yŏn-yŏ
212. Pak Sŭng-il
213. Kang Un-sŏng
214. Han Ch'ang-sun
215. Yi Sŭng-sun
216. Kim Chŏng-p'il*
217. Pang Hyo-ŭl
218. Kim Wŏn-sam*
219. Pak Yong-sŏk
220. Kye Ŭng-t'ae*
221. An Sŭng-bae
222. O Kyŏng-ae
223. Kang Po-gŭm
224. Yim Chin-gyu
225. Pak Yŏng-sŏp*
226. Chang Sam-son
227. Kim Sŏn-mo
228. Yi Chun-hwi
229. Mun Sŏng-sul
230. Yi Kye-hwan*
231. Han Su-hyŏn
232. Kim Ŭng-sang*
233. Cho Yong-p'al
234. Chŏn Pyŏng-gŭn
235. Ch'oe Pong-san
236. An Suk-yong*
237. Chŏng Il-yong
238. Kim Un-hak
239. Kim Chin-hwa
240. Yi Im-su
241. Kim Yong-bŏm
242. Cho Yŏng-mu
243. Yi Tong-jun*
244. Yi Chong-guk
245. U Yŏng-sul
246. Kim Tu-sam
247. Yi Il-ung
248. Yi Su-il
249. Kim Nam-gyo
250. Kim Sang-guk
251. Kim Pong-ch'un

252. Chŏn Ch'ang-ch'ŏl*
253. Cho Ch'ang-suk*
254. Chŏng Ch'i-ryong*
255. Kim Hŭng-il
256. Han Ki-ch'ang
257. Yi Pyŏng-bu
258. Han Ik-su*
259. Ch'oe Kŭm-san*
260. Yi Kwang-sil
261. Pak Chŏng-hyŏn*
262. Ch'oe Sa-hyŏn
263. Song Pok-ki*
264. Yi Kŭk-no
265. Pang Hak-se*
266. Kim Ch'ae-bong
267. Chŏng Kwang-nok
268. Kim Hoe-il
269. Chu In-gŏn
270. Hwang Hwa-bok
271. Yi Ki-ch'ŏl
272. Ch'oe Chung-san*
273. Kim Nŭng-il
274. Cho Chung-wŏn
275. Chŏng Ki-su
276. Chŏn Han-gyo*
277. Sŭng Ch'ang-yul
278. Kang Ch'o-sun
279. Ch'oe Ch'il-gap*
280. Ko Min-sun*
281. Yi Su-ch'ŏn
282. Chang Sang-yong
283. Yi Sun-ho*
284. Ko Chun-t'aek
285. Pak Yŏng-sun*
286. Chŏng Tong-ch'ŏl
287. Yi Yŏn*
288. Yi Kye-baek*
289. Paek Nam-un*
290. Yi Sŭng-gi*
291. Kwŏn Yun-il*
292. Kang Chŏm-gu
293. Ch'oe Sang-ŭl
294. Kang Maeng-gu*

295. Hyŏn Ch'ang-yong
296. Pak Hong-gŏl
297. Han Hyŏng-wan*
298. Kim Sŏng-gu
299. Chŏng Hŭi-ch'ŏl*
300. Pak Pong-jo
301. Chŏn Cha-ryŏn*
302. Yun Yŏn-hwan
303. Kim Mun-gŭn
304. Pak Pok-sun
305. Sin P'o-gyun*
306. Kim Yang-ch'un
307. Yi Hak-pin
308. Ch'oe Min-hwan
309. Chu Sŏng-il*
310. Chu Tu-byŏk
311. Kim Yong-t'aek*
312. Yi Chae-yun*
313. Yi Yun-do
314. An Ch'ang-hwa
315. Ham Sŏk-chun
316. Yi Ki-yŏng*
317. Han Myŏng-suk
318. Han Hubang-nyŏ*
319. Yŏ Kyŏng-gu
320. Kim Ŏin-nam*
321. Chŏng Chong-gi
322. Chŏn Chae-su
323. Mun Suk-cha*
324. Yi Chong-san
325. Pak Ch'an-je
326. O Kŭk-yŏl*
327. Yi Ch'ŏl-u
328. Ch'oe T'ae-yŏn
329. Kwŏn Yŏng-u*
330. Chŏng Tu-hwan*
331. Chin Yŏng-dong
332. Kim Wŏn-ch'an*
333. Kim Pyŏng-gyu
334. Chŏng Ki-man
335. Cho Ch'ang-sŏn
336. Ch'oe Chung-son*
337. Cho Kyŏng-suk
338. Sin Sŭng-o
339. Yi Rak-bin*
340. Kim Ok-sun*
341. Kwŏn Chŏm-du*
342. Pak Sŭng-hak
343. Yi Yong-gu
344. Yi Man-ik
345. Ch'oe Sŏng-jip
346. Ch'oe Chung-gŭk*
347. Yi Su-dŏk
348. Kim U-jin
349. Kim Yong-yŏn
350. Yi Yŏng-gi
351. Kim Ch'ŏl-man*
352. Kim Kyu-sun*
353. Ch'oe Min-ch'ŏl
354. Yi Mae-ch'un
355. Sŏ Ch'ŏl*
356. Kang Tŏk-yŏ
357. Chŏn Mun-uk
358. Hong To-hak
359. O Paek-yong*
360. Yang Chun-hyŏk
361. O T'ae-bong*
362. Kim Cha-rin
363. Yi Kye-san*
364. Yi Ŭl-sŏl*
365. O Che-ryong
366. Paek Sŏn-il
367. Song Ŏk-man
368. Kim Chong-hwa
369. Yu Pyŏng-yŏn
370. Yi Sŏng-nam
371. Kim Kŭm-sil
372. Kim Yun-sik
373. O Ki-ch'ŏn
374. Chu In-hwa
375. Sim Hyŏng-sik
376. Pak Yŏng-su*
377. Kang Hyŏn-su
378. Yi Ch'an-hwa*

379. Ch'oe Man-guk*
380. Yi Tal-yong*
381. Yi Sŏk-nam
382. Kim T'ae-hwa
383. Chu Chong-myŏng
384. Kim Wŏn-bin
385. Yim Kwi-bin
386. Ch'oe Sun-nam*
387. Yi Tu-ik*
388. Ch'u Sang-su*
389. No Su-ŏk
390. Yŏm T'ae-jun*
391. Yi Pang-gŭn*
392. O Sun-nyŏ*
393. Sŭng Sin-bŏm
394. Kim Ch'an-gwŏn
395. Kim Pong-yul*
396. Ch'oe Chae-u*
397. Chŏn Sŏn-bi
398. Pak Yŏng-sin
399. Kim Tong-hwan*
400. Kim Pong-su
401. Kim Chung-yŏ
402. Ch'a Sŏk-ho
403. Kang Uk-kuk*
404. Chŏn Mun-sŏp*
405. Yi Chin-gyu*
406. Yim Sun-nyŏ*
407. Chŏn Yong-sun
408. Yu Man-ok
409. Yi Ch'ang-jun
410. Chŏn Man-yŏng
411. Kim Kuk-t'ae
412. O T'aek-hwan*
413. T'ae Pyŏng-yŏl*
414. Chŏng Wŏl-san
415. Yim Hyŏng-gu
416. Yang Hyŏng-sŏp*
417. Yi Kŭn-mo*
418. U Sang-bok

419. Yi Pok-hyŏng
420. Yi Ho-hyŏk
421. Kim Ch'i-do
422. Pak Pyŏng-guk
423. Yi Kŭn-song*
424. O Chae-wŏn
425. O Pyŏng-dŏk*
426. Sin Su-gyŏng
427. Yim T'ae-sŏp
428. Yang Chŏng-t'ae
429. Chŏng In-sŏn
430. An Tal-su*
431. Han Yang-du
432. Kim Sŏn-uk*
433. Kim Chung-nin*
434. Cho Sun-ok
435. Ku Cha-hun*
436. Yi Mun-ja
437. Kim Sun-bok
438. Hwang Ki-sŏ
439. Yim Kye-ch'ŏl
440. Yi Ch'an-sŏn
441. Paek Hak-nim*
442. Kim Ki-sŏn*
443. Hwang Wŏn-nam*
444. Yi Chŏng-nim
445. Yun T'ae-hong
446. Ch'oe Ŏk-chun
447. Chŏn P'il-yŏ*
448. Chang Yun-p'il*
449. Ch'oe Kyu-hwan
450. Kim Ŭi-hwan
451. Chŏn No-hyŏng*
452. Yi Yŏng-sun*
453. Yim Ch'ŏl*
454. Yun Hyŏng-sik
455. Chin Mun-dŏk*
456. Yi Ch'ang-sun*
457. Kim Man-gŭm*

*Reelected to the fifth Supreme People's Assembly; 178 were reelected.

FIFTH SUPREME PEOPLE'S ASSEMBLY, DECEMBER 25–28, 1972

Officers of the Fifth Assembly[17]

President of the Republic
Kim Il Sung

Vice-Presidents of the Republic
1. Ch'oe Yong-gŏn[18]
2. Kang Yang-uk

Secretary-General
Yim Ch'un-ch'u

Central People's Committee
1. Kim Il Sung
2. Ch'oe Yong-gŏn
3. Kang Yang-uk
4. Kim Il[19]
5. Pak Sŏng-ch'ŏl
6. Ch'oe Hyŏn
7. O Chin-u
8. Kim Tong-gyu
9. Kim Yŏng-ju
10. Kim Chung-nin
11. Hyŏn Mu-gwang
12. Yang Hyŏng-sŏp
13. Chŏng Chun-t'aek
14. Kim Man-gŭm
15. Yi Kŭn-mo
16. Ch'oe Chae-u
17. Yi Chong-ok
18. Yim Ch'un-ch'u
19. Yŏn Hyŏng-muk
20. O T'ae-bong
21. Nam Il
22. Hong Wŏn-gil
23. Yu Chang-sik
24. Hŏ Tam
25. Kim Pyŏng-ha

Standing Committee
1. Hwang Chang-yŏp, chairman
2. Hong Ki-mun, vice-chairman
3. Hŏ Chŏng-suk, vice-chairman
4. Sŏ Ch'ŏl
5. Han Ik-su
6. Chŏn Ch'ang-ch'ŏl, secretary-general
7. Pak Sin-dŏk
8. Kim Yŏng-nam
9. Chŏng Chun-gi
10. Yŏm T'ae-jun
11. Kim Sŏng-ae
12. Kim I-hun
13. Yi Yŏng-bok
14. Yun Ki-bok
15. Yi Tu-ch'an
16. Kang Sŏng-san
17. O Hyŏn-ju
18. Ch'ŏn Se-bong
19. Yi Myŏng-sang

Other Committees

Bills Committee

1. O T'ae-bong, chairman
2. Yi Kil-song
3. Yi Pong-wŏn
4. Sŏ Kwan-hŭi
5. Sin Su-gŭn
6. Yi Pang-gŭn
7. Pan Il-byŏng

Budget Committee

1. Yun Ki-bok, chairman
2. Chŏng Tong-ch'ŏl
3. Pang Hak-se
4. Han Sŏk-chin
5. Kim Pyŏng-yul
6. Yi Pong-gil
7. Pak Ch'un-sik

Credentials Committee

1. Kim Tong-gyu, chairman

National Defense Commission

1. Kim Il Sung, chairman
2. Ch'oe Hyŏn, vice-chairman
3. O Chin-u, vice-chairman
4. O Paek-yong, vice-chairman

Members of the Fifth Assembly[20]

1. Yi Myŏng-je
2. Ko Yun-suk
3. Yi Yong-mu
4. Kim Ch'ŏl-man
5. Kim Chang-ch'ŏl
6. Kim Pyŏng-ha
7. Kim Sang-jin
8. Kim Ki-ha
9. Na Chŏng-hŭi
10. Cho Sŏk-ku
11. Kang Sŏng-san
12. Kang Ch'ŏ-han
13. Yi Myŏng-wŏn
14. T'ae Pyŏng-yŏl
15. Kim Yŏng-gŏl
16. Yi Chun-sil
17. Yi Cha-sŏn
18. Yang Sun-do
19. Chang Kil-yong
20. Yi Ŭng-wŏn
21. Pang T'ae-ho
22. Yang Yong-gŏn
23. Yi Chin-su
24. Kim Hŭi-in
25. Yim Nok-chae
26. Hwang Chi-ryŏp
27. Yun Pyŏng-gwŏn
28. Yi Kŭm-ok
29. Yi Tu-ch'an
30. Kim T'ae-ho
31. Pak Nam-sun
32. Pak Pok-sun
33. Kang Hŭi-wŏn
34. Kim Myŏng-sik
35. Paek Hak-nim
36. Yi Ch'un-hŭi
37. Kim Chŏng-sun
38. Yŏm Chŏng-ja
39. Kim Pyŏng-sik
40. Sŏ Kwan-hŭi
41. Hong Hak-kŭn
42. Yim Ch'ŏl

43. Sin Yong-sik
44. Hwang Myŏng-gyu
45. Kim Chŏng-hwan
46. Hŏ Pok-tŏk
47. Kwŏn T'ae-hŭp
48. Yu Suk-kŭn
49. Yun Ch'un-dŏk
50. Ch'oe Ik-kyu
51. Han An-su
52. Kim Sŏng-yun
53. Yi Se-sik
54. Chŏng Hwa-sŏp
55. Hong Sŏng-mu
56. Ch'oe Su-san
57. Pak Se-bong
58. Yi Hwa-sŏn
59. Chŏn Mun-sŏp
60. Yi Sin-ja
61. Kim Sun-yŏng
62. Ŏm Kil-yŏng
63. Kim Kyŏng-suk
64. Hŏ Ryŏn-suk
65. Yang In-gil
66. Yi Sang-hyŏn
67. Kim Sŏng-yul
68. Kim Sŏng-ok
69. Sin Su-gŭn
70. Han Se-gyŏng
71. Cho Ch'un-sam
72. Kim Ki-sŏn
73. Hŏ Tam
74. Hwang Chae-sŏn
75. Sŏ Ch'ŏl
76. Yi Chu-sŏk
77. Kye Hyŏng-sun
78. Kye Ch'un-yŏng
79. Na Chŏng-sil
80. Cho Se-ung
81. O Rye-sŏn
82. Pyŏn Ch'ang-bok
83. Pak In-su
84. Kim Kŭm-san

85. O Chae-wŏn
86. Yu Rak-chong
87. Yim Yun-sik
88. Kye Ŭng-t'ae
89. Kim Hak-sun
90. Kim Sŏk-hyŏng
91. Kim Nak-hŭi
92. Yi Kye-baek
93. No Chŏng-hŭi
94. Kim Ch'i-ryong
95. Yi Kwan-son
96. Yŏm T'ae-jun
97. Ŏm Hak-ch'ŏl
98. An Ch'ang-se
99. Chang Yun-p'il
100. Ch'oe Hyŏn-suk
101. Ch'oe Ch'ang-do
102. Kim Chin-ho
103. Ch'oe Sŭng-guk
104. Kim Wŏn-ok
105. Ch'oe Yŏng-suk
106. Pang Ch'ang-se
107. Kim Tŭk-nan
108. Kim Ch'ang-jun
109. Chŏng Tong-ch'ŏl
110. Yi Kyŏng-suk
111. Hong Nae-gŭn
112. Yi Yŏng-suk
113. Yun Ki-bok
114. Kim Ŭng-sam
115. Yi Yŏng-bu
116. Cho Mi-ri
117. Kim Po-bi
118. Chu Kil-sun
119. Han Pong-nyŏ
120. Chin Pyŏng-mu
121. Yi Yŏng-gu
122. Kim Pong-sun
123. Ch'oe Yong-gŭn
124. Kim Ch'ang-ju
125. Kim Wŏn-gŏn
126. Yang In-ho

127. Chi Kyŏng-su
128. Han Yun-ch'ang
129. No Myŏng-gŭn
130. Ch'oe Yŏng-jŏn
131. Yang Pok-wŏn
132. Kim Pyŏng-bin
133. Yang Hyŏng-sŏp
134. Yun T'ae-in
135. Ch'oe Hyŏn
136. Kim Sŭng-jo
137. Kim Ok-nyŏ
138. Kim Hak-san
139. Pak Tong-sŏn
140. Hwang Chang-yŏp
141. Kim Chun-do
142. Yi Ki-yŏng
143. Son Kyŏng-hwa
144. Kim Kuk-hun
145. Kim Chong-sŏng
146. Yi Kŭn-mo
147. Kim Se-yun
148. Ch'oe Ch'un-gil
149. Kim Yŏng-ch'ae
150. Kim Yŏng-jŏn
151. Pak Chong-i
152. Chŏn Ch'ang-ch'ŏl
153. Yi Kuk-kwŏn
154. Kim P'il-chu
155. Pak Kwan-o
156. Pak Chŏng-hyŏn
157. Pak Im-t'ae
158. Yi Sŏk-ch'un
159. No T'ae-sŏk
160. Han Chŏng-gi
161. Kim Yŏng-wŏl
162. Hong Ki-mun
163. O Hyŏn-ju
164. Hwang Sun-sin
165. Kim Tŏk-wŏn
166. Yi O-song
167. Ch'ŏn Se-bong
168. Kwŏn Yŏng-u
169. Kim Sŏng-gŏl
170. Yi Sil-ok
171. Han Ch'an-ok
172. Pak Wŏn-ha
173. Chŏng Yun-gil
174. Ch'oe Chin-sŏng
175. Kang Pong-gŭn
176. Chang Il-gyŏng
177. Kim Sŏk-ha
178. Yi Rak-bin
179. Hŏ Tong-su
180. Kim Tŏk-yong
181. Chang Ch'i-suk
182. Ch'oe Sil-tan
183. Hyŏn Chun-gŭk
184. Kong Chin-t'ae
185. Pak Yŏng-nyŏ
186. Kim Sŭng-wŏn
187. Yi Yŏng-bok
188. Kim Chŏng-hŭi
189. Chŏng Kwang-yŏn
190. Kang Yŏng-suk
191. Ch'oe Nam-hyang
192. O T'ae-bong
193. Chang Sŏn-sik
194. Kim Kyŏng-myŏng
195. Kim Kwan-sŏp
196. Kim Pong-sŏn
197. Son Sŏng-p'il
198. Yi Wŏn-sŏp
199. Na Yong-su
200. Hong Wŏn-gil
201. Cho Yŏng-suk
202. Yi Kŭm-nyŏ
203. Paek Wŏl-sŏn
204. Kim Pyŏng-yul
205. Kim Hi-jun
206. Yang Nak-kyŏng
207. Pak Sŏng-ch'ŏl
208. Ko Kŭm-sun
209. Sŏnu Pyŏng-gu
210. Chŏng Kwan-ch'ŏl

211. Paek Ŭi-myŏng
212. O Kŭk-yŏl
213. Kim In-sŏng
214. Chang Chong-yŏp
215. Kim Si-hak
216. Kim Il Sung
217. An Yŏng-bok
218. Song Ch'un-ok
219. Yun Ho-sŏk
220. Yi Pong-gil
221. Kim Ch'i-ung
222. Han Yŏng-bo
223. Han Sŏng-yong
224. Ch'oe Chong-yŏng
225. Kil Chŭng-sŭng
226. Kim Sŏk-cho
227. Chŏn Pyŏng-ch'ae
228. Yu Pyŏng-no
229. Kim Wŏn-ch'ŏng
230. Chŏn Hi-yong
231. Yang Ok-nyŏ
232. Kim Ŭn-ha
233. Yim Pong-ch'un
234. Kim Kwang-bong
235. Yi Yong-sŏn
236. Chŏng Kŭm-sŏk
237. Ch'oe Pyŏng-ho
238. Pak Hun-wŏn
239. Chang Ho-sam
240. Pang Hwan-sŏn
241. Kim Yŏng-nam
242. Ch'oe Sang-yŏl
243. Kim Ni-jun
244. Nam Ok-nyŏ
245. Pak Yŏng-sŏp
246. Paek Sang-su
247. Pang Hyo-ŭl
248. Kim Song-jŏl
249. Kim Wal-su
250. Kang Yang-uk
251. Yi Kil-song
252. Kim Wŏn-sam
253. Kim Ch'i-se
254. Yi Chong-ok
255. Yang Chong-go
256. Kim Sŏn-jun
257. Kim Hak-bŏm
258. Kim Mun-hyŏn
259. Yim Ch'un-ch'u
260. Ch'oe Rye-hwan
261. Wi Kwi-hwan
262. Han T'ae-sŏn
263. Pak Hak-sŏp
264. Chŏng Chun-t'aek
265. Yi Kye-hwan
266. Pak Ch'o-ryŏn
267. Yun Chin-sang
268. Nam Kŭm-bong
269. Pang T'ae-uk
270. Kim Chŏng-hoe
271. Yi Yŏn-suk
272. Hyŏn Ch'ŏl-gyu
273. Kim Kil-hyŏn
274. Kim P'ung-jin
275. Kim Nak-sŏp
276. Cho Chin-suk
277. Kim Chae-ryu
278. Han Hae-dong
279. Yi Tong-jun
280. An Yong-u
281. Kang Tae-sŏp
282. Ch'oe Ch'un-yong
283. Han Ik-su
284. Kim Hyŏng-su
285. Kang Sŏk-sung
286. Ch'oe Chae-hyŏp
287. Chŏng Ch'i-ryong
288. Hŏ Paek-san
289. Kim Hak-su
290. Ch'oe Hyŏn-gi
291. Cho Ch'ang-suk
292. Chŏn Yŏng-ch'un
293. Kim Hak-ch'ŏl
294. Kim Yŏng-ju
295. To Sun-mo
296. Pak Si-hyŏng

297. Yi Sun-yŏl
298. Chu To-il
299. Ch'oe Kŭm-san
300. Chin Mun-dŏk
301. Kim Yun-sŏn
302. Kim Pun-ok
303. Chŏng Kyŏng-sik
304. Yi Tong-ch'un
305. Hŏ Chŭng-ok
306. Kim Tae-ryong
307. Hwang Sun-hŭi
308. Kwŏn Hŭi-gyŏng
309. Kim Chae-ha
310. Kim Tŭk-su
311. Kim Hyŏng-sam
312. Kim Yong-ho
313. Ch'oe Chung-san
314. Ko Hak-ch'ŏn
315. Kim Il
316. Paek Wŏn-bŏm
317. Yi Hŭi-gŏl
318. Han Tŏk-su
319. Yu Hyŏng-nŭm
320. Chŏn Han-gyo
321. Pak Ch'un-myŏng
322. Ch'oe Ch'il-gap
323. Ko Min-sun
324. Hŏ Se-uk
325. Hyŏn Mu-gwang
326. Hŏ Yong-ik
327. Chin Sang-gi
328. Kim Tong-sŏn
329. Yu Su-hong
330. Song Kwan-jo
331. Yi Sŭng-gi
332. Kwŏn Yun-il
333. Ch'oe Yong-jin
334. Hŏ Chŏng-suk
335. Yi Yŏn
336. Han Sŏk-chin
337. Yi Ch'ang-do
338. Pak Yŏng-sun
339. Pak Yŏng-sŏn

340. Kim Sŏk-yong
341. Kim Chŏng-p'il
342. Kang Maeng-gu
343. Yi Wŏn-gwan
344. Yi Yong-sun
345. Kim Se-bong
346. Chŏng Song-nam
347. Kim Sin-sik
348. Pak Yong-sik
349. Yi Yang-hun
350. Yi Sun-ho
351. Mun Suk-cha
352. Kim Yun-sang
353. Ko Chun-myŏng
354. Chu Sŏng-il
355. Kim Yi-sŏk
356. Song Pok-ki
357. O Chin-u
358. Han Hyŏng-hwan
359. Han Ki-il
360. Sŏk Sun-hŭi
361. Chŏn Cha-ryŏn
362. Pak Nak-ho
363. Pan Il-byŏng
364. Yu Kwi-jin
365. Yu Kŭm-sŏn
366. Chŏng Hŭi-ch'ŏl
367. Sin Sŏng-u
368. Kim Pok-sin
369. Sin P'o-gyun
370. Cho Myŏng-sŏn
371. Kim Ŭng-sang
372. Kang Myŏn-su
373. Han Hubang-nyŏ
374. Kim Ŏin-nam
375. Kim Ki-bong
376. Han Hŭi-ho
377. Yi Chong-u
378. Yi Chun-ho
379. Yi Chae-yun
380. An Suk-yong
381. Yi Myŏn-sang
382. Kang Hak-su

383. Yi Kŭm-sŏn
384. Ch'oe Chung-gŭk
385. Chŏn Kŭm-sŏn
386. Yi Pong-gyu
387. Kim Wŏn-ch'an
388. Min Kwan-bŏm
389. Kim Kyŏng-ch'an
390. Kim Kyu-sun
391. No Se-bŏm
392. Yu Chang-sik
393. Ch'oe Yŏng-gu
394. Yi Ch'ang-sŏn
395. An T'al-sil
396. Kim Tong-gyu
397. Wŏn Hong-ch'ŏl
398. Kim Kwang-ju
399. Kim Pyŏng-ch'ŏn
400. Paek Il-bu
401. Paek Sun-ok
402. Yi Yong-gyu
403. Yu Ch'un-ok
404. O Paek-yong
405. Chang Chŏng-hwan
406. Yi Ŭn-sun
407. Song Ki-hwan
408. Nam Il
409. Hwang Yong-do
410. Yi Chin-gyu
411. Yi Hwa-yŏng
412. Chi Kŭn-su
413. Ch'oe Chung-son
414. Sin Ch'un-sŏn
415. Pak Chung-guk
416. Kim Su-dŭk
417. Chang Chae-gak
418. Ch'a Kye-ryong
419. Ch'oe In-dŏk
420. Hong Pong-su
421. Han Pong-sŏl
422. Pak Tong-gwan
423. Pyŏn Sŭng-u
424. Yi Ŭl-sŏl
425. Yi Kye-san

426. Chi Pyŏng-hak
427. Kwŏn Chŏm-du
428. Hong Si-hak
429. Cho Sun-baek
430. Pang Hak-se
431. Yun Ch'i-ho
432. Kim Chae-bong
433. Yi Wan-gi
434. Ch'oe Man-guk
435. Yi Ch'un-sŏng
436. Kang Myŏng-ok
437. Yi Chang-ch'un
438. Yun Ch'il-hwan
439. Yi Yong-ik
440. Sin Chŏng-suk
441. Cho Tong-su
442. Kim Ch'ae-yŏn
443. Pak Wal-sŏng
444. Wi Hak-sil
445. Han Chi-sŏp
446. Kim Kyŏng-yŏn
447. Yi Tu-ik
448. Kim Kwang-jin
449. Yi Pang-gŭn
450. O Sun-nyŏ
451. Kim Ch'un-gil
452. Pak Yŏng-su
453. Yi Man-gŏl
454. Kim Tong-hwan
455. Wŏn Ha-ok
456. Ch'oe Sun-nam
457. Yu Chong-yŏl
458. Yŏn Hyŏng-muk
459. Chin Ch'ang-hu
460. No U-ryong
461. Yi Ch'an-hwa
462. Ch'oe Chae-u
463. Yŏn Sŏng-yŏl
464. Yi Ch'an-dŭk
465. Sŏ Kyŏng-sil
466. Kim Kwang-jin
467. Kim Sŏng-ae
468. Yi Ch'ŏng-il

469. Yi Tal-yong
470. Ch'u Sang-su
471. Kim Chung-nyŏ
472. Ko Ch'ang-nam
473. Yi Ye-dong
474. Kang Uk-kŭk
475. Chŏng Chun-gi
476. Yim Sun-nyŏ
477. Pak Ch'un-sik
478. Kim I-hun
479. Yi In-bok
480. Yi Pong-se
481. Sŏ Yun-sŏk
482. Han Kyŏng-suk
483. Ch'oe Yong-gŏn
484. Pae Ch'ang-ho
485. O T'aek-hwan
486. Pak Sin-dŏk
487. Pang T'ae-yul
488. Yi Ŭm-jŏn
489. Kim T'aek-yong
490. Chŏng Ki-ryong
491. Kim Chung-nin
492. Han Yŏng-ok
493. Yi Chae-gon
494. Pak Sŏng-sam
495. O Sŏng-guk
496. Kim Kyŏng-in
497. Yi Kŭn-song
498. O Pyŏng-dŏk
499. Kim T'ae-hŭi
500. Chŏng Chae-p'il
501. Chu Sŭng-nam
502. Yi Hong-un
503. Chŏng Yong-t'aek
504. Kim Ok-sun
505. Pak Su-dong

506. Ch'oe Yŏl-hŭi
507. An Tal-su
508. Kim Sŏn-uk
509. Sin Kyŏng-sik
510. No Ki-sŏn
511. Kim Ik-hyŏn
512. Yi Sun-bong
513. Ku Cha-hun
514. Chang Tong-sun
515. Chi Kŭm-ju
516. Kim Hu-bun
517. Yim Nam-jae
518. Ch'oe Ch'i-sŏn
519. Hwang Wŏn-nam
520. Chŏng T'ae-hwang
521. Kim Man-gŭm
522. Yi Sun-ae
523. Yun Sŭng-gwan
524. Yi Sang-ik
525. Sin Sang-gyun
526. Yi Sŏk-chin
527. Kim Sang-ho
528. Chŏn P'il-yŏ
529. Chŏng Tu-hwan
530. Yi Pong-wŏn
531. Yi Yŏng-sun
532. Kim Yŏng-jun
533. Chŏn No-hyŏng
534. Ch'oe Yŏng-nim
535. Paek Nam-un
536. Chang In-sŏk
537. Kim Pong-yul
538. Ch'oe Wŏn-ik
539. Han Ch'ang-man
540. Kim Yong-t'aek
541. Yi Ch'ang-sun

SIXTH SUPREME PEOPLE'S ASSEMBLY, DECEMBER 15–17, 1977

Officers of the Sixth Assembly[21]

President of the Republic
   Kim Il Sung

Vice-Presidents of the Republic
1. Kim Il
2. Kang Yang-uk
3. Pak Sŏng-ch'ŏl

Secretary-General
Yim Ch'un-ch'u

Central People's Committee
1. Kim Il Sung
2. Kim Il
3. Kang Yang-uk
4. Ch'oe Hyŏn
5. Pak Sŏng-ch'ŏl
6. O Chin-u
7. Sŏ Ch'ŏl
8. Yi Chong-ok
9. Yim Ch'un-ch'u
10. O Paek-yong
11. Kye Ŭng-t'ae
12. Kim Hwan
13. Hong Si-hak
14. Kim Man-gŭm
15. No T'ae-sŏk

Standing Committee
1. Hwang Chang-yŏp, chairman
2. Hŏ Chŏng-suk, vice-chairman
3. Hong Ki-mun, vice-chairman
4. Chŏn Ch'ang-ch'ŏl, secretary-general
5. Kim Yŏng-nam
6. Chŏng Tong-ch'ŏl
7. Yun Ki-bok
8. Kim Kwan-sŏp
9. Kim Ki-nam
10. Kim Pong-ju
11. Chi Chae-ryong
12. Chang Yun-p'il
13. Kim Sŏng-ae
14. Son Sŏng-p'il
15. Ch'ŏn Se-bong

Other Committees

Bills Committee
1. Yun Ki-bok, chairman
2. Chŏng Tong-ch'ŏl
3. Yi Chin-su
4. Pang Hak-se
5. Kim Yun-hyŏk
6. Yim Sŏk-ki
7. Pyŏn Ch'ang-bok

Budget Committee
1. Hong Si-hak, chairman
2. Sŏ Kwan-hŭi
3. Kang Hyŏn-su
4. Kye Hyŏng-sun
5. Hŏ Sun
6. Kang Chung-han
7. Kim Hyŏng-sam

Credentials Committee
1. Yim Ch'un-ch'u, chairman

National Defense Commission

1. Kim Il Sung, chairman
2. Ch'oe Hyŏn, vice-chairman
3. O Chin-u, vice-chairman
4. O Paek-yong, vice-chairman

TABLES

3.1 Increase in Electoral Districts from the Second Assembly, 1957, to the Sixth Assembly, 1977
3.2 Patterns of Reelection from the First Assembly to the Sixth Assembly
3.3 Four- and Five-term Members of the Supreme People's Assembly
3.4 Chairmen and Vice-chairmen of the Assembly and Members of the Standing Committee of the Assembly
3.5 Persons with Multiple Terms as Chairman and Vice-chairman of the Assembly and as Members of the Standing Committee of the Assembly
3.6 Reelection in the Central People's Committee
3.7 Reelection in the Bills Committee
3.8 Reelection in the Budget Committee
3.9 Reelection in the Foreign Affairs Committee
3.10 Reelection in the Credentials Committee
3.11 Characteristics of Members of the Supreme People's Assembly

TABLE 3.1

Increase in Electoral Districts
from the Second Assembly, 1957, to the Sixth Assembly, 1977

	2SPA 1957	Percent	6SPA 1977	Percent	Rise in number	Percent increase
Pyongyang City	14	7	73	13	59	+6
P'yŏngan Namdo	36	17	95	16	59	-1
P'yŏngan Pukto	30	14	71	12	41	-2
Chagangdo	13	6	32	6	19	0
Hwanghae Namdo	24	11	58	10	34	-1
Hwanghae Pukto	18	8	43	7	25	-1
Kangwŏndo	17	8	43	7	26	-1
Hamgyŏng Namdo	30	14	76	14	46	0
Hamgyŏng Pukto	23	11	59	10	36	-1
Yanggando	7	3	18	3	11	0
Kaesŏng City	3	1	11	2	8	+1
Total	215	100	579	100	364	0

Electoral districts were published only for the second and sixth Assembly elections. In both cases, the districts were grouped under nine provinces and two cities. For the names of the 215 electoral districts of the Second Assembly, see *Nodong sinmun*, August 30, 1957; for the names of the 579 electoral districts of the Sixth Assembly, see *Nodong sinmun*, September 29, 1977.

TABLE 3.2

Patterns of Reelection from the First Assembly to the Sixth Assembly

1SPA	2SPA	3SPA	4SPA	5SPA	6SPA
572 ⟶	75	23	20	9*	3**
(360 south)	(13%)				
(212 north)	(35%)				
	215 ⟶	71 (33%)	49	25	
		383 ⟶	225 (59%)	101	
			457 ⟶	178 (39%)	
				541 ⟶	
					579

*They are: Ch'oe Yong-gŏn, Chŏng Chun-t'aek, Kang Yang-uk, Kim Il, Kim Il Sung, Kim Tŭk-nan, Nam Il, Paek Nam-un, and Yi Ki-yŏng.

**They are: Kang Yang-uk, Kim Il, and Kim Il Sung.

TABLE 3.3
Four- and Five-term Members of the Supreme People's Assembly

	1SPA	2SPA	3SPA	4SPA	5SPA	6SPA
Elected to five Assemblies (nine)						
Ch'oe Yong-gŏn	30	76	2	2	483	
Chŏng Chun-t'aek	29	44	17	19	264	
Kang Yang-uk	11	15	29	102	250	
Kim Il	47	119	3	3	315	
Kim Il Sung	1	21	1	1	216	120
Kim Tŭk-nan	533	55	120	183	107	
Nam Il	75	192	10	6	408	
Paek Nam-un	37	108	344	289	535	
Yi Ki-yŏng	20	26	294	316	142	
Elected to four Assemblies (thirty-two)						
An Tal-su		111	359	430	507	
Chang Yun-p'il		40	356	448	99	
Ch'oe Hyŏn		152	67	10	135	
Ch'oe Kwang	389	93	46	23		
Ch'oe Wŏn-t'aek	90	116	365	143		
Ch'oe Yong-jin		177	242	20	333	
Chŏng Il-yong	66	92	9	237		
Chŏng Tu-hwan		43	104	330	529	
Ch'u Sang-su		131	337	388	470	
Han Hubang-nyŏ		179	265	318	373	
Hong Myŏng-hŭi	9	181	4	5		
Kim Man-gŭm		20	87	457	521	
Kim Pong-sŏn	358		146	171	196	
Kim Sŏk-yong		56	117	116	340	
Kim Sŏng-yul	557		55	72	67	
Kim Yong-ho	481		133	128	312	
Ko Chun-t'aek	254	53	78	284		
Kwŏn Yŏng-u		184	374	329	168	
Pak Chŏng-ae	23	107	12	8		
Pak Mun-gyu	33	106	310	169		
Pang Hak-se	53	145		265	430	
Wŏn Hong-gu	182	71	156	85		
Yi Ch'an-hwa		125	319	378	461	
Yi Ch'ang-do		126	34	160	337	
Yi Chong-ok		142	11	7	254	
Yi Chu-yŏn	115	103	13	9		

TABLE 3.3—*Continued*

	1SPA	2SPA	3SPA	4SPA	5SPA	6SPA
Yi Kŭk-no	44	194	350	264		
Yi Kye-san		141	302	363	425	
Yi Man-gyu	56	27	77	150		
Yi Myŏn-sang		64	290	145	381	
Yi Sŭng-gi		65	250	290	331	
Yi Yong-sŏn	424		168	205	235	

Ninety-one persons were elected to three Assemblies. Those who were elected twice are marked with an asterisk in the list of Assembly members. Kang Yang-uk, Kim Il, and Kim Il Sung were elected as officers of the Sixth Assembly. The numbers in this table correspond to the numbers in the personnel registers. They represent electoral district numbers in the case of the Second, Fourth, and Fifth Assemblies and rank order in the case of the First and Third Assemblies.

TABLE 3.4

*Chairmen and Vice-chairmen of the Assembly and
Members of the Standing Committee of the Assembly*

	1SPA		2SPA		3SPA	4SPA	5SPA	6SPA
	1st sess	6th sess	1st sess	6th sess				
Chang Hae-u			18	17				
Chang Kwŏn	12	11						
Chang Sun-myŏng	11	10						
Chang Yun-p'il								12
Chi Chae-ryong								11
Cho Un	21							
Ch'oe Hyŏn					12	7		
Ch'oe Kwang						11		
Ch'oe Kyŏng-dŏk	16							
Ch'oe Wŏn-t'aek		16	C	C	C			
Ch'oe Yong-gŏn			1	1	1	1		
Ch'ŏn Se-bong							18	15
Chŏn Ch'ang-ch'ŏl							6	4
Chŏn Yun-do		19						
Chŏng Chun-gi							9	
Chŏng No-sik			15	14				
Chŏng Tong-ch'ŏl								6
Ha Ang-ch'ŏn			17	16	9			
Han Ik-su							5	
Han Sang-du			13	12				
Han Sŏl-ya			22	3				
Hŏ Chŏng-suk							3	2
Hŏ Hŏn	C							
Hŏ Pong-hak						8		
Hong Ki-hwang		VC						
Hong Ki-ju	3							
Hong Ki-mun							2	3
Hong Myŏng-hŭi					3	2		
Hong Nam-p'yo	2							
Hwang Chang-yŏp							1	1
Hyŏn Ch'il-chong			3					
Hyŏn Mu-gwang					10			
Kang Chin-gŏn	5	5	7	7				
Kang Sŏng-san							16	
Kang Sun	20							

TABLE 3.4—*Continued*

	1SPA		2SPA		3SPA	4SPA	5SPA	6SPA
	1st sess	6th sess	1st sess	6th sess				
Kang Ŭng-jin		18						
Kang Yang-uk	4	4	5	4	4	4		
Kim Ch'ang-dŏk			14	13	17			
Kim Ch'ang-jun	10	9	VC					
Kim Ch'ŏn-hae			16	15				
Kim I-hun							12	
Kim Ki-nam								9
Kim Kwan-sŏp								8
Kim Kyŏng-sŏk				21				
Kim Ok-sun					15			
Kim Pong-ju								10
Kim Pyŏng-je	18	14	9	8				
Kim Sŏng-ae							11	13
Kim Tal-hyŏn	VC							
Kim Tong-gyu						13		
Kim Tu-bong	1	1						
Kim Tŭk-nan				VC	VC	VC		
Kim Ŭng-gi		2						
Kim Wal-yong					14			
Kim Wŏn-bong				4				
Kim Yŏ-jung						15		
Kim Yŏng-ju						9		
Kim Yŏng-nam							8	5
Ko Chun-t'aek			23					
Ku Chae-su	7							
Kye Ŭng-sang			19	18	21			
Mun Tu-jae		21						
Na Sŭng-gyu	15	13						
No Ik-myŏng					16			
O Chin-u						12		
O Hyŏn-ju							17	
Paek Nam-un				22	5	C		
Pak Chŏng-ae	9	8	6	6	2	3		
Pak Kŭm-ch'ŏl					6			
Pak Mun-gyu				5	24	6		
Pak Sin-dŏk				23	11	14	7	
Pak Yun-gil	14							

TABLE 3.4—*Continued*

	1SPA		2SPA		3SPA	4SPA	5SPA	6SPA
	1st sess	6th sess	1st sess	6th sess				
Sŏ Ch'ŏl							4	
Son Sŏng-p'il								14
Sŏng Chu-sik	6	6	8					
Song Yŏng			21	20	18			
To Yu-ho					23			
Wŏn Hong-gu		17	10	9				
Yi Chae-bok					22			
Yi Hyo-sun					8			
Yi Ki-yŏng	19	15	VC	VC	VC	VC		
Yi Ku-hun	8	7						
Yi Kuk-chin						10		
Yi Kŭk-no		3	2	2				
Yi Man-gyu		22	11	10	19			
Yi Myŏn-sang			20	19	20		19	
Yi Nŭng-jong	17							
Yi Song-un			12	11				
Yi Tu-ch'an							15	
Yi Yŏng	VC	C						
Yi Yŏng-bok							13	
Yi Yŏng-ho					13	5		
Yi Yu-min		VC						
Yim Ch'un-ch'u					7			
Yŏm T'ae-jun							10	
Yu Hae-bung		20						
Yu Yŏng-jun	13	12						
Yun Ki-bok							14	7

Numbers indicate rank order in the Standing Committee.

TABLE 3.5

Persons with Multiple Terms as Chairman and Vice-chairman of the Assembly and as Members of the Standing Committee of the Assembly

	1SPA	2SPA	3SPA	4SPA	5SPA	6SPA
Elected four times (three)						
Kang Yang-uk	4	4	4	4		
Pak Sin-dŏk		23	11	14	7	
Yi Ki-yŏng	19	VC	VC	VC		
Elected three times (seven)						
Ch'oe Wŏn-t'aek	16	C	C			
Ch'oe Yong-gŏn		1	1	1		
Kim Tŭk-nan		VC	VC	VC		
Paek Nam-un		22	5	C		
Pak Mun-gyu		5	24	6		
Yi Man-gyu	22	11	19			
Yi Myŏn-sang		20	20	19		
Elected twice (twenty-one)						
Ch'oe Hyŏn			12	7		
Ch'ŏn Se-bong					18	15
Chŏn Ch'ang-ch'ŏl					6	4
Ha Ang-ch'ŏn			17	9		
Hŏ Chŏng-suk					3	2
Hong Ki-mun					2	3
Hong Myŏng-hŭi			3	2		
Hwang Chang-yŏp					1	1
Kang Chin-gŏn	5	7				
Kim Ch'ang-dŏk		14	17			
Kim Ch'ang-jun	10	VC				
Kim Pyŏng-je	18	9				
Kim Sŏng-ae					11	13
Kim Yŏng-nam					8	5
Kye Ŭng-sang		19	21			
Sŏng Chu-sik	6	8				
Song Yŏng		21	18			
Wŏn Hong-gu	17	10				
Yi Kŭk-no	3	2				
Yi Yŏng-go			13	5		
Yun Ki-bok					14	7

The remaining sixty-seven members served once

Numbers indicate rank order in the Standing Committee.

TABLE 3.6
Reelection in the Central People's Committee

	Fifth Assembly	Sixth Assembly
Ch'oe Chae-u	16	
*Ch'oe Hyŏn	6	4
Ch'oe Yong-gŏn	2	
Chŏng Chun-t'aek	13	
Hŏ Tam	24	
Hong Si-hak		13
Hong Wŏn-gil	22	
Hyŏn Mu-gwang	11	
*Kang Yang-uk	3	3
Kim Chung-nin	10	
Kim Hwan		12
*Kim Il	4	2
*Kim Il Sung	1	1
*Kim Man-gŭm	14	14
Kim Pyŏng-ha	25	
Kim Tong-gyu	8	
Kim Yŏng-ju	9	
Kye Ŭng-t'ae		11
Nam Il	21	
No T'ae-sŏk		15
*O Chin-u	7	6
O Paek-yong		10
O T'ae-bong	20	
*Pak Sŏng-ch'ŏl	5	5
Sŏ Ch'ŏl		7
Yang Hyŏng-sŏp	12	
*Yi Chong-ok	17	8
Yi Kŭn-mo	15	
*Yim Ch'un-ch'u	18	9
Yŏn Hyŏng-muk	19	
Yu Chang-sik	23	

*Asterisk indicates reelection.

TABLE 3.7
Reelection in the Bills Committee

	2SPA	3SPA	4SPA	5SPA	6SPA
Cho Yŏng	4				
Ch'oe Chong-hak	6				
Ch'oe Ki-ch'ŏl		4			
Chŏng Tong-ch'ŏl					2
Han In-sŏk	9				
Hŏ Hak-song	8				
Hŏ Pong-hak		2			
Kim Ch'ang-bok			7		
Kim Chwa-hyŏk			3		
Kim Hŭi-jun		6			
*Kim Ik-sŏn	1	1			
*Kim Kuk-hun		8	9		
Kim Si-jung		9			
Kim Sŏk-ki					6
Kim Tong-gyu		3			
Kim Yŏ-jung			1		
Kim Yong-jin	2				
Kim Yun-hyŏk					5
No Ik-myŏng		7			
O T'ae-bong				1	
Paek Hak-nim			4		
Pan Il-byŏng				7	
Pang Hak-se					4
Pyŏn Ch'ang-bok					7
Sin Nam-ch'ol	3				
Sin Su-gŭn				5	
Sŏ Kwan-hŭi				4	
Yi Chae-yŏng		5			
Yi Chin-su					3
Yi Kil-song			2		
Yi Pang-gŭn			6		
Yi Pong-wŏn			3		
Yi Rim-su			5		
Yi Sŭng-gi			8		
Yi Yong-gu			2		
Yi Yu-min	7				
Yŏm T'ae-jun			6		
Yu Ch'ŏl-mok	5				
Yun Ki-bok					1

*Only two of the thirty-nine who served in the Bills Committee from the Second to the Sixth Assembly were reelected. None was reelected more than once.

TABLE 3.8
Reelection in the Budget Committee

	2SPA	3SPA	4SPA	5SPA	6SPA
*Chang Yun-p'il	12	7	5		
Chi Chang-gŏn		12			
Ch'oe Ch'ŏl-hwan	11				
Ch'oe Ch'un-sŏp			9		
Chŏn Kyŏng-hwa		14			
Chŏn T'ae-hwan	3				
Chŏng Chong-gi		6			
Chŏng Sŏng-ŏn		3			
Chŏng Tong-ch'ŏl				2	
Chŏng Tu-hwan	5				
Chŏng Yŏn-p'yo	13				
Chu Wŏn-saeng		11			
Han Chŏng-gi			10		
Han Sŏk-chin				4	
Hŏ Sun					5
Hong Si-hak					1
Hwang Sun-ch'ŏn	10				
Hyŏn Hun	7				
Kang Chung-han					6
*Kang Hŭi-wŏn		2	2		
Kang Hyŏn-su					3
Kim Hyŏng-sam					7
Kim Mu-hoe		9			
Kim Mun-gŭn	16				
Kim Nak-hŭi			11		
Kim Pyŏng-yul				5	
Kim Sang-ch'ŏl	4				
Kim Sŏk-hyŏng			6		
Kim Tŭk-nan	6				
Kye Hyŏng-sun					4
Mun T'ae-hwa	14				
*O Che-ryong		4	3		
Paek Nam-un	2				
Pak Ch'un-sik				7	
Pak Sŭng-hŭp		10			
Pang Hak-se				3	
Sŏ Ch'un-sik	15				

TABLE 3.8—*Continued*

	2SPA	3SPA	4SPA	5SPA	6SPA
Sŏ Kwan-hŭi					2
Song Ch'ang-nyŏm	8				
Song Pong-uk	1				
Yi Chae-ch'ŏn	9				
Yi Ch'an-sŏn		5			
Yi Ch'ang-bok		8			
Yi Chong-guk			7		
Yi Pong-gil				6	
Yi Sŏk-sim		15			
Yi Wŏn-bŏm			4		
Yim Kŭn-sang	17				
*Yim Kye-ch'ŏl		1	1		
Yun Ki-bok				1	
*Yun Yŏn-hwan		13	8		

Numbers indicate rank order in the committee.

*Of fifty-one persons who served in the Budget Committee from the Second to the Sixth Assembly, only one, Chang Yun-p'il, was reelected twice, and four were reelected once, Kang Hŭi-wŏn, O Che-ryong, Yim Kye-ch'ŏl, and Yun Yŏn-hwan. These reelections were all from the Third to the Fourth Assembly.

TABLE 3.9
Reelection in the Foreign Affairs Committee

	2d Assembly	3d Assembly	4th Assembly
Ch'oe Chung-gŭk			4
Ch'oe Hak-sŏn		7	
Chŏn Ch'ang-ch'ŏl			2
Chŏng Kwang-ok		5	
Hŏ Pin	5		
Hŏ Sŏk-sŏn		3	
Hong Chŭng-sik	4		
Kim Ch'ang-man	1		
Kim Man-gŭm	2		
*Kim Ok-sun		6	3
Kim Wal-yong		2	
Kim Yŏng-su	3		
Ko Kyŏng-in	7		
O Hyŏn-ju			6
O Ki-ch'ŏn			5
*Pak Yong-guk	6	1	
Sŏ Ch'ŏl			1
Yi Yun-do			7
Yu Kŏn-yang		4	

Numbers indicate rank order in the committee.

*The Foreign Affairs Committee was in session from the Second to the Fourth Assembly and was changed to the Foreign Policy Commission of the Central People's Assembly under the 1972 constitution. Members of the Foreign Policy Commission were not announced. Only two persons, Kim Ok-sun and Pak Yong-guk, were reelected to serve twice in the Foreign Affairs Committee.

TABLE 3.10
Reelection in the Credentials Committee

	2SPA	3SPA	4SPA	5SPA	6SPA
Ch'oe Chong-gŏn			5		
Ch'oe Yong-jin		1			
Ch'u Sang-su		6			
Han Tong-baek		3			
Kim Sŏk-yong			2		
Kim T'ae-gŭn	2				
Kim Tong-gyu				1	
Kim Wŏn-bong	3				
Kim Yong-ho			3		
No Yŏng-se		7			
Pak Ch'ang-sik	6				
Pak Un-gŏl		2			
Pak Yong-t'ae	7				
Sin Hong-ye	5				
Yi Chae-yun		4			
Yi Hong-yŏl	4				
Yi Hyo-sun	1				
Yi Kuk-chin			1		
Yi Kye-san			7		
Yi Tal-yong			6		
Yim Ch'un-ch'u					1
Yim Hyŏng-gu			4		
Yu Ki-ik		5			

No one was reelected to the Credentials Committee. After the 1972 constitution, the members of this committee were not announced. Only the chairmen were known through their reports in the first session of each Assembly meeting. Numbers indicate rank order in the committee.

TABLE 3.11
Characteristics of Members of the Supreme People's Assembly

	1SPA	2SPA	3SPA	4SPA	5SPA	6SPA
Number	572	215	383	457	541	579
Background						
worker	120	84	215	292	347	248
peasant	194	68	62	70	72	64
office worker	152	60	101	95	122	267
others	106	3	5			
Imprisonment record						
none	324	154				
less than one year	68					
2 to 5 years	114					
6 to 10 years	50					
11 to 19 years	16					
imprisoned		61				
Decoration record						
decorated		180	352	412	362	301
not decorated		35	31	45	179	278
Age						
20 to 30 years	73	5	12			
31 to 40 years	223	34	99	64	96	32
41 to 50 years	174	99	181	220	280	457
51 to 60 years	77	54	71	136	126	90
61 to 70 years	21	23	20	37	39	
more than 70 years	4					
Education						
elementary	198	95				
high school	147	43	256	200	101	176
college	227	77	127	257	323	403
graduate					117	
Sex						
male	503	188	348	384	428	459
female	69	27	35	73	113	120

NOTES

1. *Chosŏn chungang yŏn'gam*, 1950 (Pyongyang: Chosŏn Chungang T'ongsin-sa, 1950), p. 12.

2. Hŏ died during the Korean war.

3. Article 48 of the constitution provides for a chairman, two vice-chairmen, one secretary-general, and seventeen members of the Standing Committee. This article was amended in the ninth session of the First Assembly in March 1955 to give flexibility in the number of people serving on the committee.

4. Hong died shortly before the Korean war.

5. *Nodong sinmun*, December 23, 1953.

6. Kang Ŭng-jin died, and Yi Man-gyu was elected to fill his post at the eighth session of the First Supreme People's Assembly, October 28–30, 1954.

7. *Chosŏn chungang yŏn'gam*, 1950, pp. 13–15.

8. *Nodong sinmun*, September 21, 1957. Hyŏn Ch'il-chong and Kim Wŏn-bong were relieved of their posts and were replaced by Han Sŏl-ya and Ko Chun-t'aek at the fourth session of the Second Supreme People's Assembly, October 1–2, 1958. Ko served only a year and was not reelected to the post at the sixth session of the Second Assembly, October 26–28, 1959.

9. Yi Kŭk-no was replaced by Paek Nam-un at the ninth session of the Second Supreme People's Assembly, March 23–25, 1961.

10. *Nodong sinmun*, August 30, 1957.

11. *Chosŏn chungang yŏn'gam*, 1963, p. 179; *Nodong sinmun*, October 23, 1962.

12. Yi Yŏng-ho was elected vice-chairman of the Standing Committee to replace Pak Kŭm-ch'ŏl

13. Yim Ch'un-ch'u was replaced by former Secretary-General Pak Mun-gyu at the fifth session of the Third Assembly, April 27–29, 1966.

14. *Nodong sinmun*, October 11, 1962.

15. *Nodong sinmun*, December 15, 1967.

16. *Nodong sinmun*, November 27, 1967.

17. *Nodong sinmun*, December 29, 1972.

18. Three officers of the Fifth Supreme People's Assembly have died since that assembly. They are: Ch'oe Yong-gŏn, Chŏng Chun-t'aek, and Hong Wŏn-gil.

19. Kim Il was elected first vice-president of the republic, a new post, at the sixth session of the Fifth Supreme People's Assembly, April 27–29, 1976. At this time, Kim Il relinquished his position as the premier of the Administration Council, and Pak Sŏng-ch'ŏl became the premier.

20. *Nodong sinmun*, December 13, 1972.

21. *Nodong sinmun*, December 18, 1977.

4

The Administration Council
1948–1980

THE CABINET OF THE DEMOCRATIC
PEOPLE'S REPUBLIC OF KOREA

Article 58 of the first constitution (September 1948) stipulated that the cabinet should be composed of a premier, vice-premiers, the chairman of the State Planning Commission, and ministers of seventeen cabinet ministries. Each ministry was designated in the constitution, but this provision was the first to be amended. Shortly after the Korean war, on April 23, 1954, at the seventh session of the first Assembly, the designation and fixed number were abolished to accommodate enlargement of ministries and commissions. The cabinet was organized by the Supreme People's Assembly, and the premier, vice-premiers, ministers, and chairmen of commissions took the oath of office before the Assembly. All cabinet members were answerable to the Assembly.

Under the revised constitution of December 1972, the cabinet was renamed the Administration Council and was put under the guidance of the newly created Central People's Committee and the office of the president of the republic (Article 107). The premier is elected by the Assembly, but ministers are appointed by the Central People's Committee on the recommendation of the premier. The premier takes the oath of office before the president of the republic. Vice-premiers and members of the Administration Council are answerable to the Central People's Committee.

The first cabinet was organized in September 1948 and served for approximately ten years. There were many changes not only in the persons serving as ministers and chairmen of commissions but also in the ministries and commissions. The first cabinet had one premier, three vice-premiers, one commission, and seventeen ministries. This was increased to one premier, six vice-premiers, twenty-three ministries, and two commissions in the second cabinet in September 1957. It was further expanded in the third cabinet in October 1962 to one premier, one first vice-premier, seven vice-premiers, twenty-three ministries, and five commissions. The fourth cabinet of December 1967 had the largest number of cabinet posts with one premier, one first vice-premier, eight vice-premiers, thirty ministries, six commissions, and four other cabinet-level secretaries and directors. With the reorganization of the government under the new constitution in the Fifth Supreme People's Assembly in December 1972, the Administration Council (the fifth cabinet) was reduced to one premier, six vice-premiers, fifteen ministries, and seven commissions. The sixth cabinet of December 1977, or the second Administration Council, had a slight increase in numbers with one premier, six vice-premiers, one secretary, twenty-one ministries, and seven commissions.

There were rapid and numerous changes of personnel during the first four cabinets from 1948 to 1972, but this trend was retarded somewhat with the fifth. Some sort of stability and continuity can be seen from the fifth to the sixth cabinet.

Aside from the offices of the premier and the vice-premiers, only four ministries and commissions established in the first cabinet are still in use in the sixth cabinet. They are the Ministries of Finance, Foreign Affairs, and Public Health and the State Planning Commission. The names of a few ministries were changed, such as the Ministry of People's Armed Forces from the Ministry of Defense and the Ministry of Labor Administration from the Ministry of Labor, but the main functions of the ministries are intact. Other changes are simple cases of structural differentiation in accordance with various functions of the ministry, such as the division of the Ministry of Agriculture and Forestry into the Ministry of Agriculture, changed ultimately to Agricultural Commission, and the Ministry of Forestry, which was later abolished altogether.

There have been extremely complicated changes in some of the cabinet posts dealing with industrial development. For example, the Ministry of Chemical Industry was first created in January 1955 from the Ministry of Chemical and Building Materials Industries, but it was merged with the Ministry of Power and Chemical Industries in August 1959, and this ministry was merged with the Heavy Industry Commission in September 1962. When the commission was abolished, the Ministry of Metal and Chemical Industries was established, and after this ministry was abolished in November 1964, the Ministry of Chemical Industry was revived in January 1965. The ministry retained its name and function in the fifth and the sixth cabinets. Similarly, the Ministry of Industry has undergone a number of changes through the Ministry of Heavy Industry, Ministry of Metal Industry, Ministry of Machine Industry, and Ministry of Machine and Chemical Industries.

Many ministries and commissions were in existence only for a short time, such as the Ministries of City Construction, City Construction Management, City and Industry Construction, City Management, Rural Management, Rural Construction, and Foodstuff and Daily Necessities Industries. A few ministries commonly found in the cabinets of other countries have been abolished, such as Ministry of Justice and Ministry of Commerce. The Ministry of Justice was abolished in August 1959 after the second cabinet, and most of the functions of justice were taken up by the Central Court and the Procurator's Office. The Ministry of Commerce was transformed into the Ministry of Internal and External Commerce, but since there is no internal commerce, ministries dealing with only external commerce were developed. There are, for example, Ministries of Foreign Trade and External Economic Affairs, but there is no Ministry of Internal Commerce. The proliferation of ministries and commissions reached an extreme at the fourth cabinet, when there were thirty ministries, six commissions, and four other cabinet-level secretaries. Throughout the six cabinets from 1948 to 1978, the North has had eighty-four different ministries, commissions, and cabinet-level offices. A total of 153 persons have served as members of the cabinet and Administration Council, and many have served concurrently in two cabinet posts in various cabinets.

Except for the members of the third cabinet, only one-third or less of the original appointees to cabinet posts were reappointed to posts in succeeding cabinets. Only seven of twenty from the first cabinet, ten of thirty from the second, twelve of the forty-seven members of the fourth cabinet, and eight of twenty-five members of the fifth cabinet were reappointed. The only exception is the fourth cabinet; twenty of thirty-three members of the third cabinet were reappointed (Table 4.1). No one has served in all six cabinets as an original appointee at the time of the formation of each cabinet. Premier Yi Chong-ok of the sixth cabinet is the only one who has served in all six cabinets, but he was not an original member of the first cabinet. Yi was appointed minister of light industry in December 1951, three years after the formation of the first cabinet.

Of the seven members of the first cabinet who were reappointed to the second cabinet, two were Premier Kim Il Sung and Vice-Premier Hong Myŏng-hŭi. No one has been reappointed to the ministry or commission to which he was originally appointed except Yi Pyŏng-nam, minister of public health. From the second to the third cabinets, out of ten who were reappointed, five were premier and vice-premiers, and among five functional ministries and commissions, only one person was reappointed to the same ministry, Kim Hoe-il, minister of transportation. This ratio improves somewhat from the third to the fourth cabinets. Of twenty who were reappointed, seven were premier, first vice-premier, and vice-premiers; and of the remaining thirteen, eight were reappointed to the same ministerial position they held in the third cabinet.

Because of the constitutional change from the cabinet to Administration Council and also because of the significant reduction in ministries and commissions, from forty-seven to twenty-five, the ratio is bad from the fourth to the fifth cabinets. Of the twelve who were reappointed, five were vice-premiers, and of the remaining seven, only three were reappointed to the same ministries. These were Kye Ŭng-t'ae of Foreign Trade, Kim Man-gŭm of the Agricultural Commission, and Yi Nak-bin of Public Health. The most remarkable ratio is from the fifth to the sixth cabinet. Of eight who were reappointed, all except one were reappointed to the same ministries they held. The exception is Yi Chong-ok, chairman of the Heavy Industry Commission in the fifth cabinet, who became premier of the sixth cabinet. This record certainly indicates some measure of stability in the political scene in recent years and also gives some idea of the turbulent nature of political appointments in the North in the past (Table 4.2).

The foremost North Korean technocrat is Yi Chong-ok, premier of the Administration Council of the Sixth Assembly. Yi is the only person who has served in all six cabinets. He has held six different cabinet positions: premier, vice-premier, light industry, state planning, heavy industry, and metal and chemical industries. He was appointed to cabinet posts twelve times (Table 4.3). The person who holds the record of being appointed to the most ministries and commissions is Chŏng Il-yong with seven different posts (Table 4.4), but Chŏng was purged. The person who served most consistently and who also was appointed to cabinet posts twelve different times, including original appointments to the first five cabinets and to the first Central People's Committee, is Chŏng Chunt'aek. Chŏng was first appointed chairman of the State Planning Commission in the first cabinet, was vice-premier from the second to the fifth cabinets, served as minister of chemical and building materials industry, chemical industry, and light industry, and was reappointed chairman of the State Planning Commission in the third and fourth cabinets. Except for Yi Chong-ok, Chŏng's service from the first to the fifth cabinet is the record for consistent service in the same post. Chŏng died on January 11, 1973, at the age of sixty-three. There are only two others who served in five different cabinet posts. They are Kim Il and Nam Il. Kim Il, the vice president of the republic, was appointed vice-premier of the first and second cabinets, first vice-premier of the third and fourth cabinets, and premier of the fifth cabinet. Nam Il, the illustrious foreign minister of the North after the Korean war, served in three cabinet posts and was concurrently vice-premier from the second to the fifth cabinets. Nam died on March 7, 1976, at the age of sixty-four. Except for Kim Il Sung and

Kim Il, who are president and vice-president of the republic, respectively, all top-ranking cabinet ministers with consistent records of reappointment have died except Yi Chong-ok, premier of the sixth cabinet.

Ministers tend to serve out their terms or stay in their positions longest when they are appointed to the Ministries of People's Armed Forces (formerly National Defense), Foreign Affairs, Public Health, Finance, and Labor Administration (formerly Labor). Of 153 who served in the six cabinets, either as the original appointees or as interim appointees to serve out the terms of the original appointees, from 1948 to 1978, more than one half, 81, served in only one cabinet; 46 served in two, and 11 served in three cabinets. Six persons served in four cabinets, 3 served in five, and only Premier Yi Chong-ok served in all six cabinets (Table 4.5). Hŏ Chŏng-suk was the only woman who ever served in the cabinet. Hŏ was the first minister of culture and propaganda and was reappointed as minister of justice in the second cabinet.

OFFICERS AND MEMBERS OF THE CABINET AND THE ADMINISTRATION COUNCIL

Each cabinet is listed as it was announced by the Supreme People's Assembly. This list includes original appointees only and does not include interim appointments.

FIRST CABINET, SEPTEMBER 9, 1948[1]

Premier	Kim Il Sung*
Vice-premier	Pak Hŏn-yŏng
Vice-premier	Hong Myŏng-hŭi*
Vice-premier	Kim Ch'aek
Chairman of the State Planning Commission	Chŏng Chun-t'aek*
Minister of National Defense	Ch'oe Yong-gŏn
Minister of State Control	Kim Wŏn-bong
Minister of Interior	Pak Il-u
Minister of Foreign Affairs	Pak Hŏn-yŏng
Minister of Industry	Kim Ch'aek
Minister of Agriculture and Forestry	Pak Mun-gyu*
Minister of Commerce	Chang Si-u
Minister of Transportation	Chu Yŏng-ha

Minister of Finance	Ch'oe Ch'ang-ik
Minister of Education	Paek Nam-un
Minister of Communications	Kim Chŏng-ju
Minister of Justice	Yi Sŭng-yŏp
Minister of Culture and Propaganda	Hŏ Chŏng-suk*
Minister of Labor	Hŏ Sŏng-t'aek*
Minister of Public Health	Yi Pyŏng-nam*
Minister of City Management	Yi Yong
Minister without Portfolio	Yi Kŭk-no

*Reappointed to the next cabinet.

SECOND CABINET, SEPTEMBER 20, 1957[2]

Premier	Kim Il Sung*
Vice-premier	Kim Il*
Vice-premier	Hong Myŏng-hŭi
Vice-premier	Chŏng Il-yong*
Vice-premier	Nam Il*
Vice-premier	Pak Ŭi-wan
Vice-premier	Chŏng Chun-t'aek*
Minister of National Defense	Kim Kwang-hyŏp*
Minister of Interior	Pang Hak-se
Minister of Foreign Affairs	Nam Il*
Minister of Justice	Hŏ Chŏng-suk
Minister of State Control	Pak Mun-gyu*
Chairman of the State Planning Commission	Yi Chong-ok*
Chairman of the State Construction Commission	Pak Ŭi-wan
Minister of Metal Industry	Kang Yŏng-ch'ang
Minister of Machine Industry	Chŏng Il-yong*
Minister of Coal Industry	Hŏ Sŏng-t'aek

Minister of Chemical Industry	Yi Ch'ŏn-ho
Minister of Agriculture	Han Chŏn-jong
Minister of Electric Powers	Kim Tu-sam
Minister of Light Industry	Mun Man-uk
Minister of Fisheries	Chu Hwang-sŏp
Minister of Transportation	Kim Hoe-il*
Minister of Construction and Building Materials Industries	Ch'oe Chae-ha
Minister of Finance	Yi Chu-yŏn*
Minister of Internal and External Commerce	Chin Pan-su
Minister of Communications	Ko Chun-t'aek
Minister of Education and Culture	Han Sŏl-ya
Minister of Public Health	Yi Pyŏng-nam
Minister of Labor	Kim Ŭng-gi
Minister of Rural Management	Chŏng Sŏng-ŏn
Minister without Portfolio	Kim Tal-hyŏn and Hong Ki-hwang

*Reappointed to the next cabinet.

THIRD CABINET, OCTOBER 23, 1962[3]

Premier	Kim Il Sung*
First Vice-premier	Kim Il*
Vice-premier	Kim Kwang-hyŏp*
Vice-premier	Kim Ch'ang-man
Vice-premier	Chŏng Il-yong*
Vice-premier	Nam Il*
Vice-premier	Yi Chong-ok*
Vice-premier	Yi Chu-yŏn*
Vice-premier	Chŏng Chun-t'aek*
Minister of National Defense	Kim Ch'ang-bong*
Minister of Public Security	Sŏk San*
Minister of Foreign Affairs	Pak Sŏng-ch'ŏl*

Chairman of the State Planning Commission   Chŏng Chun-t'aek*

Chairman of the State Construction   Nam Il*
Commission

First vice-chairman of the State Construction   Kim Ŭng-sang*

Chairman of the State Scientific and   O Tong-uk*
Technological Commission

Chairman of the Light Industry Commission   Pak Yong-sŏng

Chairman of the Agricultural Commission   Kim Man-gŭm*

Minister of Metal and Chemical Industries   Yi Chong-ok*

Minister of Power and Coal Industries   Chŏng Il-yong*

Minister of Machine Industry   Cho Tong-sŏp

Minister of Fisheries   Ch'oe Yong-jin*

Minister of Forestry   Chŏng Tong-ch'ŏl*

Minister of City and Industry Construction   Kim Pyŏng-sik

Minister of Rural Construction   Kim Pyŏng-ik

Minister of Transportation   Kim Hoe-il

Minister of Communications   Pak Yŏng-sun*

Minister of Finance   Han Sang-du*

Minister of Commerce   Kim Se-bong

Minister of Procurement and Food   Han Tae-yŏng
Administration

Minister of Foreign Trade   Yi Il-gyŏng

Minister of Labor   Paek Sŏn-il*

Minister of Interior   Pak Mun-gyu

Minister of City Management   Yŏm T'ae-jun

Minister of Higher Education   Kim Chong-hang

Minister of Common Education   Yun Ki-bok*

Minister of Culture   Pak Ung-gŏl

Minister of Public Health   Ch'oe Ch'ang-sŏk

*Reappointed to the next cabinet.

FOURTH CABINET, DECEMBER 16, 1967[4]

Premier	Kim Il Sung
First Vice-premier	Kim Il*
Vice-premier	Kim Kwang-hyŏp
Vice-premier	Pak Sŏng-ch'ŏl*
Vice-premier	Kim Ch'ang-bong
Vice-premier	Yi Chu-yŏn
Vice-premier	Nam Il*
Vice-premier	Yi Chong-ok*
Vice-premier	Ch'oe Yong-jin
Vice-premier	Chŏng Chun-t'aek*
Minister of Foreign Affairs	Pak Sŏng-ch'ŏl*
Minister of National Defense	Kim Ch'ang-bong
Minister of Public Security	Sŏk San
Chairman of the State Planning Commission	Chŏng Chun-t'aek*
Minister of Foreign Trade	Kye Ŭng-t'ae*
Chairman of the Commission for Economic Relations with Foreign Countries	Kim Kyŏng-yŏn*
Minister of Metal Industry	Kim Pyŏng-han
Minister of Mining Industry	Kim Ch'i-do
Minister of Power and Coal Industries	Kim T'ae-gŭn
Minister of Chemical Industry	Song Pok-ki
Minister of the First Ministry of Machine Industry	Hyŏn Mu-gwang*
Minister of the Second Ministry of Machine Industry	Hong Wŏn-gil*
Minister of Building Material Industry	Chŏng Il-yong
Minister of Forestry	Chŏng Tong-ch'ŏl
Minister of Fisheries	Kang Chŏm-gu
Minister of Textile and Paper Industries	Yi Yang-suk
Minister of Foodstuff and Daily Necessities Industries	Yi Ho-hyŏk

Chairman of the Agricultural Commission	Kim Man-gŭm*
Chairman of the State Construction Commission	Kim Tu-sam
Minister of Construction	Cho Kwan-ha
Minister of Railways	Kim Kap-sun
Minister of Land and Sea Transportation	O Sŏng-yŏl
Minister of Communications	Pak Yŏng-sun
Minister of Finance	Yun Ki-bok
Minister of Labor	Paek Sŏn-il
Minister of City Management	Chin Mun-dŏk
Minister of Land Administration	No Pyŏng-u
Minister of Commerce	An Sŭng-hak
Minister of Procurement and Food Administration	Pak Kwang-sŏn
Chairman of the Materials Supply Commission	Han Sang-du
Chairman of the State Scientific and Technological Commission	Kim Ŭng-sang
Minister of State Control	Kim Ik-sŏn
Minister of Higher Education	Yang Hyŏng-sŏp
Minister of Common Education	Yi Chang-su
Minister of Culture	Pak Yŏng-sin
Minister of Public Health	Yi Nak-bin*
President of Academy of Sciences	O Tong-uk
Director of the First Secretariat of the Cabinet	Ch'oe Chae-u*
Director of the Fifth Secretariat of the Cabinet	O T'ae-bong
Director of the Second Secretariat of the Cabinet	An Yong-guk

*Reappointed to the next cabinet.

ADMINISTRATION COUNCIL OF THE FIFTH SUPREME PEOPLE'S ASSEMBLY (FIFTH CABINET), DECEMBER 26, 1972[5]

Premier	Kim Il
Vice-premier	Pak Sŏng-ch'ŏl
Vice-premier	Chŏng Chun-t'aek
Vice-premier	Kim Man-gŭm
Vice-premier	Ch'oe Chae-u
Vice-premier	Nam Il
Vice-Premier	Hong Wŏn-gil
Chairman of the State Planning Commission	Ch'oe Chae-u
Minister of the People's Armed Forces	Ch'oe Hyŏn
Minister of Foreign Affairs	Hŏ Tam*
Minister of Public Security	Kim Pyŏng-ha
Chairman of Heavy Industry Commission	Yi Chong-ok*
Chairman of the Machine Industry Commission	Hong Wŏn-gil
Minister of Ship Machine Building Industry	Han Sŏng-yong
Minister of Chemical Industry	Kim Hwan
Chairman of the Light Industry Commission	Nam Il
Chairman of the Agricultural Commission	Kim Man-gŭm
Chairman of the Transportation and Communications Commission	Hyŏn Mu-gwang
Minister of Fisheries	Kim Yun-sang*
Minister of Building Materials Industry	Mun Pyŏng-il
Chairman of the People's Service Commission	Pak Sŏng-ch'ŏl
Minister of Education	Kim Sŏk-ki
Minister of Culture and Art	Yi Ch'ang-sŏn*
Minister of Finance	Kim Kyŏng-yŏn*
Minister of Foreign Trade	Kye Ŭng-t'ae*
Minister of External Economic Affairs	Kong Chin-t'ae*
Minister of Construction	Pak Im-t'ae*

Minister of Labor Administration	Chŏng Tu-hwan
Minister of Public Health	Yi Nak-bin

*Reappointed to the next cabinet.

ADMINISTRATION COUNCIL OF THE SIXTH SUPREME PEOPLE'S ASSEMBLY
(SIXTH CABINET), DECEMBER 16, 1977[6]

Premier	Yi Chong-ok
Vice-premier	Kye Ŭng-t'ae
Vice-premier	Hŏ Tam
Vice-premier	Chŏng Chun-gi
Vice-premier	Kang Sŏng-san
Vice-premier	Kong Chin-t'ae
Vice-premier	Kim Tu-yŏng
Secretary	Kim Yun-hyŏk
Minister of People's Armed Forces	O Chin-u
Minister of Foreign Affairs	Hŏ Tam
Minister of Public Security	Ch'oe Wŏn-ik
Chairman of the State Planning Commission	Hong Sŏng-yong
Chairman of the Agricultural Commission	Sŏ Kwan-hŭi
Chairman of the Mining Industry Commission	Cho Ch'ang-dŏk
Minister of Metal Industry	Yun Ho-sŏk
Minister of Power Industry	Yi Chi-ch'an
Minister of Machine Industry	Kye Hyŏng-sun
Minister of Chemical Industry	Wŏn Tong-gu
Minister of Construction	Pak Im-t'ae
Chairman of the State Construction Commission	Kim Ŭng-sang
Minister of Building Materials Industry	Kim Nam-yun
Minister of Light Industry	Hŏ Sun
Minister of Railways	Pak Yong-sŏk

Minister of Land and Sea Transportation	Yi Ch'ŏl-bong
Minister of Fisheries	Kim Yun-sang
Chairman of the People's Service Commission	Yim Hyŏng-gu
Chairman of the Education Commission	Kim Il-dae
Minister of Materials Supply	Kim T'ae-gŭk
Minister of Communications	Kim Yŏng-ch'ae
Minister of Culture and Art	Yi Ch'ang-sŏn
Minister of Finance	Kim Kyŏng-yŏn
Minister of Foreign Trade	Kye Ŭng-t'ae
Minister of External Economic Affairs	Kong Chin-t'ae
Minister of Labor Administration	Ch'ae Hŭi-jŏng
Chairman of the State Scientific and Technological Commission	Chu Hwa-jong
Minister of Public Health	Pak Myŏng-bin

MINISTRIES AND COMMISSIONS OF THE REPUBLIC

This section lists the various ministries and commissions of the republic and briefly describes the various transformations and abolitions that have taken place among them. It also includes chronological lists of the ministers, commission chairmen, and other cabinet officers. These lists include many, but not all, interim appointees; particularly from the fourth cabinet on, interim appointments ceased to be formally announced.

Abbreviations have been assigned to each ministry, commission, and office, and they are then listed in alphabetic order by the abbreviations.

Abbreviations

A	Ministry of Agriculture
AC	Agricultural Commission
AF	Ministry of Agriculture and Forestry
AS	Academy of Sciences
BM	Ministry of Building Materials Industry
C	Ministry of Commerce
CA	Ministry of Culture and Art

CB	Ministry of Chemical and Building Materials Industries
CBM	Ministry of Construction and Building Materials Industries
CC	Ministry of City Construction
CCM	Ministry of City Construction Management
CE	Ministry of Common Education
CI	Ministry of Chemical Industry
CIC	Ministry of City and Industry Construction
CM	Ministry of City Management
CO	Ministry of Construction
COI	Ministry of Coal Industry
COM	Ministry of Communications
CP	Ministry of Culture and Propaganda
CU	Ministry of Culture
E	Ministry of Education
EC	Ministry of Education and Culture
ED	Education Commission
EE	Ministry of External Economic Affairs
EF	Commission for Economic Relations with Foreign Countries
EP	Ministry of Electric Powers
F	Ministry of Finance
FA	Ministry of Foreign Affairs
FD	Ministry of Foodstuff and Daily Necessities Industries
FI	Ministry of Fisheries
FR	Ministry of Forestry
FT	Ministry of Foreign Trade
HE	Ministry of Higher Education
HI	Ministry of Heavy Industry
HIC	Heavy Industry Commission
I	Ministry of Industry
IE	Ministry of Internal and External Commerce
IT	Ministry of Interior
J	Ministry of Justice
L	Ministry of Labor
LA	Ministry of Labor Administration
LAD	Ministry of Land Administration
LI	Ministry of Light Industry
LIC	Light Industry Commission
LOA	Ministry of Local Administration
LST	Ministry of Land and Sea Transportation
MC	Ministry of Metal and Chemical Industries
MEI	Ministry of Metal Industry
MI	Ministry of Machine Industry

MIC   Machine Industry Commission
MIF   First Ministry of Machine Industry
MIS   Second Ministry of Machine Industry
MN   Ministry of Mining Industry
MNI   Mining Industry Commission
MS   Ministry of Materials Supply
MSC   Materials Supply Commission

ND   Ministry of National Defense

P   Premier
PAF   Ministry of People's Armed Forces
PCC   People's Control Commission
PCI   Ministry of Power and Chemical Industries
PCO   Ministry of Power and Coal Industries
PFA   Ministry of Procurement and Food Administration
PH   Ministry of Public Health
PI   Ministry of Power Industry
PS   Ministry of Public Security
PSC   People's Service Commission

R   Ministry of Railways
RC   Ministry of Rural Construction
RM   Ministry of Rural Management
RTC   Railway Transportation Commission

S   Secretary
SC   Ministry of State Control
SCC   State Construction Commission
SCT   State Scientific and Technological Commission
SLI   State Light Industry Commission
SMB   Ministry of Ship Machine Building Industry
SPC   State Planning Commission

T   Ministry of Transportation
TC   Transportation and Communications Commission
TP   Ministry of Textile and Paper Industries

VP   Vice-Premier
VPF   First Vice-Premier

WP   Ministry without Portfolio

A   **Ministry of Agriculture [Nongŏp sŏng]**

Established on November 29, 1952, from the Ministry of Agriculture and Forestry. Abolished to become the Agricultural Commission on October 23, 1962.

Minister	Period Served	Cabinet
Pak Mun-gyu	11/52– 3/54	
Kim Il	3/54– 9/57	
*Han Chŏn-jong	9/57– 7/59	II
Kim Man-gŭm	7/59– 8/60	
Yim Hae	8/60– 9/61	
Pak Chŏng-ae	10/61–10/62	

AC **Agricultural Commission [Nongŏp Wiwŏnhoe]**

Established on October 23, 1962, from the Ministry of Agriculture.

Chairman	Period Served	Cabinet
*Kim Man-gŭm	10/62–12/67	III
*Kim Man-gŭm	12/67–12/72	IV
*Kim Man-gŭm	12/72–12/77	V
*Sŏ Kwan-hŭi	12/77–	VI

AF **Ministry of Agriculture and Forestry [Nongnim Sŏng]**

Established in the first cabinet on September 9, 1948. Abolished to become the Ministry of Agriculture on November 29, 1952.

Minister	Period Served	Cabinet
*Pak Mun-gyu	9/48–11/52	I

AS **Academy of Sciences [Kwahagwŏn]**

President of the Academy of Sciences held a ministerial position in the fourth cabinet, December 16, 1967.

President	Period Served	Cabinet
*O Tong-uk	12/67–12/72	IV

BM **Ministry of Building Materials Industry [Kŏnjae Kongŏp Pu (Sŏng)]**

Established from the Ministry of City and Industrial Construction on January 8, 1963.

Minister	Period Served	Cabinet
Kim Pyŏng-sik	1/63– 1/65	
Kim Ŭng-sang	1/65–12/67	

*Original appointee to the post; those not marked by an asterisk were interim appointees.

Minister	Period Served	Cabinet
*Chŏng Il-yong	12/67–12/72	IV
*Mun Pyŏng-il	12/72–12/77	V
*Kim Nam-yun	12/77–	VI

C   Ministry of Commerce [Sangŏp Sŏng]

Established in the first cabinet. Merged with the Ministry of Foreign Trade and became the Ministry of Internal and External Commerce in September 1956. This was dissolved and the Ministry of Commerce was reestablished on September 29, 1958, but the ministry was abolished at the Fifth Assembly in December 1972.

Minister	Period Served	Cabinet
*Chang Si-u	9/48–10/52	I
Yi Chu-yŏn	10/52– 3/54	
Yun Kong-hŭm	3/54– 9/56	
Chin Pan-su	9/58– 5/59	
Chŏng Tu-hwan	5/59– 5/60	
Han Tae-yŏng	5/60– 2/62	
Yi Yang-suk	7/62– 8/62	
Kim Se-bong	8/62–10/62	
*Kim Se-bong	10/62–12/67	III
*An Sŭng-hak	12/67–12/72	IV

CA   Ministry of Culture and Art [Munhwa Yesul Pu]

Established at the Fifth Assembly in December 1972, succeeding the Ministry of Culture of the fourth cabinet.

Minister	Period Served	Cabinet
*Yi Ch'ang-sŏn	12/72–12/77	V
*Yi Ch'ang-sŏn	12/77–	VI

CB   Ministry of Chemical and Building Materials Industries [Hwahak Kŏnjae Kongŏp Sŏng]

Established on July 27, 1951. Renamed the Ministry of Chemical Industry in January 1955.

Minister	Period Served
Paek Hong-gwŏn	5/52– 3/54
Chŏng Chun-t'aek	3/54– 1/55

CBM **Ministry of Construction and Building Materials Industries [Kŏnsŏl Kŏnjae Kongŏp Sŏng]**

Established on August 3, 1957, from the Ministry of Construction. Renamed the Ministry of City Construction Management on November 8, 1958.

Minister	Period Served	Cabinet
*Ch'oe Chae-ha	8/57–10/58	II
Kim Pyŏng-sik	10/58–11/58	

CC **Ministry of City Construction [Tosi Kŏnsŏl Sŏng]**

Established on December 13, 1951, by renaming the Ministry of City Management. Abolished on March 24, 1954.

Minister	Period Served
Kim Sŭng-hwa	12/51– 6/53
Chu Hwang-sŏp	10/53– 3/54

CCM **Ministry of City Construction Management [Tosi Kŏnsŏl Kyŏngyŏng Sŏng]**

Established on November 8, 1958. Abolished on August 31, 1959.

Minister	Period Served
Kim Pyŏng-sik	11/58– 8/59

CE **Ministry of Common Education [Pot'ong Kyoyuk Sŏng]**

Established in December 1960 by dividing the Ministry of Education and Culture. At the Fifth Assembly, this ministry was incorporated into the Ministry of Education.

Minister	Period Served	Cabinet
Yi Il-gyŏng	1/61–11/61	
Yun Ki-bok	8/62–10/62	
*Yun Ki-bok	10/62–12/67	III
*Yi Chang-su	12/67–12/72	IV

CI **Ministry of Chemical Industry [Hwahak Kongŏp Pu (Sŏng)]**

Established in January 1955 from the Ministry of Chemical and Building Materials Industries. In August 1959, the ministry was merged with the Ministry of Power and Chemical Industries. The Ministry of Power and Chemical Industries was merged with the

Heavy Industry Commission in September 1962. When the Heavy Industry Commission was abolished, the Ministry of Metal and Chemical Industries was established, and when the Ministry of Metal and Chemical Industries was abolished in November 1964, the Ministry of Chemical Industry was revived.

Minister	Period Served	Cabinet
Chŏng Chun-t'aek	1/55– 5/56	
Yi Ch'ŏn-ho	5/56– 9/57	
*Yi Ch'ŏn-ho	9/57– 8/59	II
Song Pok-ki	1/65–12/67	
*Song Pok-ki	12/67–12/72	IV
*Kim Hwan	12/72–12/77	V
*Wŏn Tong-gu	12/77–	VI

CIC Ministry of City and Industry Construction [Tosi Mit San'ŏp Kŏn-sŏl Sŏng]

Established on October 23, 1962, from the Ministry of Construction. Dissolved on January 8, 1963.

Minister	Period Served	Cabinet
*Kim Pyŏng-sik	10/62– 1/63	III

CM Ministry of City Management [Tosi Kyŏngyŏng Sŏng]

Established in the first cabinet on September 9, 1948. Renamed the Ministry of City Construction on December 13, 1951. Reinstated as the Ministry of City Management on January 20, 1955. Incorporated into the Ministry of Rural Management on August 3, 1957. Reinstated as the Ministry of City Management in the third cabinet on October 23, 1962. Abolished on April 3, 1964. Reinstated as the Ministry of City Management in the fourth cabinet on December 16, 1967. Abolished at the Fifth Assembly in December 1972.

Minister	Period Served	Cabinet
*Yi Yong	9/48–12/51	I
Yi Ki-sŏk	1/55– 8/57	
*Yŏm T'ae-jun	10/62– 4/64	III
*Chin Mun-dŏk	12/67–12/72	IV

CO Ministry of Construction [Kŏnsŏl Pu (Sŏng)]

Established on January 20, 1955. Renamed the Ministry of Construction and Building Materials Industries on August 3, 1957.

Reestablished on January 21, 1961, as the Ministry of Construction. Renamed the Ministry of City and Industrial Construction on October 23, 1962. Revived as the Ministry of Construction in October 1967.

Minister	Period Served	Cabinet
Kim Sŭng-hwa	1/55– 8/56	
Ch'oe Chae-ha	12/56– 8/57	
Kim Pyŏng-sik	1/61–10/62	
Cho Kwan-ha	10/67–12/67	
*Cho Kwan-ha	12/67–12/72	IV
*Pak Im-t'ae	12/72–12/77	V
*Pak Im-t'ae	12/77–	VI

COI **Ministry of Coal Industry [Sŏkt'an Kongŏp Sŏng]**

Established on May 11, 1956. Merged with the Ministry of Power and Chemical Industries on August 31, 1959.

Minister	Period Served	Cabinet
Yu Ch'uk-un	5/56– 9/57	
*Hŏ Sŏng-t'aek	9/57– 9/58	II
Kim T'ae-gŭn	9/58– 8/59	

COM **Ministry of Communications [Ch'esin Pu (Sŏng)]**

Established in the first cabinet on September 9, 1948. Became a part of the Transportation and Communications Commission at the Fifth Assembly, but was reinstated at the Sixth Assembly in December 1977.

Minister	Period Served	Cabinet
*Kim Chŏng-ju	9/48– 3/53	I
Pak Il-u	3/53–11/55	
Kim Ch'ang-hŭp	11/55– 9/57	
*Ko Chun-t'aek	9/57– 4/58	II
Ch'oe Hyŏn	4/58–10/62	
*Pak Yŏng-sun	10/62–12/67	III
*Pak Yŏng-sun	12/67–12/72	IV
*Kim Yŏng-ch'ae	12/77–	VI

CP **Ministry of Culture and Propaganda [Munhwa Sŏnjŏn Sŏng]**

Established in the first cabinet on September 9, 1948. Dissolved to merge with the Ministry of Education to become the Ministry of Education and Culture in August 1957.

Minister	Period Served	Cabinet
*Hŏ Chŏng-suk	9/48– 8/57	I

CU Ministry of Culture [Munhwa Sŏng]

Established on January 21, 1961, shortly after the Ministry of Education and Culture was dissolved to become the Ministry of Higher Education and the Ministry of Common Education.

Minister	Period Served	Cabinet
Pak Ung-gŏl	1/61–10/62	
*Pak Ung-gŏl	10/62– 9/66	III
Pak Yŏng-sin	9/66–12/67	
*Pak Yŏng-sin	12/67–12/72	IV

E Ministry of Education [Kyoyuk Pu (Sŏng)]

Established in the first cabinet on September 9, 1948. The ministry was merged with the Ministry of Culture and Propaganda and became the Ministry of Education and Culture in August 1957. Revived as Ministry of Education at the Fifth Assembly, but renamed the Education Commission at the Sixth Assembly.

Minister	Period Served	Cabinet
*Paek Nam-un	9/48– 1/56	I
Kim Ch'ang-man	1/56– 5/56	
Han Sŏl-ya	5/56– 8/57	
*Kim Sŏk-ki	12/72–12/77	V

EC Ministry of Education and Culture [Kyoyuk Munhwa Sŏng]

Established in August 1957 by merging the Ministry of Education and the Ministry of Culture and Propaganda. Dissolved to become the Ministry of Higher Education and the Ministry of Common Education in April and December, respectively, of 1960.

Minister	Period Served	Cabinet
Han Sŏl-ya	8/57– 9/57	
*Han Sŏl-ya	9/57– 9/58	II
Yi Il-gyŏng	9/58– 4/60	

ED Education Commission [Kyoyuk Wiwŏnhoe]

Established at the Sixth Assembly to succeed the Ministry of Education.

Chairman	Period Served	Cabinet
*Kim Il-dae	12/77–	VI

EE **Ministry of External Economic Affairs [Taeoe Kyŏngje Saŏp Pu]**

First established at the Fifth Assembly in December 1972 to succeed the work of the Commission for Economic Relations with Foreign Countries.

Minister	Period Served	Cabinet
*Kong Chin-t'ae	12/72–12/77	V
*Kong Chin-t'ae	12/77–	VI

EF **Commission for Economic Relations with Foreign Countries [Taeoe Kyŏngje Wiwŏnhoe]**

Established on December 16, 1967, in the fourth cabinet. Renamed Ministry of External Economic Affairs at the Fifth Assembly in December 1972.

Chairman	Period Served	Cabinet
*Kim Kyŏng-yŏn	12/67–12/72	IV

EP **Ministry of Electric Power [Chŏn'gi Sŏng]**

Established on March 23, 1954. Merged with the Ministry of Power and Chemical Industries in August 1959.

Minister	Period Served	Cabinet
Kim Tu-sam	3/54– 9/57	
*Kim Tu-sam	9/57– 8/59	II

F **Ministry of Finance [Chaejŏng Pu (Sŏng)]**

Established in the first cabinet on September 8, 1948.

Minister	Period Served	Cabinet
*Ch'oe Ch'ang-ik	9/48–11/52	I
Yun Kong-hŭm	11/52– 3/54	
Ch'oe Ch'ang-ik	3/54–11/54	
Yi Chu-yŏn	11/54– 9/57	
*Yi Chu-yŏn	9/57– 4/58	II
Song Pong-uk	4/58– 8/60	
Han Sang-du	8/60–10/62	
*Han Sang-du	10/62–12/67	III
*Yun Ki-bok	12/67–12/72	IV

Minister	Period Served	Cabinet
*Kim Kyŏng-yŏn	12/72–12/77	V
*Kim Kyŏng-yŏn	12/77–	VI

FA   **Ministry of Foreign Affairs [Oemu Pu (Sŏng)]**

Established in the first cabinet on September 9, 1948.

Minister	Period Served	Cabinet
*Pak Hŏn-yŏng	9/48– 3/53	I
Nam Il	8/53– 9/57	
*Nam Il	9/57–10/59	II
Pak Sŏng-ch'ŏl	10/59–10/62	
*Pak Sŏng-ch'ŏl	10/62–12/67	III
*Pak Sŏng-ch'ŏl	12/67–12/72	IV
*Hŏ Tam	12/72–12/77	V
*Hŏ Tam	12/77–	VI

FD   **Ministry of Foodstuff and Daily Necessities Industries [Singnyo Mit Iryongp'um Kongŏp Sŏng]**

Established on January 30, 1967, but abolished by the Fifth Assembly in December 1972.

Minister	Period Served	Cabinet
Yi Ho-hyŏk	1/67–12/67	
*Yi Ho-hyŏk	12/67–12/72	IV

FI   **Ministry of Fisheries [Susan Pu (Sŏng)]**

Established on March 23, 1954. Incorporated into the Ministry of Light Industry on August 31, 1959. Reinstated on December 27, 1960.

Minister	Period Served	Cabinet
Chu Hwang-sŏp	3/54– 9/57	
*Chu Hwang-sŏp	9/57– 9/58	II
Yu Ch'ŏl-mok	9/58– 8/59	
*Ch'oe Yong-jin	12/60– 3/63	III
Kang Chŏm-gu	3/63–12/67	
*Kang Chŏm-gu	12/67–12/72	IV
*Kim Yun-sang	12/72–12/77	V
*Kim Yun-sang	12/77–	VI

FR **Ministry of Forestry [Im'ŏp Sŏng]**

Established on April 24, 1958. Abolished on April 29, 1960. Reinstated on December 27, 1960, but abolished again at the Fifth Assembly in December 1972.

Minister	Period Served	Cabinet
Ko Chun-t'aek	4/58– 9/58	
Ko Hŭi-man	10/58– 4/60	
Song Ch'ang-yŏm	1/61–10/62	
*Chŏng Tong-ch'ŏl	10/62–12/67	III
*Chŏng Tong-ch'ŏl	12/67–12/72	IV

FT **Ministry of Foreign Trade [Muyŏk Pu (Sŏng)]**

Established on October 9, 1952. Merged with the Ministry of Commerce and became the Ministry of Internal and External Commerce in September 1956. The Ministry of Internal and External Commerce was dissolved into two ministries on September 29, 1958, the Ministry of Commerce and the Ministry of Foreign Trade.

Minister	Period Served	Cabinet
Chin Pan-su	4/53– 5/56	
Yim Hae	9/58– 8/60	
Yi Chu-yŏn	8/60–11/61	
Yi Il-gyŏng	11/61–10/62	
*Yi Il-gyŏng	10/62– 4/64	III
Yi Chu-yŏn	4/64–12/67	
*Kye Ŭng-t'ae	12/67–12/72	IV
*Kye Ŭng-t'ae	12/72–12/77	V
*Kye Ŭng-t'ae	12/77–	VI

HE **Ministry of Higher Education [Kodŭng Kyoyuk Sŏng]**

Established in April 1960 when the Ministry of Education and Culture was dissolved, but was incorporated into the Ministry of Education at the Fifth Assembly.

Minister	Period Served	Cabinet
Kim Chong-hang	4/60–10/62	
*Kim Chong-hang	10/62–11/67	III
*Yang Hyŏng-sŏp	12/67–12/72	IV

HI   **Ministry of Heavy Industry [Chung Kongŏp Sŏng]**

Established in November 1951 when the Ministry of Industry was divided into three separate ministries, the Ministry of Heavy Industry, the Ministry of Light Industry, and the Ministry of Chemical and Building Materials Industries. Dissolved on June 25, 1955, to become the Ministry of Metal Industry.

Minister	Period Served
Chŏng Il-yong	11/51–11/52
Kim Tu-sam	11/52– 3/54
Chŏng Il-yong	3/54– 6/55

HIC   **Heavy Industry Commission [Chung Kongŏp Wiwŏnhoe]**

Established on April 4, 1960. Formerly the Ministry of Metal Industry. Dissolved in September 1962, but reinstated in the Administration Council of the 1972 constitution. At the Sixth Supreme People's Assembly the commission was dissolved, and the Ministry of Metal Industry was reinstated.

Chairman and vice-chairman; vice-chairman also held ministerial rank.

Chairman	Period Served	Cabinet
Yi Chong-ok	4/60– 9/62	
*Yi Chong-ok	12/72–12/77	V

Vice-chairman	Period Served
Ch'oe Chae-u	9/61– 8/62
Chŏng Yu-ho	4/60–11/60
Han Sang-du	11/60– 8/62
Kim Tu-sam	4/60– 8/60
No T'ae-sŏk	4/60–10/61

I   **Ministry of Industry [San'ŏp Sŏng]**

Established in the first cabinet. Dissolved on July 27, 1951, to become three separate ministries, the Ministry of Heavy Industry, the Ministry of Light Industry, and the Ministry of Chemical and Building Materials Industries.

Minister	Period Served	Cabinet
*Kim Ch'aek	9/48– 1/51	I
Chŏng Il-yong	2/51– 7/51	

IE   **Ministry of Internal and External Commerce [Taenae Taeoe Sangŏp Sŏng]**

Established on September 11, 1956. Dissolved to become the Ministry of Commerce and the Ministry of Foreign Trade on September 29, 1958.

Minister	Period Served	Cabinet
Chin Pan-su	9/56– 9/57	
*Chin Pan-su	9/57– 9/58	II

IT   **Ministry of Interior [Naemu Sŏng]**

Established in the first cabinet on September 9, 1948. Incorporated into the Ministry of Land Administration on April 3, 1964.

Minister	Period Served	Cabinet
*Pak Il-u	9/48–10/52	I
Pang Hak-se	10/52– 9/57	
*Pang Hak-se	9/57–11/60	II
Sŏk San	11/60–10/62	
*Pak Mun-gyu	10/62– 4/64	III

J   **Ministry of Justice [Sabŏp Sŏng]**

Established in the first cabinet on September 9, 1948. Abolished in August 1959.

Minister	Period Served	Cabinet
*Yi Sŭng-yŏp	9/48–12/51	I
Yi Yong	12/51–12/53	
Hong Ki-ju	12/53– 7/57	
Hŏ Chŏng-suk	8/57– 9/57	
*Hŏ Chŏng-suk	9/57– 8/59	II

L   **Ministry of Labor [Nodong Sŏng]**

Established in the first cabinet on September 9, 1948. Abolished on August 31, 1959, but reinstated on February 28, 1961. The ministry was changed to the Ministry of Labor Administration in December 1972 at the Fifth Assembly.

Minister	Period Served	Cabinet
*Hŏ Sŏng-t'aek	9/48– 5/52	I
Kim Wŏn-bong	5/52– 9/57	
*Kim Ŭng-gi	9/57– 8/59	II

Minister	Period Served	Cabinet
Yang T'ae-gŭn	2/61–10/62	
*Paek Sŏn-il	10/62–12/67	III
*Paek Sŏn-il	12/67–12/72	IV

LA   **Ministry of Labor Administration [Nodong Haengjŏng Pu]**

Succeeded the Ministry of Labor and was established at the Fifth Assembly in December 1972.

Minister	Period Served	Cabinet
*Chŏng Tu-hwan	12/72–12/77	V
*Ch'ae Hŭi-jŏng	12/77–	VI

LAD   **Ministry of Land Administration [Kukt'o Kwalli Sŏng]**

Established on December 4, 1964. Abolished at the Fifth Assembly in December 1972.

Minister	Period Served	Cabinet
Pak Mun-gyu	1/65–12/67	
*No Pyŏng-u	12/67–12/72	IV

LI   **Ministry of Light Industry [Kyŏng Kongŏp Pu (Sŏng)]**

Established on July 27, 1951. Dissolved to become the Light Industry Commission on April 4, 1960. Reinstated at the Sixth Assembly in December 1977.

Minister	Period Served	Cabinet
Yi Chong-ok	12/51– 3/54	
Pak Ŭi-wan	3/54– 1/55	
Yi Chong-ok	1/55–11/55	
Mun Man-uk	11/55– 9/57	
*Mun Man-uk	9/57– 4/60	II
*Hŏ Sun	12/77–	VI

LIC   **Light Industry Commission [Kyŏng Kongŏp Wiwŏnhoe]**

Established on April 4, 1960. Dissolved to become the State Light Industry Commission in January 1964. Revived under the Administration Council of the Fifth Supreme People's Assembly in December 1972, but reverted to the Ministry of Light Industry at the Sixth Assembly.

Chairman and vice-chairman; vice-chairman also held ministerial rank.

Chairman	*Period Served*	*Cabinet*
Chŏng Chun-t'aek	4/60–12/60	
Yim Kye-ch'ŏl	12/60–10/62	
*Pak Yong-sŏng	10/62– 1/64	III
*Nam Il	12/72– 3/76	V

Vice-chairman	*Period Served*
Mun Man-uk	4/60– 1/64
Pak Yong-sŏng	9/60–10/62

LOA **Ministry of Local Administration [Chibang Haengjŏng Sŏng]**

Established in May 1959, after the Ministry of State Control was abolished. Dissolved in August 1959.

Minister	*Period Served*
Pak Mun-gyu	5/59– 8/59

LST **Ministry of Land and Sea Transportation [Yugun Mit Haeun Pu (Sŏng)]**

Established in the fourth cabinet on December 16, 1967. Abolished at the Fifth Assembly, but reinstated at the Sixth Assembly in December 1977.

Minister	*Period Served*	*Cabinet*
*O Sŏng-yŏl	12/67–12/72	IV
*Yi Ch'ŏl-bong	12/77–	VI

MC **Ministry of Metal and Chemical Industries [Kŭmsok Hwahak Kongŏp Sŏng]**

Established in September 1962. Abolished in November 1964.

Minister	*Period Served*	*Cabinet*
Yi Chong-ok	9/62–10/62	
*Yi Chong-ok	10/62–11/64	III

MEI **Ministry of Metal Industry [Kŭmsok Kongŏp Pu (Sŏng)]**

Established on June 25, 1955. Formerly the Ministry of Heavy Industry. The ministry changed its name to the Heavy Industry Commission on April 4, 1960. In September 1962, it was changed again to the Ministry of Metal and Chemical Industry. In November 1964, the Ministry of Metal and Chemical Industry was separated into two ministries, the Ministry of Metal Industry and the

Ministry of Chemical Industry, and the Ministry of Metal Industry was reinstated. The ministry was changed again at the Fifth Assembly in December 1972 to the Heavy Industry Commission, but was reinstated at the Sixth Assembly in December 1977.

Minister	Period Served	Cabinet
Chŏng Il-yong	6/55–11/55	
Kang Yŏng-ch'ang	11/55– 9/57	
*Kang Yŏng-ch'ang	9/57– 9/58	II
Han Sang-du	9/58– 4/60	
Yi Chae-yŏng	1/65–12/67	
*Kim Pyŏng-han	12/67–12/72	IV
*Yun Ho-sŏk	12/77–	VI

MI   **Ministry of Machine Industry [Kigye Kongŏp Pu (Sŏng)]**

Established on May 11, 1956. Merged with the Heavy Industry Commission on April 4, 1960. Reinstated on October 23, 1962. Dissolved to become the Machine Industry Commission on July 30, 1963. Renamed the Ministry of Machine Industry on December 4, 1964. The ministry was split into the First and Second Ministries of Machine Industry on January 30, 1967. Reinstated at the Sixth Assembly in December 1977.

Minister	Period Served	Cabinet
Pak Ch'ang-ok	5/56– 9/56	
*Chŏng Il-yong	9/57– 2/58	II
Ch'oe Chae-u	2/58– 4/60	
*Cho Tong-sŏp	10/62– 7/63	III
Hyŏn Mu-gwang	12/64– 1/67	
*Kye Hyŏng-sun	12/77–	VI

MIC   **Machine Industry Commission [Kigye Kongŏp Wiwŏnhoe]**

Renamed to this commission from the Ministry of Machine Industry on July 30, 1963. Abolished and renamed the Ministry of Machine Industry on December 4, 1964. Reestablished under the Administration Council of the Fifth Supreme People's Assembly in 1972, but reverted to the Ministry of Machine Industry in the Sixth Assembly.

Chairman	Period Served	Cabinet
Hyŏn Mu-gwang	7/63–12/64	
*Hong Wŏn-gil	12/72–12/77	V

MIF **First Ministry of Machine Industry [Cheil Kigye Kongŏp Sŏng]**

Established on January 30, 1967, but abolished at the Fifth Assembly in December 1972. Reinstated at the Sixth Assembly as the Ministry of Machine Industry, combining the First and the Second Ministries.

Minister	Period Served	Cabinet
Hyŏn Mu-gwang	1/67–12/67	
*Hyŏn Mu-gwang	12/67–12/72	IV

MIS **Second Ministry of Machine Industry [Chei Kigye Kongŏp Sŏng]**

Established on January 30, 1967, by dividing the Ministry of Machine Industry. Abolished at the Fifth Assembly in December 1972, but reinstated at the Sixth Assembly, combining the First and Second Ministries.

Minister	Period Served	Cabinet
Hong Wŏn-gil	10/67–12/67	
*Hong Wŏn-gil	12/67–12/72	IV

MN **Ministry of Mining Industry [Kwangŏp Sŏng]**

Since the fourth cabinet, December 16, 1967. The ministry was abolished at the Fifth Assembly, but was reinstated as the Mining Industry Commission in the Sixth Assembly in December 1977.

Minister	Period Served	Cabinet
*Kim Ch'i-do	12/67–12/72	IV

MNI **Mining Industry Commission [Kwangŏp Wiwŏnhoe]**

Reinstated the former Ministry of Mining Industry at the Sixth Assembly in December 1977.

Chairman	Period Served	Cabinet
*Cho Ch'ang-dŏk	12/77–	VI

MS **Ministry of Materials Supply [Chajae Konggŭp Pu]**

Established as a ministry at the Sixth Assembly in December 1977 to succeed the Materials Supply Commission of the fourth cabinet.

Minister	Period Served	Cabinet
*Kim T'ae-gŭk	12/77–	VI

MSC **Materials Supply Commission [Chajae Konggŭp Wiwŏnhoe]**

Established on January 30, 1967. Some sources indicate that the commission was established as early as November 20, 1966. This was abolished at the Fifth Assembly. Reinstated as a Ministry of Materials Supply in the Sixth Assembly in December 1977.

Chairman	Period Served	Cabinet
*Han Sang-du	12/67–12/72	IV

ND **Ministry of National Defense [Minjok Powi Sŏng]**

Established at the time of the first cabinet on September 9, 1948. Abolished to become the Ministry of People's Armed Forces under the 1972 constitution in December 1972.

Minister	Period Served	Cabinet
*Ch'oe Yong-gŏn	9/48– 9/57	I
*Kim Kwang-hyŏp	9/57–10/62	II
*Kim Ch'ang-bong	10/62–12/67	III
*Kim Ch'ang-bong	12/67–12/72	IV

P **Premier [susang, ch'ongni]**

Premier	Period Served	Cabinet
*Kim Il Sung	9/48– 9/57	I
*Kim Il Sung	9/57–10/62	II
*Kim Il Sung	10/62–12/67	III
*Kim Il Sung	12/67–12/72	IV
*Kim Il	12/72– 4/76	V
Pak Sŏng-ch'ŏl	4/76–12/77	
*Yi Chong-ok	12/77–	VI

PAF **Ministry of People's Armed Forces [Inmin Muryŏk Pu]**

Established under the new Administration Council December 26, 1972, to succeed the Ministry of National Defense.

Minister	Period Served	Cabinet
*Ch'oe Hyŏn	12/72–12/77	V
*O Chin-u	12/77–	VI

PCC **People's Control Commission [Inmin Kŏmyŏl Wiwŏnhoe]**

Established from the Ministry of State Control by renaming the ministry on May 8, 1952. The commission was again renamed the Ministry of State Control and dissolved on January 20, 1955.

Chairman	Period Served
Yi Sŭng-yŏp	5/52– 3/53
Yi Ki-sŏk	3/53– 1/55

PCI **Ministry of Power and Chemical Industries [Tongyŏk Hwahak Kongŏp Sŏng]**

Established on August 31, 1959. Merged with the Heavy Industry Commission in April 1960.

Minister	Period Served
Kim Tu-sam	8/59– 4/60

PCO **Ministry of Power and Coal Industries [Chŏn'gi Sŏkt'an Kongŏp Sŏng]**

Since the third cabinet, October 23, 1962. It was abolished at the Fifth Assembly in December 1972, but was reinstated as the Ministry of Power Industry in 1977.

Minister	Period Served	Cabinet
*Chŏng Il-yong	10/62–12/64	III
Kim T'ae-gŭn	12/64–12/67	
*Kim T'ae-gŭn	12/67–12/72	IV

PFA **Ministry of Procurement and Food Administration [Sumae Yang-jŏng Sŏng]**

Established on May 11, 1956. Abolished on August 3, 1957, to become the Ministry of Rural Management. Reestablished in November 1958, but merged with the Ministry of Commerce in August 1959. Reestablished once again on July 11, 1962, but abolished at the Fifth Assembly in December 1972.

Minister	Period Served	Cabinet
O Ki-sŏp	5/56– 8/57	
Chŏng Sŏng-ŏn	11/58– 8/59	
Han Tae-yŏng	7/62–10/62	
*Han Tae-yŏng	10/62–12/67	III
*Pak Kwang-sŏn	12/67–12/72	IV

PH **Ministry of Public Health [Pogŏn Pu (Sŏng)]**

Since the first cabinet, September 1948.

Minister	Period Served	Cabinet
*Yi Pyŏng-nam	9/48– 9/57	I
*Yi Pyŏng-nam	9/57–10/59	II
Ch'oe Ch'ang-sŏk	5/60–10/62	
*Ch'oe Ch'ang-sŏk	10/62–12/67	III
*Yi Nak-bin	12/67–12/72	IV
*Yi Nak-bin	12/72–12/77	V
*Pak Myŏng-bin	12/77–	VI

PI **Ministry of Power Industry [Chŏllyŏk Kongŏp Pu]**

Reestablished to succeed the Ministry of Power and Coal Industries in December 1977 at the Sixth Assembly.

Minister	Period Served	Cabinet
*Yi Chi-ch'an	12/77–	VI

PS **Ministry of Public Security [Sahoe Anjŏn Pu (Sŏng)]**

Established on March 6, 1951. Incorporated into the Ministry of Interior in December 1952. Reestablished on October 23, 1962.

Minister	Period Served	Cabinet
Pang Hak-se	3/51–12/52	
*Sŏk San	10/62–12/67	III
*Sŏk San	12/67–12/72	IV
*Kim Pyŏng-ha	12/72–12/77	V
*Ch'oe Wŏn-ik	12/77–	VI

PSC **People's Service Commission [Inmin Pongsa Wiwŏnhoe]**

First established at the Fifth Assembly in December 1972.

Chairman	Period Served	Cabinet
Pak Sŏng-ch'ŏl	12/72–12/77	V
Yim Hyŏng-gu	12/77–	VI

R **Ministry of Railways [Ch'ŏlto Pu (Sŏng)]**

Established on July 13, 1951, by renaming the Ministry of Transportation. Abolished to reinstate the Ministry of Transportation on December 19, 1953. Reestablished as the Ministry of Railways on February 4, 1964. Abolished and became the Transportation and Communications Commission in December 1972, but reinstated at the Sixth Assembly in December 1977.

Minister	Period Served	Cabinet
Pak Ŭi-wan	7/51– 7/53	
Kim Hoe-il	7/53–12/53	
Kim Hoe-il	2/64– 9/66	
*Kim Kap-sun	12/67– 1/69	IV
*Pak Yong-sŏk	12/77–	VI

RC **Ministry of Rural Construction [Nongch'on Kŏnsŏl Sŏng]**

Established on September 1, 1961. Abolished on January 8, 1963.

Minister	Period Served	Cabinet
Kim Pyŏng-ik	9/61–10/62	
*Kim Pyŏng-ik	10/62– 1/63	III

RM **Ministry of Rural Management [Chibang Kyŏngni Sŏng]**

Established on August 3, 1957, but abolished in November 1958.

Minister	Period Served	Cabinet
Chŏng Sŏng-ŏn	8/57– 9/57	
*Chŏng Sŏng-ŏn	9/57–11/58	II

RTC **Railway Transportation Commission [Kyot'ong Unsu Wiwŏnhoe]**

Established on February 4, 1964, when the Ministry of Transportation was abolished. Abolished on November 17, 1965.

Chairman	Period Served
Ch'oe Yong-jin	2/64–11/65

S **Secretary [samujang]**

Sometime after the formation of the third cabinet the directors of the first, the second, and the fifth secretariats of the cabinet were given ministerial rank, and this was formally announced in the formation of the fourth cabinet. These were abolished with the new constitution in 1972. The sixth cabinet in December 1977 revived the post of secretary of the cabinet.

Director	Period Served	Cabinet
Ch'oe Chae-u (First Secretariat)	4/62–12/67	
*Ch'oe Chae-u (First Secretariat)	12/67–12/72	IV

Director	Period Served	Cabinet
O T'ae-bong		
(Fifth Secretariat)	9/62–12/67	
*O T'ae-bong		
(Fifth Secretariat)	12/67–12/72	IV
*An Yong-gak		
(Second Secretariat)	12/64–12/72	IV
Chŏng Yu-ho	7/63– 6/66	
Yi Kŭn-mo	7/63–12/63	
Yŏm T'ae-jun	4/64–12/67	
Pak Yong-sŏng	1/64–12/67	

Secretary	Period Served	Cabinet
*Kim Tu-yŏng	12/77–	VI

SC   Ministry of State Control [Kukka Kŏmyŏl Sŏng]

Established in the first cabinet on September 9, 1948. Abolished to become the People's Control Commission on May 8, 1952. Reinstated as the Ministry of State Control on January 20, 1955. Abolished once again to become the Ministry of Local Administration in May 1959. Reinstated once again as the Ministry of State Control in September 1966, but abolished at the time of the Fifth Assembly in December 1972.

Minister	Period Served	Cabinet
*Kim Wŏn-bong	9/48– 5/52	I
Ch'oe Ch'ang-ik	1/55– 8/55	
Yi Hyo-sun	8/55–11/55	
Kim Ik-sŏn	11/55– 5/56	
Pak Mun-gyu	5/56– 9/57	
*Pak Mun-gyu	9/57– 5/59	II
Kim Ik-sŏn	9/66–12/67	
*Kim Ik-sŏn	12/67–12/72	IV

SCC   State Construction Commission [Kukka Kŏnsŏl Wiwŏnhoe]

Established on June 8, 1953. At the time of the third cabinet this commission had a post of first vice-chairman in addition to the chairman. Both chairman and first vice-chairman carried ministerial rank. It was abolished at the Fifth Assembly in December 1972, but was reinstated at the Sixth Assembly in December 1977.

Chairman	Period Served	Cabinet
Kim Sŭng-hwa	6/53– 1/55	
Pak Ŭi-wan	1/55– 9/57	
*Pak Ŭi-wan	9/57–12/57	II
Kim Ŭng-sang	12/57– 8/60	
Nam Il	8/60–10/62	
*Nam Il	10/62–12/62	III
Kim Tu-sam	12/62–12/67	
*Kim Tu-sam	12/67–12/72	IV
*Kim Ŭng-sang	12/77–	VI

First Vice-chairman	Period Served	Cabinet
*Kim Ŭng-sang	8/60– 1/65	III

SCT **State Scientific and Technological Commission [Kukka Kwahak Kisul Wiwŏnhoe]**

Established on July 11, 1962, but abolished at the Fifth Assembly. Reactivated at the Sixth Assembly in December 1977.

Chairman	Period Served	Cabinet
O Tong-uk	7/62–10/62	
*O Tong-uk	10/62–12/67	III
*Kim Ŭng-sang	12/67–12/72	IV
*Chu Hwa-jong	12/77–	VI

SLI **State Light Industry Commission [Kukka Kyŏng Kongŏp Wiwŏnhoe]**

Established in January 1964. Dissolved to become the Ministry of Light Industry on January 10, 1966.

Chairman and vice-chairman; vice-chairman also had ministerial rank.

Chairman	Period Served
Yim Kye-ch'ŏl	1/64– 1/66

Vice-chairman	Period Served
Mun Man-uk	1/64– 1/66

SMB **Ministry of Ship Machine Building Industry [Sŏnbak Kigye Kongŏp Pu]**

Established at the Fifth Assembly in December 1972, but was not revived in the sixth cabinet.

Minister	Period Served	Cabinet
*Han Sŏng-yong	12/72–12/77	V

SPC   **State Planning Commission [Kukka Kyehoek Wiwŏnhoe]**

Since the first cabinet, September 9, 1948.

Chairman	Period Served	Cabinet
*Chŏng Chun-t'aek	9/48– 3/54	I
Pak Ch'ang-ok	3/54– 1/56	
Yi Chong-ok	1/56– 9/57	
*Yi Chong-ok	9/57– 7/59	II
Yim Kye-ch'ŏl	7/59–12/60	
Chŏng Chun-t'aek	12/60–10/62	
*Chŏng Chun-t'aek	10/62–12/67	III
*Chŏng Chun-t'aek	12/67–12/72	IV
*Ch'oe Chae-u	12/72–12/77	V
*Hong Sŏng-yong	12/77–	VI

T   **Ministry of Transportation [Kyot'ong Sŏng]**

Established in the first cabinet on September 9, 1948. Abolished to be named the Ministry of Railways on July 13, 1951. Renamed the Ministry of Transportation on December 19, 1953. Abolished on February 4, 1964, to become two separate ministries, the Ministry of Railway and the Railway Transportation Commission.

Minister	Period Served	Cabinet
*Chu Yŏng-ha	9/48–10/48	I
Pak Ŭi-wan	11/48– 7/51	
Kim Hoe-il	12/53– 9/57	
*Kim Hoe-il	9/57–10/62	II
*Kim Hoe-il	10/62– 2/64	III

TC   **Transportation and Communications Commission [Kyot'ong Ch'esin Wiwŏnhoe]**

Newly established at the Fifth Assembly in December 1972, combining several ministries, but this commission was disbanded to revert to various ministries in the Sixth Assembly in December 1977.

Minister	Period Served	Cabinet
Hyŏn Mu-gwang	12/72–12/77	V

TP **Ministry of Textile and Paper Industries [Pangjik Cheji Kongŏp Sŏng]**

Established on January 30, 1967, but abolished at the Fifth Assembly in December 1972.

Minister	Period Served	Cabinet
Yi Yang-suk	1/67–12/67	
*Yi Yang-suk	12/67–12/72	IV

VP **Vice-Premier [pususang, puch'ongni]**

First cabinet, September 9, 1948, to September 20, 1957. Three original appointees.

Vice-Premier	Period Served	Cabinet
*Pak Hŏn-yŏng	9/48– 3/53	I
*Hong Myŏng-hŭi	9/48– 9/57	I
*Kim Ch'aek	9/48– 1/51	I
Hŏ Ka-i	11/51– 3/53	
Ch'oe Ch'ang-ik	11/52– 9/56	
Ch'oe Yong-gŏn	11/52– 5/56	
Ch'oe Yong-gŏn	7/53– 9/57	
Pak Ŭi-wan	7/53– 9/57	
Pak Ch'ang-ok	3/54– 9/56	
Kim Il	3/54– 9/57	
Chŏng Chun-t'aek	5/56– 9/57	

Second cabinet, September 20, 1957, to October 23, 1962. Six original appointees. This number increased to seven on October 20, 1960.

Vice-Premier	Period Served	Cabinet
*Kim Il	9/57– 1/59	II
*Hong Myŏng-hŭi	9/57–10/62	II
*Chŏng Il-yong	9/57–10/62	II
*Nam Il	9/57–10/62	II
*Pak Ŭi-wan	9/57– 3/58	II
*Chŏng Chun-t'aek	9/57–10/62	II
Yi Chu-yŏn	3/58–10/62	
Yi Chong-ok	1/60–10/62	
Kim Kwang hyŏp	10/60–10/62	

Third cabinet, October 23, 1962, to December 16, 1967. Seven original appointees.

Vice-Premier	Period Served	Cabinet
*Kim Kwang-hyŏp	10/62–12/67	III
*Kim Ch'ang-man	10/62– 1/66	III
*Chŏng Il-yong	10/62–12/64	III
*Nam Il	10/62–12/67	III
*Yi Chong-ok	10/62–12/67	III
*Yi Chu-yŏn	10/62–12/67	III
*Chŏng Chun-t'aek	10/62–12/67	III
Ch'oe Yong-jin	7/64–12/67	
Ko Hyŏk	9/66– 3/67	
Pak Sŏng-ch'ŏl	10/66–12/67	
Kim Ch'ang-bong	10/66–12/67	

Fourth cabinet, December 16, 1967, to December 26, 1972. Eight original appointees.

Vice-Premier	Period Served	Cabinet
*Kim Kwang-hyŏp	12/67– 1968	IV
*Pak Sŏng-ch'ŏl	12/67–12/72	IV
*Kim Ch'ang-bong	12/67– 1968	IV
*Yi Chu-yŏn	12/67– 8/69	IV
*Nam Il	12/67–12/72	IV
*Yi Chong-ok	12/67–12/72	IV
*Ch'oe Yong-jin	12/67–12/72	IV
*Chŏng Chun-t'aek	12/67–12/72	IV

Fifth cabinet, December 26, 1972, to December 16, 1977. Six original appointees.

Vice-Premier	Period Served	Cabinet
*Pak Sŏng-ch'ŏl	12/72– 4/76	V
*Chŏng Chun-t'aek	12/72– 1/73	V
*Kim Man-gŭm	12/72–12/77	V
*Ch'oe Chae-u	12/72–12/77	V
*Nam Il	12/72– 3/76	V
*Hong Wŏn-gil	12/72–12/77	V

Sixth cabinet, December 16, 1977 - . Six original appointees.

Vice-Premier	Period Served	Cabinet
*Kye Ŭng-t'ae	12/77–	VI
*Hŏ Tam	12/77–	VI
*Chŏng Chun-gi	12/77–	VI
*Kang Sŏng-san	12/77–	VI
*Kong Chin-t'ae	12/77–	VI

Vice-Premier	Period Served	Cabinet
*Kim Tu-yŏng	12/77–	VI
No T'ae-sŏk	8/78–12/79	

VPF   First Vice-Premier [cheil pususang]

Office was created on January 20, 1959, but was abolished at the Fifth Assembly in December 1972.

First Vice-Premier	Period Served	Cabinet
Kim Il	1/59–10/62	
*Kim Il	10/62–12/67	III
*Kim Il	12/67–12/72	IV

WP   Ministry without Portfolio [Muimso Sŏng]

Established in the first cabinet, September 9, 1948. This ministry ceased to exist from the third cabinet, October 23, 1962.

Minister	Period Served	Cabinet
*Yi Kŭk-no	9/48–12/53	I
Chu Hwang-sŏp	7/53–10/53	
Yi Yong	12/53– 3/55	
Kim Tal-hyŏn	12/53– 9/57	
*Kim Tal-hyŏn	9/57– 3/59	II
*Hong Ki-hwang	9/57– 3/59	II

TABLES

4.1   Pattern of Reappointment from the First Cabinet to the Sixth Cabinet (Original Appointees Only)

4.2   Persons Who Served in the Same Post in More Than Two Cabinets (Original Appointees Only)

4.3   Number of Appointments to Cabinet Posts (Including Replacement Appointments, Concurrent Appointments, and Reappointments to the Same Ministry)

4.4   Number of Different Cabinet Posts Held (Including Replacement Appointments)

4.5   Records of Cabinet Service, 1948–1978 (Including Replacement Appointments)

4.6   Members of the Cabinets and Administration Councils (Including Interim Appointments)

For the abbreviations used in this section, see the abbreviations of ministries and commissions in the preceding section.

TABLE 4.1

Pattern of Reappointment from the First Cabinet to the Sixth Cabinet (Original Appointees Only)

First Cabinet	Second Cabinet	Third Cabinet	Fourth Cabinet	Fifth Cabinet	Sixth Cabinet
20 →	7* →	3 →	2 →	1 →	0
		Chŏng Chun-t'aek → **	Chŏng Chun-t'aek → ***		
		Kim Il Sung → **	Kim Il Sung → ***		
		Pak Mun-gyu			
	30 →	10* →	8 →	4 →	1
			Chŏng Chun-t'aek → **	Chŏng Chun-t'aek → ***	
			Chŏng Il-yong → **		
			Kim Il		
			Kim Il Sung		
			Kim Kwang-hyŏp		
			Nam Il → **		
			Yi Chong-ok → **		
			Yi Chu-yŏn		
		33 →	20* →	6 →	1
				Chŏng Chun-t'aek	
				Kim Il	
				Kim Man-gŭm	
				Nam Il	
				Pak Sŏng-ch'ŏl	
				Yi Chong-ok → **	
			47 →	12* →	3
					Kim Kyŏng-yŏn
					Kye Ŭng-t'ae
					Yi Chong-ok
				25 →	8*
					33

*An asterisk indicates the number of original appointees reappointed to the following cabinet as original appointees. For the names of these persons, see the listings of cabinet ministers by cabinets. The next number indicates how many of those reappointed were appointed for the third time, and their names are listed here. Those reappointed for the fourth time are indicated by two asterisks (**), and for the fifth time by three asterisks (***).

TABLE 4.2

Persons Who Served in the Same Post in More Than Two Cabinets
(original appointees only)

	Cabinet Post	Cabinets
Served four times		
Chŏng Chun-t'aek	vice-premier	II, III, IV, V
Kim Il Sung	premier	I, II, III, IV
Nam Il	vice-premier	II, III, IV, V
Served three times		
Chŏng Chun-t'aek	SCP	I, III, IV
Kim Man-gŭm	AC	III, IV, V
Kye Ŭng-t'ae	FT	IV, V, VI
Served twice		
Chŏng Il-yong	VP	II, III
Chŏng Tong-ch'ŏl	FR	III, IV
Hŏ Tam	FA	V, VI
Hong Myŏng-hŭi	VP	I, II
Kim Ch'ang-bong	ND	III, IV
Kim Hoe-il	T	II, III
Kim Il	VPF	III, IV
Kim Kwang-hyŏp	VP	III, IV
Kim Kyŏng-yŏn	F	V, VI
Kim Ŭng-sang	SCC	III, VI
Kim Yun-sang	FI	V, VI
Kong Chin-t'ae	EE	V, VI
Paek Sŏn-il	L	III, IV
Pak Im-t'ae	CO	V, VI
Pak Sŏng-ch'ŏl	FA	III, IV
Pak Sŏng-ch'ŏl	VP	IV, V
Pak Yŏng-sun	COM	III, IV
Sŏk San	PS	III, IV
Yi Ch'ang-sŏn	CA	V, VI
Yi Chong-ok	VP	III, IV
Yi Chu-yŏn	VP	III, IV
Yi Nak-bin	PH	IV, V
Yi Pyŏng-nam	PH	I, II

TABLE 4.3

Number of Appointments to Cabinet Posts (Including Replacement Appointments, Concurrent Appointments, and Reappointments to the Same Ministry)

Number of times appointed		Number of persons
1		68
2		37
3		20
4		10
5	Ch'oe Chae-u	8
	Han Sang-du	
	Hyŏn Mu-gwang	
	Kim Man-gŭm	
	Kim Pyŏng-sik	
	Kim Tu-sam	
	Kim Ŭng-sang	
	Mun Man-uk	
6	Kim Hoe-il	2
	Pak Ŭi-wan	
7	Kim Il	2
	Pak Mun-gyu	
8	Pak Sŏng-ch'ŏl	2
	Yi Chu-yŏn	
9	Nam Il	1
10	Chŏng Il-yong	1
11	----------------	----
12	Chŏng Chun-t'aek	2
	Yi Chong-ok	
	Total	153

TABLE 4.4
Number of Different Cabinet Posts Held
(Including Replacement Appointments)

Number of cabinet posts		Cabinet post	Number of persons
1			91
2			35
3			13
4	Han Sang-du	MEI, F, HIC, MSC	7
	Hyŏn Mu-gwang	MIC, MI, MIF, TC	
	Kim Il	A, VP, VPF, P	
	Kim Tu-sam	HI, EP, HIC, PCI	
	Nam Il	FA, VP, SCC, LIC	
	Pak Sŏng-ch'ŏl	FA, VP, PSC, P	
	Yi Chu-yŏn	C, F, VP, FT	
5	Ch'oe Chae-u	MI, HIC, S, VP, SPC	4
	Chŏng Chun-t'aek	SPC, CB, CI, VP, LIC	
	Kim Pyŏng-sik	CBM, CCM, CO, CIC, BM	
	Pak Ŭi-wan	T, R, VP, LI, SCC	
6	Pak Mun-gyu	AF, SC, A, LOA, IT, LAD	2
	Yi Chong-ok	LI, SPC, HIC, VP, MC, P	
7	Chŏng Il-yong	I, HI, VP, MEI, ME, PCO, BM	1
		Total	153

TABLE 4.5
Records of Cabinet Service, 1948---1978
(Including Replacement Appointments)

	Cabinet
Served in six cabinets (one)	
Yi Chong-ok	I, II, III, IV, V, VI
Served in five cabinets (three)	
Chŏng Chun-t'aek	I, II, III, IV, V
Kim Il	I, II, III, IV, V
Nam Il	I, II, III, IV, V
Served in four cabinets (six)	
Chŏng Il-yong	I, II, III, IV
Kim Il Sung	I, II, III, IV
Kim Man-gŭm	II, III, IV, V
Kim Ŭng-sang	II, III, IV, VI
Pak Sŏng-ch'ŏl	II, III, IV, V
Yi Chu-yŏn	I, II, III, IV
Served in three cabinets (sixteen)	
Ch'oe Chae-u	II, IV, V
Han Sang-du	II, III, IV
Hong Wŏn-gil	III, IV, V
Hyŏn Mu-gwang	III, IV, V
Kim Hoe-il	I, II, III
Kim Ik-sŏn	I, III, IV
Kim Kwang-hyŏp	II, III, IV
Kim Kyŏng-yŏn	IV, V, VI
Kim T'ae-gŭn	II, III, IV
Kye Ŭng-t'ae	IV, V, VI
Mun Man-uk	I, II, III
O Tong-uk	II, III, IV
Pak Mun-gyu	I, II, III
Sŏk San	II, III, IV
Yi Yang-suk	II, III, IV
Yun Ki-bok	II, III, IV
Served in two cabinets	
Forty-six persons	
Served in one cabinet	
Eighty-one persons	

TABLE 4.6

Members of the Cabinets and Administration Councils
(Including Interim Appointments)

	First Cabinet	Second Cabinet	Third Cabinet	Fourth Cabinet	Fifth Cabinet	Sixth Cabinet
An Sŭng-hak				C*		
An Yong-gak				S*		
Ch'ae Hŭi-jŏng						LA*
Chang Si-u	C*					
Chin Mun-dŏk				CM*		
Chin Pan-su	FT, IE	IE*, C				
Cho Ch'ang-dŏk						MNI*
Cho Kwan-ha			CO	CO*		
Cho Tong-sŏp			MI*			
Ch'oe Chae-ha	CO	CBM*				
Ch'oe Chae-u		MI, HIC		S*	VP*, SPC*	
Ch'oe Ch'ang-ik	F*, VP F, SC					
Ch'oe Ch'ang-sŏk		PH, COM	PH*			
Ch'oe Hyŏn		COM			PAF*	
Ch'oe Wŏn-ik						PS*
Ch'oe Yong-gŏn	ND*, VP					
Ch'oe Yong-jin			FI*, VP RTC	VP*		
Chŏng Chun-gi						VP*
Chŏng Chun-t'aek	SPC*, CB CI, VP	VP*, LIC SPC	VP* SPC*	VP* SPC*	VP*	
Chŏng Il-yong	I, HI VP, HI MEI	VP* ME*	VP* PCO*	BM*		
Chŏng Sŏng-ŏn	RM	RM*, PFA				
Chong Tong-ch'ŏl			FR*	FR*		
Chŏng Tu-hwan		C			LA*	
Chŏng Yu-ho		HIC	S			
Chu Hwa-jong						SCT*
Chu Hwang-sŏp	WP, FI CC	FI*				
Chu Yŏng-ha	T*					
Han Chŏn-jong		A*				

TABLE 4.6—*Continued*

	First Cabinet	Second Cabinet	Third Cabinet	Fourth Cabinet	Fifth Cabinet	Sixth Cabinet
Han Sang-du		MEI, F HIC	F*	MSC*		
Han Sŏl-ya	E, EC	EC*				
Han Sŏng-yong					SMB*	
Han Tae-yŏng		C, PFA	PFA*			
Hŏ Chŏng-suk	CP*, J	J*				
Hŏ Ka-i	VP					
Hŏ Sŏng-t'aek	L*	COI*				
Hŏ Sun						LI*
Hŏ Tam					FA*	VP*, FA*
Hong Ki-hwang		WP				
Hong Ki-ju	J					
Hong Myŏng-hŭi	VP*	VP*				
Hong Sŏng-yong						SPC
Hong Wŏn-gil			MIS	MIS*	VP*, MIC*	
Hyŏn Mu-gwang			MIC, MI MIF	MIF*	TC*	
Kang Chŏm-gu			FI	FI*		
Kang Sŏng-san						VP*
Kang Yŏng-ch'ang	MEI	MEI*				
Kim Ch'aek	I*, VP*					
Kim Ch'ang-bong			ND*, VP	VP*, ND*		
Kim Ch'ang-hŭp	COM					
Kim Ch'ang-man	E		VP*			
Kim Ch'i-do				MN*		
Kim Chong-hang		HE	HE*			
Kim Chŏng-ju	COM*					
Kim Hoe-il	R, T	T*, R	T*, R			
Kim Hwan					CI*	
Kim Ik-sŏn	SC		SC	SC*		
Kim Il	A, VP	VP*, VPF	VPF*	VPF*	P*	
Kim Il-dae						ED*
Kim Il Sung	P*	P*	P*	P*		
Kim Kap-sun				R*		
Kim Kwang-hyŏp		ND*, VP	VP*	VP*		
Kim Kyŏng-yŏn				EF*	F*	F*
Kim Man-gŭm		A	AC*	AC*	AC*, VP*	
Kim Nam-yun						BM*

TABLE 4.6—*Continued*

	First Cabinet	Second Cabinet	Third Cabinet	Fourth Cabinet	Fifth Cabinet	Sixth Cabinet
Kim Pyŏng-ha					PS*	
Kim Pyŏng-han				MEI*		
Kim Pyŏng-ik		RC	RC*			
Kim Pyŏng-sik		CBM	CIC*, BM			
		CCM, CO				
Kim Se-bong		C	C*			
Kim Sŏk-ki					E*	
Kim Sŭng-hwa	CC, SCC					
	CO					
Kim T'ae-gŭk						MS*
Kim T'ae-gŭn		COI	PCO	PCO*		
Kim Tal-hyŏn	WP	WP*				
Kim Tu-sam	HI, EP	EP*, PCI				
		HIC				
Kim Tu-yŏng						VP*
Kim Ŭng-gi		L*				
Kim Ŭng-sang		SCC	SCC*	SCT*		SCC*
			BM			
Kim Wŏn-bong	SC*, L					
Kim Yŏng-ch'ae						COM*
Kim Yun-hyŏk						SR*
Kim Yun-sang					FI*	FI*
Ko Chun-t'aek		COM*, FR				
Ko Hŭi-man		FR				
Ko Hyŏk			VP			
Kong Chin-t'ae					EE*	VP*, EE*
Kye Hyŏng-sun						MI*
Kye Ŭng-t'ae				FT*	FT*	FT*, VP*
Mun Man-uk	LI	LI*, LIC	LIC, SLI			
Mun Pyŏng-il					BM*	
Nam Il	FA	FA*, VP*	SCC*	VP*	VP*, LIC*	
		SCC	VP*			
No Pyŏng-u				LAD*		
No T'ae-sŏk		HIC				
O Chin-u						PAF*
O Ki-sŏp	PFA					
O Sŏng-yŏl				LST*		
O T'ae-bong				S*		

TABLE 4.6—*Continued*

	First Cabinet	Second Cabinet	Third Cabinet	Fourth Cabinet	Fifth Cabinet	Sixth Cabinet
O Tong-uk		SCT	SCT*	AS*		
Paek Hong-gwŏn	CB					
Paek Nam-un	E*					
Paek Sŏn-il			L*	L*		
Pak Ch'ang-ok	VP, SPC MI					
Pak Chŏng-ae		A				
Pak Hŏn-yŏng	VP*, FA*					
Pak Il-u	IT* COM					
Pak Im-t'ae					CO*	CO*
Pak Kwang-sŏn				PFA*		
Pak Mun-gyu	AF*, SC A	LOA SC*	IT* LAD			
Pak Myŏng-bin						PH*
Pak Sŏng-ch'ŏl		FA	FA* VP	FA* VP*	VP*, P PSC*	
Pak Ŭi-wan	T, R, VP LI, SCC	SCC*				
Pak Ung-gŏl		CU	CU			
Pak Yŏng-sin			CU	CU*		
Pak Yong-sŏk					R*	
Pak Yong-sŏng		LIC	LIC*, S			
Pak Yŏng-sun			COM*	COM*		
Pang Hak-se	PS, IT	IT*				
Sŏ Kwan-hŭi						AC*
Sŏk San		IT	PS*	PS*		
Song Ch'ang-nyŏm		FR				
Song Pok-ki			CI	CI*		
Song Pong-uk		F				
Wŏn Tong-gu						CI*
Yang Hyŏng-sŏp				HE*		
Yang T'ae-gŭn		L				
Yi Chae-yŏng			MEI			
Yi Ch'ang-sŏn					CA*	CA*
Yi Chang-su				CE*		
Yi Chi-ch'an					PI*	
Yi Ch'ŏl-bong					LST*	

TABLE 4.6—*Continued*

	First Cabinet	Second Cabinet	Third Cabinet	Fourth Cabinet	Fifth Cabinet	Sixth Cabinet
Yi Chong-ok	LI, LI SPC	SPC*, VP HIC, MC	VP*, MC*	VP*	HIC*	P*
Yi Ch'ŏn-ho	CI	CI*				
Yi Chu-yŏn	C, F	F*, VP FT	FT, VP*	VP*		
Yi Ho-hyŏk			FD	FD*		
Yi Hyo-sun	SC					
Yi Il-gyŏng		EC, CE FT	FT*			
Yi Ki-sŏk	PCC, CM					
Yi Kŭk-no	WP*					
Yi Kŭn-mo			S			
Yi Nak-bin				PH*	PH*	
Yi Pyŏng-nam	PH*	PH*				
Yi Sŭng-yŏp	J*					
Yi Yang-suk		C	TP	TP*		
Yi Yong	CM*, J WP					
Yim Hae		FT, A				
Yim Hyŏng-gu						PSC*
Yim Kye-ch'ŏl		SPC, LIC	SLI			
Yŏm T'ae-jun			CM*, S			
Yu Ch'ŏl-mok		FI				
Yu Ch'uk-un	COI					
Yun Ho-sŏk						MEI*
Yun Ki-bok		CE	CE	F*		
Yun Kong-hŭm	F, C					

*Original appointee to the post; those without asterisks were interim appointees.

NOTES

1. *Chosŏn chungang yŏn'gam, 1950* (Pyongyang: Chosŏn Chungang T'ongsin-sa, 1950), p. 12.

2. *Nodong sinmun*, September 21, 1957.

3. *Nodong sinmun*, October 24, 1962.

4. *Nodong sinmun*, December 17, 1967.

5. *Nodong sinmun*, December 29, 1972.

6. *Nodong sinmun*, December 18, 1977.

5

The Central Court and the Central Procurator's Office

THE JUDICIARY

Under the 1948 constitution, the highest judicial organ in the North was the Supreme Court, but the name was changed in the 1972 constitution to the Central Court. Despite the change in the name, the structure and functions of the court more or less remained the same. In addition to the Central Court there are the Provincial Courts, the People's Court, and the Special Courts. The People's Court is the lowest court, and its decisions can be appealed to the Provincial Court. However, decisions of the Provincial Court are final, and there is no appeal from there. An emergency case may be submitted for review to the Central Court from the Provincial Court, but this is an exception rather than the rule. The Special Court hears cases concerning military personnel and railway and water transportation workers. Thus, the Special Courts consist of the Military Court and the Traffic and Transportation Court (not to be confused with the traffic court dealing with automobile traffic). The Central Court hears those cases involving criminal and civil offenses of nationwide importance. It also reviews those exceptional cases that are appealed from the Provincial Court, but these are rare.

The Central Court is accountable to the Supreme People's Assembly, the president of the republic, and the Central People's Committee; and the local courts are similarly answerable to the respective local People's Assemblies. The Central Court, however, supervises the judicial work of all courts. Each court must have at least one judge and two people's assessors to hear a case. The party sets policy and guides judicial work. All hearings must be held in public and in the Korean language, and the accused has the right to a defense counsel. All judges and people's assessors are elected by the Standing Committee of the Supreme People's Assembly.

In the past thirty years, the committee has elected six chief justices and two presidents of the Central Court. The 1972 constitution changed the name of chief justice of the Supreme Court to president of the Central Court. Kim Ik-sŏn, who served thirteen years from the First to the Third Assembly at various intervals, was in the position for the longest period. President Pang Hak-se, who has served since the Fifth Assembly, is next with six years. All others served for relatively short periods, and several were purged, including Cho Sŏng-mo, Hwang Se-hwan, and Kim Ha-un. From the First to the Third Assembly, the Standing Committee elected several chief justices to replace those purged, but since the Fourth Assembly, chief justices have served out their terms. It is interesting to note that a number of chief justices served concurrently in functional committees in the Assembly, most commonly the Legislative Committee.

In contrast to the chief justice and president of the Central Court, the procurator-general of the Central Procurator's Office is appointed by the Supreme People's Assembly, and all other procurators are appointed by the procurator-general. The office of the procurator-general is responsible to the Assembly, the president of the republic, and the Central People's Committee; and the Provincial, City, County, and Special Procurators' offices are accountable to the Central Procurator's Office. The constitution provides that the procurators perform the functions of general surveillance, investigation, preliminary examination, and ultimate prosecution of criminals and offenders and take appropriate legal sanctions to preserve the laws and implement policies set by the party.

As in the case of the chief justices, many procurators-general were removed before their terms were up during the First and the Third Assembly, but from the Fourth Assembly on the procurators-general began to serve out their terms of office. Nine persons served as procurator-general, but many were purged. Pak Se-ch'ang, who served the longest, from 1957 to 1964, was also purged. None of the procurators-general served concurrently in any functional committees of the Assembly until the Sixth Assembly. Yi Chin-su, who was appointed procurator-general in the Sixth Assembly, is also a member of the Legislative Committee of the Assembly. It is interesting to note that several people served the republic both as chief justice and as procurator-general. For example, Cho Sŏng-mo, who was the second chief justice of the Central Court from 1955 to 1956, left the post to become procurator-general from 1956 to 1957, and Yi Kuk-chin, who was appointed procurator-general in 1964 and served two years, was elected chief justice in 1966.

Since 1967, both chief justices and procurators-general have served out their terms of office, and this may be indicative of a rather stable political atmosphere in the North.

CHIEF JUSTICES AND PRESIDENTS OF THE CENTRAL COURT

FIRST SUPREME PEOPLE'S ASSEMBLY. SEPTEMBER 2–10, 1948.

Kim Ik-sŏn   September 1948–March 1955
Cho Sŏng-mo   March 1955–March 1956
(elected at the ninth session of the Standing Committee, March 9–11, 1955)
Hwang Se-hwan March 1956–September 1957
(elected at the eleventh session of the Standing Committee, March 10–13, 1956)

SECOND SUPREME PEOPLE'S ASSEMBLY. SEPTEMBER 18–20, 1957.

Kim Ha-un   September 1957–October 1959
Hŏ Chŏng-suk October 1959–November 1960
(elected at the sixth session of the Standing Committee, October 26–28, 1959)
Kim Ik-sŏn   November 1960–October 1962
(elected at the eighth session of the Standing Committee, November 19–24, 1960)

THIRD SUPREME PEOPLE'S ASSEMBLY. OCTOBER 22–23, 1962.

Kim Ik-sŏn   October 1962–September 1966
Yi Kuk-chin   September 1966–December 1967
(There is no official report on the election of Yi Kuk-chin by the Standing Committee. He is said to have assumed the post on September 30, 1966, but neither the fifth nor the sixth session of the Standing Committee, in April and November, 1966, respectively, reported the change. It is assumed that Yi served out the term of Kim Ik-sŏn from the Third Assembly.)

FOURTH SUPREME PEOPLE'S ASSEMBLY. DECEMBER 14–16, 1967.

Yi Yong-gu   December 1967–December 1972

FIFTH SUPREME PEOPLE'S ASSEMBLY. DECEMBER 25–28, 1972.

Pang Hak-se   December 1972–December 1977

SIXTH SUPREME PEOPLE'S ASSEMBLY. DECEMBER 15–17, 1977.

Pang Hak-se   December 1977–

PROCURATORS-GENERAL
OF THE CENTRAL PROCURATOR'S OFFICE

FIRST SUPREME PEOPLE'S ASSEMBLY. SEPTEMBER 2–10, 1948.

Chang Hae-u   September 1948–June 1952

Yi Song-un   June 1952–March 1956
(appointed during the fifth and sixth sessions of the First Assembly, toward the end of the Korean war)

Cho Sŏng-mo   March 1956–September 1957
(appointed at the eleventh session of the Standing Committee, March 10–13, 1956)

SECOND SUPREME PEOPLE'S ASSEMBLY. SEPTEMBER 18–20, 1957.

Pak Se-ch'ang   September 1957–October 1962

THIRD SUPREME PEOPLE'S ASSEMBLY. OCTOBER 22–23, 1962.

Pak Se-ch'ang   October 1962–March 1964

Yi Kuk-chin   March 1964–September 1966
(appointed at the third session of the Standing Committee, March 26–28, 1964)

Yi Song-un   September 1966–December 1967
(There is no official record of Yi Song-un's appointment. Yi Kuk-chin was appointed chief justice of the Central Court, and Yi Song-un served the remainder of Yi Kuk-chin's term.)

FOURTH SUPREME PEOPLE'S ASSEMBLY. DECEMBER 14–16, 1967.

Yun T'ae-hong   December 1967–December 1972

FIFTH SUPREME PEOPLE'S ASSEMBLY. DECEMBER 25–28, 1972.

Chŏng Tong-ch'ŏl   December 1972–December 1977

SIXTH SUPREME PEOPLE'S ASSEMBLY. DECEMBER 15–17, 1977.

Yi Chin-su   December 1977–

6

The Constitution and the Bylaws

THE CONSTITUTIONS OF THE REPUBLIC

The socialist constitution that is in force today is only the second constitution of the republic. It was adopted in December 1972 at the Fifth
Supreme People's Assembly. The first constitution of the republic came
into force even before the formal establishment of the government in the
North. A draft constitution was adopted at a special session of the People's Assembly of North Korea on April 28, 1948. This was the work of a
forty-nine-member committee to draft the constitution under the chairmanship of Kim Tu-bong. This draft constitution was adopted on September 8, 1948, at the First Supreme People's Assembly and became the
constitution of the Democratic People's Republic of Korea. It had 10
chapters and 104 articles and had provisions on basic principles, rights
and duties of citizens, central and local legislative and executive organs,
courts, budgets, national defense, amendment procedures, and the state
emblem and capital.[1]

During the twenty-four years of the life of the first constitution from
1948 to 1972, it was amended on six different occasions. The amendments all came during the first fourteen years.

The first revision was made on April 23, 1954, at the time of the
seventh session of the First Supreme People's Assembly and dealt with
two articles, Article 37, paragraph 8, and Article 58. Article 37 dealt
with the abolition of the *myŏn* as an administrative subdivision, maintaining only province, city, county, and *ri* administrative districts. Article 58 was revised to accommodate newly established and reorganized
cabinet ministries and committees. The constitution provided a fixed
number of cabinet posts, and this was changed to meet the needs of the
growing cabinets and ministerial commissions.

The second revision was in the same year, October 30, 1954, at the
eighth session of the First Assembly, and dealt with Article 36 and arti-

cles concerning the local organizations. The amendment of Article 36 extended the term of the representatives for one year, from three to four years. By this time, the representatives had already served for six years from 1948. No sessions were held during the Korean war, 1950–1953, and perhaps this accounts for the extension of their terms. Since the Second Supreme People's Assembly was not convened until 1957, the representatives of the First Supreme People's Assembly, in fact, served for nine years.

The revision of Articles 68–81 in Chapter 5 dealt with the delegation of legislative functions to the People's Assembly and administrative functions to the People's Committee in local organizations. Formerly the People's Committee performed both functions in local organizations from province to *ri*. This amendment was only a partial application of the principle of differentiated function of the People's Committee, because there were several other provisions in the constitution that dealt with this problem. Failure to amend all provisions related to this problem prompted another revision in the following session of the Assembly.

The third amendment involved six articles, Articles 2, 3, 48, 53, 58, and 83. Of these, Articles 2, 3, and 83 dealt with the redesignation of the local People's Assembly from what was called a local People's Committee. Article 48 involved the organization of the Standing Committee of the Supreme People's Assembly. The original article stipulated seventeen committee members, but this was amended to allow more flexibility in the composition of the Standing Committee by eliminating the exact number of members. The amendment to Article 53 involved only a change of wording: the word "directives" *(chisi)* was changed to read "orders" *(myŏngyŏng)*. The article stipulated that the cabinet had the power to issue "orders" (instead of "directives"). The full meaning of this change is difficult to understand, unless it was intended to implement more forcefully the decisions of the cabinet. Article 58 dealt with the composition of the cabinet and was being amended for the second time. At this time a separate law concerning the formation of various cabinet ministries was passed, but details of the law were not made public.

The fourth amendment involved the lowering of the voting age from twenty to eighteen years. This time the Supreme People's Assembly merely went through the motions of legalizing what had already been approved in the Standing Committee in September 1956. This was formally approved at the twelfth session of the First Supreme People's Assembly on November 7, 1956.

The content of the fifth amendment is not known. The agenda of the third session of the Second Supreme People's Assembly, held June 9–11,

1958, included organization of a committee to draft an amendment and supplement to the constitution. This was proposed by Hŏ Chŏng-suk and approved, but it is not known what this committee did. The work of the committee was never reported, and there is no record of an amendment or supplement to the constitution resulting from the work of the committee.

The sixth amendment was approved on October 22, 1962, at the time of the Third Supreme People's Assembly. It amended Articles 35, 57, 58, and 59 and abolished Article 61. Article 35 deals with the ratio of representatives to the Supreme People's Assembly, and the amendment set the new ratio at one representative for each 30,000 population. Formerly the ratio was one for each 50,000. Articles 57, 58, and 59 all deal with the formation of the cabinet and its operation. Precise changes in these articles were not announced, and any supplements to these articles were not revealed in subsequent meetings. Article 61, which was abolished, stipulated that the premier, vice-premiers, and ministers must take an oath of office before the Supreme People's Assembly with the wording provided in the constitution.

The North Koreans have not made public an amended version of the constitution since November 1956. Most available versions of the first constitution incorporated the amendments up to November 1956; there is none available that incorporates the amendments of June 1958 or October 1962. In fact, the North Koreans did not publish an edition of the constitution in the 1960s.[2]

The new constitution, much lengthier than the first one, has 11 chapters and 149 articles. The basic format and a number of features are similar to the first constitution. In the fields of the rights and duties of citizens, the supreme legislative organs, the local organizations, the courts, the emblem and flag, among others, the provisions are similar to those in the first constitution. However, there were drastic changes in the Administrative Organs of the State, and the section dealing with Basic Principles of the Republic was expanded. The administrative changes included the creation of the office of the president of the republic, the Central People's Committee, the Administration Council, and others. The basic principle of the constitution was expanded to incorporate political, economic, and cultural aspects that are fundamental to understanding the republic. Several redundant chapters of the first constitution were left out, such as those chapters and provisions dealing with the national budget, national security, and amendment to the constitution. Other than these major changes, there were a few minor changes, such as the lowering of the voting age from eighteen to seventeen and changing of the capital of the republic from Seoul to Pyongyang.

The two major changes, the basic principles and the administrative restructuring, are adjustments to the growth of the republic. The elaborate explanation of the basic principles in three chapters seems to reflect the incorporation of the North Korean campaign of three revolutions—the ideological, technical, and cultural revolutions—in addition to the long campaign to be self-reliant. While such lofty ideals are explained in detail, the administrative restructuring of the state organization is patterned after that of the People's Republic of China. These changes notwithstanding, the present constitution can be said to have grown out of the first constitution, and many provisions of the first constitution were kept in the present constitution.

The text of the constitution presented here is the North Korean translation with minor corrections.[3]

TEXT OF THE SOCIALIST CONSTITUTION OF 1972

Chapter I

POLITICS

Article 1. The Democratic People's Republic of Korea is an independent socialist State representing the interests of all the Korean people.

Article 2. The Democratic People's Republic of Korea rests on the politico-ideological unity of the entire people based on the worker-peasant alliance led by the working class, on the socialist relations of production and the foundation of an independent national economy.

Article 3. The Democratic People's Republic of Korea is a revolutionary State [power] which has inherited the brilliant traditions formed during the glorious revolutionary struggle against the imperialist aggressors and for the liberation of the homeland and for the freedom and well-being of the people.

Article 4. The Democratic People's Republic of Korea is guided in its activity by the *chuch'e* idea of the Workers' Party of Korea, a creative application of Marxism-Leninism to the conditions of our country.

Article 5. The Democratic People's Republic of Korea strives to achieve the complete victory of socialism in the northern half, drive out foreign forces on a national scale, reunify the country peacefully on a democratic basis and attain complete national independence.

Article 6. In the Democratic People's Republic of Korea class antagonisms and all forms of exploitation and oppression of man by man have been eliminated forever.

The State defends and protects the interests of the workers, peasants, soldiers and working intellectuals freed from exploitation and oppression.

Article 7. The sovereignty of the Democratic People's Republic of Korea rests with the workers, peasants, soldiers and working intellectuals.

The working people exercise power through their representative organs—the Supreme People's Assembly and local People's Assemblies at all levels.

Article 8. The organs of State [power] at all levels from the county People's Assembly to the Supreme People's Assembly are elected on the principle of universal, equal and direct suffrage by secret ballot.

Deputies to the organs of State [power] at all levels are accountable to the electors for their activities.

Article 9. All State organs in the Democratic People's Republic of Korea are formed and run in accordance with the principle of democratic centralism.

Article 10. The Democratic People's Republic of Korea exercises the dictatorship of the proletariat and pursues class and mass lines.

Article 11. The State defends the socialist system against the subversive activities of hostile elements at home and abroad and revolutionizes and "working-classicizes" the whole [of] society by intensifying the ideological revolution.

Article 12. The State, in all its work, thoroughly implements the great Ch'ŏngsalli spirit and Ch'ŏngsalli method that assist the work of the lower echelon by the upper echelon, respect the public opinion, and arouse self-conscious enthusiasm of the masses by giving priority to political work and work with the people.

Article 13. The Ch'ŏllima Movement in the Democratic People's Republic of Korea is the general line in the building of socialism.

The State accelerates socialist construction to the maximum by constantly developing the Ch'ŏllima Movement in depth and breadth.

Article 14. The Democratic People's Republic of Korea is based on the all-people, nationwide system of defense and carries through a self-defense military line.

It is the mission of the armed forces of the Democratic People's Republic of Korea to protect the interests of the workers, peasants and other working people, defend the socialist system and revolutionary gains and safeguard the freedom and independence of the country and peace.

Article 15. The Democratic People's Republic of Korea protects the democratic, national rights of Koreans overseas and their legitimate rights under international law.

Article 16. The Democratic People's Republic of Korea is completely equal and independent in its relations with foreign countries.

The State establishes diplomatic as well as political, economic and cultural relations with all friendly countries, on the principles of complete equality, independence, mutual respect, noninterference in each other's internal affairs and mutual benefit.

The State, in accordance with the principles of Marxism-Leninism and proletarian internationalism, unites with the socialist countries, unites with all peoples of the world opposed to imperialism and actively supports and encourages their national-liberation and revolutionary struggles.

Article 17. The law of the Democratic People's Republic of Korea reflects the will and interests of the workers, peasants and other working people, and it is consciously observed by all State organs, enterprises, social cooperative organizations and citizens.

Chapter II

ECONOMY

Article 18. In the Democratic People's Republic of Korea the means of production are owned by the State and cooperative organizations.

Article 19. The property of the State belongs to the whole people.

There is no limit to the properties that the State may own.

All natural resources of the country, major factories and enterprises, ports, banks, transport and communication establishments are owned solely by the State.

State property plays a leading role in the economic development of the Democratic People's Republic of Korea.

Article 20. The property of cooperative organizations is collectively owned by the working people involved in the cooperative economy.

Land, draught animals, farm implements, fishing boats, buildings, as well as small and medium factories and enterprises may be owned by cooperative organizations.

The State protects the property of cooperative organizations by law.

Article 21. The State strengthens and develops the socialist cooperative economic system and gradually transforms the property of cooperative organizations into the property of all the people on the basis of the voluntary will of the entire membership.

Article 22. Personal property is property for the personal uses of the working people.

The personal property of the working people is derived from socialist distribution according to work done and from additional benefits granted by the State and society.

The products from the inhabitants' supplementary husbandry including those from the small plots of cooperative farmers are also personal property.

The State protects the working people's personal property by law and guarantees their right to inherit it.

Article 23. The State regards it as the supreme principle of its activities to steadily improve the material and cultural standards of the people.

The constantly increasing material wealth of society in the Democratic People's Republic of Korea is used entirely to promote the well-being of the working people.

Article 24. The foundation of an independent national economy in the Democratic People's Republic of Korea is the material guarantee of the prosperity and development of the country and the improvement of the people's well-being.

In the Democratic People's Republic of Korea the historic task of industrialization has been accomplished successfully.

The State strives to consolidate and develop the successes in industrialization and further strengthen the material and technical foundations of socialism.

Article 25. The State accelerates the technical revolution to eliminate the distinctions between heavy and light labor and between agricultural and industrial labor, free the working people from arduous labor and gradually narrow the difference between physical and mental labor.

Article 26. The State enhances the role of the county and strengthens its guidance and assistance to the countryside in order to eliminate the difference between town and country and class distinction between workers and peasants.

The State undertakes at its own expense the building of production facilities for the cooperative farms and modern houses in the countryside.

Article 27. The working masses are the makers of history. Socialism and communism are built by the creative labor of millions of working people.

All the working people of the country take part in labor, and work for the country and the people and for their own benefit by displaying conscious enthusiasm and creativity.

The State correctly applies the socialist principle of distribution according to the quantity and quality of work done, while constantly raising the political and ideological consciousness of the working people.

Article 28. The working day is eight hours. The State may reduce the length of the working day depending upon the difficulties and special categories of work.

The State guarantees that working hours are fully utilized through the proper organization of labor and the strengthening of labor discipline.

Article 29. In the Democratic People's Republic of Korea the minimum age for starting work is 16 years.

The State prohibits the employment of children under working age.

Article 30. The State directs and manages the nation's economy through the Taean work system, an advanced socialist form of economic management whereby the economy is operated and managed scientifically and rationally on the basis of the collective strength of the producer masses, and through the new system of agricultural guidance whereby agricultural management is done by industrial methods.

Article 31. The national economy of the Democratic People's Republic of Korea is a planned economy.

In accordance with the laws of economic development of socialism, the State draws up and carries out the plans for the development of the national economy so that the balance of accumulation and consumption can be maintained correctly, economic construction accelerated, the people's living standards steadily raised and the nation's defense potential strengthened.

The State ensures a high rate of growth in production and a proportionate development of the national economy by implementing a policy of unified and detailed planning.

Article 32. The Democratic People's Republic of Korea compiles and implements the State budget according to the national economic development plan.

The State systematically increases its accumulation and expands and develops socialist property by intensifying the struggle for increased production and economy, and by exercising strict financial control in all fields.

Article 33. The State abolishes taxation, a relic of the old society.

Article 34. In the Democratic People's Republic of Korea foreign trade is conducted by the State or under its supervision.

The State develops foreign trade on the principles of complete equality and mutual benefit.

The State pursues a tariff policy in order to protect the independent national economy.

Chapter III

CULTURE

Article 35. In the Democratic People's Republic of Korea all people study and a socialist national culture flourishes and develops fully.

Article 36. The Democratic People's Republic of Korea, by thoroughly carrying out the cultural revolution, trains all the working people to be builders of socialism and communism who are equipped with a profound knowledge of nature and society and a high level of culture and technology.

Article 37. The Democratic People's Republic of Korea builds a true people's revolutionary culture which serves the socialist working people.

In building a socialist national culture, the State opposes the cultural infiltration of imperialism and the tendency to return to the past and protects the heritage of national culture and takes over and develops it in keeping with socialist reality.

Article 38. The State eliminates the way of life left over from the old society and introduces the new socialist way of life in all fields.

Article 39. The State carries into effect the principles of socialist pedagogy and brings up the rising generation to be steadfast revolutionaries who fight for society and the people, to be men of a new communist mould who are knowledgeable, virtuous and healthy.

Article 40. The State gives top priority to public education and the training of cadres for the nation and blends general education with technological education, and education with productive labor.

Article 41. The State introduces universal compulsory ten-year senior middle school education for all young people under working age.

The State grants to all pupils and students education free of charge.

Article 42. The State trains competent technicians and experts by developing the general educational system as well as different forms of part-time education for those at work.

The students of higher educational institutions and higher specialized schools are granted scholarships.

Article 43. The State gives all children a compulsory one-year preschool education.
The State brings up all children of preschool age in creches and kindergartens at State and public expense.

Article 44. The State accelerates the nation's scientific and technological progress by thoroughly establishing *chuch'e* in scientific research and strengthening creative cooperation between scientists and producers.

Article 45. The State develops a *chuch'e*-oriented, revolutionary literature and art, national in form and socialist in content.
The State encourages the creative activities of writers and artists and draws the broad masses of workers, farmers and other working people into literary and artistic activities.

Article 46. The State safeguards our language from the policy of the imperialists and their stooges aimed at destroying it, and develops it to meet present-day needs.

Article 47. The State steadily improves the physical fitness of the working people.
The State fully prepares the entire people for work and national defense by popularizing physical culture and sports and developing physical training for national defense.

Article 48. The State consolidates and develops the system of universal free medical service and pursues a policy of preventive medical care so as to protect people's lives and promote the health of the working people.

Chapter IV

FUNDAMENTAL RIGHTS AND DUTIES OF CITIZENS

Article 49. In the Democratic People's Republic of Korea the rights and duties of citizens are based on the collectivist principle of "One for all and all for one."

Article 50. The State effectively guarantees genuine democratic rights and liberties as well as the material and cultural well-being of all citizens.
In the Democratic People's Republic of Korea the rights and freedoms

of citizens increase with the consolidation and development of the socialist system.

Article 51. Citizens all enjoy equal rights in the political, economic and cultural and all other spheres of State and public activity.

Article 52. All citizens who have reached the age of 17 have the right to elect and be elected, irrespective of sex, race, occupation, length of residence, property status, education, party affiliation, political views and religion.

Citizens serving in the armed forces also have the right to elect and be elected.

Those who are deprived by a Court decision of the right to vote and insane persons are denied the right to elect and be elected.

Article 53. Citizens have freedom of speech, the press, assembly, association and of demonstration.

The State guarantees conditions for the free activities of democratic political parties and social organizations.

Article 54. Citizens have freedom of religious belief and freedom of anti-religious propaganda.

Article 55. Citizens are entitled to make complaints and submit petitions.

Article 56. Citizens have the right to work.

All able-bodied citizens can choose occupations according to their desire and skills and are provided with stable jobs and working conditions.

Citizens work according to their ability and receive remuneration according to the quantity and quality of work done.

Article 57. Citizens have the right to rest. This right is ensured by the eight-hour working day, paid leave, accommodation at health resorts and holiday homes at State expense and by an ever-expanding network of cultural facilities.

Article 58. Citizens are entitled to free medical care, and persons who have lost the ability to work because of old age, sickness or deformity, old people and children without guardian have the right to material assistance. This right is ensured by free medical care, a growing network of hospitals, sanatoria and other medical institutions, and the State social insurance and security system.

Article 59. Citizens have the right to education. This right is ensured by an advanced educational system, free compulsory education and other State educational measures for the people.

Article 60. Citizens have freedom of scientific, literary and artistic pursuits.

The State grants benefits to innovators and inventors.

Copyright and patent rights are protected by law.

Article 61. Revolutionary fighters, the families of revolutionary and patriotic martyrs, the families of People's Armymen, and disabled soldiers enjoy the special protection of the State and society.

Article 62. Women are accorded equal social status and rights with men.

The State affords special protection to mothers and children through maternity leave, shortened working hours for mothers of large families, a wide network of maternity hospitals, creches and kindergartens and other measures.

The State frees women from the heavy burden of household chores and provides every condition for them to participate in public life.

Article 63. Marriage and the family are protected by the State.

The State pays great attention to consolidating the family, the cell of society.

Article 64. Citizens are guaranteed inviolability of the person and the home and privacy of correspondence.

No citizen can be placed under arrest except by law.

Article 65. All Korean citizens in foreign lands are legally protected by the Democratic People's Republic of Korea.

Article 66. The Democratic People's Republic of Korea extends the right of asylum to foreign citizens persecuted for fighting for peace and democracy, national independence and socialism, or for the freedom of scientific and cultural pursuits.

Article 67. Citizens must strictly observe the laws of the State and the socialist norms of life and the socialist rules of conduct.

Article 68. Citizens must display a high degree of collectivist spirit.

Citizens must cherish their collective and organization and develop the revolutionary trait of working devotedly for the good of society and the people and for the interests of the homeland and the revolution.

Article 69. It is the sacred duty and honor of citizens to work.

Citizens must voluntarily and honestly participate in work and strictly observe labor discipline and working hours.

Article 70. Citizens must take good care of State and communal property, combat all forms of misappropriation and wastage and run the nation's economy assiduously with the attitude of masters.

The property of the State and social cooperative organizations is inviolable.

Article 71. Citizens must heighten their revolutionary vigilance against the maneuvers of the imperialists and all hostile elements opposed to our country's socialist system, and must strictly preserve State secrets.

Article 72. National defense is a supreme duty and honor for citizens.

Citizens must defend the country and serve in the army as stipulated by law.

Treason against the country and the people is the most heinous of crimes.

Those who betray the country and the people are punishable with all the severity of the law.

Chapter V

THE SUPREME PEOPLE'S ASSEMBLY

Article 73. The Supreme People's Assembly is the highest organ of State [power] in the Democratic People's Republic of Korea.

Legislative power is exercised exclusively by the Supreme People's Assembly.

Article 74. The Supreme People's Assembly is composed of deputies elected on the principle of universal, equal and direct suffrage by secret ballot.

Article 75. The Supreme People's Assembly is elected for a term of four years.

A new Supreme People's Assembly is elected according to the decision of the Standing Committee of the Supreme People's Assembly prior to the expiry of its term of office. When unavoidable circumstances render the election impossible, the term of office is prolonged until the election.

Article 76. The Supreme People's Assembly has the authority to:

1. adopt or amend the constitution, laws and ordinances;

2. establish the basic principles of domestic and foreign policies of the State;

3. elect the President of the Democratic People's Republic of Korea;

4. elect or recall the Vice-Presidents of the Democratic People's Republic of Korea, and the Secretary and members of the Central People's

Committee on the recommendation of the President of the Democratic People's Republic of Korea;

5. elect or recall members of the Standing Committee of the Supreme People's Assembly;

6. elect or recall the Premier of the Administration Council on the recommendation of the President of the Democratic People's Republic of Korea;

7. elect or recall the Vice-Chairmen of the National Defense Commission on the recommendation of the President of the Democratic People's Republic of Korea;

8. elect or recall the President of the Central Court and appoint or remove the Procurator-General of the Central Procurator's Office;

9. approve the State plan for the development of the national economy;

10. approve the State budget;

11. decide on questions of war and peace.

Article 77. The Supreme People's Assembly holds regular and extraordinary sessions.

The regular session is convened once or twice a year by the Standing Committee of the Supreme People's Assembly.

The extraordinary session is convened when the Standing Committee of the Supreme People's Assembly deems it necessary, or at the request of a minimum of one-third of the total number of deputies.

Article 78. The Supreme People's Assembly needs more than half the total number of deputies to meet.

Article 79. The Supreme People's Assembly elects its Chairman and Vice-Chairmen.

The Chairman presides over the session.

Article 80. Items to be considered at the Supreme People's Assembly are submitted by the President of the Democratic People's Republic of Korea, the Central People's Committee, the Standing Committee of the Supreme People's Assembly and the Administration Council. Items can also be presented by deputies.

Article 81. The first session of the Supreme People's Assembly elects a Credentials Committee and on hearing the Committee's report, adopts a decision confirming the credentials of deputies.

Article 82. The laws, ordinances and decisions of the Supreme People's Assembly are adopted when more than half of the deputies present give approval by a show of hands.

The Constitution is adopted or amended with the approval of more than two-thirds of the total number of deputies to the Supreme People's Assembly.

Article 83. The Supreme People's Assembly can appoint a Budget Committee, a Bills Committee and other necessary Committees.

The Committees of the Supreme People's Assembly assist in the work of the Supreme People's Assembly.

Article 84. Deputies to the Supreme People's Assembly are guaranteed inviolability as such.

No deputy to the Supreme People's Assembly can be arrested without the consent of the Supreme People's Assembly or, when it is not in session, without the consent of its Standing Committee.

Article 85. The Standing Committee of the Supreme People's Assembly is a permanent body of the Supreme People's Assembly.

Article 86. The Standing Committee of the Supreme People's Assembly consists of the Chairman, Vice-Chairmen, Secretary and members.

The Chairman and Vice-Chairmen of the Supreme People's Assembly are concurrently the Chairman and Vice-Chairmen of its Standing Committee.

Article 87. The Standing Committee of the Supreme People's Assembly has the duties and authority to:

1. examine and decide on bills in the intervals between sessions of the Supreme People's Assembly and obtain the approval of the next session of the Supreme People's Assembly;

2. amend current laws and ordinances when the Supreme People's Assembly is not in session and obtain the approval of the next session of the Supreme People's Assembly;

3. interpret current laws and ordinances;

4. convene the session of the Supreme People's Assembly;

5. conduct the election of deputies to the Supreme People's Assembly;

6. work with the deputies to the Supreme People's Assembly;

7. work with the Committees of the Supreme People's Assembly in the intervals between sessions of the Supreme People's Assembly;

8. organize the elections of deputies to the local People's Assemblies;

9. elect or recall the Judges and People's Assessors of the Central Court.

Article 88. The Standing Committee of the Supreme People's Assembly adopts decisions.

Chapter VI

THE PRESIDENT OF THE DEMOCRATIC PEOPLE'S REPUBLIC OF KOREA

Article 89. The President of the Democratic People's Republic of Korea is the Head of State and represents State [power] in the Democratic People's Republic of Korea.

Article 90. The President of the Democratic People's Republic of Korea is elected by the Supreme People's Assembly.

The term of office of the President of the Democratic People's Republic of Korea is four years.

Article 91. The President of the Democratic People's Republic of Korea directly guides the Central People's Committee.

Article 92. The President of the Democratic People's Republic of Korea, when necessary, convenes and presides over meetings of the Administration Council.

Article 93. The President of the Democratic People's Republic of Korea is the supreme commander of all the armed forces of the Democratic People's Republic of Korea and the Chairman of the National Defense Commission, and commands all the armed forces of the State.

Article 94. The President of the Democratic People's Republic of Korea promulgates the laws and ordinances of the Supreme People's Assembly, the decrees of the Central People's Committee and the decisions of the Standing Committee of the Supreme People's Assembly.

The President of the Democratic People's Republic of Korea issues edicts.

Article 95. The President of the Democratic People's Republic of Korea exercises the right of granting special pardon.

Article 96. The President of the Democratic People's Republic of Korea ratifies or abrogates treaties concluded with other countries.

Article 97. The President of the Democratic People's Republic of Korea receives the letters of credence and recall of diplomatic representatives accredited by foreign states.

Article 98. The President of the Democratic People's Republic of Korea is accountable to the Supreme People's Assembly for his activities.

Article 99. The Vice-Presidents of the Democratic People's Republic of Korea assist the President in his work.

Chapter VII

THE CENTRAL PEOPLE'S COMMITTEE

Article 100. The Central People's Committee is the highest leadership organ of State [power] in the Democratic People's Republic of Korea.

Article 101. The Central People's Committee is headed by the President of the Democratic People's Republic of Korea.

Article 102. The Central People's Committee consists of the President and Vice-Presidents of the Democratic People's Republic of Korea and the Secretary and members of the Central People's Committee.
The term of office of the Central People's Committee is four years.

Article 103. The Central People's Committee has the duties and authority to:
1. draw up the home and foreign policies of the State;
2. direct the work of the Administration Council and the local People's Assemblies and People's Committees;
3. direct the work of judicial and procuratorial organs;
4. guide the work of national defense and State political security;
5. ensure the observance of the Constitution, the laws and ordinances of the Supreme People's Assembly, the edicts of the President of the Democratic People's Republic of Korea and the decrees, decisions and directives of the Central People's Committee, and annul the decisions and directives of State organs which contravene them;
6. establish or abolish Ministries, respective executive bodies of the Administration Council;
7. appoint or remove Vice-Premiers, Ministers and other members of the Administration Council on the recommendation of the Premier of the Administration Council;
8. appoint or recall ambassadors and ministers;
9. appoint or remove high-ranking officers and confer military titles of generals;
10. institute decorations, titles of honor, military titles and diplomatic ranks and confer decorations and titles of honor;
11. grant general amnesties;
12. institute or change administrative districts;
13. proclaim a state of war and issue orders for mobilization in case of emergency.

Article 104. The Central People's Committee adopts decrees and decisions and issues directives.

Article 105. The Central People's Committee establishes a Domestic Policy Commission, a Foreign Policy Commission, a National Defense Commission, a Justice and Security Commission, and other respective Commissions to assist it in its work.

The members of the Commissions of the Central People's Committee are appointed or removed by the Central People's Committee.

Article 106. The Central People's Committee is accountable to the Supreme People's Assembly for its activities.

Chapter VIII

THE ADMINISTRATION COUNCIL

Article 107. The Administration Council is the administrative and executive body of the highest organ of State [power].

The Administration Council works under the guidance of the President of the Democratic People's Republic of Korea and the Central People's Committee.

Article 108. The Administration Council consists of the Premier, Vice-Premiers, Ministers and other necessary members.

Article 109. The Administration Council has the duties and authority to:

1. direct the work of Ministries, organs directly under its authority and local administrative committees;

2. establish or abolish organs directly under its authority;

3. draft the State plan for the development of the national economy and adopt measures to put it into effect;

4. compile the State budget and adopt measures to implement it;

5. organize and execute the work of industry, agriculture, home and foreign trade, construction, transport, communications, land administration, municipal administration, science, education, culture, health service, etc.;

6. adopt measures to strengthen the monetary and banking system;

7. conclude treaties with foreign countries and conduct external affairs;

8. build up the people's armed forces;

9. adopt measures to maintain public order, protect the interests of the State, and safeguard the rights of citizens;

10. annul the decisions and directives of the State administrative organs which run counter to the decisions and directives of the Administration Council.

Article 110. The Administration Council convenes the Plenary Meeting and the Permanent Commission.

The Plenary Meeting consists of all members of the Administration Council. The Permanent Commission consists of the Premier, Vice-Premiers and other members of the Administration Council appointed by the Premier.

Article 111. The Plenary Meeting of the Administration Council discusses and decides on new, important problems arising in the State administration.

The Permanent Commission of the Administration Council discusses and decides on matters entrusted to it by the Plenary Meeting of the Administration Council.

Article 112. The Administration Council adopts decisions and issues directives.

Article 113. The Administration Council is accountable for its activities to the Supreme People's Assembly, the President of the Democratic People's Republic of Korea and the Central People's Committee.

Article 114. The Ministry is a departmental executive body of the Administration Council.

The Ministry issues directives.

Chapter IX

THE LOCAL PEOPLE'S ASSEMBLY, PEOPLE'S COMMITTEE AND ADMINISTRATIVE COMMITTEE

Article 115. The People's Assembly of the province (or municipality directly under central authority), city (or district) and county is the local organ of State [power].

Article 116. The local People's Assembly consists of deputies elected on the principle of universal, equal and direct suffrage by secret ballot.

Article 117. The term of office of the People's Assembly of the province (or municipality directly under central authority) is four years, and that of the People's Assembly of the city (or district) and county is two years.

Article 118. The local People's Assembly has the duties and authority to:

1. approve the local plan for the development of the national economy;

2. approve the local budget;

3. elect or recall the Chairman, Vice-Chairmen, Secretary and members of the People's Committee at the corresponding level;

4. elect or recall the Chairman of the Administrative Committee at the corresponding level;

5. elect or recall the Judges and People's Assessors of the Court at the corresponding level;

6. annul inappropriate decisions and directives of the People's Committee at the corresponding level and the People's Assemblies and People's Committees at the lower levels.

Article 119. The local People's Assembly convenes regular and extraordinary sessions.

The regular session is convened once or twice a year by the People's Committee at the corresponding level.

The extraordinary session is convened when the People's Committee at the corresponding level deems it necessary or at the request of a minimum of one-third of the total number of deputies.

Article 120. The local People's Assembly needs more than half the total number of deputies to meet.

Article 121. The local People's Assembly elects its Chairman.

The Chairman presides over the session.

Article 122. The local People's Assembly adopts decisions.

The decision of the local People's Assembly is announced by the Chairman of the People's Committee at the corresponding level.

Article 123. The People's Committee of the province (or municipality directly under central authority), city (or district) and county exercises the function of the local organ of State power when the People's Assembly at the corresponding level is not in session.

Article 124. The local People's Committee consists of the Chairman, Vice-Chairmen, Secretary and members.

The term of office of the local People's Committee is the same as that of the corresponding People's Assembly.

Article 125. The local People's Committee has the duties and authority to:

1. convene the session of the People's Assembly;

2. organize work for the election of deputies to the People's Assembly;

3. work with the deputies to the People's Assembly;

4. adopt measures to implement the decisions of the corresponding People's Assembly and the People's Committees at higher levels;

5. direct the work of the Administrative Committee at the corresponding level;

6. direct the work of the People's Committees at lower levels;

7. direct the work of the State institutions, enterprises and social cooperative organizations within the given area;

8. annul inappropriate decisions and directives of the Administrative Committee at the corresponding level and the People's Committees and Administrative Committees at lower levels, and suspend the implementation of inappropriate decisions of the People's Assemblies at lower levels;

9. appoint or remove the Vice-Chairmen, Secretary and members of the Administrative Committee at the corresponding level.

Article 126. The local People's Committee adopts decisions and issues directives.

Article 127. The local People's Committee is accountable for its activities to the corresponding People's Assembly and the People's Committees at higher levels.

Article 128. The Administrative Committee of the province (or municipality directly under central authority), city (or district) and county is the administrative and executive body of the local organ of State [power].

Article 129. The local Administrative Committee consists of the Chairman, Vice-Chairmen, Secretary and members.

Article 130. The local Administrative Committee has the duties and authority to:

1. organize and carry out all administrative affairs in the given area;

2. carry out the decisions and directives of the People's Assembly and People's Committee at the corresponding level and of the organs at higher levels;

3. draft the local plan for the development of the national economy and adopt measures to implement it;

4. compile the local budget and adopt measures for its implementation;

5. adopt measures to maintain public order, protect the interests of the State, and safeguard the rights of citizens in the given area;

6. guide the work of the Administrative Committees at lower levels;

7. annul inappropriate decisions and directives of the Administrative Committees at lower levels.

Article 131. The local Administrative Committee adopts decisions and issues directives.

Article 132. The local Administrative Committee is accountable for its activities to the People's Assembly and People's Committee at the corresponding level.

The local Administrative Committee is subordinate to the higher Administrative Committees and to the Administration Council.

Chapter X

THE COURT AND THE PROCURATOR'S OFFICE

Article 133. Justice is administered by the Central Court, the Court of the province (or municipality directly under central authority), the People's Court and the Special Court.

Verdict is delivered in the name of the Democratic People's Republic of Korea.

Article 134. The Judges and People's Assessors of the Central Court are elected by the Standing Committee of the Supreme People's Assembly.

The Judges and People's Assessors of the Court of the province (or municipality directly under central authority) and the People's Court are elected by the People's Assembly at the corresponding level.

The term of office of Judges and People's Assessors is the same as that of the People's Assembly at the corresponding level.

Article 135. The Chairman and Judges of the Special Court are appointed or removed by the Central Court.

The People's Assessors of the Special Court are elected by servicemen and employees at their respective meetings.

Article 136. The functions of the Court are to:

1. protect through judicial activities the power of the workers and peasants and the socialist system established in the Democratic People's Republic of Korea, the property of the State and social cooperative organizations, personal rights as guaranteed by the Constitution, and the lives and property of citizens against all infringements;

2. ensure that all State institutions, enterprises, social cooperative organizations and citizens strictly observe State laws and actively struggle against class enemies and all law-breakers;

3. give judgements and findings with regard to property and conduct notarial work.

Article 137. Justice is administered by the Court consisting of one Judge and two People's Assessors. In special cases there may be three Judges.

Article 138. Court cases are heard in public and the accused is guaranteed the right of defense.

Hearings may be closed to the public as stipulated by law.

Article 139. Judicial proceedings are conducted in the Korean language.

Foreign citizens may use their own language during court proceedings.

Article 140. In administering justice, the Court is independent, and judicial proceedings are carried out in strict accordance with the law.

Article 141. The Central Court is the highest judicial organ of the Democratic People's Republic of Korea.

The central Court supervises the judicial activities of all the Courts.

Article 142. The Central Court is accountable for its activities to the Supreme People's Assembly, the President of the Democratic People's Republic of Korea and the Central People's Committee.

The Court of the province (or municipality directly under central authority) and the People's Court are accountable for their activities to the respective People's Assembly.

Article 143. Investigation and prosecution are conducted by the Central Procurator's Office, the Procurator's Offices of the province (or municipality directly under central authority), city (or district) and county and Special Procurator's Office.

Article 144. The functions of the Procurator's Office are to:

1. ensure the strict observance of State laws by State institutions, enterprises, social cooperative organizations and by citizens;

2. ensure that decisions and directives of State organs conform with the Constitution, the laws and ordinances of the Supreme People's Assembly, the edicts of the President of the Democratic People's Republic of Korea, the decrees, decisions and directives of the Central People's Committee, the decisions of the Standing Committee of the Supreme People's Assembly and with the decisions and directives of the Administration Council;

3. expose and institute legal proceedings against criminals and offenders so as to safeguard the power of the workers and peasants and the socialist system from all forms of encroachment, and protect the property of the State and social cooperative organizations and personal rights as guaranteed by the Constitution and the lives and property of citizens.

Article 145. Investigation and prosecution are conducted under the coordinated leadership of the Central Procurator's Office, and all Procurator's Offices are subordinated to their higher offices and the Central Procurator's Office.

Procurators are appointed or removed by the Central Procurator's Office.

Article 146. The Central Procurator's Office is accountable for its activities to the Supreme People's Assembly, the President of the Democratic People's Republic of Korea and the Central People's Committee.

Chapter XI

EMBLEM, FLAG AND CAPITAL

Article 147. The national emblem of the Democratic People's Republic of Korea is adorned with the design of a grand hydroelectric power plant under the beaming light of a five-pointed red star, ovally framed with ears of rice bound with a red band bearing the inscription "The Democratic People's Republic of Korea."

Article 148. The national flag of the Democratic People's Republic of Korea has a red panel across the middle, bordered above and below in sequence by a thin white stripe and a broad blue stripe. On the red panel near the staff is depicted a five-pointed red star within a white circle.

The ratio of width to length is 1:2.

Article 149. The capital of the Democratic People's Republic of Korea is Pyongyang.

THE BYLAWS OF THE PARTY

The first bylaws of the party were introduced by Kim Yong-bŏm, chairman of the committee to draft the bylaws, on the third day of the first party congress of the Workers' Party of North Korea, August 30, 1946. It was a simple document of four chapters and forty-one articles with provisions for general principles, rights and duties of the members, central and local party organs, and other rules of the party.[4]

During the first two decades after its founding, each succeeding party congress amended the bylaws, improving and adding articles to the original document. However, since the early 1960s the party has seldom mentioned the bylaws. The latest amendment was on October 13, 1980, at the time of the sixth party congress.

The first effort to amend the bylaws was made during the second party congress in March 1948. Four major amendments were introduced by Chu Yŏng-ha, then vice-chairman of the party.[5] The first one dealt with the incorporation of the Central Inspection Committee into the Central Committee of the party. The first bylaws provided that the members of the Central Inspection Committee be elected by the party congress and that the committee be an organ of the congress. This amendment renamed the committee the Inspection Committee and made it part of the Central Committee, with members to be elected by the Central Committee. The second amendment dealt with changes in the number of members on important committees, such as the Political Committee, with five members, and the Standing Committee, with eleven to thirteen members. The numbers were removed to give greater flexibility and to accommodate the needs of each committee. The third change dealt with the creation of candidate membership to the Central Committee. The original bylaws specified only the regular members, and the first party congress elected only regular members of the Central Committee. This amendment made it possible to elect candidate members to fill vacancies in the committee. The fourth amendment dealt with the creation of the Central Auditing Committee to take care of party finance. Members of the committee were to be elected by the party congress and were to be responsible directly to the congress. There were other minor changes in the local organizations, and the wording of some of the duties of party members was changed to improve the bylaws.

Since the merger of the Workers' Parties of North and South Korea was not completed until June 1949, the amended bylaws of the second party congress remained the bylaws of the Workers' Party of North Korea. Its South Korean counterpart, the Workers' Party of South Korea, also had its own bylaws, which were adopted at the time of the founding congress in Seoul on November 23, 1946.[6] It is not clear how the parties reconciled the two sets of bylaws when they merged in June 1949. No separate party congress was held for the merger of the two parties, and there is no record of any amendment to either bylaws at the time of the merger. It is most likely that the bylaws of the North Korean party were used even after the merger.

The second amendment took place at the sixth joint plenum, August 4–6, 1953, shortly after the Korean war. A fifteen-member committee headed by Kim Il Sung and Pak Chŏng-ae was elected to amend the bylaws. The members of this committee included a few members of the Workers' Party of South Korea, such as Yi Ki-sŏk, Kang Mun-sŏk, and Hwang T'ae-sŏng. The amendments of this committee were never reported, and it is not known which provisions were amended to what extent. In her report to the third party congress in 1956, Pak Chŏng-ae said that the bylaws had already been amended twice prior to the third party congress.[7]

The third amendment was an extensive one. Almost-new and much-expanded bylaws of ten chapters and sixty-two articles were adopted on April 28, 1956, at the third party congress.[8] Pak Chŏng-ae gave three reasons for the amendment: (1) the new task of the party to build social-ism in the northern half of the republic, (2) the need to accommodate the growth of the party, and (3) significant changes in the relationship of the party to fraternal socialist and Communist parties.

In addition to the original four chapters of the first party, the new by-laws had a separate chapter on candidate members of the party and were expanded to include separate chapters for the provincial, city and county, and basic party organizations in addition to the central organs of the party. A new chapter was created to provide for the special rela-tionship the party had with the government and other social organiza-tions. It also had a separate chapter to specify the schedule of dues to be collected from the members of the party. These bylaws were widely cir-culated, and books were written to explain and study their nature. There are indications that the party perhaps followed the provisions of these bylaws more closely than any other. The holding of party conferences two years from the party congresses, the holding of party congresses every five years, and the election of members of various important com-mittees within the party give clues to the effort to faithfully observe the bylaws.

These bylaws were again amended five years later at the fourth party congress. Only brief mention was made of the amendments on the last day of the congress, September 18, 1961. There was no separate report or lengthy discussion, but the bylaws subsequently published incorpor-ate the amendments of this party congress. The number of chapters was reduced from ten to nine, but the number of articles was increased from sixty-two to seventy.[9]

The amended bylaws have a preamble. The separate chapter on can-didate members was eliminated and relevant articles on candidate mem-bers were incorporated in the chapter on membership (chapter 1). Five chapters dealt with the principles (chapter 2) and structure of the organi-zation and the central (chapter 3), provincial (chapter 4), city and coun-ty (chapter 5), and basic organizations (chapter 6) of the party. There were two separate chapters on the relationships of the party with the League of Socialist Working Youth (chapter 7) and with the Korean Peo-ple's Army (chapter 8). The last chapter repeated the schedule of dues of party members.

The fifth amendment was made on the last day of the fifth party con-gress on November 13, 1970.[10] The amendment was introduced by Kim Yŏng-ju, a representative from the Pyongyang City Party Organization Committee, and was unanimously approved. However, there was no of-ficial announcement of the provisions amended, nor were the amended bylaws published. The report suggested that a portion of the bylaws was amended to conform with the development of the party and that a few new articles were added to improve the bylaws.

The amended bylaws of November 1970 are printed below. The English translation is from an unofficial Korean version of the bylaws, and there may be a few inaccuracies, but this is the best available outside of North Korea. This version includes the amended provisions of the fifth amendment at the time of the fifth party congress. The bylaws have ten chapters and sixty articles, an increase of one chapter and decrease of ten articles. Many redundant articles were eliminated, and Chapter 7 on the Party and the League of the Socialist Working Youth was renamed the Party and Organizations of the Working Masses. The chapter was expanded to include other organizations such as the General Federation of Trade Unions, the Union of Agricultural Working People, and the Democratic Women's Union. A new chapter on political bureaus was added.

As with the constitution, which was rewritten in 1972, the time has long passed to overhaul the bylaws of the party. The party was expected to bring out new bylaws at its sixth congress, but since the revised bylaws were neither discussed nor made public at the time of the sixth congress, it is not clear whether the party adopted entirely new bylaws or made amendments to the existing ones.

TEXT OF THE BYLAWS OF NOVEMBER 1970

PREAMBLE

The Workers' Party of Korea is the vanguard organization of the working class and the entire working masses of our country, and it is the highest form of revolutionary organization among all organizations of the working masses.

The Workers' Party of Korea represents the interests of the Korean nation and the Korean people.

The Workers' Party of Korea is organized with progressive fighters from among the workers, peasants, and the working intellectuals who fight for the interests of the working masses and the victory of the great work of socialism and communism.

The Workers' Party of Korea is the direct successor of the glorious revolutionary tradition established by the Korean Communists in the anti-Japanese armed struggle. The Workers' Party of Korea is guided in its activities by Marxism and Leninism and the *chuch'e* idea of Comrade Kim Il Sung, which is the creative application of Marxism and Leninism to the reality of our country.

The Workers' Party of Korea opposes revisionism, dogmatism, and all kinds of opportunism and bourgeois ideologies that appeared in the international Communist movement and the labor movement, and fights for the purity of Marxism and Leninism.

The immediate purpose of the Workers' Party of Korea is the assurance of the complete victory of socialism in the northern half of the republic and the development of the revolutionary tasks of national liberation and the people's democracy in the entire region of the republic. The ultimate purpose is the establishment of a Communist society.

The Workers' Party of Korea holds the monolithic ideological system as its basic principle in the party work and in carrying out the revolutionary tasks of the party.

The Workers' Party of Korea strengthens the dictatorship of the proletariat, which is a powerful weapon in the establishment of socialism and communism, and develops with full force the Ch'ŏllima movement, which is the general line in the establishment of socialism.

The Workers' Party of Korea promotes the leadership role of the working class and fights for the strengthening of the united front of all segments of patriotic, democratic forces based upon the worker-peasant alliance.

The Workers' Party of Korea holds as its highest task to upgrade the material and cultural life of the people.

The Workers' Party of Korea holds as its basic task work with the people.

The Workers' Party of Korea holds as its basic task the class line and the mass line.

The Workers' Party of Korea carries out Ch'ŏngsalli spirit and the Ch'ŏngsalli method in the party work.

The Workers' Party of Korea firmly establishes the monolithic ideological system in the party members and the workers, reforms and revolutionizes the entire society after the examples set by the working class, strengthens the revolutionary ranks with political thoughts, strengthens the proletarian dictatorship against enemies of the class, develops the economic and defense establishments with the revolutionary spirit of self-resuscitation, further strengthens the socialist system established in the northern half of the republic, and fights for the complete victory of socialism.

The Workers' Party of Korea carries out an independent, peaceful line for the unification of the fatherland, drives out the American imperialists, the enemies of the Korean people, from South Korea, opposes the Japanese militarists, and directly supports the anti-American and anti-puppet-regime struggles of the South Korean people to overthrow the puppet regime of landlords, capitalists, and reactionary bureaucrats.

The Workers' Party of Korea cooperates with socialist countries and struggles for the strengthening of the international Communist movement based upon the principles of Marxism and Leninism and proletarian internationalism, develops friendly relations with newly independent countries of Asia, Africa, and Latin America, supports the anti-imperialist national liberation movement of the people everywhere and the revolutionary struggles of the working class and the people of capitalist countries against monopoly capitalism, develops the broad anti-imperialist and anti-American united front, opposes international capitalism by cutting off the four limbs of American imperialism, and fights for peace, democracy, national independence, and victory of joint struggles of socialist countries.

CHAPTER 1. PARTY MEMBERS

1. Members of the Workers' Party of Korea are revolutionaries who fight for the fatherland, the people, and the ultimate victory of socialism and communism.

2. Members of the Workers' Party of Korea are citizens of Korea armed with the monolithic ideological system, who accept the platform and the bylaws of the party and resolutely fight for the realization of its objectives, and who work within the party organization and carry out decisions of the party.

3. Members of the Workers' Party of Korea are recruited from among candidate members who have fulfilled a specified probationary period. However, in special cases, an applicant may be accepted as a member without the probationary period. One is eligible for admission at the age of eighteen. The admission procedure is as follows.

   a. One who is applying for admission as a candidate member must submit an application form and letters of recommendation from two members of the party to the party cell concerned. In case of a member of the League of Socialist Working Youth, a recommendation from the city or county committee of the league may be substituted for a recommendation from one party member. In case of a candidate member applying for membership, the application form and recommendation are not necessary. However, when the party cell deems it necessary, a new recommendation must be submitted.

   b. A recommending person must have been a party member for more than two years. One must know the past and present social and political activities of the candidate well. One is responsible to the party for one's recommendation.

   c. Each application is investigated separately. It is discussed and acted upon in the general meeting of the party cell with the applicant participating, and the decision must be approved by the city or county party committee. A recommending person need not be present at the meeting. The city or county party committee must act on the decision of the party cell within a month.

d. An application for admission from those who work under special circumstances is considered under special procedures and rules of the Central Committee of the party.

e. An application for admission from those who were expelled from other parties must include three letters of recommendation from those who have been members of the party for more than three years. It must be approved by the city or county party committee for a regular member, and by the Central Committee for officers above the city or county levels.

f. The probationary period of a candidate member is one year. The party cell should give assistance to candidate members to qualify for membership within the specified period. The general meeting of the party cell should decide on an application of a candidate member for membership at the end of the probationary period. In special cases, a candidate member may be accepted as a member before the end of the probationary period. The probationary period may be extended for another year for a candidate member not fully qualified for membership. For those who failed to qualify for membership at the end of the probationary period, the general meeting of the party cell must decide on expulsion. The extension of the probationary period or the expulsion of candidate members should be approved by the city or county party committee.

g. The date of admission to the party is when the general meeting of the party cell decides on the membership of a candidate member, or for one who is admitted without the probationary period, the date when such decision is made by the general meeting of the party cell.

4. The duties of a party member are as follows.

a. A party member should stand firmly on the monolithic ideological system of the party. The party member should be armed with the monolithic ideological system, and unconditionally accept, preserve, and carry out the party line and policies. The party member should study, preserve, and promote the revolutionary tradition of the party. The party member should fight against all antiparty and antirevolutionary lines of revisionism, dogmatism, bourgeois ideologies, feudalistic Confucianism, factionalism, provincialism, and nepotism that are contrary to the monolithic ideological system and should protect the unity of the party based upon the *chuch'e* idea.

b. A party member should actively participate in the organizational life of the party, be trained in the party spirit, and revolutionize and "working-classize" oneself after the examples set by the working class. The party member should actively participate in party meetings and study groups, carry out the assigned work of the party, review one's party life daily, actively carry out ideological struggle through self-criticism, and transform himself into a revolutionary. The party member should observe the bylaws of the party that apply to all members, irrespective of rank and accomplishments, and fight against the violators of the bylaws.

c. A party member should have revolutionary study habits and continuously upgrade one's political, ideological, and cultural standards. The party member should study the party line, policies, revolutionary tradition; upgrade one's ideological and theoretical standards by studying the general principles of Marxism and Leninism; correctly analyze current problems based upon correct understanding of the party policies; and make efforts to upgrade cultural standards by studying the problems of socialist economic management and advanced science and technology.

d. A party member should carry out the revolutionary mass line and must always work with the masses. The party member should always explain the party line and policies to the masses, educate and transform them, organize them around the party and mobilize them for party work, and meet their demands in time by correctly understanding the masses.

e. A party member should set an example for the masses, always think of revolutionary tasks, and be a vanguard. The party member should have a higher standard of political awareness and be an example in the tasks of revolution. The party member should love to work, should voluntarily observe regulations, and should set an example by taking on difficult work as well as the assigned work. The party member should fight against conservatism and negativism, actively participate in the technical revolutionary movement, increase the level of production, participate in the management of enterprises, preserve and protect social properties of the state, and be thrifty.

f. A party member should possess lofty Communist moral character, love one's organization and groups, and sacrifice individual gains for the benefit of the organization. The party member should always be frugal, humble, unselfish, and frank before the party, humane, and culturally oriented and voluntarily observe the social order and social morality.

g. A party member should defend the socialist fatherland. The party member should always be alert and be ready to be mobilized, learn about the military, defend the revolutionary gains against enemy intrusions, and be determined to fight in the war of fatherland unification.

h. A party member should obey orders of the revolutionary system, fight against indolence and maintain vigilance at all times, and keep secrets of the party and state.

i. A party member should report problems arising from the party work and party life to the party. The party member should fight against shortcomings and negative tendencies not only in the phenomena contrary to the monolithic ideological system, but also in general work and life, and should report them in time to appropriate party organizations up to the Central Committee.

j. A party member should pay a determined amount of dues each month.

5. The rights of a party member are:

a. A party member has the right to express opinions in party meetings and in party publications for the purpose of carrying out party policies and doing party work.

b. A party member has the right to elect and to be elected in every party leadership organization.

c. A party member has the right to criticize any member in party meetings for cause, and has the right to refuse any order contrary to the monolithic ideological system of the party.

d. A party member has the right to demand participation in any party meeting that deliberates and decides on one's own behavior and work.

e. A party member has the right to initiate a request or appeal to every party committee including the Central Committee and demand investigation.

f. The duties of a candidate member are the same as those of a party member. The rights of candidate members are the same as those of party members except for the right to elect and to be elected.

g. A party member who violates the bylaws shall be punished by the party.

(i) A party member who acts contrary to the monolithic ideological system of the party, forms factions against the party line and policies, cooperates with enemies, and seriously harms the party shall be expelled from the party.

(ii) A party member who has not committed an offense serious enough to warrant expulsion from the party, may receive, depending on the seriousness of the offense, a reprimand, warning, or temporary suspension of rights in the party.

(iii) The purpose of a reprimand is to educate the party member. The party must seriously consider the motive and cause of the offense and thoroughly explain the results of the investigation.

(iv) The appropriate punishment should be discussed and decided upon at a general meeting of the party cell to which the member belongs and with the participation of the member. On special occasions, the punishment can be decided upon without the participation of the member. The Central Committee, the provincial, city, or county committees can directly punish party members for violation of the bylaws. The decision of the party cell to punish a party member should be approved by the provincial party committee. Except for special cases, a party member should be allowed to participate in party activities and the member's party card should not be lifted until the decision of the party cell is approved.

(v) The penalty for members and candidate members of the Central Committee should be decided upon in the plenary meeting of the Central Committee, and the penalty for members and candidate members of the provincial, city, or county party committees should be decided upon in the plenary meetings of the committees concerned. The party cell may submit a recommendation to the committees concerned when members and candidate members of the Central Committee, provincial, city, and county committees violate the bylaws. However, when the offenses committed by members and candidate members of the provincial, city, or county committees have no direct relevance to the work of the committee concerned, the party cell may decide on the penalty, up to a warning, and such decision must be approved by the committee concerned.

6. Investigation of party disciplinary problems of party members who participate in factions and other factional activities, shall be as follows. The provincial committee shall investigate members and officers of the county committee, and the Central Committee shall investigate members and officers of the provincial and county committees.

7. The Central Committee, the provincial, city, or county committees should promptly investigate and solve problems related to party discipline requested by a member.

8. The party cell should always help punished members, and when such members recant and correct errors and reform themselves, the party cells should decide on the removal of the punishment. The decision of the party cell to remove the punishment must be approved by the city or county committees. The removal of the punishment of members and candidate members must be approved by the committee that made the final decision.

9. For a party member who fails to participate in party activities for more than six months without reason, the general meeting of the party cell may decide to remove the member from the party, and such decision must be approved by the city or county committees.

10. The transfer of party members should follow the rules and procedures set by the Central Committee of the party.

CHAPTER 2. ORGANIZATION PRINCIPLES AND STRUCTURES OF THE PARTY

11. The party shall be organized on the principle of democratic centralism.
   a. Every leadership organization of the party shall be democratically elected, and the elected leadership organization shall report its work periodically to party organizations.
   b. Party members shall obey the party organizations, the minority shall obey the majority, the lower party organization shall obey the higher party organization, and all party organizations shall absolutely obey the Central Committee of the party.
   c. All party organizations should unconditionally support and carry out the party line and policies, and the lower party organizations must execute dutifully the decisions of the higher party organizations. The higher party organizations shall systematically direct and inspect the work of the lower party organizations, and the lower party organizations shall periodically report their work to the higher party organizations.

12. Every party organization is organized in accordance with region or production units. The regional party organization is the highest organization of all party organizations of the region, and the party organization in charge of party affairs that affect the entire region is the highest party organization in party work.

13. Every party committee is the supreme leadership organization and headquarters of the region or the production units it represents. Each party committee must execute decisions that were collectively discussed and decided upon by the party organization, and must carry out the decisions by combining initiative and responsibility. The party committee may discuss and decide independently the problems of

the region, but such decisions should not be in conflict with the party line or policies.

14. The supreme leadership organization of the party is as follows:

    a. For the entire party, it is the party congress, and between party congresses, it is the Central Committee elected by the party congress. For the provincial, city, or county party organizations, it is the party conference, and between party conferences, it is the appropriate party committees elected by the party conference. For the primary party organizations, it is the general meeting of the party or the party conference, and between the general meetings of the party or the party conferences, it is the appropriate party committee elected by the general meeting of the party or the party conference.

    b. Representatives to the party congress or the party conference shall be elected by the party congress or the party conferences of the lower party organizations. The ratio of elected representatives to the party congress is determined by the Central Committee. The ratio of elected representatives to the provincial, city, or county party organization is determined by the appropriate party committee in accordance with the ratio established by the Central Committee. The number of members and candidate members of the Central Committee is determined by the party congress. The number of members and candidate members of the provincial, city, or county committees and the number of executive committee members of the primary party committees are determined by the appropriate party conferences or the general meetings of the party in accordance with the standards set by the Central Committee.

    Members and candidate members of the Central Committee, provincial, city or county committees are elected from the core members who directly engage in production work. Election in each leadership organization is conducted in accordance with the election rules set by the Central Committee.

15. Interim election or expulsion of members and candidate members of the Central Committee, provincial, city, or county committees are conducted by the plenary meetings of the appropriate party committees. When there is a vacancy in the membership of the Central Committee, provincial, city, or county committees, a number of members equal to the number of vacancies is elected from candidate members of the appropriate party committee.

    In case of party members who are not candidate members, the election must follow the rules and procedures set by the Central Committee. Interim election or expulsion of members of leadership organizations of the primary-level party organizations are conducted by the appropriate general meeting or conference of the party. When there is a vacancy in the higher party organizations, the lower party committees may send their secretary. Candidate members of every party organization may participate in the plenary meeting but may not vote.

16. The quorum for any party meeting is two-thirds of the members and candidate members of the particular party organization, and the decision of the meeting is made by a simple majority of the members participating in the meeting.

17. Each party committee may have departments within the committee. The right to establish and dissolve any such department is in the Central Committee.

18. Establishment and dissolution of any provincial, city, or county committees on the same level performing similar functions should be approved by the Central Committee. The establishment and dissolution of primary party committees or sections of primary party committees should be approved by the provincial committee. The establishment and dissolution of a primary party committee with a small number of members, a sectional party committee, and party cells should be approved by the city or county committees. The provincial, city, or county committees should report such establishment and dissolution to the Central Committee.

19. The Central Committee may dissolve any party organization that violates the platform and the bylaws of the party or fails to carry out party policies, investigate members individually, or reorganize them under a new organization.

20. For important regions under special political, economic, and military considerations, the Central Committee may establish a separate organization, prescribe operational methods, and decide on other problems of the party.

CHAPTER 3. CENTRAL ORGANIZATION OF THE PARTY

21. The highest organ of the party is the party congress. The party congress is convened once every four years by the Central Committee of the party. The Central Committee may, when necessary, convene earlier or later than the four-year period. The Central Committee of the party must announce the date and agenda of the party congress three months in advance.

22. The functions of the party congress are:
    a. report the work of the Central Committee and the Central Auditing Committee.

   b. amend or supplement the platform and bylaws of the party.

   c. decide on the party line and policies and on basic problems of strategy and tactics.

   d. elect members of the Central Committee and the Central Auditing Committee of the party.

23. The Central Committee directs the work of the party between party congresses. The Central Committee firmly establishes the monolithic ideological system for the entire party and organizes and directs the party to carry out party policies. It strengthens the ranks and prepares the auxiliary forces and directs the organizational life of members. Following the examples of the working class, it revolutionizes and "working-classizes" the entire society and unites members and directs their ideological works. It establishes the party committees of every level and directs and inspects their activities; establishes the party organization and directs and inspects its administration and economic works; and organizes revolutionary armed forces and assures the safety of the people. It also represents the party in its external relations with other political parties within and outside of the country. It manages the finances of the party.

24. The Central Committee shall convene a plenary meeting of the Central Committee at least once every six months. The plenary meeting of the Central Committee discusses and decides important issues of the party, elects the general secretary, secretaries, and members of the Political Committee, organizes the Secretariat of the party, and elects members of the Military Affairs Committee and the Inspection Committee.

25. The Political Committee of the Central Committee shall organize and direct all party work in behalf of the Central Committee between the plenary meetings. The Political Committee of the Central Committee shall meet at least once every month.

26. The Secretariat of the Central Committee periodically discusses and decides on the problems of cadres, internal problems of the party, and other tasks of the party, and directs the execution of its decisions.

27. The Military Affairs Committee of the Central Committee discusses and decides on the party's military policy and methods of its execution; organizes work to strengthen military industries, the people's army, and all armed forces; and directs the military forces of our country.

28. The Inspection Committee of the Central Committee investigates members who commit antiparty, antirevolutionary factional activities and other activities contrary to the monolithic ideological system of the party, and who fail to observe the platform and bylaws or vio-

late other rules of the party. It also examines and resolves cases appealed by individual party members and proposals from the provincial committees related to problems of party discipline.

29. The Central Auditing Committee shall audit the finances and accounting work of the party.
30. The Central Committee may convene a party conference between party congresses. The election procedures and ratio of representatives to the party conference are decided by the Central Committee. The party conference shall discuss and decide on urgent problems of policies, tactics, and strategies of the party and shall recall those members and candidate members of the Central Committee who fail to perform their duties and elect new members and candidate members.

CHAPTER 4. PARTY ORGANIZATION OF THE PROVINCES

31. The highest organization of the provincial party organization is the provincial party conference. The provincial party conference is convened once in every two years by the Provincial Committee. When necessary, the provincial party conference may be convened earlier or later than the two-year period. The Provincial Committee must notify its subordinate organizations of the date and agenda of the conference two months prior to the conference.
32. The functions of the provincial party conference are:
    a. review the work of the Provincial Committee and the provincial Inspection Committee.
    b. elect members of the Provincial Committee and the provincial party Inspection Committee.
    c. elect representatives to the party congress.
33. The functions of the Provincial Committee are:
    The committee organizes and directs the work to firmly establish the monolithic ideological system in party members and working masses. The committee struggles against revisionism, dogmatism, bourgeois ideology, and feudalistic Confucianism contrary to the party's monolithic ideological system; fights against antiparty and antirevolutionary ideas of factionalism, provincialism, and nepotism; and protects the unity and consolidation of the party based upon the *chuch'e* idea. The committee strengthens the rank and file and auxiliaries, organizes the forces of the party, assigns revolutionary tasks to the members, and directs their party life. The committee directs and inspects the activities of the city or county committees, primary party committees, and party cells in factories, enterprises, and institutions of higher learning. Following the examples of the

working class, the committee revolutionizes the working masses, reforms them, consolidates their strength around the party, and organizes and directs the ideological work of members. The committee strengthens the social organizations of workers and directs and inspects their work so that they can successfully carry out the assigned work on their own, and it performs a leadership role in administrative and economic works to assure successful completion of revolutionary tasks. The committee strengthens the Worker-Peasant Red Guards, assures military mobilization, and upgrades their strategic forces. The committee manages the finances of the Provincial Committee and periodically reports the financial situation to the Central Committee.

34. The Provincial Committee shall convene a plenary meeting at least once every four months. The Provincial Committee discusses and decides on the methods of implementing the party line and policies. The committee elects the general secretary and secretaries of the Standing Committee of the Provincial Committee, organizes the Secretariat, and elects members of the Military Committee and the Inspection Committee of the Provincial Committee. The Standing Committee of the Provincial Committee shall meet at least once a month. The Secretariat of the Provincial Committee discusses internal party problems and cadre work and organizes and directs implementation of decisions. The Military Committee of the Provincial Committee discusses and decides on military policy and organizes and directs its implementation.

35. The Inspection Committee of the Provincial Committee investigates members who commit antiparty or antirevolutionary factionalist activities or other activities contrary to the monolithic ideological system of the party and those who violate the party bylaws. It also approves decisions related to party discipline and expulsion of members submitted by the city and county committees and resolves appeals from members on problems related to party discipline.

CHAPTER 5. PARTY ORGANIZATIONS OF CITY (DISTRICT), COUNTY

36. The highest organization of the city, county party organization is the city, county party conference. The city, county party conference is convened once in every two years by the City, County Committee. When necessary, the city, county conference may be convened earlier or later than the two-year period. The City, County Committee must notify its subordinate organizations of the date and agenda of the conference two months prior to the conference.

37. The functions of the city, county conference are:
    a. report the work of the City, County Committee and the Central Auditing Committee.
    b. elect members of the City, County Committee and the City, County Inspection Committee.
    c. elect representatives to be sent to the Provincial Committee.
38. The functions of the City, County Committee are:
    The committee organizes and directs the work to firmly establish the monolithic ideological system in party members and the working masses. The committee struggles against revisionism, dogmatism, bourgeois ideology, and feudalistic Confucianism contrary to the party's monolithic ideological system; fights against antiparty and antirevolutionary ideas of factionalism, provincialism, and nepotism; and protects the unity and consolidation of the party based upon the *chuch'e* idea. The committee strengthens the rank and file and auxiliaries, organizes the forces of the party, assigns the revolutionary tasks to the members, and directs their party life. The committee finds the core of the party and increases the ranks, organizes and directs recruitment of party members, assigns party strengths, and educates members and candidate members of the party. Following the examples of the working class, the committee revolutionizes the working masses, reforms them, consolidates their strength around the party, and organizes and directs the ideological work of members. The committee strengthens the social organizations of the workers, directs and inspects their work so that they can successfully carry out the assigned work on their own, and performs a leadership role in administrative and economic works to assure successful completion of revolutionary tasks. The committee strengthens the Worker-Peasant Red Guards, assures military mobilization, and upgrades their strategic forces. The committee manages the finances of the City, County Committee and periodically reports the financial situation to the higher party committee.
39. The City, County Committee shall convene a plenary meeting at least once every three months. The City, County Committee discusses and decides on the methods of implementing the party line and policies. The committee elects the general secretary and secretaries of the Standing Committee of the City, County Committee, organizes the Secretariat, elects members of the Military Committee and the Inspection Committee of the City, County Committee. The Standing Committee of the City, County Committee shall meet at least twice a month. The Secretariat of the City, County Committee discusses internal party problems and cadre work and organizes and directs im-

plementation of decisions. The Military Committee of the City, County Committee discusses and decides on military policy and organizes and directs its implementation.

40. The Inspection Committee of the City, County Committee investigates members who commit antiparty or antirevolutionary factionalist activities or other activities contrary to the monolithic ideological system of the party and those who violate the party bylaws. It also approves decisions related to party discipline and expulsion of members submitted by the party cells and resolves appeals from members on problems related to party discipline.

CHAPTER 6. BASIC ORGANIZATION OF THE PARTY

41. The basic organization of the party is a party cell. The party cell is the starting point of party life, and it is a fighting unit that carries out the party line and policies. The party cell is organized from administration and production units with more than five party members.

42. The organization methods of the basic units are:
   a. A unit with five to fifteen party members organizes the party cell. A unit with fewer than five party members and candidate members may belong to the party cell of a neighboring administration and production unit, or two such units may form one party cell. In special cases, a unit with fewer than five members or more than fifteen members may organize a party cell. A unit with fewer than three members may organize a small party unit with a chairman appointed by the City or County Committee.
   b. A unit with more than sixteen members shall organize a primary party committee.
   c. An administration and production unit with more than sixteen members may organize a sectional party committee between the party cell and the primary party committee.
   d. When it is not possible to organize an administration and production unit with the organization formula for a primary party committee, a sectional party committee, or a party cell, a primary party committee may be organized between the primary party committee and the sectional party committee.

43. The highest organization of the primary party organizations is the general meeting.
   a. A general meeting of the party cell shall be convened at least once per month.
   b. General meetings of the primary party committee and the sectional party committee shall be convened at least once in three months. A primary party organization that has more than 500

members, or whose units are widely dispersed, may convene a party general meeting once in six months.

44. The primary party organization shall elect members of an executive organization with one-year terms.

   a. The general meeting of the party cell shall elect a secretary and a deputy secretary.

   b. Members of the primary party committee, the subprimary party committee, and the sectional party committee shall be elected by the appropriate party general meeting, and the secretary and deputy secretary shall be elected by the appropriate party committee. The primary party committee, when necessary, may organize an executive committee. The primary party committee, the subprimary party committee, and the sectional party committee shall convene its meetings at least three times per month, and the primary party committee that has organized an executive committee shall convene its meetings at least once per month.

   c. A party leadership committee may be organized in the primary party organization of cabinets and other central organizations.

45. The duties of the primary party organization are:

   a. Firmly establish the monolithic ideological system in party members and in working masses, have them accept the system unconditionally, and help them to carry out the party line and policies. Fight against revisionism, dogmatism, bourgeois ideology, feudalistic Confucianism contrary to the party's monolithic ideological system, and all kinds of antiparty, antirevolutionary ideas of factionalism, provincialism, and nepotism. Arm party members and working masses with our party's *chuch'e* idea to maintain the unity of the party.

   b. Systematically strengthen the rank and file of the lower party organizations, find and educate the core of the party, and continuously increase and strengthen them.

   c. Strengthen the party life of members, train their party spirit, organize regular studies of the bylaws, make them always think about the revolutionary tasks, assign them party work so as to play a vanguard role, conduct party meetings on a high level of political awareness, understand fully the party life of members, reform them for revolution, develop ideological struggle through self-criticism, investigate the mistakes of members, and help them to correct their mistakes.

   d. Find prospective party members, investigate and train them systematically, and help the newly recruited members and candidate members of the party.

e. Following the examples of the working class, revolutionize the working masses, reform them and consolidate their strength around the party, organize and direct their ideological work to accomplish revolutionary tasks, humbly accept the opinions and demands of the working masses, solve their problems in time, upgrade the level of material and cultural life, establish order and system in all administration and production units, and strengthen the fight against antirevolutionary elements.

f. Strengthen the ideological training work of members and working masses. Strengthen the educational work, revolutionary tradition, class consciousness, and patriotic socialism that are the basis of Communist education.

g. Strengthen social organizations of the workers, point out the direction of their work, and lead them to correctly carry out their duties.

h. Continuously change work methods to adapt to new environments, put political work ahead of all other work, assure successful completion of revolutionary tasks, show correct leadership in administration and economic work, direct party members and working masses to faithfully carry out their revolutionary tasks, continuously revitalize production, directly participate in the Ch'ŏllima movement and the competitive socialist movement, strengthen the technical revolution, increase labor production capabilities, strengthen the labor regulations, and be thrifty with social and state properties.

i. Thoroughly strengthen the Worker-Peasant Red Guards, strengthen their ideological, political, and military education, and prepare them for the call of the party.

j. Educate members and candidate members of the party, collect dues, and regularly report activities to higher party committees.

Chapter 7. Party Organization in the Korean People's Army

46. The Korean People's Army is the true army of the people, and it is the revolutionary armed forces of the Workers' Party of Korea in the glorious tradition of the anti-Japanese armed struggle.

47. A party organization shall be organized in every unit of the Korean People's Army, and the Korean People's Army Party Committee shall be organized to encompass all the party organizations within the Korean People's Army. The Korean People's Army Party Committee shall be directly under the Central Committee of the Workers' Party of Korea, work under its direction, and regularly report its activities to the Central Committee.

48. The functions of every party organization within the Korean People's Army are:

Firmly establish the monolithic ideological system of the party in party members and soldiers, strengthen officers and educate soldiers, organize and direct the party life of members, and strengthen and enlarge the party ranks. Revolutionize members and soldiers, reform them by the examples set by the working class, consolidate their forces around the party, strengthen the organization of the League of Socialist Working Youth in the Korean People's Army, direct them to improve their capabilities, strengthen the party leadership in military works, carry out military policy of the party, directly develop the Red Flag Company movement, arm the military with the revolutionary spirit of one against one hundred enemies, and lead them to show the traditional spirit of unity of the officers, soldiers, and people of the anti-Japanese armed guerrillas.

49. Each unit in the Korean People's Army operates in accordance with directives and approved principles of the Central Committee and the bylaws of the Workers' Party of Korea.

50. Each party unit of the Korean People's Army should have a close relationship with local party organizations. With the approval of the Central Committee of the party, the Korean People's Army Party Committee may recommend political and military cadres to become members of the provincial, city, or county party committees or the primary party committee where they are stationed.

Chapter 8. Political Bureaus

51. The Central Committee of the party, when necessary, shall organize Political Bureaus in important sectors of the political, economic, and military fields. The Political Bureaus organized in the cabinet and central organizations and other political bureaus direct the political educational work of members and perform the function of an executive group of party committees in that unit. The General Political Bureau of the Korean People's Army exercises the functions of a political unit of the appropriate party committee and directs the political work of party organizations.

52. Each party organization belonging to the General Political Bureau of the Korean People's Army works under the leadership of the higher-level party organization, and the party organization at each level belonging to the cabinet and central organization works under the joint leadership of the higher-level party organization and local party committees.

53. The Political Bureau of the cabinet and central organization shall

have close working relationships with local party committees when directing the work of the lower-level party organizations.

54. The Political Bureau may convene party activists conferences for the purpose of mobilizing members and working masses to carry out the party line and policies.

55. The Political Bureau operates under the principles and directions approved by the Central Committee and the bylaws of the Workers' Party of Korea.

CHAPTER 9. THE PARTY AND ORGANIZATIONS OF THE WORKING MASSES

56. The organizations of the working masses are political and supporting organizations of the party succeeding the glorious revolutionary tradition of the anti-Japanese guerrilla struggles. The organizations of the working masses are ideological training organizations of the masses and the party's faithful helpers that tie the party to the masses. The League of Socialist Working Youth is the revolutionary organization of the youth that directly inherits revolutionary tasks and is the party's fighting rearguard unit. The organizations of the working masses operate under the direction of the party.

57. The organizations of the working masses consolidate the strength of members around the monolithic ideological system of the party, revolutionize and "working-classize" them in accordance with the examples set by the working class, strengthen the rank and file and their ideological, educational work, develop the Ch'ŏllima movement and socialist competition, and directly mobilize the members to the revolution and construction.

   a. The General Federation of Trade Unions develops ideological, technical, and cultural revolution among members, achieves or overachieves the goals of economic plans, has members participate in production management, and must work to insure the living conditions of the working masses.

   b. The League of Agricultural Working People develops ideological, technical, and cultural revolution among members, carries out the goals set forth in the "Theses for the Socialist Agrarian Question in Our County," continuously increases agricultural production, improves the capacity of labor production, and works to insure living conditions of the agricultural working people.

   c. The League of Socialist Working Youth prepares members to become members of the rearguard units of the party; continuously educates them for the party and the fatherland; prepares students and youth to become faithful builders of socialism and communism; prepares them to become learned, morally upright, physically strong, and politically ready members of the shock troops; helps them to support and protect the Central Committee with their lives; and educates them to voluntarily participate in the holy task of the defense of the fatherland.

  d. The Democratic Women's Union of Korea actively develops the work to upgrade the political ideology and cultural levels of its members, further upgrades the role of women in the socialist construction, educates their sons and daughters to become faithful successors of our revolution, and revolutionizes their family.

58. Each party organization must strengthen the rank and file of the working masses, establish the working system of the masses through organizations of the working masses, correctly devise methods in accordance with special characteristics of the masses, and lead them to voluntarily participate in completing their duties.

CHAPTER 10. PARTY FINANCES

59. Party finance consists of dues from the members of the party, income from party organizations and party enterprises, and other income.

60. Party dues of members and candidate members of the party are 2 percent of their monthly income.

NOTES

1. The text of the first constitution is available in almost every yearbook published by the North. See, for example, *Chosŏn chungang yŏn'gam*, 1950 (Pyongyang: Chosŏn Chungang T'ongsinsa, 1950), pp. 2–11.

2. For the latest version of the first constitution, incorporating most of the amendments, see *Chosŏn minju chuŭi inmin konghwaguk, hŏnbŏp* (Tokyo: Hagu Sŏbang, 1960), pp. 127–40.

3. The text of the constitution is available in *Kim Il Sung chŏjak sŏnjip* (Pyongyang: Chosŏn Nodongdang Ch'ulp'ansa, 1974), 6: 370–91. For an English version and commentary on the constitution, see *On the Socialist Constitution of the Democratic People's Republic of Korea* (Pyongyang: Foreign Languages Publishing House, 1975).

4. The text of the bylaws is available in Korean in the collection of documents of the first party congress. *Pukchosŏn nodongdang ch'angnip taehoe* (n.p.: Pukchosŏn Nodongdang Chungang Ponbu, n.d.), pp. 47–56.

5. The details of the amendment and the speech by Chu are available in *Pukchosŏn nodongdang che ich'a chŏndang taehoe hoeŭirok* (n.p.: Pukchosŏn Nodongdang Chungang Ponbu, n.d.), pp. 191–213.

6. Kim Nam-sik, *Namnodang* (Seoul: Sin Hyŏnsilsa, 1975), p. 310.

7. Pak Chŏng-ae, "Chosŏn nodongdang kyuyak kaejŏng e kwanhan pogo," in

Chosŏn nodongdang che samch'a taehoe munhŏnjip (Pyongyang: Chosŏn Nodongdang Ch'ulp'ansa, 1956), pp. 405–38.

8. The text of the 1956 bylaws is available in Japanese, English, and Korean. See the explanation of the bylaws in *Chosŏn nodongdang kyuyak haesŏl* (Tokyo: Hagu Sŏbang, 1960), p. 264.

9. *Nodong sinmun*, September 19, 1961. The Korean text of the latest bylaws is in *Pukhan ch'onggam, 1945–1968* (Seoul: Kongsan'gwŏn Munje Yŏn'guso, 1968), pp. 671–78.

10. *Nodong sinmun*, November 14, 1971.

7

Standard Terms of the Political System

FOR STANDARD TERMS

Problems of standard terminology are complex, both in the process of establishing the standard and in the popular subscription and usage of the terms. In the case of North Korean terminology, there is neither a standard nor any systematic practice. This is due in part to the indiscriminate translation of Korean terms into English by scholars in both North and South Korea and in the United States. In the course of the past thirty years, some measure of stability has begun to emerge from the North, and it is now perhaps an appropriate time to put a few basic terms in order.

Approximately two hundred terms, primarily of the political system of the North, are presented here in the hope that they will be accepted and used. The terms follow closely the practice of the North Koreans, who have somewhat regularized their usage during the past ten years or so as they have begun to translate their materials into English in earnest and with regularity. The list consists of the names of political organizations, the names of ministries and commissions, and a few political terms, somewhat unusual but commonly found in the writings of Kim Il Sung.

In many cases, it is difficult to rationalize the North Korean practice. For example, they use the word *league* to designate the youth organization (League of the Socialist Working Youth) and *union* for the peasant organization (Union of Agricultural Working People), while both terms come from the same Korean word, *tongmaeng*. Similarly, it is *committee* for some organizations and *commission* for others for the same Korean word, *wiwŏnhoe*, for example, the Central Committee and the Heavy Industry Commission.

This is also true in the positioning of the word *Korea* in translation. For example, it is the Democratic People's Republic of Korea for the official designation of the state, but it is the Korean People's Army for the armed forces. Both designations begin with the Korean word, *Chosŏn*; Chosŏn Minju Chuŭi Inmin Konghwaguk and Chosŏn Inmin'gun. Similarly, it is Korean Central News Agency for Chosŏn Chungang T'ongsinsa, but it is the Workers' Party of Korea for Chosŏn Nodongdang. In all these cases, the North Korean practice that has been regularized in their English translations has been followed. It is important to establish a standard for these terms and to conform to the standard. It is the Workers' Party of Korea and not the Korean Workers' Party, and it is the Korean People's Army and not the People's Army of Korea.

Under the 1972 constitution, the North Koreans have changed some of the names of their organizations; for example, the Supreme Court has become the Central Court, and the chief justice of the Supreme Court has become the president of the Central Court. The designation of ministries and commissions remained the same in English, but the Korean designation of ministry was changed from *sŏng* to *pu*, and the minister from *sang* to *pujang*. All the past and present names of ministries and commissions are included here, but there are many nonministerial organizations that have ceased to exist, and they are not included here unless the organization played an important role in the development of the North and is mentioned often in subsequent writings. A number of organizations changed their names in the course of their development, and important ones are included here, for example, the Democratic Youth League of Korea, which changed its name at the fifth congress to the League of Socialist Working Youth.

It is also important to distinguish the same or similar terms in English that have different terms in Korean and represent different political organizations. For example, the secretary of the Administration Council is *samujang* in Korean, and the secretary of the Workers' Party of Korea is *pisŏ* in Korean. Similarly, the premier of the first four cabinets was called *susang* in Korean, but the premier under the 1972 constitution is called *ch'ongni*. The president of the republic is now called *chusŏk*, and the president of the Central Court is called *sojang*. The secretary-general of the Central People's Committee is called *sŏgijang*, and *ch'ong pisŏ* of the Workers' Party of Korea is called general secretary and not secretary-general.

As to common English terms, only a few political terms that are frequently used, particularly those describing expressions of ideas such as mysticism, dogmatism, and flunkeyism, and some that involve uncommon usage of terms, such as departmentalism and formalism, are included here. For a more comprehensive list of the terms for translation purposes, there is a glossary of North Korean terms published by the

Joint Publication Research Service in May 1973. There are some North Korean inventions of terms that did not exist in the English language, such as *closed-doorism* for *kwanmun chuŭi* and *working-classization* for *nodong kyegŭphwa*. These are controversial terms and they are not included, for more appropriate terms may be devised and regularized in the future.

Other terms should be added, of course, but it is hoped that the following list of simple but basic terms will be subscribed to by scholars and its usage regularized in scholarly writings about North Korea.

LIST OF TERMS

ENGLISH-KOREAN

Academy of Sciences	Kwahagwŏn
Administration Council (AC)	Chŏngmuwŏn
Administrative Committee	Haengjŏng wiwŏnhoe
Agricultural Commission	Nongŏp wiwŏnhoe
Bills Committee (of the SPA)	Pŏban simŭi wiwŏnhoe
Budget Committee (of the SPA)	Yesan simŭi wiwŏnhoe
bureaucratism	kwallyo chuŭi
candidate member	hubo wiwŏn
Central Auditing Committee	Chungang kŏmsa wiwŏnhoe
Central Committee (CC)	Chungang wiwŏnhoe
Central Court	Chungang chaep'anso
Central Party School	Chungang tang hakkyo
Central People's Committee (CPC)	Chungang inmin wiwŏnhoe
Central Procurator's Office	Chungang kŏmch'also
Ch'ŏllima rider	Ch'ŏllima ŭi kisu
Ch'ŏllima Workteam Movement	Ch'ŏllima chagŏppan undong
Ch'ŏndogyo Young Friends Party	Ch'ŏndogyo ch'ŏngudang
class spirit	kyegŭpsŏng
collectivism	chiptan chuŭi
colonel	sangjwa
colonel-general	sangjang
Commission for Economic Relations with Foreign Countries	Taeoe kyŏngje wiwŏnhoe
Committee for the Peaceful Reunification of the Fatherland	Choguk p'yŏnghwa t'ongil wiwŏnhoe
Confederal Republic of Koryŏ	Koryŏ yŏnbang konghwaguk
County Cooperative Farm Management Committee	Kun hyŏptong nongjang kyŏngyŏng wiwŏnhoe
Credentials Committee (of the SPA)	Chagyŏk simsa wiwŏnhoe
democratic centralism	minju chuŭi chungang chipkwŏnje
Democratic Front for the Reunification of the Fatherland	Choguk t'ongil minju chuŭi chŏnsŏn

Democratic Lawyers Association of Korea — Chosŏn minju pŏmyulga hyŏphoe

Democratic National United Front — Minju chuŭi minjok t'ongil chŏnsŏn

Democratic People's Republic of Korea (DPRK) — Chosŏn minju chuŭi inmin konghwa- guk

Democratic Scientists Association of Korea — Chosŏn minju kwahakcha hyŏphoe

Democratic Women's Union of Korea — Chosŏn minju yŏsŏng tongmaeng

Democratic Youth League of Korea (DYL) — Chosŏn minju ch'ŏngnyŏn tongmaeng

departmentalism — kigwan bonwi chuŭi

dogmatism — kyojo chuŭi

Domestic Policy Commission (of the CPC) — Taenae chŏngch'aek wiwŏnhoe

Education Commission — Kyoyuk wiwŏnhoe

enlarged plenary meeting (of the WPK) — hwaktae chŏnwŏn hoeŭi

factionalism — chongp'a chuŭi

First Ministry of Machine Industry — Cheil kigye kongŏp sŏng

first vice-premier — cheil pususang

Five-Point Policy of Nature Re- making — Chayŏn kaejo odae pangch'im

flunkeyism — sadae chuŭi

Foreign Affairs Committee (of the SPA) — Oegyo wiwŏnhoe

Foreign Policy Commission (of the CPC) — Taeoe chŏngch'aek wiwŏnhoe

formalism — hyŏngsik chuŭi

General Association of Korean Resi- dents in Japan — Chae ilbon chosŏn in ch'ong yŏnhap- hoe

General Federation of Literature and Arts of Korea — Chosŏn munhak yesul ch'ong tong- maeng

General Federation of Science and Technology — Kwahak kisul ch'ong yŏnmaeng

General Federation of Trade Unions — Chigŏp ch'ong tongmaeng

general secretary (of the WPK) — ch'ong pisŏ

Heavy Industry Commission — Chung kongŏp wiwŏnhoe

independence — chaju

Inspection Committee (of the CC) — Kŏmyŏl wiwŏnhoe

junior lieutenant — sowi

Justice and Security Commission (of the CPC) — Sabŏp anjŏn wiwŏnhoe

Juvenile Corps — Sonyŏndan

Korean Central News Agency (KCNA) — Chosŏn chungang t'ongsinsa

Korean Communist Party (KCP) — Chosŏn kongsandang

Korean Democratic Party — Chosŏn minjudang

Korean Journalists Union   Chosŏn kija tongmaeng
Korean People's Army (KPA)   Chosŏn inmin'gun
League of Socialist Working Youth   Sahoe chuŭi nodong ch'ŏngnyŏn
  (LSWY)   tongmaeng
liberalism   chayu chuŭi
Light Industry Commission   Kyŏng kongŏp wiwŏnhoe
Machine Industry Commission   Kigye kongŏp wiwŏnhoe
Manpower Administration   Nodong haengjŏng
marshal   wŏnsu
Materials Supply Commission   Chajae konggŭp wiwŏnhoe
Meritorious War Service Medal   Kun'gong medal
Military Armistice Commission   Kunsa chŏngjŏn wiwŏnhoe
Mining Industry Commission   Kwangŏp wiwŏnhoe
Ministry of Agriculture   Nongŏp sŏng
Ministry of Agriculture and Forestry   Nongnim sŏng
Ministry of Building Materials Industry   Kŏnjae kongŏp pu (sŏng)
Ministry of Chemical and Building   Hwahak kŏnjae kongŏp sŏng
  Materials Industries
Ministry of Chemical Industry   Hwahak kongŏp pu (sŏng)
Ministry of City and Industry Con-   Tosi mit san'ŏp sŏng
  struction
Ministry of City Construction   Tosi kŏnsŏl sŏng
Ministry of City Construction Man-   Tosi kŏnsŏl kyŏngyŏng sŏng
  agement
Ministry of City Management   Tosi kyŏngyŏng sŏng
Ministry of Coal Industry   Sŏkt'an kongŏp sŏng
Ministry of Commerce   Sangŏp sŏng
Ministry of Common Education   Pot'ong kyoyuk sŏng
Ministry of Communications   Ch'esin pu (sŏng)
Ministry of Construction   Kŏnsŏl pu (sŏng)
Ministry of Construction and   Kŏnsŏl kŏnjae kongŏp sŏng
  Building Materials Industries
Ministry of Culture   Munhwa sŏng
Ministry of Culture and Art   Munhwa yesul pu
Ministry of Culture and Propaganda   Munhwa sŏnjŏn sŏng
Ministry of Education   Kyoyuk pu (sŏng)
Ministry of Education and Culture   Kyoyuk munhwa sŏng
Ministry of Electric Power   Chŏn'gi sŏng
Ministry of External Economic   Taeoe kyŏngje saŏp pu
  Affairs
Ministry of Finance   Chaejŏng pu (sŏng)
Ministry of Fisheries   Susan pu (sŏng)
Ministry of Foodstuff and Daily   Singnyo mit iryongp'um kongŏp sŏng
  Necessities Industries
Ministry of Foreign Affairs   Oemu pu (sŏng)

Ministry of Foreign Trade	Muyŏk pu (sŏng)
Ministry of Forestry	Imŏp sŏng
Ministry of Heavy Industry	Chung kongŏp sŏng
Ministry of Higher Education	Kodŭng kyoyuk sŏng
Ministry of Industry	Sanŏp sŏng
Ministry of Interior	Naemu sŏng
Ministry of Internal and External Commerce	Taenae taeoe sangŏp sŏng
Ministry of Justice	Sabŏp sŏng
Ministry of Labor	Nodong sŏng
Ministry of Labor Administration	Nodong haengjŏng pu
Ministry of Land Administration	Kukt'o kwalli sŏng
Ministry of Land and Sea Transportation	Yugun mit haeun pu (sŏng)
Ministry of Light Industry	Kyŏng kongŏp pu (sŏng)
Ministry of Local Administration	Chibang haengjŏng sŏng
Ministry of Machine Industry	Kigye kongŏp pu (sŏng)
Ministry of Materials Supply	Chajae konggŭp pu
Ministry of Metal and Chemical Industries	Kŭmsok hwahak kongŏp sŏng
Ministry of Metal Industry	Kŭmsok kongŏp pu (sŏng)
Ministry of Mining Industry	Kwangŏp sŏng
Ministry of National Defense	Minjok powi sŏng
Ministry of People's Armed Forces	Inmin muryŏk pu
Ministry of Power and Chemical Industries	Tongyŏk hwahak kongŏp sŏng
Ministry of Power and Coal Industries	Chŏn'gi sŏkt'an kongŏp sŏng
Ministry of Power Industry	Chŏllyŏk kongŏp pu
Ministry of Procurement and Food Administration	Sumae yangjŏng sŏng
Ministry of Public Health	Pogŏn pu (sŏng)
Ministry of Public Security	Sahoe anjŏn pu (sŏng)
Ministry of Railways	Ch'ŏlto pu (sŏng)
Ministry of Rural Construction	Nongch'on kŏnsŏl sŏng
Ministry of Rural Management	Chibang kyŏngni sŏng
Ministry of Ship Machine Building Industry	Sŏnbak kigye kongŏp pu
Ministry of State Control	Kukka kŏmyŏl sŏng
Ministry of Textile and Paper Industries	Pangjik cheji kongŏp sŏng
Ministry of Transportation	Kyot'ong sŏng
Ministry without Portfolio	Muimso sŏng
monolithic ideological system	yuil sasang ch'egye
monolithic ideology	yuil sasang
mysticism	sinbi chuŭi

National Defense Commission (of the CPC) — Kukpang wiwŏnhoe

national nihilism — minjok hŏmu chuŭi

negativism — sogŭk chuŭi

nepotism — kajok chuŭi

North Korean Branch Bureau (of the KCP) — Pukchosŏn pun'guk

North Korean Provisional People's Committee (NKPPC) — Pukchosŏn imsi inmin wiwŏnhoe

North-South Coordination Committee — Nambuk chojŏl wiwŏnhoe

opportunism — kihoe chuŭi

Order of Labor — Noryŏk hunjang

Order of National Flag — Kukki hunjang

Organization Committee (of the WPK) — Chojik wiwŏnhoe

parochialism — chibang chuŭi

party cadre — tang kanbu

party center — tang chungang

party conference — tang taep'yoja hoeŭi

party congress — tang taehoe

party spirit — tangsŏng

People's Assembly — Inmin hoeŭi

People's Assembly of North Korea (PANK) — Pukchosŏn inmin hoeŭi

People's Assessor — Inmin ch'amsimwŏn

People's Committee — Inmin wiwŏnhoe

People's Constabulary — Inmin kyŏngbidae

People's Control Commission — Inmin kŏmyŏl wiwŏnhoe

People's Court — Inmin chaep'anso

People's Service Commission — Inmin pongsa wiwŏnhoe

Permanent Commission — Sangmu hoeŭi

plenary meeting — chŏnwŏn hoeŭi

Political Committee (of the WPK) — Chŏngch'i wiwŏnhoe

popular spirit — inminsŏng

premier — susang

premier (of the AC) — ch'ongni

president of the Central Court — chungang chaep'anso sojang

president of the republic — kukka chusŏk

procurator-general of the Central Procurator's Office — chungang kŏmch'also sojang

Provincial Court — To chaep'anso

provincialism — chibang ponwi chuŭi

Railway Transportation Commission — Kyot'ong unsu wiwŏnhoe

Red Young Guards — Pulgun ch'ŏngnyŏn kŭnwidae

restorationism — pokko chuŭi

revisionism — sujŏng chuŭi

Revolutionary Party for Reunification (RPR) T'ongil hyŏngmyŏngdang

secretary (of the AC and SPA) samujang

secretary (of the WPK) pisŏ

secretary-general (of the CPC) sŏgijang

Second Ministry of Machine Industry Chei kigye kongŏp sŏng

self-defense chawi

self-sustenance charip

senior colonel taejwa

senior lieutenant sangwi

Special Court T'ŭkpyŏl chaep'anso

Standing Committee (of the SPA) Sangsŏl hoeŭi

Standing Committee (of the WPK) Sangim wiwŏnhoe

State Construction Commission Kukka kŏnsŏl wiwŏnhoe

State Light Industry Commission Kukka kyŏng kongŏp wiwŏnhoe

State Scientific and Technological Commission Kukka kwahak kisul wiwŏnhoe

State Planning Commission Kukka kyehoek wiwŏnhoe

subjectivism chugwan chuŭi

Supreme Court Ch'oego chaep'anso

Supreme People's Assembly (SPA) Ch'oego inmin hoeŭi

Taean Work System Taean ŭi saŏp ch'egye

Three Major Tasks of Technical Revolution Samdae kisul hyŏngmyŏng

Three-Revolution Red Flag Movement Samdae hyŏngmyŏng pulgun'gi chaengch'wi undong

Three-Revolution Team Samdae hyŏngmyŏng sojo

Transportation and Communication Commission Kyot'ong ch'esin wiwŏnhoe

Union of Agricultural Working People (UAWP) Nongŏp kŭlloja tongmaeng

vice-marshal ch'asu

vice-premier pususang

vice-premier (of the AC) puch'ongni

vice-president of the republic kukka pujusŏk

Worker-Peasant Red Guards Nonong chŏgwidae

Workers' Party of Korea (WPK) Chosŏn nodongdang

Workers' Party of North Korea Pukchosŏn nodongdang

Workers' Party of South Korea Namchosŏn nodongdang

KOREAN-ENGLISH

Chae ilbon chosŏnin ch'ong yŏnhap-hoe General Association of Korean Residents in Japan

Chaejŏng pu (sŏng) Ministry of Finance

Chagyŏk simsa wiwŏnhoe Credentials Committee (of the SPA)

Chajae konggŭp pu	Ministry of Materials Supply
Chajae konggŭp wiwŏnhoe	Materials Supply Commission
chaju	independence
charip	self-sustenance
ch'asu	vice-marshal
chawi	self-defense
Chayŏn kaejo odae pangch'im	Five-Point Policy of Nature Remaking
chayu chuŭi	liberalism
Chei kigye kongŏp sŏng	Second Ministry of Machine Industry
Cheil kigye kongŏp sŏng	First Ministry of Machine Industry
cheil pususang	first vice-premier
Ch'esin pu (sŏng)	Ministry of Communications
chibang chuŭi	parochialism
Chibang haengjŏng sŏng	Ministry of Local Administration
Chibang kyŏngni sŏng	Ministry of Rural Management
chibang ponwi chuŭi	provincialism
Chigŏp ch'ong tongmaeng	General Federation of Trade Unions
chiptan chuŭi	collectivism
Ch'oego chaep'anso	Supreme Court
Ch'oego inmin hoeŭi	Supreme People's Assembly (SPA)
Choguk p'yŏnghwa t'ongil wiwŏnhoe	Committee for the Peaceful Reunification of the Fatherland
Choguk t'ongil minju chuŭi chŏnsŏn	Democratic Front for the Reunification of the Fatherland
Chojik wiwŏnhoe	Organization Committee (of the WPK)
Ch'ŏllima chagŏppan undong	Ch'ŏllima Workteam Movement
Ch'ŏllima ŭi kisu	Ch'ŏllima rider
Chŏllyŏk kongŏp pu	Ministry of Power Industry
Ch'ŏlto pu (sŏng)	Ministry of Railways
Ch'ŏndogyo ch'ŏngudang	Ch'ŏndogyo Young Friends Party
ch'ong pisŏ	general secretary (of the WPK)
Chŏngch'i wiwŏnhoe	Political Committee (of the WPK)
Chŏn'gi sŏkt'an kongŏp sŏng	Ministry of Power and Coal Industries
Chŏn'gi sŏng	Ministry of Electric Power
Chŏngmuwŏn	Administration Council (AC)
ch'ongni	premier (of the AC)
chongp'a chuŭi	factionalism
chŏnwŏn hoeŭi	plenary meeting
Chosŏn chungang t'ongsinsa	Korean Central News Agency (KCNA)
Chosŏn inmin'gun	Korean People's Army (KPA)
Chosŏn kija tongmaeng	Korean Journalists Union
Chosŏn kongsandang	Korean Communist Party (KCP)
Chosŏn minju ch'ŏngnyŏn tongmaeng	Democratic Youth League of Korea (DYL)

Chosŏn minju chuŭi inmin konghwaguk
Chosŏn minju kwahakcha hyŏphoe

Chosŏn minju pŏmyulga hyŏphoe

Chosŏn minju yŏsŏng tongmaeng
Chosŏn minjudang
Chosŏn munhak yesul ch'ong tong-
   maeng
Chosŏn nodongdang
chugwan chuŭi
Chungang chaep'anso
chungang chaep'anso sojang
Chungang inmin wiwŏnhoe
Chungang kŏmch'also
chungang kŏmch'also sojang

Chungang kŏmsa wiwŏnhoe
Chung kongŏp sŏng
Chung kongŏp wiwŏnhoe
Chungang tang hakkyo
Chungang wiwŏnhoe
Haengjŏng wiwŏnhoe
hubo wiwŏn
Hwahak kŏnjae kongŏp sŏng

Hwahak kongŏp pu (sŏng)
hwaktae chŏnwŏn hoeŭi

hyŏngsik chuŭi
Imŏp sŏng
Inmin chaep'anso
Inmin ch'amsimwŏn
Inmin hoeŭi
Inmin kŏmyŏl wiwŏnhoe
Inmin kyŏngbidae
Inmin muryŏk pu
Inmin pongsa wiwŏnhoe
Inmin wiwŏnhoe
inminsŏng
kajok chuŭi
kigwan bonwi chuŭi
Kigye kongŏp pu (sŏng)
Kigye kongŏp wiwŏnhoe
kihoe chuŭi
Kodŭng kyoyuk sŏng

Democratic People's Republic of
   Korea (DPRK)
Democratic Scientists Association of
   Korea
Democratic Lawyers Association of
   Korea
Democratic Women's Union of Korea
Korean Democratic Party
General Federation of Literature and
   Arts of Korea
Workers' Party of Korea (WPK)
subjectivism
Central Court
president of the Central Court
Central People's Committee (CPC)
Central Procurator's Office
procurator-general of the Central
   Procurator's Office
Central Auditing Committee
Ministry of Heavy Industry
Heavy Industry Commission
Central Party School
Central Committee (CC)
Administrative Committee
candidate member
Ministry of Chemical and Building
   Materials Industries
Ministry of Chemical Industry
enlarged plenary meeting (of the
   WPK)
formalism
Ministry of Forestry
People's Court
People's Assessor
People's Assembly
People's Control Commission
People's Constabulary
Ministry of People's Armed Forces
People's Service Commission
People's Committee
popular spirit
nepotism
departmentalism
Ministry of Machine Industry
Machine Industry Commission
opportunism
Ministry of Higher Education

Kŏmyŏl wiwŏnhoe | Inspection Committee (of the CC)
Kŏnjae kongŏp pu (sŏng) | Ministry of Building Materials Industry

Kŏnsŏl pu (sŏng) | Ministry of Construction
Kŏnsŏl kŏnjae kongŏp sŏng | Ministry of Construction and Building Materials Industries

Koryŏ yŏnbang konghwaguk | Confederal Republic of Koryŏ
kukka chusŏk | president of the republic
Kukka kŏmyŏl sŏng | Ministry of State Control
Kukka kŏnsŏl wiwŏnhoe | State Construction Commission
Kukka kwahak kisul wiwŏnhoe | State Scientific and Technological Commission

Kukka kyehoek wiwŏnhoe | State Planning Commission
Kukka kyŏngkongŏp wiwŏnhoe | State Light Industry Commission
kukka pujusŏk | vice-president of the republic
Kukki hunjang | Order of National Flag
Kukpang wiwŏnhoe | National Defense Commission (of the CPC)

Kukt'o kwalli sŏng | Ministry of Land Administration
Kŭmsok hwahak kongŏp sŏng | Ministry of Metal and Chemical Industries

Kŭmsok kongŏp pu (sŏng) | Ministry of Metal Industry
Kun hyŏptong nongjang kyŏngyŏng wiwŏnhoe | County Cooperative Farm Management Committee
Kun'gong medal | Meritorious War Service Medal
Kunsa chŏngjŏn wiwŏnhoe | Military Armistice Commission
Kwahak kisul ch'ong yŏnmaeng | General Federation of Science and Technology

Kwahagwŏn | Academy of Sciences
kwallyo chuŭi | bureaucratism
Kwangŏp sŏng | Ministry of Mining Industry
Kwangŏp wiwŏnhoe | Mining Industry Commission
kyegŭpsŏng | class spirit
kyojo chuŭi | dogmatism
Kyŏng kongŏp pu (sŏng) | Ministry of Light Industry
Kyŏng kongŏp wiwŏnhoe | Light Industry Commission
Kyot'ong ch'esin wiwŏnhoe | Transportation and Communication Commission

Kyot'ong sŏng | Ministry of Transportation
Kyot'ong unsu wiwŏnhoe | Railway Transportation Commission
Kyoyuk pu (sŏng) | Ministry of Education
Kyoyuk munhwa sŏng | Ministry of Education and Culture
Kyoyuk wiwŏnhoe | Education Commission
minjok hŏmu chuŭi | national nihilism
Minjok powi sŏng | Ministry of National Defense
minju chuŭi chungang chipkwŏnje | democratic centralism

Minju chuŭi minjok t'ongil chŏnsŏn   Democratic National United Front
Muimso sŏng   Ministry without Portfolio
Munhwa sŏng   Ministry of Culture
Munhwa sŏnjŏn sŏng   Ministry of Culture and Propaganda
Munhwa yesul pu   Ministry of Culture and Art
Muyŏk pu (sŏng)   Ministry of Foreign Trade
Naemu sŏng   Ministry of Interior
Nambuk chojŏl wiwŏnhoe   North-South Coordination Commission

Namchosŏn nodongdang   Workers' Party of South Korea
Nodong haengjŏng   Manpower Administration
Nodong haengjŏng pu   Ministry of Labor Administration
Nodong sŏng   Ministry of Labor
Nongch'on kŏnsŏl sŏng   Ministry of Rural Construction
Nongnim sŏng   Ministry of Agriculture and Forestry
Nongŏp kŭlloja tongmaeng   Union of Agricultural Working People (UAWP)

Nongŏp sŏng   Ministry of Agriculture
Nongŏp wiwŏnhoe   Agricultural Commission
Nonong chŏgwidae   Worker-Peasant Red Guards
Noryŏk hunjang   Order of Labor
Oegyo wiwŏnhoe   Foreign Affairs Committee (of the SPA)

Oemu pu (sŏng)   Ministry of Foreign Affairs
Pangjik cheji kongŏp sŏng   Ministry of Textile and Paper Industries

pisŏ   secretary (of the WPK)
Pŏban simŭi wiwŏnhoe   Bills Committee (of the SPA)
Pogŏn pu (sŏng)   Ministry of Public Health
pokko chuŭi   restorationism
Pot'ong kyoyuk sŏng   Ministry of Common Education
puch'ongni   vice-premier (of the AC)
Pukchosŏn inmin hoeŭi   People's Assembly of North Korea (PANK)

Pukchosŏn imsi inmin wiwŏnhoe   North Korean Provisional People's Committee (NKPPC)

Pukchosŏn nodongdang   Workers' Party of North Korea
Pukchosŏn pun'guk   North Korean Branch Bureau (of the KCP)

Pulgun ch'ŏngnyŏn kŭnwidae   Red Young Guards
pususang   vice-premier
Sabŏp anjŏn wiwŏnhoe   Justice and Security Commission (of the CPC)

Sabŏp sŏng   Ministry of Justice
sadae chuŭi   flunkeyism
Sahoe anjŏn pu (sŏng)   Ministry of Public Security

Sahoe chuŭi nodong ch'ŏngnyŏn tongmaeng — League of Socialist Working Youth (LSWY)

Samdae hyŏngmyŏng pulgun'gi chaengch'wi undong — Three-Revolution Red Flag Movement

Samdae hyŏngmyŏng sojo — Three-Revolution Team

Samdae kisul hyŏngmyŏng — Three Major Tasks of Technical Revolution

samujang — secretary (of the AC and SPA)

Sangim wiwŏnhoe — Standing Committee (of the WPK)

sangjang — colonel-general

sangjwa — colonel

Sangmu hoeŭi — Permanent Commission

Sangŏp sŏng — Ministry of Commerce

Sangsŏl hoeŭi — Standing Committee (of the SPA)

sangwi — senior lieutenant

Sanŏp sŏng — Ministry of Industry

sinbi chuŭi — mysticism

Singnyo mit iryongp'um kongŏp sŏng — Ministry of Foodstuff and Daily Necessities Industries

sŏgijang — secretary-general (of the CPC)

sogŭk chuŭi — negativism

Sŏkt'an kongŏp sŏng — Ministry of Coal Industry

Sŏnbak kigye kongŏp pu — Ministry of Ship Machine Building Industry

Sonyŏndan — Juvenile Corps

sowi — junior lieutenant

sujŏng chuŭi — revisionism

Sumae yangjŏng sŏng — Ministry of Procurement and Food Administration

Susan pu (sŏng) — Ministry of Fisheries

susang — premier

Taean ŭi saŏp ch'egye — Taean Work System

taejwa — senior-colonel

Taenae chŏngch'aek wiwŏnhoe — Domestic Policy Commission (of the CPC)

Taenae taeoe sangŏp sŏng — Ministry of Internal and External Commerce

Taeoe chŏngch'aek wiwŏnhoe — Foreign Policy Commission (of the CPC)

Taeoe kyŏngje saŏp pu — Ministry of External Economic Affairs

Taeoe kyŏngje wiwŏnhoe — Commission for Economic Relations with Foreign Countries

tang chungang — party center

tang kanbu — party cadre

tang taehoe — party congress

tang taep'yoja hoeŭi	party conference
tangsŏng	party spirit
To chaep'anso	Provincial Court
T'ongil hyŏngmyŏngdang	Revolutionary Party for Reunification (RPR)
Tongyŏk hwahak kongŏp sŏng	Ministry of Power and Chemical Industries
Tosi kŏnsŏl kyŏngyŏng sŏng	Ministry of City Construction Management
Tosi kŏnsŏl sŏng	Ministry of City Construction
Tosi kyŏngyŏng sŏng	Ministry of City Management
Tosi mit san'ŏp sŏng	Ministry of City and Industry Construction
T'ŭkpyŏl chaep'anso	Special Court
wŏnsu	marshal
Yesan simŭi wiwŏnhoe	Budget Committee (of the SPA)
Yugun mit haeun pu (sŏng)	Ministry of Land and Sea Transportation
yuil sasang	monolithic ideology
yuil sasang ch'egye	monolithic ideological system

Name Index

Adassi, N., 171
Aini, Mohsin Ahmed Al, 183
Ali, Salem Rubaya, 198
Ali Bhutto, Sulfikar, 210
Allende, Salvador, 176
An Chae-sŭng, 407
An Ch'an-su, 303
An Ch'ang-hwa, 416
An Ch'ang-se, 303, 413, 420
An Hŭi-nam, 399
An Ki-sŏng, 289, 398
An Kil, 317
An Myŏng-ch'ŏl, 331
An Pae-ok, 329, 346
An Pyŏng-su, 403
An Sang-ch'un, 412
An Se-hun, 399
An Si-do, 397
An Sin-ho, 396
An Suk-yong, 408, 415, 423
An Sŭng-bae, 415
An Sŭng-hak, 303, 327, 331, 334, 352,
    409, 414, 453, 460, 489
An T'al-sil, 424
An Tal-su, 403, 411, 417, 425, 430
An Yŏng, 326, 410, 414
An Yŏng-bok, 422
An Yong-gak, 478, 489
An Yŏng-gil, 396
An Yong-guk, 453
An Yŏng-hwan, 413
An Yŏng-il, 396
An Yŏng-muk, 397
An Yong-u, 422
Antaku Tsunehiko, 225
Assad, Hafez Al, 197

Bagaza, Jean-Baptiste, 225
Balout, Ali, 172
Banga, Mobutu Sese Seko Kuku Ngbendu
    Wa Za, 199

Barre, Mohamed Siad, 181
Beavogui, Lansana, 185
Berlinguer, Enrico, 228
Bokassa, the First, 220
Bongo, El Hadj Omar, 214
Boumedienne, Houari, 192, 203
Bulganin, N. A., 125
Burchett, Wilfred, 207
Burham, Linden Forbes Sampson, 220

Cabral, Luiz, 227
Carillo, Santiago, 184
Ceausescu, Nikolae, 176, 203, 221, 222,
    228
Ch'a Chi-hun, 397
Ch'a Kye-ryong, 424
Ch'a Sŏk-ho, 417
Ch'a Sun-ch'ŏl, 321
Ch'ae Chun-sŏk, 395
Ch'ae Hŭi-jŏng, 327, 335, 410, 456, 470,
    489
Ch'ae Ki-ok, 400
Ch'ae Kyu-hyŏng, 321
Ch'ae Paek-hŭi, 396
Chang Chae-gak, 424
Chang Ch'i-suk, 421
Chang Ch'ŏl, 320, 331, 335, 346, 350,
    397
Chang Chŏng-hwan, 410, 414, 424
Chang Chong-sik, 318
Chang Ch'ŏng-t'aek, 409
Chang Chong-yŏp, 422
Chang Chun, 397
Chang Ha-il, 324
Chang Ha-myŏng, 400
Chang Hae-u, 320, 346, 364, 394, 401,
    402, 432, 498
Chang Ho-sam, 422
Chang Hŭi-do, 412
Chang Il-gyŏng, 414, 421
Chang In-sŏk, 334, 425

Chang Ki-uk, 398
Chang Kil-yong, 396, 419
Chang Kuk-ch'an, 308, 334
Chang Kuk-chin, 303
Chang Kwŏn, 393, 432
Chang Kyŏng-sun, 408
Chang Myŏng-jun, 408
Chang P'yŏng-san, 324, 402
Chang Pyŏng-su, 410
Chang Sam-son, 303, 415
Chang Sang-bong, 398
Chang Sang-yong, 415
Chang Si-u, 289, 317, 320, 393, 448,
    460, 489
Chang Sŏk-ha, 413
Chang Sŏn-sik, 421
Chang Sŏng-u, 334
Chang Sun-myŏng, 126, 289, 317, 320,
    346, 358, 393, 432
Chang Tong-sun, 425
Chang U-uk, 395
Chang Wi-sam, 321
Chang Yun-p'il, 297, 303, 327, 330, 334,
    352, 391, 401, 402, 406, 410, 412,
    417, 420, 426, 430, 432, 438, 439
Che Guevara, 166
Chi Chae-ryong, 308, 426, 432
Chi Chang-gŏn, 406, 407, 413, 438
Chi Ch'ang-ik, 308, 335
Chi Kŭm-ju, 425
Chi Kŭn-su, 424
Chi Kyŏng-su, 421
Chi Myŏng-gwan, 408
Chi Pyŏng-hak, 327, 330, 411, 413, 424
Chin Ch'ang-hu, 303, 385, 424
Chin Mun-dŏk, 417, 423, 453, 462, 489
Chin Pan-su, 317, 319, 320, 323, 340,
    346, 404, 450, 460, 467, 469, 489
Chin Pyŏng-mu, 408, 413, 420
Chin Sang-gi, 423
Chin Ŭng-wŏn, 164
Chin Yŏng-dong, 416
Cho Chae-han, 395
Cho Ch'ang-dŏk, 308, 334, 385, 455,
    473, 489
Cho Ch'ang-sŏn, 416
Cho Ch'ang-suk, 415, 422
Cho Chin-suk, 422
Cho Ch'ŏl-jun, 335
Cho Chŏng-hyŏn, 404
Cho Ch'un-sam, 413, 420
Cho Chung-gon, 397
Cho Chung-gwang, 394
Cho Chung-wŏn, 415
Cho Han-yŏng, 282
Cho Hi-yŏng, 282, 395

Cho Hŭi-wŏn, 334
Cho Hun, 324
Cho Il-myŏng, 288
Cho In-guk, 403
Cho Kŭm-sŏng, 397
Cho Kwan-ha, 414, 453, 463, 489
Cho Kyŏng-hŭi, 384
Cho Kyŏng-suk, 416
Cho Man-sik, 35, 41
Cho Mi-ri 420
Cho Myŏng-hwa, 407, 414
Cho Myŏng-nok, 334, 336
Cho Myŏng-sŏn, 331, 334, 352, 423
Cho Pok-ae, 399
Cho Pok-nye, 289, 396
Cho Pŏm-gu, 395
Cho Se-ung, 332, 333, 342, 383, 420
Cho Sŏk-ku, 419
Cho Sŏng-gyu, 398
Cho Sŏng-mo, 118, 325, 373, 404, 496,
    497, 498
Cho Sun-baek, 334, 424
Cho Sun-ok, 417
Cho Sun-yong, 297
Cho T'ae-u, 397
Cho Tong-sŏk, 400
Cho Tong-sŏp, 408, 451, 472, 489
Cho Tong-su, 424
Cho U-bang, 399
Cho Un, 393, 432
Cho Ŭng-sŏp, 408
Cho Wŏn-suk, 399
Cho Yŏng, 292, 320, 324, 399, 401, 405,
    437
Cho Yŏng-mu, 415
Cho Yŏng-nae, 396
Cho Yong-p'al, 415
Cho Yong-se, 394
Cho Yŏng-suk, 384, 421
Ch'oe Chae-gon, 303
Ch'oe Chae-ha, 404, 450, 461, 463, 489
Ch'oe Chae-hyŏp, 422
Ch'oe Chae-rin, 320
Ch'oe Ch'ae-ryŏng, 413
Ch'oe Chae-u, 305, 327, 330, 333, 342,
    352, 383, 384, 410, 417, 418, 424,
    436, 453, 454, 468, 472, 477, 480,
    482, 486, 487, 488, 489
Ch'oe Ch'ang-do, 407, 413, 420
Ch'oe Ch'ang-gŏl, 408
Ch'oe Ch'ang-gwŏn, 303, 330
Ch'oe Ch'ang-hwan, 331, 336
Ch'oe Ch'ang-ik, 117, 127, 283, 289, 317,
    319, 320, 322, 323, 340, 343, 344,
    348, 356, 357, 369, 370, 371, 449,
    465, 478, 481, 489

Ch'oe Ch'ang-sŏk, 297, 327, 407, 451,
476, 489
Ch'oe Ch'ang-yong, 414
Ch'oe Ch'i-sŏn, 336, 425
Ch'oe Ch'il-gap, 409, 415, 423
Ch'oe Chin-sŏng, 302, 331, 334, 352, 421
Ch'oe Ch'ol-hwan, 324, 401, 403, 438
Ch'oe Chŏng, 409
Ch'oe Chong-gŏn, 327, 331, 350, 412,
441
Ch'oe Chŏng-gŭn, 334
Ch'oe Chong-hak, 130, 292, 324, 401,
404, 437
Ch'oe Chong-yŏng, 422
Ch'oe Ch'un-gil, 421
Ch'oe Ch'un-sŏp, 407, 412, 413, 438
Ch'oe Chun-yŏng, 394
Ch'oe Ch'ŭn-yong, 422
Ch'oe Chung-gŭk, 412, 416, 424, 440
Ch'oe Chung-san, 409, 415, 423
Ch'oe Chung-sŏk, 409
Ch'oe Chung-son, 416, 424
Ch'oe Hak-sŏn, 327, 406, 409, 440
Ch'oe Han-ch'ŏl, 398
Ch'oe Han-gil, 384
Ch'oe Han-sik, 400
Ch'oe Hyŏn, 324, 326, 328, 329, 332,
333, 336, 340, 344, 348, 404, 405,
407, 411, 412, 418, 419, 421, 426,
427, 430, 432, 435, 436, 454, 463,
474, 489
Ch'oe Hyŏn-gi, 383, 422
Ch'oe Hyŏn-gyu, 303
Ch'oe Hyŏn-suk, 420
Ch'oe Ik-han, 394
Ch'oe Ik-kyu, 382, 420
Ch'oe Il, 324
Ch'oe In, 399
Ch'oe In-dŏk, 330, 334, 412, 424
Ch'oe Ka-ma, 398
Ch'oe Ki-ch'ŏl, 326, 406, 409, 437
Ch'oe Ki-nam, 397
Ch'oe Ki-wŏn, 408
Ch'oe Kŭm-bok, 397
Ch'oe Kŭm-nyŏ, 414
Ch'oe Kŭm-san, 415, 423
Ch'oe Kwan-yong, 397
Ch'oe Kwang, 4, 89, 324, 326, 328, 332,
333, 342, 344, 347, 352, 356, 398,
403, 407, 411, 412, 430, 432
Ch'oe Kwang-yŏl, 321
Ch'oe Kyŏng-dŏk, 317, 320, 393, 432
Ch'oe Kyŏng-hu, 413
Ch'oe Kyŏng-hwi, 402
Ch'oe Kyu-hwan, 417
Ch'oe Man-guk, 332, 410, 417, 424

Ch'oe Man-hyŏn, 335
Ch'oe Min-ch'ŏl, 327, 416
Ch'oe Min-hwan, 409, 416
Ch'oe Mun-sŏn, 334
Ch'oe Myŏng-ch'ŏl, 336
Ch'oe Nam-hyang, 384, 421
Ch'oe Ŏk-chun, 411, 417
Ch'oe Pong-san, 409, 415
Ch'oe Pong-su, 321, 394, 405
Ch'oe Pong-sun, 409
Ch'oe Pyŏng-ho, 336, 422
Ch'oe Rin-bŏm, 414
Ch'oe Rye-hwan, 422
Ch'oe Sa-hyŏn, 415
Ch'oe San-hwa, 399
Ch'oe Sang-hwa, 402, 407
Ch'oe Sang-uk, 334, 336
Ch'oe Sang-ŭl, 409, 415
Ch'oe Sang-yŏl, 335, 422
Ch'oe Sil-tan, 421
Ch'oe Sŏk-sun, 397
Ch'oe Sŏn-bi, 397
Ch'oe Sŏn-gyu, 324, 395
Ch'oe Sŏn-ja, 395
Ch'oe Sŏng-hwan, 395
Ch'oe Song-jip, 410, 416
Ch'oe Song-nak, 409
Ch'oe Su-san, 420
Ch'oe Suk-yang, 320, 399
Ch'oe Sun-nam, 410, 417, 424
Ch'oe Sŭng-guk, 420
Ch'oe Sŭng-hŭi, 396, 403
Ch'oe T'ae-sŏn, 408
Ch'oe T'ae-yŏn, 416
Ch'oe Ton-gŭn, 323, 325, 346
Ch'oe Tu-ch'an, 403
Ch'oe Un-hak, 407, 412
Ch'oe Ŭng-nok, 335
Ch'oe Ŭng-yŏ, 395
Ch'oe Wŏl-sŏng, 400
Ch'oe Wŏn-ik, 385, 425, 455, 476, 489
Ch'oe Wŏn-t'aek, 282, 289, 314, 318,
322, 324, 326, 330, 344, 348, 393,
394, 400, 401, 403, 405, 411, 414,
430, 432, 435
Ch'oe Yŏl-hŭi, 384, 425
Ch'oe Yong-dal, 73, 317, 346, 395
Ch'oe Yong-gŏn, 292, 296, 313, 314, 323,
325, 326, 328, 329, 338, 339, 340,
343, 344, 348, 377, 381, 393, 400,
401, 403, 405, 406, 411, 412, 418,
425, 429, 430, 432, 435, 436, 443,
448, 474, 481, 489
Ch'oe Yŏng-gu, 424
Ch'oe Yong-gŭn, 420
Ch'oe Yong-jin, 297, 324, 326, 329, 334,

348, 352, 378, 404, 406, 409, 412,
423, 430, 441, 451, 452, 466, 477,
482, 489
Ch'oe Yŏng-jŏn, 421
Ch'oe Yŏng-nim, 330, 333, 342, 425
Ch'oe Yŏng-suk, 420
Ch'oe Yun-ok, 364, 396
Ch'oe Yun-su, 303, 330, 381
Chŏn Cha-ryŏn, 409, 416, 423
Chŏn Chae-bong, 330, 335
Chŏn Chae-su, 416
Chŏn Ch'an-bae, 395
Chŏn Ch'ang-ch'ŏl, 302, 326, 329, 333,
348, 407, 412, 415, 418, 421, 426,
432, 435, 440
Chŏn Che-ha, 336
Ch'ŏn Ch'i-ok, 292
Chŏn Chin-su, 335
Chŏn Chong-hyŏk, 308
Chŏn Chŏng-il, 398
Chŏn Chung-hak, 398
Chŏn Ha-ch'ŏl, 303, 331, 336, 350
Chŏn Hak-su, 415
Chŏn Han-gyo, 415, 423
Chŏn Hi-yong, 422
Chŏn Ho-sŏn, 297
Chŏn Hŭi, 412
Chŏn Hŭi-jŏng, 334
Chŏn Kap-sun, 398
Chŏn Kŭm-sŏn, 424
Chŏn Kyŏng-hwa, 406, 407, 438
Chŏn Man-yŏn, 410, 417
Chŏn Mun-sŏp, 326, 330, 332, 333, 336,
340, 348, 410, 417, 420
Chŏn Mun-uk, 330, 334, 416
Chŏn Myŏng-sim, 385
Chŏn Myŏng-su, 335
Chŏn No-hyŏng, 417, 425
Chŏn P'il-yŏ, 417, 425
Chŏn Pok-chin, 396
Chŏn Pong-hwa, 399
Chŏn Pyŏng-ch'ae, 303, 422
Chŏn Pyŏng-gi, 398
Chŏn Pyŏng-gŭn, 415
Chŏn Pyŏng-ho, 331, 334, 352
Chŏn Sang-gŏn, 404
Ch'ŏn Se-bong, 331, 334, 352, 418, 421,
426, 432, 435
Chŏn Sŏn-bi, 417
Chŏn Sŏng-hwa, 318
Ch'ŏn Sŏng-ok, 400
Chŏn Suk-cha, 396
Chŏn T'ae-hwan, 401, 403, 438
Chŏn Yŏng-ch'un, 422
Chŏn Yŏng-gi, 396
Chŏn Yŏng-hŭi, 331

Chŏn Yong-sun, 417
Chŏn Yŏng-uk, 397
Chŏn Yun-do, 393, 400, 432
Chŏng Chae-p'il, 425
Chŏng Chae-sŏn, 399
Chŏng Chi-hwan, 327, 408
Chŏng Ch'i-ryong, 415, 422
Chŏng Ch'il-sŏng, 325, 395, 403
Chŏng Chin-sŏp, 399
Chŏng Ch'ŏl, 335, 395
Chŏng Chong-gi, 406, 409, 416, 438
Chŏng Chŏng-man, 410
Chŏng Chong-sik, 395
Chŏng Chu-gyŏng, 395
Chŏng Chu-ha, 400
Chŏng Chun-gi, 302, 330, 333, 342, 381,
383, 384, 385, 418, 425, 432, 455,
482, 489
Chŏng Ch'un-sil, 385
Chŏng Chun-t'aek, 291, 297, 302, 319,
320, 323, 326, 329, 340, 342, 348,
367, 368, 370, 382, 393, 402, 407,
412, 418, 422, 429, 436, 443, 447,
448, 449, 450, 451, 452, 454, 460,
462, 471, 480, 481, 482, 484, 485,
486, 487, 488, 489
Chŏng Hŭi-ch'ŏl, 303, 416, 423
Chŏng Hwa-sŏp, 420
Chŏng Il-yong, 289, 303, 319, 320, 322,
323, 325, 326, 338, 340, 343, 344,
348, 394, 403, 406, 415, 430, 447,
449, 450, 451, 452, 459, 468, 472,
475, 481, 482, 484, 485, 486, 487,
488, 489
Chŏng In-ch'ul, 399
Chŏng In-sŏk, 397
Chŏng In-sŏn, 411, 417
Chŏng Ki-hwan, 410
Chŏng Ki-man, 410, 416
Chŏng Ki-ryong, 425
Chŏng Ki-su, 415
Chŏng Kil-sŏng, 397
Chŏng Kŭm-sŏk, 422
Chŏng Kwan-ch'ŏl, 421
Chŏng Kwan-yul, 333
Chŏng Kwang-nok, 406, 409, 415
Chŏng Kwang-ok, 440
Chŏng Kwang-yŏn, 421
Chŏng Kwang-yul, 346
Chŏng Kye-rak, 292
Chŏng Kyŏng-bok, 328, 344, 412
Chŏng Kyŏng-hŭi, 329, 333, 342
Chŏng Kyŏng-sik, 303, 332, 423
Chŏng Mok, 325
Chŏng Myŏng-yong, 329, 346
Chŏng Nak-sŏn, 405

Chŏng Nam-jo, 397
Chŏng No-sik, 319, 325, 394, 401, 403, 432
Chŏng Paek, 395
Chŏng Pyŏng-gap, 327, 407, 413
Chŏng Se-ho, 396
Chŏng Se-yŏl, 396
Chŏng Sin-hyŏk, 308
Chŏng Sin-hyŏn, 397
Chŏng Song-nam, 335, 423
Chŏng Sŏng-ŏn, 324, 394, 403, 406, 411, 415, 438, 475, 477, 489
Chŏng T'ae-hwang, 383, 425
Chŏng T'ae-sik, 292
Chŏng Tae-sŏk, 395
Chŏng Tal-hyŏn, 73
Chŏng Tong-ch'ŏl, 328, 330, 333, 409, 415, 419, 420, 426, 432, 437, 438, 451, 452, 467, 485, 489, 498
Chŏng Tu-hwan, 324, 326, 332, 336, 352, 354, 401, 402, 408, 416, 425, 430, 438, 455, 460, 470, 489
Chŏng Tu-hyŏn, 317, 320
Chŏng Un-bok, 404
Chŏng Un-yŏng, 395
Chŏng Wŏl-san, 410, 470
Chŏng Wŏn-gyo, 335
Chŏng Yŏn-p'yo, 324, 402, 438
Chŏng Yŏn-t'ae, 396
Chŏng Yong-t'aek, 383, 425
Chŏng Yŏng-yŏl, 413
Chŏng Yu-ho, 468, 470, 489
Chŏng Yun, 319
Chŏng Yun-gil, 421
Chou En-lai (Zhou Enlai), 101, 117, 142, 148, 173, 226
Chu Ch'ang-bok, 331, 333, 335, 346, 350
Chu Ch'ang-jun, 411
Chu Ch'ang-sŏn, 397
Chu Chin-hwang, 398
Chu Chong-myŏng, 410, 417
Chu Chun-il, 303
Chu Hae, 395
Chu Hang-sŏp, 395, 404, 450, 489
Chu Ho-sun, 413
Chu Hwa-jong, 308, 336, 456, 479, 489
Chu Hwang-sŏp, 461, 466, 483
Chu In-gŏn, 415
Chu In-hwa, 416
Chu Kil-bon, 335
Chu Kil-sun, 413, 420
Chu Kyu-ch'ang, 331, 335, 350
Chu Man-sul, 399
Chu Pyŏng-sŏn, 402
Ch'u Sang-su, 404, 406, 410, 417, 425, 430, 441

Chu Sŏng-il, 409, 416, 423
Chu Sŭng-nam, 425
Chu To-il, 330, 334, 336, 411, 413, 423
Chu Tu-byŏk, 416
Chu Wŏn-saeng, 406, 409, 438
Chu Yŏng-ha, 289, 316, 317, 319, 320, 338, 340, 367, 393, 448, 480, 489, 522
Ch'u Yun-yŏp, 405
Chung, Arthur, 214
Cleaver, Eldridge, 6

DaCosta, Manuel Pinto, 208
Daddah, Moktar Ould, 160, 196, 204
Deba, Alfonse Massamba, 154

Eyadema, Gnassiugbe, 196

Fuse Michio, 153

Gomi Mitsuo, 208

Ha Ang-ch'ŏn, 292, 321, 323, 326, 342, 352, 401, 403, 405, 407, 432, 435
Ha P'il-wŏn, 400
Ha Yŏng-suk, 398
Ham Ik-nok, 395
Ham Se-tŏk, 396
Ham Sŏk-chun, 416
Ham To-gyŏm, 396
Han An-su, 420
Han Ch'an-ok, 407, 413, 421
Han Ch'ang-gyo, 399
Han Chang-ho, 399
Han Ch'ang-man, 425
Han Chang-su, 335, 399
Han Ch'ang-sun, 297, 410, 415
Han Chi-sŏp, 424
Han Chŏn-jong, 324, 403, 450, 459, 489
Han Chŏng-gi, 412, 414, 421, 438
Han Chŏng-hŏn, 414
Han Chong-su, 398
Han Ch'un-yŏ, 397
Han Hae-dong, 422
Han Hong-sik, 410
Han Hubang-nyŏ, 404, 409, 416, 425, 430
Han Hŭi-ho, 423
Han Hŭng-guk, 321
Han Hyo-sam, 394
Han Hyŏng-ho, 413
Han Hyŏng-hwan, 416, 423
Han Ik-su, 326, 329, 338, 340, 382, 408, 415, 418, 422, 432
Han Il-mu, 317, 320, 324, 348, 358, 395, 403
Han Il-su, 394

Han In-hwan, 385
Han In-sŏk, 401, 403, 437
Han Ki-ch'ang, 296, 409, 415
Han Ki-il, 423
Han Kil-yong, 404
Han Kwan-ok, 403
Han Kyŏng-su, 399
Han Kyŏng-suk, 327, 425
Han Kyu-p'al, 336
Han Myŏng-suk, 416
Han P'il-hwa, 303
Han Pin, 317
Han Pong-nyŏ, 383, 420
Han Pong-sŏl, 424
Han Pyŏng-yong, 303
Han Sang-du, 126, 292, 297, 323, 326,
    342, 400, 401, 405, 407, 412, 432,
    451, 453, 465, 468, 472, 474, 486,
    487, 488, 490
Han Sang-gyu, 335, 385
Han Sang-muk, 394
Han Sang-sun, 408
Han Se-gyŏng, 420
Han Sŏk-chin, 419, 423, 438
Han Sŏk-kwan, 333, 346
Han Sŏl-ya, 289, 292, 297, 317, 320, 323,
    326, 348, 371, 376, 395, 401, 404,
    432, 443, 450, 464, 490
Han Sŏng-yong, 335, 422, 454, 480, 490
Han Su-dong, 409
Han Su-hyŏn, 409, 415
Han Sŭng-gyŏm, 302
Han Sŭng-un, 408
Han T'ae-ryong, 413
Han T'ae-sŏn, 422
Han T'ae-suk, 414
Han Tae-yŏng, 297, 327, 408, 451, 460,
    475, 490
Han Tŏk-su, 413, 423
Han Tong-baek, 403, 406, 407, 441
Han Yang-du, 417
Han Yang-ŭl, 398
Han Yŏng-bo, 383, 422
Han Yŏng-gyu, 398
Han Yŏng-hak, 330
Han Yŏng-ok, 334, 408, 425
Han Yŏng-uk, 318
Han Yun-ch'ang, 421
Hanrouche, Abdel Hamid Ahmed, 169
Harrison, Selig S., 182
Hŏ Ch'ang-suk, 331, 336, 350
Hŏ Chŏng-suk, 317, 320, 324, 333, 347,
    348, 375, 377, 382, 385, 394, 405,
    418, 423, 426, 432, 435, 448, 464,
    469, 490, 497, 500
Hŏ Chun, 399

Hŏ Chŭng-ok, 423
Hŏ Ha-baek, 398
Hŏ Hak-song, 323, 327, 346, 401, 405,
    410, 437
Hŏ Hŏn, 32, 282, 313, 314, 318, 322,
    339, 344, 367, 392, 393, 432
Hŏ Ka-i, 286, 287, 288, 317, 319, 320,
    321, 322, 339, 340, 344, 358, 394,
    481, 490
Hŏ Kuk-bong, 325
Hŏ Man-ho, 399
Hŏ Min-sŏn, 336
Hŏ Nam-hŭi, 395
Hŏ Paek-san, 413, 422
Hŏ P'il-su, 409
Hŏ Pin, 324, 402, 404, 440
Hŏ Pok-tŏk, 420
Hŏ Pong-hak, 326, 328, 339, 344, 356,
    406, 407, 411, 412, 432, 437
Hŏ Ryŏn-suk, 382, 420
Hŏ Se-uk, 423
Hŏ Sin, 396
Hŏ Sŏk-sŏn, 327, 406, 410, 440
Hŏ Sŏng-t'aek, 319, 323, 324, 346, 394,
    405, 449, 463, 469, 490
Hŏ Sun, 335, 426, 438, 455, 470, 490
Hŏ Tam, 302, 308, 330, 332, 333, 342,
    381, 383, 385, 418, 420, 436, 454,
    455, 466, 482, 485, 490
Hŏ Tong-su, 421
Hŏ Yŏn-suk, 331
Hŏ Yong-ik, 423
Honecker, Erich, 218
Hong Chin, 400
Hong Ch'ŏl-hŭi, 400
Hong Chŭng-sik, 398, 402, 403, 440
Hong Hak-kŭn, 419
Hong Ho-sik, 385
Hong In-bŏm, 336
Hong Ki-hwang, 292, 393, 394, 402, 432,
    450, 483, 490
Hong Ki-ju, 118, 373, 392, 393, 432,
    469, 490
Hong Ki-mun, 334, 398, 418, 421, 426,
    432, 435
Hong Kwang-jun, 396
Hong Myŏn-hu, 395
Hong Myŏn-ok, 397
Hong Myŏng-hŭi, 74, 367, 370, 393, 404,
    405, 406, 411, 412, 430, 432, 435,
    446, 448, 449, 481, 485, 490
Hong Nae-gŭn, 413, 420
Hong Nam-p'yo, 319, 392, 393, 432
Hong Pong-su, 424
Hong Si-hak, 303, 330, 332, 333, 338,
    383, 385, 409, 414, 424, 426, 436, 438

Hong Sŏn-u, 397
Hong Sŏng-mu, 420
Hong Sŏng-nam, 334
Hong Sŏng-u, 318
Hong Sŏng-yong, 307, 334, 455, 480, 490
Hong Sŭng-guk, 396
Hong To-hak, 410, 416
Hong Tŏk-yu, 318
Hong Wŏn-gil, 303, 328, 329, 352, 382, 414, 418, 421, 436, 443, 452, 454, 472, 473, 482, 488, 490
Hong Yu-bok, 414
Hua Kuo-feng (Hua Guofeng), 221
Hwang Chae-sŏn, 407, 413, 420
Hwang Chang-yŏp, 302, 308, 330, 332, 333, 338, 381, 385, 410, 418, 421, 426, 432, 435
Hwang Chi-ryŏp, 413, 419
Hwang Ch'ŏl, 404
Hwang Chung-ŏp, 405, 407, 413
Hwang Hae-yŏng, 328
Hwang Hwa-bok, 409, 415
Hwang Il-bo, 398
Hwang Ki-sŏ, 417
Hwang Myŏng-gyu, 420
Hwang Myŏng-jong, 404
Hwang Se-hwan, 118, 325, 374, 496, 497
Hwang Sun-ch'ŏn, 401, 405, 438
Hwang Sun-hŭi, 327, 330, 334, 352, 407, 412, 423
Hwang Sun-sin, 421
Hwang T'ae-sŏng, 289, 394, 523
Hwang T'ae-yŏl, 396
Hwang Tae-yŏn, 303
Hwang Uk, 395
Hwang Un-bong, 398
Hwang Wŏn-bo, 326, 327, 346, 410
Hwang Wŏn-jun, 410
Hwang Wŏn-nam, 411, 417, 425
Hwang Wŏn-t'aek, 408, 414
Hwang Yong-do, 424
Hyŏn Ch'ang-sin, 382
Hyŏn Ch'ang-yong, 331, 408, 416
Hyŏn Ch'il-chong, 321, 325, 354, 376, 400, 404, 432, 443
Hyŏn Ch'ŏl-gyu, 330, 422
Hyŏn Chŏng-min, 292, 324, 404
Hyŏn Chun-gŭk, 334, 421
Hyŏn Chun-hyŏk, 280
Hyŏn Hun, 397, 401, 403, 438
Hyŏn Mu-gwang, 298, 303, 326, 329, 333, 338, 342, 348, 385, 405, 407, 412, 418, 423, 432, 436, 452, 454, 472, 473, 480, 486, 487, 488, 490
Hyŏn Po-yŏl, 399
Hyŏn Sŭng-gap, 398

Hyŏn Tong-uk, 282
Hyŏn U-hyŏn, 319

Iwamoto Kiyoshi, 153

Juvenal, Habyarimana, 222

Kaganovich, L., 125
Kang Chae-wŏn, 413
Kang Chang-su, 383
Kang Ch'il-yong, 297
Kang Chin-gŏn, 317, 320, 324, 326, 348, 392, 393, 400, 401, 402, 432, 435
Kang Ch'ŏ-han, 419
Kang Ch'o-sun, 404, 409, 415
Kang Ch'ŏl, 398
Kang Chŏm-gu, 308, 336, 415, 452, 466, 490
Kang Chong-gŭn, 414
Kang Chun-guk, 402, 407
Kang Chun-sam, 395
Kang Chung-han, 336, 408, 426, 438
Kang Chung-yŏn, 408
Kang Hak-su, 423
Kang Ho-sin, 408
Kang Hŭi-wŏn, 326, 330, 334, 348, 406, 407, 412, 413, 419, 438, 439
Kang Hyŏn-su, 330, 334, 416, 426, 438
Kang In-gŏl, 398
Kang In-gyu, 399
Kang Kŏn, 320, 394
Kang Kyu-ch'an, 398
Kang Maeng-gu, 415, 423
Kang Mun-sŏk, 289, 314, 318, 319, 322, 344, 394, 523
Kang Myŏn-su, 423
Kang Myŏng-ok, 424
Kang Po-gŭm, 415
Kang Pong-gŭn, 421
Kang Sin-u, 399
Kang Sŏk-san, 328
Kang Sŏk-sung, 335, 422
Kang Sŏng-jae, 399
Kang Sŏng-san, 303, 308, 330, 332, 333, 340, 382, 383, 384, 385, 418, 419, 432, 455, 482, 490
Kang Sun, 393, 432
Kang Sŭng-hwan, 308
Kang T'ae-hŭi, 303
Kang T'ae-mu, 404
Kang Tae-sŏp, 422
Kang Tŏk-il, 324
Kang Tŏk-yŏ, 404, 410, 416
Kang U-sik, 408, 414
Kang Uk-kŭk, 410, 417, 425

Kang Un-sŏng, 408, 415
Kang Ŭng-jin, 393, 394, 433, 443
Kang Wi-jun, 407, 413
Kang Yang-uk, 297, 302, 308, 367, 372,
    376, 382, 390, 392, 393, 400, 401,
    402, 405, 407, 411, 413, 418, 422,
    426, 429, 430, 433, 435, 436
Kang Yŏng-ch'ang, 291, 321, 324, 326,
    352, 403, 409, 449, 472, 490
Kang Yŏng-suk, 414, 421
Kang Yŏng-sun, 400
Kang Yun-wŏn, 396
Kaunda David Kenneth, 227
Keita, Modibo, 148
Kerekou, Mathiew, 211–212
Khruschechev, N. S., 125
Ki Sŏk-bok, 319, 320, 340
Kieu Sampan, 205
Kil Chae-gyŏng, 335
Kil Chin-sŏp, 398
Kil Chŭng-sŭng, 422
Kil Wŏn-p'al, 396
Kim Cha-rin, 328, 416
Kim Chae-bong, 335, 424
Kim Ch'ae-bong, 415
Kim Chae-gu, 410
Kim Chae-ha, 292, 423
Kim Chae-hŭng, 414
Kim Chae-mun, 335
Kim Chae-rok, 395
Kim Chae-ryong, 317, 346
Kim Chae-ryu, 422
Kim Chae-suk, 411
Kim Chae-uk, 317, 319, 320, 340, 394
Kim Chae-ŭl, 400
Kim Chae-un, 408, 414
Kim Ch'ae-yŏn, 382, 424
Kim Chae-yong, 331, 399
Kim Ch'aek, 148, 317, 319, 320, 322,
    340, 344, 366, 367, 393, 448, 468,
    481, 490
Kim Ch'an, 317, 321, 346, 394
Kim Ch'an-gwŏn, 417
Kim Ch'ang-bok, 303, 331, 411, 414, 437
Kim Ch'ang-bong, 324, 326, 328, 344,
    352, 356, 407, 412, 450, 452, 474,
    482, 485, 490
Kim Chang-ch'ŏl, 419
Kim Ch'ang-dŏk, 324, 326, 327, 346,
    401, 402, 406, 410, 433, 435
Kim Ch'ang-gŏl, 102
Kim Chang-gwŏn, 330, 335
Kim Ch'ang-han, 399
Kim Ch'ang-ho, 336
Kim Ch'ang-hŭp, 325, 463, 490
Kim Ch'ang-hwan, 333. 346

Kim Ch'ang-ju, 420
Kim Ch'ang-jun, 393, 400, 403, 407, 433
Kim Ch'ang-jun, 371, 393, 407, 413, 420,
    435
Kim Ch'ang-man, 289, 292, 296, 300,
    317, 323, 325, 326, 338, 339, 340,
    342, 343, 347, 348, 402, 404, 406,
    440, 450, 464, 482, 490
Kim Ch'ang-nok, 398
Kim Che-wŏn, 53, 370, 398
Kim Ch'i-do, 417, 452, 473, 490
Kim Ch'i-gu, 332, 334
Kim Chi-ha, 198
Kim Ch'i-hyŏk, 92
Kim Ch'i-ryong, 420
Kim Ch'i-se, 385, 422
Kim Ch'i-ung, 422
Kim Chik-hyŏng, 320, 324
Kim Chin-guk, 319
Kim Chin-ho, 400, 420
Kim Chin-hwa, 409, 415
Kim Chin-hyŏk, 308
Kim Chin-sŏn, 297
Kim Chin-t'ae, 292
Kim Chin-yŏ, 321
Kim Ch'ŏl-ho, 397
Kim Ch'ŏl-hun, 303
Kim Ch'ŏl-man, 330, 333, 336, 342, 410,
    416, 419
Kim Ch'ŏl-min, 385
Kim Ch'ŏl-su, 397
Kim Ch'ŏl-u, 325
Kim Ch'ŏm-gwŏn, 397
Kim Ch'ŏn-hae, 288, 323, 401, 404, 433
Kim Ch'ŏn-hwang, 408, 414
Kim Chŏng-ae, 400
Kim Chong-hang, 297, 326, 407, 451,
    467, 490
Kim Chŏng-hoe, 422
Kim Chŏng-hong, 282
Kim Chŏng-hŭi, 421
Kim Chong-hwa, 416
Kim Chŏng-hwan, 420
Kim Chŏng-hyŏk, 403
Kim Chŏng-il, 332, 333, 336, 338, 340
Kim Chŏng-ju, 394, 449, 463, 490
Kim Chŏng-p'il, 415, 423
Kim Chong-sŏng, 303, 308, 336, 421
Kim Chŏng-sun, 383, 399, 419
Kim Chong-t'ae, 171
Kim Chŏng-t'ae, 413
Kim Ch'ŏng-yong, 330, 335
Kim Chu-yŏng, 335
Kim Chun-do, 421
Kim Ch'un-gil, 424
Kim Ch'un-sŏng, 408

Kim Ch'ung-gyu, 395
Kim Chung-nin, 302, 308, 327, 329, 332, 333, 338, 339, 340, 352, 381, 408, 417, 418, 425, 436
Kim Chung-nyŏ, 425
Kim Chung-yŏ, 417
Kim Chwa-hyŏk, 327, 330, 334, 346, 348, 410, 411, 413, 437
Kim Dae-jung, 198
Kim Ha-un, 375, 376, 496, 497
Kim Hae-ch'ŏn, 395
Kim Hae-jin, 396, 403
Kim Hak-bŏm, 422
Kim Hak-ch'ŏl, 422
Kim Hak-chong, 396
Kim Hak-san, 421
Kim Hak-su, 422
Kim Hak-sun, 303, 383, 409, 420
Kim Han-il, 396
Kim Han-jung, 321, 398
Kim Han-ung, 396
Kim Hi-jun, 410, 421
Kim Ho-gyŏng, 308
Kim Ho-sun, 396
Kim Ho-yŏng, 396
Kim Hoe-il, 54, 297, 324, 327, 330, 334, 348, 403, 409, 415, 446, 450, 451, 477, 480, 485, 486, 488, 490
Kim Hong-gi, 400
Kim Hong-gwan, 297, 327, 331, 350
Kim Hong-ok, 328, 332, 354
Kim Hong-wŏn, 384
Kim Hu-bun, 425
Kim Hu-nam, 405
Kim Hŭi-in, 419
Kim Hŭi-jun, 383, 406, 437
Kim Hŭng-il, 405, 409, 415
Kim Hwak-sil, 296
Kim Hwan, 332, 333, 338, 340, 426, 436, 454, 462, 490
Kim Hwang-il, 289, 320, 322, 323, 344, 394, 404
Kim Hyo-wŏn, 400
Kim Hyŏk-ch'ŏl, 330, 335
Kim Hyŏn-bong, 324
Kim Hyŏn-gŭk, 396
Kim Hyŏn-su, 407
Kim Hyŏng-bong, 331, 335, 350
Kim Hyŏng-gŏn, 395
Kim Hyŏng-hae, 385
Kim Hyŏng-sam, 327, 423, 426, 438
Kim Hyŏng-sŏn, 318
Kim Hyŏng-su, 422
Kim Hyŏng-t'ae, 397
Kim I-hun, 303, 330, 382, 418, 425, 433
Kim I-sun, 409

Kim Ik-hyŏn, 330, 425
Kim Ik-sŏn, 296, 323, 324, 326, 328, 342, 344, 346, 347, 373, 377, 378, 391, 401, 404, 406, 412, 437, 453, 478, 488, 490, 496, 497
Kim Il, 4, 89, 289, 290, 292, 296, 297, 301, 302, 303, 304, 313, 314, 317, 319, 320, 322, 323, 325, 326, 328, 329, 332, 333, 338, 339, 340, 343, 344, 348, 379, 380, 381, 382, 383, 384, 385, 390, 394, 404, 406, 412, 418, 423, 426, 429, 430, 436, 443, 447, 448, 449, 450, 452, 454, 474, 481, 483, 484, 485, 486, 487, 488, 490
Kim Il-ch'ŏl, 334, 336
Kim Il-ch'ŏng, 395
Kim Il-dae, 334, 385, 456, 465, 490
Kim Il-sŏn, 400, 403
Kim Il Sung, 1–273, 280, 281, 284, 285, 286, 287, 288, 289, 290, 291, 293, 294, 295, 296, 297, 298, 299, 300, 301, 302, 303, 304, 305, 306, 307, 308, 309, 313, 314, 316, 317, 319, 320, 321, 322, 323, 325, 326, 328, 329, 332, 333, 336, 338, 339, 340, 342, 344, 348, 356, 368, 381, 383, 386, 390, 393, 402, 406, 412, 418, 419, 421, 425, 426, 427, 429, 430, 436, 446, 447, 448, 449, 450, 452, 474, 484, 485, 488, 490, 523
Kim In-bae, 399
Kim In-ch'ŏl, 413
Kim In-sŏng, 422
Kim Kang-hwan, 333, 336, 342
Kim Kap-sun, 414, 453, 477, 490
Kim Ki-bong, 423
Kim Ki-do, 394
Kim Ki-du, 327
Kim Ki-ha, 419
Kim Ki-ju, 292
Kim Ki-jun, 403
Kim Ki-nam, 308, 333, 400, 426, 433
Kim Ki-sŏn, 331, 334, 352, 411, 417, 420
Kim Ki-su, 397, 409
Kim Ki-t'aek, 399
Kim Ki-u, 91
Kim Kil-hyŏn, 422
Kim Kil-su, 396
Kim Ko-mang, 320, 346
Kim Ku, 41, 69, 73, 81
Kim Kuk-hun, 302, 328, 331, 334, 384, 391, 406, 407, 411, 414, 421, 437
Kim Kuk-t'ae, 302, 330, 333, 417
Kim Kŭm-ch'ŏl, 303, 332
Kim Kŭm-ok, 331, 383
Kim Kŭm-san, 407, 413, 420

Kim Kŭm-sil, 410, 416
Kim Kwan-sŏp, 327, 331, 333, 350, 352, 408, 421, 426, 433
Kim Kwan-su, 384
Kim Kwang-bin, 321
Kim Kwang-bong, 422
Kim Kwang-guk, 331
Kim Kwang-hyŏp, 289, 291, 297, 300, 320, 322, 323, 324, 325, 326, 328, 339, 340, 344, 348, 356, 379, 402, 406, 412, 449, 450, 452, 474, 481, 482, 484, 485, 488, 490
Kim Kwang-jin, 335, 424
Kim Kwang-jin, 424
Kim Kwang-ju, 424
Kim Kwang-jun, 399
Kim Kwang-su, 168, 289, 319, 394
Kim Kwang-t'aek, 292
Kim Kye-hwan, 383
Kim Kye-hyŏn, 331, 414
Kim Kye-rim, 282, 296, 315, 319, 325, 328, 354, 396
Kim Kyo-yŏng, 317, 320, 325
Kim Kyŏng-ch'an, 424
Kim Kyŏng-hoe, 409
Kim Kyŏng-in, 410, 425
Kim Kyŏng-myŏng, 414, 421
Kim Kyŏng-sŏk, 297, 320, 324, 326, 348, 376, 401, 433
Kim Kyŏng-suk, 420
Kim Kyŏng-yŏn, 330, 333, 382, 383, 384, 424, 452, 454, 456, 465, 466, 484, 485, 488, 490
Kim Kyu-sik, 73, 81
Kim Kyu-sun, 416, 424
Kim Man-guk, 335
Kim Man-gŭm, 302, 324, 326, 329, 334, 342, 348, 402, 407, 417, 418, 425, 426, 430, 436, 440, 447, 451, 453, 454, 455, 459, 482, 484, 485, 486, 488, 490
Kim Man-jung, 399
Kim Man-su, 400
Kim Min-san, 289, 318, 320, 325, 358, 394
Kim Mu-hoe, 406, 408, 414, 438
Kim Mu-sam, 396
Kim Mun-gŭm, 404
Kim Mun-gŭn, 402, 409, 416, 438
Kim Mun-hwa, 296
Kim Mun-hwan, 399
Kim Mun-hyŏn, 422
Kim Myŏng-gŏn, 327
Kim Myŏng-gyŏng, 408
Kim Myŏng-gyun, 404
Kim Myŏng-ho, 405, 411
Kim Myŏng-hwan, 397

Kim Myŏng-jun, 402
Kim Myŏng-ni, 398
Kim Myŏng-ok, 414
Kim Myŏng-sik, 419
Kim Myŏng-sŏk, 395
Kim Myŏng-sŏng, 297
Kim Myŏng-suk, 413
Kim Nak-chin, 400
Kim Nak-hŭi, 292, 303, 331, 336, 402, 407, 412, 413, 420, 438
Kim Nak-sŏp, 422
Kim Nak-to, 398
Kim Nam-ch'ŏn, 395
Kim Nam-gyo, 415
Kim Nam-yun, 490
Kim Nanju-hwa, 397
Kim Ni-jun, 422
Kim Nŭng-il, 331, 415
Kim O-sŏng, 289, 318, 319, 344, 394
Kim Ŏin-nam, 416, 423
Kim Ok-bin, 394
Kim Ok-chun, 408
Kim Ok-nyŏ, 421
Kim Ŏk-sim, 297
Kim Ŏk-su, 410
Kim Ok-sun, 327, 382, 391, 405, 406, 409, 412, 416, 425, 433, 440
Kim On, 398
Kim Ŏp-tol, 400
Kim Paek-tong, 395
Kim P'il-chu, 397, 421
Kim Po-bi, 420
Kim Po-ok, 413
Kim Po-p'ae, 399
Kim Pok-chin, 404
Kim Pok-sil, 303
Kim Pok-sin, 382, 423
Kim Pok-sŏn, 413
Kim Pong-ch'un, 415
Kim Pong-ju, 335, 426, 433
Kim Pong-sŏn, 397, 408, 414, 421, 430
Kim Pong-su, 417
Kim Pong-sun, 420
Kim Pong-yul, 324, 335, 410, 417, 419, 425
Kim Pun-ok, 385, 423
Kim P'ung-jin, 422
Kim Pyŏng-bin, 414, 421
Kim Pyŏng-ch'ŏn, 424
Kim Pyŏng-gyu, 416
Kim Pyŏng-ha, 330, 333, 418, 419, 436, 454, 476, 491
Kim Pyŏng-han, 414, 454, 472, 491
Kim Pyŏng-ik, 411, 414, 451, 477, 491
Kim Pyŏng-je, 393, 404, 435
Kim Pyŏng-je, 397, 400, 401, 404, 410, 433

Kim Pyŏng-ju, 399
Kim Pyŏng-mo, 408
Kim Pyŏng-mun, 398
Kim Pyŏng-sam, 327, 331, 350
Kim Pyŏng-sik, 407, 413, 419, 451, 459, 461, 462, 463, 486
Kim Pyŏng-sik, 297, 327, 413, 487, 491
Kim Pyŏng-sŏn, 403
Kim Pyŏng-su, 291, 297, 328, 407
Kim Pyŏng-sun, 409
Kim Pyŏng-yŏn, 405
Kim Pyŏng-yul, 308, 330, 334, 383, 421, 438
Kim Sam-yong, 314, 318, 319, 321, 322, 339, 344, 394
Kim Sang-ch'ŏl, 320, 324, 394, 401, 403, 438
Kim Sang-guk, 409, 415
Kim Sang-hae, 292
Kim Sang-ho, 425
Kim Sang-hwan, 407
Kim Sang-hyŏk, 319, 324, 394, 404
Kim Sang-jin, 412, 419
Kim Sang-ju, 395
Kim Sang-mun, 303
Kim Sang-sin, 403
Kim Sang-sun, 400
Kim Se-bong, 328, 332, 354, 382, 409, 423, 451, 460, 491
Kim Se-hwal, 303, 332
Kim Se-yul, 396, 403
Kim Se-yun, 383, 421
Kim Si-gyŏm, 398
Kim Si-hak, 331, 334, 422
Kim Si-jung, 406, 410, 437
Kim Si-yŏp, 397
Kim Sin-sik, 423
Kim Sŏ-ho, 321
Kim Sŏk-bong, 296
Kim Sŏk-cho, 422
Kim Sŏk-ha, 421
Kim Sŏk-hwa, 382
Kim Sŏk-hwan, 330
Kim Sŏk-hyŏng, 382, 383, 408, 414, 420, 438
Kim Sŏk-ki, 384, 437, 454, 464, 491
Kim Sŏk-man, 408, 414
Kim Sŏk-t'ae, 410
Kim Sŏk-yong, 403, 408, 412, 413, 423, 430, 441
Kim Sŏn-ch'o, 398
Kim Sŏn-gil, 395
Kim Sŏn-jun, 422
Kim Sŏn-mo, 415
Kim Sŏn-uk, 417, 425
Kim Sŏng-ae, 330, 334, 418, 424, 426, 433, 435

Kim Sŏng-ch'ŏl, 408
Kim Sŏng-do, 414
Kim Sŏng-gŏl, 335, 421
Kim Sŏng-gu, 416
Kim Sŏng-guk, 331, 413
Kim Sŏng-gŭn, 327, 383
Kim Sŏng-gyu, 394
Kim Sŏng-hak, 395
Kim Song-jŏl, 422
Kim Sŏng-mun, 403
Kim Sŏng-ok, 395, 420
Kim Sŏng-su, 73, 81
Kim Sŏng-yŏn, 413
Kim Sŏng-yul, 382, 383, 400, 407, 413, 420, 430
Kim Sŏng-yun, 420
Kim Su-bok, 296, 407
Kim Su-dŭk, 303, 330, 382, 424
Kim Su-hyŏn, 395
Kim Su-il, 396
Kim Sun-bok, 297, 417
Kim Sun-il, 396
Kim Sun-nam, 397
Kim Sun-p'il, 385
Kim Sun-yŏng, 420
Kim Sŭng-do, 405
Kim Sŭng-hun, 317, 346
Kim Sŭng-hwa, 115, 123, 289, 320, 322, 324, 344, 461, 463, 479, 491
Kim Sŭng-hyŏn, 395
Kim Sŭng-jo, 421
Kim Sŭng-mo, 395
Kim Sŭng-wŏn, 408, 414, 421
Kim T'ae-bong, 399
Kim T'ae-gŭk, 335, 456, 473, 491
Kim T'ae-gŭn, 126, 292, 324, 326, 352, 402, 405, 411, 414, 441, 452, 463, 475, 488, 491
Kim T'ae-ho, 419
Kim Tae-hong, 326, 330, 410, 414
Kim T'ae-hong, 397
Kim T'ae-hŭi, 425
Kim T'ae-hwa, 321, 417
Kim T'ae-hyŏn, 303, 327, 407, 413
Kim T'ae-ja, 397
Kim T'ae-jun, 319
Kim T'ae-ryŏn, 320, 423
Kim Tae-ryong, 320, 398, 408
Kim T'ae-sŏng, 398
Kim T'aek-yong, 297, 425
Kim T'ak, 397
Kim Tal-chun, 408
Kim Tal-hyŏn, 84, 292, 392, 393, 404, 433, 450, 483, 491
Kim Tal-sam, 399
Kim To-man, 326, 328, 339, 410
Kim To-sŏng, 399

Kim Tŏk-bok, 408
Kim Tŏk-hŭng, 396
Kim Tŏk-wŏn, 414, 421
Kim Tŏk-yong, 421
Kim Tŏk-yŏng, 324, 403
Kim Tong-gyu, 303, 326, 328, 329, 338,
   340, 344, 381, 382, 383, 406, 407,
   411, 412, 418, 419, 424, 433, 436,
   437, 441
Kim Tong-hwan, 417, 424
Kim Tong-hyŏk, 409
Kim Tong-hyŏn, 409
Kim Tong-il, 396
Kim Tong-sik, 408
Kim Tong-sŏn, 423
Kim Tong-yŏn, 413
Kim Tu-bong, 117, 118, 281, 282, 289,
   291, 313, 316, 317, 319, 320, 322,
   323, 338, 339, 340, 343, 344, 348,
   365, 366, 367, 392, 393, 402, 433, 499
Kim Tu-nam, 334
Kim Tu-sam, 292, 324, 332, 402, 415,
   450, 453, 465, 468, 475, 479, 486,
   487, 491
Kim Tu-yong, 310, 321
Kim Tu-yŏng, 308, 333, 455, 478, 483,
   491
Kim Tŭk-nan, 382, 400, 401, 403, 405,
   408, 411, 414, 420, 429, 430, 433,
   435, 438
Kim Tŭk-su, 423
Kim U-jin, 416
Kim Ŭi-hwan, 411, 417
Kim Ŭi-su, 397
Kim Ŭi-sun, 303, 331, 398
Kim Uk-chin, 317
Kim Ŭn-ha, 422
Kim Un-hak, 415
Kim Ŭn-han, 399
Kim Un-suk, 332
Kim Ŭn-sun, 297
Kim Ung, 87, 320
Kim Ŭng-bin, 289
Kim Ŭng-gi, 289, 320, 324, 346, 359,
   393, 394, 403, 433, 450, 469, 491
Kim Ŭng-sam, 331, 336, 350, 420
Kim Ŭng-sang, 327, 335, 365, 407, 415,
   423, 453, 455, 457, 459, 479, 485,
   486, 488
Kim Ŭng-yul, 399
Kim Wa-ryong, 403, 408
Kim Wal-su, 297, 422
Kim Wal-yong, 297, 326, 405, 409, 433,
   440
Kim Wan-gŭn, 396
Kim Wŏl-song, 318

Kim Wŏn-bin, 407, 417
Kim Wŏn-bong, 324, 376, 393, 404, 443
Kim Wŏn-bong, 376, 400, 402, 404, 433,
   441, 448, 469, 478, 491
Kim Wŏn-ch'an, 416, 424
Kim Wŏn-ch'ŏng, 408, 414, 422
Kim Wŏn-gŏn, 420
Kim Wŏn-gyu, 403
Kim Wŏn-hyŏng, 395, 409
Kim Wŏn-jŏm, 407, 413
Kim Wŏn-jŏn, 407
Kim Wŏn-muk, 297
Kim Wŏn-ok, 420
Kim Wŏn-p'ung, 292
Kim Wŏn-sam, 408, 415, 422
Kim Wŏn-sŏl, 408
Kim Yang-ch'un, 409, 416
Kim Yang-yul, 408
Kim Ye-p'il, 317
Kim Yi-ch'ang, 335
Kim Yi-sŏk, 423
Kim Yŏ-jung, 323, 328, 329, 346, 347,
   409, 411, 414, 433, 437
Kim Yŏl, 89, 286, 289, 317, 319, 320,
   322, 340, 344, 358, 394
Kim Yŏn-p'il, 400
Kim Yŏn-yŏ, 415
Kim Yong-am, 318, 319, 344
Kim Yong-bŏm, 280, 317, 346, 415, 522
Kim Yŏng-ch'ae, 334, 413, 421, 456, 463,
   491
Kim Yŏng-ch'ang, 297
Kim Yŏng-ch'un, 335
Kim Yong-dam, 394
Kim Yŏng-gŏl, 419
Kim Yong-guk, 397
Kim Yŏng-hak, 303
Kim Yong-ho, 399, 408, 412, 414, 423,
   430, 441
Kim Yŏng-ho, 413
Kim Yong-hŭi, 398
Kim Yong-hyŏn, 335
Kim Yŏng-jae, 319, 394
Kim Yong-jin, 324, 401, 403, 437
Kim Yŏng-jŏn, 421
Kim Yŏng-ju, 314, 326, 328, 329, 338,
   339, 340, 344, 407, 411, 412, 418,
   422, 433, 436, 524
Kim Yŏng-jun, 425
Kim Yŏng-jung, 150, 158
Kim Yŏng-nam, 308, 330, 332, 333, 338,
   340, 418, 422, 426, 433, 435
Kim Yŏng-nan, 308
Kim Yŏng-sik, 413
Kim Yong-sŏk, 327
Kim Yŏng-sŏp, 397

Kim Yŏng-su, 320, 325, 394, 402, 404, 440
Kim Yong-sun, 334
Kim Yŏng-t'ae, 317
Kim Yong-t'aek, 416, 425
Kim Yong-uk, 399
Kim Yŏng-uk, 408, 414
Kim Yong-un, 334
Kim Yŏng-ŭn, 400
Kim Yŏng-wan, 394
Kim Yŏng-wŏl, 421
Kim Yong-wŏn, 400
Kim Yŏng-yŏl, 303
Kim Yong-yŏn, 331, 335, 416
Kim Yŏng-yun, 396
Kim Yu-hun, 383
Kim Yu-sun, 335
Kim Yu-t'ae, 397
Kim Yu-yŏng, 396
Kim Yun-gŏl, 395
Kim Yun-hyŏk, 334, 426, 437, 455, 491
Kim Yun-sang, 334, 423, 454, 456, 466, 485, 491
Kim Yun-sik, 416
Kim Yun-sŏn, 330, 412, 423
Kim Yun-yong, 302
Ko Ch'an-bo, 318, 319, 344
Ko Ch'ang-nam, 398, 425
Ko Chin-hŭi, 399
Ko Ch'ŏl-u, 398
Ko Chŏng-ik, 407
Ko Chŏng-sik, 308, 334, 385
Ko Chun-myŏng, 423
Ko Chun-t'aek, 376, 396, 403, 407, 415, 430, 433, 443, 450, 463, 467, 491
Ko Han-ch'ŏn, 336, 423
Ko Hŭi-man, 324, 394, 404, 467, 491
Ko Hyŏk, 329, 407, 491
Ko In-gŏl, 408, 414
Ko Kŭm-sun, 383, 408, 414, 421
Ko Kwang-han, 400
Ko Kyŏng-in, 325, 399, 402, 405, 440
Ko Min-sun, 409, 415, 423
Ko Pong-gi, 289, 291, 321, 324, 352
Ko Sŏk-hwan, 396
Ko T'ae-ŭn, 336
Ko Yŏng-ja, 292
Ko Yŏng-sŏn, 308
Ko Yun-suk, 303, 383, 419
Kong Chin-t'ae, 308, 333, 342, 421, 454, 456, 465, 482, 485, 491
Kosygin, Alexei N., 151
Kozlov, F. L., 296
Krehler, Alfred, 296
Ku Cha-hun, 417, 425
Ku Cha-sŏng, 403

Ku Chae-su, 282, 289, 318, 319, 344, 392, 393, 433
Kuno Chuji, 225
Kwak Chu-sŏk, 396
Kwak Tae-hong, 303
Kwak Yŏng-ho, 336
Kwŏn Chŏm-du, 416, 424
Kwŏn Hŭi-gyŏng, 335, 423
Kwŏn O-gil, 403
Kwŏn O-jik, 289, 398
Kwŏn Pyŏng-ch'ŏl, 396
Kwŏn Sŏng-nin, 335
Kwŏn T'ae-bong, 400
Kwŏn T'ae-hŭp, 420
Kwŏn Ŭn-hae, 398
Kwŏn Yŏng-ju, 397
Kwŏn Yŏng-t'ae, 327, 407
Kwŏn Yŏng-u, 404, 411, 416, 421, 430
Kwŏn Yun-il, 409, 415, 423
Kye Ch'un-yŏng, 413, 420
Kye Hyŏng-sun, 303, 331, 336, 350, 385, 420, 426, 438, 455, 472, 491
Kye Tong-sŏn, 321, 396
Kye Ŭng-sang, 401, 403, 405, 408, 433, 435
Kye Ŭng-t'ae, 308, 330, 332, 333, 340, 385, 415, 420, 426, 447, 452, 454, 455, 456, 467, 482, 484, 485, 488, 491

Larsen, Reidar, 172
Lenin, V. I., 31, 109, 173–174
Li Yuk-sa, 6, 8

Ma Chong-hwa, 398
Ma Tong-hŭi, 179
Machel, Samora Moises, 221
Maeng T'ae-ho, 308
Maeng Tu-ŭn, 396
Malenkov, G. M., 100, 103, 125
Manian, 87
Mao Tse-tung (Mao Zedong), 2, 98
Midorikawa Touru, 190, 207
Min Hyŏk-cho, 395
Min Ki-wŏn, 398
Min Kwan-bŏm, 424
Miyamoto Kenji, 165, 296
Molotov, V. M., 125
Mu Chŏng, 89, 317, 320
Mugabe, Robert G., 228–229
Mun Ch'ang-sŏk, 409
Mun Ch'i-hwa, 399
Mun Chŏng-suk, 296, 407, 413
Mun Hong-gi, 397
Mun Ki-sŏp, 303
Mun Man-uk, 292, 324, 403, 450, 470, 471, 479, 486, 488, 491

Mun Min-un, 399
Mun Ok-sun, 396
Mun Pyŏng-il, 454, 459, 491
Mun Sang-jik, 397
Mun Sŏng-sul, 334, 409, 415
Mun Suk-cha, 416, 423
Mun T'ae-hwa, 401, 404, 438
Mun Tong-yong, 396
Mun Tu-jae, 393, 398, 433
Mun Ŭi-sok, 397
Myŏng Hi-jo, 317

Na Chŏng-hŭi, 419
Na Chŏng-sil, 420
Na Sŭng-gyu, 393, 402, 433
Na Yong-su, 421
Na Yun-ch'ul, 398, 404
Nam Ch'un-hwa, 410
Nam Il, 289, 292, 297, 303, 321, 322,
    323, 325, 326, 329, 340, 344, 348,
    352, 372, 376, 394, 405, 406, 412,
    418, 424, 429, 430, 436, 447, 449,
    450, 451, 452, 454, 466, 471, 479,
    481, 482, 484, 485, 486, 487, 488, 491
Nam Kŭm-bong, 422
Nam Kyŏng-hun, 318
Nam Ok-nyŏ, 422
Nam Sŏn-ok, 408, 414
Ndong, Maie Nguema Biyogo Negue, 217
Ne Win, U, 217
N'gouabi, Marien, 189, 222
Nimeri, Gaafar Mohamed, 174
No Chin-han, 394
No Chŏng-hŭi, 420
No Ik-myŏng, 329, 406, 407, 433, 437
No Ki-sŏn, 425
No Myŏng-gŭn, 333, 421
No Myŏng-hwan, 398
No Pyŏng-u, 303, 330, 414, 453, 470,
    491
No Se-bŏm, 384, 424
No Sŏk-kwi, 395
No Su-ŏk, 326, 410, 417
No T'ae-sŏk, 327, 330, 352, 421, 426,
    436, 468, 483, 491
No U-yong, 303, 424
No Yong-sam, 327
No Yŏng-se, 403, 406, 408, 441
Nyerere, Julius K., 165

O Chae-il, 398
O Chae-wŏn, 330, 334, 417, 420
O Chae-yŏng, 394
O Che-hong, 399
O Che-ryong, 297, 327, 406, 410, 412,
    416, 438, 439
O Che-yŏng, 404

O Chin-u, 302, 324, 326, 328, 329, 332,
    333, 336, 338, 340, 344, 348, 352,
    382, 410, 411, 412, 418, 419, 423,
    426, 427, 433, 436, 455, 474, 491
O Ch'ol-chu, 397
O Ch'un-gyŏng, 384
Ŏ Han-sang, 403
O Ho-sŏk, 398
O Hyŏn-ju, 297, 327, 336, 410, 412, 413,
    418, 421, 433, 440
O Ik-hwan, 383
O Ki-ch'ŏn, 303, 412, 416, 440
O Ki-ok, 396
O Ki-sŏp, 57, 73, 121, 280, 310, 317,
    320, 324, 348, 395, 404, 475, 491
O Kŭk-yŏl, 308, 331, 332, 333, 336, 340,
    416, 422
O Kyŏng-ae, 408, 415
O Kyŏng-hun, 331
O Myŏng-sŏp, 413
O Ok-byŏl, 399
O Paek-yong, 326, 329, 332, 333, 336,
    340, 348, 408, 416, 419, 424, 426,
    427, 436
O Pyŏng-dŏk, 417, 425
O Rye-sŏn, 407, 420
O Sin-nam, 397
O Sŏng-guk, 425
O Sŏng-yŏl, 303, 453, 471, 491
O Sŏng-yun, 22
O Suk-hŭi, 330
O Sun-nyŏ, 417, 424
O T'ae-bong, 327, 330, 352, 383, 407,
    416, 418, 419, 421, 436, 437, 453,
    478, 491
O T'ae-yŏng, 399
O T'aek-hwan, 417, 425
O Tong-uk, 324, 327, 330, 352, 407, 414,
    451, 453, 459, 479, 488, 492
O Yŏng, 318, 396
O Yong-bang, 331, 335, 336, 350
O Yŏng-bong, 326, 329, 346, 347
Ok Mun-hwan, 398
Ok Pong-nin, 325
Ok Yŏng-ja, 395
Ŏm Aeng-gwan, 398
Ŏm Hak-ch'ŏl, 420
Ŏm Kil-yŏng, 420
Ŏm Sang-il, 303, 332
Orego, Carlos A., 176
Oyama Ikuo, 103

Pae Ch'ang-ho, 425
Pae Ch'ŏl, 288
Pae Ch'ol-u, 335
Pae Hyŏng-han, 400
Pae Ki-jun, 328, 410

Pae Sŭng-hyŏk, 330
Paek Chong-hŭp, 413
·Paek Hak-nim, 327, 330, 331, 333, 336,
340, 352, 411, 417, 419, 437
Paek Hong-gwŏn, 324, 460, 492
Paek Hyŏng-gi, 308
Paek Il-bu, 424
Paek In-jun, 308
Paek Kŏn-sa, 414
Paek Nak-yŏng, 396
Paek Nam-un, 325, 326, 330, 352, 373,
377, 394, 401, 403, 405, 410, 411,
415, 425, 429, 430, 433, 435, 438,
443, 449, 464, 492
Paek P'a, 399
Paek Pŏm-su, 308, 331, 334, 352
Paek Pong-gwan, 292
Paek Pong-sŏn, 395
Paek Pyŏng-ik, 395
Paek Saeng-gŭm, 405
Paek Sang-su, 422
Paek Sŏn-il, 327, 331, 350, 408, 416,
451, 453, 470, 485, 492
Paek Sŏng-guk, 409
Paek Sŏng-hak, 409, 415
Paek Sun-jae, 292, 325
Paek Sun-ok, 424
Paek Ŭi-myŏng, 407, 413, 422
Paek Ŭng-yŏp, 398
Paek Wŏl-sŏn, 421
Paek Wŏn-bŏm, 423
Pak Chae-p'il, 410
Pak Chae-ro, 382
Pak Chae-sŏp, 400
Pak Ch'an-hyŏk, 397
Pak Ch'an-je, 410, 416
Pak Ch'ang-gu, 397
Pak Ch'ang-ok, 115, 127, 130, 288, 289,
290, 319, 320, 322, 323, 339, 340,
344, 356, 357, 359, 371, 394, 472,
480, 481, 492
Pak Ch'ang-sik, 317, 325, 340, 394, 402,
403, 441
Pak Ch'ang-sil, 320
Pak Ch'i-ho, 395
Pak Ch'i-hwa, 397
Pak Chin-hong, 398
Pak Ch'o-ryŏn, 422
Pak Ch'ŏl, 397
Pak Chŏng-ae, 288, 289, 291, 292, 297,
317, 319, 320, 322, 323, 325, 326,
338, 339, 341, 343, 344, 348, 372,
373, 375, 392, 393, 400, 401, 403,
405, 406, 411, 412, 430, 433, 459,
492, 523, 524
Pak Chŏng-gŭn, 410
Pak Chŏng-hyŏn, 396, 415, 421

Pak Chong-i, 383, 421
Pak Chong-t'ae, 397
Pak Chŏng-yŏl, 409
Pak Ch'un-hyŏk, 326, 346
Pak Ch'un-myŏng, 423
Pak Ch'un-ŏn, 399
Pak Ch'un-sik, 331, 382, 419, 425, 438
Pak Ch'un-sŏk, 317, 346
Pak Chun-yŏng, 395
Pak Chung-guk, 335, 424
Pak Hae-gwŏn, 331
Pak Hak-sŏp, 423
Pak Hŏn-yŏng, 107, 109, 110, 281, 287,
289, 314, 318, 321, 322, 339, 344,
367, 368, 393, 448, 466, 481, 492
Pak Hong-gŏl, 409, 415
Pak Hong-sun, 409
Pak Hun, 381
Pak Hun-il, 318, 320, 323, 348, 358, 394
Pak Hun-wŏn, 422
Pak Hyo-sam, 317, 320, 325, 341
Pak Hyŏng-suk, 327
Pak Hyŏng-uk, 399
Pak Il-u, 109, 283, 317, 318, 319, 320,
322, 341, 345, 358, 393, 448, 463,
469, 492
Pak Il-yŏng, 323, 395
Pak Im-t'ae, 336, 383, 385, 421, 454,
455, 463, 485, 492
Pak In-hyŏk, 327
Pak In-su, 420
Pak Ki-ho, 395
Pak Ki-sŏ, 331, 335, 350
Pak Ki-t'aek, 413
Pak Kŏn-byŏng, 399
Pak Kŭk-ch'ŏl, 348
Pak Kŭm-ch'ŏl, 289, 290, 292, 293, 294,
296, 321, 322, 323, 325, 326, 328,
338, 339, 341, 345, 359, 404, 405,
406, 433, 443
Pak Kŭm-ok, 407
Pak Kŭn-mo, 398
Pak Kwan-o, 421
Pak Kwan-sun, 413
Pak Kwang-hŭi, 324
Pak Kwang-sŏn, 407, 413, 453, 475, 492
Pak Kwi-nyŏ, 403
Pak Kyŏng-su, 289
Pak Kyŏng-suk, 407, 414
Pak Kyŏng-sun, 411
Pak Mu, 320, 324, 402
Pak Mun-gyu, 282, 319, 324, 327, 330,
349, 376, 393, 401, 403, 410, 411,
414, 430, 433, 435, 443, 448, 449,
451, 459, 469, 470, 471, 478, 484,
486, 487, 488, 492
Pak Mun-sun, 398

Pak Myŏng-bin, 335, 385, 456, 476, 492
Pak Nae-su, 292
Pak Nak-ho, 423
Pak Nam-sun, 413, 419
Pak P'il-hwan, 399
Pak Po-ok, 399
Pak Pok-cho, 397
Pak Pok-sun, 303, 382, 416, 419
Pak Pong-jo, 409, 416
Pak Pong-ju, 336
Pak Pong-u, 397
Pak Pyŏng-guk, 410, 417
Pak Pyŏng-jik, 398
Pak Sang-jun, 394
Pak Sang-sun, 396
Pak Se-bong, 420
Pak Se-ch'ang, 327, 375, 378, 407, 496,
  498
Pak Se-yŏng, 394
Pak Si-hyŏng, 335, 422
Pak Si-yun, 397
Pak Sin-dŏk, 297, 302, 376, 390, 401,
  405, 407, 411, 413, 418, 425, 433, 435
Pak Sŏl-hŭi, 336
Pak Sŏn-gyun, 303, 331
Pak Sŏng-ch'ŏl, 302, 304, 326, 328, 329,
  332, 333, 341, 345, 349, 377, 379,
  381, 382, 384, 408, 412, 418, 421,
  426, 436, 443, 450, 452, 454, 466,
  474, 476, 482, 484, 485, 486, 487,
  488, 492
Pak Sŏng-guk, 402, 407, 413
Pak Sŏng-ok, 398
Pak Sŏng-sam, 425
Pak Su-bŏm, 336, 413
Pak Su-dong, 302, 330, 332, 333, 338
Pak Sŭng-gŭk, 397
Pak Sŭng-hak, 410, 416
Pak Sŭng-hŭp, 406, 410, 438
Pak Sŭng-il, 415
Pak Sŭng-sŏ, 409
Pak Sŭng-wŏn, 288
Pak T'ae-jin, 327, 410
Pak Tae-sŏp, 303
Pak To-hwa, 402
Pak Tong-ch'o, 321
Pak Tong-gwan, 408, 414, 424
Pak Tong-sŏn, 421
Pak U-sŏp, 327
Pak Ŭi-wan, 117, 123, 292, 323, 342,
  404, 449, 470, 477, 479, 480, 481,
  486, 487, 492
Pak Un-gŏl, 441
Pak Ŭn-sŏng, 399
Pak Ung-gŏl, 327, 406, 411, 451, 464,
  492

Pak Ŭng-ik, 317, 346
Pak Wal-sŏng, 424
Pak Wŏn-ha, 421
Pak Wŏn-jun, 396
Pak Wŏn-sul, 321
Pak Yŏng-bin, 130, 288, 289, 290, 322,
  339, 345, 359
Pak Yŏng-ch'an, 336
Pak Yŏng-ch'ŏl, 308, 336
Pak Yong-guk, 292, 324, 326, 328, 339,
  345, 352, 391, 402, 406, 407, 440
Pak Yong-han, 395
Pak Yŏng-hwa, 321
Pak Yong-myŏn, 336
Pak Yŏng-nyŏ, 421
Pak Yong-sik, 303, 423
Pak Yŏng-sin, 303, 331, 402, 410, 417,
  453, 464, 492
Pak Yŏng-sŏk, 330, 334, 385, 415, 455,
  477, 492
Pak Yŏng-sŏn, 286, 319, 320, 341, 345,
  358, 423
Pak Yong-sŏng, 409, 451, 471, 478, 492
Pak Yŏng-sŏng, 394
Pak Yŏng-sŏp, 402, 415, 422
Pak Yŏng-su, 410, 416, 424
Pak Yong-suk, 118
Pak Yŏng-sun, 303, 326, 330, 334, 349,
  407, 415, 423, 451, 453, 463, 485, 492
Pak Yong-t'ae, 402, 405, 441
Pak Yun-gil, 393, 433
Pan Il-byŏng, 419, 423, 437
Pang Ch'ang-se, 420
Pang Ch'ol-gap, 335
Pang Ch'ol-ho, 335
Pang Hak-se, 320, 323, 330, 334, 346,
  347, 348, 394, 404, 415, 419, 424,
  426, 430, 437, 438, 449, 469, 476,
  492, 496, 497
Pang Ho-san, 109
Pang Hwan-sŏn, 422
Pang Hyo-ŭl, 415, 422
Pang Ki-yŏng, 336
Pang T'ae-ho, 419
Pang T'ae-uk, 384, 422
Pang T'ae-yul, 425
Pang U-yong, 317, 346
Park Chung Hee, 150, 182, 195, 197
P'eng Teh-huai, 100
Phomvihane, Kaysone, 215
P'i Ch'ang-nin, 292, 296, 303, 327, 330
Pol Pot, 217–218
Pyŏn Ch'ang-bok, 302, 333, 382, 385,
  420, 426, 437
Pyŏn Ki-ch'ang, 398
Pyŏn Sŭng-u, 335, 424

Rahman, Ziaur, 223
Ratsiraka, Didier, 211, 222–223
Rene, Albert, 221, 228
Rhee Syngman, 41, 45, 73, 81

Sakai Tatsuo, 153
Salisbury, Harrison, 181
Senghor, Leopold Sedar, 194
Sihanouk, Norodom, 155, 174, 177, 181,
    184, 187, 188, 193, 199, 202, 205,
    206–207, 225, 381
Sim Ch'ang-wan, 331, 334, 352
Sim Hyŏng-sik, 410, 416
Sim Kyŏng-ch'ŏl, 330, 335
Sim Sang-ŭi, 410
Sin Chin-sik, 411
Sin Chin-sun, 331, 335, 350
Sin Chin-u, 396
Sin Chŏng-hŭi, 382
Sin Chŏng-suk, 424
Sin Ch'un-sŏn, 424
Sin Chung-sun, 403, 407
Sin Hong-ye, 402, 403, 441
Sin Hyŏn-u, 398
Sin In-ha, 335
Sin Ko-song, 411
Sin Kyŏng-sik, 425
Sin Myŏng-ch'ŏl, 411
Sin Nam-ch'ŏl, 395, 401, 403, 437
Sin Paek-hyŏn, 399
Sin P'o-gyŭn, 416, 423
Sin Pong-hyŏn, 403
Sin Sang-dong, 400
Sin Sang-gyun, 335, 425
Sin Sang-hun, 400
Sin Sang-yun, 336
Sin Sŏng-u, 303, 423
Sin Su-gŭn, 303, 308, 419, 420, 437
Sin Su-gyŏng, 417
Sin Sun-jik, 399
Sin Sun-ye, 399
Sin Sŭng-o, 416
Sin Tae-sik, 326
Sin Tong-hwan, 336
Sin Yong-bok, 395
Sin Yong-sik, 413, 420
Sŏ Chae-hong, 335
Sŏ Ch'ang-nam, 331
Sŏ Ch'ang-sŏp, 397
Sŏ Ch'ŏl, 303, 308, 325, 326, 329, 332,
    333, 341, 346, 349, 352, 408, 412,
    416, 418, 420, 426, 434, 436, 440
Sŏ Ch'un-sik, 291, 324, 401, 403, 438
Sŏ Hwi, 323
Sŏ Kap-sun, 395

Sŏ Kwan-hŭi, 333, 385, 413, 419, 426,
    437, 439, 455, 459, 492
Sŏ Kyŏng-sil, 424
Sŏ Man-sul, 308
Sŏ Pyŏng-sik, 297
Sŏ Pyŏng-su, 396
Sŏ Sŏn-ch'il, 336
Sŏ Ŭl-hyŏn, 126, 408
Sŏ Yun-sŏk, 308, 331, 333, 342, 352, 425
Sŏk Ch'il-bo, 408, 414
Sŏk San, 324, 326, 328, 339, 345, 352,
    356, 408, 412, 450, 452, 469, 476,
    485, 488, 492
Sŏk Sun-hŭi, 423
Sŏk T'ae-ryong, 400
Sŏl Pyŏng-ho, 396
Son Ch'ŏl, 404
Son Chong-yŏl, 399
Son Kyŏng-hwa, 421
Son Kyŏng-jun, 303, 308, 331, 335, 352
Son Sŏng-p'il, 331, 335, 421, 426, 434
Sŏn Tong-gi, 395
Son Tu-hwan, 399
Son Wŏn-dong, 407
Song Chae-ch'ŏl, 397
Song Chae-hyŏn, 399
Song Ch'ang-nyŏm, 292, 327, 401, 405,
    408, 439, 467, 492
Song Che-jun, 320
Song Chong-gŭn, 398
Song Chu-sik, 392, 393, 400, 404, 434,
    435
Song Chun-ho, 399
Song Ch'un-ok, 422
Song Ki-hwan, 424
Song Kŭm-ae, 400
Song Kŭm-sun, 332, 336, 354
Song Kwan-jo, 336, 413, 423
Song Kyu-hwan, 395
Song Myŏng-hŏn, 395
Song Ŏk-man, 416
Song Ŏn-p'il, 397
Song Pok-ki, 327, 330, 336, 352, 383,
    415, 423, 452, 462, 492
Song Pong-uk, 324, 367, 394, 401, 404,
    439, 465, 492
Song Sŏng-ch'ŏl, 399
Song Sŏng-p'il, 302, 382
Song T'ae-jun, 398
Song T'ae-rae, 398
Song Tŏk-hun, 407, 412
Song Ŭl-su, 318, 319, 324, 345, 394, 405
Song Wan-sŏk, 396
Song Yŏng, 328, 401, 402, 406, 407, 414,
    434, 435
Sŏng Yu-gyŏng, 319

Sŏnu Pyŏng-gu, 421
Stalin, Joseph V., 4, 31, 70, 78, 81, 82,
   91, 96, 97, 99, 100, 101
Sukarno, 148
Sŭng Ch'ang-yul, 415
Sŭng Sin-bŏm, 410, 417
Sŭng So-il, 414

T'ae Ch'ang-am, 384
T'ae Chong-su, 308, 335
T'ae Pyŏng-yŏl, 327, 330, 333, 336, 352,
   407, 417, 419
T'ae Sŏng-su, 317, 320, 358, 394
T'ak Ch'ang-hyŏk, 394
Teng Hsiao-p'ing (Deng Xiaoping), 296
Teng Ying-ch'ao (Deng Yingchao), 226
Tito, Josip Broz, 83, 204, 210, 216, 228
To Chong-ho, 409
To Pong-sŏp, 404
To Sun-mo, 422
To Yu-ho, 406, 407, 434
Tokko Mun-hŭng, 414
Tong Min-gwang, 335
Tong Sun-mo, 383
Toure, Sekou, 185, 227, 228
Traore, Moussa, 210

U Pong-un, 395
U Sang-bok, 417
U Yŏng-sul, 415

Vassilievsky, A., 99, 100

Wang Ok-hwan, 331, 336, 350
Watanabe Michio, 98
Wi Hak-sil, 424
Wi Kwi-hwan, 422
Wŏn Ch'ŏn-jun, 396
Wŏn Ha-ok, 424
Wŏn Ho-sun, 395
Wŏn Hong-ch'ŏl, 424
Wŏn Hong-gu, 393, 395, 400, 401, 403,
   408, 413, 430, 434, 435
Wŏn Man-su, 395
Wŏn Myŏng-gyun, 335
Wŏn Tal-sik, 336
Wŏn Tong-gu, 334, 385, 455, 462, 492

Yang Chae-il, 414
Yang Chong-go, 414, 422
Yang Chŏng-t'ae, 303, 407, 417
Yang Chun-hyŏk, 410, 416
Yang Ch'ung-gyŏm, 328, 331, 350, 409
Yang Ho-jae, 412
Yang Hong-ju, 395

Yang Hyŏng-sŏp, 302, 305, 329, 333,
   338, 342, 381, 384, 409, 417, 418,
   421, 436, 453, 467, 492
Yang In-gil, 414, 420
Yang In-ho, 420
Yang Kun-ok, 326, 330
Yang Kye, 324
Yang Man-ch'ŏl, 330
Yang Nak-kyŏng, 421
Yang Ok-nyŏ, 414, 422
Yang Po-hyŏn, 396
Yang Pok-wŏn, 409, 421
Yang Sin-yŏng, 403
Yang Sun-do, 381, 419
Yang T'ae-gŭn, 328, 332, 354, 409, 470,
   492
Yang T'aek-kŏn, 408, 414
Yang Wŏn-mo, 399
Yang Yong-gŏn, 383, 419
Yang Yong-gyŏk, 334
Yang Yŏng-sun, 321
Yasue Ryosuke, 207, 209, 224
Yhomby-opango, Joachim, 222
Yi Cha-sŏn, 382, 383, 419
Yi Chae-bok, 406, 407, 413, 434
Yi Chae-ch'ŏn, 324, 401, 402, 439
Yi Chae-gon, 385, 425
Yi Chae-gŭn, 409
Yi Chae-hyang, 396
Yi Chae-nam, 319
Yi Chae-yŏng, 397, 437, 492
Yi Chae-yŏng, 292, 297, 327, 395, 406,
   410, 472, 492
Yi Chae-yun, 296, 308, 327, 334, 347,
   406, 409, 416, 423, 441
Yi Ch'an-dŭk, 424
Yi Ch'an-hwa, 404, 410, 416, 424, 430
Yi Ch'an-sŏn, 334, 406, 408, 417, 439
Yi Ch'ang-bin, 399
Yi Ch'ang-bok, 406, 407, 413, 439
Yi Chang-ch'un, 424
Yi Ch'ang-do, 382, 404, 407, 414, 423,
   430
Yi Ch'ang-gyu, 396
Yi Ch'ang-ha, 396
Yi Ch'ang-jun, 303, 410, 417
Yi Ch'ang-sŏn, 334, 424, 454, 456, 460,
   485, 492
Yi Chang-su, 327, 331, 414, 453, 461,
   492
Yi Ch'ang-su, 398
Yi Ch'ang-sun, 296, 411, 417, 425
Yi Che-jin, 413
Yi Chi-ch'an, 308, 321, 325, 328, 330,
   334, 350, 352, 385, 397, 455, 476, 492

Yi Ch'il-sŏng, 395
Yi Chin, 397
Yi Chin-gŭn, 397
Yi Chin-gyu, 384, 417, 424
Yi Chin-su, 302, 308, 333, 419, 426, 437, 496, 498
Yi Chin-suk, 398
Yi Ch'ŏl, 396
Yi Ch'ŏl-bong, 331, 335, 456, 471, 492
Yi Ch'ŏl-u, 416
Yi Chŏm-sun, 394
Yi Ch'ŏn-ho, 325, 403, 450, 462, 493
Yi Ch'ŏn-jin, 289
Yi Chŏng-bae, 334
Yi Chŏng-do, 336
Yi Chŏng-gu, 398
Yi Chong-guk, 412, 415, 439
Yi Chong-gwŏn, 398
Yi Chŏng-hwan, 318
Yi Chong-ik, 318, 320, 346
Yi Ch'ŏng-il, 331, 424
Yi Chong-man, 394, 402
Yi Chong-mok, 335
Yi Chong-myŏng, 397
Yi Chŏng-nim, 417
Yi Chong-ok, 291, 294, 297, 308, 323, 325, 326, 332, 333, 341, 342, 347, 349, 377, 385, 404, 406, 412, 418, 422, 426, 430, 436, 446, 447, 448, 449, 450, 451, 452, 454, 455, 468, 470, 471, 474, 480, 481, 482, 484, 485, 486, 487, 488, 493
Yi Chŏng-sam, 407
Yi Chong-san, 416
Yi Chŏng-sik, 336
Yi Ch'ŏng-song, 396
Yi Chŏng-suk, 397, 402, 407
Yi Chŏng-sun, 303, 384
Yi Chong-u, 335, 423
Yi Chong-wan, 399
Yi Ch'ŏng-wŏn, 289, 292, 324
Yi Chŏng-yŏl, 396
Yi Chŏng-yong, 333
Yi Chu-ha, 318, 319, 345, 395
Yi Chu-sang, 289
Yi Chu-sŏk, 420
Yi Chu-yŏn, 103, 291, 292, 297, 315, 321, 325, 326, 342, 354, 372, 373, 377, 394, 403, 406, 412, 430, 450, 452, 460, 465, 467, 481, 482, 484, 485, 486, 487, 488, 493
Yi Ch'un-am, 317
Yi Ch'un-bal, 414
Yi Chun-ho, 383, 423
Yi Ch'un-hŭi, 419

Yi Chun-hwi, 415
Yi Chun-sil, 414, 419
Yi Ch'un-sŏng, 424
Yi Ch'un-su, 396
Yi Ch'un-yong, 408
Yi Chung-gŭn, 320
Yi Chung-nin, 302
Yi Ha-il, 334
Yi Hae-su, 397
Yi Hak-pin, 409, 416
Yi Hi-bong, 398
Yi Ho-ch'ŏl, 328
Yi Ho-hyŏk, 303, 336, 417, 466, 493
Yi Ho-je, 399
Yi Hong-gyun, 297, 327, 331, 350
Yi Hong-un, 425
Yi Hong-yŏl, 394, 402, 404, 441
Yi Hong-yŏn, 396
Yi Hu-gil, 302
Yi Hŭi-gŏl, 423
Yi Hŭi-jun, 320, 325
Yi Hun, 87, 397
Yi Hwa-sŏn, 335, 420
Yi Hwa-sŏp, 404
Yi Hwa-sun, 308, 385
Yi Hwa-yŏng, 334, 410, 424
Yi Hwan-gi, 397
Yi Hwan-sam, 303, 336
Yi Hyo-sun, 297, 321, 323, 325, 326, 328, 338, 339, 341, 342, 345, 346, 353, 402, 403, 405, 406, 434, 441, 478, 493
Yi Hyŏk-yŏng, 395
Yi Hyŏn-muk, 413
Yi Hyŏn-sang, 318, 319, 345
Yi Hyŏng, 303
Yi Il-gyŏng, 292, 297, 323, 326, 402, 408, 451, 461, 464, 467, 493
Yi Il-ung, 415
Yi Im-su, 415
Yi In-bok, 425
Yi In-dŏk, 335
Yi In-dong, 324, 394, 404
Yi In-gi, 308
Yi In-gyu, 397
Yi Kang-guk, 288, 395
Yi Kang-mu, 398
Yi Ki-ch'ŏl, 409, 415
Yi Ki-hwan, 399
Yi Ki-sŏk, 282, 289, 318, 339, 345, 359, 394, 405, 462, 475, 493, 523
Yi Ki-yŏng, 390, 393, 400, 401, 402, 405, 410, 411, 416, 421, 429, 430, 434, 435
Yi Kil-song, 303, 308, 330, 334, 384, 419, 422, 437

Yi Kŏn-il, 331
Yi Ku-hun, 392, 393, 434
Yi Kuk-chin, 327, 409, 411, 412, 434,
    441, 496, 497, 498
Yi Kuk-kwŏn, 414, 421
Yi Kŭk-no, 377, 393, 394, 400, 401, 405,
    410, 415, 431, 434, 435, 443, 449,
    483, 493
Yi Kŭm-nyŏ, 414, 421
Yi Kŭm-ok, 419
Yi Kŭm-sŏn, 424
Yi Kŭn-mo, 327, 330, 333, 342, 353,
    382, 383, 417, 418, 421, 436, 478, 493
Yi Kŭn-song, 410, 417, 425
Yi Kŭn-u, 398
Yi Kwan-son, 420
Yi Kwan-sul, 398
Yi Kwang-han, 336
Yi Kwang-p'il, 329, 346
Yi Kwang-sil, 297, 327, 409, 415
Yi Kwang-sŏn, 409
Yi Kwang-su, 68
Yi Kwang-u, 297
Yi Kwŏn-mu, 87, 289, 320, 324, 404
Yi Kye-baek, 415, 420
Yi Kye-hwan, 415, 422
Yi Kye-san, 404, 410, 412, 416, 424, 431,
    441
Yi Kyŏng-dong, 400
Yi Kyŏng-hŭi, 282
Yi Kyŏng-sŏk, 331
Yi Kyŏng-sŏn, 334
Yi Kyŏng-sŏp, 303
Yi Kyŏng-suk, 384, 420
Yi Kyŏng-yong, 409
Yi Kyu-ho, 404
Yi Kyu-hŭi, 397
Yi Kyu-hwan, 321, 325, 350
Yi Mae-ch'un, 410, 416
Yi Man-gŏl, 424
Yi Man-gyu, 394, 400, 401, 402, 406,
    407, 414, 431, 434, 435, 443
Yi Man-ik, 410, 416
Yi Man-su, 396, 403
Yi Min-su, 326, 330, 346, 408, 414
Yi Min-yong, 398
Yi Mun-hwan, 395
Yi Mun-il, 324
Yi Mun-ja, 417
Yi Myŏn-hong, 399
Yi Myŏn-sang, 303, 327, 330, 334, 353,
    401, 403, 406, 410, 414, 418, 423,
    431, 434, 435
Yi Myŏng-je, 419
Yi Myŏng-wŏn, 413, 419

Yi Nak-bin, 303, 308, 332, 336, 354, 447,
    453, 455, 476, 485, 493
Yi Nam-i, 402
Yi Nam-yŏn, 405
Yi Nŭng-jong, 393, 434
Yi O-song, 421
Yi Ok-sang, 385
Yi Pang-gŭn, 417, 419, 424, 437
Yi P'il-gyu, 324
Yi P'il-sŏng, 331
Yi Po-yŏl, 398
Yi Pok-hyŏng, 417
Yi Pok-ki, 399
Yi Pŏm-sŏk, 81
Yi Pong-ch'un, 404
Yi Pong-gil, 330, 334, 419, 422, 439
Yi Pong-gyŏm, 331, 413
Yi Pong-gyu, 303, 424
Yi Pong-nam, 397, 409
Yi Pong-nyŏ, 414
Yi Pong-nyŏn, 396
Yi Pong-se, 425
Yi Pong-sŏp, 331
Yi Pong-su, 328
Yi Pong-wŏn, 331, 334, 336, 353, 419,
    425, 437
Yi Pong-yong, 303
Yi Puk-myŏng, 320, 325, 327, 347, 353
Yi Pyŏng-bu, 409, 415
Yi Pyŏng-ho, 397
Yi Pyŏng-hŭi, 397
Yi Pyŏng-il, 399
Yi Pyŏng-je, 115, 394
Yi Pyŏng-nam, 394, 404, 446, 449, 450,
    476, 485, 493
Yi Pyŏng-no, 399
Yi Pyŏng-sik, 413
Yi Pyŏng-uk, 335
Yi Rak-bin, 416, 421
Yi Rim, 324, 404
Yi Rim-su, 303, 331, 411, 437
Yi Sang-ch'un, 403
Yi Sang-gap, 399
Yi Sang-ho, 398
Yi Sang-hun, 396
Yi Sang-hyŏn, 420
Yi Sang-ik, 425
Yi Sang-in, 396
Yi Sang-jo, 325
Yi Sang-jun, 394
Yi Sang-sun, 395
Yi Sang-un, 328, 409
Yi Se-sik, 420
Yi Si-ha, 404
Yi Si-wŏn, 331

Yi Sik, 394
Yi Sil-ok, 421
Yi Sin-ja, 420
Yi Sŏ-hyang, 399
Yi Sŏ-un, 399
Yi Sŏk-bo, 394
Yi Sŏk-chin, 425
Yi Sŏk-chong, 297
Yi Sŏk-ch'un, 421
Yi Sŏk-ha, 400
Yi Sŏk-ku, 318
Yi Sŏk-nam, 404, 410, 417
Yi Sŏk-sim, 406, 411, 439
Yi Sŏk-sung, 397
Yi Sŏn-bi, 412
Yi Sŏn-hwa, 330
Yi Sŏn-jae, 395
Yi Sŏn-sil, 333, 342
Yi Sŏng-baek, 398
Yi Sŏng-bok, 335
Yi Song-jŏng, 398
Yi Sŏng-nam, 410, 416
Yi Song-un, 291, 321, 324, 326, 349,
    400, 401, 402, 407, 434, 498
Yi Song-yŏn, 409
Yi Su-ch'ŏn, 415
Yi Su-dŏk, 416
Yi Su-il, 415
Yi Su-wŏl, 336
Yi Suk-kyŏng, 396
Yi Suk-yŏ, 400
Yi Sul-chin, 395
Yi Sun-ae, 425
Yi Sun-bong, 384, 425
Yi Sun-gŭn, 317, 320, 325, 336
Yi Sun-ho, 415, 423
Yi Sun-jŏ, 396
Yi Sun-nam, 413
Yi Sun-sin, 131
Yi Sun-yŏl, 423
Yi Sun-yŏng, 410, 413
Yi Sŭng-gi, 130, 297, 382, 409, 411, 415,
    423, 431, 437
Yi Sŭng-sun, 415
Yi Sŭng-u, 326, 347
Yi Sŭng-yŏp, 109, 118, 288, 314, 318,
    321, 322, 339, 345, 367, 394, 449,
    469, 475, 493
Yi T'ae-hwa, 291, 325
Yi T'ae-sŏng, 395
Yi T'ae-u, 408
Yi Tal-chin, 324
Yi Tal-yong, 412, 417, 425, 441
Yi Tal-yŏng, 410
Yi Tan, 408, 413

Yi Tŏk-hyŏn, 327, 408
Yi Tong-ch'un, 330, 334, 423
Yi Tong-gŭn, 396
Yi Tong-ho, 334
Yi Tong-hwa, 317, 320, 347, 394, 403
Yi Tong-il, 413
Yi Tong-jun, 415, 422
Yi Tong-sŏn, 398
Yi Tong-sŏng, 409
Yi Tong-t'ak, 397
Yi Tong-yŏng, 395
Yi Tu-ch'an, 334, 413, 418, 419, 434
Yi Tu-ik, 330, 334, 336, 410, 417, 424
Yi Tu-san, 396
Yi Tu-wŏn, 397
Yi Uk, 396
Yi Ŭl-sŏl, 330, 334, 336, 410, 416, 424
Yi Ŭm-jŏn, 425
Yi Ŭm-sŏn, 384
Yi Un-jŏn, 303
Yi Ŭn-sun, 384, 424
Yi Ŭng-wŏn, 407, 413, 419
Yi Wan-gi, 335, 424
Yi Wŏn-bŏm, 334, 412, 414, 439
Yi Wŏn-gwan, 423
Yi Wŏn-il, 395
Yi Wŏn-jun, 408
Yi Wŏn-sŏp, 421
Yi Yang-hun, 423
Yi Yang-suk, 327, 335, 409, 413, 414,
    452, 460, 481, 488, 493
Yi Ye-dong, 425
Yi Yŏ-sŏng, 394, 404
Yi Yŏn, 409, 415, 423
Yi Yŏn-suk, 422
Yi Yong, 394, 449, 462, 469, 483, 493
Yi Yŏng, 392, 393, 402, 434
Yi Yŏng-bok, 382, 418, 421, 434
Yi Yong-bu, 420
Yi Yong-dŏk, 397
Yi Yŏng-gi, 347, 416
Yi Yŏng-go, 435
Yi Yŏng-gu, 409, 414, 420, 497
Yi Yong-gu, 296, 411, 416, 437
Yi Yŏng-gyu, 382, 424
Yi Yŏng-ho, 324, 326, 328, 345, 356,
    379, 405, 407, 411, 412, 434, 443
Yi Yong-hŭi, 413
Yi Yŏng-hwa, 321
Yi Yong-ik, 330, 334, 424
Yi Yong-jin, 398
Yi Yŏng-ju, 400
Yi Yŏng-jun, 394
Yi Yong-mo, 333, 347
Yi Yong-mu, 330, 419

Yi Yong-nin, 329, 347
Yi Yŏng-nin, 347
Yi Yŏng-sŏm, 289, 321, 395
Yi Yong-sŏn, 398, 408, 414, 422, 431
Yi Yŏng-suk, 413, 420
Yi Yong-sun, 336, 423
Yi Yŏng-sun, 410
Yi Yŏng-sun, 327, 411, 417, 425
Yi Yŏng-uk, 318
Yi Yu-min, 321, 324, 393, 394, 401, 404, 434, 437
Yi Yu-sŏp, 414
Yi Yun-do, 412, 416, 440
Yim Chae-yŏng, 396
Yim Chin-gyu, 327, 408, 415
Yim Ch'ŏl, 327, 330, 417, 419
Yim Chŏng-sun, 398
Yim Ch'un-ch'u, 4, 89, 328, 330, 332, 333, 341, 345, 385, 405, 409, 418, 422, 426, 434, 436, 441, 443
Yim Hae, 292, 317, 320, 323, 341, 349, 405, 459, 467, 493
Yim Ho-gun, 333
Yim Hyŏng-gu, 331, 334, 353, 412, 417, 441, 456, 476, 493
Yim Kŭn-sang, 402, 439
Yim Kwi-bin, 410, 417
Yim Kye-ch'ŏl, 297, 303, 326, 334, 347, 406, 408, 412, 417, 439, 471, 479, 480, 493
Yim Nam-jae, 425
Yim Nok-chae, 335, 419
Yim Pong-ch'un, 422
Yim Pong-ŏn, 408
Yim P'ung-wŏn, 399
Yim Sang-sun, 397
Yim Sŏk-ki, 426
Yim Su-man, 330, 334
Yim Sun-nyŏ, 410, 417, 425
Yim T'ae-sŏp, 417
Yim T'aek, 399, 403
Yim To-jun, 317
Yim Tong-uk, 399
Yim Wŏn-sang, 385
Yim Yŏng-gyun, 408
Yim Yun-sik, 407, 413, 420
Yŏ Ch'un-sŏk, 335
Yŏ Kyŏng-gu, 409, 466
Yŏ Un-ch'ŏl, 339
Yŏ Un-hyŏng, 32, 35, 47, 282
Yŏm Chae-man, 334, 414
Yŏm Chŏng-gwŏn, 395
Yŏm Chŏng-ja, 419
Yŏm Ki-sun, 335
Yŏm Kyŏng-jae, 407

Yŏm Sang-gi, 327
Yŏm T'ae-jun, 327, 330, 334, 353, 382, 407, 411, 417, 418, 420, 434, 437, 451, 462, 478, 493
Yŏm Ŭi-hyŏn, 400
Yŏm Ŭi-jae, 327
Yŏn Hyŏng-muk, 302, 330, 332, 333, 338, 341, 414, 418, 424, 436
Yŏn Pok-kil, 408
Yŏn Sŭng-yŏl, 424
Yu Chae-hun, 409
Yu Chae-hwa, 336
Yu Ch'ang-gwŏn, 327, 409, 413
Yu Chang-sik, 330, 414, 418, 424, 436
Yu Chin-yŏng, 397
Yu Ch'ol-mok, 292, 324, 401, 403, 437, 466, 493
Yu Ch'ŏl-sŭng, 325
Yu Chŏng-suk, 330, 334
Yu Chong-yŏl, 332, 424
Yu Ch'uk-un, 289, 292, 323, 402, 463, 493
Yu Ch'un-ok, 424
Yu Hae-bung, 393, 394, 434
Yu Hyŏn-gyu, 402
Yu Hyŏng-gyu, 396
Yu Hyŏng-nŭm, 423
Yu Ki-ik, 406, 407, 441
Yu Ki-sŏp, 394
Yu Kŏn-yang, 406, 408, 440
Yu Kŭm-bong, 399
Yu Kŭm-sŏn, 382, 384, 423
Yu Kwang-yŏl, 291, 404
Yu Kwi-jin, 423
Yu Kye-ryang, 90
Yu Kyŏng-sam, 404
Yu Kyŏng-su, 87, 324, 404
Yu Man-ok, 403, 410, 417
Yu Mun-hwa, 321, 325, 354
Yu Myŏng-ho, 408
Yu Myŏng-sŏk, 398
Yu Pyŏng-no, 422
Yu Pyŏng-yŏn, 410, 416
Yu Rak-chong, 408, 414, 420
Yu Sŏk-kyun, 399
Yu Sŏng-hun, 402
Yu Su-hong, 423
Yu Su-yŏn, 402
Yu Suk-kŭn, 420
Yu Sun-hŭi, 330
Yu Sun-sik, 292
Yu Sŭng-nam, 330
Yu Tong-yŏl, 395
Yu Ŭl-sam, 303
Yu Yŏn-hwa, 325

Yu Yŏng-gi, 317
Yu Yŏng-jun, 318, 319, 345, 393, 405, 434
Yu Yong-sang, 399
Yu Yŏng-sŏp, 408
Yu Yŏng-yun, 396
Yun Chae-bong, 398
Yun Ch'ang-sun, 327
Yun Ch'i-ho, 335, 424
Yun Ch'i-il, 402
Yun Ch'il-hwan, 424
Yun Chin-sang, 422
Yun Ch'un-dŏk, 420
Yun Chŭng-u, 394, 403
Yun Haeng-jung, 394
Yun Ho-sŏk, 334, 385, 422, 455, 472, 493
Yun Hŭi-gu, 400
Yun Hyŏng-sik, 289, 374, 394, 411, 417
Yun Il-chu, 318
Yun In-yŏng, 398
Yun Ki-bok, 303, 330, 332, 333, 338, 342, 380, 381, 409, 418, 419, 420, 426, 434, 435, 437, 439, 451, 453, 461, 465, 488, 493

Yun Ki-ho, 404
Yun Ki-jŏng, 335
Yun Kong-hŭm, 317, 324, 347, 460, 465, 493
Yun Kyŏng-ja, 414
Yun Myŏng-gŭn, 336
Yun Pong-gu, 414
Yun Pong-jin, 402
Yun Pyŏng-gwan, 397
Yun Pyŏng-gwŏn, 407, 413, 419
Yun Sang-man, 396
Yun Sang-yŏl, 397
Yun Su, 395
Yun Sun-dal, 288
Yun Sŭng-gwa, 296
Yun Sŭng-gwan, 425
Yun T'ae-hong, 328, 417, 498
Yun T'ae-in, 421
Yun Ŭng-yong, 323, 347
Yun Yŏn-hwan, 406, 409, 412, 416, 439
Yun Yŏng-gyŏng, 410
Yun Yong-jun, 400
Yun Yong-muk, 303

Zhivkov, Todor, 190–191, 204

Subject Index

Academy of Sciences, 98, 185, 459
Administration Council, 444–448; members, fifth Supreme People's Assembly, 454–455; members, sixth Supreme People's Assembly, 455–456; premier and vice-premiers, 444. *See also* cabinet
Agricultural Commission, 459
Agricultural Cooperative Farm movement, 171
agriculture, 128, 137, 213, 225, 236–237; agrarian law, 220; agrarian problems, 145, 222; agrarian reform, 39; agrarian revolution, 145; agrarian sector, 158–159; agrarian theses, 198–199; agrarian workers, 8, 100, 168; agricultural cooperatives, 112, 124; agricultural management, 84, 107, 112, 124, 136, 163, 189, 290, 291; agricultural production, 189
Agriculture, Ministry of, 458–459
Agriculture and Forestry, Ministry of, 459
Algeria, Democratic People's Republic of, 192, 203
anti-Japanese guerrillas, 10, 13, 20, 131, 162, 173, 206
Anti-Japanese United Army, 127
architects and technicians, 105, 110
Argentina, 196
arts and literature, 42, 64, 71, 89, 92, 94, 148, 157, 172–173, 247–248
Asahi shinbun, 11, 177
Asian Economic Seminar, 147
athletics, 172
August 15th incident, 197
August 15th liberation, 46, 62–63, 76–77, 102, 129, 250; fifth anniversary, 87; sixth anniversary, 92–93; seventh anniversary, 97; tenth anniversary, 109; seventeenth anniversary, 138; eighteenth anniversary, 142; twentieth anniversary, 154
Australia, 198

Bangladesh, People's Republic of, 223
banks, 136, 224; banking system, 143–144; Central Bank, 144, 211; Peasant Bank, 211
Benin, People's Republic of, 211–212, 226
Bills Committee, Supreme People's Assembly, 391; members, second assembly, 401; members, third assembly, 406; members, fourth assembly, 411; members, fifth assembly, 419; members, sixth assembly, 426
Budget Committee, Supreme People's Assembly, 391; members, second assembly, 401–402; members, third assembly, 406; members, fourth assembly, 412; members, fifth assembly, 419; members, sixth assembly, 426
Building Materials Industry, Ministry of, 459
Bulgarian People's Republic, 190, 204
bureaucracy, 95, 108, 126, 149, 157, 161, 218, 290
Burma, 217
Burundi, 225

cabinet, 444–448; abbreviations, 456–458; members, first cabinet, 448–449; members, second cabinet, 449–450; members, third cabinet, 450–451; members, fourth cabinet, 452–454. *See also* Administration Council, members
Cambodia, 155, 174, 180, 181, 184, 187, 188, 193, 199, 206–207. *See also* Kampuchea
Central Africa, 220
Central Auditing Committee, Workers' Party of Korea, 273, 277, 286, 315; members, second congress, 321; members, third congress, 325; members, fourth congress, 328; members, fifth congress, 332; members, sixth congress 336; personnel, 309–315

Central Bank, 144, 211. See also banks
Central Committee, the Workers' Party of
    Korea, 10, 57, 66, 68, 71, 273–274;
    members and candidate members, 312;
    method of election, 310–312; officers,
    313–314; personnel, 309–315
—First Congress: chairman and vice-
    chairmen, 316; members, 317–318; of-
    ficers, 316–318; plenums, 275–276,
    283–286
—Second Congress: chairman and vice-
    chairmen, 319; members and candidate
    members, 319–321; officers, 319–320;
    plenums, 276, 285–291
—Third Congress: chairman and vice-
    chairmen, 322–323; members and
    candidate members, 323–325; officers,
    322–323; plenums, 276, 291–296
—Fourth Congress: chairman and vice-
    chairmen, 325; members and candidate
    members, 326–328; officers, 325–326;
    officers in 1966, 328; plenums,
    276–277, 298–302, 328
—Fifth Congress: members and candidate
    members, 329–332; officers, 329;
    plenums, 277, 303–307; secretaries,
    329
—Sixth Congress: members and candidate
    members, 333–336; officers, 332; secre-
    taries, 332
Central Court, 495, 496; chief justices
    and presidents, 497
Central Election Committee, 363
Central Inspection Committee, 309–310,
    358n22; members, first congress,
    317–318
Central Party School, 42, 45, 60–61, 62,
    96–97, 121
Central People's Committee, Supreme Peo-
    ple's Assembly, 4, 388–389, 444; mem-
    bers, fifth assembly, 418; members,
    sixth assembly, 426; reelection rate,
    390
Central Procurator's Office, 496;
    Procurators-General, 498
Central Security School, 78
Chemical and Building Materials Indus-
    tries, Ministry of, 460
chemical industry, 130, 132
Chemical Industry, Ministry of, 461–462
Chilean Socialist Party, 176
China. See People's Republic of China
Chinese Communist Party, 202, 226
Chinese Volunteer Army, 89, 90, 95, 97,
    98, 99, 100, 101, 104, 117, 118
Ch'ŏllima movement, 9, 130, 131

Ch'ŏllima speed, 191
Ch'ŏllima Workteam Movement, 164, 299
Ch'ŏndogyo Ch'ŏngudang (Ch'ŏndogyo
    Young Friends Party), 84, 93, 297,
    308, 387
chŏngch'i sajŏn, 2
ch'ongnyŏn. See Chōsōren; General Asso-
    ciation of Korean Residents in Japan;
    Korean Resident's Association in Japan
Ch'ŏngsalli, 128, 298
Chosŏn Yosŏng, 47
Chōsōren, 175, 189. See also General As-
    sociation of Korean Residents in Japan;
    Korean Resident's Association in Japan
chuch'e, 8, 69, 109–110, 111, 128, 141,
    151, 152, 153, 155, 161, 165, 175,
    178, 180, 183, 184, 185, 192, 195,
    196, 198, 204, 206, 211, 220, 223,
    226, 229
City and Industry Construction, Ministry
    of, 462
City Construction, Ministry of, 461
City Construction Management, Ministry
    of, 461
City Management, Ministry of, 462
Coal Industry, Ministry of, 463
Cominform, 83
Comintern, 32
Commerce, Ministry of, 460
Common Education, Ministry of, 461
Communication, Ministry of, 463
Communist Youth Groups, 19, 20–21
Communist Youth League, 280
Confederal Republic of Koryŏ, 188, 209
Congo, Brazzaville Republic of, 154
Congo, People's Republic of, 189, 222
Constitution of the Democratic People's
    Republic of Korea, 76, 185, 304, 305,
    367, 499; amendment, 372, 499–501;
    draft of 1948, 366, 499; first constitu-
    tion, 499; first to sixth revisions,
    499–501; text of 1972, 502–522
construction, 110, 115, 123–124,
    140–141, 144–145, 152, 293
Construction, Ministry of, 462–463
Construction and Building Materials In-
    dustries, Ministry of, 461
consumer goods, 120, 137, 173
Control Commission, members, sixth con-
    gress, 333
Costa Rica, 201
County Cooperative Farm Management
    Committee, 134, 140, 145–146
courts. See Central Court
Credentials Committee, Supreme People's
    Assembly, 367, 391; members, second

assembly, 402; members, third assembly, 406; members, fourth assembly, 412; members, fifth assembly, 419; members, sixth assembly, 426
Credentials Committee, Workers' Party of Korea, 308
Cuba, 131, 153–154, 158, 176, 223
Cultural Revolution, 186–187
culture, 247–248
Culture, Ministry of, 464
Culture and Art, Ministry of, 460
Culture and Propaganda, Ministry of, 463–464
currency reform, 67

Dahomey, 196, 207
Democratic Front for Fatherland Unification, 82, 287
Democratic National United Front, 44, 45, 46, 47, 53, 54, 57, 61, 65, 71, 72, 82, 280, 282
Democratic Party. *See* Korean Democratic Party
Democratic People's Republic of Korea: agreements with the Soviet Union, 81, 85; anniversaries, 82, 88, 98, 122, 142, 148, 165, 189–190, 223; delegations, 81, 202; establishment, 78; national budgets, 366, 369, 370, 371–372, 372–373, 377, 379, 383, 384; policies, 177, 180; political programs, 77, 161; state system, 185, 233–234; tasks, 8, 139. *See also* Administration Council; cabinet; Central People's Committee; Constitution of the Democratic People's Republic of Korea; Korean People's Army
Democratic Women's League, 33, 154, 178
Democratic Youth League, 29, 30, 32, 33, 34, 42, 49, 71, 90, 111, 137, 147, 280
dictatorship of proletariat, 159

economic and cultural cooperation: North Korea and People's Republic of China, 103; North Korea and U.S.S.R., 100
Economic Relations with Foreign Countries, Commission for, 465
economy, 235–239; management of, 33, 149, 186; rural, 9, 136; theoretical problems, 168–169. *See also* People's Economic Plan
Ecuador, 198
education, 27, 55, 110, 122–123, 132, 133, 137, 139, 141, 153, 163, 166, 247–248, 373; cadres, 212; compulsory, 179, 201; encyclopedia and maps,

146; higher education, 300; nursery schools, 158; reforms, 29, 56, 141, 144, 151, 179, 194, 195; socialist education theses, 216–217, 223–224, 306; teachers, 179
Education, Ministry of, 464
Education and Culture, Ministry of, 464
Education Commissions, 464–465
Electric Powers, Ministry of, 465
Equadorial Guinea, 217
External Economic Affairs, Ministry of, 465

factionalism, 21, 28, 73
Fatherland Restoration Association, 22
finance, 167, 211, 224
Finance, Ministry of, 465–466
fisheries, 75–76, 84, 112, 113, 126, 136, 164, 169, 214, 293
Fisheries, Ministry of, 466
Foodstuff and Daily Necessities Industries, Ministry of, 466
Foreign Affairs, Ministry of, 466
Foreign Affairs Committee, Supreme People's Assembly, 391; members, second assembly, 402; members, third assembly, 406; members, fourth assembly, 412
Foreign Ministers' Conference, 33
Foreign Trade, Ministry of, 467
forestry, 84, 106
Forestry, Ministry of, 467
480-minute work-day, 150, 160, 301
4-19 student demonstration, 295
French Communist Party, 205

Gabon, 214
General Association of Korean Residents in Japan, 292, 308. *See also* Chōsōren; Korean Resident's Association in Japan
General Federation of Trade Unions, 171. *See also* trade unions
German Democratic Republic, 218
Guinea, Republic of, 185, 227
Guinea-Bissau, 227
Guinean Revolutionary People's Republic, 228
Guyana, 214, 220

Heavy Industry, Ministry of, 468
Heavy Industry Commission, 468
Higher Education, Ministry of, 151, 467
Hwanghae Steel Mill, 67, 138, 150

ideological revolution, 186–187
Industrial Bank, 211

industries, 237–239. *See also* economy; People's Economic Plan
Industry, Ministry of, 468
Inspection Committee, the Workers' Party of Korea, 273, 277, 283, 286, 289; election of members, 281; members, second congress, 320; members, third congress 323; members, fourth congress, 326; members, fifth congress, 329; members, Workers' Party of South Korea, 318–319
intellectuals, 30, 49, 110, 164–165, 185
Interim People's Committee, 280
Interior, Ministry of, 469
Internal and External Commerce, Ministry of, 469
international aid, 103
international relations, 241–242
International Trade Union, 98. *See also* trade unions
International Women's League, 92
interviews of Kim Il Sung, 244–246
Iraq, 169, 178
Italian Communist Party, 192, 228

Japan, 5, 103, 114, 123, 153, 180, 181, 190, 197
Japanese Communist Party, 165, 182
judiciary, 495–496
Justice, Ministry of, 469
justices. *See* Central Court
Juvenile Corps, 20–21, 156, 211

Kampuchea, Democratic Republic of, 217–218, 225
Kampuchea, National United Front of, 177, 187. *See also* Cambodia
Kansan Uutiset, 170
Kim Ch'aek Polytechnic Institute, 166
Kim Il Sung Military Academy, 143
Kim Il Sung University, 47, 65, 78, 83, 84, 119, 212
Korea Focus, 194–195
Korean Central News Agency, 5, 15, 82
Korean Coast Guard, 162
Korean Communist Party, 4, 310; agendas in North Korea, 279–281; agendas in South Korea, 281–282; draft declaration, 281; North Korean Branch Bureau, 26, 27, 28, 29, 31, 32, 34, 39, 44–45, 274
Korean Democratic Party, 308, 387
Korean People's Army, 4, 8, 48, 65, 66, 69, 70, 71, 86, 88, 90, 91, 93, 95, 96, 99, 101, 190; air force, 31; anniversaries, 90, 95, 99, 162, 186; anti-Japanese armed struggle, 117; instructors, 122–

123; intelligence officers, 104; military-political cadres, 107; orders, 87, 89, 90, 91, 93, 95, 96, 97, 99, 101, 102, 104, 105; political education and work, 130, 141; self-defense policy, 143; seventh congress of agitators, 218; supreme commander, 86, 87, 88, 90, 91, 93; units and divisions, 117, 130, 162; veternas, 119, 120, 126, 127, 135, 159
Korean People's Party, 35, 43
Korean People's Revolutionary Army, 21, 22, 23–25
Korean Resident's Association in Japan, 175. *See also* Chōsōren; General Association of Korean Residents in Japan
Korean Revolutionary Army, 20, 23–24
Korean War, 5, 7, 93, 97, 182, 241; cease-fire agreement, 101–102; decorated veterans, 119, 120, 126, 127, 135, 159; prisoners-of-war, 92, 101; radio address, 86
Kuwait, 198
Kyodo News Agency, 153, 177

Labor, Ministry of, 469
Labor Administration, Ministry of, 470
Labor Law, 43, 226
Land Administration, Ministry of, 470
Land and Sea Transportation, Ministry of, 471
Land Law, 214
land reform, 27, 29, 37, 39–40, 56, 57, 280, 363
Language, Korean, 144, 156
Lao, People's Democratic Republic of, 215
Le Monde, 215
League of Korean Youth in Japan, 197
League of the Socialist Working Youth, 8, 147, 156, 175, 177, 213. *See also* youth
Lebanon, 172
Liberal Democratic Party of Japan, 225
light industries, 116–117, 135, 173
Light Industry, Ministry of, 116–117, 470
Light Industry Commission, 470–471
Local Administration, Ministry of, 471
local budget system, 201
local industries, 173
local organization, 95

machine industry, 114, 215, 216
Machine Industry, First Ministry of, 473
Machine Industry, Ministry of, 472
Machine Industry, Second Ministry of, 473
Machine Industry Commission, 472

Madagascar, Democratic Republic of, 211, 222–223
Mainichi shinbun, 7, 11, 183
Mali, Republic of, 210
Mangyŏngdae Revolutionary Family School, 80
manpower administration, 160, 167, 168, 301
March First Movement, 36
Marxism and Leninism, 9, 19, 83, 95, 108, 143, 153, 173, 183
Materials Supply, Ministry of, 473
Materials Supply Commission, 474
Mauritania, Islamic Republic of, 196
Mauritania, Republic of, 160, 204
May 10 election, 75, 76
May 30 riot, 9, 19
Metal and Chemical Industries, Ministry of, 149, 471
Metal Industry, Ministry of, 151, 471
military, 143, 239–241
Military Affairs Committee, Workers' Party of Korea, 130, 273–274
Military Commission, members, sixth congress, Workers' Party of Korea, 336
Military Court, 495
Mining Industry, Ministry of, 473
Mining Industry Commission, 473
Ministry without Portfolio, 483
Minju Chosŏn, 42–43, 50
Mozambique, People's Republic of, 221

National Congress of Agriculture, 191, 200, 225
National Defense, Ministry of, 474
National Defense Commission, Supreme People's Assembly, 391; members, fifth assembly, 419; chairman and vice-chairmen, sixth assembly, 427
National Youth General League, 163
New China News Agency, 90
New Democratic Party, 275, 281, 310
New York Times, 7, 181
Nihon keizai shinbun, 153
nonaligned countries, 142, 174, 204–205, 208, 210, 217, 218, 229. *See also* third-world countries
North Korean Provisional People's Committee, 360, 362–363; first, second, and third plenums, 363; founding congress, 363
North Korean Yearbook, 15
North-South Coordination Committee, 186, 187, 190
Norwegian Communist Party, 172
November 3 election, 67
Nuclear Test Ban Treaty, 142

Organization Committee, Workers' Party of Korea, 289; members, in 1949, 322; members, second congress, 320; members, third congress, 323

Pakistan, Islamic Republic of, 210
Panama, 195
Peasant Bank, 38. *See also* banks
Peasants' Union, 147
People's Armed Forces, Ministry of, 474
People's Assembly of North Korea, 56, 70, 77, 360, 363; first congress, 363–364; first to fifth sessions, 365–366
People's Committee, 48, 49, 51, 52, 55–56, 58, 59, 61, 64, 67, 72, 75, 76, 364, 365
People's Control Commission, 474–475
People's Court, 495
People's Economic Plan: 1947 plan, 55, 60, 70, 284, 366; 1948 plan, 70, 76, 366, 368; two-year plan, 80–81, 84–85; three-year plan, 102, 107, 110, 371; five-year plan, 114, 117, 120, 294, 375; six-year plan, 174, 175, 180, 193, 198, 204, 205, 207, 209, 213–214, 302, seven-year plan, 132, 148, 150, 152, 155, 213–214, 297; second seven-year plan, 219–220, 307, 385; planning system, 170; shortcomings, 85
People's Party, 281
People's Republic of China, 97, 106, 109, 117, 123, 127, 133, 173, 202, 221, 501
People's Service Commission, 476
Peru, 194, 204–205
Poch'ŏnbo, 23, 120
Politbureau, Workers' Party of Korea, 278; alternate members, sixth congress, 332–338; members, sixth congress, 332–333; presidium members, sixth congress, 332
Political Committee, Workers' Party of Korea, 133, 140, 143, 159, 171, 186, 187, 188, 273, 288, 289, 309; members, first congress, 317; members, second congress, 319; members, 1949, 322; members, 1953, 322; members and candidate members, fourth congress, 325–326; members and candidate members, 1966, 328; members and candidate members, fifth congress, 329
postwar recovery and reconstruction, 104, 105, 106
Power and Chemical Industries, Ministry of, 475
Power and Coal Industries, Ministry of, 475

Power Industry, Ministry of, 476
Pravda, 11, 97, 173
Premier, 474
procurators-general, 368, 496, 498
Procurement and Food Administration, Ministry of, 475
pro-Japanese collaborators, 37
proletarian internationalism, 83, 96
provincial court, 495
Provisional People's Committee of North Korea, 35–36, 37, 38, 39, 43, 45, 46, 55, 56
public health, 8, 60, 72, 75, 94, 119, 126, 132, 163, 248–250, 293
Public Health, Ministry of, 158, 163, 476
Public Security, Ministry of, 476
Pueblo, U.S.S., 162, 163
P'yŏngbuk sinbo, 40
Pyongyang City People's Committee, 87
Pyongyang Hagwŏn, 30, 36, 40, 65
Pyongyang School for the Families of the Revolutionaries, 66
Pyongyang Times, 15
Pyongyang Worker-Peasant Political Institute, 26

Railway Transportation Commission, 477
Railways, Ministry of, 476–477
reunification. *See* unification
Revolutionary Party for Reunification, 308
Romanian Communist Party, 221–222
Romanian Socialist Republic, 176–177, 203, 228
Rural Construction, Ministry of, 477
Rural Management, Ministry of, 477
Rwanda, Republic of, 222

Sao Tome and Principe, 208
science and technology, 184–185
scientists, 96
secretary, 477
security, 239–241
security cadres, 59, 66, 95
Sekai, 184, 207, 209, 224
Selected Works of Kim Il Sung, 3–4
self-reliant posture, 3, 150
Senegal, Republic of, 194, 195
Seoul Sinmum, 33
Seychelles, 221, 228
Ship Machine Building Industry, Ministry of, 479–480
Sino-Japanese Peace Treaty, 224
Sino-Soviet dispute, 146, 152, 154, 156–157, 169–170, 172, 178, 215
social scientists, 8

Socialist constitution of 1972, 11, 185; bylaws, 522–544; text, 502–522
socialist construction, 108, 111–112, 114, 118, 122, 127–128, 152, 163, 164, 166, 167, 168, 192, 193, 196, 197, 200–201, 206, 211, 223, 224, 293, 295
socialist pedagogy, 179, 216
socialist rural question, 145
Somalia, 181
South Korea, 85, 109, 146, 152, 153, 170, 177, 180, 190, 197; leaders, 73; national assembly, 386; newspaper reporters, 73; Seoul liberation, 86; unilateral election, 75
Soviet Union, 3, 10, 36, 39, 41, 43, 72, 87, 100, 101, 102–103, 106, 109, 115, 125, 133, 138, 142, 147, 151, 165, 291, 294; agreement with North Korea, 85; aid to North Korea, 81, 83; army, 97; Communist Party of, 100, 115, 124–125, 298; economic and cultural cooperation, 91; October revolution, 94, 115–116, 293; ten-year treaty with North Korea, 81
Spanish Communist Party, 184
Special Court, 495
standard terms, 546–548; list of, 548–559
Standing Committee, Supreme People's Assembly, members, first assembly, 393; members, 1953, 393; members, second assembly, 400–401; members, 1957, 401; members, third assembly, 405–406; members, fourth assembly, 411; members, fifth assembly, 418; members, sixth assembly, 426; reelection rate, 390
Standing Committee, Workers' Party of Korea, 60, 62, 63, 64, 66, 68, 273, 277, 283, 289, 361; meetings, first congress, 356–357; meetings, third congress, 357; members, first congress, 317; members, second congress, 319; members and candidate members, third congress, 323; members, 1953, 322
State Construction Commission, 152, 478–479
State Control, Ministry of, 479
State Light Industry Commission, 479
State Planning Commission, 155, 480
State Scientific and Technological Commission, 479
steel production, 151
Sudan, Democratic Republic of, 174, 193
Supreme Court, 365, 368, 374, 495. *See also* Central Court
Supreme People's Assembly, 3, 10, 12, 14,

153; agendas, 361–386; cabinet organization, 444–445; citations, 91; election, 77, 80, 286; functional committees, 388; laws, 219; meetings, 360–361; membership, 388, 391. *See also* Bills Committee; Budget Committee; Credentials Committee; Foreign Affairs Committee; National Defense Committee; Standing Committee
—First Assembly, 80, 386; chairman and vice-chairmen, 392, 393; members, 393–400; officers, 393; sessions, first to thirteenth, 76, 77, 81, 82, 85, 103, 367–374
—Assembly in 1953: chairman and vice-chairmen, 393; officers, 393
—Second Assembly, 387–388; chairman and vice-chairmen, 400, 401; members, 402–405; officers, 400–401; sessions, first to eleventh, 114, 120, 374–378
—Assembly in 1959; chairman and vice-chairmen, 400–401; officers, 401–402
—Third Assembly, 388; chairman and vice-chairmen, 405; members, 406–411; officers, 405–406; sessions, first to seventh, 139, 378–380
—Fourth Assembly, 388; chairman and vice-chairmen, 411–412; members, 412–417; officers, 411–412; sessions, first to sixth, 161, 380–381
—Fifth Assembly, 388–389; members, 419–425; officers, 418–419; president and vice-presidents, 418; secretary-general, 418; sessions, first to seventh, 185, 198, 201, 209, 214, 381–384
—Sixth Assembly, 389; officers, 426–427; president and vice-presidents, 426; secretary-general, 426; sessions, first to sixth, 219, 385–386
Syrian Arab Republic, 171, 197

Taean electric factory, 133, 134
Taean work system, 139–140, 219
Tanzania, Republic of, 165
tax law, 365
technological revolution, 129, 141, 161, 176, 186, 187, 198–199
terminology, 546–547. *See also* standard terms
terms, list, 548–559
Textile and Paper Industries, Ministry of, 481
third-world countries, 148, 152, 160, 192, 194, 195, 196, 199, 201, 202, 206, 207, 217, 221, 222. *See also* non-aligned countries

Three-revolution Team Council, 187
three revolutions, 168, 185, 197, 200, 205, 206, 207, 222, 229, 305, 502
Togo, Republic of, 196
Trade, Ministry of, 150
trade unions, 8, 67, 83, 150, 179
Traffic and Transportation Court, 495
transportation, 58, 105, 106, 145, 167, 301
Transportation, Ministry of, 84, 480
Transportation and Communications Commission, 480
trusteeship, 33, 34, 84
Twenty-point platform, 38

unification (reunification), 72–73, 75, 80, 82, 84, 97, 102, 108, 114, 132, 143, 146, 149, 152, 153, 161, 165, 174, 177, 178, 180, 182, 183, 188, 190, 195, 196, 197, 198, 203, 206, 210, 218, 223, 226, 229, 234–235, 290, 297, 299, 304, 376, 379
Union of Agricultural Working People, 147, 180
United Arab Republic, 154, 169
United Front, 27, 28, 32, 33, 42, 43, 53, 60, 71, 82
United Nations, 72, 73, 88, 178, 182, 183, 188, 190, 192–193, 197, 203, 368
United States, 6–7, 61, 72, 73, 83, 85, 87, 89, 93, 123, 135, 142, 148, 154, 155, 160, 165, 166, 170, 171, 176, 180, 181, 182, 190, 196

vice-premier, 481–483; first vice-premier, 483
vinylon, 130, 132
visitors to the North, 242–244

Washington Post, 182
weapons manufacturing, 82
women, 248–250
Women's League, 33, 41, 47, 66
Workers' Party of Korea, 4, 14, 192, 273–359; agendas, 281–309; anniversaries, 63, 155, 205–206; bylaws, 297, 308, 356, 522–525, 525–545; cadres, 164, 179; city and county committees, 166; class education, 108, 290; factory committee, 138; fatherland liberation, 96; founding date, 274–275; ideological work, 136; judicial policy, 118; local party organizations, 232; members, 108, 164, 309; nominating council, 311; organization work, 93; party conferences, 117, 156–157, 273–274, 275,

293, 300; party congresses, 10, 230, 273, 274–275, 275–276, 309–310; party work, 195; policies, 113, 164–165, 177; reform, 118; "shock troop," 101; shortcomings, 126. *See also* Central Auditing Committee; Central Committee; Central Inspection Committee; Central People's Committee; Credentials Committee; Inspection Committee; Military Affairs Committee; Organization Committee; Politbureau; Political Committee; Standing Committee; Workers' Party of North Korea; Workers' Party of South Korea
—First Congress, agendas, 282–283, 356n8
—Second Congress, 72; agendas, 285–286, 357n13
—1949 officers, 321–322
—1953 officers, 322
—Third Congress, 111; agendas, 291–292
—Fourth Congress, 132; agendas, 296–298; plenums, 136, 145–146, 147, 149, 153, 156, 160, 167, 169
—Fifth Congress, 174–175; agendas, 296–298; plenums (sessions), 178, 183, 184, 192, 200, 201, 208, 212, 213, 216, 217, 218–219
—Sixth Congress, 229, 278, 358n19; agendas, 308–309
Workers' Party of North Korea, 46–47, 48, 54, 55, 275
Workers' Party of South Korea, 48, 275; chairman and vice-chairmen, 318; Inspection Committee, 314; members, Central Committee, 318–319; members, Political Committee, 318; members, Standing Committee, 318; officers, 318
Works of Kim Il Sung, 1–18; Chinese version, 3; complete works, 3; English collections, 4; first edition, 4; Russian version, 5; second edition, 5–6; third edition, 6; topical collections, 7–9
Writings of Kim Il Sung: alleged, 9; articles, 10–11; authenticity, 1; bibliography, 15–18; Chronological Index, 251–271; functional speeches, 10; interviews, 11; itemization, 12–13; language use, 13–14; literature and arts, 9; metaphors, 13; military, 11; open letters, 10, 246–247; party, 11; post-1945, 10–11; pre-1945, 10, 250; prolixity, 12; statistics, 12; styles, 11–14; Subject Index, 230–250; theses, 10–11

Yemen, Arab Republic of, 183
Yemen, Democratic People's Republic of, 198
Yomiuri shinbun, 7, 180, 205, 213
youth, 79, 118, 132, 248–250; carry forward, 177; development center, 146–147; problems, 8, 75; South Korean, 30; Youth Corps, 176
Yugoslavia, Socialist Republic of, 192, 204

Zaire, Republic of, 199
Zambia, 227
Zimbabwe, Republic of, 228